THE OCEAN
OF WISDOM

The most comprehensive compendium of
worldly and spiritual wisdom this century

DEDICATION

*For Laura, Keith, Graham, Jacob,
Hannah, Sarah and Jack*

ACKNOWLEDGEMENTS

The Author and publisher wish to thank all those contributors and copyright holders too numerous to mention who have given their permission for an extract to appear. If, however, there are any omissions the author and publisher will be pleased to correct the matter in any future editions.

To Michael Mann for suggesting the compilation of this anthology.

To the helpful staff and great resources of the British Library without whom this book would not have been possible.

To my dear wife Jane for her continual interest and support.

To Catharine Elliott for painstakingly typing the manuscript.

THE OCEAN
OF WISDOM

The most comprehensive compendium of
worldly and spiritual wisdom this century

Compiled by
ALAN JACOBS

BOOKS

WINCHESTER UK
NEW YORK USA

Copyright © 2005 O Books
O Books is an imprint of The Bothy, John Hunt Publishing Ltd.,
Deershot Lodge, Park Lane, Ropley, Hants, SO24 0BE, UK
office@johnhunt-publishing.com
www.O-books.net

Distribution in:
UK
Orca Book Services
orders@orcabookservices.co.uk
Tel: 01202 665432 Fax: 01202 666219 Int. code (44)

USA and Canada
NBN
custserv@nbnbooks.com
Tel: 1 800 462 6420 Fax: 1 800 338 4550

Australia
Brumby Books
sales@brumbybooks.com
Tel: 61 3 9761 5535 Fax: 61 3 9761 7095

New Zealand
Peaceful Living
books@peaceful-living.co.nz
Tel: 64 7 57 18105 Fax: 64 7 57 18513

Singapore
STP
davidbuckland@tlp.com.sg
Tel: 65 6276 Fax: 65 6276 7119

South Africa
Alternative Books
altbook@global.co.za
Tel: 27 011 792 7730 Fax: 27 011 972 7787

Text: © compiler Alan Jacobs 2005

Design: Infograf, London

ISBN 1 905047 07 X

Scripture quotes are taken from the Authorised King James Version
unless otherwise indicated.

The rights of Alan Jacobs as editor and compiler have been asserted
in accordance with the Copyright, Designs and Patents Act 1988.

A CIP catalogue record for this book is available from the British
Library.

Printed in the USA by Maple-Vail Manufacturing Group

contents

preface

What Wisdom is, and how she came into being, I will relate;
I will conceal no mysteries from you,
but will track her from her first beginnings
and bring the knowledge of her into the open.
Wisdom of Solomon 8:22

Wisdom is the principal thing; therefore get wisdom: and with all
thy getting get understanding.
Proverbs 3:7

"They tell me that you possess the pearl of divine knowledge: either
give it me or sell it." Junayd answered: "I cannot sell it, for you
have not the price thereof; and if I give it you, you will have gained
it cheaply. You do not know its value. Cast yourself headlong, like
me, into this ocean, in order that you may win the pearl by waiting
patiently."
Shibli

Thou knowest not where is the Ocean of thought;
Yet when thou seest fair waves of speech,
Thou knowest there is a glorious Ocean beneath them.
When waves of thought arise from the Ocean of Wisdom,
They assume the forms of sound and speech.
These forms of speech are born and die again,
These waves cast themselves back into the Ocean.
RUMI, from *The Mathnawi*

foreword

The Eternal Question - What is Wisdom? - is an enigma that has baffled mankind since the dawn of history.

There is firstly a Higher Wisdom and secondly an Earthly Wisdom. The Higher Wisdom consists of accurate pointers, signposts on the life journey, which will eventually lead to knowledge of Metaphysical Truth.

The Earthly Wisdom consists of intelligent skills that can be applied to different areas of everyday life.

Both are for pondering, but their perspectives are very different. Fortunately for us the Goddess of Wisdom is invariably lightened by her younger, and less respected handmaiden, 'Wit'.

The quotations I have selected come from a vast library of sources. In many cases, in the numerous books to which I have referred, the exact references have not been given. The aim of this anthology is to stimulate a love and an interest in Wisdom for every man and woman rather than be regarded as a scholarly work.

I have arranged many themes with carefully chosen quotations covering both the Transcendental Wisdom for the Soul along with the practical Wisdom for Life. The well honed and crafted aphorisms, epigrams and poetry about our astounding world, by highly intelligent and gifted individuals, genii, poets and sages are the pearls found in the oyster bed on the floor of this ocean. It could well happen that an attentive reader will suddenly find him or herself resonating strongly with a particular extract. This could well lead him or her to a deeper study and a new interest in investigating the author and diving more deeply.

In my selections I have tried to find a balance between the Metaphysical and Earthly Wisdom. The number of possibilities appeared to be endless. I found as I proceeded that new themes would be needed to maintain the equilibrium and some had to be omitted to avoid repetition of similar themes in different guises.

For example, Taoism is included because it is still a working methodology for many people in the East and in the West. At the same time it is a forerunner of the popular Zen Buddhism, many of whose ideas have found their way into our popular cultural mainstream Confucianism, a near neighbour, but which has been omitted because I found that its emphasis on family and ancestral values were covered elsewhere as in Relationship, and today its aphorisms often appear antique. Nevertheless Confucian quotations are often included wherever appropriate.

Alan Jacobs
London, 2004

ONE

WISDOM

If you are wise you will show
yourself
rather as a reservoir than a
canal. For
a canal spreads abroad the
water it
receives, but a reservoir waits
until it
is filled before overflowing,
and thus
shares without loss to itself
its superabundance of water.
ST. BERNARD OF
CLAIRVAUX

A man can be so busy
making a living that he
forgets to make a life.
WILLIAM BARCLAY

A wise man makes his
own decisions.
An ignorant man follows
public
opinions.
CHINESE PROVERB

By thoughtfulness, by restraint
and self-control, the wise man
may make for himself an
island which no flood can
overwhelm.
From *The Dhammapada*

The highest wisdom has but
once science - the science of
the whole - the science
explaining the whole creation
and man's place in it.
LEO TOLSTOY, *War and
Peace*, Book V, Chapter 2

When one turns inside and
urgently quests
"Where hides the 'I
Thought's' deeply buried
Source?"
False ego topples down, this
way is best;
Thus our Search for Wisdom
is engaged with force.
RAMAHA MAHARSHI

He who understands others
Is learned.
He who knows himself
Is wise.
He who conquers others
Has muscular strength,
He who subdues himself
Is strong.
He who is content
Is wealthy,
He who does not lose
His Soul
Will endure.
LAO-TSE

She is pure and full of light,
crowning grey hairs with
lustre,
And kindling the eye of youth

with a fire not its own:
And her words, whereunto
canst thou liken them? for
earth cannot show their peers:
They be grains of the diamond
sand, the radiant floor of
heaven,
Rising in sunny dust behind
the chariot of God;
They be flashes of the day-
spring from on high, shed
from the windows of the skies;
They be streams of living
waters, fresh from the fountain
of Intelligence:
Such, and so precious, are the
words which the lips of
Wisdom utter.
MARTIN TUPPER

Even the severed branch
grows again,
and the sunken moon
returns:
wise men
who ponder this
are not troubled
in adversity.
BHARTRHARI

"A wise person is one who
watches over himself and
restraints himself from that
which is harmful and strives
for that which will confront
him after death; and a foolish

one is he who gives rein to his
cravings and seeks from Allah
the fulfilment of his vain
desires."
From *Forty Hadith, Tirmidhi:
Nawawi*, (1974), *op.cit.*, page 21

A thousand reasons
for worry,
a thousand reasons
for anxiety
oppress
day after day
the fool,
but not the
wise man.
HITOPADESA OF
NARAYANA

When danger
encircles you,
show yourself
steadfast and
undaunted,
but when the winds
are too favourable,
fail not to show
wise caution and
haul in the
billowing sail.
HORACE

Fools follow vanity; but the
wise man prizes his
thoughtfulness as a treasure.
From *The Dhammapada*

There is this difference
between a wise man and a fool;
the wise man expects future
things,
but does not depend upon
them,
and in the meantime enjoys
the present
remembering the past with
delight
but the life of the fool is
wholly carried on in the
future.
EPICURIES

O thriftfulness of dream and
guess!
O wisdom which is
foolishness!
Why idly seek from outward
things
The answer inward silence
brings?
WITTIER from
Questions of Life

The clouds may drop down
Titles and estates;
Wealth may seek us;
Wisdom must be sought;
Sought before all;
But how unlike all else
We seek on earth!
'Tis never sought in vain.
YOUNG, Night Thoughts,
Night VIII line 62

Of all the gifts of GOD,
Wisdom is chiefest. Wisdom
ordereth the mind. She
directeth the life, and ruleth
the works thereof; teaching
what ought to be done, and
what to be left undone:
without which no man may be
safe.

Wisdom teacheth to do, as
well as to speak.

Of all the gifts of GOD,
Wisdom is [the] most
excellent. She giveth
goodness to the good; and
forgiveth the wicked their
wickedness.

To men of low degree,
Wisdom is an honour; and
Foolishness is a shame to men
of high degree.

Wisdom garnisheth [adorneth]
Riches; and shadoweth
[casteth into the shadow]
Poverty.

Wisdom is the defence of the
Soul, and the mirror of
Reason; and therefore blessed
is he that travaileth [labours]
to get her: for she is the
ground and root of all noble

deeds. By her, we obtain the Chief Good, that is, Eternal Felicity.
PLATO from *The Sayings of the Wise*, William Baldwin, (AD 1555)

The library of wisdom is more precious than all riches, and nothing that can be wished for is worthy to be compared with it. Whosoever therefore acknowledges himself to be a zealous follower of truth, of happiness, of wisdom, of science, or even of the faith, must of necessity make himself a lover of those books.
RICHARD DE BURY (in 1344)

Have we not, then, perhaps the right to say that he treads the path of wisdom who, having weighed the worldly opinions and achievements of men, can smile tolerantly upon their pretensions as compared with the charm and abiding interest of the simple manifestations of life - the mystic loveliness of Nature, the comparative wisdom of all living things according to their needs, the One Spirit permeating all - and who by his profoundest intuition finds himself in unity and harmony with all things.

Knowledge is proud that he has learned so much;
Wisdom is humble that he knows not more.
WILLIAM COWPER

He who cannot see the workings of a Divine Wisdom in the order of the heavens, the change of the seasons, the flowing of the tides, the operations of the wind and other elements, the structure of the human body, the circulation of the blood through a variety of vessels wonderfully arranged and conducted, the instincts of beasts, their tempers and dispositions, the growth of plants, and their many effects for meat and medicine; he who cannot see all these, and many other things, as the evident contrivances of a Divine wisdom, is sottishly blind, and unworthy of the name of a man.
REVEREND WILLIAM JONES OF NAYLAND

How happy is the man who
finds wisdom,
The man who gains
understanding!
For her income is better than
income of silver,
And her revenue than gold.
She is more precious than
corals,
And none of your heart's
desires can compare with her.
Long life is in her right hand,
In her left are riches and
honour.
Her ways are ways of
pleasantness,
And all her paths are peace.
She is a tree of life to those
who grasp her,
And happy is every one who
holds her fast.

The LORD by wisdom
founded the earth,
By reason he established the
heavens;
By his knowledge the depths
are broken up,
And the clouds drop down
dew.

My son, keep guard on
wisdom and discretion,
Let them not slip from your
sight;
They will be life to you,
And an ornament round your
neck.
Then you may go your way in
security,
Without striking your foot on
a stone;
When you rest, you will not
be afraid,
When you lie down, your
sleep will be sweet;
You will fear no sudden terror,
Nor the storm that falls on the
wicked;
For the LORD will be your
confidence,
And will keep your foot from
the snare.
Proverbs 3:13-26

All that the prophets brought
of sciences is clothed in forms
which are accessible to the
most ordinary intellectual
capacities, so that he who
does not go to the heart of
things stops at this clothing
and takes it for what which is
the most beautiful, whereas
the man of subtle
comprehension, the diver who
fishes for pearls of Wisdom,
knows how to indicate for
what reason such or such a
Divine Truth is clothed in
terrestrial form; he evaluates
the robe and the material of

which it is made, and knows by that, all that it covers, attaining thus to a science which remains inaccessible to those who do not have knowledge of this order.
(*ibid.*, page 106)
IBN ARABI from *Wisdom of the Prophets*

It takes years and maturity to make the discovery that the power of faith is nobler than the power of doubt; and that there is a celestial wisdom in the ingenuous propensity to trust, which belongs to honest and noble natures.
STOWE, *Orr's Island*, XXIV

Whereas mental starvation is catastrophic to the wise, too much thinking and too much counsel suffocate the fool; mental fatigue claims him without a blow being struck. Some men die because they have sense; others live because they have none. Learning is life to the wise and slow death to the fool. The wise man never knows enough and will only offer advice when asked; the fool believes he knows too much and has advice for anyone who will listen.

However, both fool and wise man fall victim when the nourishing of their respective needs becomes excessive.
BALTASAR GRACIAN

He hath slender worldly wisdom, and no knowledge of himself,
Who fancieth men care for him, as a study worth their musing;
A little of their idlest curiosity is all he need expect;
Even if the man hath won a name, and set it high in honour.
We may be mountains to ourselves, but are molehills to most others,
And there is a wise humility in judging of oneself as nought;
Yet there is greatness in each one of us, depth, and height, and breadth,
And it were a folly to forget our values to be vast and individual;
Only let each as to himself count over his just responsibilities,
Giving his neighbour credit for the like internal sense -
A sense, most personal to each of us, and yearning little

over others,
Selfish and unheedful if ye
will; but the stringent law of
our being -
That each man is the centre
for his either-world
circumference,
And everything to self,
although as nothing to his
neighbour.
MARTIN TUPPER

Wisdom itself requires to go
through a certain probation of
folly, in order to acquire the
degree of knowledge which
shall teach what folly is - what
shape it takes, and how it will
affect us.
SIMMS, Woodcraft, XIX

Wisdom is a fox who, after
long hunting, will at last cost
you the pains to dig out: 'tis a
cheese, which by how much
the richer, has the thicker, the
homelier, and the coarser
coat; and whereof to a
judicious palate, the maggots
are best. 'Tis a sack posset,
wherein the deeper you go,
you'll find it the sweeter.
Wisdom is a hen, whose
cackling we must value and
consider, because it is
attended with an egg. But

lastly, 'tis a nut, which unless
you choose with judgement,
may cost you a tooth, and pay
you with nothing but a worm.
DEAN SWIFT

He who learns the rules of
wisdom without conforming
to them in his life is like a
man who ploughs in his field
but does not sow.
SADI

Dare to be wise! Energy of
spirit is needed to overcome
the obstacles which indolence
of nature as well as cowardice
of heart oppose to our
instruction.
FRIEDRICH VON SHILLER

There are days when
everything goes right for some,
and with little effort, and
when everything goes wrong
for others. For those whose
star is in the ascendant the
spirit is well disposed, the
mind is alert, and all they
touch turns to gold. This is
the hour to strike, and not to
squander the least advantage.
But each man must recognise
his unlucky days, for even the
strongest mind has its periods
of uncertainty. No man is

wise at all hours, since, at times, it takes luck even to think straight. On days when nothing goes right, even though the game may change, the bad luck may not. It is a time not to throw the dice, not to press for decisions. It is a time to retreat and inwardly regroup, and to draw on the power of your internal compass for the alignment of the stars in your favour.
From *The Wisdom of Baltasar Gracian*

Cultivate the habit of attention and try to gain opportunities to hear wise men and women talk. Indifference and inattention are the two most dangerous monsters that you ever meet. Interest and attention will insure to you an education.
ROBERT A MILLIKAN

[King] Solomon has made it clear that the need for preliminary studies is a necessity and that it is impossible to attain true wisdom except after having been trained. For he says: "If the iron be blunt, and he do not whet the edge, then must he put to more strength; but even more preparation is needed for wisdom."
[Ecclesiastes 10:10] And he also says: "Hear counsel and receive instruction that thou mayest be wise in thy latter end."
Proverbs 19:20

MOSES MAIMONIDES
Wisdom is the principal thing; therefore get wisdom; and with all thy getting get understanding.
Proverbs 4:7

The finest quality in man is that he should be an inquirer.
From *The Wisdom of Ibn Gabirol*

The wise man is a greater asset to a nation than is a king.
From *The Philosophy of Maimonides*

Thoughtful among the thoughtless, and awake among slumberers, the wise man advances like a racer.
From *The Dhammapada*

As far as we can discern, the sole purpose of human existence is to kindle a light

in the darkness of mere being.
C.G. JUNG, (1875-1961),
Memories, Dreams, Reflections,
Chapter 11

Giving up past, present and
future, the wise man crosses to
the farther shores. Being freed
he will not come to rebirth.
From *The Wisdom of Buddhism*

Hear this, all you peoples;
Give heed, all you dwellers in
the world,
Sons of men, and all mankind,
Both rich and poor.
My mouth speaks wisdom,
And my heart's meditation is
insight.
I incline my ear to proverb;
I solve my riddle on the lyre …
Even wise men die;
The fool and the brutish alike
perish,
And leave their wealth to
others.
Their graves are their
everlasting home,
Their dwelling throughout the
ages,
Though lands are named after
them.
But man is an ox without
understanding;
He is like the beasts that
perish.

This is the fate of those who
are self-sufficient,
And the end of those who are
satisfied with their own words.
Like sheep they are appointed
to Sheol …
Psalm 49

The wisdom of life consists in
a careful culture of your
capacities, a large expansion
of your sympathies, a loving
acknowledgement of your
surroundings, a quick eye for
opportunity, and a dextrous
use of circumstances.
BLACKIE

Rabban Gamaliel used to say:
"Get yourself a teacher, and
keep away from doubtful
matters, and never tithe by
guesswork."

Simeon, his son, said: "All my
life I have grown up among
the wise, and I have found
nothing better than silence.
The chief thing is not to study
but to do. And he who says
too much, encourages sin."

Rabban Simeon ben Gamaliel
said: "The world rests on three
things - Truth, Law and
Peace."

Rabban Gamaliel, the son of Rabbi Jehudah the Prince, said: "It is good to follow a workaday occupation as well as to study the Torah, for between the two one forgets to sin... Beware of the [Roman] authorities, for they make no advances to a man except for their own purposes. They seem friendly when it is to their advantage, but desert a man when he is in trouble."

Rabban Jochanan ben Zakki used to say: "Don't feel self-righteous if you have learned much Torah, because that is what you were created for." He said to his disciples: "Go and discover what [best helps] a man to find the right way of life." Rabbi Eliezer answered: "A good eye." Rabbi Jehoshua answered: "A good comrade." Rabbi Jose answered: "A good neighbour." Rabbi Simeon answered: "Foresightedness."
Wisdom from The Mishna

The noblest of the gifts which God bestowed on His human creatures ... is Wisdom. This constitutes the life of their spirit, the lamp of their intellect. It secures them the favours of God, and saves them from His wrath both here and hereafter ...

Wisdom falls into three divisions. The first division is the science of created things ... and deals with the essential and accidental properties of material bodies. The second division consists of the ancillary sciences; for instance, arithmetic, geometry, astronomy and music. The third department is the science of theology, and treats of the knowledge of God, blessed be He, and of the knowledge of His law, and so forth.

All the sciences are gates which the Creator has opened to rational beings, through which they may attain to a comprehension of religion and of the world. But while some sciences are more adapted to the needs of religion, others are more requisite for secular interests. The sciences specially required in secular affairs form the lowest division; whereas the one essential to religion is the highest science, Theology ...
From *The Ethics of Bahya*

Avert thy face from world deceptions; mistrust thy senses, they are false. But within thy body, the shrine of thy sensations, seek in the impersonal for the 'Eternal Man', and having sought him out, look inward; thou art Buddha.

From *The Wisdom of Buddhism*

The indisputable evidences of Divine Wisdom in the Universe can be classified under seven heads. The first is to be seen in the order of the cosmos itself. The Earth, we observe, is at the centre; close to it and above it is water; close to the water is the atmosphere; above all is fire in a just and unchanging balance and measure. Each of these elements maintains the proper position appointed for it. The ocean bed, with the waters imprisoned therein, stays in its place and does not pass beyond its boundaries, notwithstanding the roaring of the waves and the ragings of the winds, as it is written (Job 38:9-11), "And I prescribed for it my decree, and set bars and doors; and said: 'Thus far shalt thou come, but no further, and here shall thy proud waves be stayed.'"

The second evidence of wisdom is apparent in the human species - a universe on a small scale that completes the ordered series of creation, and constitutes its crowning beauty, glory, and perfection. David, peace be to him, referred to Man when he exclaimed: "O Eternal, our Lord, how glorious is Thy name in all the earth."

The third evidence of wisdom is apparent in the formation of the individual human being - his physical structure, the faculties of his mind and the light of reason with which the Creator has distinguished him and thus given him superiority over other living creatures that are irrational. Man resembles the large universe, being like it fundamentally and in its original elements...

The fourth evidence is seen in other species of living creatures, from the least to the greatest - those that fly or swim or creep or move on four feet, with their various qualities, pleasures and uses ...

The fifth is displayed in plants and other natural products [e.g., minerals] that have been provided for the improvement of the human race, because of their usefulness to man in various ways, according to their natures, constitutions and virtues ...

The sixth is discernible in the sciences, arts, and crafts which the Creator, blessed be He, provided for man, to contribute to his improvement, to enable him to obtain a livelihood and gain other benefits of a general and particular character. This mark of Divine Wisdom is referred to in the texts (Job 38:36), "Who hath put wisdom in the inward parts? Or who hath given understanding to the mind?" and again (Prov. 2:6), "For the Lord giveth wisdom; out of His mouth cometh knowledge and discernment."

The seventh evidence in the appointment of the Torah and its statutes, to teach us how to serve the Creator and secure for one who consistently lives according to their dictates, immediate happiness here, and recompense in the life to come hereafter ... To this should be added the customs by which the government of other nations is regulated together with their useful features. For those nations, these customs take the place of the Torah, though only in secular matters ...

Some are of the opinion that when the wise man said (*Proverbs* 9:1), "Wisdom hath built her house; she hath hewn out her seven pillars," he had in mind the seven evidences which we have just mentioned.
From *The Ethics of Bahya*

Between two worlds life hovers like a star
'Twixt night and morn upon the horizon's verge.
How little do we know that which we are!
How less what we may be!
The eternal surge
Of time and tide rolls on and bears afar

Our bubbles. As the old burst,
new emerge,
Lashed from the foam of ages;
while the graves
Of empires heave but like
some passing waves.
From *The Sayings of Lord Byron*

I do not know what I may
appear to the world; but to
myself I seem to have been
only like a boy playing on the
seashore, and diverting myself
in now and then finding a
smoother pebble or a prettier
shell than ordinary, whilst the
great ocean of truth lay all
undiscovered before me.
SIR ISAAC NEWTON

Of all the good gifts of God,
wisdom is the purest. She
giveth goodness to good
people; and obtaineth for the
wicked pardon for their
wickedness. She maketh the
poor rich; and the rich
honourable: and such as
unfeignedly embrace her, she
maketh like to God.

Wisdom and Justice are
honourable, both to God and
man.
Intelligence is King both of
heaven and earth.

Wisdom is the messenger of
Reason.
WILLIAM BALDWIN from
The Sayings of the Wise, (1555
AD), HERMES

Then I saw that wisdom
excelleth folly
As far as light excelleth
darkness
The wise man's eyes are in his
head
The fool walketh in darkness
One event happens to them
all.
Ecclesiastes 2: 13-14

There is more wisdom in
Your body
Than in your deepest
Philosophy
FRIEDRICH NIETZSCHE
(1844-1900), From *Human All
Too Human*, Part II

Knowledge dwells
in heads replete with thoughts
of other men;
Wisdom in minds attentive
to their own.
WILLIAM COWPER (1731-
1800) from *The Task*

The first man knew her
(wisdom) not perfectly: no
more shall the last find her out.

For her thoughts are more
than the sea,
And her counsels profounder
than the great deep.
I also came out as a brook
from a river,
And as a conduit into a
garden
I said, "I will water my best
garden
And will water abundantly my
garden-bed.
And lo! my brook became a
river
And my river became a sea.
ECCLESIASTICUS

We're not a wisdom society -
we're a knowledge society;
knowledge becomes outdated
very
quickly, and therefore old
people
become obsolete.
RAM DAS from *One Liners*

To be surprised, to wonder, is
to begin to understand.
JOSÉ ORTEGA Y GASSET,
The Revolt of the Masses,
(1930)

The wise man is but a clever
infant, spelling letters from a
hieroglyphical book, the
lexicon of which lies in

Eternity.
THOMAS CARLYLE

Be not wise in your own
conceits.
Romans 12:16

Human wisdom is the
aggregate of all human
experience, constantly
accumulating and selecting,
and re-organising its own
materials.
JUDGE STORY

Learn wisdom from the
experience of others; and from
their failings you will be able
to correct your own faults ...

The first step towards
being wise is to know that you
are ignorant; and if you wish
to be esteemed in the
judgement of others, cast off
the folly of trying to appear
wise. As a plain garment best
adorns a beautiful woman, so
is modest behaviour the
greatest ornament of wisdom.

True wisdom is less
presuming than folly: the wise
man doubts often, and
changes his mind; but the fool

is obstinate and does not doubt - he knows all things except his own ignorance!

The pride of emptiness is an abomination, and to talk much is the foolishness of folly. Nevertheless, it is part of wisdom to bear with fools; to hear their absurdities with patience - and to pity their weakness. Do not become puffed-up, neither boast of superior understanding; for the clearest human knowledge is but little better than blindness.

The wise man knows his own imperfections. But the fool peeps into the shallow stream of his own mind and is pleased with the pebbles which he sees at the bottom; he brings them up, and shows them as pearls, and the applause of other fools delights him.
DANDEMIS

A fool may associate with a wise man all his life, but perceive the truth as little as the spoon perceives the taste of soup. An intelligent man may associate with a wise man

one minute, and perceive the truth as the tongue perceives the taste of soup.
From *The Dhamanpeda*

God has chosen the foolish things of the world with which to confound the wise; and he has chosen the weak things of the world with which to confound the mighty.
I *Corinthians* 1:27

Wisdom is the olive that springeth from the heart, bloometh on the tongue, and beareth fruit in the action.
GRYMESTONE

It is far easier to be wise for others than to be so for oneself.
LA ROCHEFOCAULD

Wisdom is the only thing which can relieve us from the sway of the passions and the fear of danger, and which can teach us to bear the injuries of fortune itself with moderation, and which shows us all the ways which lead to tranquillity and peace.
CICERO

There is not a man in the world, but desires to be, or to be thought to be, a wise man; and yet if he considered how little he contributes himself thereunto, he might wonder to find himself in any tolerable degree of understanding.
CLARENDON

The first step to wisdom is to be exempt from folly.
HORACE

If he, a teacher, is indeed wise he does not bid you enter the house of his wisdom, but rather leads you to the threshold of your own mind.
THE PROPHET KAHLIL GIBRAN, *Of Teaching*

Mixing one's wines may be a mistake, but old and new wisdom mix admirably.
BERTOLD BRECHT from *The Caucasian Chalk Circle*, (1944), from Prologue

If one is too lazy to think,
Too vain to do a thing badly,
Too cowardly to admit it,
One will never attain wisdom.
CYRIL CONNOLLY, *The Unquiet Grave*, (1945)

Be ye therefore wise as serpents, and harmless as doves.
JESUS CHRIST, *Matthew* 10:16

We become wise by adversity; prosperity destroys our appreciation of the right.
SENECA, *Letter to Lucilium* XCIV

The wisdom of a learned man
Cometh by opportunity of leisure:
He that has little business shall become wise.
How can he get wisdom
Who holds the plough,
Glories in the goad,
Drives oxen,
Is occupied in their labours,
Whose talk is of bullocks?
Ecclesiastes 9:17

The wisdom of the Deity, as testified in the works of creation, surpasses all idea we have of wisdom drawn from the highest intellectual operation of the highest of intelligent beings with whom we are acquainted.
WILLIAM PALEY

Wisdom is that which makes men judge what are the best ends, and what the best means to attain them, and gives a man advantages of counsel and direction.
SIR W. TEMPLE

Learning sleeps and snores in libraries, but wisdom is everywhere, wide awake, on tiptoes.
JOSH BILLINGS

The wise man is informed in what is right. The inferior man is informed in what will pay.
CONFUCIUS

A single conversation across the table with a wise man is better than ten years' mere study of books.
LONGFELLOW, Hyperion (1839), line 7

O thriftfulness of dream and guess!
O wisdom which is foolishness!
Why idly seek from outward things
The answer inward silence brings:
WITTIER from Questions of Life

A wise man among the ignorant is as a beautiful girl in the company of blind men.
SAADI (Sufi Poet)

Not by constraint or severity shall you have access to true wisdom, but by abandonment, and childlike mirthfulness. If you would know aught, be cheerful before it.
HENRY DAVID THOREAU, Journal

The attempt to combine wisdom and power has only rarely been successful and then only for a short while.
ALBERT EINSTEIN, Ideas and Opinions

The truest sayings are paradoxical.
LAO-TSE

As the arrow-maker makes straight his arrow, so the wise man makes straight the trembling and unsteady thought which is difficult to control and difficult to hold back.
From The Dhammapada

Wisdom, at the beginning, seemeth a great wonder.

Wisdom is like a thing fallen into the water; which no man can find, except he search [for] it at the bottom.

Wisdom thoroughly learned, will never be forgotten.

Science is got by diligence; but Discretion and Wisdom cometh of God.
WILLIAM BALDWIN from The Sayings of the Wise, (AD 1555), PYTHAGORAS

The wise man adapts himself appropriately to each situation. He does not desire to make it different.
When he finds himself amid wealth and dignity, he conducts himself as one who is worthy and esteemed.
When he finds himself among the poor and despised, he behaves in ways appropriate to poverty and disdain.
When he finds himself in a foreign civilisation, he adapts himself to foreign customs.
When he finds himself in distress and affliction, he acts as one who is distressed or afflicted.
Thus the wise man is willing to accept every appropriate kind of behaviour as his own.
When in a high position, he does not regard his inferiors with contempt. When in a low position, he does not flatter his superiors.
He always acts appropriately of his own accord, and needs no guidance by others.
Hence, he does not feel himself imposed upon. He neither grumbles about his cosmic fate nor complains about his treatment by men.
Thus the wise man is serene and confident, trusting the future. But the foolish man risks troubles, hoping for more than he deserves. The wise man is like an archer. When the archer fails to hit the target, he reflects and looks for the cause of his failure within himself.
CONFUCIUS

It is better to weep with wise men than to laugh with fools.
SPANISH PROVERB

I am: yet what I am none cares, or knows.
JOHN CLARE, (1793-1864), *I am*

Were there not a need-be of
wisdom, nothing would be as
it is,
For essence without necessity
argueth a moral weakness.
We look through a glass
darkly, we catch but glimpses
of truth;
But, doubtless, the sailing of a
cloud hath Providence to its
pilot,
Doubtless, the root of an oak
is gnarled for a special
purpose,
The foreknown station of a
rush is as fixed as the station
of a king,
And chaff from the hand of
the winnower, steered as the
stars in their courses.
Man liveth only in himself,
but the Lord liveth in all
things;
And his pervading unity
quickeneth the whole
creation.
Man doeth one thing at once,
nor can he think two thoughts
together;
But God compasseth all
things, mantling the globe like
air:
And we render homage to his
wisdom, seeing use in all his
creatures,
For, perchance, the universe
would die, were not all things
as they are.
MARTIN TUPPER

How profusely do invisible
powers manifest their
influence!
When we look for them, we
cannot see them. Yet they are
present everywhere, and
nothing is without them.
They move masses of people
to fast and to purify
themselves and to bedeck
themselves with their finest
raiment in order to sacrifice to
them. The world seems
flooded with them, both
above and on all sides.
In the *Book of Verses* it is
written: 'The invisible powers
come upon us unawares. Yet
they cannot be ignored.'
Such is the way in which the
invisible is expressed. And
such is the impossibility of
restraining expressions of
faith.
CONFUCIUS

Wisdom, which is the worker
of all things, taught me;
For in her is an understanding
spirit,
Holy, one only, manifold,
subtle,

Lively, clear, undefiled,
Plain, not subject to hurt,
loving the thing that is good,
quick,
Which cannot be letted, ready
to do good, kind to man,
Steadfast, sure, free from care,
Having all power, overseeing
all things,
And going through all
understanding, pure and most
subtle.
For wisdom is more moving
than any motion,
She passeth and goeth
through all things by reason of
her pureness,
For she is the breath of the
power of God,
And a pure influence flowing
from the glory of the
Almighty,
Therefore can no defiled thing
fall into her
For she is the brightness of the
everlasting light,
The unspotted mirror of the
power of God
And the image of His
goodness.
And being but one, she can
do all things,
And remaining in herself, she
maketh all things new,
And in all ages, entering into
holy souls,

She maketh them friends of
God and prophets.
For God loveth none
But him that dwelleth with
wisdom.
For she is more beautiful than
the sun
And above all the order of the
stars:
Being compared with the
light, she is found before it.
For after this cometh night,
But vice shall not prevail
against wisdom.
Wisdom reacheth from one
end to another mightily:
And sweetly doth she order all
things.
I loved her and sought her out
from my youth
I desired to make her my
spouse,
And I was a lover of her
beauty …
O send her out of Thy holy
heavens
And from the throne of Thy
glory
That being present she may
labour with me,
For the thoughts of mortal
men are miserable
And our devices are but
uncertain
For the corruptible body
presseth down the soul,

And the earthly tabernacle
weigheth down the mind that
museth upon many things,
And hardly do we guess aright
at things that are upon earth,
And with labour do we find
the things that are before us,
But the things that are in
heaven who hath searched
out?
And Thy counsel who hath
known, except Thou give
wisdom

And send Thy Holy Spirit
from above?
For so the ways of them which
lived on the earth were
reformed,
And men were taught the
things that are pleasing unto
Thee,
And were saved through
wisdom.
WISDOM OF SOLOMON

TWO

ACTION

The reason why people so ill know how to do their duty on great occasions, is, that they will not be diligent in doing their duty on little occasions.
HARE GUENOS AL TRUE, *Augustus & Julius*, (1866)

When we act according to our duty, we commit the event to Him by whose laws our actions are governed, and who will suffer none to be finally punished for obedience. But when, in prospect of some good, whether natural or moral, we break the rules prescribed to us, we withdraw from the direction of superior wisdom, and take all consequences upon ourselves.
DR. JOHNSON, *Rasselas*

Acceptance says, True, this is my situation at the moment. I'll look unblinkingly at the reality of it. But I'll also open my hands to accept willingly whatever a loving Father sends.
CATHERINE WOOD MARSHALL

Think that day lost whose (low) descending Sun, Views from thy hand no noble action done.
JACOB BOBART

Attempt the end and never stand to doubt, Nothing's so hard but search will find it out.
HERRICK

What can suppress the tendencies of these but firmness of mind! Do not be inconstant and changeful, not knowing why, lest you escape from yourself and see not how. Be incapable of change from that which is right; and men will rely upon you. See that your principles are just; then will you be inflexible in carrying them out. Do not let your passions have rule over you; so shall your constancy ensure to you the good you possess.
DANDEMIS, Indian, (3 BC)

The Empire has ever been won by letting things take their course. He who must always be doing is unfit to obtain the Empire.
LAO-TSE

I have always thought the actions of men the best

interpreters of their thoughts.
LOCKE

Every man feels instinctively that all the beautiful sentiments in the world weigh less than a single lovely action.
LOWELL

Accept the fact that you are accepted.
PAUL TILLICH

Only the actions of the just Smell sweet and blossom in the dust.
SHIRLEY

What one has, one ought to use; and whatever he does, he should do with all his might.
CICERO

Peace comes not by establishing a calm outward setting so much as by inwardly surrendering to whatever the setting.
HUBERT VAN ZELLER

The bell never rings of itself; unless someone handles it or moves it, it is dumb.
PLAUTUS

Do not do what is already done.
TERENCE

So to conduct one's life as to Realise Oneself - this seems to me the highest attainment possible to a human being. It is the task of one and all of us, but most of us bungle it.
IBSEN

I hate to see things done by halves: if it be right, do it boldly, if it be wrong; leave it undone.
GILPIN

As you sow, y'are like to reap.
BUTLER

What you would not have done to yourselves, never do unto others.
ALEXANDER SEVERUS

I will give them singleness of heart and action, so that they will always fear me for their own good and the good of their children after them.
Jeremiah 32:39 NIV

Thought is the seed of action.
RALPH WALDO EMERSON

Thinking is easy, acting is difficult, and to put one's thoughts into action is the most difficult thing in the world.
GOETHE

Strong reasons make strong actions.
WILLIAM SHAKESPEARE

All worthwhile men have good thoughts, good ideas and good intentions - but precious few of them ever translate those into action.
J.H. FIELD

Our faculties become dull and soon lose their power if they are not exercised.
O.S. MARDEN

A man who has to be convinced to act before he acts is not a man of action ... You must act as you breathe.
CLEMENCEAU

Action makes more fortunes than caution.
VAUVENARGUES

It is by action and not by faith alone that a man is justified.
James 2.24

Tsze-kung asked what constituted a superior man. The Master said, "He acts before he speaks, and afterwards speaks according to his actions."
CONFUCIUS

The great end of life is not knowledge but action.
ALDOUS HUXLEY

If I rest, I rust.
MARTIN LUTHER

How can the actions of a man be right who has no rule of life?
DANDEMIS, Indian, (3rd century BC)

Our problem is not that we take refuge from action in spiritual things, but that we take refuge from spiritual things in action.
MONICA FURLONG

Think it over, yes, but don't dawdle until someone else has thought it over, worked it out, and put it over.
WILFRED PETERSON

Let us be tried by our actions.
MOTTO (Anon)

Take time to deliberate; but
when the time for action
arrives, stop thinking and go
in.
ANDREW JACKSON

Thy actions, and thy actions
alone, determine thy worth.
FICHTE

Follow diligently the Way in
your own heart, but make no
display of it to the world.
LAO-TSE

I find the doing of the will of
God leaves me no time for
disputing about His plans.
GEORGE MAC DONALD

In action, a great heart is the
chief qualification; in work, a
great head.
SCHOPENHAUER

Belief in God and in
immortality thus gives us the
moral strength and the ethical
guidance we need for virtually
every action in our daily lives.
WERNHER VON BRAUN

A tree is known by its fruit; a
man by his deeds.
ST. BASIL

Elijah went up to the people
and said, "How much longer
will it take you to make up
your minds? If the Lord is
God, worship him; but if Baal
is God, worship him!"
1 *King* 18.21

Our duties hang in such a
chain, one from the other, and
all from heaven, that he who
fulfils the highest is likely to
fulfil the rest; while he who
neglects the highest whereby
alone the others are upheld,
will probably let the rest
draggle in the mire.
HARE GUENOS AL TRUE,
Augustus & Julius, (1866)

A good deed is never lost; he
who sows courtesy reaps
friendship, and he who plants
kindness gathers love.
ST. BASIL

Deeds are fruits - words are
leaves.
GASPARD DOUGHET

Go on in new deeds of valour,
my son! That is the way to
the stars.
VIRGIL

Between saying and doing
there is a great distance.
F.W. ROBERTSON

How far that little candle
throws his beams! So shines a
good deed in a naughty world.
WILLIAM SHAKESPEARE

Let me thank you with deeds,
not with words.
KERNER

When a man dies they who
survive him ask what property
he has left behind. The angel
who bends over the dying
man asks what good deeds he
has sent before him.
The Koran

We make our decisions, and
then our decisions turn
around and make us.
FRANCIS WILLIAM (F.W.)
BOREHAM

By your works ye shall be
known.
The Holy Bible

We live in deeds, not years; in
thoughts, not breaths.
P.J. BAILEY

Life's no resting, but a
moving; Let thy life be deed
on deed.
GOETHE

A life spent worthily should
be measured by deeds, not
years.
RICHARD BRINSLEY
SHERIDAN

Give me the ready hand
rather than the ready tongue.
GARIBALDI

How often men decide to do
good and noble deeds but
never accomplish them,
because they spend so much
time in thinking of doing
these things that they never
do them until it is too late.
This noble and generous deed,
this kind and encouraging
word that you were
contemplating, should be
carried into action now.
H.F. KLEITZING

Our deeds still travel with us
from afar, And what we have
been makes us what we are.
GEORGE ELIOT

Do not esteem an action
because it is done with noise

and pomp; for the noblest soul
is he who does great things
quietly.
DANDEMIS, Indian, (3rd
century BC)

Good actions ennoble us, we
are the sons of our own deeds.
CERVANTES

We should believe only in
deeds; words go for nothing
everywhere.
ROJAS

Reflect on the issue and
decide who to involve.
Review the evidence.
Make a self assessment of
strengths and weaknesses.
Describe the ideal future state
of affairs.
State the school objective
concisely and recognisably.
Select key features for use as
indicators and evaluation
headings.
Generate a list of options for
actions to be taken to lead to
the objective.
Select a limited, related, set of
these actions.
Cost the actions proposed.
Show plans for acquiring or
allocating further resources.
Define tasks, targets and

responsible individuals,
resource allocation and dates
for completion.
Complete a project planning
chart to show how different
tasks are related.
Choose an evaluator and
agree stages, and audiences,
for reports on progress.
Produce the public version of
the plan in summary form.
RUSSELL & SWEETMAN,
Management Plan

In morals, as in art, saying is
nothing, doing is all.
RENAN

When we cannot act as we
wish, we must act as we can.
TERENCE

All heaven's glory is within
and so is hell's fierce burning.
You must yourself decide in
which direction you are
turning.
ANGELUS SILESIUS

All our actions are divided
into those which have a value,
and those which have no
value at all in the face of
death. If I were told that I
had to die tomorrow, I should
not go out for a ride on

horseback; but if I were about
to die this moment, and
Levochka here fell and burst
into tears, I should run to him
and pick him up. We are all
in the position of passengers
from a ship which has reached
an island. We have gone on
shore, we walk about and
gather shells, but we must
always remember that, when
the whistle sounds all the
little shells will have to be
thrown away and we must run
to the boat.
LEO TOLSTOY

He that humbles himself shall
be preserved entire. He that
bends shall be made straight.
He that is empty shall be
filled. He that is worn out
shall be renewed. He who has
little shall succeed. He who
has much shall go astray.
LAO-TSE

Time hath, my lord, a wallet
at his back,
Wherein he puts alms for
oblivion,
A great-sized monster of
ingratitudes:
Those scraps are good deeds
past; which are devour'd
As fast as they are made,

forgot as soon
As done: perseverance, dear
my lord,
Keeps honour bright: to have
done is to hang
Quite out of fashion, like a
rusty mail
In monumental mockery.
WILLIAM SHAKESPEARE,
Ulysses, Troilus and Cressida,
Act III, Scene iii

Never waste time and
energywishing you were
somewhere else.
Accept your situation and
realise you are
where you are, doing what you
are doing,
for a very specific reason.
Realise that nothing is
by chance, that you have
certain lessons to learn
and that the situation you are
in has been given
to you to enable you to learn
those lessons
as quickly as possible, so that
you can move
onward and upward along this
spiritual path.
EILEEN CADDY from *Pearls
of Wisdom*

Once you make the
fundamental

choice to be the predominant creative force
in your life, any approach you choose to take
for your own growth and development can work.
And you will be especially attracted to those
approaches which will work particularly well for you.
ROBERT FRITZ

The Sage occupies himself with inaction, and conveys instruction without words.
LAO-TSE

To live is not merely to breathe: it is to act; it is to make use of our organs, senses, faculties - of all those parts of ourselves which give us the feeling of existence.
ROUSSEAU

Religions, philosophies, formulas, projects, blueprints, programmes, plans are inert until action infuses them with power.
WILFRED PETERSON

Words are good, but there is something better. The best is not to be explained by words. The spirit in which we act is the chief matter. Action can only be understood and represented by the spirit.
GOETHE

Judge not of actions by their mere effect;
Dive to the centre, and the cause detect.
Great deeds from meanest springs may take their course,
And smallest virtues from a mighty source.
ALEXANDER POPE

In private places, among sordid objects, an act of truth or heroism seems at once to draw to itself the sky as its temple, the sun as its cradle. Nature stretches out her arms to embrace man, only let his thoughts be of equal greatness.
RALPH WALDO EMERSON

Indeed, what is this Infinite of Things itself, which men name Universe, but an Action, a sum-total of Actions and Activities? The living ready-made sum-total of these three - which Calculation cannot aid, cannot bring on its tablets; yet the sum, we say, is written visible: All that has been done, All that is doing,

All that will be done!
Understand it well, the Thing
thou beholdest, that Thing is
an Action, the product and
expression of exerted Force:
the All of Things is an
infinite conjugation of the
verb To Do.

Shoreless Fountain - Ocean of
Force, of power to Do;
wherein force rolls and circles,
billowing, many-streamed,
harmonious; wide as
Immensity, deep as Eternity;
beautiful and terrible, not to
be comprehended: this is what
man names Existence and
Universe; this thousand-tinted
flame-image, at once veil and
revelation, reflex such as he,
in his poor brain and heart,
can paint of One
Unnameable, dwelling in
inaccessible light! From
beyond the Star-galaxies, from
before the Beginning of Days,
it billows and rolls - round
thee, nay, thyself art of it, in
this point of Space where
thou now standest, at this
moment.
THOMAS CARLYLE

I hate to see a thing done by
halves: if it be right, do it
boldly; if it be wrong, leave it
undone.
BERNARD GILPIN

A conference is a gathering of
important people who singly
can do nothing, but together
can decide that nothing can
be done.
FRED ALLEN

When you do good, do it
because it is good - not
because men praise it; and
when you avoid evil, avoid it
because it is evil - not because
men speak against it.
DANDEMIS, Indian, (3rd
century BC)

Our life is composed greatly
from dreams, from the
unconscious, and they must be
brought into connection with
action. They must be woven
together.
ANAÏS NIN, *The Diaries of
Anaïs Nin*, Volume IV

Arouse yourself, gird your
loins, put aside idleness, grasp
the nettle, and do some hard
work.
SAINT BERNARD OF
CLAIRVAUX, *Letters*

Conditions are never just right. People who delay action until all factors are favourable are the kind who do nothing.
WILLIAM FEATHER, *The Business of Life*

My experience of the world is that things left to themselves don't get right.
THOMAS HENRY HUXLEY, *Aphorisms and Reflections*

Considering the chaos and disorder in the world - both outwardly and inwardly - seeing all this misery, starvation, war, hatred, brutality - many of us have asked what one can do... One feels one must be committed... When you commit yourself, you are committed to a part and therefore the part becomes important and that creates division. Whereas, when one is involved completely, totally with the whole problem of living, action is entirely different. Then action is not only inward, but also outward; it is in relationship with the whole problem of life.
J. KRISHNAMURTI, *You Are the World*

What you theoretically know, vividly realize.
FRANCIS THOMPSON, *Works*, Shelley, Volume III

Say well is good, but do well is better;
Do well seems the spirit, say well is the letter;
Say well is godly and helps to please,
But do well is godly and gives the world ease;
Say well to silence is sometimes bound,
But do well is free on every ground;
Say well has friends, some here, some there,
But do well is welcome everywhere.
By say well man to God's word cleaves,
But for lack of do well it often leaves.
If say well and do well were bound in one frame,
Then all were done, all were won, and gotten were gain.
ANON

It is not book learning young men need, nor instruction about this and that, but a stiffening of the vertebrae which will cause them to be

loyal to a trust, to act promptly, concentrate their energies, do a thing - "carry a message to Garcia."
ELBERT HUBBARD, *Carry a Message to Garcia*

He who grasps, lets slip.
LAO-TSE

Nobody can become perfect by merely ceasing to act.
Bhagavad Gita

Tsze-Kung asked what constituted a superior man. The Master said, "He acts before he speaks, and afterwards speaks according to his actions."
CONFUCIUS

A man who has to be convinced to act before he acts is *not* a man of action. It's as if a tennis player before returning the ball began to question himself as to the physical and moral value of tennis. You must act just as you breathe.
GEORGES CLÉMENCEAU

The smallest good deed is better than the grandest good intention.
GASPARD DOUGHET

Our actions are not altogether our own; they depend less upon us than upon chance. They are given to us from every hand; we do not always deserve them.
ANATOLE FRANCE

Action, indeed, is always easy, and when presented to us in its most aggravated, because more continuous, form, which I take to be that of real industry, becomes simply the refuge of people who have nothing whatever to do.
OSCAR WILDE

The more perfection anything has, the more active and the less passive it is; and contrariwise, the more active it is, the more perfect it becomes.
SPINOZA

Adapt yourself to the things among which your lot has been cast and love sincerely the fellow creatures with whom destiny has ordained that you shall live.
MARCUS AURELIUS

Be honest for love of honesty, and you will be uniformly so;

for he who does it without
principle is but a waverer.
The inconstant man has no
peace in his soul: neither has
any one who concerns himself
with him Today he is a
tyrant; tomorrow, more
humble than a servant. Why?
He does not know! Today he
is profuse; tomorrow, he
grudges even his own mouth
that which it should eat.
Today, he loves you;
tomorrow, he detests you.
Why? He does not know!
DANDEMIS, Indian, (3rd
century BC)

How could there be any
question of acquiring or
possessing, when the one
thing needful for a man is to
become - to *be* at last, and to
die in the fullness of his being.
ANTOINE DE SAINT-
EXUPÉRY, *The Wisdom of the
Sands*, 38, (1948)

Accursed greed for gold,
To what dost thou not drive
the heart of man?
VIRGIL, *Aeneid*, 3.56, (30-19 BC)

Action should culminate in
wisdom.
Bhagavad Gita, 4

We often do not know
ourselves the grounds
On which we act, though
plain to others.
BERTOLT BRECHT,
Roundheads and Peakheads, 4,
(1933)

Who is there that can make
muddy water clear? But if
allowed to remain still, it will
gradually become clear of
itself. Who is there that can
secure a state of absolute
repose? But let time go on,
and the state of repose will
gradually arise.
LAO-TSE

In our era, the road to
holiness necessarily passes
through the world of action.
DAG HAMMARSKJÖLD,
"1955" *Markings* (1964)

We cannot withdraw our cards
from the game. Were we as
silent and as mute as stones, our
very passivity would be an act.
JEAN-PAUL SARTRE,
Situations, Présentation des
'Temps Modernes', (1947-49)

Action will remove the doubt
that theory cannot solve.
TEHYI HSIEH

Renunciation and activity
both liberate,
but to work is better than to
renounce.
Bhagavad Gita, 5

One cannot manage too many
affairs: like pumpkins in the
water, one pops up while you
try to hold down the other.
CHINESE PROVERB

The worshipper of energy is
too physically energetic to see
that he cannot explore certain
higher fields until he is still.
CLARENCE DAY, *This
Simian World*, 5, (1920)

He that is everywhere is
nowhere.
THOMAS FULLER, M.D.,
Gnomologia, 2176, (1732)

What is the use of running
when we are not on the right
road?
GERMAN PROVERB

Unreal is action without
discipline, charity without
sympathy, ritual without
devotion.
Bhagavad Gita, 17

Determine never to be idle.
No person will have occasion
to complain of the want of
time who never loses any. It
is wonderful how much may
be done if we are always
doing.
THOMAS JEFFERSON,
letter to Martha Jefferson,
May 5, 1787

There is no kind of idleness by
which we are so easily seduced
as that which dignifies itself
by the appearance of business.
SAMUEL JOHNSON, *The
Idler*, 48, (1758-60)

There are people who want to
be everywhere at once and
they seem to get nowhere.
CARL SANDBURG,
Complete Poems, Anywhere
and Everywhere People, (1950)

Men need some kind of
external activity, because they
are inactive within.
SCHOPENHAUER, *Parerga
and Paralipomena*, Further
Psychological Observations,
(1851

Every one has time if he likes.
Business runs after nobody:
people cling to it of their own

free will and think that to be busy is a proof of happiness.
SENECA, *Letters to Lucilius*, 106.1, (1st Century)

Where most of us end up there is no knowing,
But the hellbent get where they are going.
JAMES THURBER, *Further Fables for Our Time*, (1956)

Sow an act and you reap a habit; sow a habit and you reap a character; sow a character and you reap a destiny.
FRANCES E. WILLARD (1905)

I've arrived at this outermost edge of my life by my own actions. Where I am is thoroughly unacceptable. Therefore, I must stop doing what I've been doing.
ALICE KOLLER, *An Unknown Woman*, (1982)

I think one's feelings waste themselves in words; they ought all to be distilled into actions which bring results.
FLORENCE NIGHTINGALE, *The Cause*, (1928)

We should do only those righteous actions which we cannot stop ourselves from doing.
SIMONE WEIL, *Gravity and Grace*, (1947)

One never notices what has been done; one can only see what remains to be done.
MARIE CURIE, (1894)

There can be no happiness if the things we believe in are different from the things we do.
FREYA STARK, *The Lycian Shore*, (1956)

All progressive legislation has always had its genesis in the mind of one person... One can do much. And one and one and one can move mountains.
JOAN WARD-HARRIS, *Creature Comforts*, (1979)

A small group of thoughtful people could change the world. Indeed, it's the only thing that ever has.
MARGARET MEAD, in *The Utne Reader*, (1992)

The ocean is made of drops.
MOTHER TERESA, *Love Until It Hurts*, (1980)

If you're not living on the edge, you're taking up too much room.
LORRAINE TEEL, *Minnesota Press*

It is always thus with those who know not constancy. Who shall say that the chameleon is black, when a moment afterwards the colour of the grass overspreads him? Who can say of the inconstant: "He is joyful," when his next breath is spent in sighing? What is the life of such a man but the phantom of a dream? In the morning he rises happy: at noon he is on the rack. This hour he is a god: the next, beneath a worm. One moment he laughs: the next he is weeping. Now he wills: in an instant he will will it not; and in another instant he will not know whether he wills or no.
DANDEMIS, Indian, (3rd century BC)

The softest things in the world override the hardest. That which has no substance enters where there is no crevice. Hence I know the advantage of inaction.
LAO-TSE

Action is worry's worst enemy.
AMERICAN PROVERB, mid 20th century

If it ain't broke, don't fix it.
Late 20th century

Iron rusts from disuse; stagnant water loses its purity and in cold weather becomes frozen; even so does inaction saps the vigour of the mind.
LEONARDO DA VINCI, (1452-1519)

We have left undone those things which we ought to have done;
And we have done those things which we ought not to have done;
And there is no health in us.
The Book of Common Prayer, (1662), Morning Prayer General Confession

They also serve who only stand and wait.
JOHN MILTON, (1608-74), *When I consider how my light is spent*, (1673)

Think nothing done while aught remains to do.
SAMUEL ROGERS, (1763-1855), *Human Life*, (1819)

I grew up in the Thirties with our unemployed father. He did not riot, he got on his bike and looked for work.
NORMAN TEBBIT

From the moment of birth we are immersed in action, and can only fitfully guide it by taking thought.
A.N. WHITEHEAD, Science *and the Modern World*, (1925)

Action springs not from thought, but from a readiness for responsibility.
DIETRICH BONHOEFFER, *Letters and Papers from Prison*

The world can only be grasped by action not by contemplation. The hand is more important than the eye.
JACOB BRONOWSKI, *The Ascent of Man*, (1973)

Through ages, through eternity, what you have done for God, that, and only that, you are. Deeds never die.
F.W. ROBERTSON

Barking dogs seldom bite.
PROVERB

Suit the action to the word, the word to the action; with this special observance, that you o'erstep not the modesty of nature.
WILLIAM SHAKESPEARE, (1564-1616), *Hamlet*, Act III, Scene ii

Now, *here*, you see, it takes all the running *you* can do, to stay in the same place. If you want to get somewhere else, you must run at least twice as fast as that!
LEWIS CARROLL, (1832-98), *Through the Looking Glass*, Chapter 2

Meetings are indispensable when you don't want to do anything.
J.K. GALBRAITH, (1908), *Ambassador's Journal*, Chapter 5

I wish to preach, not the doctrine of ignoble ease, but the doctrine of the strenuous life.
THEODORE ROOSEVELT, (1858-1919), speech at Chicago, 10 April 1899

But men must know, that in this theatre of man's life it is reserved only for God and angels to be lookers-on.
FRANCIS BACON, (1561-1626), The Advancement of Learning, II.xx.8

The dreadful burden of having nothing to do.
NICHOLAS BOILEAU, (1636-1711), Epistle XI, 86

The hand is more important than the eye... that hand is the cutting edge of the mind.
J. BRONOWSKI, (1908-74), The Ascent of Man, 3

Deliberation is the work of many men. Action of one alone.
GENERAL DE GAULLE, (1890-1970), War Memoirs, Volume II, Unity, Chapter 5

Everyone knows that it is much harder to turn word into deed than deed into word.
MAXIM GORKY, (1868-1936), from 'On Plays', in USSR (1937)

Clay lies still, but blood's a rover;
Breath's a ware that will not keep.
Up, lad: when the journey's over
There'll be time enough for sleep.
A.E. HOUSEMAN, (1859-1936), A Shropshire Lad, 4, Reveille

Activity conquers cold, but stillness conquers heat. Purity and stillness are the correct principles for mankind.
LAO-TSE

A categorical imperative would be one which represented an action as objectively necessary in itself, without reference to any other purpose.
IMMANUEL KANT, (1724-1804), Fundamental Principles of Morals, 2

Trust no Future, howe'er pleasant
Let the dead Past bury its dead!
Act - act in the living Present!
Heart within, and God o'erhead!
H.W. LONGFELLOW, (1807-82), A Psalm of Life

Think nothing done while aught remains to do.
SAMUEL ROGERS, (1763-1855), *Human Life*, 49

Trust the man who hesitates in his speech and is quick and steady in action, but beware of long arguments and long beards.
GEORGE SANTAYANA, (1863-1952), *Soliloquies in England*

Between the acting of a
dreadful thing
And the first motion, all the
interim is
Like a phantasma or a hideous
dream;
The genius and the mortal
instruments
Are then in council; and the
state of man,
Like to a little kingdom,
suffers then
The nature of an insurrection.
WILLIAM SHAKESPEARE,
(1564-1616), *Julius Caesar*,
Act II, Scene I, line 63

Be resolute, and direct an even and an uninterrupted course; so shall your foot be upon the earth, and your head above the clouds. Though obstacles appear in your path, do not deign to look down to them, but proceed with resolution, guided by right, and mountains shall sink beneath your tread. Storms may roar against your shoulders, but they will not shake you. Thunder will burst over your head in vain; the lightning will but serve to show the glory of your soul.
DANDEMIS, Indian, (3rd century BC)

Footprints on the sands of time are not made by sitting down.
PROVERB

Death closes all: but
something ere the end,
Some work of noble note, may
yet be done,
Not unbecoming men that
strove with God.
ALFRED, LORD
TENNYSON, (1809-92),
Ulysses, 51

O! what men dare do! what men may do! what men daily do, not knowing what they do!
WILLIAM SHAKESPEARE, *Much Ado About Nothing*, Act IV, Scene I, line 19

Talking of the effects of drinking, he said: Drinking may be practised with great prudence: a man who exposes himself when he is intoxicated has not the art of getting drunk.
SAMUEL JOHNSON
(quoted in Boswell's *Life of Johnson*)

Take care to get what you like or you will be forced to like what you get.
G. BERNARD SHAW, *Man and Superman* (Maxims)

"I apply myself with diligence to every kind of study," said the son of Confucius to the great Chinese philosopher, "and neglect nothing that can render me clever and ingenious, but still I do not advance." "Omit some of your pursuits," replied Confucius, "and you will get on better." Among those who travel constantly on foot have you ever observed any who run? It is essential to do everything in order, and only grasp that which is within reach of your arm, for otherwise you give yourself useless trouble. Those who, like yourself, desire to do everything in one day, do nothing to the end of their lives; while others, who steadily adhere to one pursuit, find they have accomplished their purpose.
ANON

THREE

ADOLESCENCE

When all the world is young,
lad,
And all the trees are green;
And every goose a swan, lad,
And every lass a queen:
Then hey for boot and horse,
lad,
And round the world away;
Young blood must have its
course, lad,
And every dog his day.
CHARLES KINGSLEY

Bliss was it in that dawn to be
alive,
But to be young was very
Heaven!
WILLIAM
WORDSWORTH, *The
Prelude*, Book XI

Bestow thy youth so that thou
mayst have comfort to
remember it, when it hath
forsaken thee, and not sigh
and grieve at the account
thereof. Whilst thou art
young thou wilt think it will
never have an end; but behold
the longest day hath his
evening, and that thou shalt
enjoy it but once, that it
never returns again; use it
therefore as the spring-time,
which soon departeth, and
wherein thou oughtest to
plant and sow all provisions
for a long and happy life.
SIR WALTER RALEIGH

How can we more essentially
benefit our country, than by
instructing and giving a
proper direction to the minds
of our youth.
CICERO

The best rules to form a young
man, are, to talk little, to hear
much, to reflect alone upon
what has passed in company;
to distrust one's own opinions,
and value others that deserve it.
SIR WILLIAM TEMPLE

The Lord satisfieth thy mouth
with good things; so that thy
youth is renewed like the
eagle's.
Psalms 3:5

Youth, what man's age is like
to be, doth show;
We may our ends by our
beginnings know.
DENHAM, *On Prudence*, line
225

Meek young men grow up in
libraries believing it their duty
to accept the views which
Cicero, which Locke, which

Bacon have given; forgetful that Cicero, Locke and Bacon were only young men in libraries when they wrote these books.
RALPH WALDO EMERSON

Remember not the sins of my youth, nor my transgressions: according to thy mercy remember thou me for thy goodness' sake, O Lord.
Psalms 25.7

Would you remain always young, and would you carry all the joyousness and buoyancy of youth into your maturer years? Then have care concerning one thing - how you live in the thought world.
HENRY DAVID THOREAU

A young man cannot be perfectly wise. For Wisdom requireth Experience; which for lack of time, young men may not have.
ARISTOTLE

Proficiency at billiards is proof of a misspent youth.
HERBERT SPENCER, (1820-1903), attributed

Better is a poor and a wise child than an old and foolish king, who will no more be admonished.
Ecclesiastes 4:13

The young always have the same problem - how to rebel and conform at the same time. They have now solved this by defying their parents and copying one another.
QUENTIN CRISP, (circa 1910-), *The Naked Civil Servant*

Almost everything that is great has been done by youth.
BENJAMIN DISRAELI, (1804-81), *Coningsby*, Book III, Chapter 1

Let no one despise your youth, but set the believers an example in speech and conduct, in love, in faith, in purity.
1 *Timothy* 4:12 (NRSV)

Young men make great mistakes in life; for one thing, they idealize love too much.
BENJAMIN JOWETT, (1817-93), British Theologian

It is good for a man that he bear the yoke in his youth.
Lamentations 3:27

One starts to get young at the age of sixty and then it is too late.
PABLO PICASSO, (1881-1973)

The youth who daily farther from the east
Must travel, still is Nature's priest,
And by the vision splendid
Is on his way attended:
At length the man perceives it die away,
And fade into the light of common day.
WILLIAM WORDSWORTH, (1770-1850), Ode, Intimations of Immortality, 5

Ah, but I was so much older then,
I'm younger than that now.
BOB DYLAN, (1941-), song, My Back Pages

Behold the child, by nature's kindly law
Pleased with a rattle, tickled with a straw:
Some livelier plaything gives his youth delight,
A little louder, but as empty quite:
Scarfs, garters, gold, amuse his riper stage,
And beads and prayer books are the toys of age:
Pleased with this bauble still, as that before;
Till tired he sleeps, and life's poor play is o'er.
ALEXANDER POPE, (1688-1744), An Essay on Man, II.275

For in my youth I never did apply
Hot and rebellious liquors to the blood...
Therefore my age is as the lusty winter,
Frosty, but kindly.
WILLIAM SHAKESPEARE, (1564-1616), As You Like It, Act II, Scene iii, line 48

Remember now thy Creator in the days of thy youth, while the evil days come not, nor the years draw nigh, when thou shalt say, I have no pleasure in them.
Ecclesiastes 12.1

My salad days
When I was green in judgement.
WILLIAM SHAKESPEARE, (1564-1616), Antony and Cleopatra, Act I, verse 73

I think what is happening to me is so wonderful, and not only what can be seen on my body, but all that is taking place inside. I never discuss myself or any of these things with anybody; that is why I have to talk to myself about them.
ANNE FRANK, (1929-45), *Diary of a Young Girl*

All evil comes from the old. They grow fat on ideas and young men die of them.
JEAN ANOUILH, *Catch as Catch Can*, (1960)

If age, which is certainly
As wicked as youth, looks any wiser
It is only that youth is still able to believe
It will get away with anything, while age
Knows only too well that it has got away with nothing.
W.H. AUDEN, *The Sea and the Mirror*, (1945)

Flee the evil desires of youth, and pursue righteousness, faith, love and peace, along with those who call on the Lord out of a pure hart.
2 Timothy 2:22 (NIV)

Americans began by loving youth and now, out of self-pity, they worship it.
JACQUES BARZUN, *The House of Intellect*, (1959)

I never dared be radical when young, for fear it would make me conservative when old.
ROBERT FROST, *Precaution*

Let us feel that we are still alive, instead of constantly going around in deedless admiration for the conventional.
CARL NIELSEN, *My Childhood*

As a result of all his education, from everything he sees and hears around him, the child absorbs such a lot of lies and foolish nonsense, mixed in with essential truths, that the first duty of the adolescent who wants to be a healthy man is to disgorge it all.
ROMAIN ROLLAND, *Jean Christophe*, (1912)

It is the highest creatures who take the longest to mature, and are the most helpless during their immaturity.
GEORGE BERNARD SHAW, *Back to Methuselah*, (1922)

I remember the gleams and
glooms that dart
Across the school-boy's brain;
The song and the silence in
the heart,
That in part are prophecies,
and in part
Are longings wild and vain.

And the voice of that fitful
song
Sings on, and is never still:
"A boy's will is the wind's will,
And the thoughts of youth are
long, long thoughts."
CHARLES KINGSLEY

Heroics are not easily had for
the young in our times.
Perhaps that is why they go to
such extremes to create their
own dangers.
GAIL GODWIN, *False Lights*

Youth has a quickness of
apprehension, which it is very
apt to mistake for an acuteness
of penetration.
HANNAH MORE, *Essays on
Various Subjects*, (1777)

This is a youth-oriented
society, and the joke is on
them because youth is a
disease from which we all
recover.

DOROTHY FULDHEIM, *A
Thousand Friends*

I shall die very young ...
maybe seventy, maybe eighty,
maybe ninety. But I shall be
very young.
JEANNE MOREAU

The hatred of the youth
culture for adult society is not
a disinterested judgement but
a terror-ridden refusal to be
hooked into the ... ecological
chain of birthing, growing,
and dying. It is the demand,
in other words, to remain
children.
MIDGE DECTER

Who would ever think that so
much can go on in the soul of
a young girl?
ANNE FRANK, *The Diary of
a Young Girl*, (1952)

Bringing up teenagers is like
sweeping back ocean waves
with a frazzled broom - the
inundation of outside
influences never stops.
Whatever the lure - cars, easy
money, cigarettes, drugs,
booze, sex, crime - much that
glitters along the shore has a
thousand times the appeal of a

parent's lecture.
MARY ELLEN
SNODGRASS, *Motherhood or
Bust*

We thought we were running
away from the grownups, and
now we are the grownups.
MARGARET ATWOOD,
Cat's Eye, (1988)

We have created a child who
will be so exposed to the
media that he will be lost to
his parents by the time he is
12.
DAVID BOWIE, (1947-)

Young men are fitter to invent
than to judge, fitter for
execution than for counsel,
and fitter for new projects
than for settled business.
FRANCIS BACON, (1561-
1626), *Essays*, Of Youth and
Age, (1625)

Heaven lies about us in our
infancy!
Shades of the prison-house
begin to close
Upon the growing boy,
WILLIAM
WORDSWORTH, *Ode,
Intimations of Immortality*

I'm not young enough to
know everything.
J.M. BARRIE, (1860-1937),
The Admirable Crichton

Youth would be an ideal state
if it came a little later in life.
HERBERT HENRY
ASQUITH, (1852-1928)

The force that through the
green fuse drives the flower
Drives my green age.
DYLAN THOMAS, (1914-
53)

Adults who do not like and
respect adolescents - and this
includes a large proportion of
those who make a career of
working with them - are badly
frightened by the increasingly
democratic relationships
between adolescents and
adults that are coming to
prevail in our society.
EDGAR Z. FRIEDENBERG,
The Vanishing Adolescent

As for boys and girls, it is one
of the sorriest of mistakes to
talk down to them: almost
always your lad of fifteen
thinks more simply, more
fundamentally than you do;
and what he accepts as good

coin is not facts or precepts, but feelings and convictions.
DAVID GRAYSON, *The Friendly Road*

People sometimes say to youth, "The world is at your feet!" But this is not true unless heaven is in your heart.
P. AINSWORTH

Young people will respond if the challenge is tough enough and hard enough. Youth wants a master and a controller. Young people were built for God, and without God as the centre of their lives they become frustrated and confused, desperately grasping for and searching for security.
BILLY GRAHAM

You yourself know how slippery is the path of youth - a path on which I myself have fallen, and which you are now travelling not without fear.
Saint JEROME

One other thing stirs me when I look back at my youthful days, the fact that so many people gave me something or were something to me without knowing it.
ALBERT SCHWEITZER

Nothing great was ever achieved without enthusiasm.
RALPH WALDO EMERSON

The old are trying to be young, as they always have, as we all do, youth being the model. But the young are not trying to be old.
MARTIN AMIS, *London Fields*, 14

Whenever the older generation has lost its bearings, the younger generation is lost with it.
BRUNO BETTELHEIM, *The Sexual Wilderness*

Any given generation gives the next generation advice that the given generation should have been given by the previous one but now it's too late.
ROY BLOUNT, JR

The arrogance of age must submit to be taught by youth.
EDMUND BURKE, *letter to Fanny Burney*

Adolescence is an intermediary stage linking the

paradise of childhood to the inferno of failure.
E.M. CIORAN, *Tears and Saints*

The task and yearning of youth is to become, whereas the mature man's task is to give himself away.
HERMANN HESSE, *Reflections*, 660

The forties are the old age of youth and the fifties the youth of old age.
EDWARD HOAGLAND, in *Learning to Eat Soup*

I hope you have lost your good looks for while they last any fool can adore you, and the adoration of fools is bad for the soul. No, give me a ruined complexion and a lost figure and sixteen chins on a farmyard of crow's feet and an obvious wig. Then you shall see me come out strong.
GEORGE BERNARD SHAW, *letter to Mrs. Pat Campbell*

It would seem that for some of the mind's creations, the winter of the body is the spring of the soul.
JOSEPH JOUBERT, *Thoughts and Maxims*

No one renounces what he knows; we renounce only what we do not know. That is why the young are less egotistical than adults or old men.
CESARE PAVESE, *This Business of Living*

Old and young, we are all on our last cruise.
ROBERT LOUIS STEVENSON, *Virginibus Puerisque*

The moral is this - that a right way of looking at things will see through almost anything.
SAMUEL BUTLER

'Tis a maxim with me to be young as long as one can: there is nothing can pay one for that invaluable ignorance which is the companion of youth; those sanguine groundless hopes, and that lively vanity, which make all the happiness of life. To my extreme mortification I grow wiser every day.
LADY MARY WORTLEY MONTAGU

Many might go to heaven
with half the labour they go to
hell, if they would venture
their industry the right way.
BEN JOHNSON, Timber,
Random Thoughts, (1640)

Money is sullen
And wisdom is sly,
But youth is the pollen
That blows through the sky
And does not ask why.
STEPHEN VINCENT
BENÉT, John Brown's Body, 1,
(1928)

The excesses of our youths are
drafts upon our old age,
payable with interest, about
thirty years after date.
CHARLES CALEB
COLTON, Lacon, line 76,
(1825)

A youth is to be regarded with
respect. How do you know
that his future will not be
equal to our present?
CONFUCIUS, Analects, 9.22,
(6th century BC)

Those who love the young
best stay young longest.
EDGAR Z. FRIEDENBERG,
The Vanishing Adolescent

A wild colt may become a
sober horse.
THOMAS FULLER, M.D.,
Gnomologia, (1732)

Give me those days with heart
in riot,
The depths of bliss that
touched on pain,
The force of hate, and love's
disquiet -
Ah, give me back my youth
again!
GOETHE, Faust: Part 1,
Prelude in the Theatre,
(1808)

The imagination of a boy is
healthy, and the mature
imagination of a man is
healthy; but there is a space of
life between, in which the
soul is in a ferment, the
character undecided, the way
of life uncertain, the ambition
thicksighted.
JOHN KEATS, Endymion,
Preface, (1818)

Youth is perpetual
intoxication; it is a fever of
the mind.
LA ROCHEFOUCAULD,
Maxims, (1665)

It is, indeed, one of the capital tragedies of youth - and youth is the time of real tragedy - that the young are thrown mainly with adults they do not quite respect.
H.L. MENCKEN, The Baltimore Evening Sun, Travail, Oct. 8, 1928

Immature is the love of the youth, and immature his hatred of man and earth. His mind and the wings of his spirit are still tied down and heavy.
FRIEDRICH NIETZSCHE, Thus Spoke Zarathustra, On Free Death, (1883-92)

The ripeness of adolescence is prodigal in pleasures, skittish, and in need of a bridle.
PLUTARCH, Moralia, The Education Children, (AD 100)

We cannot always build the future for our youth, but we can build our youth for the future.
FRANKLIN D. ROOSEVELT

In early youth, as we contemplate our coming life, we are like children in a theatre before the curtain is raised, sitting there in high spirits and eagerly waiting for the play to begin.
SCHOPENHAUER, Parerga and Paralipomena, (1851)

The right way to begin is to pay attention to the young, and make them just as good as possible.
SOCRATES, in Plato's Euthyphro, (4-3rd century BC)

For youthful faults ripe virtues shall atone.
WILLIAM WORDSWORTH, Artegal and Elidure, (1815)

Pollytics and bankin' is th' on'y two games where age has th' best iv it. Youth has betther things to attind to, an' more iv thim.
FINLEY PETER DUNNE, Observations by Mr. Dooley, Avarice and Generosity, (1902)

When a man is young he is so wild he is insufferable. When he is old he plays the saint and becomes insufferable again.
NIKOLAI GOGOL, Gamblers, (1842)

He that would pass the latter part of life with honour and decency must, when he is young, consider that he shall one day be old; and remember, when he is old, that he has once been young.
SAMUEL JOHNSON, *The Rambler*, 50, (1750-52)

The passions of the young are vices in the old.
JOSEPH JOUBERT, *Pensées*, (1842)

Most men spend the first half of their lives making the second half miserable.
LA BRUYÈRE, *Characters*, 11. 102, (1688)

Youth is incautious.
Wisdom learns to tread softly.
Valuing moments.
AMY LOWELL, *What's O'Clock*, The Anniversary, (1925)

If you will be cherished when you are old, be courteous while you be young.
JOHN LYLY, *Euphues: The Anatomy of Wit*, (1579)

The young man who has not wept is a savage, and the older man who will not laugh is a fool.
GEORGE SANTAYANA, *Dialogues in Limbo*, (1925)

FOUR

ADULTHOOD

Is not old wine wholesomest,
old pippins toothsomest, old
wood burn brightest, old linen
wash whitest? Old soldiers,
sweetheart, are surest, and old
lovers are soundest.
JOHN WEBSTER, *Westward
Ho*, Act II, Scene ii

Adam: Though I look old, yet
I am strong and lusty;
For in my youth I never did
apply
Hot and rebellious liquors in
my blood;
Nor did not with unbashful
forehead woo
The means of weakness and
debility;
Therefore my age is as a lusty
winter,
Frosty, but kindly.
WILLIAM SHAKESPEARE,
As You Like It, Act II, Scene
iii , line 47

The man of wisdom is the
man of years.
YOUNG, *Night Thoughts*,
Night 5, 1. 775

To know how to grow old is
the masterwork of wisdom,
and one of the most difficult
chapters in the great art of
living.

AMIEL, *Journal*, Sept 14,
1874

We do not count a man's
years, until he has nothing
else to count.
RALPH WALDO
EMERSON, *Society and
Solitude*, Old Age

In ageing, our minds are often
permeated by memories of the
past
or worries about the future.
What gets missed is the
present -
and right there in the moment
is the
doorway into timelessness.
ANON

If a young or middle-aged
man, when leaving a
company, does not recollect
where he laid his hat, it is
nothing; but if the same
inattention is discovered in an
old man, people will shrug up
their shoulders, and say, "His
memory is going."
SAMUEL JOHNSON: quoted
in Boswell's *Life of Johnson*

Do people conform to the
instructions of us old ones?
Each thinks he must know

best about himself, and thus many are lost entirely.
GOETHE, quoted in Johann Peter Eckermann's *Conversations with Goethe*, Sept. 18, 1823

In youth I used to look for the hidden genius in every man; in mature age I have to struggle against looking for the hidden man in every genius.
NICKOLAYAVITCH PANIN (1855)

Adults are children who have failed to find a substitute for the charm they lost.
IRVING LAYTON, *The Whole Bloody Bird*, aphs

I sometimes think we all die at twenty-five and after that are nothing but walking corpses, with gramophones inside.
GEORGE SANTAYANA, *The Letters*

God never destroys the work of his own hands, he removes what would pervert it, that is all. Maturity is the stage where the whole life has been brought under the control of God.
OSWALD CHAMBERS

As we grow older ... we discover that the lives of most human beings are worthless except in so far as they contribute to the enrichment and emancipation of the spirit ... No one over thirty-five is worth meeting who has not something to teach us - something more than we could learn by ourselves, from a book.
CYRIL CONNOLLY, *The Unquiet Grave*

The whole business of marshalling one's energies becomes more and more important as one grows older.
HUME CRONYN, *Showcase* by Roy Newquist

At middle age the soul should be opening up like a rose, not closing up like a cabbage.
JOHN ANDREW HOLMES, *Wisdom in Small Doses*

Honesty consists of the unwillingness to lie to others; maturity, which is equally hard to attain, consists of the unwillingness to lie to oneself.
SYDNEY J. HARRIS

The Indian Summer of life should be a little sunny and a little sad, like the season, and infinite in wealth and depth of tone - but never hustled.
HENRY ADAMS, *The Education of Henry Adams*, 35, (1907)

The years between fifty and seventy are the hardest. You are always being asked to do things, and yet you are not decrepit enough to turn them down.
T.S. ELIOT, *Time*, October 23, 1950

Whoever, in middle age, attempts to realise the wishes and hopes of his early youth, invariably deceives himself. Each ten years of a man's life has its own fortunes, its own hopes, its own desires.
GOETHE, *Elective Affinities*, 30, (1809)

The youth gets together materials for a bridge to the moon, and at length the middle-aged man decides to make a woodshed with them.
HENRY DAVID THOREAU

Spiritual maturity comes, not by erudition, but by compliance with the known will of God.
D.W. LAMBERT

Perhaps middle age is, or should be, a period of shedding shells; the shell of ambition, the shell of material accumulations and possessions, the shell of the ego.
ANNE MORROW LINDBERGH

The Indian Red Jacket, when the young braves were boasting their deeds, said: But the sixties have all the twenties and forties in them.
RALPH WALDO EMERSON, *Old Age*

Age is not all decay; it is the ripening, the swelling, of the fresh life within, that withers and bursts the husk.
GEORGE MACDONALD

It is well to be taught, even by an enemy.
OVID, *Metamorphoses*, Book 4

Unless a serpent eats a serpent it will not become a dragon.
LATIN (MEDIEVAL) PROVERB

Falstaff: Your lordship, though not clean past your youth, hath yet some smack of age in you, some relish of the saltness of time; and I most humbly beseech your lordship to have a reverend care of your health.
WILLIAM SHAKESPEARE, *Henry IV*, Act I, Scene ii, line 91

It is usual to associate age with years only because so many men and women somewhere along in what is called middle age stop trying.
HENRY FORD

Maturity begins to grow when you can sense your concern for others outweighing your concern for yourself.
JOHN MAC NAUGHTON

A young physician fattens the churchyard.
PROVERB

One should try everything once, except incest and folk-dancing.
ARNOLD BAX, (1883-1953), *Farewell to My Youth*

Poverty of mind as a spiritual attitude is a growing willingness to recognise the incomprehensibility of the mystery of life. The more mature we become the more we will be able to give up our inclination to grasp, catch, and comprehend the fullness of life and the more we will be ready to let life enter into us.
HENRI J.M. NOUWEN

A moment's insight is sometimes worth a life's experience.
OLIVER WENDELL HOLMES, *The Professor at the Breakfast Table*, Chapter 10

Experience is never limited, and it is never complete; it is an immense sensibility, a kind of huge spider-web of the finest silken threads suspended in the chamber of consciousness, and catching every air-borne particle in its tissue.
HENRY JAMES, (1843-1916), *Partial Portraits*

Experience is the mother of wisdom.
PROVERB

All experience is an arch wherethro'

Gleams that untravelled
world, whose margin fades
For ever and for ever when I
move.
ALFRED LORD
TENNYSON, *Ulysses*

He is only advancing in life,
whose heart is getting softer,
his blood warmer, his brain
quicker, and his spirit entering
into living peace.
JOHN RUSKIN

You don't set a fox to
watching the chickens just
because he has a lot of
experience in the hen house.
HARRY S. TRUMAN

I have learned
To look on nature, not as in
the hour
Of thoughtless youth; but
hearing often-times
The still, sad music of
humanity.
WILLIAM
WORDSWORTH, *Lines
Composed above Tintern Abbey*

An expert is a man who has
made all the mistakes, which
can be made, in a very narrow
field.
NIELS BOHR

One of the marks of spiritual
maturity is the quiet
confidence that God is in
control... without the need to
understand why he does what
he does.
CHARLES R. SWINDOLL

It is not you or I that is
important, neither what sort
we might be nor how we came
to be each where we are.
What is important is anyone's
coming awake and discovering
a place... What is important
is the moment of opening a
life and feeling it touch - with
an electric hiss and cry - this
speckled mineral sphere, our
present world.
ANNIE DILLARD, *An
American Childhood*

Metellus: O, let us have him,
for his silver hairs
Will purchase us a good
opinion,
And buy men's voices to
commend our deeds:
It shall be said his judgement
ruled our hands;
Our youths and wildness shall
no whit appear,
But all be buried in his
gravity.
WILLIAM SHAKESPEARE,

Julius Caesar, Act II, Scene i, line 144

I compare human life to a large mansion of many apartments, two of which I can only describe, the doors of the rest being as yet shut upon me.
JOHN KEATS, *letter to J.H. Reynolds*

If you want knowledge, you must take part in the practice of changing reality. If you want to know the taste of a pear, you must change the pear by eating it yourself.
MAO ZEDONG, *On Practice*, July 1937

The mark of the immature man is that he wants to die nobly for a cause, while the mark of the mature man is that he wants to live humbly for one.
WILHELM STEKEL, (1868-1940)

Grace is given of God, but knowledge is bought in the market.
ARTHUR HUGH CLOUGH, (1819-61), *The Bothie of Toberna-Vuolich*, (1848)

Experience is not what happens to a man; it is what a man does with what happens to him.
ALDOUS HUXLEY, (1894-1963), *Texts and Pretexts*, (1932)

We had the experience but missed the meaning.
T.S.ELIOT, (1888-1965), *Four Quartets*, The Dry Salvages, (1941)

I learned ... that one can never go back, that one should not ever try to go back - that the essence of life is going forward. Life is really a One Way Street.
AGATHA CHRISTIE, (1890-1976), *At Bertram's Hotel*, (1965)

How many roads must a man walk down
Before you can call him a man?...
The answer, my friend, is blowin' in the wind,
The answer is blowin' in the wind.
BOB DYLAN, 1941-, *Blowin' in the Wind*, (1962 song)

Never send a boy to do a
man's job.
PROVERB

And so, from hour to hour, we
ripe and ripe,
And then from hour to hour,
we rot and rot:
And thereby hangs a tale.
WILLIAM SHAKESPEARE,
1564-1616, *As You Like It*,
(1599)

Every human being on this
earth is born with a tragedy,
and it isn't original sin. He's
born with the tragedy that he
has to grow up ... He has to
lose everything that is lovely
and fight for a new loveliness
of his own making, and it's a
tragedy. A lot of people don't
have the courage to do it.
HELEN HAYES, *Showcase*,
(1966)

Adventure can be an end in
itself. Self-discovery is the
secret ingredient that fuels
daring.
GRACE LICHTENSTEIN,
Machisma, (1981)

Grown up, and that is a
terribly hard thing to do. It is
much easier to skip it and go
from one childhood to
another.
F. SCOTT FITZGERALD,
The Crack-Up, (1936)

The process of maturing is an
art to be learned, an effort to
be sustained. By the age of
fifty you have made yourself
what you are and if it is good
it is better than your youth.
MARYA MANNES, *More in
Anger*, (1958)

One does not discover new
lands without consenting to
lose sight of the shore for a
very long time.
ANDRÉ GIDE, *The
Counterfeiters*, (1926)

Without adventure
civilisation is in full decay.
A.N. WHITEHEAD,
Adventures of Ideas, (1933)

FIVE

ANCIENT GREECE

Among those who say that the first principle is one and mobile and boundless is to be reckoned Anaximander of Miletus, the son of Praxiades, the successor and follower of Thales. He said that "the boundless" was the first principle and element of the things that are, being the first to make use of this term in describing the first principle ... That from which things take their origin, into that again they pass away, as destiny orders.

Theophr. Fr. 2 ap. Simplic. Phys. 24 (Dox. 476; R.P. 12).

There is one god, supreme among gods and men; resembling mortals neither in form nor in mind. The whole of him sees, the whole of him thinks, the whole of him hears. Without toil he rules all things by the power of his mind. And he stays always in the same place, nor moves at all, for it is not seemly that he wander about now here, now there.

XENOPHANES, *The Fragments*

Listen, and I will instruct thee - and thou, when thou hearest, shalt ponder -

What are the sole two paths of research that are open to thinking.
One path is: That Being doth be, and Non-Being is not:
This is the way of Conviction, for Truth follows hard in her footsteps.
Th' other path is: That Being is not, and Non-Being must be;
This one, I tell thee in truth, is an all-incredible pathway.
For thou never canst know what is not (for none can conceive it),
Nor canst thou give it expression, for one thing are Thinking and Being.

PARAMENEDES

This Word is everlasting, but men are unable to comprehend it before they have heard it or even after they have heard it for the first time. Although everything happens in accordance with this Word, they behave like inexperienced men whenever they make trial of words and deeds such as I declare as I analyse each thing according to its nature and show what it is. But other men have no idea what they are doing when awake, just as they

forget what they do when they are asleep. One ought to follow the lead of that which is common to all men. But although the Word is common to all, yet most men live as if each had a private wisdom of his own.
HERACLITUS

Nothing comes into being without a reason, but everything arises from a specific ground and driven by necessity.
LEUCIPPUS from 2, Diels

Sophistic is nothing but apparent wisdom in no wise real, and the Sophist is only eager to get rich off his apparent wisdom which is not the true. Evidently these fellows seek rather to appear wise than to be wise without so appearing.

Of men some possess genuine health, others have the appearance only and are puffed up and deck themselves like victims for the altar. The former are fair in virtue of their own beauty; the latter look fair - when they have made their toilet.

The Sophist is a speculator in sham wisdom.
ARISTOTLE

When some one asked him what object of study he thought best for a man, he replied, 'Good conduct.' When he asked him again whether he thought 'good fortune' an object of study, he answered, 'Fortune' and 'Conduct' I think entirely opposed; for, for a person to light on anything that he wants without seeking it, I consider to be 'good fortune', but to achieve anything successfully by learning and study, I regard as 'good conduct' and those who make this their object of study appear to me to do well.

The best men, and those most beloved by the gods, he observed, were those who, in agriculture, performed their agricultural duties well, those who, in medicine, performed their medical duties well, and those who, in political offices, performed their public duties well; but he who did nothing well, he said, was neither useful for any purpose, nor

acceptable to the gods.
XENOPHON, *Memorabilia*,
III. 9, 14

There are two things that one
would rightly attribute to
Socrates: inductive reasoning
and universal definition. And
in fact these two things are
the very foundations of
knowledge. But Socrates did
not give his universals, or his
definitions, separate existence.
Others, however, did, and
called such reals 'ideas'.
ARISTOTLE, *Met.* 12, 4,
1078 b

You, Antipho, seem to think
that happiness consists in
luxury and extravagance; but I
think that to want nothing is
to resemble the gods, and that
to want as little as possible is
to make the nearest approach
to the gods; that the Divine
nature is perfection, and that
to be nearest to the Divine
nature is to be nearest to
perfection.
XENOPHON, *Memorabilia*, I.
6, 10

You may say generally that all
desire of good and happiness is
only the great and subtle

power of love; but they who
are drawn toward him by any
other path, whether the path
of money-making or
gymnastics or philosophy, are
not called lovers - the name of
the whole is appropriated to
those whose affection takes
one form only - they alone are
said to love, or to be lovers.
PLATO

Let me tell you then why the
Creator made this world of
generation. He was good, and
the good can never have any
jealousy of anything. And
being free from jealousy, he
desired that all things should
be as like himself as they
could be. This is in the truest
sense the origin of creation
and of the world, as we shall
do well in believing on the
testimony of wise men: God
desired that all things should
be good and nothing bad, so
far as this was attainable.
TIMÆUS

And he observed that the
expression 'to reason', had its
origin in people's practice of
meeting together to reason on
matters, and distinguishing
them, according to their

several kinds. It was the duty of every one, therefore, he thought, to make himself ready in this art, and to study it with the greatest diligence; for that men, by the aid of it, became most accomplished, most able to guide others, and most acute in discussion.
XENOPHON, *Memorabilia*, IV. 5, 18

"Imagine a number of men living in an underground cavernous chamber, with an entrance open to the light, extending along the entire length of the cavern, in which they have been confined, from their childhood, with their legs and necks so shackled that they are obliged to sit still and look straight forward, because their chains render it impossible for them to turn their heads round; and imagine a bright fire burning some way off, above and behind them, and an elevated roadway passing between the fire and the prisoners, with a low wall built along it, like the screens which conjurers put up in front of their audience, and above which they exhibit their wonders."

"I have it," he replied.
"Also figure to yourself a number of persons walking behind this wall, and carrying with them statues of men, and images of other animals, wrought in wood and stone and all kinds of materials, together with various other articles, which overtop the wall; and, as you might expect, let some of the passers-by be talking, and others silent."
"You are describing a strange scene, and strange prisoners."
"They resemble us," I replied. "For let me ask you, in the first place, whether persons so confined could have seen anything of themselves or of each other, beyond the shadows thrown by the fire upon the part of the cavern facing them?"
"Certainly not, if you suppose them to have been compelled all their lifetime to keep their heads unmoved."
"And is not their knowledge of the things carried past them equally limited?"
"Unquestionably it is."
"And if they were able to converse with one another, do you not think that they would

be in the habit of giving names to the objects which they saw before them?"

"Doubtless they would."

"Again: if their prison-house returned an echo from the part facing them, whenever one of the passers-by opened his lips, to what, let me ask you, could they refer the voice, if not to the shadow which was passing?"

"Unquestionably they would refer it to that."

"Then surely such persons would hold the shadows of those manufactured articles to be the only realities."

"Without doubt they would."

"Now consider what would happen if the course of nature brought them a release from their fetters, and a remedy for their foolishness, in the following manner: Let us suppose that one of them has been released, and compelled suddenly to stand up, and turn his neck round and walk with open eyes toward the light; and let us suppose that he goes through all these actions with pain, and that the dazzling splendour renders him incapable of discerning those objects of which he used formerly to see the shadows. What answer should you expect him to make, if some one were to tell him that in those days he was watching foolish phantoms, but that now he is somewhat nearer to reality, and is turned toward things more real, and sees more correctly; above all, if he were to point out to him the several objects that are passing by, and question him, and compel him to answer what they are? Should you not expect him to be puzzled, and to regard his old visions as truer than the objects now forced upon his notice?"

"Yes, much truer."

"And if he were further compelled to gaze at the light itself, would not his eyes, think you, be distressed, and would he not shrink and turn away to the things which he could see distinctly, and consider them to be really clearer than the things pointed out to him?"

"Just so."

"And if some one were to drag him violently up the rough and steep ascent from the cavern, and refuse to let him go till he had drawn him out into the light of the sun, would he not, think you, be vexed and indignant at such treatment, and on reaching the light, would he not find his eyes so dazzled by the glare as to be incapable of making out so much as one of the objects that are now called true?"

"Yes, he would find it so at first."

"Hence, I suppose, habit will be necessary to enable him to perceive objects in that upper world. At first he will be most successful in distinguishing shadows; then he will discern the reflections of men and other things in water, and afterward the realities; and after this he will raise his eyes to encounter the light of the moon and stars, finding it less difficult to study the heavenly bodies and the heaven itself by night, than the sun and the sun's light by day."

"Doubtless."

"Last of all, I imagine, he will be able to observe and contemplate the nature of the sun, not as it appears in water or on alien ground, but as it is in itself in its own territory."

"Of course."

"His next step will be to draw the conclusion, that the sun is the author of the seasons and the years, and the guardian of all things in the visible world, and in a manner the cause of all those things which he and his companions used to see."

"Obviously, this will be his next step."

"What then? When he recalls to mind his first habitation, and the wisdom of the place, and his old fellow-prisoners, do you not think he will congratulate himself on the change, and pity them?"

"Assuredly he will."

"And if it was their practice in those days to receive honour and commendations one from another, and to give prizes to him who had the keenest eye for a passing object, and who remembered best all that used to precede and follow and accompany it, and from these data divined most ably what was going to come next, do you fancy that he will covet these prizes, and envy those who receive honour and exercise authority among them? Do you not rather imagine that he will feel what Homer describes, and wish extremely

    'To drudge on the lands of a master,

    Under a portionless wight,' and be ready to go through anything, rather than entertain those opinions, and live in that fashion?

"For my own part," he replied, "I am quite of that opinion. I believe he would consent to go through anything rather than live in that way."

"And now consider what would happen if such a man were to descend again and seat himself on his old seat? Coming so suddenly out of the sun, would he not find his eyes blinded with the gloom of the place?"

"Certainly, he would."

"And if he were forced to deliver his opinion again, touching the shadows aforesaid, and to enter the lists against those who had always been prisoners, while his sight continued dim, and his eyes unsteady, - and if this process of initiation lasted a considerable time, would he not be made a laughing-stock, and would it not be said of him, that he had gone up only to come back again with his eyesight destroyed, and that it was not worth while even to attempt the ascent? And if any one endeavoured to set them free and carry them to the light, would they not go so far as to put him to death, if they could only manage to get him into their power?"

"Yes, that they would."

"Now this imaginary case, my dear Glaucon, you must apply in all its parts to our former statements, by comparing the region which the eye reveals to the prison-house, and the light of the fire therein to the power of the sun: and if, by the upward ascent and the contemplation of the upper world, you understand the mounting of the soul into the intellectual region, you will hit the tendency of my own surmises, since you desire to be told what they are; though, indeed, God only knows whether they are correct. But, be that as it may, the view which I take of the subject is to the following effect: In the world of knowledge, the essential Form of Good is the limit of our inquiries, and can barely be perceived; but, when perceived, we cannot help concluding that it is in every case the source of all that is bright and beautiful, - in the visible world giving birth to light and its master, and in the intellectual world dispensing, immediately and with full authority, truth and reason; and that, whosoever would act wisely, either in private or in public, must set this Form of Good before his eyes."

"To the best of my power," said he, "I quite agree with you."

"That being the case," I continued, "pray agree with me on another point, and do not be surprised that those who have climbed so high are unwilling to take a part in the affairs of men, because their souls are ever loath to desert that upper region. For how could it be otherwise, if the preceding simile is indeed a correct representation of their case?"

"True, it could scarcely be otherwise."

"Well: do you think it a marvellous thing, that a person who has just quitted the contemplation of divine objects for the study of human infirmities should betray awkwardness, and appear very ridiculous, when with his sight still dazed, and before he has become sufficiently habituated to the darkness that reigns around, he finds himself compelled to contend in courts of law, or elsewhere, about the shadows of justice, or images which throw the shadows, and to enter the lists in questions involving the arbitrary suppositions entertained by those who have never yet had a glimpse of the essential features of justice?"

"No, it is anything but marvellous."

"Right: for a sensible man will recollect that the eyes may be confused in two distinct ways and from two distinct causes - that is to say, by sudden transitions either from light to darkness, or from darkness to light. And, believing the same idea to be applicable to the soul, whenever such a person sees a case in which the mind is perplexed and unable to distinguish objects, he will not laugh irrationally, but he will examine whether it has just quitted a brighter life, and has been blinded by the novelty of darkness, or whether it has come from the depths of ignorance into a more brilliant life, and has been dazzled by the unusual splendour; and not till then will he congratulate the one upon its life and condition, and compassionate the other; and if he chooses to laugh at it, such laughter will be less ridiculous than that which is raised at the expense of the soul that has descended from the light of a higher region."

"You speak with great judgement."

"Hence, if this be true, we cannot avoid adopting the belief, that the real nature of education is at variance with the account given of it by certain of its professors, who pretend, I believe, to infuse into the mind a knowledge of which it was destitute, just as sight might be instilled into blinded eyes."

"True; such are their pretensions."

"Whereas, our present argument shows us that there is a faculty residing in the soul of each person, and an instrument enabling each of us to learn; and that, just as we might suppose it to be

impossible to turn the eye round from darkness to light without turning the whole body, so must this faculty, or this instrument, be the perishing world, until it be enabled to endure the contemplation of the real world and the brightest part thereof, which, according to us, is the Form of Good. Am I not right?"

"You are."

"Hence," I continued, "this very process of revolution must give rise to an art, teaching in what way the change will most easily and most effectually be brought about. Its object will not be to generate in the person the power of seeing. On the contrary, it assumes that he possesses it, though he is turned in a wrong direction, and does not look toward the right quarter; and its aim is to remedy this defect."

PLATO, From *The Republic*

Science arises whenever from a number of notions derived from experience a universal conception is formed comprising all similar cases.

ARISTOTLE

Irresistible power and great
wealth may, up to a certain
point, give us security as far as
men are concerned; but the
security of men in general
depends upon the tranquillity
of their souls, and their
freedom from ambition.
EPICURUS

God is beneficial. Good is
also beneficial. It should
seem, then, that where the
essence of God is, there too is
the essence of good. What
then is the essence of God -
flesh? By no means. An
estate? Fame? By no means.
Intelligence: Knowledge?
Right reason? Certainly.
Here, then, without more ado,
seek the essence of good.
EPICTETUS

Now I assert that the mind
and the soul are kept together
in close union and make up a
single nature, but that the
directing principle, which we
call mind and understanding,
is the head so to speak and
reigns paramount in the whole
body. It has a fixed seat in the
middle region of the breast:
here throb fear and
apprehension, about these

spots dwell soothing joys;
therefore here is the
understanding or mind. All
the rest of the soul
disseminated through the
whole body obeys and moves
at the will and inclination of
the mind. It by itself alone
knows for itself, rejoices for
itself, at times when the
impression does not move
either soul or body together
with it.
LUCRETIUS

Nevertheless we think that
knowledge and understanding
are properties of science rather
than of experience, and we
hold men of science to be
wiser than men of experience
on the ground that in every
case wisdom is to be ascribed
to one in proportion to the
extent of his knowledge. And
the reason why we do this is
because the former know the
reason why, the latter do not;
men of experience know the
fact, men of science know the
wherefore of the fact ...

In general the mark of
knowledge is ability to impart
what one knows to others; and
this is why we hold science to

be a higher form of knowledge than experience, men of science being able, men of experience being unable to impart their knowledge to others.
ARISTOTLE

For which reason, when he was framing the universe, he put intelligence in soul, and soul in body, that he might be the creator of a work which was by nature fairest and best. Wherefore, using the language of probability, we may say that the world became a living creature truly endowed with soul and intelligence by the providence of God.
PLATO

The riches of nature are defined and easily procurable; but vain desires are insatiable.
EPICURUS

Man, we might say, is not something simple, but has within him a soul. He has also a body attached to him, it may be as an instrument, it may be in some other capacity. Let us then distinguish the soul from the body and have a look at the nature and character of them both. Evidently a body which is composite cannot in reason be lasting. Moreover our senses perceive its dissolution and disintegration and liability to corruption of every sort, the reversion of its ingredients each to its proper nature, the destruction of one part by another, and their change and corruption into things other than they were. This is particularly noticeable whenever the soul, which puts them in accord, is not present in a mass of matter.

It follows that if the body be a part of us, the whole of us is not immortal. And if it be an instrument, it must be given to us for a certain time as such. But the dominant part and the essential man himself would bear the same relation to the body as form to matter, or as a man to the instrument he uses.

In either case, however, the soul is the man's real Self.
PLOTINUS, *Enneads*, IV. 7, 1

All men understand as the object of what is called wisdom knowledge of ultimate causes and first principles, so that, as we said before, the man of experience is superior in point of wisdom to the man who merely trusts his senses, whatever the sense may be, and the man of science is superior to the man of experience, the architect to the manual labourer, theory to practice. It is evident from all this that wisdom is the knowledge of causes and first principles of some kind or other.

ARISTOTLE, *Criticism of the Theory of Ideas*

The happiest men are they who have arrived at the point of having nothing to fear from those who surround them.

EPICURUS

But you are a primary existence. You are a distinct portion of the essence of God, and contain a certain part of him in yourself. Why then are you ignorant of your noble birth? Why do not you consider whence you came? Why do not you remember, when you are eating, who you are who eat, and whom you feed? When you are in the company of women, when you are conversing, when you are exercising, when you are disputing, do not you know that it is the Divine you feed, the Divine you exercise? You carry a God about with you, poor wretch, and know nothing of it. Do you suppose I mean some god without you of gold or silver? It is within yourself that you carry him; and you do not observe that you profane him by impure thoughts and unclean actions. If the mere external image of God were present, you would not dare to act as you do; and when God himself is within you, and hears and sees all, are not you ashamed to think and act thus - insensible of your own nature, and at enmity with God?

But we are anxious about this paltry body or estate of ours, or about what Caesar thinks, and not at all about anything internal.

EPICTETUS, *Ench.* XXXI. *Disc.* II. 13

Everything which exists, both primary existences and whatsoever is in any way spoken of as being, exists by

virtue of its unity. For what would a thing be were it not one thing? Take away its unity and it is no longer what we define it to be.
PLOTINUS, *Enneads*, VI. 9, 1, 757 A (C. p. 1385; V. II. 518)

Justice has no independent existence; it results from mutual contracts, and establishes itself wherever there is a mutual engagement to guard against doing or sustaining mutual injury.
EPICURUS

But why then do we not remain in the vision? I reply, because we have never wholly come forth from our earthly selves. But there shall come a time for us when the vision will be unbroken, and we are no longer disturbed by any unrest of the body. It is not the faculty of vision which is disturbed but some other, when the seer leaves the vision unaccomplished, but deserts not the knowledge which lies in demonstration and belief and the dialectical operation of the soul. The seer and his seeing, however,

are no longer reason and reasoning, but superior to reason and prior to reason and extraneous to reason, even as is the object of the vision.
PLOTINUS, *Enneads*, VI. 9, 1

The just man is the freest of all men from disquietude; but the unjust man is a perpetual prey to all.
EPICURUS

Wonder is the feeling of a philosopher, and philosophy begins in wonder.
PLATO, *Theaetetus*, xi, (Socrates)

The soul then has naturally a love of God and desires to be united with him with the love which a virgin bears to a noble father. But when she has betaken herself to creation, deceived as it were in her nuptials, she exchanges her former love for mortal love, and is bereft of her father and becomes wanton. Still if she begin again to hate the wantonness of earth, she is purified and turns once more to her father and all is well with her. Those to whom this heavenly love is unknown may get some conception of it from earthly love, and what joy it is to obtain possession of what one loves most. Let him then reflect that these objects of his love are mortal and perishable, mere shadows for his love to feed upon, and soon turned to loathly things, because they are not the true beloved, nor our good, nor what we seek; whereas in the higher world we find the true beloved with whom it is possible for us to unite ourselves when we have seized and held it, because it is not clothed with flesh and blood.

He who has beheld this beloved knows the truth of what I say, how the soul then receives a new life when she has gone forth to it, and come to it and participated in it, so that in her new condition she knows that the giver of true life is beside her, and that she needs nothing else. Such an one knows also, however, that we must put all else away, and abide in the beloved alone, and become only it, stripping off all else that wraps us about; and hence that we must hasten to come forth from the things of this world, and be wroth at the bonds which bind us to them, to the end that we may embrace the beloved with all our soul, and have no part of us left with which we do not touch God. It is possible for us even while here in the body to behold both him and ourselves in such wise as it is lawful for us to see. Ourselves we see illumined, full of the light of the intelligible, or rather as that very light itself, pure, without heaviness, upward rising. Verily we see ourselves as made, nay, as being God himself. Then it is that we are kindled. But when we again sink to earth, we are, as it were, put out.
PLOTINUS, *Enneads*, VI. 9, 768 C (C. p. 1406, 1. 10; V. II. 521, line 20)

Of all the things which wisdom provides for the happiness of the whole life, by far the most important is the acquisition of friendship.
EPICURUS

SIX

ART

We must never forget that art is not a form of propaganda; it is a form of truth.
PRESIDENT JOHN F. KENNEDY, address, Amherst College

Art enlarges experience by admitting us to the inner life of others.
WALTER LIPPMANN, *The Golden Rule and After*

Real art is religion, a search for the beauty of God deep in all things.
EMILY CARR, (1935), *Hundreds and Thousands*, (1966)

The dignity of the artist lies in his duty of keeping awake the sense of wonder in the world. In this long vigil he often has to vary his methods of stimulation; but in this long vigil he is also himself striving against a continual tendency to sleep.
G.K. CHESTERTON, *Generally Speaking*, On Maltreating Words (1928)

Without tradition, art is a flock of sheep without a shepherd. Without innovation, it is a corpse.
SIR WINSTON CHURCHILL, *Time*, May 11, 1953

All art constantly aspires towards the condition of music.
WALTER PATER, *Studies in the History of the Renaissance*, Giorgione

Great art is precisely that which never was, nor will be taught, it is pre-eminently and finally the expression of the spirits of great men.
JOHN RUSKIN

Art must take reality by surprise. It takes those moments which are for us merely a moment, plus a moment, plus another moment, and arbitrarily transforms them into a special series of moments held together by a major emotion.
FRANCOISE SAGAN, interview, *Writers at Work*

The basic unit for contemporary art is not the idea, but the analysis of and extension of sensations.
SUSAN SONTAG, *One Culture and the New Sensibility*

Art, if it is to be reckoned as one of the great values of life, must teach men humility, tolerance, wisdom and magnanimity. The value of art is not beauty, but right action.
W. SOMERSET MAUGHAM

God is so very much, and so essentially an artist that there must be something wrong with those who despise art, even when they are pious and believe.
THEODOR HAECKER, Journal in the Night

If it's bad art, it's bad religion, no matter how pious the subject.
MADELEINE L'ENGLE, Walking on Water, (1980)

The most immoral and disgraceful and dangerous thing that anybody can do in the arts is knowingly to feed back to the public its own ignorance and cheap tastes.
EDMUND WILSON, Memoirs of Hecate County

The essence of all beautiful art, all great art, is gratitude.
FRIEDRICH NIETZSCHE

Everyone wants to understand art. Why not try to understand the song of a bird? Why does one love the night, flowers, everything around one, without trying to understand them? But in the case of a painting people have to understand ... People who try to explain pictures are usually barking up the wrong tree.
PABLO PICASSO, Artists on Art

The man who has honesty, integrity, the love of inquiry, the desire to see beyond, is ready to appreciate good art. He needs no one to give him an art education; he is already qualified.
ROBERT HENRI, The Art Spirit

A work of art has an author and yet, when it is perfect, it has something which is essentially anonymous about it.
SIMONE WEIL, Gravity ad Grace

The people who stand most stubbornly in the way of progress in any art are generally the very people who know most about it.
DEEMS TAYLOR

Criticism is powerless to reach art. Art proceeds itself in a region quite beyond the reach of other expression save itself.
JOHN JAY CHAPMAN, *Memories and Milestones*

We are all heirs to the loveliness of the visible world, but only by process of art can we be inducted into possession of this large estate.
C.E. MONTAGUE, *A Writer's Notes on His Trade*

This is the thing that I don't think you can come back to often enough; the tremendous importance of art to make one realize in the gravel of one's gizzard what otherwise might become simply an abstraction in the head.
ARCHIBALD MACLEISH

Great art is cathartic; it is always moral.
JOYCE CAROL OATES

Art is only a means to life, to the life more abundant. It merely points the way, something which is overlooked not only by the public, but very often by the artist himself. In becoming an end it defeats itself.
HENRY MILLER, *The Wisdom of the Heart*

Art flourishes when there is a sense of adventure, a sense of nothing having been done before, of complete freedom to experiment; but when caution comes in you get repetition, and repetition is the death of art.
ALFRED NORTH WHITEHEAD, *Dialogues of Alfred North Whitehead*

A painter told me that nobody could draw a tree without in some sort becoming a tree.
RALPH WALDO EMERSON, *Essays*, History

It needs a certain purity of spirit to be an artist, of any sort ... An artist may be a profligate and, from the social point of view, a scoundrel. But if he can paint a nude woman, or a couple of apples, so that they are a living image, then he was pure in spirit, and, for the time being, his was the kingdom of heaven.
D.H. LAWRENCE

That thrill of creation which we experience when we see a masterpiece is not unlike the feeling of the artist who created it; such a work is a fragment of the world which he has annexed and which belongs to him alone.
ANDRÉ MALRAUX, *The Voices of Silence*

There is only one difference between a madman and me. I am not mad.
SALVADOR DALI

True artists are the antennae of nature. Coming nature casts its artists before it.
A.R. ORAGE, *Essays and Aphorisms*

Being an artist means, not reckoning and counting, but ripening like the tree which does not force its sap and stands confident in the storms of spring without the fear that after them may come no summer. It does come. But it comes only to the patient, who are there as though eternity lay before them, so unconcernedly still and wide.
RAINER MARIA RILKE, *Letters to a Young Poet*

The ideal artist is he who knows everything, feels everything, experiences everything, and retains his experience in a spirit of wonder and feeds upon it with creative lust.
GEORGE BELLOWS, *Artists on Art*

The creative life is often a groping, a terrible stumbling until the artist finds himself doing what his subconscious has demanded all along.
ANDREW TURNBULL, *Thomas Wolfe*

Beauty is the ultimate principle and the highest aim of Art.
GOETHE

Many artists have said that when life itself becomes fully conscious, art as we know it will vanish. Art is only a stopgap, an imperfect effort to wrest meaning from an environment where nearly everyone is sleepwalking.
MARILYN FERGUSON, *The Aquarian Conspiracy*, (1980)

Arts may be learned by application - proportions and

attitudes may be studied and repeated - mathematical principles may be, and have been, comprehended and adopted; but yet there has not been hewn from the marble a second Apollo, and no measuring by compasses will ever give the secret of its power. The ideal dwelt in the Sculptor's mind, and his hands fashioned it.
JOHN RUSKIN

The greatest productions of art, whether painting, music, sculpture or poetry, have invariably this quality - something approaching the work of God.
D.T. SUZUKI

Thoroughly to know oneself, is above all art, for it is the highest art.
THEOLOGIA GERMANICA

In every block of marble I see a statue as plain as though it stood before me, shaped and perfect in attitude and action. I have only to hew away the rough walls that imprison the lovely apparition to reveal it to other eyes as mine see it.
MICHELANGELO

What quality is shared by all objects that provoke our aesthetic emotions? What quality is common to Sta. Sophia and the windows at Chartres, Mexican sculpture, a Persian bowl, Chinese carpets, Giotto's frescoes at Padua, and the masterpieces of Poussin, Piero della Francesca, and Cézanne? Only one answer seems possible - significant form. In each, lines and colours combined in a particular way, certain forms and relations of forms, stir our aesthetic emotions. These relations and combinations of lines and colours, these aesthetically moving forms, I call 'Significant Form'; and 'Significant Form' is the one quality common to all works of visual art.
CLIVE BELL, Art, page 8

A work of art may be simple, though that is not necessary. There is no logical reason why the camel of great art should pass through the needle of mob intelligence.
REBECCA WEST, Battlefield and Sky

All arts are brothers, each is a light to the other.

AMERICAN PROVERB, mid 19th Century

Painting is silent poetry, poetry is eloquent painting.
SIMONIDES, (circa 556-468 BC), Plutarch, *Moralia*

The poet ranks far below the painter in the representation of visible things, and far below the musician in that of invisible things.
LEONARDO DA VINCI, (1452-1519), from the *Notebooks of Leonardo da Vinci*

Artists are exposed to great temptations: their eyes see paradise before their souls have reached it, and that is a great danger.
PHYLLIS BOTTOME, *Innocence and Experience*, (1934)

God help the Minister that meddles with art!
LORD MELBOURNE, (1779-1848)

Art for art's sake is an empty phrase. Art for the sake of the true, art for the sake of the good and the beautiful, that is the faith I am searching for.
GEORGE SAND, (1804-76)

Artists are the antennae of the race, but the bullet-headed many will never learn to trust their great artists.
EZRA POUND, *Literary Essays*, (1954)

Historians make men wise; poets, witty; the mathematics, subtile; natural philosophy, deep; moral, grave; logic and rhetoric, able to contend.
FRANCIS BACON, (1561-1626), *Essays*, Of Studies, (1625)

Every good poem, in fact, is a bridge built from the known, familiar side of life over into the unknown. Science too, is always making expeditions into the unknown. But this does not mean that science can supersede poetry. For poetry enlightens us in a different way from science; it speaks directly to our feelings or imagination. The findings of poetry are no more and no less true than science.
C. DAY-LEWIS, (1904-72), *Poetry for You*, (1944)

Perfectionism is the enemy of art. Since art is essentially divine play, not dogged work, it often happens that as one

becomes more professionally driven one also becomes less capriciously playful.
ERICA JONG, *Parachutes & Kisses*, (1984)

True men of action in our time, those who transform the world, are not the politicians and statesmen, but the scientists. Unfortunately poetry cannot celebrate them, because their deeds are concerned with things, not persons, and are, therefore, speechless. When I find myself in the company of scientists, I feel like a shabby curate who has strayed by mistake into a drawing room full of dukes.
W.H. AUDEN, (1907-73), *The Dyer's Hand*, (1963)

Scientists are explorers, philosophers are tourists.
RICHARD FEYNMAN, (1918-88)

Without a strong cup to carry the emotion, it is only a curiosity. Great art can come to us only in strong cups. Without emotion, there is nothing to carry.
NADIA BOULANGER

A part of all art is to make silence speak. The things left out in painting, the note withheld in music, the void in architecture - all are as necessary and as active as the utterance itself.
FREYA STARK, *On Silence*

Art is the expression of a man's life, of his mode of being, of his relations with the universe, since it is, in fact, man's inarticulate answer to the universe's unspoken message.
VERNON LEE, *Renaissance Fancies and Studies*, (1895)

"Organic" is a word I'll stick by. It means the work is an extension of your blood and body; it has the rhythm of nature. This is something artists don't talk about much and it's not even well understood: the fact that there exists a state of feeling and that when you reach it, when you hit it, you can't go wrong.
NELL BLAINE, in *Originals*

Art attempts to find in the universe, in matter as well as in the facts of life, what is fundamental, enduring,

essential.
SAUL BELLOW, (1970)

I wanted to become a work of
art myself, and not an artist.
BERNARD BERENSON,
Diaries, (1947-58)

Abstract art? A product of
the untalented, sold by the
unprincipled to the utterly
bewildered.
AL CAPP, Li'l Abner
cartoonist

Deliver me from writers who
say the way they live doesn't
matter. I'm not sure a bad
person can write a good book.
If art doesn't make us better,
then what on earth is it for?
ALICE WALKER, (1986)

What was any art but an effort
to make a sheath, a mould, in
which to imprison for a
moment the shining, elusive
element which is life itself.
WILLA CATHER, The Song
of the Lark, (1915)

Art is the unceasing effort to
compete with the beauty of
flowers - and never
succeeding.
MARC CHAGALL, (1977)

In our daily lives - eating,
dressing, working, or seeking
amusement - art, good or bad,
is always with us. For most of
us, most of the time, it is bad art.
R.L. DUFFUS, North
American Review, (Sept 1936)

I do not think abstract art can
ever be as good as the art of a
religious age. It stands on a
different level of human
aspiration.
SIR ERNEST GOMBRICH

Great art is the expression of a
solution of the conflict
between the demands of the
world without and that
within.
EDITH HAMILTON, The
Greek Way, (1930)

The finest works of art are
precious, among other reasons,
because they make it possible
for us to know, if only
imperfectly and for a little
while, what it actually feels
like to think subtly and feel
nobly.
ALDOUS HUXLEY, Ends and
Means, (1937)

Our feeling for a work of art is
rarely independent of the

place it occupies in art history.
ANDRÉ MALRAUX, *The Voices of Silence*, (1951)

In those days, as a little child, I was living in Paradise and had no need of the arts, which at best are only a shadow of Paradise.
JOHN MASEFIELD, *So Long To Learn*

Another unsettling element in modern art is that common symptom of immaturity, the dread of doing what has been done before.
EDITH WHARTON, *The Writing of Fiction*, (1925)

The artist does not tinker with the universe; he re-creates it out of his own experience and understanding of life.
HENRY MILLER, *The Cosmological Eye*, (1939)

We are the heirs to the loveliness of the visible world, but only by the process of art can we be inducted into possession of this large estate.
C.E. MONTAGUE, *A Writer's Notes On His Trade*, (1930)

People don't learn to enjoy pictures because they seldom look at them; and they seldom look at pictures because they have never learnt to enjoy them.
RAYMOND MORTIMER

Great art is as irrational as great music. It is mad with its own loveliness.
GEORGE JEAN NATHAN, *House of Satan*

If your man says of some picture, "Yes but what does it mean?" ask him and keep on asking him, what his carpet means, or the circular patterns on his rubber shoe-soles. Make him lift up his foot to look at them.
STEPHEN POTTER, *One-Upmanship*, (1952)

Artistic genius in its reactions is like those extremely high temperatures which have the power to disintegrate combinations of atoms which they proceed to combine afresh in a diametrically opposite order.
MARCEL PROUST, *Remembrance of Things Past*, (1913-27)

A work of art is good if it has sprung from necessity.
RAINER MARIA RILKE, *Letter to a Young Poet*, (1903)

Nothing is so poor and melancholy as art that is interested in itself and not in its subject.
GEORGE SANTAYANA, *The Life of Reason*, Reason in Art, (1905)

Abstract art: a construction site for high fashion, for advertising, for furniture.
ADRIENNE MONNIER, (1939)

If it is art it is not for all, and if it is for all it is not art.
ARNOLD SCHOENBERG

The arts are an even better barometer of what is happening in our world than the stock market or debates in Congress.
HENRIK WILLEM VAN LOON, *The Arts*

A work of art has an author and yet, when it is perfect, it has something which is anonymous about it.
SIMONE WEIL, *Gravity and Grace*, (1927)

Art for art's sake is a philosophy of the well-fed.
CAO YU, Chinese playwright

Art is our chief means of breaking bread with the dead.
W.H. AUDEN, (1907-73)

Art and Religion are, then, two roads by which men escape from circumstances to ecstasy.
CLIVE BELL, *Art*, Part II.1

For me that is the definition of a great work - a landscape painted so well that the artist disappears in it.
PIERRE BOULEZ

Art is meant to disturb. Science reassures.
GEORGES BRAQUE, *Day and Night*, Notebooks, (1882-1963)

Blest be the art that can immortalise.
WILLIAM COWPER, (1731-1800)

Art is the only thing you cannot punch a button for. You must do it the old-fashioned way. Stay up and really burn the midnight oil.

There are no compromises.
LEONTYNE PRICE, *I Dream a World*, (1989)

Yes, the work comes out more beautiful from a material that resists the process, verse, marble, onyx, or enamel.
THÉOPHILE GAUTIER, *L'Art*, (1811-72)

Science is spectral analysis. Art is light synthesis.
KARL KRAUS, *Riddles*, (1874-1936)

Art is not a mirror to reflect the world, but a hammer with which to shape it.
VLADIMIR MAYAKOVSKY, (1893-1930)

All art deals with the absurd and aims at the simple. Good art speaks truth, indeed *is* truth, perhaps the only truth.
IRIS MURDOCH, *The Black Prince*

The artist must create himself or be born again.
DENISE LEVERTOV, *The Jacob's Ladder*, (1961)

Art comes to you proposing frankly to give nothing but the highest quality to your moments as they pass, and simply for those moments' sake.
WALTER PATER, *The Renaissance*, (1839-94)

Art is a lie which makes us realise the truth.
PABLO PICASSO, (1881-1973)

Conception, my boy, *fundamental brain-work*, is what makes the difference in all art.
GABRIEL ROSSETTI, (1828-82)

A work of art is a corner of creation seen through a temperament.
EMILE ZOLA, (1840-1902)

The artist is extremely lucky who is presented with the worst possible ordeal which will not actually kill him.
JOHN BERRYMAN, (1914-72)

Art is an affirmation of life, a rebuttal of death. And here we blunder into paradox

again, for during the creation of any form of art, which affirms the value and the holiness of life, the artist must die. To serve a work of art, great or small, is to die, to die to self.
MADELEINE L'ENGLE, *Walking on Water*, (1980)

That is what the title of artist means: one who perceives more than his fellows, and who records more than he has seen.
EDWARD GORDON CRAIG, *On the Art of the Theatre*

The more perfect the artist, the more completely separate in him will be the man who suffers and the mind which creates.
T.S. ELIOT, in *Palinurus*, (1888-1965)

The artist in his work ought to be like God in creation, invisible and all powerful; everywhere felt but nowhere visible.
GUSTAVE FLAUBERT, (1821-80)

Only he is an artist who can make a riddle out of a solution.
KARL KRAUS, *Riddles*, (1874-1936)

The most demanding part of living a lifetime as an artist is the strict discipline of forcing oneself to work steadfastly along the nerve of one's own most intimate sensitivity.
ANNE TRUITT, *Daybook*, (1982)

The artist's egoism is outrageous; it must be: he is by nature a solipsist and the world exists only in his imagination
W. SOMERSET MAUGHAM, *The Summing Up*, Chapter 61

The artist, like the idiot or clown, sits on the edge of the world, and a push may send him over it.
OSBERT SITWELL, *The Scarlet Tree*, (1892-1969)

All art constantly aspires towards the condition of music.
WALTER PATER, attributed to Schopenhauer

Fine art is that in which the hand, the head, and the heart of man go together.
JOHN RUSKIN, *The Two Paths*, Lecture II

Skill without imagination is craftsmanship and gives us many useful objects such as wickerwork picnic baskets. Imagination without skill gives us modern art.
TOM STOPPARD, *Artist Ascending a Staircase*, (1937-)

Art is the imposing of a pattern on experience, and our aesthetic enjoyment is recognition of the pattern.
A.N. WHITEHEAD, *Dialogues*, 228, (1861-1947)

Media saturation is probably very destructive to art. New movements get overexposed and exhausted before they have a chance to grow, and they turn to ashes in a short time. Some degree of time and obscurity is often very necessary to artists.
JOYCE JOHNSON, *Writing for Your Life*, (1992)

Poets and painters are outside the class system, or rather they constitute a special class of their own, like the circus people and the gipsies.
GERALD BRENAN, *Thoughts in a Dry Season*, Writing

One of the reasons why medieval and renaissance architecture is so much better than our own is that the architects were artists. Bernini, one of the great artists of seventeenth-century Rome, was a sculptor.
KENNETH CLARK, *Civilisation*, (1903-83)

Every man's work, whether it be literature or music or pictures or architecture or anything else, is always a portrait of himself.
SAMUEL BUTLER, *The Ways of All Flesh*, Chapter 14

The excellence of every art is its intensity, capable of making all disagreeables evaporate, from their being in close relationship with beauty and truth.
JOHN KEATS, Letter to G. and T. Keats, 21st December 1817

The whole of art is an appeal
to a reality which is not
without us but in our minds.
DESMOND MAC CARTHY,
Theatre, Modern Drama,
(1877-1952)

Music begins to atrophy when
it departs too far from the
dance ... poetry begins to
atrophy when it gets too far
from music.
EZRA POUND, *ABC of
Reading*, (1885-1972)

It would follow that
'significant form' was form
behind which we catch a
sense of ultimate reality.
CLIVE BELL, *Art*, Part I,
Chapter 3, (1881-1964)

Art is not a pastime, but a
priesthood.
JEAN COCTEAU, (1889-1963)

It is the artists who make the
true value of the world,
though at times they may
have to starve to do it. They
are like earthworms, turning
up the soil so things can grow,
eating dirt so that the rest of
us may eat green shoots.
ERICA JONG, *Serenissima*,
(1987)

Works of art, in my opinion,
are the only objects in the
material universe to possess
internal order, and that is why,
though I don't believe that
only art matters, I do believe
in Art for Art's sake.
E.M. FORSTER

I rarely draw what I see. I
draw what I feel in my body.
BARBARA HEPWORTH

But the Devil whoops, as he
whooped of old: "It's clever,
but is it art?"
RUDYARD KIPLING,
Conundrum of the Workshops,
(1865-1936)

The successful artist is one
who, among other things,
finds by luck, labour, instinct,
or whatever a form and image
to reflect in power (never in
literal representation) the
original sensory experiences
that were received by the
[child's] innocent mind. And
by contrast, a failed or weak
artist would then be one for
whom, among other things,
the way back is lost or
confused or the reflecting
image a counterfeit one or
mechanically imitative.

ELEANOR MUNRO,
Originals, (1979)

Art is not a special sauce
applied to ordinary cooking; it
is the cooking itself if it is
good.
W.R. LETHABY, *Art and
Workmanship*, (1857-1931)

Art is more godlike than
Science. Science discovers:
but Art creates.
JOHN OPIE

SEVEN

BEAUTY

I am of opinion that there is nothing so beautiful, but that there is something still more beautiful, of which this is the mere image or expression - a something which can neither be perceived by the eyes, the ears, nor any of the senses.
CICERO

I pray Thee, O God, that I may be beautiful within.
SOCRATES

Beauty - a living Presence of the Earth, surpassing the most ideal fair forms which craft of delicate spirits hath composed from Earth's materials - waits upon my steps, an hourly neighbour.

Paradise, and groves Elysian, why should they be a history only of departed things, or a mere fiction of what never was? for the discerning intellect of man, when wedded to this goodly Universe in love and holy passion, shall find these a simple produce of the common day.
WILLIAM WORDSWORTH

The soul enamoured of beauty, and pursuing it, cannot achieve its quest in selfishness and isolation; it must be purified by active sympathy with others.
SIR SYDNEY COLVIN

Why do we seek this lurking beauty in skies, in poems, in drawings? Ah! because there we are safe, there we neither sicken nor die. I think we fly to Beauty as an asylum from the terrors of finite nature. We are made immortal by the kiss, by the contemplation of beauty.
RALPH WALDO EMERSON, *Journals of Ralph Waldo Emerson*

The hours when the mind is absorbed by beauty are the only hours when we really live.
RICHARD JEFFERIES, *Pageant of Summer*

After a lovely day out of doors by myself I saw that a single act of admiration is of little use. We must live with beauty, without any straining effort to admire, quietly attentive, absorbent, until by degrees the beauty becomes

one with us and alters our blood.
MARK RUTHERFORD, *Last Pages from a Journal*

I feel more and more that the instinct for beauty (spiritual and moral as well as natural) is the most trustworthy of all instincts, and the surest sign of the nearness of God.
A.C. BENSON, Excerpts from the *Letters of Dr. A.C. Benson to M.E.A*

What I care for is the beautiful itself and the vision of the beautiful, in so far as they manage to exist, or to be suggested: and this frail, intermittent, but actual realization of the beautiful I call the spiritual sphere. All life is, intrinsically, a part of it; but horribly interrupted and perturbed.
GEORGE SANTAYANA, *The Letters of George Santayana*

If we were charged so much a head for sunsets, if God sent round a drum before the hawthorn came in flower, what a work should we make about their beauty.

ROBERT LOUIS STEVENSON, *An Inland Voyage*

I find beauty in all things, even in the eyes that are blind to beauty.
KAHLIL GIBRAN, *Sand and Foam*

On the other hand a sense of beauty, although mutilated, distorted, and soiled, remains rooted in the heart of men as a powerful incentive. It is present in all the preoccupations of secular life. If it were made true and pure, it would sweep all secular life in a body to the feet of God.
SIMONE WEIL, *Waiting for God*

The most beautiful things in the world are those from which all excess weight has been removed.
HENRY FORD

Anyone who keeps the ability to see beauty never grows old.
FRANZ KAFKA

Beauty is a fruit which we look at without trying to seize it.
SIMONE WEIL, *Gravity and Grace*

We are conscious of beauty
when there is a harmonious
relation between something in
our nature and the quality of
the object which delights us.
PASCAL

Beauty is a manifestation of
secret natural laws, which
otherwise would have been
hidden from us forever.
GOETHE

A little beauty is preferable to
much wealth.
SA'DI, *Gulistan* (1258), 3.28

A passion for the manifold
beauties of earth is in its
nature identical with the
passion for transcendental
beauty.
SIR SYDNEY COLVIN

Beauty is nothing other than
the promise of happiness.
STENDHAL, *On Love*, 17

O Beauty, find thyself in love,
not in the flattery of thy
mirror.
RABINDRANATH
TAGORE, *Stray Birds*, 28

Beauty is truth, truth beauty,
- that is all ye know on earth,

and all ye need to know.
JOHN KEATS, *Ode on a
Grecian Urn*, (1819)

Anything in any way beautiful
derives its beauty from itself,
and asks nothing beyond
itself. Praise is no part of it,
for nothing is made worse or
better by praise.
MARCUS AURELIUS,
Meditations, (2nd century),
4.20

A thing of beauty is a joy for
ever:
Its loveliness increases; it will
never
Pass into nothingness; but still
will keep
A bower quiet for us, and a
sleep
Full of sweet dreams, and
health, and quiet breathing.
Therefore, on every morrow,
are we wreathing
A flowery band to bind us to
the earth,
Spite of despondence, of the
inhuman dearth
Of noble natures, of the
gloomy days,
Of all the unhealthy and o'er-
darkened ways
Made for our searching: yes, in
spite of all,

Some shape of beauty moves
away the pall
From our dark spirits. Such
the sun, the moon,
Trees old, and young,
sprouting a shady boon
For simple sheep; and such are
daffodils
With the green world they
live in; and clear rills.
JOHN KEATS, from
Endymion, (1817)

EIGHT

BIRTH

Do as your great progenitors
have done,
And, by their virtues, prove
yourself their son.
DRYDEN, *Wife of Bath*, line
398

We brought nothing into this
world, and it is certain we can
carry nothing out.
1 *Timothy* 6:7

Believing, hear what you
deserve to hear:
Your birthday as my own to
me is dear.
Blest and distinguish'd days!
which we should prize
The first, the kindest bounty
of the skies.
But yours gives most; for mine
did only lend
Me to the world; yours gave to
me a friend.
MARTIAL, *Epigrams*, Book
IX, Epigram 53

Not only around our infancy
Doth heaven with all its
splendors lie;
Daily, with souls that cringe
and plot,
We Sinias climb and know it
not.
LOWELL, *The Vision of Sir
Launfal*, Prelude to Part First

Our birth is but a sleep and a
forgetting;
The soul that rises with us,
our life's star,
Hath had elsewhere its
setting,
And cometh from afar:
Not in entire forgetfulness,
And not in utter nakedness,
But trailing clouds of glory do
we come
From God, who is our home:
Heaven lies about us in our
infancy!
Shades of the prison-house
begin to close
Upon the growing boy,
But he beholds the light, and
whence it flows;
He sees it in his joy.
WILLIAM
WORDSWORTH, *Ode on
Immortality*, Stanza 5

The infant, as soon as Nature
with great pangs of travail
hath sent it forth from the
womb of its mother into the
regions of light, lies, like a
sailor cast out from the waves,
naked upon the earth, in utter
want and helplessness, and
fills every place around with
mournful wailings and piteous
lamentations, as is natural for
one who has so many ills of

life in store for him, so many
evils which he must pass
through and suffer.
FRANCIS BACON, *De
Rerum Natura*, v. 223

I see the sleeping babe,
nestling the breast of its
mother;
The sleeping mother and
babe-hushed,
I study them long and long.
WALT WHITMAN, *Leaves of
Grass*, Mother and Babe

Lear: Thou must be patient:
we came crying hither;
Thou know'st the first time
that we smell the air
We wawl and cry, -
When we are born, we cry,
that we are come
To this great stage of fools.
WILLIAM SHAKESPEARE,
King Lear, Act IV, Scene vi,
line 182

A child is helpless in inverse
ratio to his age. He is at the
zenith of his powers while he
is an infant in arms. What on
earth is more powerful than a
very young baby?
ALINE KILMER, *Hunting a
Hair Shirt*

She ventured slowly down
that shadowed lane,
Now bright with wonder and
now dark with pain...
The trembling thread of life
stretched taut and thin,
But softly then, new radiance
filtered in.
LYDIA B. ATKINSON, *The
Answering Radiance*, Birth

Last night my child was born -
a very strong boy, with large
black eyes... If you ever
become a father, I think the
strangest and strongest
sensation of your life will be
hearing for the first time the
thin cry of your own child.
For a moment you have the
strange feeling of being
double; but there is something
more, quite impossible to
analyze - perhaps the echo in
a man's heart of all the
sensations felt by all the
fathers and mothers of his race
at a similar instant in the past.
It is a very tender, but also a
very ghostly feeling.

LAFCADIO HEARN,
*Lafcadio Hearn: Life and
Letters*, Volume 2

When one becomes a father, then first one becomes a son. Standing by the crib of one's own baby, with that world-old pang of compassion and protectiveness toward this so little creature that has all its course to run, the heart flies back in yearning and gratitude to those who felt just so towards one's self. Then for the first time one understands the homely succession of sacrifices and pains by which life is transmitted and fostered down the stumbling generations of men.
CHRISTOPHER MORLEY,
Mince Pie

We are born, so to speak, twice over; born into existence and born into life; born a human being and born a man.
JEAN-JACQUES
ROUSSEAU, *Émile*, Book 4

Except a man be born again, he cannot see the kingdom of God.
John 3:3

NINE

BUDDHISM

A Truth-finder, monks, one perfected, fully awakened, causes a Way to arise which had not arisen before; he brings about a Way not brought about before; he proclaims a Way not proclaimed before. He is a knower of the Way, understander of the Way, skilled in the Way. And now his disciples, monks, are wayfarers who follow after him. This is the distinction, the specific feature which distinguishes a Truth-finder, a perfected one, a fully awakened one, from a monk who is freed by wisdom.
THE BUDDHA

Cease to do evil;
Learn to do good;
Cleanse your own heart;
This is the teaching of the Buddhas.
H.P. BLAVATSKEY, From *Voice of the Silence*

All that we are is the result of what we have thought: it is founded on our thoughts and made up of our thoughts. If a man speak or act with a good thought, happiness follows him like a shadow that never leaves him.
OLD WISDOM SCHOOL

A warrior must only take care that his spirit is never broken.
SHISSAI

It is the 'Noble Eight-fold Path', the way that leads to the Cessation of Suffering, namely:
(1) Right Understanding.
(2) Right Mindedness.
(3) Right Speech.
(4) Right Action.
(5) Right Living.
(6) Right Effort.
(7) Right Attentiveness.
(8) Right Concentration.

This, Brothers, is the Middle Path which the Perfect One has found out, which makes one both to see and to know; which leads to peace, to discernment, to enlightenment, and to Nibbana which is free from suffering, free from torment, free from lamentation, free from pain, leading right onwards.

Give ear then, Brothers, for the Immortal is found. I reveal, I set forth the Truth.

As I reveal it to you, so act,
and you shall in no long time
see, face to face, realise, and
win, even in this life, to that
goal (Nibbana) for the sake of
which sons of good families
forsake their home for the
homeless life, and manifest,
realise, and obtain the
perfection of holiness even in
this life.
BUDDHA

The perfect way knows no
difficulties
Except that it refuses to make
preferences;
Only when freed from hate
and love
It reveals itself fully and
without disguise;
A tenth of an inch's difference,
And heaven and earth are set
apart.
If you wish to see it before
your own eyes
Have no fixed thoughts either
for or against it.
THIRD ZEN PATRIARCH

Our body is the Bodhi-tree,
And our mind a mirror bright.
Carefully we wipe them hour
by hour
And let no dust alight.
There is no Bodhi-tree

Nor stand of mirror bright.
Since all is Void,
Where can the dust alight?
HUI NENG

He who clings to the Void
And neglects Compassion,
Does not reach the highest
stage.
But he who practises only
Compassion
Does not gain release from
toils of existence.
He, however, who is strong in
practice of both,
Remains neither in Samsara
nor in Nirvana.
SARAHA

You yourself must make the
effort. Buddhas only point the
way. Those who have entered
the path and who meditate
will be free from the fetter of
illusion.
THE OLD WISDOM
SCHOOL

All wrong-doing arises
because of mind. If mind is
transformed can wrong-doing
remain?
BUDDHA

I have often been asked what I
thought was the secret of

Buddha's smile. It is - it can only be - that he smiles at himself for searching all those years for what he already possessed.
PAUL BRUNTON

Song of Meditation
Sentient beings are primarily all Buddhas;
It is like ice and water,
Apart from water no ice can exist;
Outside sentient beings, where do we find the Buddhas?
Not knowing how near the Truth is,
People seek it far away - what a pity!
They are like him who, in the midst of water,
Cries in thirst so imploringly;
They are like the son of a rich man
Who wandered away among the poor.
The reason why we transmigrate through the six worlds
Is because we are lost in the darkness of ignorance;
Going astray further and further in the darkness,
When are we able to get away from birth-and-death?
As regards the Meditation practised in the Mahayana,
We have no words to praise it fully:
The virtues of perfection such as charity, morality, etc.,
And the invocation of the Buddha's name, confession, and ascetic discipline,
And many other good deeds of merit, -
All these issue from the practice of Meditation;
Even those who have practised it for just one sitting
Will see all their evil karma wiped clean;
Nowhere will they find the evil paths,
But the Pure Land will be near at hand.
With a reverential heart, let them to this Truth
Listen even for once.
And let them praise it, and gladly embrace it,
And they will surely be blessed most infinitely.
For such as, reflecting within themselves,
Testify to the truth of Self-nature,
To the truth that Self-nature is no-nature,
They have really gone beyond the ken of sophistry.
For them opens the gate of

oneness of cause and effect,
And straight runs the path of
non-duality and non-trinity.
Abiding with the not-
particular which is in
particulars,
Whether going or returning,
they remain for ever
unmoved;
Taking hold of the no-thought
which lies in thoughts,
In every act of theirs they hear
the voice of the truth.
How boundless the sky of
Samadhi unfettered!
How transparent the perfect
moon-light of the fourfold
Wisdom!
At that moment what do they
lack?
As the Truth eternally calm
reveals itself to them,
This very earth is the Lotus
Land of Purity,
And this body is the body of
the Buddha.
HAKUIN

We are what we think. All
that we are arises with our
thoughts. With our thoughts
we make the world.
BUDDHA

Do not be idolatrous about or
bound to any doctrine, theory,
or ideology, even Buddhist
ones. Buddhist systems of
thought are guiding means;
they are not absolute truth.
VIETNAMESE BUDDHIST
PRECEPT

Your work is to discover your
work and then with all your
heart to give yourself to it.
BUDDHA

The point we emphasize is
strong confidence in our
original nature.
SHUNRYU SUZUKI

If I keep a green bough in my
heart, the singing bird will
come.
CHINESE PROVERB

Carpenters bend wood;
fletchers bend arrows; wise
men fashion themselves.
BUDDHA

This then, is the human
problem; there is a price to be
paid for every increase in
consciousness. We cannot be
more sensitive to pleasure
without being more sensitive
to pain.
ALAN WATTS

Zen is the game of insight, the game of discovering who you are beneath the social masks.
R.H. BLYTH

To be a warrior is to learn to be genuine in every moment of your life.
CHÖGYAM TRUNGPA

Mankind's role is to fulfil his heaven-sent purpose through a sincere heart that is in harmony with all creation and loves all things.
MORIHEI UESHIBA

The truth of Zen, just a little bit of it, is what turns one's humdrum life, a life of monotonous, uninspiring commonplaceness, into one of art, full of genuine inner creativity.
D.T. SUZUKI

If you can't meditate in a boiler room, you can't meditate.
ALAN WATTS

We become contemplative when God discovers Himself in us.
THOMAS MERTON

Those who seek the truth by means of intellect and learning only get further and further away from it.
HUANG-PO

The wisdom of enlightenment is inherent in every one of us. It is because of the delusion under which our mind works that we fail to realize it ourselves, and that we have to seek the advice and the guidance of enlightened ones.
HUI-NENG

Not knowing how near the truth is,
People seek it far away, what a pity!
They are like him who, in the midst of water,
Cries in thirst so imploringly.
HAKUIN

If we walk
The true Way
In our inmost heart,
Even without praying,
God will be with us!
TAKUAN

Within the domain of our mind there is a Tathagata of Enlightenment who sends forth a powerful light which illumines externally the six gates (of sensation) and purifies them. This light is strong enough to pierce through the six heavens of desire, and when it is turned inwardly to the Essence of Mind it eliminates at once the three poisonous elements, purges away our sin which might lead us to the hells, and enlightens us thoroughly within and without.

Within our mind there is a Buddha, and that Buddha within is the real Buddha. If Buddha is not to be sought within our mind, where shall we find the real Buddha? Doubt not that a Buddha is within your mind, apart from which nothing can exist.

Avert thy face from world deceptions; mistrust thy senses, they are false. But within thy body, the shrine of thy sensations, seek in the impersonal for the 'Eternal Man', and having sought him out, look inward; thou art Buddha.

OLD BUDDHIST TEXT

TEN

BUSINESS

Few people do business well who do nothing else.
LORD CHESTERFIELD

Business is really more agreeable than pleasure; it interests the whole mind, the aggregate nature of man more continuously, and more deeply.
WALTER BAGEHOT

It is not by any means certain that a man's business is the most important thing he has to do.
ROBERT LOUIS STEVENSON

Not a tenth of us who are in business are doing as well as we could if we merely followed the principles that were known to our grandfathers.
WILLIAM FEATHER

Never trust the advice of a man in difficulties.
AESOP, *Fables*, The Fox and the Goat, (6th century BC?)

He that hath little business shall become wise.
ECCLESIASTICUS 38

A man often thinks he has given up business, when he has only exchanged it for another.
MONTAIGNE

Economists set themselves too easy, too useless a task if in tempestuous seasons they can only tell us that when the storm is long past the ocean is flat again.
JOHN MAYNARD KEYNES, *A Tract on Monetary Reform*, Chapter 3

If all economists were laid end to end, they would not reach a conclusion.
GEORGE BERNARD SHAW (attributed)

Every business has a belief system - and it is at least as important as its accounting system or its authority system.
ALVIN TOFFLER, *The Adaptive Corporation*, Chapter 2

Buying and selling is good and necessary; it is very necessary and it may, possibly, be very good; but it cannot be the noblest work of man.
ANTHONY TROLLOPE, *Dr. Thorne*, Chapter 1
In the multitude of counsellors there is safety.

Proverbs 11:14 and 24:6

A completely planned economy ensures that when no bacon is delivered, no eggs are delivered at the same time.
LEO FRAIN, in the *Sunday Telegraph*, January 1965

If I had to give a definition of capitalism I would say: the process whereby American girls turn into American women.
CHRISTOPHER HAMPTON, *Savages*, Scene 16

Regarded as a means the business man is tolerable; regarded as an end he is not so satisfactory.
JOHN MAYNARD KEYNES, *Essays in Persuasion*, 4

He who builds to every man's advice will have a crooked house.
DANISH PROVERB

The playthings of our elders are called business.
ST. AUGUSTINE, *Conf.*, Book 1
You Irish gentlemen (said the attorney) are rather in too great a hurry in doing business. Business, sir, is a thing that must be done slowly to be done well.

MISS EDGEWORTH, *Essays on Irish Bulls*, Chapter 3

A business that makes nothing but money is a poor kind of business.
HENRY FORD, (1919)

A man without a smiling face must not open a shop.
CHINESE PROVERB

Try novelties for salesman's bait, for novelty wins everyone.
GOETHE, *Faust*, Part 1

In democracies, nothing is more great or more brilliant than commerce: it attracts the attention of the public, and fills the imagination of the multitude; all energetic passions are directed towards it.
ALEXIS DE TOCQUEVILLE, *Democracy in America*

The world is too much with us; late and soon,
Getting and spending, we lay

waste our powers:
Little we see in Nature that is
ours;
We have given our hearts
away, a sordid boon!
WILLIAM
WORDSWORTH, *The World
Is Too Much With Us*, (1807)

Everything which is properly
business we must keep
carefully separate from *life*.
Business requires earnestness
and method; life must have a
freer handling.
GOETHE, *Elective Affinities*,
4, (1809)

There are two times in a man's
life when he should not
speculate: when he can't
afford it, and when he can.
MARK TWAIN, *Pudd'nhead
Wilson's New Calendar*,
Following the Equator, 2.20,
(1897)

To be at ease is better than to
be at business.
BALTASAR GRACIAN

The advertisements in a
newspaper are more full of
knowledge in respect to what
is going on in a state or
community than the editorial
columns are.
HENRY WARD BEECHER,
Proverbs from Plymouth Pulpit,
(1887)

A bank is a place that will
lend you money if you can
prove that you don't need it.
BOB HOPE, *Life in the Crystal
Palace*, (1959)

We are all wise for other
people, none for himself.
RALPH WALDO
EMERSON, *Journals*, (1834)

Three women make a market.
GEORGE HERBERT, *Jacula
Prudentum*

Regarded as a means the
business man is tolerable;
regarded as an end he is not so
satisfactory.
JOHN MAYNARD KEYNES,
Essays in Persuasion, 4, A
Short View of Russia

Every business has a belief
system - and it is at least as
important as its accounting
system or its authority system.
ALVIN TOFFLER, *The
Adaptive Corporation*, Chapter 2

Live together like brothers,

and do business like strangers.
ARABIC PROVERB

Most are engaged in business
the greater part of their lives,
because the soul abhors a
vacuum and they have not
discovered any continuous
employment for man's nobler
faculties.
HENRY DAVID THOREAU

Time is the measure of
business.
FRANCIS BACON, *Essays*,
Of Dispatch, (1625)

Fuel is not sold in a forest, nor
fish on a lake.
CHINESE PROVERB

Boldness in business is the
first, second, and third thing.
THOMAS FULLER, M.D.,
Gnomologia, 1006, (1732)

A corporation is an artificial
being, invisible, intangible,
and existing only in
contemplation of law.
JOHN MARSHALL, *Trustees
of Dartmouth College v.
Woodward*, (1819)

A man who is always ready to
believe what is told him will
never do well, especially a

businessman.
PETRONIUS, *Satyricon*, (1st
century)

There are two fools in every
market: one asks too little,
one asks too much.
RUSSIAN PROVERB

You will always find some
Eskimos ready to instruct the
Congolese on how to cope
with heat waves.
STANISLAW LEC, *Unkempt
Thoughts*, (1962)

A false balance is
abomination to the Lord: but
a just weight is his delight.
Proverbs 11:1

Man does not only sell
commodities, he sells himself
and feels himself to be a
commodity.
ERICH FROMM, *Escape from
Freedom*, 4, (1941)

He who findeth fault meaneth
to buy.
THOMAS FULLER, M.D.,
Gnomologia, 2383, (1732)

A miser and a liar bargain
quickly.
GREEK PROVERB

The buyer needs a hundred eyes, the seller not one.
GEORGE HERBERT, *Jacula Prudentum*, (1651)

When a man is trying to sell you something, don't imagine he is that polite all the time.
EDGAR WATSON HOWE, *Country Town Sayings*, (1911)

Ours is the country where, in order to sell your product, you don't so much point out its merits as you first work like hell to sell yourself.
LOUIS KRONENBERGER, *Company Manners*, 3.3, (1954)

One beats the bush, another catches the bird.
GERMAN PROVERB

Pleasing ware is half sold.
GEORGE HERBERT, *Jacula Prudentum*, (1651)

A hundred sage counsels are lost upon one who cannot take advice; a hundred bits of wisdom are lost upon the unintelligent.
Panchatantra, 1, (circa 5th century)

Fetters of gold are still fetters, and silken cords pinch.
ENGLISH PROVERB

All of us, at certain moments of our lives, need to take advice and to receive help from other people.
ALEXIS CARREL, *Reflections on Life*

Advertising may be described as the science of arresting the human intelligence long enough to get money from it.
STEPHEN LEACOCK

It is far easier to write ten passably effective Sonnets, good enough to take in the not too inquiring critic, than one effective advertisement that will take in a few thousand of the uncritical buying public.
ALDOUS HUXLEY, *On the Margin*

If we define pornography as any message from any communication medium that is intended to arouse sexual excitement, then it is clear that most advertisements are covertly pornographic.
PHILIP SLATER, The Pursuit of Loneliness

ELEVEN

CHILDHOOD

Whosoever therefore shall humble himself as this little child, the same is greatest in the kingdom of heaven.
Matthew 17:4

When I was a child, I spake as a child, I understood as a child, I thought as a child; but when I became a man, I put away childish things.
I *Corinthians* 13:11

They are idols of hearts and of households;
They are angels of God in disguise;
The sunlight still sleeps in their tresses,
His glory still gleams in their eyes;
These truants from home and from Heaven,
They have made me more manly and mild;
And I know now how Jesus could liken
The kingdom of God to a child.
CHARLES M. DICKINSON,
The Children

Lo, children are a heritage of the Lord: and the fruit of the womb is his reward. As arrows are in the hand of a mighty man; so are children of the youth. Happy is the man that hath his quiver full of them.
Psalms 127:3-5

Children are to be won to follow liberal studies by exhortations and rational motives and on no account to be forced thereto by whipping.
PLUTARCH, *Of the Training of Children*

Train up a child in the way he should go; and when he is old, he will not depart from it.
Proverbs 22:6

Better a little chiding than a great deal of heart-break.
WILLIAM SHAKESPEARE,
The Merry Wives of Windsor,
Act V, Scene 3, line 11

It were better for him that a millstone were hanged about his neck, and he cast into the sea, than that he should offend one of these little ones.
Luke 17:2

Suffer the little children to come unto me, and forbid them not; for of such is the kingdom of God.
Mark 10:14

While others early learn to swear,
And curse, and lie, and steal;
Lord, I am taught Thy name to fear,
And do Thy holy will.
ISAAC WATTS, *Praise for Mercies Spiritual and Temporal*

Your children were vexation to your youth,
But mine shall be a comfort to your age.
WILLIAM SHAKESPEARE, *Richard III*, Act IV, Scene iv, line 305

There is in most men's minds a secret instinct of reverence and affection towards the days of their childhood. They cannot help sighing with regret and tenderness when they think of it.
SAINT AILRED OF RIEVAULX, *Christian Friendship*

If there is anything that we wish to change in the child, we should first examine it and see whether it is not something that could better be changed in ourselves.
C.G. JUNG, *Psychological Reflections*

The discontented child cries for toasted snow.
ARAB PROVERB

Innocence is the child, and forgetfulness, a new beginning, a game, a self-rolling wheel, a first movement, a holy Yea.
FRIEDRICH NIETZSCHE, *Thus Spake Zarathustra*

No one who has ever brought up a child can doubt for a moment that love is literally the life-giving fluid of human existence.
DR. SMILEY BLANTON, *Love or Perish*

The hearts of small children are delicate organs. A cruel beginning in this world can twist them into curious shapes.
CARSON McCULLERS, *The Member of the Wedding*

"To become as little children." Everyone bows his head in silence when this utterance is repeated. But no one truly believes it. And parents will always be the last to believe.
HENRY MILLER, *The Books in My Life*

We of this self-conscious, incredulous generation, sentimentalize our children, analyse our children, think we are endowed with a special capacity to sympathize and identify ourselves with children. And the result is that we are not more childlike, but our children are less childlike.
FRANCIS THOMPSON, *Works*, Volume III

That energy which makes a child hard to manage is the energy which afterward makes him a manager of life.
HENRY WARD BEECHER, *Proverbs from Plymouth Pulpit*, (1887)

Children need models rather than critics.
JOSEPH JOUBERT, *Pensées*, (1842)

Children are God's apostles, day by day sent forth to preach of love, and hope, and peace.
JAMES RUSSELL LOWELL, *On the Death of a Friend's Child*, (1844)

Children know the grace of God better than most of us.

They see the world the way the morning brings it back to them, new and born and fresh and wonderful.
ARCHIBALD MACLEISH, *JB*, 1, (1958)

A child is not frightened at the thought of being patiently transmuted into an old man.
ANTOINE DE SAINT-EXUPÉRY, *Flight to Arras*, (1942), 4

If men to not keep on speaking terms with children, they cease to be men, and become merely machines for eating and for earning money.
JOHN UPDIKE, *Assorted Prose*, A Foreword for Younger Readers, (1965)

Your children are not your children. They are the sons and daughters of Life's longing for itself ... you may strive to be like them, but seek not to make them like you.
KAHLIL GIBRAN, *The Prophet*, Of Children

There is always one moment in childhood when the door opens and lets the future in.
GRAHAM GREENE, *The*

Power and the Glory, Part 1, Chapter 1

Childhood's a risk we all take.
DAVID HUGHES, *The Pork Butcher*, page 114

Children have neither past nor future; and unlike us, they enjoy the present.
JEAN DE LA BRUYÈRE, *Characters*, Of Man, 51

Nothing is astonishing when everything is astonishing: that is the condition of the child.
ANTOINE DE RIVAROL, *Notes, réflexions et maximes*, Philosophe

It's never too late to have a happy childhood.
TOM ROBBINS, *Still Life with Woodpecker*, Epilogue

The most infallible way to make your child miserable is to accustom him to obtain everything he desires.
JEAN JACQUES ROUSSEAU, quoted in *Aphorisms on Education*, 82, (1800)

A child becomes an adult when he realizes that he has a right not only to be right but also to be wrong.
THOMAS. S. SZASZ, *The Second Sin*, Childhood

Children's talent to endure stems from their ignorance of alternatives.
MAYA ANGELOU, (1928-), *I Know Why the Caged Bird Sings*, (1969)

Eighteen is a good time for suffering. One has all the necessary strength, and no defences.
WILLIAM GOLDING, (1911-93), *The Pyramid*, page 12

TWELVE

CHRISTIANITY

Ye are the light of the world. A city that is set on an hill cannot be hid. Neither do men light a candle, and put it under a bushel, but on a candlestick; and it giveth light unto all that are in the house. Let your light so shine before men, that they may see your good works, and glorify your Father which is in heaven.
Matthew 5: 14-16

Jesus said: When you make the two One, you will become Sons of man, and if you say: "Mountain, move away," it shall move.
St. Thomas 106 P

A real 'transformation of consciousness' occurs in the individual subject from an awareness of his false self, or empirical ego, to the true self or person. Now the individual is no longer conscious of himself as an isolated ego, but sees himself in his inmost ground of being as dependent on Another or as being formed through relationships, particularly his relationship with God. By forgetting himself both as subject and as object of reflection, man finds his real self hidden with Christ in God. And so, as his self-consciousness changes, the individual is transformed; his self is no longer its own centre; it is now centred on God.
THOMAS MERTON

Come unto me, all ye that labour and are heavy laden, and I will give you rest. Take my yoke upon you, and learn of me; for I am meek and lowly in heart: and ye shall find rest unto your souls. For my yoke is easy, and my burden is light.
Matthew 11:28-30

And why call ye me, Lord, Lord, and do not the things which I say? Whosoever cometh to me, and heareth my sayings, and doeth them, I will shew you to whom he is like: he is like a man which built an house, and digged deep, and laid the foundation on a rock: and when the flood arose, the stream beat vehemently upon that house, and could not shake it: for it was founded upon a rock. But he that heareth, and doeth not, is like a man that without

a foundation built an house
upon the earth; against which
the stream did beat
vehemently, and immediately
it fell; and the ruin of that
house was great.
Luke 6:46-49

There is one Mind, one
omnipresent Mind,
Omnific. His most holy name
is Love.
Truth of subliming import!
with the which
Who feeds and saturates his
constant soul,
He from his small particular
orbit flies
With blest outstarting! From
himself he flies,
Stands in the sun, and with
no partial gaze
Views all creation; and he
loves it all,
And blesses it, and calls it
very good!
This is indeed to dwell with
the Most High!
Cherubs and rapture-
trembling Seraphim
Can press no nearer to the
Almighty's throne.
S.T. COLERIDGE from
Religious Musings

Blessed are the peacemakers:
for they shall be called the
children of God.
Matthew 5:9

Jesus said: Let him who seeks
not cease from seeking until
he finds; and when he finds,
he will be turned around; and
when he is turned around, he
will marvel, and he shall reign
over the All.
St. Thomas 2 2N

Blessed are they which do
hunger and thirst after
righteousness: for they shall be
filled.
Matthew 5:6

Are not five sparrows sold for
two farthings, and not one of
them is forgotten before God?
Luke 12:6

Then said Jesus to those Jews
which believed on him, If ye
continue in my word, then are
ye my disciples indeed; and ye
shall know the truth, and the
truth shall make you free.
John 8:31-32

Blessed are the pure in heart:
for they shall see God.
Matthew 5:8

The Corn was Orient and Immortal Wheat, which never should be reaped, nor was ever sown. I thought it had stood from Everlasting to Everlasting. The Dust and Stones of the Street were as Precious as GOLD. The Gates were at first the End of the World, The Green Trees when I saw them first through one of the Gates Transported and Ravished me; their Sweetnes and unusual beauty made my Heart to leap, and almost mad with Exstasie ... I knew no Churlish Proprieties*, nor Bounds nor Divisions: but all Properties and Divisions were mine... So that with much adoe I was corrupted; and made to learn the Dirty Devices of this World. Which now I unlearn, and becom as it were a little Child again, that I may enter into the Kingdom of God.
*i.e. properties, possessions
THOMAS TRAHERNE, Century III

Lay not up for yourselves treasures upon earth, where moth and rust doth corrupt, and where thieves break through and steal: but lay up for yourselves treasures in heaven, where neither moth nor rust doth corrupt, and where thieves do not break through nor steal: for where your treasure is, there will your heart be also.
Matthew 6:19-21

For whosoever shall do the will of God, the same is my brother, and my sister, and mother.
Mark 3:35

Let not your heart be troubled: ye believe in God, believe also in me. In my Father's house are many mansions: if it were not so, I would have told you. I go to prepare a place for you.
John 14:1-2

And he said, A certain man had two sons: and the younger of them said to his father, Father, give me the portion of goods that falleth to me. And he divided unto them his living. And not many days after the younger son gathered all together, and took his journey into a far country, and there wasted his substance with riotous living. And when he had spent all, there arose a mighty famine in that land; and he began to be in want. And he went and joined himself to a citizen of that country; and he sent him into his fields to feed swine. And he would fain have filled his belly with the husks that the swine did eat: and no man gave unto him. And when he came to himself, he said, How many hired servants of my father's have bread enough and to spare, and I perish with hunger! I will arise and go to my father, and will say unto him, Father, I have sinned against heaven, and before thee, and am no more worthy to be called thy son: make me as one of thy hired servants. And he arose, and came to his father ...

Luke 15:11-20

But when he was yet a great way off, his father saw him, and had compassion, and ran, and fell on his neck, and kissed him. And the son said unto him, Father, I have sinned against heaven, and in thy sight, and am no more worthy to be called thy son. But the father said to his servants, Bring forth the best robe, and put it on him; and put a ring on his hand, and shoes on his feet: and bring hither the fatted calf, and kill it; and let us eat, and be merry: for this my son was dead, and is alive again; he was lost, and is found. And they began to be merry. Now his elder son was in the field: and as he came and drew nigh to the house, he heard musick and dancing. And he called one of the servants, and asked what these things meant. And he said unto him, Thy brother is come; and thy father hath killed the fatted calf, because he hath received him safe and sound ...

Luke 15:20-27

And he was angry, and would not go in: therefore came his father out, and intreated him. And he answering said to his father, Lo, these many years do I serve thee, neither transgressed I at any time thy commandment: and yet thou never gavest me a kid, that I might make merry with my friends: but as soon as this thy son was come, which hath devoured thy living with

harlots, thou hast killed for him the fatted calf. And he said unto him, Son, thou art ever with me, and all that I have is thine. It was meet that we should make merry, and be glad: for this thy brother was dead, and is alive again; and was lost, and is found.
Luke 15:28-32

No man can serve two masters: for either he will hate the one, and love the other; or else he will hold to the one, and despise the other. Ye cannot serve God and mammon.
Matthew 6:24

Jesus said: If those who guide your Being say to you: "Behold the Kingdom is in the heaven," then the birds of the sky will precede you; if they say to you: "It is in the sea," then the fish will precede you. But the Kingdom is in your centre and is about you. When you know your Selves then you will be known, and you will be aware that you are the sons of the Living Father. But if you do not know yourselves then you are in poverty, and you are the poverty.
St. Thomas 3 7N

The only true joy is to escape from the prison of our own selfhood ... and enter by love into union with the Life Who dwells and sings within the essence of every creature and in the core of our minds.
THOMAS MERTON

Therefore I say unto you, Take no thought for your life, what ye shall eat, or what ye shall drink; nor yet for your body, what ye shall put on. Is not the life more than meat, and the body than raiment? Behold the fowls of the air: for they sow not, neither do they reap, nor gather into barns; yet your heavenly Father feedeth them. Are ye not much better than they?
Matthew 6:25-26

Be ye therefore merciful, as your Father also is merciful.
Luke 6:36

In the last day, that great day of the feast, Jesus stood and cried, saying, If any man thirst, let him come unto me,

and drink. He that believeth on me, as the scripture hath said, out of his belly shall flow rivers of living water.
John 7:37-38

Let your loins be girded about, and your lights burning; and ye yourselves like unto men that wait for their lord, when he will return from the wedding; that when he cometh and knocketh, they may open unto him immediately. Blessed are those servants, whom the lord when he cometh shall find watching: verily I say unto you that he shall gird himself, and make them to sit down to meat, and will come forth and serve them.
Luke 12:35-37

From the beginning to the end, I had two manners of beholding. The one was endless, continuant love, with secureness of keeping and blissful salvation, for of us this was all the shewing. The other was of the common teaching of Holy Church in which I was afore informed and grounded, and with all my will having in use and understanding. And the beholding of this went not from me: for by the shewing I was not stirred nor led therefrom in no manner of point, but I had therein teaching to love it and like it: whereby I might, by the help of our Lord and His grace, increase and rise to more heavenly knowing and higher loving.
JULIAN OF NORWICH

Ye are the salt of the earth: but if the salt have lost his savour, wherewith shall it be salted? it is thenceforth good for nothing, but to be cast out, and to be trodden under foot of men.
Matthew 5:13

Woman has the same spiritual dignity as man. Both of them have the same God, the same Teacher, the same Church. They breathe, see, hear, know, hope and love in the same way. Beings who have the same life, grace and salvation are called ... to the same manner of being.
CLEMENT OF ALEXANDRIA, *Tutor*, 1, 4

Woman is in the image of God equally with man. The sexes are of equal worth. Their virtues are equal, their struggles are equal … Would a man be able to compete with a woman who lives her life to the full?
GREGORY OF NYSSA, *Let us make Man in our Image and Likeness*, 2nd discourse

But Jesus said unto him, Follow me; and let the dead bury their dead.
Matthew 8:22

Labour not for the meat which perisheth, but for that meat which endureth unto everlasting life, which the Son of man shall give unto you: for him hath God the Father sealed.
John 6:27

Because God has become man, man can become God. He rises by divine steps corresponding to those by which God humbled himself out of love for men, taking on himself without any change in himself the worst of our condition.
MAXIMUS THE CONFESSOR, *Theological and Economic Chapters*

The wind bloweth where it listeth, and thou hearest the sound thereof, but canst not tell whence it cometh, and whither it goeth: so is every one that is born of the Spirit.
John 3:8

And as ye would that men should do to you, do ye also to them likewise.
Luke 6:31

Behold I send you forth as sheep in the midst of wolves: be ye therefore wise as serpents, and harmless as doves.
Matthew 10:16

Amid the tumult of outward cares, inwardly a great peace and calm is reigning, in love.
GREGORY THE GREAT, *Commentary on the Book of Job*

For whosoever will save his life shall lose it: and whosoever will lose his life for my sake shall find it. For what is a man profited, if he shall gain the whole world, and lose his own soul? or what

shall a man give in exchange
for his soul?
Matthew 16:25-26

God's love is by its nature
warmth. When it lights on
someone without any limit, it
plunges the soul into ecstasy.
That is why the heart of one
who has felt it cannot bear to
be deprived of it. But he
gradually undergoes a strange
alteration in proportion to the
love that enters into him.
These are the signs of that
love: his face becomes
inflamed with joy and his
body is filled with warmth...
His thought is in continual
dialogue with the Other.
ISAAC OF NINEVEH,
Ascetic Treatises, 24

Then said Jesus, Father,
forgive them: for they know
not what they do. And they
parted his raiment, and cast
lots.
Luke 23:34

Watch and pray, that ye enter
not into temptation: the spirit
indeed is willing, but the flesh
is weak.
Matthew 26:41

Peace I leave with you, my
peace I give unto you: not as
the world giveth, give I unto
you. Let not your heart be
troubled, neither let it be
afraid.
John 14:27

Jesus said: If a blind man
guides the Being of a blind
man, both of them fall to the
bottom of a pit.
St. Thomas 34 N

When perfect love has driven
out fear, or fear has been
transformed into love, then
everything that has been
saved will be a unity growing
together through the one and
only Fullness, and everyone
will be, in one another, a
unity in the perfect Dove, the
Holy Spirit... In this way,
encircled by the unity of the
Holy Spirit as the bond of
peace, all will be one body
and one spirit... But it would
be better to quote the very
words of the Gospel literally:
'That they may all be one;
even as thou, Father, art in me
and I in thee, that they also
may be in us' (John 17.21).
Now the bond of this unity is
glory. And that this glory is

the Holy Spirit, anyone familiar with Scripture will agree if he is attentive to the word of the Lord: 'The glory which thou hast given me, I have given to them' (John 17.22). He has indeed really given them such glory when he said: 'Receive the Holy Spirit' (John 20.22).
GREGORY OF NYSSA,
Homilies on the Song of Songs, 15

After this manner therefore pray ye: Our Father which art in heaven, hallowed be thy name. Thy kingdom come. Thy will be done in earth, as it is in heaven. Give us this day our daily bread. And forgive us our debts, as we forgive our debtors. And lead us not into temptation, but deliver us from evil: for thine is the kingdom, and the power, and the glory, for ever. Amen.
Matthew 6:9-13

Jesus said unto him, If thou canst believe, all things are possible to him that believeth.
Mark 9:23

It is better to keep silent and to be, rather than to speak but not to be. One who truly possesses Christ's words can also hear his silence in order to be perfect... Nothing is hidden from the Lord but our very secrets are close to him. Let us do everything in him who dwells in us so that we may become his temples.
IGNATIUS OF ANTIOCH,
Epistle to the Ephesians, 15, 1-3

Jesus saith unto him, Thomas, because thou hast seen me, thou hast believed: blessed are they that have not seen, and yet have believed.
John 20:29

'The kingdom of God is within you' (Luke 17:21). From this we learn that by a heart made pure... we see in our own beauty the image of the godhead ... You have in you the ability to see God. He who formed you put in your being an immense power. When God created you he enclosed in you the image of his perfection, as the mark of a seal is impressed on wax. But your straying has obscured Gods image ... You are like a metal coin: on the whetstone the rust disappears. The coin

was dirty, but now it reflects the brightness of the sun and shines in its turn. Like the coin, the inward part of the personality, called the heart by our Master, once rid of the rust that hid its beauty, will rediscover the first likeness and be real ... So when people look at themselves they will see in themselves the One they are seeking. And this is the joy that will fill their purified hearts. They are looking at their own translucency and finding the model in the image. When the sun is looked at in a mirror, even without any raising of the eyes to heaven, the sun's brightness is seen in the mirror exactly as if the sun's disc itself were being looked at. You cannot contemplate the reality of the light; but if you rediscover the beauty of the image that was put in you at the beginning, you will obtain within yourself the goal of your desires ...
The divine image will shine brightly in us in Christ Jesus our Lord, to whom be glory throughout all ages.
GREGORY OF NYSSA,
Homilies on the Beatitudes, 6

And all things, whatsoever ye shall ask in prayer, believing, ye shall receive.
Matthew 21:22

I say unto you, that likewise joy shall be in heaven over one sinner that repenteth, more than over ninety and nine just persons, which need no repentance.
Luke 15:7

And he said, So is the kingdom of God, as if a man should cast seed into the ground; and should sleep, and rise night and day, and the seed should spring and grow up, he knoweth not how. For the earth bringeth forth fruit of herself; first the blade, then the ear, after that the full corn in the ear. But when the fruit is brought forth, immediately he putteth in the sickle, because the harvest is come.
Mark 4:26-29

Fear not the coming of your God; fear not his friendship. He will not straiten you when he comes; rather he will enlarge you. So that you might know that he will enlarge you he not only

promised to come, saying, 'I will dwell with them,' but he also promised to enlarge you, adding, 'and I will walk with them.' You see then, if you love, how much room he gives you. Fear is a suffering that oppresses us. But look at the immensity of love. 'God's love has been poured into our hearts' (Romans 5.5).
AUGUSTINE OF HIPPO, *Sermons*, 23, 7

And Jesus said unto him, No man, having put his hand to the plough, and looking back, is fit for the kingdom of God.
Luke 9:62

And said, Verily I say unto you, Except ye be converted, and become as little children, ye shall not enter into the kingdom of heaven. Whosoever therefore shall humble himself as this little child, the same is greatest in the kingdom of heaven.
Matthew 18:3-4

For anyone who reflects, the appearances of beauty become the themes of an invisible harmony. Perfumes as they strike our senses represent spiritual illumination. Material lights point to that immaterial light of which they are the images.
DIONYSIUS THE AREOPAGITE, *Celestial Hierarchy*, I, 3

The world is one … for the spiritual world in its totality is manifested in the totality of the perceptible world, mystically expressed in symbolic pictures for those who have eyes to see. And the perceptible world in its entirety is secretly fathomable by the spiritual world in its entirety, when it has been simplified and amalgamated by means of the spiritual realities. The former is embodied in the latter through the realities; the latter in the former through the symbols. The operation of the two is one.
MAXIMUS THE CONFESSOR, *Mystagogia*, 2

For they all saw him, and were troubled. And immediately he talked with them, and saith unto them, Be of good cheer: it is I; be not afraid.
Mark 6:50

TWELVE - CHRISTIANITY   151

And when Jesus had cried with a loud voice, he said, Father, into thy hands I commend my spirit: and having said thus, he gave up the ghost.
Luke 23:46

Not every one that saith unto me, Lord, Lord, shall enter into the kingdom of heaven; but he that doeth the will of my Father which is in heaven.
Matthew 7:21

Believe me that I am in the Father, and the Father in me: or else believe me for the very works' sake.
John 14:11

All things are delivered unto me of my Father: and no man knoweth the Son, but the Father; neither knoweth any man the Father, save the Son, and he to whomsoever the Son will reveal him.
Matthew 11:27

I tell you that he will avenge them speedily. Nevertheless when the Son of man cometh, shall he find faith on the earth?
Luke 18:8

God's love for humanity wraps the spiritual in the perceptible, the superessential in the essence. It gives form… to what is formless and, through a variety of symbols, it multiplies and shapes Simplicity that has no shape.
DIONYSIUS THE AREOPAGITE, *Divine Names*, I, 4

He that is of God heareth God's words: ye therefore hear them not, because ye are not of God.
John 8:47

Then said Jesus unto his disciples, Verily I say unto you, That a rich man shall hardly enter into the kingdom of heaven. And again I say unto you, It is easier for a camel to go through the eye of a needle, than for a rich man to enter into the kingdom of God.
Matthew 19:23-24

Our Father who art in heaven: these are the words of those who enjoy intimacy with God, like a son in the bosom of his father.

Hallowed by thy name: that is to say, may it, being glorified through our witness, be hallowed among us, by people who will say: these are true servants of God.

Thy Kingdom come: the Kingdom of God is the Holy Spirit. We pray that he may be sent down upon us.

Thy will be done on earth as it is in heaven: the will of God is the salvation of every soul. What is accomplished among the powers of heaven we pray may come about for us on earth.

Our bread for tomorrow is what we shall inherit from God. We pray that we may have an earnest of it today, that is, that his sweetness may make itself felt in us in this world, causing a burning thirst.

EVAGRIUS OF PONTUS, *Cantenae on the Gospels,* Coptic documents

And Jesus said unto them, I am the bread of life: he that cometh to me shall never hunger; and he that believeth on me shall never thirst.
John 6:35

Every Christian, even if he lacks any education, knows that every place is a part of the universe and that the universe itself is the temple of God. He prays in every place with the eyes of his senses closed and those of his soul awake, and in this way he transcends the whole world. He does not stop at the vault of heaven but reaches the heights above it, and, as though out of this world altogether, he offers his prayer to God, led by God's Spirit.
ORIGEN, *Against Celsus*, 7, 44

Another parable put he forth unto them, saying, The kingdom of heaven is like to a grain of mustard seed, which a man took, and sowed in his field: which indeed is the least of all seeds: but when it is grown, it is the greatest among herbs, and becometh a tree, so that the birds of the air come and lodge in the branches thereof.
Matthew 13:31-32

And I say unto you, Ask, and it shall be given you: seek, and ye shall find; knock, and it shall be opened unto you.
Luke 11:9

While ye have light, believe in the light, that ye may be the children of light. These things spake Jesus, and departed, and did hide himself from them.
John 12:36

By prayer I mean not that which is only in the mouth, but that which springs up from the bottom of the heart. In fact, just as trees with deep roots are not shattered or uprooted by storms... in the same way prayers that come from the bottom of the heart, having their roots there, rise to heaven with complete assurance and are not knocked off course by the assault of any thought. That is why the psalm says: 'Out of the deep have I called unto thee, O Lord' (Psalm 130.1).
JOHN CHRYSOSTOM, *On the Incomprehensibility of God*, Sermon 5

It is the spirit that quickeneth; the flesh profiteth nothing: the words that I speak unto you, they are spirit, and they are life.
John 6:63

Again, the kingdom of heaven is like unto treasure hid in a field; the which when a man hath found, he hideth, and for joy thereof goeth and selleth all that he hath, and buyeth that field.
Matthew 13:44

And which of you with taking thought can add to his stature one cubit?
Luke 12:25

Again, the kingdom of heaven is like unto a merchant man, seeking goodly pearls: who, when he had found one pearl of great price, went and sold all that he had, and bought it.
Matthew 13:45-46

For the Father himself loveth you, because ye have loved me, and have believed that I came out from God.
John 16:27

But he answered and said, It is written, Man shall not live by bread alone, but by every word that proceedeth out of the mouth of God.
Matthew 4:4

And take heed to yourselves, lest at any time your hearts be overcharged with surfeiting, and drunkenness, and cares of this life, and so that day come upon you unawares. For as a snare shall it come on all them that dwell on the face of the whole earth.
Luke 21:34-35

Take therefore no thought for the morrow: for the morrow shall take thought for the things of itself. Sufficient unto the day is the evil thereof.
Matthew 6:34

But whosoever drinketh of the water that I shall give him shall never thirst; but the water that I shall give him shall be in him a well of water springing up into everlasting life.
John 4:14

And why take ye thought for raiment? Consider the lilies of the field, how they grow; they toil not, neither do they spin: and yet I say unto you, That even Solomon in all his glory was not arrayed like one of these. Wherefore, if God so clothe the grass of the field, which to day is, and to morrow is cast into the oven, shall he not much more clothe you, O ye of little faith?
Matthew 6:28-30

Jesus saith unto him, I am the way, the truth, and the life: no man cometh unto the Father, but by me.
John 14:6

Then Jesus answering said unto them, Go your way, and tell John what things ye have seen and heard; how that the blind see, the lame walk, the lepers are cleansed, the deaf hear, the dead are raised, to the poor the gospel is preached.
Luke 7:22

And Jesus said unto them, Because of your unbelief: for verily I say unto you, If ye have faith as a grain of mustard seed, ye shall say unto this mountain, Remove hence to yonder place; and it shall remove; and nothing shall be impossible unto you.
Matthew 17:20-21

And Jesus answered him, The first of all the commandments

is, Hear, O Israel; The Lord our God is one Lord: and thou shalt love the Lord thy God with all thy heart, and with all thy soul, and with all thy mind, and with all thy strength: this is the first commandment. And the second is like, namely this, Thou shalt love thy neighbour as thyself. There is none other commandment greater than these.
Mark 12:29-31

And why beholdest thou the mote that is in thy brother's eye, but considerest not the beam that is in thine own eye?
Matthew 7:3

Jesus answered them, and said, My doctrine is not mine, but his that sent me. If any man will do his will, he shall know of the doctrine, whether it be of God, or whether I speak of myself.
John 7:16-17

Enter ye in at the strait gate: for wide is the gate, and broad is the way, that leadeth to destruction, and many there be which go in thereat: Because stait is the gate, and narrow is the way, which leadeth unto life, and few there be that find it.
Matthew 7:13-14

And when he was demanded of the Pharisees, when the kingdom of God should come, he answered them and said, The kingdom of God cometh not with observation: neither shall they say, Lo here! or, lo there! for, behold, the kingdom of God is within you.
Luke 17:20-21

Jesus answered and said unto him, Verily, verily, I say unto thee, Except a man be born again, he cannot see the kingdom of God... Jesus answered, Verily, verily, I say unto thee, Except a man be born of water and of the Spirit, he cannot enter into the kingdom of God.
John 3:3,5

Beware of false prophets, which come to you in sheep's clothing, but inwardly they are ravening wolves.
Matthew 7:15

Jesus said: He who has in his hand, to him shall be given;

and he who does not have,
even the little that he has
shall be taken from him.
St. Thomas 41 P

How think ye? if a man have
an hundred sheep, and one of
them be gone astray, doth he
not leave the ninety and nine,
and goeth into the mountains,
and seeketh that which is
gone astray? And if so be that
he find it, verily I say unto
you, he rejoiceth more of that
sheep, than of the ninety and
nine which went not astray.
Even so it is not the will of
your Father which is in
heaven, that one of these
little ones should perish.
Matthew 18:12-14

Then spake Jesus again unto
them, saying, I am the light of
the world: he that followeth
me shall not walk in darkness,
but shall have the light of life.
John 8:12

Either what woman having
ten pieces of silver, if she lose
one piece, doth not light a
candle, and sweep the house,
and seek diligently till she
find it? And when she hath
found it, she calleth her

friends and her neighbours
together, saying, Rejoice with
me; for I have found the piece
which I had lost. Likewise, I
say unto you, there is joy in
the presence of the angels of
God over one sinner that
repenteth.
Luke 15:8-10

Jesus said unto them, Verily,
verily, I say unto you, Before
Abraham was, I am.
John 8:58

First one should know, and it
is indeed obvious, that man
has in himself a twofold
nature: body and spirit.
Hence a learned work says:
"Whoever knows himself
knows all creatures, for all
creatures are either body or
spirit." Hence also the
Scriptures say of humanity
that there is in us one man
outwardly and another man
inwardly.
Everything belongs to the
outer man which clings to the
soul, although enclosed by and
mixed with the flesh, and it
has a common activity with
each and every member
physically, such as the eye, the
ear, the tongue, the hand and

the like. And the Scriptures call all this the old man, the earthly man, the outer man, the hostile man, the servile man.

The second man that is in us is the inward man, whom the Scriptures call the new man, the heavenly man, the young man, the friend and the nobleman. This is what our Lord means when he says: "A nobleman went out into a far country and received for himself a kingdom and returned."
MASTER ECKHART

But Jesus answered them, My Father worketh hitherto, and I work.
John 5:17

But the very hairs of your head are all numbered.
Matthew 10:30

And he said unto his disciples, Therefore I say unto you, take no thought for your life, what ye shall eat; neither for the body, what ye shall put on. The life is more than meat, and the body is more than raiment. Consider the ravens: for they neither sow nor reap;

which neither have storehouse nor barn; and God feedeth them: how much more are ye better than the fowls? And which of you with taking thought can add to his stature one cubit? If ye then be not able to do that thing which is least, why take ye thought for the rest?
Luke 12:22-26

Our Lord says in the Gospel: "A nobleman went out into a far country to receive for himself a kingdom and returned." Our Lord teaches us in these words how nobly man is constituted by nature, and how divine is the state to which he can come by grace, and also how man can attain this. In addition, a large part of Holy Scripture is affected by these words.

When our endeavour and will are one with the will of God, then we attain the first step on the ladder of love and the holy life.

A good will is the foundation of all virtue; wherefore saith the prophet David: *O Lord, to thee have I*

fled, teach me to do thy will, for thou art my God. Thy good spirit shall lead me into the right land; that is, truth and virtue. A good will, united to the will of God, overcomes the devil and all sins, for it is full of God's grace; and it is the first offering that we should and must make to God, if we would live for Him. The man of good will follows and desires God that he may love and serve Him, now and for all eternity. This is his life and inward worship, which makes him to rejoice in peace with God, himself, and every other thing. And so the angels on the night when Christ was born, sang *Glory to God in the highest: and on earth peace to men of good will.* And never can good will fail of good actions, for, as our Lord saith, *A good tree bringeth forth good fruit.*
BLESSED JAN VAN RUYSBROECK

Take heed that ye despise not one of these little ones; for I say unto you, behold the face of my Father which is in heaven.
Matthew 18:10

For we walk by faith, not by sight.
2 Corinthians 17

And said unto them that sold doves, Take these things hence; make not my Father's house an house of merchandise.
John 2:16

Give not what is pure to dogs, lest they cast it on the dung-heap. Throw not pearls to swine lest they pollute them.
St. Thomas 93 N

Then saith Jesus unto him, Get thee hence, Satan: for it is written, Thou shalt worship the Lord thy God, and him only shalt thou serve.
Matthew 4:10

And he spake a parable unto them, saying, The ground of a certain rich man brought forth plentifully: and he thought within himself, saying, What shall I do, because I have no room where to bestow my fruits? And he said, This will I do: I will pull down my barns, and build greater; and there will I bestow all my fruits and my goods. And I

will say to my soul, Soul thou
hast much goods laid up for
many years; take thine ease,
eat, drink, and be merry. But
God said unto him, Thou fool,
this night thy soul shall be
required of thee: then whose
shall those things be, which
thou hast provided? So is he
that layeth up treasures for
himself, and is not rich toward
God.
Luke 12:16-21

I am the good shepherd: the
good shepherd giveth his life
for the sheep.
John 10:11

And the disciples were
astonished at his words. But
Jesus answereth again, and
saith unto them, Children,
how hard is it for them that
trust in riches to enter into
the kingdom of God! It is
easier for a camel to go
through the eye of a needle,
than for a rich man to enter
into the kingdom of God.
Mark 10:24-25

Behold the fowls of the air: for
they sow not, neither do they
reap, nor gather into barns;
yet your heavenly Father
feedeth them. Are ye not
much better than they?
Matthew 6:26

THIRTEEN

CIVILISATION

While nations ascend in civilisation, governments descend in administration.
JULES D'AUREVILLY

Civilisation does but dress men... Inside the civilised man stands the savage still in the place of honour.
HENRY DAVID THOREAU

Christianity has carried civilisation along with it, whithersoever it has gone; and, as if to show that the latter does not depend on physical causes, some of the countries the most civilised in the days of Augustus, are now in a state of hopeless barbarism.
ARCHBISHOP HARE

The true civilisation is where every man gives to every other every right that he claims for himself.
R.G. INGERSOLL

Every prison is the exclamation point and every asylum is the question mark in the sentences of civilisation.
S.W. DUFFIELD, Essays: Righteousness

The true test of civilisation is, not the census, nor the size of cities, nor the crops, - no, but the kind of man the country turns out.
RALPH WALDO EMERSON, Society and Solitude: Civilisation

Jesus wept; Voltaire smiled. Of that divine tear and of that human smile is composed the sweetness of the present civilisation.
VICTOR HUGO, Centenary Oration on Voltaire, 30 May 1878

It is perhaps hardly too much to say that the future of English fiction may rest with this Unknown Public - a reading public of three millions which lies right out of the pale of true literary civilisation - which is now waiting to be taught the difference between a good book and a bad.
WILKIE COLLINS, (1824-89)

It's certainly difficult to think of a better symbol of civilisation than books.
PHILIP LARKIN, (1922-85), Required Writing (1983)

It takes an old civilisation to set a novelist in motion - a proposition that seems to me so true as to be a truism. It is on manners, customs, usages, habits, forms, upon all these things matured and established, that a novelist lives - they are the very stuff his work is made of.
HENRY JAMES, (1843-1916)

The most fundamental of divisions is that between the intellect, which can only do its work by saying continually "thou fool," and the religious genius which makes all equal. That is why we have discovered that the mountain top and the monastery are necessary to civilisation. Civilisation dies of all those things that feed the soul, and both die if the Remnant refuses the wilderness.
W.B. YEATS, *Autobiography*

Because I see so many weak ones trodden down, I greatly doubt the sincerity of much that is called progress and civilisation. I do believe in civilisation, but only in the kind that is founded on real humanity. That which costs human life I think cruel, and I do not respect it.
VINCENT VAN GOGH from *Dear Theo*

Civilisation does not lie in a greater or lesser degree of refinement, but in an awareness shared by a whole people. And this awareness is never refined. It is even quite simple and straightforward.
ALBERT CAMUS, *Notebooks 1935-1942*

I say civilisation, but in reality I mean a *few men*, a few great, extraordinary individuals whose spiritual development has so far outstripped that of the ordinary man that they remain unique and exert over the great majority of men a tyranny which is to all intents and purposes obsessive. The cold, sterile crystallisation of the truths which they have perceived and acted upon forms the framework of what is called civilisation.
HENRY MILLER, *The Cosmological Eye*

The Widow Douglas she took me for her son, and allowed she would sivilize me; but it

was rough living in the house all the time, considering how dismal regular and decent the widow was in all her ways; and so when I couldn't stand it no longer I lit out.
MARK TWAIN

Neither St. Francis, nor Dante, nor Blake, nor Cézanne, nor Dostoyevsky was completely civilised, nor, given his work and all its implications, could he have been.
CLIVE BELL

By being civilised we mean that there is a certain list of things about which we permit a man to have an opinion different from ours. Usually they are things which we have ceased to care about: for instance, the worship of God.
AUBREY MENEN

We must not stay as we are, doing always what was done last time, or we shall stick in the mud. Yet neither must we undertake a new world as catastrophic Utopians, and wreck our civilisation in our hurry to mend it.
GEORGE BERNARD SHAW

A decent provision for the poor is the true test of civilisation.
SAMUEL JOHNSON

Civilisation is a limitless multiplication of unnecessary necessaries.
MARK TWAIN

Civilisation, in the real sense of the term, consists not in the multiplication, but in the deliberate and voluntary reduction of wants. This alone promotes real happiness and contentment, and increases the capacity for service.
MAHATMA GANDHI

Many clever men like you have trusted to civilisation. Many clever Babylonians, clever Egyptians, many clever men at the end of Rome. Can you tell me, in a world that is flagrant with the failures of civilisation, what there is particularly immortal about yours?
G.K. CHESTERTON

It is only an uncivilised world which would worship civilisation.
HENRY S. HASKINS

Civilisation is the lamb's skin in which barbarism masquerades.
THOMAS BAILEY ALDRICH, Leaves from a Notebook, Ponkapog Papers (1903)

The crimes of extreme civilisation are probably worse than those of extreme barbarism, because of their refinement, the corruption they presuppose, and their superior degree of intellectuality.
JULES BARBEY D'AUREVILLY, La vengeance d'une femme, Les Diaboliques (1874)

The civilisation of one epoch becomes the manure of the next.
CYRIL CONNOLLY, The Unquiet Grave (1945), 2

There is held to be no surer test of civilisation than the increase per head of the consumption of alcohol and tobacco. Yet alcohol and tobacco are recognisably poisons, so that their consumption has only to be carried far enough to destroy civilisation altogether.
HAVELOCK ELLIS, The Dance of Life (1923), 7

The social moulds civilisation fits us into have no more relation to our actual shapes than the conventional shapes of the constellations have to real star patterns.
THOMAS HARDY, Jude the Obscure (1895)

In the dust where we have buried the silent races and their abominations we have buried so much of the delicate magic of life.
D.H. LAWRENCE, quoted in Stewart L. Udall's The Quiet Crisis (1963), 1

Why build these cities glorious
If man unbuilded goes?
In vain we build the world, unless
The builder also grows.
EDWIN MARKHAM, Man Making (1920)

You can't say civilisation don't advance... for every war they kill you a new way.
WILL ROGERS, The Autobiography of Will Rogers (1949), 14

The passage from the state of nature to the civil state produces a very remarkable change in man, by substituting justice for instinct in his conduct.
ROUSSEAU, *The Social Contract* (1762), 1.8

Theory of true civilisation. It does not consist in gas or steam or turntables. It consists in the diminution of Original Sin.
CHARLES BAUDELAIRE, *Intimate Journals*, My Heart Laid Bare, 32

Civilisations are remembered by their artefacts, not their bank-rates.
STEPHEN BAYLEY, in the *Observer*, 9 March 1986

The English, on the strength of a few mechanical discoveries, have mistaken comfort for civilisation.
BENJAMIN DISRAELI, in W.R. Inge, *The End of an Age*, Chapter 7

Civilisation is the art of living in cities of such size that everyone does not know everyone else.
JULIAN JAYNES, *The Origin of Consciousness in the Breakdown of the Bicameral Mind*, Book 2, Chapter 1

FOURTEEN

CONDUCT

Our ingress into the world
Was naked and bare;
Our progress through the
world
Is trouble and care;
Our egress from the world
Will be nobody knows where:
But if we do well here
We shall do well there.
LONGFELLOW, *Tales of a
Wayside Inn*, Part 2

From another's evil qualities a
wise man corrects his own.
PUBILIUS SYRUS

To the real artist in humanity,
what are called bad manners
are often the most picturesque
and significant of all.
WALT WHITMAN, *Notes
Left Over* (1881), Emerson's
Books

It may be a good working
guide to conduct might be
framed on this ideal of living
to the fullest here and now.
STEPHEN MACKENNA,
*Journal and Letters of Stephen
Mackenna*

I am a firm believer in the
theory that the strongest
motive, whether we are
conscious of it or not, rules

our conduct.
ELLEN GLASGOW, *Letters of
Ellen Glasgow*

The ultimate test for us of
what a truth means is the
conduct it dictates or inspires.
WILLIAM JAMES

Be not afraid of going slowly,
be afraid only of standing still.
CHINESE PROVERB

The society of women is the
foundation of good manners.
(*Der Umgang mit Fraues ist das
Element guter Sitten.*)
JOHANN WOLFGANG
VON GOETHE, *Die
Wahlverwandtschaften*, Bk.ii, Ch. 5

The great secret is not having
bad manners or good manners
or any other particular sort of
manners, but having the same
manners for all human souls.
BERNARD SHAW,
Pygmalion, Act V

Training is everything. The
peach was once a bitter
almond; cauliflower is nothing
but cabbage with a college
education.
MARK TWAIN, *Pudd'nhead
Wilson's Calendar*

He that hath more manners
than he ought,
Is more a fool than he
thought.
THOMAS D'URFEY,
Quixote, Act II, Scene i

A fool beholdeth only the
beginning of his works, but a
wise man taketh heed to the
end.
UNKNOWN, *Dialogues of
Creatures*, CCVII (1535)

Conduct is three-fourths of
our life and its largest
concern.
MATTHEW ARNOLD,
Literature and Dogma,
Chapter 1

The sum of behaviour is to
retain a man's own dignity,
without intruding upon the
liberty of others.
FRANCIS BACON,
*Advancement of Learning: Civil
Knowledge*, Section 3

Acting without design,
occupying oneself without
making a business of it,
finding the great in what is
small and the many in the
few, repaying injury with
kindness, effecting difficult

things while they are easy, and
managing great things in their
beginnings, this is the method
of Tao.
LAO-TSZE, *The Simple Way*

What a man does, not what
he feels, thinks or believes, is
the universal yardstick of
behaviour.
BENJAMIN C. LEEMING,
Imagination

I see the right, and I approve
it, too;
Condemn the wrong, and yet
the wrong pursue.

(*Video meliora proboque*,
Deteriora sequor.)
OVID, *Metamorphoses*, Book
VII, line 20

Hast thou named all the birds
without a gun?
Loved the wood-rose and left
it on its stalk?
At rich men's tables eaten
bread and pulse?
Unarmed, faced danger with a
heart of trust?
And loved so well a high
behaviour,
In man or maid, that thou
from speech refrained,
Nobility more nobly to repay?

O, be my friend, and teach me
to be thine!
RALPH WALDO
EMERSON, *Forbearance*

Let every man be swift to
hear, slow to speak, slow to
wrath.
James 1:19

If not seemly, do it not; if not
true, say it not.
MARCUS AURELIUS,
Meditations, Book XII,
Section 17

My code of life and conduct is
simply this: work hard; play to
the allowable limit; disregard
equally the good and bad
opinion of others; never do a
friend a dirty trick;... never
grow indignant over anything;
... live the moment to the
utmost of its possibilities...
and be satisfied with life
always, but never with oneself.
GEORGE JEAN NATHAN,
Testament of a Critic, page 14

Love thyself last: cherish those
hearts that hate thee:
Corruption wins not more
than honesty.
Still in thy right hand carry
gentle peace,

To silence envious tongues.
Be just, and fear not:
Let all the ends thou aim'st at
be thy country's,
Thy God's and truth's.
WILLIAM SHAKESPEARE,
Henry VIII, Act III, Scene ii,
line 443

Be not careless in deeds, nor
confused in words, nor
rambling in thought.
MARCUS AURELIUS,
Meditations, Book VIII,
Section 51

Four things a man must learn
to do
If he would make his record
true:
To think without confusion
clearly;
To love his fellow-men
sincerely;
To act from honest motives
purely;
To trust in God and Heaven
securely.
HENRY VAN DYKE, *Four
Things*

Do all the good you can,
In all the ways you can,
In all the places you can,
At all the times you can,
To all the people you can,

As long as ever you can.
JOHN WESLEY, *Rules of Conduct*

What once were vices, are now the manners of the day.
SENECA, *Epistolae Ad Lucilium*, XXXIX

True is, that whilome that good poet sayd,
The gentle mind by gentle deeds is knowne;
For a man by nothing is so well bewray'd
As by his manners.
SPENSER, *The Faerie Queene*, Book VI, Canto iii, Stanza 1

Behaviour is a mirror in which every one shows his image.
GOETHE, *Die Wahlverwandtschaften*, II. 5

Whatever he did, was done with so much ease,
In him alone 'twas natural to please.
DRYDEN, *Absalom and Achitophel*, Part I, line 27

Manners must adorn knowledge, and smooth its way through the world. Like a great rough diamond, it may do very well in a closet by way of curiosity, and also for its intrinsic value; but it will never be worn, nor shine, if it is not polished.
CHESTERFIELD, *Letters*, 1 July 1748

Attention is like a narrow-mouthed vessel; pour into it what you have to say cautiously, and, as it were, drop by drop.
JOSEPH JOUBERT, *Pensées* (1842), 21.45

FIFTEEN

CRISIS

Courage is not simply one of
the virtues but the form of
every virtue at the resting
point, which means at the
point of highest reality.
C.S. LEWIS

Courage is the price
that life exacts
for granting peace,
the soul that knows it not,
knows no release
from little things;
knows not the livid loneliness
of fear,
nor mountain heights
where bitter joy can hear
the sound of wings.
AMELIA EARHART, U.S.
AVIATOR, From *The Sound
of Wings*, Chapter 1

The soul, secured in her
existence,
Smiles at the drawn dagger
And defies its point.
THOMAS ADDISON - *Cato*,
Act I, Scene iv

Be steadfast as a tower
That doth not bend
Its stately summit
To the tempest's shock.
DANTE – *Purgatorio*, verse 14

The people I respect must

behave as if they were
immortal and as if society was
eternal.
E.M. FORSTER, *Two Cheers
for Democracy* 1951

Life is mostly froth and bubble
Two things stand like stone
Kindness in another's trouble
Courage in your own.
ADAM LINDSAY GORDON
(1833-1870) *Ye Wearie
Wayfarer, Fytte*, 8

Every act of courage
Is a manifestation
Of the ground of being,
However questionable
The content of the act may
be.
PAUL TILLICH, *The Courage
to Be*

What is more mortifying than
to feel that you have missed
the plum for want of courage
to shake the tree?
LOGAN PEARSALL
SMITH, *Afterthoughts*

Courage is required not only
in a person's occasional crucial
decision for his own freedom,
but in the little hour-to-hour
decisions which place the
bricks in the structure of his

building of himself into a
person who acts with freedom
and responsibility.
ROLLO MAY, *Man's Search
for Himself*

We learn courageous actions
by going forward whenever
fear urges us back. A little
boy was asked how he learned
to skate. "Oh, by getting up
every time I fell down," he
answered.
DAVID SEABURY, *How to
Worry Successfully*

We must assume our existence
as broadly as we in any way
can; everything, even the
unheard-of, must be possible
in it. That is at bottom the
only courage that is demanded
of us: to have courage for the
most extraordinary, the most
singular and the most
unexplicable that we may
encounter.
RAINER MARIA RILKE,
Letters to a Young Poet

It is contrary to human nature
to court privations. We know
that the saints did court them,
and valued them as avenues to
grace ... We ourselves are not
hunting assiduously for

hardships; but which of us has
not summoned up courage
enough to laugh in the face of
disaster?
AGNES REPPLIER,
Americans and Others

Courage is rightly esteemed
the first of human qualities
because it is the quality which
guarantees all others.
WINSTON S. CHURCHILL.

He that climbs the tall tree
has won right to the fruit.
He that leaps the wide gulf
should prevail in his suit.
SIR WALTER SCOTT,
Blondel's Song, *Talerina*,
Chapter 26

Screw your courage to the
sticking-place,
And we'll not fail.
WILLIAM SHAKESPEARE,
Macbeth, Act I, Scene vii,
line 60

My dear thing, it all comes
back, as everything always
does, simply to personal pluck.
It's only a question, no matter
when or where, of having
enough.
HENRY JAMES, *The
Awkward Age*

The highest courage is not to
be found in the instinctive
acts of men who risk their
lives to save a friend or slay a
foe; the physical fearlessness of
a moment or an hour is not to
be compared with immolation
of months or years for the sake
of wisdom or art.
JOSEPH H. ODELL,
Unmailed Letters

Pick yourself up,
Dust yourself down,
And start all over again.
FRANK SINATRA

What do you mean by guts?
DOROTHY PARKER

Grace under pressure.
ERNEST HEMINGWAY

If the Creator had
a purpose in equipping
us with a neck,
He surely meant us
to stick it out.
ARTHUR KOESTLER,
Encounter, May 1970

The great virtue in life
is real courage,
that knows how to face facts
and live beyond them.
D.H. LAWRENCE, *Selected
Letters*

No coward soul is mine,
No trembler in the world's
storm-
troubled sphere:
I see Heaven's glories shine,
And faith shines equal,
arming me
from fear.
EMILY BRONTE, POETESS
AND NOVELIST (1812-
1848), from *No Coward Soul is
Mine*, (1846)

A heart full of courage and
cheerfulness needs a little
danger from time to time, or
the world gets unbearable.
FRIEDRICH NIETZSCHE

Courage, in the final analysis,
is nothing but an affirmative
answer to the shocks of
existence, which must be
borne for the actualization of
one's own nature.
DR. KURT GOLDSTEIN,
quoted in *Man's Search for
Himself* by Rollo May

We have short memories for
the many dangerous storms
before which we have sailed
without taking harm.
ANONYMOUS (HENRY S.
HASKINS), *Meditations in
Wall Street*

The fascination of danger is at the bottom of all great passions.
ANATOLE FRANCE, *The Anatole France Calendar*, selected by A.S. Rappoport

The peril of the hour moved the British to tremendous exertions, just as always in a moment of extreme danger things can be done which had previously been thought impossible. Mortal danger is an effective antidote for fixed ideas.
FIELD MARSHAL ERWIN ROMMEL, *The Rommel Papers*

No emotional crisis is wholly the product of outward circumstances. These may precipitate it. But what turns an objective situation into a subjectively critical one is the interpretation the individual puts upon it - the meaning it has in his emotional economy; the way it affects his self-image.
BONARO OVERSTREET, *Understanding Fear in Ourselves and Others*

The beauty of the soul shines out when a man bears with composure one heavy mischance after another, not because he does not feel them, but because he is a man of high and heroic temper.
ARISTOTLE, *Nicomachean Ethics* (4th century BC), line 10

The misfortune of the wise is better than the prosperity of the fool.
EPICURUS (3rd century BC), quoted in *Diogenes Laertius' Lives and Opinions of Eminent Philosophers* (3rd century AD)

That which does not kill me makes me stronger.
FRIEDRICH NIETZSCHE, "Maxims and Missiles," 8, *Twilight of the Idols* (1888)

Let us be of good cheer, however, remembering that the misfortunes hardest to bear are those which never come.
JAMES RUSSELL LOWELL, "Democracy," *Democracy and Other Addresses* (1887)

Sweet are the uses of adversity, which, like the toad, ugly and venomous, wears yet

a precious jewel in his head.
WILLIAM SHAKESPEARE,
As You Like It (1599-1600)
Act II, Scene i, line 12

This is courage in a man: to
bear unflinchingly what
heaven sends.
EURIPIDES, *Heracles* (circa
422 BC)

For an extraordinary situation,
extraordinary measures, and
sacrifices in proportion.
GRAFFITO WRITTEN
DURING FRENCH
STUDENT REVOLT, May
1968

When written in Chinese, the
word "crisis" is composed of
two characters - one
represents danger and the
other represents opportunity.
JOHN F. KENNEDY, address,
United Negro College Fund
Convocation, Indianapolis,
Ind., April 12, 1959

That oft the cloud that wraps
the present hour
Serves but to brighten all our
future days!
JOHN BROWN, *Barbarossa*,
Act V, Scene iii

Adversity is the first path to
truth.
BYRON, *Don Juan*, Canto
XII, Stanza 50

If aught can teach us aught,
Affliction's looks,
(Making us pry into ourselves
so near),
Teach us to know ourselves,
beyond all books,
Or all the learned schools that
ever were.
SIR JOHN DAVIES, *Nosce
Teipsum*: Introduction, Section
I, Stanza 38

Muster your wits: stand in
your own defence;
Or hide your heads like
cowards, and fly hence.
WILLIAM SHAKESPEARE,
Love's Labour's Lost, Act V,
Scene ii, line 85

I have chosen thee in the
furnace of affliction.
Isaiah 17:10

Adversity reminds men of
religion.
LIVY, *History*, Book V,
Chapter 51

Should the whole frame of
nature round him break

In ruin and confusion hurled,
He, unconcerned, would hear
the mighty crack,
And stand secure amidst a
falling world.
HORACE, *Odes*, III, iii

Once I ha' laughed at the
power of Love and twice at
the grip of the Grave,
And thrice I ha' patted my
God on the head that men
might call me brave.
RUDYARD KIPLING,
Tomlinson, line 65

A man should stop his ears
against paralysing terror, and
run the race that is set before
him with a single mind.
R.L. STEVENSON, *Virginibus
Puerisque: Æs Triplex*

We have hard work to do, and
loads to lift;
Shun not the struggle - face it;
'tis God's gift.
MALTBIE BABCOCK, *Be
Strong*

Be steadfast as a tower that
doth not bend
Its stately summit to the
tempest's shock.
(Sta come torre ferma, che
non crolla

Giammai la cima per soffiar
de' venti.)
DANTE, *Purgatorio*, Canto V,
line 14

O friends, be men, and let
your hearts be strong,
And let no warrior in the heat
of fight
Do what may bring him
shame in others' eyes;
For more of those who shrink
from shame are safe
Than fall in battle, while with
those who flee
Is neither glory nor reprieve
from death.
HOMER, *Iliad*, Book V, line
663

Oh fear not in a world like
this,
And thou shalt know erelong,
Know how sublime a thing it is
To suffer and be strong.
LONGFELLOW, *The Light of
Stars*, Stanza 9

Over a long period of time
you have been warned,
prepared and fortified to meet
violence and disorder; it is,
therefore, like good soldiers of
the Prince of Peace that you
find yourselves on duty. Do
not let a thought touched by

cynicism penetrate your armour; do not wonder that a Prince of Peace should need an army, for 'an armed man keepeth his goods in peace' and the servants of Christ are defending the citadels of the Spirit which giveth Life and not death. The sword of the Spirit frees all men because its discipline is upon the man who bears it.

And now a high resolve is essential. Prepare yourselves for inward strength, a refuge within undisturbed, a realm august, the kingdom of heaven within your own consciousness, and let no destructive human emotion draw you from it.
Every individual has, within himself, a great part to play, and let no one think he is too small, too insignificant. For the power of the kingdom of heaven, when man makes way for it to pour through him as a channel in the stillness of disciplined and controlled emotion, cannot be measured, and there is nothing too great, nothing too small.
MARY STRONG

Awake, arise, or be for ever fall'n!
MILTON, *Paradise Lost*, Book I, line 330

Gloucester, 'tis true that we are in great danger;
The greater therefore should our courage be.
WILLIAM SHAKESPEARE, *Henry V*, Act IV, Scene 1, line 1

He that leaves nothing to chance will do few things ill, but he will do very few things.
MARQUIS OF HALIFAX

Experience is the best teacher; but the school fees are heavy.
G.W.F. HEGEL

One stroke fells not an oak.
He that stays does the business.
Step after step the ladder is ascended.
He who goes slowly goes safely, he who goes safely goes far.
He that endures is not overcome.
ITALIAN PROVERBS

Demosthenes writes of King Philip of Macedon - "I beheld

Philip himself with whom we were at war for power and dominion, with one eye torn out by an arrow, his collar bone broken, his hand and leg maimed, ready to give up whatever part of his body fortune might choose to take, so that he might live in future with respect and honour."
AG, II, 27

Remember that there is nothing stable in human affairs; therefore avoid undue elation in prosperity, or undue depression in adversity.
SOCRATES

We have not wings, we cannot soar;
But we have feet to scale and climb,
By slow degrees, by more and more,
The cloudy summits of our time.

The mighty pyramids of stone
That, wedge-like, cleave the desert airs,
When nearer seen, and better known,
Are but gigantic flights of stairs.

The distant mountains, that uprear
Their solid bastions to the skies,
Are crossed by pathways, that appear
As we to higher levels rise.

The heights by great men reached and kept,
Were not attained by sudden flight,
But they while their companions slept,
Were toiling upwards in the night.
LO., *Ladder of St. Augustine*

Present suffering is not enjoyable, but life would be worth little without it. The difference between iron and steel is fire, but steel is worth all it costs. Iron ore may think itself senselessly tortured in the furnace, but when the watch-spring looks back, it knows better.
BABCOCK

Why then, you princes, do you with cheeks abashed behold our works, and think them shames, which are, indeed, nought else but the protractive trials of great Jove,

to find persistive constancy in
men? The fineness of which
metal is not found in fortune's
love: for the bold and coward,
the wise and fool, the artist
and unread, the hard and soft,
seem all affined and kin: but,
in the wind and tempest of
her frown, distinction, with
the broad and powerful fan,
puffing at all, winnows the
light away; and what hath
mass, or matter, by itself lies,
rich in virtue, and unmingled.
WILLIAM SHAKESPEARE

Times of great calamity and
confusion have ever been
productive of the greatest
minds. The purest ore is
produced from the hottest
furnace, and the brightest
thunderbolt is elicited from
the darkest storm.
COLTON

In adversity man sees himself
abandoned by others; he finds
that all his hopes are centred
within himself; he rouses his
soul; he encounters his
difficulties, and they yield
before him.
In prosperity he fancies
himself safe: he thinks he is
beloved by all who smile upon

him; he grows careless and
remiss; he does not see the
dangers before him; he trusts
to others, and, in the end,
they deceive him.
Better is the sorrow that leads
to contentment, than the joy
that renders a man unable to
endure distress and afterwards
plunges him into it.
Be upright in your whole life:
be content in all its changes.
And remember that he who
despairs of the end shall never
attain unto it.
DANDEMIS

'Tis good for men to love their
present pains
Upon example; so the spirit is
eased.
WILLIAM SHAKESPEARE

The higher moral courage can
look danger in the face
unawed and undismayed; can
encounter loss of ease, of
wealth, of friends, of your own
good name; can face a world
full of howling and of scorn -
aye, of loathing and of hate;
can see all this with a smile,
and, suffering it all, can still
hold on, conscious of the
result, yet fearless still.
PARKER

Perils, misfortune, want, pain, and injury come the way of every man who comes into the world; therefore, you should fortify your mind with courage and patience from your youth up, that you may bear with resolution any part of calamity that may come your way.

Let courage sustain you in the instant of danger, so that the steadiness of your mind shall carry you through; for calmness alleviates the weight of misfortunes, and by constancy you are able to surmount them.

In the hour of danger be not embarrassed; and in the day of misfortune, do not let despair overwhelm your soul.
DANDEMIS

Courage consists not in blindly overlooking danger, but in seeing it, and conquering it.
RICHTER

What he can brave, who, born and nurst
In danger's path, has dared her worst!
Upon whose ear the signal word
Of strife and death is hourly breaking;
Who sleeps with head upon the sword
His fever'd hand must grasp in waking.
MOORE

The firmest friendships have been formed in mutual adversity, as iron is most strongly welded by the fiercest fire.
WILLIAM SHAKESPEARE

That man who has never been in danger cannot answer for his courage.
LA ROCHEFOUCAULD

True valour, friends, on virtue founded strong,
Meets all events alike.
MALLET

Adversity's sweet milk, Philosophy.
WILLIAM SHAKESPEARE

He holds no parley with unmanly fears,
Where duty bids he confident steers,
Faces a thousand dangers at her call,

And, trusting to his God,
surmounts them all.
WILLIAM COWPER

Rocks have been shaken from
their solid base,
But what shall move a firm
and dauntless mind?
JOANNA BAILLIE

He is the most wretched of
men who has never felt
adversity.
WILLIAM SHAKESPEARE

Adversity borrows its sharpest
sting from our impatience.
BISHOP HORNE

Sweet are the uses of
adversity,
Which like the toad, ugly and
venomous,
Wears yet a precious jewel in
his head;
And this our life, exempt from
public haunt,
Find tongues in trees, books in
the running brooks,
And good in everything.
WILLIAM SHAKESPEARE

The important thing
is to pull yourself up by your
own hair
to turn yourself inside out

and see the whole world with
fresh eyes.
PETER WEISS, *Marat/Sade*
(1964), line 13

The coward and the small in
soul scarce do live.
One generous feeling, one
great thought, one deed
Of good, ere night would
make life longer seem
Than if each year might
number a thousand days,
Spent as is this by nations of
mankind.
We live in deeds, not years; in
thoughts, not breaths;
In feelings; not in figures on a
dial,
We should count time by
heart-throbs. He most lives
Who thinks most, feels the
noblest, acts the best.
Life's but a means unto an
end; that end,
To those who dwell in Him,
He most in them,
Beginning, mean and end to
all things, God.
PHILIP JAMES BAILEY from
Festus

He's truly valiant that can
wisely suffer
The worst that man can
breathe, and make his wrongs

His outside's; to wear them
like his raiment, carelessly;
And ne'er prefer his injuries to
his heart
To bring it into danger.
WILLIAM SHAKESPEARE

It is true, you cannot for a
moment be fearful, it is not
the role for a soldier. Attack
without fear and you will be
given courage for each
fraction of a moment.
Courage is what will steady
you; you need to bite into
courage and hold tight then
you will be free from the drill
sergeant of discipline. Only
the fearful are disciplined;
keep far ahead of your fears,
then you will be calm,
protected and completely safe.

Only the confident are quiet
and full of success, only they
can poke out their tongues at
the drill sergeant who is so full
of wind. Courage is a matter
of elan. When again in the
battle smoke where all things
swell big to frighten the child
in you, take out your little
drum and beat it hard and
armies of heroes will gallop
with the glint of eternal
valour on their helmets, for is
it not an eternal truth that a
child shall lead them?
Brave men are childlike.
MARY STRONG

SIXTEEN

DEATH

Death levels all things in his
march,
Nought can resist his mighty
strength;
The palace proud - triumphal
arch,
Shall mete their shadows
length;
The rich, the poor, one
common bed
Shall find, in the unhonour'd
grave,
Where weeds shall crown
alike the head
Of tyrant and of slave.
MARVEL

The body being only the
covering of the soul, at its
dissolution we shall discover
the secrets of nature - the
darkness shall be dispelled,
and our souls irradiated with
light and glory; a glory
without a shadow, a glory that
shall surround us; and from
whence we shall look down,
and see day and night beneath
us; and as now we cannot lift
up our eyes towards the sun
without dazzling, what shall
we do when we behold the
divine light in its illustrious
original.
SENECA

If I must die
I will encounter darkness as a
bride
And hug it in my arms.
WILLIAM SHAKESPEARE

When I lived, I provided for
everything but death; now I
must die, and am unprepared.
BORGIA

Die when I may, I want it said
of me by those who knew me
best that I always plucked a
thistle and planted a flower
wherever I thought a flower
would grow.
LINCOLN

Either death is a state of
nothingness, or there is a
change and migration of the
soul from this world to
another ... If death is the
journey to another place - and
there, as men say, all the dead
are - what good can be greater
than this? If, indeed, when
the pilgrim arrives there, he is
delivered from the professors
of justice in this world, and
finds the true judges... and
other sons of God who were
righteous in their own life -
that pilgrimage will be worth
making. Above all, I shall

then be able to continue my search into true and false knowledge. And I shall find out who is wise and who pretends to be wise and is not ... Wherefore, be of good cheer about death, and know of a certainty that no evil can happen to a good man, either in this life or after death. He and his are not neglected by the gods, nor has my own approaching end happened by mere chance ... The hour of my departure has arrived, and we go our ways - I to die and you to live. Which is better, God only knows.
SOCRATES

As the production of the metal proves the work of the refiner, so is death the test of our lives; the assay which shows the standard of all our actions.
The terrors of death are not terrors to those who have done good; therefore, restrain your hand from evil, and your soul will have nothing to fear. If you would learn to die nobly, let your vices die first; then, when your hour comes, you will be happy from having nothing to regret.

Man is not punished for the good that he has done; therefore, to the man of virtue, there is nothing in death to fear.
DANDEMIS

We sometimes congratulate ourselves at the moment of waking from a troubled dream: we shall probably congratulate ourselves the moment after death.
HAWTHORNE

Men fear death as children fear to go in the dark.
FRANCIS BACON

When a man dies they who survive him ask what property he has left behind. The angel who bends over the dying man asks what good deeds he has done.
MAHOMET

We read that at the death of Alexander, a golden sepulchre was constructed, and that a number of philosophers assembled round it. One said: "Yesterday, Alexander made a treasure of gold, and now gold makes a treasure of him." Another observed: "Yesterday,

the whole world was not enough to satiate his ambition; today, three or four ells of cloth are more than sufficient." A third said: "Yesterday, Alexander commanded the people; today, the people command him." Another said: "Yesterday, Alexander could enfranchise thousands; today, he cannot free himself from the bonds of death." Another remarked: "Yesterday, he pressed the earth; today, it oppresses him." "Yesterday," said another, "all men feared Alexander; today, men refuse him nothing." Another said: "Yesterday, Alexander had a multitude of friends; today, not one." Another said, "Yesterday, Alexander led an army; today that army bears him to the grave."
Gesta Romanorum

Thou knowest not what time he will come; wait always, that because thou knowest not the time of his coming, thou mayest be prepared against the time he cometh. And for this, perchance, thou knowest not the time, because thou mayest be prepared against all times.
ST. AUGUSTINE

Bridge players have no nationality. They have no friends, no enemies ... no nothing except thirteen fanned cards and a score block. When they hear the last trump they will bid two no-trumps and die smiling.
STEPHEN LISTER, *In Search of Paradise*

It is better to live and be done with it, than to die daily in the sickroom ... even if the doctor does not give you a year, even if he hesitates about a month, make one brave push and see what can be accomplished in a week.
R.L. STEVENSON, *Aes Triplex*

What is death, but a ceasing to be what we were before? We are kindled, and put out, we die daily; nature that begot us expels us, and a better and safer place is provided for us.
SENECA

Death is a commingling of eternity with time; in the death of a good man, eternity is seen looking through time.
GOETHE

Ephemera die all at sunset,
and no insect of this class has
ever sported in the beams of
the morning sun. Happier are
ye, little human ephemera! Ye
played only in the ascending
beams, and in the early dawn,
and in the eastern light; ye
drank only of the prelibations
of life; hovered for a little
space over a world of freshness
and of blossoms; and fell
asleep in innocence before yet
the morning dew was exhaled.
RICHTER

Believe that each day is the
last to shine upon thee.
HORACE

A true philosopher
Makes death his common
practice, while he lives,
And every day by
contemplation strives
To separate the soul, far as he
can,
From off the body.
MAY

He that always waits upon
God, is ready whensoever He
calls. Neglect not to set your
accounts even; he is a happy
man who so lives, as that
death at all times may find

him at leisure to die.
FELTHAM

Here is my journey's end, here
is my birth,
And very sea-mark of my
utmost sail.
WILLIAM SHAKESPEARE

The last enemy that shall be
destroyed is death.
1 *Corinthians* 15:26

The sleeping and the dead
Are but as pictures: 'tis the
eye of childhood
That fears a painted devil.
WILLIAM SHAKESPEARE

A death-like sleep,
A gentle wafting to immortal
life.
MILTON

Who knows that 'tis not life
which we call death,
And death our life on earth?
EURIPIDES, *Phrixus*,
Fragment 11

Death,
The undiscover'd country,
from whose bourn
No traveller returns.
WILLIAM SHAKESPEARE,
Hamlet, Act III, Scene i, line 79

He but sleeps
The holy sleep; say not the
good man dies.
CALLIMACHUS,
Epigrammata, X, 1

Death, the gate of life.
MILTON, *Paradise Lost*, Book
XII, line 571

Death but entombs the body;
life the soul;
Life makes the soul dependent
on the dust;
Death gives her wings to
mount above the spheres.
YOUNG, *Night Thoughts*,
Night III, 1ine 458

The grave itself is but a
covered bridge,
Leading from light to light,
through a brief darkness!
LONGFELLOW,
The Golden Legend

So when this corruptible shall
have put on incorruption, and
this mortal shall have put on
immortality, then shall be
brought to pass the saying that
is written, Death is swallowed
up in victory.
O death, where is thy sting?
O grave, where is thy victory?
St Paul in 1 *Corinthians* 15:54- 55

Every moment dies a man,
Every moment one is born.
ALFRED, LORD
TENNYSON,
The Vision of Sin

If we only knew the real value
of a day, nothing would
contribute more to put us in
possession of ourselves ...
Once a man fully realises that
he can mould only the day he
has, or if other days, only
through it, he will begin both
to take things easily and to do
them well, and these two have
a closer connection than most
people seem to imagine.
JOSEPH FARRELL, *Lectures
of a Certain Professor*

One always dies too soon - or
too late. And yet one's whole
life is complete at that
moment, with a line drawn
neatly under it, ready for the
summing up.
JEAN-PAUL SARTRE,
No Exit

Since the death instinct exists
in the heart of everything that
lives, since we suffer from
trying to repress it, since
everything that lives longs for
rest, let us unfasten the ties

that bind us to life, let us cultivate our death wish, let us develop it, water it like a plant, let it grow unhindered. Suffering and fear are born from the repression of the death wish.
EUGÈNE IONESCO,
Fragments of a Journal

Once I give form to my thought, I must free myself from it. For the time being, it seems to me that I want absolute freedom to create new forms for new ideas. I am sure physical death has the same meaning for us - the creative impulse of our soul must have new forms for its realisation. Death can continue to dwell in the same sepulchre, but life must unceasingly outgrow its dwelling-place; otherwise the form gets the upper hand and becomes a prison.
RABINDRANATH TAGORE, *Letters to a Friend*

The dark background which death supplies brings out the tender colours of life in all their purity.
GEORGE SANTAYANA,
Soliloquies in England

Have pity upon every man, Lord in that hour when he has finished his task and stands before Thee like a child whose hands are being examined.
PAUL CLAUDEL, quoted in *The Soul Afire*

Death cancels everything but truth.
ANON

Dust thou art, and unto dust shalt thou return.
Genesis 3:19

Death, so called, is a thing which makes men weep, And yet a third of Life is passed in sleep.
BYRON, *Don Juan*, (1819-24), 14.3

Any man's death diminishes me, because I am involved in mankind; and therefore never send to know for whom the bell tolls; it tolls for thee.
JOHN DONNE, *Devotions* (1624), 17

Why, do you not know, then, that the origin of all human evils, and of baseness, and cowardice, is not death, but rather the fear of death?

EPICTETUS, *Discourses* (2nd century AD) 3.26

Death, the most dreaded of evils, is therefore of no concern to us; for while we exist death is not present, and when death is present we no longer exist.
EPICURUS, Letter to Menoeceus (3rd century BC)

Strange - is it not? - that of the myriads who
Before us passed the door of Darkness through,
Not one returns to tell us of the road
Which to discover we must travel too.
OMAR KHAYYAM, *Rubaiyat*, Stanza 68

In the nineteenth century the problem was that God is dead; in the twentieth century the problem is that man is dead.
ERICH FROMM, *The Sane Society*, Chapter 9

Die before you die. There is no chance after.
C.S. LEWIS, *Till We Have Faces*, Book 2, Chapter 2

When a person dies the angels say, "What has he sent in advance?" but human beings say, "What has he left behind?"
MUHAMMAD

For death is no more than a turning of us over from time to eternity.
WILLIAM PENN, *Reflections and Maxims*, line 503

The birth you are afraid to take becomes your death.
CHUCK SPEZZANO, *Awaken the Gods*, page 158

Death: a trick played by the inconeivable on the conceivable.
PAUL VALÉRY, *Rhumbs*, Moralities

Death. An instantaneous state, without past or future. Indispensable for entering eternity.
SIMONE WEIL, *Gravity and Grace*, Decreation

The dying man looks at himself in the mirror and says, "We won't be seeing each other any more."
PAUL BOWLES, quoted in Ned Rorem, *The Paris Diary*, Part 1

We can be certain that more than a hundred thousand persons die in the world every day. So that a man who has only lived for thirty years has escaped this tremendous destruction about one thousand, four hundred times.
NICHOLAS-SÉBASTIEN CHAMFORT, *Maxims and Considerations*, 18

I think the dying pray at the last not please but thank you as a guest thanks his host at the door.
ANNIE DILLARD, *Pilgrim at Tinker Creek*, Chapter 15

Claudio: If I must die,
I will encounter darkness as a bride
and hug it in my arms.
WILLIAM SHAKESPEARE, *Measure for Measure*, Act III, Scene i, line 83

What good can come from meeting death with tears? ...
If a man is sorry for himself, he doubles death.
EURIPIDES, *Iphigenia in Tauris*, (circa 414-12 BC)

Death is the next step after the pension - it's perpetual retirement without pay.
JEAN GIRAUDOUX, *The Enchanted*, 3, (1933)

To die is to go into the Collective unconscious, to lose oneself in order to be transformed into form, pure form.
HERMANN HESSE

One should part from life as Odysseus partedfrom Nausicaa - blessing it rather than in love with it.
FRIEDRICH NIETZSCHE, *Beyond Good and Evil* (1886), 96

There is no death! what seems so is transition;
This life of mortal breath
Is but a suburb of the life Elysian
Whose portal we call death.
LONGFELLOW, *Resignation*

Man imagines that it is death he fears; but what he fears is the unforeseen, the explosion. What man fears is himself, not death.
ANTOINE DE SAINT-EXUPÉRY, *Flight to Arras* (1942), 19

Death is stronger than all the governments because the governments are men and men die and then death laughs: now you see 'em, now you don't.
CARL SANDBURG, From *Death Snips Proud Men*, (1950)

The sense of death is most in apprehension,
And the poor beetle that we tread upon
In corporal sufferance finds a pang as great
As when a giant dies.
WILLIAM SHAKESPEARE, *Measure for Measure*, (1604-05), Act III, Scene i, line 78

One should die proudly when it is no longer possible to live proudly.
FRIEDRICH NIETZSCHE, *Twilight of the Idols* (1888)

Nobody knows, in fact, what death is, nor whether to man it is not perchance the greatest of all blessings; yet people fear it as if they surely knew it to be the worst of evils.
SOCRATES, in Plato's *Apology* (4th century BC)

The sand of the sea, the drops of rain, and the days of eternity - who can count them?
Apocrypha, Ecclesiasticus 1:2

Eternity for bubbles proves at last
A senseless bargain.
WILLIAM COWPER, *The Garden*, 175

He that dies pays all debts.
WILLIAM SHAKESPEARE, *The Tempest* (1611-12), Act III, Scene ii, line 40

This is the promise that He hath promised us, even eternal life.
I *John* 2:25

The time will come when every change shall cease,
This quick revolving wheel shall rest in peace:
No summer then shall glow, nor winter freeze;
Nothing shall be to come, and nothing past,
But an eternal now shall ever last.
PETRARCH, *The Triumph of Eternity*, line 117

Think not thy time short in this world, since the world itself is not long. The created world is but a small parenthesis in eternity, and a short interposition, for a time, between such a state of duration as was before it and may be after it.
SIR THOMAS BROWNE, *Christian Morals*, Part III, xxix

The fear of death is more to be dreaded than death itself.
SYRUS, *Maxim* 511

A Power is passing from the earth
To breathless Nature's dark abyss;
But when the great and good depart,
What is it more than this -
That man, who is from God sent forth,
Doth yet again to God return?
Such ebb and flow must ever be;
Then wherefore should we mourn?
WILLIAM WORDSWORTH, *Lines at Grasmere* (1806)

Death is the crown of life.
YOUNG, *Night Thoughts*, 3

Let me die the death of the righteous, and let my last end be like his!
Numbers 23:10

A Moment's Halt, - a momentary taste
Of BEING from the Well amid the Waste, -
And, Lo! the phantom Caravan has reached
The NOTHING it set out from. Oh make haste!
OMAR KHAYYAM, *Rubaiyat*, Stanza xiviii

Remember that man's life lies all within this present as 'twere but a hair's breadth of time: as for the rest, the past is gone, the future yet unseen. Short, therefore, is man's life, and narrow is the corner of the earth wherein he dwells.
MARCUS AURELIUS, *Meditations*, 10

'Tis the divinity that stirs within us;
'Tis heaven itself, that points out an hereafter,
And intimates eternity to man.
THOMAS ADDISON, *Cato*, Act V, Scene i

Beyond the stars, and all this
passing scene,
Where change shall cease, and
Time shall be no more.
KIRKE WHITE, *Time*, line
726

And call not those who are
slain in the way of Allah
'dead'. Nay, they are living,
only ye perceive not.
Qur'ân, II, 154

The attitude of the Indian
toward death, the test and
background of life, is entirely
consistent with his character
and philosophy. Death has no
terrors for him; he meets it
with simplicity and perfect
calm, seeking only an
honourable end as his last gift
to his family and descendants.
OHIYESA

... My wishes be
To leave this life, not loving
it, but Thee.
ROBERT HERRICK

Seek not for life on earth or in
heaven. Thirst for life is
delusion. Knowing life to be
transitory, wake up from this
dream of ignorance and strive
to attain knowledge and

freedom before death shall
claim thee. The purpose of
this mortal life is to reach the
shore of immortality by
conquering both life and
death.
Srimad Bhagavatam, XI. xiii

Say to my brethren when they
see me dead,
and weep for me, lamenting
me in sadness:
'Think ye I am this corpse ye
are to bury?
I swear by God, this dead one
is not I.
When I had formal shape,
then this, my body,
Served as my garment. I
wore it for a while.'
AL-GHAZALI, Ode
composed on his deathbed

Why mourn the dead? They
are free from bondage.
Mourning is the chain forged
by the mind to bind itself to
the dead.
SRI RAMANA MAHARSHI

Chuang-tse said, "Were I to
prevail upon God to allow
your body to be born again,
and your bones and flesh to be
renewed, so that you could
return to your parents, to your

wife, and to the friends of your youth, - would you be willing?

At this, the skull opened its eyes wide and knitted its brows and said, "How should I cast aside happiness greater than that of a king, and mingle once again in the toils and troubles of mortality?"
CHUANG-TSE, Chapter XVIII

We can die gladly if God will live and work in us ... We die, 'tis true, but 'tis a gentle death.
ECKHART

Your fear of death is really fear of yourself: see what it is from which you are fleeing!
RUMI

As Tullius says, in his *De Senectute*, "Natural death is, as it were, our haven after a long voyage, and our repose." And as a good sailor, when he nears the harbour, lowers his sails, and gently and with feeble headway enters it, so should we lower the sails of our worldly occupations, and return to God with all our mind and heart, so that we may enter our haven with all gentleness and all peace. And our own nature teaches us much as to the gentleness (of natural death); because in such a death there is no pain, nor any bitterness; but as a ripe apple lightly and without violence detaches itself from the bough, so our soul, without pain, leaves the body in which it has been. Wherefore Aristotle, in his *Youth and Old Age*, says that the death which comes to old age is a death without sadness.
DANTE, *Il Convito*, IV, xxviii, 1

Indomitable faith combined with supreme serenity of mind are indispensable at the moment of death.
GAMPOPA

Death is a bridge whereby the lover is joined to the Beloved.
ABD AL-'AZIZ B. SULAYMÀN

Courage is but being fearless of the death which is but the parting of the Soul from the body, an event which no one can dread whose delight is to be his unmingled Self.
PLOTINUS

Zen has no secrets other than seriously thinking about birth-and-death.
TAKEDA SHINGEN

Strive after the Good before thou art in danger, before pain masters thee and thy mind loses its keenness.
KULÂRNAVA TANTRA, line 27

Everyone is aware of the eternal Self. He sees so many dying but still believes himself eternal. Because it is the Truth. Unwillingly the natural Truth asserts itself. The man is deluded by the intermingling of the conscious Self with the insentient body. This delusion must end.
SRI RAMANA MAHARSHI

Learn now to die to the world, that thou mayest then begin to live with Christ.
The Imitation of Christ, I, xxiii

Against his will he dieth that hath not learned to die. Learn to die and thou shalt learn to live, for there shall none learn to live that hath not learned to die.
The Book of the Craft of Dying

The Prince of mankind (Muhammad) said truly that no one who has passed away from this world
Feels sorrow and regret for having died; nay, but he feels a hundred regrets for having missed the opportunity,
Saying to himself, "Why did I not make death my object - death which is the store-house of all fortunes and riches ...?"
The grief of the dead is not on account of death; it is because they dwelt on the phenomenal forms of existence.
RUMI

Man must wholly die to Self-hood in the death, and give himself up in the resigned will wholly into the obedience of God, as a new child of a new will; ... without this there is only the form, the history that was once brought to pass, and that a man need only accept of it, and comfort himself therewith; but this will remains without, for it will be a child of an assumed grace, and not wholly die to its Self-hood in the grace, and become a child of grace in the resigned will.
JACOB BOEHME

SIXTEEN - DEATH   201

He who does not become an
expert in annihiliation shall
not discover the beautiful face
of the bride.
ABU 'L-MAWÂHIB ASH-
SHÂDHILI

The childish go after outward
pleasures;
They walk into the net of
widespread death.
But the wise, knowing
immortality,
Seek not the stable among
things which are unstable
here.
Katha Upanishad, IV, 2

It is the character only of a
good man to be able to deny
and disown himself, and to
make a full surrender of
himself unto God; forgetting
himself, and minding nothing
but the will of his Creator;
triumphing in nothing more
than in his own nothingness,
and in the allness of the
Divinity. But indeed this, his
being nothing, is the only way
to be all things; this, his
having nothing, the truest way
of possessing all things.
JOHN SMITH THE
PLATONIST

Verily, verily, I say unto you,
Except a corn of wheat fall
into the ground and die, it
abideth alone: but if it die, it
bringeth forth much fruit. He
that loveth his life shall lose
it; and he that hateth his life
in this world shall keep it unto
life eternal.
John 12:24-25

Those who cling to life die,
and those who defy death live.
UYESUGI KENSHIN

To sue to live, I find I seek to
die,
And, seeking death, find life.
WILLIAM SHAKESPEARE,
Measure for Measure, Act III.
Scene i, line 42

Kâhn have I bought, the price
he asked, I gave.
Some cry, "'Tis great," and
others jeer, "'Tis small" -
I gave in full, weighed to the
utmost grain,
My love, my life, my soul, my
all.
MIRÂ BÂÎ

The *Double* only *seems*, but
The One *is*,
Thy-self to Self-annihilation
give

That this false *Two* in that
true *One* may live.
ATTÂR

There's a special providence
in the fall of a sparrow. If it
be now, 'tis not to come; if it
be not to come, it will be now;
if it be not now, yet it will
come: the readiness is all.
Since no man has aught of
what he leaves, what is't to
leave betimes?
WILLIAM SHAKESPEARE,
Hamlet, Act V, Scene ii, line
232

"What if anyone is dead?
What if any one is ruined? Be
dead yourself - be ruined
yourself." In that sense there
is no pain after one's death.
What is meant by this sort of
death? Annihilation of the
ego, though the body is alive.
SRI RAMANA MAHARSHI

Thou bringest forth the living
from the dead, and Thou
bringest forth the dead from
the living.
Qur'ân, III. 27

SEVENTEEN

EDUCATION

Animals can learn, but it is not by learning that they become dogs, cats, or horses. Only man has to learn to become what he is supposed to be.
ERIC HOFFER, *Between the Devil and the Dragon*, Part 1, Introduction

The world's great men have not commonly been scholars, nor its great scholars great men.
OLIVER WENDELL HOLMES, *The Autocrat of the Breakfast Table*, Chapter 6

Learn: To add to one's ignorance by extending the knowledge we have of the things that we can never know.
ELBERT HUBBARD, *The Roycroft Dictionary*

Ignorance is like a delicate exotic fruit; touch it and the bloom is gone. The whole theory of modern education is radically unsound. Fortunately in England, at any rate, education produces no effect whatsoever.
OSCAR WILDE, *The Importance of Being Earnest*, Act 1

By nature all men are alike, but by education widely different.
CHINESE PROVERB

How is it that little children are so intelligent and men so stupid? It must be education that does it.
ALEXANDRE DUMAS FILS, quoted in L. Treich's *L'Esprit d'Alexandre Dumas*

Only the educated are free.
EPICTETUS, *Discourses* (2nd century AD) 2.1.

Education is the ability to listen to almost anything without losing your temper or your self-confidence.
ROBERT FROST

On one occasion Aristotle was asked how much educated men were superior to those uneducated: "As much," said he, "as the living are to the dead."
DIOGENES LAERTIUS, *Aristotle*, XI

The direction in which education starts a man, will determine his future life.
PLATO, *The Republic* (4th century BC), 4

It is only the ignorant who despise education.
PUBLILIUS SYRUS, *Moral Sayings* (1st century BC), 571

Education is the leading of human souls to what is best, and making what is best out of them; and these two objects are always attainable together, and by the same means; the training which makes men happiest in themselves also makes them most serviceable to others.
JOHN RUSKIN, *The Stones of Venice* (1851-53), 3

What does education often do? It makes a straight-cut ditch of a free, meandering brook.
THOREAU, *Journal*, 1850

They that sow in tears shall reap in joy.
Psalms 126:5

By labour fire is got out of a stone.
DUTCH PROVERB

The bitter and the sweet come from the outside, the hard from within, from one's own efforts.
ALBERT EINSTEIN, *Out of My Later Years* (1950), 2

Education bewildered me with knowledge and facts in which I was only mildly interested.
CHARLES CHAPLIN, *My Autobiography*

A little learning is a dang'rous thing;
Drink deep, or taste not the Pierian spring:
There shallow draughts intoxicate the brain,
And drinking largely sobers us again.
ALEXANDER POPE, *An Essay on Criticism*, 215

He who can, does. He who cannot, teaches.
GEORGE BERNARD SHAW, *Man and Superman*

A teacher should have maximal authority and minimal power.
THOMAS S. SZASZ, *The Second Sin*, Education

Education is an admirable thing. But it is as well to remember from time to time that nothing that is worth knowing can be taught.

OSCAR WILDE, *For the Instruction of the Over-educated*

Academic questions are interlopers in a world where so few of the real ones have been answered.
HENRY S. HASKINS, *Meditations in Wall Street*

The great thing, then, in all education, is to make our nervous system our ally instead of our enemy.
WILLIAM JAMES, *The Principles of Psychology,* Chapter 4

If you educate a man you educate a person, but if you educate a woman you educate a family.
RUBY MANIKAN, echoing Bishop Fénélon's *Treatise on the Education of Girls*

A young man who is not a radical about something is a pretty poor risk for education.
JACQUES BARZUN, *Teacher in America*

All education is a continuous dialogue - questions and answers that pursue every problem to the horizon. That

is the essence of academic freedom.
WILLIAM O. DOUGLAS, *Wisdom*, October 1956

From the very beginning of his education, the child should experience the joy of discovery.
ALFRED NORTH WHITEHEAD, *The Aims of Education*

Unfortunately, we are inclined to talk of man as it would be desirable for him to be rather than as he really is ... True education can proceed only from naked reality, not from any ideal illusion about man, however attractive.
C.G. JUNG, *Psychological Reflections*

We now spend a good deal more on drink and smoke than we spend on education. This, of course, is not surprising. The urge to escape from selfhood and the environment is in almost everyone almost all the time. The urge to do something for the young is strong only in parents, and in them only for the few years during which

their children go to school.
ALDOUS HUXLEY, *The Doors of Perception*

It is hard to convince a high-school student that he will encounter a lot of problems more difficult than those of algebra and geometry.
E.W. HOWE, *Country Town Sayings*

A classroom, any classroom, is an awesome place of shadows and shifting colours, a place of unacknowledged desires and powers, a magic place. Its inhabitants are tamed. After years of unnecessary repetition, they will be able to perform their tricks - reading, writing, arithmetic and their more complex derivatives. But they are tamed only in the manner of a cage full of jungle cats. Let the right set of circumstances arise, the classroom will explode.
GEORGE B. LEONARD, *Education and Ecstasy*

The great desideratum of human education is to make all men aware that they are gods in the making, and that they can all walk upon water

if they will.
DON MARQUIS, *The Almost Perfect State*

Children who are treated as if they are uneducable almost invariably become uneducable.
KENNETH B. CLARK, *Dark Ghetto*

No one knows what is in him till he tries, and many would never try if they were not forced to.
BASIL W. MATURIN, *Laws of the Spiritual Life*

Every educated man should write verse, even if he cannot paint a picture.
LORD HAILSHAM, 1907, attributed, 1962

One chief aim of any true system of education must be to impart to the individual the courage to play the game against any and all odds, the nerve to walk into the ambushes of existence, the hardness to face the most despicable truth about himself and not let it daunt him permanently; it must armour him with an ultimate

carelessness.
DON MARQUIS, *The Almost Perfect State*

A teacher affects eternity; he can never tell where his influence stops.
HENRY ADAMS, *The Education of Henry Adams*, Chapter 20

Very different sorts of eternal students: those who always have their nose in a dictionary, and those who keep searching the books of wisdom. But there are also some who prefer to dissolve wisdom with the help of a dictionary.
ELIAS CANETTI, *The Secret Heart of the Clock*, 1981

The richest soil, if uncultivated, produces the rankest weeds.
PLUTARCH, *Coriolanus*

The great secret of education is to secure that bodily and mental exercises shall always serve to relax one another.
ROUSSEAU

An educated villain has all the more tools at command

with which to do evil.
C.H. SPURGEON, *Salt-Cellars*

Educate men without religion and you make them but clever devils.
DUKE OF WELLINGTON, *Sayings*

Satan keeps school for neglected children.
Quoted as a saying in C.H. SPURGEON'S *Salt-Cellars*

With half an hour's reading in bed every night as a steady practice, the busiest man can get a fair education before the plasma sets in the periganglionic spaces of his grey cortex.
SIR WILLIAM OSLER

Education is the process of casting false pearls before real swine.
IRWIN EDMAN in Frank Muir, *The Frank Muir Book*

The true purpose of education is to cherish and unfold the seed of immortality already sown within us; to develop, to their fullest extent, the capacities of every kind with

which the God who made us has endowed us.
ANNA JAMESON, *Education*

Observation more than books, experience rather than persons, are the prime educators.
A.B. ALCOTT, *Table Talk*, Part II

The roots of education are bitter, but the fruit is sweet.
ARISTOTLE, from DIOGENES LAERTIUS, *Aristotle*, Section 18

Gie me ae spark o' Nature's fire!
That's a' the learning I desire.
ROBERT BURNS, *First Epistle to J. Lapraik*, Stanza 13

Natural gifts without education have more often attained to glory and virtue than education without natural gifts.
CICERO, *Pro Archia Poeta*, Chapter VII, Section 15

Education is an ornament in prosperity and a refuge in adversity.
ARISTOTLE, from DIOGENES LAERTIUS, *Aristotle*, 19

We are faced with the paradoxical fact that education has become one of the chief obstacles to intelligence and freedom of thought.
BERTRAND RUSSELL, *Sceptical Essays*, page 163

No education deserves the name unless it develops thought, unless it pierces down to the mysterious spiritual principle of mind, and starts that into activity and growth.
WHIPPLE

The human intellect can only grow by its own action. Every man must, therefore, educate himself. His books and teacher are but helps; the work is his. A man is not educated until he has the ability to summon, in an emergency, his mental powers in vigorous exercise to effect its proposed object.
DANIEL WEBSTER

The aim of education should be to teach us rather how to think than what to think.
BEATTIE

The sentiments of an adult are compounded of a kernel of instinct surrounded by a vast husk of education.
BERTRAND RUSSELL,
Sceptical Essays, page 206

Whatever expands the affections, or enlarges the sphere of our sympathies, whatever makes us feel our relation to the universe, must unquestionably refine our nature and elevate us in the scale of being.
CHANNING

A college education shows a man how little other people know.
HALIBURTON

All of us who are worth anything, spend our manhood in unlearning the follies, or expiating the mistakes of our youth.
PERCY BYSSHE SHELLEY

The noblest employment of the mind of man is the study of the works of his Creator. Cast your eyes towards the clouds. Do you not find the heavens full of wonders? Look down at the earth. Does not the worm proclaim to you: "Could less than Omnipotence have formed me?" The planets follow their courses and the sun remains in his place; the comet wanders through Space and returns to his destined road again. What but an Infinite Wisdom could have appointed them their laws? Look down upon the Earth and see her produce; examine under the surface, and behold what it contains. Has not Wisdom and Power ordained the whole? Can the meanest fly create itself? - could you have fashioned it? You, who see the whole as admirable as its parts, cannot better employ your eye than in tracing out your Creator's greatness; or your mind than in examining the wonders of Creation.

What is the study of words compared with this? Wherein lies Knowledge, but in the study of Nature! For the rest, whatever science is most useful, and whatever knowledge has least vanity, is to be preferred. All other sciences are vain; and all other knowledge is boast unless it makes a man more good and more honest.

Adoration of your God, and benevolence to your fellow-creatures: are they not your great studies? Who shall teach you the one, or who shall inform you of the other, like unto the study of His works!
DANDEMIS

In exalting the faculties of the soul, we annihilate, in a great degree, the delusion of the senses.
AIMI MARTEN

If you suffer your people to be ill-educated, and their manner to be corrupted from their infancy, and then punish them for those crimes to which their first education disposed them - you first make thieves, and then punish them.
SIR THOMAS MOORE

Every man has two educations - that which is given to him, and the other, that which he gives to himself. Of the two kinds, the latter is by far the most valuable. Indeed all that is most worthy in a man, he must work out and conquer for himself. It is that, that constitutes our real and best nourishment. What we are merely taught, seldom nourishes the mind like that which we teach ourselves.
RICHTER

EIGHTEEN

GENIUS

As diamond cuts diamond,
and one hone smooths a
second, all the parts of
intellect are whetstones to
each other; and genius, which
is but the result of their
mutual sharpening, is
character too.
C.A. BARTOL, *Radical
Problems: Individualism*

Every man who observes
vigilantly and resolves
steadfastly, grows
unconsciously into genius.
BULWER-LYTTON,
Caxtoniana, Essay 21

Genius, cried the commuter,
As he ran for the 8.13,
Consists of an infinite
capacity
For catching trains.
CHRISTOPHER MORLEY,
An Ejaculation

Of the three requisites of
genius, the first is soul, and
the second, soul, and the
third, soul.
E.P. WHIPPLE, *Literature and
Life: Genius*

Many men of genius must
arise before a particular man
of genius can appear.

ISAAC D'ISRAELI, *Literary
Character of Men of Genius*,
Chapter 12

The lamp of genius burns
more rapidly than the lamp of
life.
SCHILLER, *Fiesco*, Act II,
Scene 17

There are two kinds of genius.
The first and highest may be
said to speak out of the eternal
to the present, and must
compel its eternal to the
present, and must compel its
age to understand it; the
second understands its age,
and tells it what it wishes to
be told.
J.R. LOWELL, *My Study
Windows: Pope*

Talent convinces - Genius but
excites;
This tasks the reason, that the
soul delights.
Talent from sober judgement
takes its birth,
And reconciles the pinion to
the earth;
Genius unsettles with desires
the mind,
Contented not till earth be
left behind;
Talent, the sunshine on a

cultured soil,
Ripens the fruit, by slow
degrees, for toil;
Genius, the sudden Iris of the
skies,
On cloud itself reflects its
wondrous dyes:
Talent gives all that vulgar
critics need -
And frames a horn-book for
the Dull to read;
Genius, the Pythian of the
Beautiful,
Leaves its large truths a riddle
to the Dull -
From eyes profane a veil the
Isis screens,
And fools on fools still ask -
"What Hamlet means?"
BULWER-LYTTON, *Talent
and Genius*

There is no work of genius
which has not been the
delight of mankind, no word
of genius to which the human
heart and soul have not
sooner or later responded.
JEAN JACQUES
ROUSSEAU

There was never yet a truly
great man that was not at the
same time truly virtuous.
BENJAMIN FRANKLIN, *The
Busy-body*, No. 3

Great men are they who see
that spiritual is stronger than
any material force, that
thoughts rule the world.
RALPH WALDO
EMERSON, *Letters and Social
Aims*, Progress of Culture

Great men are too often
unknown, or, what is worse,
misknown.
THOMAS CARLYLE, *Sartor
Resartus*, Book I, Chapter iii

The world knows nothing of
its greatest men.
HENRY TAYLOR, *Philip Van
Artevelde*, Act I, Scene 5

Great truths are portions of
the soul of man;
Great souls are portions of
eternity.
LOWELL, *Sonnet VII*

Passion holds up the bottom
of the universe and genius
paints up its roof.
CHANG CH'AO

God did not rest after the six
days of creation: He is still
continuously at work, as on
the first day. Surely it
wouldn't have been much fun
for Him to build this

lumbering world out of simple elements and let it roll about in the sunshine year in, year out, if He hadn't had the plan to build upon this material basis a training ground for higher spirits. And so He is continually at work in great geniuses, so as to pull the common people *up*.
GOETHE

When thou seest an eagle, thou seest a portion of genius; lift up thy head!
WILLIAM BLAKE

Genius is a promontory jutting out into the future.
VICTOR HUGO

Every man of genius is considerably helped by being dead.
ROBERT LYND

It is the nature of a great mind to be calm and undisturbed, and ever to despise injuries and misfortunes.
SENECA, *De Clementia*, 1, 5

Be not afraid of greatness. Some men are born great, some achieve greatness, and some have greatness thrust

upon them.
WILLIAM SHAKESPEARE, *Twelfth Night*, Act II, Scene v

Through love, through hope, and faith's transcendent dower,
We feel that we are greater than we know.
WILLIAM WORDSWORTH, *River Duddon*

You cannot create genius. All you can do is nurture it.
NINETTE DE VALOIS, *Time*, September 26, 1960

Sensibility alters from generation to generation in everybody, whether we will or no; but expression is only altered by a man of genius.
T.S. ELIOT

Genius always finds itself a century too early.
RALPH WALDO EMERSON, *Journals*, (1840)

The definition of genius is that it acts unconsciously; and those who have produced immortal works have done so without knowing how or why.
WILLIAM HAZLITT, *The Plain Speaker* (1826)

Genius is gifted with a vitality which is expended in the enrichment of life through the discovery of new worlds of feeling.
HANS HOFMANN, *Search for the Real* (1967)

A person of genius should marry a person of character. Genius does not herd with genius.
OLIVER WENDELL HOLMES, SR., *The Professor at the Breakfast Table* (1860), 11

Everyone is a genius at least once a year. The real geniuses simply have their bright ideas closer together.
GEORG CHRISTOPH LICHTENBERG, *Aphorisms* (1764-99)

There are two types of genius: one which above all begets and wants to beget, and another which prefers being fertilized and giving birth.
FRIEDRICH NIETZSCHE, *Beyond Good and Evil* (1886), 248

We should like to have some towering geniuses, to reveal us to ourselves in colour and fire, but of course they would have to fit into the pattern of our society and be able to take orders from sound administrative types.
J.B. PRIESTLEY

The deep waters of time will flow over us: only a few men of genius will lift a head above the surface, and though doomed eventually to pass into the same silence, will fight against oblivion and for a long time hold their own.
SENECA, *Letters to Lucilius* (1st century AD), 21.5

Nature never sends a great man into the planet without confiding the secret to another soul.
RALPH WALDO EMERSON, *Uses of Great Men*

The persecution of genius fosters its influence.
TACITUS, *Annals* (AD 115-117?), 4.35

The public is wonderfully tolerant. It forgives everything except genius.
OSCAR WILDE, *Intentions*, The Critic as Artist (1891)

In every man of genius a new strange force is brought into the world.
HAVELOCK ELLIS, *Selected Essays*

The highest endowments do not create - they only discover. All transcendent genius has the power to make us know this as utter truth. Shakespeare, Beethoven - it is inconceivable that they have *fashioned* the works of their lives; they only saw and heard the universe that is opaque and dumb to us.
RUTH BENEDICT, *An Anthropologist at Work* by Margaret Mead

But the genius, as with the birds, discovers within himself that which never need be sought. "I do not seek, I find," Picasso says, and before him, Cézanne spoke, "I am the primitive of my way."
LOUIS DANZ, *Dynamic Dissonance*

I know now that revelation is from the Self, but from that age-long memoried Self, that shapes the elaborate shell of the mollusc and the child in the womb, that teaches the birds to make their nest; and that genius is a crisis that joins that buried Self for certain moments to our trivial daily mind.
W.B. YEATS, *Autobiography*

All men of genius that we have ever heard of have triumphed over adverse circumstances, but that is no reason for supposing that there were not innumerable others who succumbed in youth.
BERTRAND RUSSELL, *The Conquest of Happiness*

The essential definition of a genius, I think, is that he is a man who not only knows the laws of things, but experiences them in himself with self-evident certainty. This experience of pure being transcends even love.
OSWALD SCHWARZ, *The Psychology of Sex*

Genius not only hears more sounds in the rushing tumult of life, but selects more harmonious strains from the din.
RADOSLAV A. TSANOFF, *The Ways of Genius*

Beauty, truth, power, God, all these come without searching, without effort. The struggle is not for these; the struggle is deeper than that. The struggle is to synchronize the potential being with the actual being, to make a fruitful liaison between the man of yesterday and the man of tomorrow. It is the process of growth which is painful, but unavoidable. We either grow or we die, and to die while alive is a thousand times worse than to "shuffle off this mortal coil."
HENRY MILLER, *The Cosmological Eye*

The works of genius are watered with its tears.
HONORÉ DE BALZAC, 1799-1850, *Lost Illusions* (1837-43)

What is genius - but the power of expressing a new individuality?
ELIZABETH BARRETT BROWNING, (1806-61)

Genius, all over the world, stands hand in hand, and one shock of recognition runs the whole circle round.
HERMAN MELVILLE, 1819-91, *Hawthorne and His Mosses* (1850)

Genius does what it must, and Talent does what it can.
OWEN MEREDITH, 1831-91, *Last Words of a Sensitive Second-Rate Poet* (1868)

Unless one is a genius, it is best to aim at being intelligible.
ANTHONY HOPE, 1863-1933, *The Dolly Dialogues* (1894)

If a man is going to behave like a bastard, he'd better be a genius.
JILL CRAIGIE, on *Bookmark* (BBC2)

There is a great man who makes every man feel small. But the real great man is the man who makes every man feel great.
G.K. CHESTERTON, *Charles Dickens*

Wisdom is like electricity. There is no permanently wise man, but men capable of wisdom, who being put into certain company, or other

favourable conditions, become wise for a short time, as glasses rubbed acquire electric power for a while.
RALPH WALDO EMERSON, *Society and Solitude (Clubs)*

To display the greatest powers, unless they are applied to great purposes, makes nothing for the character of greatness. To throw a barleycorn through the eye of a needle, to multiply nine figures by nine in the memory, argues definite dexterity of body and capacity of mind, but nothing comes of either ... A mathematician who solves a profound problem, a poet who creates an image of beauty in the mind that was not there before, imparts knowledge and power to others, in which his greatness and his fame consists, and in which it reposes ... A great chess player is not a great man, for he leaves the world as he found it. No act terminating in itself constitutes greatness.
HA, *Indian Jugglers*

The three indispensables of genius are understanding, feeling, and perseverance. The three things that enrich genius, are contentment of mind, the cherishing of good thoughts, and exercising the memory.
SOUTHEY

Time, place and action, may with pains be wrought,
But genius must be born, and never can be taught.
DRYDEN

To carry on the feelings of childhood into the powers of manhood, to combine the child's sense of wonder and novelty with the appearances which every day has rendered familiar, this is the character and privilege of genius, and one of the marks which distinguish genius from talent.
SAMUEL TAYLOR COLERIDGE

No enemy is so terrible as a man of genius.
DISRAELI

Men of genius are often dull and inert in society, as a blazing meteor when it descends to earth, is only a stone.
LONGFELLOW

The lamp of genius, though by
nature lit,
If not protected, pruned, and
fed with care,
Soon dies, or runs to waste,
with fitful glare.
WILCOX

To be endowed with strength
by nature, to be actuated by
the powers of the mind, and
to have a certain spirit almost
Divine infused into you.
CICERO

There is no great genius free
from some tincture of
madness.
SENECA

Thy genius, for a minister it is
Unto the throne of Fate.
Draw to thy soul,
And centralise the rays which
are around
Of the Divinity.
BAILEY

Genius, without religion, is
only a lamp on the outer gate
of a palace. It may serve to
cast a gleam of light on those
that are without, while the
inhabitant sits in darkness.
HANNAH MORE

When a true genius appears in
the world you may know him
by this sign, that the dunces
are all in confederacy against
him.
SWIFT

He only is great of heart who
floods the world with a great
affection. He only is great of
mind who stirs the world with
great thoughts. He only is
great of will who does
something to shape the world
to a great career. And he is
greatest who does the most of
these things, and does them
best.
HITCHCOCK

The greatest man is he who
chooses the right with
invincible resolution, who
resists the sorest temptations
from without and within, who
bears the heaviest burdens
cheerfully, who is calmest in
storms and most fearless under
menace and frowns.
CHANNING

He who comes up to his own
idea of greatness must always
have had a very low standard
of it in his mind.
HAZLITT

The less people speak of their greatness, the more we think of it.
FRANCIS BACON

Great minds have purposes, others have wishes. Little minds are tamed and subdued by misfortune; but great minds rise above them.
IRVING

He is great who feeds other minds. He is great who inspires others to think for themselves. He is great who tells you the things you already know, but which you did not know you knew until he told you. He is great who shocks you, irritates you, affronts you, so that you are jostled out of your wonted ways, pulled out of your mental ruts, and lifted out of the mire of the commonplace.
HUBBARD

NINETEEN

GOD

The Lord is always good and full of love; He never abandons those who put their trust in Him.
SWAMI RAMDAS

General, natural religion requires no faith. The persuasion that a great creating, regulating, and guiding Being conceals himself, as it were, behind Nature, to make himself comprehensible to us - such a conviction forces itself on us all.
GOETHE, *Autobiography*, Book 4

If all the light of the world were to be extinguished, still we should know what light is - for it is God.
IBSEN, *Love's Comedy*, Act 3 (1862)

There is practically nothing that men do not prefer to God. A tiresome detail of business, an occupation utterly pernicious to health, the employment of time in ways one does not dare to mention. Anything rather than God.
FRANÇOIS DE FÉNELON

Whosoever keepeth his duty to Allah, Allah will appoint a way out for him, and will provide for him in a way that he cannot foresee. And whosoever putteth his trust in Allah, He will suffice him. Lo! Allah bringeth His command to pass. Allah hath set a measure for all things.
Qur'ân, LXV, 2,3

From the invisible he made all things visible, himself being invisible.
2 *Enoch*, XLVIII. 5

Faith is the belief of the heart in that knowledge which comes from the Unseen.
MUHAMMAD B. KHAF'IF

How calmly may we commit ourselves to the hands of Him who bears up the world - of Him who has created, and who provides for the joy even of insects, as carefully as if He were their Father!
RICHTER

He hath made the earth by His power, He hath established the world by His wisdom, and hath stretched out the heavens by His

discretion.
Jeremiah 10:12

Thou dread source,
Prime, self-existing cause and
end of all
That in the scale of being fill
their place;
Above our human region or
below
Set and sustain'd. Thou, thou
alone, O! Lord,
Art everlasting.
WILLIAM WORDSWORTH

Of old hast thou laid the
foundation of the earth: and
the heavens are the work of
Thy hands. They shall perish,
but thou shalt endure: yea all
of them shall wax old like a
garment: as a vesture shalt
Thou change them, and they
shall be changed, but thou art
the same, and thy years shall
have no end.
Psalms 102:25

Faith is the substance of
things hoped for, the evidence
of things not seen... Through
faith we understand that the
worlds were framed by the
word of God, so that things
which are seen were not made
of things which do appear...

He that cometh to God must
believe that he is, and that he
is a rewarder of them that
diligently seek him.
Hebrews 11:1,3 6,7

No one has the capacity to
judge God. We are drops in
that limitless ocean of mercy.
MAHATMA GANDHI

Everyone, whether he is self-
denying or self-indulgent, is
seeking after the Beloved.
Every place may be the shrine
of love, whether it be mosque
or synagogue.
HÂFIZ, ghazals from the
Divan (14th century), 8

He who created us without
our help will not save us
without our consent.
ST. AUGUSTINE (attributed)

Nothing human can be done
without reference to the
divine, and conversely.
MARCUS AURELIUS,
Meditations, Book 3, 13

God is the eternal confidant,
in that tragedy of which each
of us is the hero.
CHARLES BAUDELAIRE,
Intimate Journals

The world of sense and colour
... is a narrow prison.
The cause of narrowness is
compoundness and number
(plurality): the senses are
moving towards composition.
Know that the world of
Unification lies beyond sense:
if you want Unity, march in
that direction.
RUMI

Acquaint thyself with God, if
thou wouldst taste his works.
WILLIAM COWPER

Even if God did not exist,
religion would still be holy
and divine. God is the only
being who, in order to rule,
does not even need to exist.
CHARLES BAUDELAIRE,
Intimate Journals

He to whom you pray is nearer
to you than the neck of your
camel.
MUHAMMAD

Whoever knocks persistently,
ends by entering.
'ALI

The soul of Man to God is as
the flower to the sun; it opens
at its approach and shuts

when it withdraws.
BENJAMIN WHICHCOAT

Sometimes God acts as the
magnet and the devotee as the
needle. God attracts the
needle to Himself. Again,
sometimes the devotee acts as
the magnet and God as the
needle. Such is the attraction
of the devotee that God
comes to him, unable to resist
his magnetism.
SRI RAMAKRISHNA

The thing we tell of can never
be found by seeking, yet only
seekers find it.
BÂYAZÎD AL-BISTÂMÎ

All things work together for
good to them that love God,
to them who are the called
according to his purpose.
Romans 8:28

We love God with his own
love; awareness of it deifies us.
ECKHART

No life can express, nor
tongue so much as name what
this enflaming all-conquering
love of God is. It is brighter
than the sun; it is sweeter
than anything that is called

sweet, it is stronger than all strength; it is more nutrimental than food; more cheering to the heart than wine, and more pleasant than all the joy and pleasantness of this world. Whoever obtaineth it, is richer than any monarch on earth; and he who getteth it, is nobler than any emperor can be, and more potent and absolute than all power and authority.
BOEHME

A disciple asked his teacher, "Sir, please tell me how I can see God." "Come with me," said the guru, "and I shall show you." He took the disciple to a lake, and both of them got in the water. Suddenly the teacher pressed the disciple's head under the water. After a few moments he released him and the disciple raised his head and stood up. The guru asked him, "How did you feel?" The disciple said, "Oh! I thought I should die; I was panting for breath." The teacher said, "When you feel like that for God, then you will know you haven't long to wait for His vision."
SRI RAMAKRISHNA

As the hart panteth after the water brooks, so panteth my soul after thee, O God.
Psalms 42:1

When God's nearness takes possession of a man's heart, it overwhelms all else, both the inward infiltrations of the purposes and the outward motions of the members. Thereafter the man continues, going or coming, taking or giving: there prevails in him the purpose which has ruled his mind, namely, the love of God and His nearness.
AHMAD B. 'ÎSÂ AL-KHARRÂZ

A single atom of the love of God in a heart is worth more than a hundred thousand paradises.
BÂYAZÎD AL-BISTÂMÎ

An atheist is a man who has no invisible means of support.
JOHN BUCHAN

When men make gods, there is no God.
EUGENE O'NEILL, *Lazarus Laughed* (1927), 2.2

It is the heart which experiences God, and not the reason.
PASCAL, *Pensées* (1670), 278

I need God to take me by force, because if death, doing away with the shield of the flesh, were to put me face to face with him, I should run away.
SIMONE WEIL, *Gravity and Grace*

Fear God, yes, but don't be afraid of Him.
J.A. SPENDER, *The Comments of Bagshot*

Whatever your conception of God may be, believe Him to be your Friend.
DR. FRANK CRANE, *Essays*

Thine, O Lord, is the greatness, and the power, and the glory, and the victory, and the majesty: for all that is in the heaven and in the earth, is Thine; Thine is the kingdom, O Lord, and thou art exalted as head above all.
1 *Chronicles* 29:11

Many are the means described for the attainment of the highest good, such as love, performance of duty, self-control, truthfulness, sacrifices, gifts, austerity, charity, vows, observance of moral precepts. I could name more. But of all I could name, verily love is the highest: love and devotion that make one forgetful of everything else, love that unites the lover with me. What ineffable joy does one find through love of me, the blissful Self! Once that joy is realised, all earthly pleasures fade into nothingness.
SRIMAD BHAGAVATAM, XI, viii

The soul, having conquered the multiple heavens and possessed herself of the mysterious power, is plunged into the unity of the motionless heaven, called fire or the empyrean, not because it is burning but because it is enlightening, all who are in the heaven being ablaze with the cherubic light of divine love.
ECKHART

We are pieces of steel, and thy love is the magnet.
DÎVÂNI SHAMSI TABRIZ, XXXII

As a devotee cannot live without God, so also God cannot live without His devotee. (Thus?) the devotee becomes the sweetness, and God its enjoyer. The devotee becomes the (nectar?) and God the bee. It is the Godhead that has become these two in order to enjoy Its (unclear) Bliss. That is the significance of the episode of Râdhâ and Krishna.
SRI RAMAKRISHNA

My children, mark me, I pray you. Know! God loves my soul so much that his very life and being depend upon his loving me, whether he would or no. To stop God loving me would be to rob him of his Godhood: for God is love no less than he is truth; as he is good, so is he love as well. It is the absolute truth, as God lives...

If anyone should ask me what God is, I should answer: God is love, and so altogether lovely that creatures all with one accord essay to love his loveliness, whether they do so knowingly or unbeknownst, in joy or sorrow.
ECKHART

Nor Aught nor Nought existed: yon bright sky
Was not, nor Heaven's broad woof outstretched above.
What covered all? what sheltered? what concealed?
Was it the water's fathomless abyss?
There was not Death: yet was there nought immortal.
There was no confine betwixt day and night:
The only ONE breathed breathless by Itself.
Other than It there was nothing since has been.
Darkness there was, and all at first was veiled
In gloom profound - an ocean without light -
The Germ that still lay covered in the husk
Burst forth, one nature, from the fervent heat.
Then first came love upon it, the new spring
Of mind - yea poets in their hearts discerned,
Pondering, this bond between created things
And uncreated. Comes this spark from Earth
Piercing and all-pervading, or from Heaven?
Then seeds were sown, and mighty powers arose -

Nature below, and power and
will above -
Who knows the secret? Who
proclaimed it here,
Whence, whence this
manifold creation sprang?
He from whom all this great
creation came,
Whether His will created or
was mute,
The Most High Seer that is in
highest heaven,
He knows it - or perchance
even He knows not.
CREATION HYMN from the
Rig-Veda

He that loveth not knoweth
not God: for God is love...
He that dwelleth in love
dwelleth in God, and God in
him.
I *John* 4:8,16

Thou hast put salt in our
mouths that we may thirst for
Thee.
SAINT AUGUSTINE,
Confessions

One who says no to himself
cannot say yes to God.
HERMANN HESSE,
Reflections, 289, Religion and
the Church

God is within us: He is that
inner presence which makes
us admire the beautiful, which
rejoices us when we have
done right and consoles us for
not sharing the happiness of
the wicked.
EUGÈNE DELACROIX

God is our expression for all
forces and powers which we
do not understand, or with
which we are unfamiliar.
SAMUEL BUTLER

God is that indefinable
something which we all feel
but which we do not know.
To me God is truth and love,
God is ethics and morality,
God is fearlessness, God is the
source of light and life and yet
He is above and beyond all
these. God is conscience. He
is even the atheism of the
atheist.
GANDHI

The foundation of all
foundations, the pillar
supporting all wisdoms, is the
recognition of the reality of
God.
MOSES MAIMONIDES

Those who attempt to search into the majesty of God will be overwhelmed with its glory.
THOMAS À KEMPIS

Belief in God is an instinct as natural to man as walking on two legs.
G.C. LICHTENBERG

To stand on one leg and prove God's existence is a very different thing from going on one's knees and thanking Him.
SÖREN KIERKEGAARD

Truth seeth God, and Wisdom beholdeth God, and of these two cometh the third: that is a holy marvelling delight in God; which is Love. Where Truth and Wisdom are verily, there is Love verily, coming of them both.
JULIAN OF NORWICH

The perfect love of God knoweth no difference between the poor and the rich.
PACUVIUS

God moves in a mysterious way
His wonders to perform;
He plants His footsteps in the sea,
And rides upon the storm.
WILLIAM COWPER

When God reveals His march through Nature's night
His steps are beauty, and His presence light.
MONTGOMERY

He who waits for God fails to understand that he possesses Him. Believe that God and happiness are one, and put all your happiness in the present moment.
ANDRÉ GIDE

Who guides below, and rules above:
The great Disposer, and the mighty King.
Than He none greater, next Him none,
That can be, is, or was:
Supreme, He singly fills the throne.
HORACE

Love is my bait; you must be caught by it; it will put its hook into your heart and (teach?) you to know that of all strong things nothing is so strong, so irresistible, as divine love.

It brought forth all the creation; it kindles all the life of Heaven; it is the song of all (the?) angels of God. It has redeemed all the world; it seeks for every sinner upon earth and embraces all the enemies of God. It has redeemed all the world; it seeks for every sinner upon earth (unclear) embraces all the enemies of God; and from the beginning to the end of time the one (unclear) of Providence is the one work of love.
WILLIAM LAW

It is a hard and steely heart that is not softened by the divine presence and not attracted [by] its sweetness.
RICHARD OF SAINT-VICTOR

God is one. And he that is one is nameless: for he does not need a name, since he is alone.
HERMES, *Fragments*, 3

I believe in god as I believe in my friends, because I feel the breath of His affection, feel His invisible and intangible hand drawing me, leading me, grasping me; because I possess an inner consciousness of a particular providence and of a universal mind that marks out for me the course of my own destiny.
MIGUEL DE UNAMUNO

There is nothing that stands fast, nothing fixed, nothing free from change, among the things which come into being, neither among those in heaven nor among those on earth. God alone stands unmoved, and with good reason; for he is self-contained, and self-derived, and wholly self-centred, and in him is no deficiency or imperfection. He stands fast in virtue of his own immobility, nor can he be moved by any force impinging on him from without, seeing that in him are all things, and that it is he alone that is in all things.
HERMES, *Heterod*, Introduction

People ought to talk about God only naturally.
ANDRÉ GIDE

But I always think that the
best way to know God is to
love many things.
VINCENT VAN GOGH
from *Dear Theo*

Wretched is the man that
knows every thing but God.
BISHOP THOMAS
WILSON, *Maxims of Piety and
Christianity*

A clear understanding of God
makes one want to follow the
direction of things, the
direction of one's Self.
ANDRÉ GIDE, *Journals,*
Volume I

All in One as One, and One
in All as All, and One and all
Good, is loved through the
One in One, and for the sake
of the One, for the love that
man hath to the One.
Theologia Germanica, XLIII

There is a reality even prior to
heaven and earth:
Indeed, it has no form, much
less a name:
Eyes fail to see it:
It has no voice for ears to detect:
To call it Mind or Buddha
violates its nature.
DAI-O KOKUSHI

Before the One, what is there
to count?
SEFER YETSIRAH

Behind the facts there must be
the man, and *the man must be
with God,* must talk like God
Almighty.
HENRY MILLER, *The
Cosmological Eye*

God often visits us, but most
of the time we are not at
home.
JOSEPH ROUX, *Meditations
of a Parish Priest*

Why should I wish to see God
better than this day?
I see something of God each
hour of the twenty-four, and
each moment then,
In the faces of men and
women I see God, and in my
own face in the glass,
I find letters from God dropt
in the street, and every one is
sign'd by God's name,
And I leave them where they
are, for I know that whereso'er
I go,
Others will punctually come
for ever and ever.
WALT WHITMAN, *Leaves of
Grass,* Song of Myself

Everything in these depths of
the Holy Spirit is beyond
understanding or explanation.
ST. SIMEON THE NEW
THEOLOGIAN

His greatness is unsearchable.
Psalms 145:3

God has made all things out
of nothing, and that same
nothing is himself.
BOEHME

... Him whom neither being
nor understanding can
contain.
DIONYSIUS

If we fail to find God it is
because we seek in semblance
what has no resemblance...
On merging into the Godhead
all definition is lost.
ECKHART

His being cannot be
accurately described by any of
the names we call him.
HERMES

The soul is a creature
receptive to everything
named, but the nameless she
cannot receive until she is
gotten so deep into God that
she is nameless herself. And
then none can tell if it is she
that has gotten God or God
has gotten her.
ECKHART

Conscious of this, the Sacred
Writers celebrate It by every
Name while yet they call It
Nameless.
DIONYSIUS, *Reality*, 775

All that which we call the
attributes of God are only so
many human ways of our
conceiving that abyssal All
which can neither be spoken
nor conceived by us.
WILLIAM LAW

Now mark! God is nameless:
no one can know or say
anything of him.
ECKHART

It is infinite,
incomprehensible,
immeasurable, it exceeds our
powers, and is beyond our
scrutiny. The place of it, the
whither and the whence, the
manner and quality of its
being, are unknown to us. It
moves in absolute stability,
and its stability moves within it.
HERMES

St. Augustine says, "The soul
has a private door into
divinity where for her all
things amount to naught."
There she is ignorant with
knowing, will-less with
willing, dark with
enlightenment.
ECKHART

Do you seek God? Well, seek
Him in man!
His divinity is manifest more
in man than in
any other object. Look
around you for a man
with a love of God that
overflows,
a man who yearns for God, a
man
intoxicated with His love. In
such a man
God has incarnated Himself.
SURI RAMAKRISHNA

Acquaint thyself with God, if
thou would'st taste
His works. Admitted once to
his embrace,
Thou shalt perceive that thou
wast blind before:
Thine eye shall be instructed;
and thine heart,
Made pure, shall relish, with
divine delight
Till then unfelt, what hands

divine have wrought.
Brutes graze the mountain-
top, with faces prone
And eyes intent upon the
scanty herb
It yields them; or, recumbent
on its brow,
Ruminate heedless of the
scene outspread
Beneath, beyond, and
stretching far away
From inland regions to the
distant main.
Man views it, and admires;
but rests content
With what he views. The
landscape has his praise,
But not its author.
Unconcern'd who form'd
The paradise he sees, he finds
it such,
And such well-pleas'd to find
it, asks no more.
Not so the mind that has been
touch'd from heav'n,
And in the school of sacred
wisdom taught
To read his wonders, in whose
thought the world,
Fair as it is, existed ere it was.
Not for its own sake merely,
but for his
Much more who fashion'd it,
he gives it praise;
Praise that, from earth
resulting, as it ought,

To earth's acknowledg'd
sov'reign, finds at once
Its only just proprietor in
Him.
The soul that sees him, or
receives sublim'd
New faculties, or learns at
least t' employ
More worthily the pow'rs she
own'd before;
Discerns in all things, what,
with stupid gaze
Of ignorance, till then she
overlook'd -
A ray of heav'nly light, gilding
all forms
Terrestrial in the vast and the
minute;
The unambiguous footsteps of
the God
Who gives its lustre to an
insect's wing,
And wheels his throne upon
the rolling worlds.
Much conversant with heav'n,
she often holds
With those fair ministers of
light to man,
That fill the skies nightly with
silent pomp,
Sweet conference: inquires
what strains were they
With which heav'n rang,
when ev'ry star, in haste
To gratulate the new-created
earth,

Sent forth a voice and all the
sons of God
Shouted for joy. Tell me, ye
shining hosts,
That navigate a sea that
knows no storms,
Beneath a vault unsullied with
a cloud,
If from your elevation, whence
ye view
Distinctly scenes invisible to
man,
And systems of whose birth
no tidings yet
Have reach'd this nether
world, ye spy a race
Favour'd as our's; transgressors
from the womb,
And hasting to a grave, yet
doom'd to rise.
WILLIAM COWPER from
The Task

TWENTY

GOVERNMENT

To be acquainted with the merit of a ministry, we need only observe the condition of the people.
JUNIUS, *Letters*, Letter 1

What government is the best? That which teaches us to govern ourselves.
GOETHE, *Sprüche in Prosa*, Part III

Nothing appears more surprising to those who consider human affairs with a philosophical eye, than the easiness with which the many are governed by the few.
HUME, *Essays: First Principles of Government*

Unjust rule never endures perpetually.
SENECA, *Medea*, line 196

They that govern best make least noise.
JOHN SELDEN

In the long-run every government is the exact symbol of its people, with their wisdom and unwisdom.
THOMAS CARLYLE, *Past and Present* (1843), 4.4

I believe and confess that a people can value nothing more highly than the dignity and liberty of its existence. This it must defend these to the last drop of its blood. That there is no higher duty to fulfil, no higher law to obey. That the shameful blot of cowardly submission can never be erased. That this drop of poison in the blood of a nation is passed on to posterity, crippling and eroding the strength of future generations. That the honour of the king and government are one with the honour of the people, and the sole safeguard of its well-being. That a people courageously struggling for its liberty is invincible. That even the destruction of liberty after a bloody and honourable struggle assures the people's rebirth. It is the seed of life, which one day will bring forth a new, securely rooted tree.
PAUL CLAUSEWITZ

It is a maxim of wise government to deal with men not as they ought to be but as they are.
GOETHE

That government is not best which best secures mere life and property - there is a more valuable thing - manhood.
MARK TWAIN, *Notebook* (1935)

He shall rule them with a rod of iron.
Revelation 2:27

That to live by one man's will became the men's misery.
RICHARD HOOKER, *Ecclesiastical Policy*, Book 1

Our object in the construction of the state is the greatest happiness of the whole, and not that of any one class.
PLATO, *Republic*, IV, 1

My experience in government is that when things are non-controversial, beautifully coordinated and all the rest, it must be that there is not much going on.
PRESIDENT JOHN F. KENNEDY

No government is safe unless buttressed by goodwill.
CORNELIUS NEPOS, *Dion*

Nothing is so galling to a people, not broken in from the birth, as a paternal, or, in other words, a meddling government, a government which tells them what to read, and say, and eat, and drink, and wear.
MACAULAY, *Southey's Colloquies*

Do not move unless it is advantageous.
Do not execute unless it is effective.
Do not challenge unless it is critical.

An intense View is not a reason to launch an opposition.
An angry leader is not a reason to initiate a challenge.

If engagement brings advantage, move.
If not, stop.

Intensity can cycle back to fondness.
Anger can cycle back to

satisfaction.
But an extinct organisation
cannot cycle back to survival.
And those who are destroyed
cannot cycle back to life.

Thus, a Brilliant Ruler is
prudent;
A Good Leader is on guard.

Such is the Tao of a Stable
Organisation and a Complete
Force.
SUN TZU

Local self-government is the
life-blood of liberty.
J.L. MOTLEY, Rise of Dutch
Republic, Part 6, Chapter 1

You do not know, my son,
with how little wisdom men
are governed.
COUNT AXEL
OXENSTIERNA OF
SWEDEN, (1583-1654)

The axiom of power united to
philosophy is in every way
true: That neither a state nor
a man can ever be happy
unless by leading a life of
prudence in subjection always
to justice.
PLATO, Epistle 7

Both the USA and Modern
Russia have been built by
robber barons. The difference
is that the Barons of America
made it whereas the Russian
ones have bought it.
TONY RENTON

Where there is not modesty,
nor regard for law, nor
religion, reverence, good faith,
the kingdom is insecure.
SENECA, Thyesles, Act II,
215

Fear not the tyrants shall rule
for ever,
Or the priests of the bloody
faith;
They stand on the brink of
that mighty river,
Whose waves they have
tainted with death.
PERCY BYSSHE SHELLEY,
Rosalind

Fascism is not in itself a new
order of society. It is the
future refusing to be born.
ANEURIN BEVAN

Syracusans, above all things
turn your regard to laws not
designed merely for money-
making and wealth. There are

three things, soul, body, and worldly prosperity. Put the worth of the soul first; that of the body second; but third and last that of wealth, as being the servant of both body and soul.
PLATO, *Epistle 8*

Dead dictators are my speciality. I discovered to my horror that all the political figures most featured in my writing - Mrs. G, Sanjay Gandhi, Bhutto, Zia - have now come to sticky ends. It's the grand slam really. This is a service I can perform, perhaps. A sort of literary contract.
SALMAN RUSHDIE, (1947)

One person calls it a democracy, another by another name, as he pleases. But it is in truth a government by the best, combined with a good opinion of the people.
PLATO, *Menexenus, 8*

I really do inhabit a system in which words are capable of shaking the entire structure of government, where words can prove mightier than ten military divisions.
VÀCLAV HAVEL, (1989)

Those who govern, having much business on their hands, do not generally like to take the trouble of considering and carrying into execution new projects. The best public measures are therefore seldom adopted from previous wisdom, but forced by the occasion.
BENJAMIN FRANKLIN, *Autobiography* (1791), 2

A compassionate government keeps faith with the trust of the people and cherishes the future of their children. Through compassion for the plight of one individual, government fulfils its purpose as the servant of all the people.
LYNDON B. JOHNSON, (1964)

The best of all rulers is but a shadowy presence to his subjects.
Next comes the ruler they love and praise;
Next comes one they fear;
Next comes one with whom they take liberties.

When there is not enough faith, there is lack of good faith.
Hesitant, he does not utter words lightly.
When his task is accomplished and his work done
The people all say, "It happened to us naturally."
LAO-TSE, *Tao Te Ching*, I. XVII

Render therefore unto Caesar the things which are Caesar's; and unto God the things that are God's.
Matthew 22:21

When Tzu Lu asked about the art of government, the Master replied: "Be in advance of the people; show them how to work." On his asking for something more, the Master added: "Untiringly."
SAYINGS OF CONFUCIUS

As if an individual could only share in the life of the state by taking the business of government directly to heart; as if this feverish desire to manage everything were not in fact a kind of sickness; as if,

even when such active participation is guaranteed, it did not finally come down to a few restless souls in the capital and the commercial centres, with the mass of people remaining spectators in the streets. But the masses will also be aroused, of course, and their passions will swing back and forth; yet this back and forth is precisely the problem.
If the subject is to be linked properly with the state, he must understand its main interests. These must be great and permanent, and the citizen's support of this permanent direction must constitute his participation. The government must be so organised that it deserves his confidence. This confidence need not be blind or absolute. He can evaluate the government's actions, and his heart can give them greater or lesser approval. In this judgement and greater or lesser approval on the part of the subject, the government can recognise the stars that guide it and enable it to travel more easily and quickly.
PAUL CLAUSEWITZ

Government is a contrivance
of human wisdom to provide
for human wants. Men have a
right that these wants should
be provided by this wisdom.
EDMUND BURKE,
*Reflections on the French
Revolution*

You can only govern men by
serving them. The rule is
without exception.
VICTOR COUSIN

I will govern according to the
commonweal, but not
according to the common will.
JAMES I OF ENGLAND,
(1621)

A wise man neither suffers
himself to be governed, nor
attempts to govern others.
LA BRUYÈRE, *Les Caractères*

He that would govern others,
first should be
The master of himself.
PHILIP MASSINGER, *The
Bondman*, Act I, Scene iii

When the government is
muddled
The people are simple;
When the government is alert

The people are cunning.
It is on disaster that good
fortune perches;
It is beneath good fortune that
disaster crouches.
Who knows the limit? Does
not the straightforward exist?
The straightforward changes
again into the crafty, and the
good changes again into the
monstrous.
Indeed, it is long since the
people were perplexed.
Therefore the sage is square-
edged but does not scrape,
Has corners but does not jab,
Extends himself but not at the
expense of others,
Shines but does not dazzle.
LAO-TSE, *Tao Te Ching*, II.
LVIII

Where five economists gather
together, there you will find
six opinions, two of them
Maynard Keynes's, and one
Milton Freedman's.
ANON

The proper function of a
government is to make it easy
for people to do good, and
difficult for them to do evil.
GLADSTONE

Nothing is politically right
which is morally wrong.
O'CONNELL

The philosopher is he who has
in his mind the perfect pattern
of justice, beauty, and truth;
his is the knowledge of the
eternal; he contemplates all
time, and all existence. I need
no longer hesitate to say that
we must make our guardians
philosophers. Our test must
be thorough, for the soul must
be trained up by the pursuit of
all kinds of knowledge to the
capacity for the pursuit of the
highest - higher than justice
and wisdom - the idea of the
good. Our rulers must possess
every endowment of mind and
body, all cultivated to the
highest degree. From the
select we must again select, at
twenty, those who are most fit
for the next ten years' course
of education; and from them,
at thirty, we shall choose
those who can, with
confidence, be taken to face
the light: who have been
tested and found to be
absolutely steadfast, not
shaken by having got beyond
the conventional view of

things. We will give them
five or six years of philosophy;
then fifteen years of
responsible office in the State;
and at fifty they shall return to
philosophy to take up the
duties of educating their
successors.
SOCRATES

It is better for a city to be
governed by a good man than
by good laws.
ARISTOTLE

Leaders are those who protect
the organisation.
If the protection is complete,
the organisation will be strong.
If the protection is flawed, the
organisation will be
vulnerable.

A Ruler can bring adversity to
the Force in three ways:

By not understanding that the
Force is unable to advance
And calling for an advance;
Or not understanding that the
Force is unable to retreat,
And calling for a retreat.
This is called hobbling the
Force.

By not understanding the
Work of the Entire Force
And aligning the Entire Force
along political lines.
As a result, individuals in the
Force become doubtful.
By not understanding the
natural authority of the Entire
Force
And aligning the Entire Force
with appointed officials.
As a result, individuals in the
Force become skeptical.

When the Entire Force is
doubtful, and moreover,
skeptical,
Other leaders can cause
serious problems.

This is what is meant by a
disordered Force leading to
another's triumph.
SUN TZU

It seems to me a great truth,
that human things cannot
stand on selfishness,
mechanical utilities,
economies, and law courts;
that if there be not a religious
element in the relations of
men, such relations are
miserable, and doomed to
ruin.
THOMAS CARLYLE

When any of the four pillars
of government are mainly
shaken, or weakened (which
are religion, justice, counsel,
and treasure,) men had need
to pray for fair weather.
FRANCIS BACON

Ill can he rule the great that
cannot reach the small.
SPENSER, *Faerie Queene*,
Book V, Canto ii, Stanza 43

Govern a great nation as you
would fry small fish.
LAO-TSE

But who can penetrate man's
secret thought,
The quality and temper of his
soul,
Till by high office put to
frequent proof,
And execution of the laws?
SOPHOCLES, *Antigone*

The Athenians govern the
Greeks; I govern the
Athenians; you, my wife,
govern me; your son governs
you.
THEMISTOCLES.
(PLUTARCH, *Lives:
Themistocles*, Chapter 18,
Section 5)

The care of human life and
happiness, and not their
destruction, is the first and
only legitimate object of good
government.
THOMAS JEFFERSON,
Notes on Virginia: Writings,
Volume III, page 263

TWENTY-ONE

HAPPINESS

To seek happiness, identifying the Self with the body, is like trying to cross a river on the back of a crocodile. When the ego rises, the mind is separated from its Source, the Self, and is restless like a stone thrown up into the air, or like the waters of a river. When the stone or the river reaches its place of origin, the ground or the ocean, it comes to rest. So too the mind comes to rest and is happy when it returns to and rests in its Source. As the stone and the river are sure to return to their starting place, so too the mind will inevitably - at some time - return to its Source.

Happiness is your own nature. Hence it is not wrong to desire it. What is wrong is seeking it outside, because it is inside.
SRI RAMANA MAHARSHI

In tranquillity, in stillness, in the unconditioned, in inaction, we find the levels of the universe, the very constitution of TAO...
CHUANG-TSE , Action, Chapter XV, 358

"Peace be with you" was the salutation of him who was the salvation of man. For it was meet that the supreme saviour should utter the supreme salutation.
DANTE, De Monarchia, IV

Sorrow and happiness are the heresies of virtue; joy and anger lead astray from TAO; love and hate cause the loss of virtue. The heart unconscious of sorrow and happiness, - this is perfect virtue. ONE, without change, - that is perfect repose.
CHUANG-TSE ,
Renunciation, ch. XV, 136

No one has ever attained to the grandeur or glory
Of the Soul which has not established repose in his or her heart.
ANGELUS SILESIUS

Justice is the only worship.
Love is the only priest.
Ignorance is the only slavery.
Happiness is the only good.
The time to be happy is now.
The place to be happy is here.
The way to be happy is to make other people happy.
INGERSOLL

Happiness grows at our own fireside, and is not to be picked up in strangers' gardens.
JERROLD

Nature has granted to all to be happy, if we did but know how to use her benefits.
CLAUDIAN

True happiness is a thing that never gives rise to satiety.
HERMES

If solid happiness we prize, within our breast this jewel lies; and they are fools who roam. The world has nothing to bestow; from our own selves our joys must flow, and that dear hut - our home.
COTTON

A man does not seek to see himself in running water, but in still water. For only what is itself still can impart stillness into others.
CHUANG-TSE, *Knowledge*, Chapter V, 749

What is the best thing of all for a man, that he may ask from the Gods?
"That he may be always at peace with himself."
Contest of Homer and Hesiod

The peace of God, which passeth all understanding, shall keep your hearts and minds.
Philippians 4:7

All real and wholesome enjoyments possible to man have been just as possible to him as they are now; and they are possible to him chiefly in peace. To watch the corn grow and the blossom set, to draw hard breath over plough-share or spade, to read, to think, to love, to hope, to pray - these are the things to make men happy.
RUSKIN

You traverse the world in search of happiness, which is within the reach of every man: a contented mind confers it on all.
HORACE

Hume's doctrine was that the circumstances vary, the amount of happiness does not; that the beggar cracking fleas in the sunshine under a hedge, and the duke rolling by in his

chariot, the girl equipped for her first Ball, and the orator returning triumphant from the debate, all had different means, but the same quality of pleasant excitement.
RALPH WALDO EMERSON

The rich should not presume in his riches, nor the poor despond in his poverty; for the providence of God gives happiness to both of them - and the distribution of happiness between them is more equally divided than the fool would believe.
DANDEMIS

I wish but for the thing I have.
WILLIAM SHAKESPEARE, *Romeo and Juliet*, Act II, Scene ii, line 132

Do not envy the appearance of happiness in any man, for you do not know his secret griefs.
DANDEMIS

Nothing is left to Saichi.
Except a joyful heart nothing is left to him.
Neither good nor bad has he, all is taken away from him:
Nothing is left to him!

To have nothing - how completely satisfying!
Everything has been carried away,
He is thoroughly at home with himself.
SAICHI

This Divine Name is in truth a mine of riches, it is the fount of the highest holiness and the secret of the greatest happiness that a man can hope to enjoy on this Earth.
E.D.M., *The Wonders of the Holy Name*

The Prayer of my heart gave me such consolation that I felt there was no happier person on earth than I, and I doubted if there could be greater and fuller happiness in the kingdom of Heaven. Not only did I feel this in my own soul, but the whole outside world also seemed to me full of charm and delight.
Everything drew me to love and thank God. People, trees, plants, animals, I saw them all as my kinsfolk. I found on all of them the magic of the Name of Jesus. Sometimes I felt as light as though I had no body and was floating happily

through the air instead of walking. Sometimes when I withdrew into myself I ... was filled with wonder at the wisdom with which the human body is made.
THE RUSSIAN PILGRIM,
Introduction on Holiness

Men are made for happiness, and anyone who is completely happy has a right to say to himself: "I am doing God's will on earth."
ANTON CHEKHOV

A happiness that is sought for ourselves alone can never be found: for a happiness that is diminished by being shared is not big enough to make us happy.
THOMAS MERTON, *No Man Is an Island*

Happiness is not a horse; you cannot harness it.
RUSSIAN PROVERB

For the last year I have been happy for the first time in my life - happy not in the outward shadow part of me, but in my soul which is clear and radiant out of a long darkness.
ELLEN GLASGOW, *Letters*

The conventional notions of happiness cannot possibly be taken seriously by anyone whose intellectual or moral development has progressed beyond that of a three-week-old puppy.
JOHN W. GARDNER, in *No Easy Victories*

You cannot make people happy, only create the conditions for them to be happy in.
JONAS CABAL

Just as a cautious businessman avoids investing all his capital in one concern, so wisdom would probably admonish us also not to anticipate all our happiness from one quarter alone.
SIGMUND FREUD,
Civilisation and Its Discontents

I think that all happiness depends on the energy to assume the mask of some other self; that all joyous or creative life is a rebirth as something not oneself, something which has no memory and is created in a moment and perpetually renewed.
W.B. YEATS, *Autobiography*

I have never looked upon ease and happiness as ideals in themselves - this ethical basis I call the ideal of the pigsty.
ALBERT EINSTEIN, *Ideas and Opinions*

I have come to know happy individuals by the way, who are happy only because they are whole. Even the lowliest, provided he is whole, can be happy and in his own way perfect.
GOETHE, *Wisdom and Experience*

Happiness is a great love and much serving.
OLIVE SCHREINER, quoted in A *Diary for the Thankful-Hearted*

We haven't time to be ourselves. All we have time for is happiness.
ALBERT CAMUS, *Notebooks*, 1935-1942

Very few people can stand conditions of life that are too happy; the great majority become stultified by them. Life is only felt to be real when it is creatively active. Thus people who appear to outsiders to be exceptionally happy, because of their freedom from care, are as a rule the least satisfied.
COUNT HERMANN KEYSERLING, *The Book of Marriage*

Happiness comes, I know, from within a man - from some curious *adjustment* to life. The happiest people I have known in this world have been the Saints - and, after these, the men and women who get immediate and conscious enjoyment from little things.
HUGH WALPOLE, *Roman Fountain*

The happiness that is genuinely satisfying is accompanied by the fullest exercise of our faculties, and the fullest realization of the world in which we live.
BERTRAND RUSSELL, *The Conquest of Happiness*

The secret of happiness (and therefore of success) is to be in harmony with existence, to be always calm, always lucid, always willing "to be joined to the universe without being

more conscious of it than an idiot," to let each wave of life wash us a little farther up the shore.
CYRIL CONNOLLY, *The Unquiet Grave*

The bird of paradise alights only upon the hand that does not grasp.
JOHN BERRY, *Flight of White Crows*, 1961

He who binds to himself a joy
Does the winged life destroy;
But he who kisses the joy as it flies
Lives in eternity's sunrise.
WILLIAM BLAKE, *Eternity*, (1793-99)

Whose happiness is so firmly established that he has no quarrel from any side with his estate of life?
BOETHIUS, *The Consolation of Philosophy* (AD 524), 2

You are forgiven for your happiness and your successes only if you generously consent to share them.
ALBERT CAMUS, *The Fall*, (1956)

Happiness is like a sunbeam, which the least shadow intercepts.
CHINESE PROVERB

Happiness, that grand mistress of the ceremonies in the dance of life, impels us through all its mazes and meanderings, but leads none of us by the same route.
CHARLES CALEB COLTON, *Lacon* (1825), 2. 109

Happiness lies in the fulfilment of the spirit through the body.
CYRIL CONNOLLY, *The Unquiet Grave* (1945), 1

Eden is that old-fashioned House
We dwell in every day
Without suspecting our abode
Until we drive away.
EMILY DICKINSON, *Poems* (c. 1862-86)

True joy is the earnest which we have of heaven, it is the treasure of the soul, and therefore should be laid in a safe place, and nothing in this world is safe to place it in.
JOHN DONNE, *Sermons*, No. 28, (1624-25?)

What we call happiness in the strictest sense comes from the (preferably sudden) satisfaction of needs which have been dammed up to a high degree.
SIGMUND FREUD, *Civilization and Its discontents,* (1930), 2

I have the happiness of the passing moment, and what more can mortal ask?
GEORGE GISSING, *The Private Papers of Henry Ryecroft,* (1903)

Happiness is a thing of gravity. It seeks for hearts of bronze, and carves itself there slowly; pleasure startles it away by tossing flowers to it. Joy's smile is much more close to ears than it is to laughter.
VICTOR HUGO, *Hernani* (1830), 5.3

It is neither wealth nor splendour, but tranquillity and occupation, which give happiness.
THOMAS JEFFERSON, letter, 1788

Wherein lies happiness? In that which becks

Our ready minds to fellowship divine,
A fellowship with essence; till we shine,
Full alchemized, and free of space. Behold
The clear religion of heaven!
JOHN KEATS, Endymion, 1.777

When one door of happiness closes, another opens; but often we look so long at the closed door that we do not see the one which has been opened for us.
HELEN KELLER, *We Bereaved* (1929)

Happiness is itself a kind of gratitude.
JOSEPH WOOD KRUTCH, *The Twelve Seasons,* October, (1949)

That thou art happy, owe to God;
That thou continuest such, owe to thyself,
That is, to thy obedience.
MILTON, *Paradise Lost* (1667), Book V, line 520

We should consider every day lost on which we have not danced at least once. And we

should call every truth false
which was not accompanied
by at least one laugh.
FRIEDRICH NIETZSCHE,
Thus Spoke Zarathustra, On old
and New Tablets, (1883-92), 3

There are many roads
to happiness, if the gods
assent.
PINDAR, *Odes* (5th century
BC), Olympia 8

Happiness is indeed a
Eurydice, vanishing as soon as
gazed upon. It can exist only
in *acceptance*, and succumbs as
soon as it is laid claim to.
DENIS DE ROUGEMONT,
Love in the Western World
(1939), 7.4

Most people ask for happiness
on condition. Happiness can
only be felt if you don't set
any condition.
ARTHUR RUBINSTEIN,
(1956)

A string of excited, fugitive,
miscellaneous pleasures is not
happiness; happiness resides in
imaginative reflection and
judgement, when the picture
of one's life, as of human life,
as it truly has been or is,

satisfies the will, and is gladly
accepted.
GEORGE SANTAYANA,
The Middle Span (1945), 1

Our happiness depends
on wisdom all the way.
SOPHOCLES, *Antigone* (442-
41 BC)

Those undeserved joys which
come uncalled and make us
more pleased than grateful are
they that sing.
THOREAU, *Journal*, (1842)

A wise man sings his joy in
the closet of his heart.
TIBULLUS, *Elegies* (1st
century BC), 3.19

The hidden harmony is better
than the obvious.
HERACLITUS, *Fragments*
(circa 500 BC), 116

It is indeed from the
experience of beauty and
happiness, from the occasional
harmony between our nature
and our environment, that we
draw our conception of the
divine life.
GEORGE SANTAYANA,
The Sense of Beauty, (1896)

Prosperity is not without many fears and distastes; and adversity is not without comforts and hopes.
FRANCIS BACON, Essays, Of Adversity

Everyone chases after happiness
But happiness is running after them.
BERTOLT BRECHT, The Song of the Super-inadequacy of Human Striving

Much is won if we succeed in transforming hysterical misery into common unhappiness.
SIGMUND FREUD

Happiness Makes up in Height What It Lacks in Length.
ROBERT FROST

The happiest man is one who can link the end of his life with its beginning.
JOHANN WOLFGANG VON GOETHE, Maxims and Reflections

Happiness can be possessed only as long as it is unseen.
HERMANN HESSE, Reflections, 601

If a man talks of his misfortunes, there is something in them that is not disagreeable to him.
DR. SAMUEL JOHNSON, Boswell, Life of Johnson, (1780)

Happiness comes uninvited; and the moment you are conscious that you are happy, you are no longer happy.
J. KRISHNAMURTI, Krishnamurti Reader, Questions and Answers

Men who are unhappy, like men who sleep badly, are always proud of the fact.
BERTRAND RUSSELL, The Conquest of Happiness, Chapter 1

Who never knew the price of happiness will not be happy.
YEVGENY YEVTUSHENKO, Lies

There is this in common between the lives or ordinary men and of saints, that they all aspire to happiness; they differ only in the object where they place it.
PASCAL, Pensées

Really high-minded people are indifferent to happiness, especially other people's.
BERTRAND RUSSELL, *The Conquest of Happiness*

There is a time when a man distinguishes the idea of felicity from the idea of wealth; it is the beginning of wisdom.
RALPH WALDO EMERSON, *Journals of Ralph Waldo Emerson*

If happiness hae not her seat
And centre in the breast,
We may be wise or rich or great,
But never can be blest.
ROBERT BURNS, *Epistle to Davie*, Stanza 5

Now the heart is so full that a drop overfills it;
We are happy now because God wills it.
LOWELL, *Vision of Sir Launfal*, Prelude to Part I, line 61

Happiness depends, as Nature shows,
Less on exterior things than most suppose.
WILLIAM COWPER, *Table Talk*, line 246

The foolish man seeks happiness in the distance;
The wise man grows it under his feet.
JAMES OPPENHEIM, *The Wise*

Joy, joy for ever! - my task is done -
The gates are pass'd, and Heaven is won!
MOORE, *Lalla Rookh: Paradise and the Peri*

From harmony, from heavenly harmony,
This universal frame began:
From harmony to harmony
Through all the compass of the notes it ran,
The diapason closing full in Man.
DRYDEN, *A Song for St. Cecilia's Day*, line 11

Perfect happiness is the absence of the striving for happiness; perfect renown is the absence of concern for renown.
CHUANG-TSE

It is the chiefest point of happiness that a man is willing to be what he is.
ERASMUS

If an Arab in the desert were suddenly to discover a spring in his tent, and so would always be able to have water in abundance, how fortunate he would consider himself - so too, when a man, who as a physical being is always turned toward the outside, thinking that his happiness lies outside him, finally turns inward and discovers that the source is within him; not to mention his discovery that the source is his relation to God.
SÖREN KIERKEGAARD

Some of us might find happiness if we would quit struggling so desperately for it.
WILLIAM FEATHER

I have always been impressed by the fact that the most studiously avoided subject in western philosophy is that of happiness.
LIN YUTANG

No one praises happiness, as one praises justice, but we call it "a blessing", deeming it something higher and more divine than things we praise.
ARISTOTLE, Nicomachean Ethics, Book I, Chapter 12, Section 4

Whoever does not regard what he has as most ample wealth, is unhappy, though he be master of the world.
EPICURUS, Fragments, No. 474

He is not happy who does not think himself so.
PUBILIUS SYRUS, Sententiae, No. 984

We're born to be happy, all of us.
ALFRED SUTRO, The Perfect Lover, Act II

Happiness is a by-product of an effort to make some one else happy.
GRETTA PALMER, Permanent Marriage

Happiness and Beauty are by-products.
BERNARD SHAW, Maxims for Revolutionists

Happiness is a way-station between too little and too much.
CHANNING POLLOCK, Mr. Moneypenny

Happiness lies in the consciousness we have of it,

TWENTY-ONE - HAPPINESS 259

and by no means in the way
the future keeps its promises.
GEORGE SAND, *Handsome
Lawrence*, Chapter 3

The happiness of a man
consisteth not in having
temporal things in abundance,
but a moderate competency
sufficeth.
THOMAS À KEMPIS, *De
Imitatione Christi*, Part I,
Chapter 22

There is that in me - I do not
know what it is - but I know it
is in me ...
I do not know it - it is without
name - it is a word unsaid;
It is not in any dictionary,
utterance, symbol.
Something it swings on more
than the earth I swing on.
To it the creation is the friend
whose embracing awakes me...
It is not chaos or death - it is
form, union, plan - it is
eternal life - it is Happiness.
WALT WHITMAN, *Song of
Myself*, Section 50

The days that make us happy
make us wise.
JOHN MASEFIELD,
Biography

Nature has given the
opportunity of happiness to
all, knew they but how to use it.
CLAUDIAN, *In Rufinum*,
Book I, line 215

Happiness is not steadfast but
transient.
EURIPIDES, *Phoenissae*, line
558

The highest happiness, the
purest joys of life, wear out at
last.
GOETHE, *Iphigenia auf Tauris*,
Act IV, Scene v, line 9

One is never as happy or as
unhappy as one thinks.
LA ROCHEFOUCAULD,
Maximes, No. 49

The rays of happiness, like
those of light, are colourless
when unbroken.
LONGFELLOW, *Kavanagh*,
Chapter 13

My cup runneth over.
Psalms 23:5

There is no duty we so much
under-rate as the duty of being
happy.
R.L. STEVENSON, *An
Apology for Idlers*

So long as we can lose any happiness, we possess some.
BOOTH TARKINGTON,
Looking Forward, page 172

Inwardness, mildness, and self-renouncement do make for man's happiness.
MATTHEW ARNOLD,
Literature and Dogma,
Chapter 3

To be happy here is man's chief end,
For to be happy he must needs be good.
KIRKE WHITE, To
Contemplation

Who is the happiest of men?
He who values the merits of others.
ANON

There is in man a higher than love of happiness; he can do without happiness, and instead thereof find blessedness.
THOMAS CARLYLE, Sartor Resartus, The Everlasting Yea

I do not understand what the man who is happy wants in order to be happier.
CICERO, Tusculanarum

Disputationum, Book V,
Chapter 8, Section 23

The eternal not ourselves which makes for happiness.
MATTHEW ARNOLD,
Literature and Dogma,
Chapter 8

All beings desire happiness always, happiness without a tinge of sorrow. At the same time every body loves himself best. The cause for love is only happiness. So, that happiness must lie in one. Further that happiness is daily experienced by every one in sleep, when there is no mind. To attain that natural happiness one must know oneself. For that Self-Enquiry 'Who am I?' is the chief means.

Happiness is the nature of the Self. They are not different. The only happiness there is, is of the Self. That is the truth. There is no happiness in any object of the world. Because of our ignorance we imagine we derive happiness from them.

If, as a man generally imagines, his happiness is due

to external causes, it is reasonable to conclude that his happiness must increase with the increase of possessions and diminish in proportion to their diminution. Therefore, if he is devoid of possessions his happiness should be nil. What, however, is the real experience of man? Does it confirm this view? In deep sleep the man is devoid of all possessions, including his own body. Instead of being unhappy he is quite happy. Every one desires to sleep soundly. The conclusion therefore is that happiness is inherent in man and is not due to external causes. One must realise his Self in order to open the store of unalloyed happiness.

RAMANA MAHARSHI

TWENTY-TWO

HEALTH

The common ingredients of
health and long life are:
Great temp'rance, open air,
Easy labour, little care.
SIR PHILIP SIDNEY

In these days, half our diseases
come from the neglect of the
body in the overwork of the
brain. In this railway age, the
wear and tear of labour and
intellect go on without pause
or self-pity. We live longer
than our forefathers, but we
suffer more from a thousand
artificial anxieties and cares.
They fatigued only the
muscles, we exhaust the finer
strength of the nerves.
BULWER-LYTTON

Health is the greatest of all
possessions, and 'tis a maxim
with me, that a hale cobbler is
a better man than a sick king.
BICKERSTAFF

Health,
Thou chiefest good,
Bestow'd by heaven, but
seldom understood.
LUCAN

He who has health has hope,
and he who has hope has
everything.
ARABIAN PROVERB

Plain living and high thinking
will secure health for most of
us.
AVEBURY

Health and good estate of
body are above all gold, and a
strong body above infinite
wealth.
Apocrypha Ecclesiasticus 30, 15

Health is the most natural
thing in the world. It is
natural to be healthy, because
we are a part of Nature - we
are Nature. Nature tries hard
to keep us well... To centre
on one's-self, and forget one's
relationship to society, is to
summon misery; and misery
means disease. Misery is an
irritant. It affects the heart-
beats of circulation first; then
the digestion; and then the
person is ripe for two hundred
and nineteen diseases and six
hundred and forty-two
complications. What we call
diseases are principally
symptoms of mental
conditions. Our bodies are
automatic, and thinking about
our digestion does not aid us:
rather it hinders. If we are
worried enough, digestion will
stop absolutely.

The moral is obvious:
Don't worry.

The recipe for good health
is: Forget it!
HUBBARD

If all be well with belly, feet,
and sides,
A king's estate no greater
good provides.
HORACE, *Epistles*, Book1,
Epistle 12, line 5. Quoted by
Montaigne, *Essays*, Book 1,
Chapter 42

All health is better than
wealth.
SCOTT, *Familiar Letters*,
Volume 1, page 255

A good wife and good health
is a man's best wealth.
C.H. SPURGEON, *John
Ploughman*, Chapter 16

A man's own observation,
what he finds good of and
what he finds hurt of, is the
best physic to preserve health.
FRANCIS BACON, *Essays*,
Of Regimen of Health

The first was called Doctor
Diet, the second Doctor
Quiet, the third Doctor

Merryman.
WILLIAM BULLEIN,
Government of Health, Fo. 51
(1558)

Diet cures more than doctors.
A.B. CHEALES, *Proverbial
Folk-Lore*, No. 82

Nature, time and patience are
the three great physicians.
H.G. BOHN, *Hand-Book of
Proverbs*, 457

The surest road to health, say
what they will,
Is never to suppose we shall be
ill.
Most of those evils we poor
mortals know
From doctors and imagination
flow.
CHARLES CHURCHILL,
Night, line 69

Say you are well, or all is well
with you,
And God shall hear your
words and make them true.
ELLA WHEELER WILCOX,
Speech

People who are always taking
care of their health are like
misers, who are hoarding a
treasure which they have

never spirit enough to enjoy.
LAWRENCE STERNE

The only way for a rich man
to be healthy is, by exercise
and abstinence, to live as if he
were poor.
SIR W. TEMPLE

Ruddy Health the loftiest
Muse.
Live in the sunshine, swim the
sea,
Drink the wild air's salubrity.
RALPH WALDO
EMERSON, *Conduct of Life*,
Considerations by the Way

He that goes to bed thirsty
rises healthy.
GEORGE HERBERT, *Jacula
Prudentum*

Reason's whole pleasure, all
the joys of sense,
Lie in three words - Health,
Peace and Competence.
But health consists with
temperance alone,
And peace, O Virtue! peace is
all thy own.
ALEXANDER POPE, *Essay
on Man*, Epistle IV, line 79

Hold fast, then, to this sound
and wholesome rule of life:

indulge the body only so far as
is needful for health.
SENECA, *Epistulae ad
Lucilium*, Epistle VIII,
Section 5

When Health, affrighted,
spreads her rosy wing,
And flies with every changing
gale of spring.
BYRON, *Childish Recollections*,
1. 3

Oh, powerful bacillus,
With wonder how you fill us,
Every day!
While medical detectives,
With powerful objectives,
Watch your play.
W.T. HELMUTH, *Ode to the
Bacillus*

No man can have a peaceful
life who thinks too much
about lengthening it.
SENECA, *Epistulae ad
Lucilium*, Epistle IV, Section 4

He destroys his health by
labouring to preserve it.
VIRGIL, *Aeneid*, Book XII,
line 46

Health - silliest word in our
language, and one knows so
well the popular idea of

health. The English country gentleman galloping after a fox - the unspeakable in full pursuit of the uneatable.
OSCAR WILDE, A *Woman of No Importance*, Act I

Some reckon he killed himself with purgations.
CHARLES WRIOTHESLEY, *Chronicle*, Volume 1, page 16 (1560)

In psychoanalysis nothing is true except the exaggerations.
THEODOR ADORNO, *Minima Memoralia*, Part 1, 29

The new definition of psychiatry is the care of the id by the odd.
ANON, in M.B. Strauss, *Familiar Medical Quotations*

Honour a physician with the honour due unto him for the uses which you may have of him: for the Lord hath created him.
Apocrypha Ecclesiasticus, 38, 1

A fool is he, of little skill,
Who tests the urine of the ill
And says, "Wait, sir, and be so kind,
The answer in my books I'll find."

And while he thumbs the folios,
The patient to the bone yard goes.
SEBASTIAN BRANT, *The Ship of Fools*, 55

The paranoid is on his way to nowhere. Everything external becomes a part of his inner labyrinth. He cannot escape himself. He loses himself without forgetting himself.
ELLAS CANETTI, *The Secret Heart of the Clock*, (1983)

Psychoanalysis is a permanent fad.
PETER DE VRIES, *Forever Panting*

Much Virtue in Herbs, little in Men.
BENJAMIN FRANKLIN, *Poor Richard's Almanack*, 1755

A man too busy to take care of his health is like a mechanic too busy to take care of his tools.
SPANISH PROVERB

Be careful to preserve your health. It is a trick of the devil, which he employs to deceive good souls, to incite

them to do more than they are able, in order that they may no longer be able to do anything.
SAINT VINCENT DE PAUL

Must be out-of-doors enough to get experience of wholesome reality, as a ballast to thought and sentiment. Health requires this relaxation, this aimless life.
HENRY DAVID THOREAU, *Journal*

A man needs a purpose for real health.
SHERWOOD ANDERSON, *Letters*

The cult of physical health is simply absurd nowadays. Health has a relative value, like other things. That value is very low, if your health is to be used by somebody else for his benefit.

Again, doctor's health is only a special kind and takes no account of the mental activity of the patient which may be stimulated by a different physical state.
FREDERICK GOODYEAR, *Letters and Remains*

Health is the first muse, and sleep is the condition to produce it.
RALPH WALDO EMERSON, *Uncollected Lectures*, Resources

Do the best you can, without straining yourself too much and too continuously, and leave the rest to God. If you strain yourself too much you'll have to ask God to patch you up. And for all you know, patching you up may take time that it was planned to use some other way.
DON MARQUIS, *The Almost Perfect State*

It is true that I am carrying out various methods of treatment recommended by doctors and dentists in the hope of dying in the remote future in perfect health.
GEORGE SANTAYANA, *Letters*

All sorts of bodily diseases are produced by half-used minds.
GEORGE BERNARD SHAW, *On the Rocks*

Good or bad health makes our philosophy.
CHAULIEU

I honour health as the first
muse, and sleep as the
condition of health.
RALPH WALDO
EMERSON, Inspiration

The trouble about always
trying to preserve the health
of the body is that it is so
difficult to do without
destroying the health of the
mind.
G.K. CHESTERTON, Come
to Think of It (1930)

If you mean to keep as well as
possible, the less you think
about your health the better.
OLIVER WENDELL
HOLMES, SR., Over the
Teacups (1891), 8

A sound mind in a sound
body, is a short but full
description of a happy state in
this world.
JOHN LOCKE, Some
Thoughts Concerning Education
(1693), 1

Oh, the powers of nature!
She knows what we need, and
the doctors know nothing.
BENVENUTO CELLINI,
Autobiography (1558-66)

If th' Christyan Scientists had
some science an' th' doctors
more Christyanity, it wudden't
make anny diff'rence which ye
called in - if ye had a good
nurse.
FINLEY PETER DUNNE, Mr.
Dooley's Opinions, (1901)

The general order of things
that takes care of fleas and
moles also takes care of men,
if they will have the same
patience that fleas and moles
have, to leave it to itself.
MONTAIGNE, Essays

Medicine being a
compendium of the successive
and contradictory mistakes of
medical practitioners, when
we summon the wisest of
them to our aid, the chances
are that we may be relying on
a scientific truth the error of
which will be recognised in a
few years' time.
MARCEL PROUST,
Remembrance of Things Past:
The Guermantes Way, (1913-27)

It is medicine, not scenery, for
which a sick man must go
searching.
SENECA, Letters to Lucilius,
(1st century AD), 104.18

Health and cheerfulness
mutually beget each other.
ADDISON, *The Spectator*, No.
387

A healthy body is the guest-
chamber of the soul; a sick, its
prison.
FRANCIS BACON,
Augmentis Scientiarum:
Valetudo

Health is indeed a precious
thing, to recover and preserve
which we undergo any misery,
drink bitter potions, freely
give our goods; restore a man
to his health, his purse lies
open to thee.
ROBERT BURTON, *Anatomy*
of Melancholy, Part III, Section
i, mem, 2, subsection 1

The health of the people is
really the foundation upon
which all their happiness and
all their powers as a State
depend.
BENJAMIN DISRAELI,
(1877)

Physicians must discover the
weaknesses of the human
mind, and even condescend to
humour them, or they will
never be called in to cure the
infirmities of the body.
CHARLES CALEB
COLTON, *Lacon* (1825), line
482

A patient in th' hands iv a
doctor is like a hero in th'
hands iv a story writer. He's
goin' to suffer a good dale, but
he's goin' to come out all right
in th' end.
FINLEY PETER DUNNE,
Going to See the Doctor, (1919)

The best surgeon is he that
hath been hacked himself.
ENGLISH PROVERB

Every physician almost hath
his favourite disease.
HENRY FIELDING, *Tom*
Jones, (1749), 2.9

God heals, and the doctor
takes the fees.
BENJAMIN FRANKLIN,
Poor Richard's Almanack
(1732-57)

Yesterday Dr. Marcus went to
see the statue of
Zeus.
Though Zeus,
& though marble,
We're burying the statue
today.

Greek Anthology, (7th century BC - 10th century AD), 11.113

The dignity of a physician requires that he should look healthy, and as plump as nature intended him to be; for the common crowd consider those who are not of this excellent bodily condition to be unable to take care of themselves.
HIPPOCRATES, *The Physician* (circa 400 BC)

A physician can sometimes parry the scythe of death, but has no power over the sand in the hourglass.
HESTER LYNCH PIOZZI, letter to Fanny Burney, Nov. 12, 1781

The best doctor in the world is the Veterinarian. He can't ask his patients what is the matter - he's got to just know.
WILL ROGERS, *Autobiography*, (1949), 12

A man too busy to take care of his health is like a mechanic too busy to take care of his tools.
SPANISH PROVERB

Men who are occupied in the restoration of health to other men, by the joint exertion of skill and humanity, are above all the great of the earth. They even partake of divinity, since to preserve and renew is almost as noble as to create.
VOLTAIRE, *Philosophical Dictionary*, Physicians, (1764)

I don't think of work, only of gradually regaining my health through reading, rereading, reflecting.
RAINER MARIA RILKE, 1875-1926, letter circa 1911; Donald Prater, *A Ringing Glass* (1986)

TWENTY-THREE

HINDUISM

So let the enlightened toil,
sense-freed, but set
To bring the world
deliverance, and its bliss;
Not sowing in those simple,
busy hearts
Seed of despair. Yea! let each
play his part
In all he finds to do, with
unyoked soul.
All things are everywhere by
Nature wrought
In interaction of the qualities.
The fool, cheated by self,
thinks, "This I did"
And, "That I wrought;" but -
ah, thou strong-armed Prince!
-
A better-lessoned mind,
knowing the play
Of visible things within the
world of sense,
And how the qualities must
qualify,
Standeth aloof even from his
acts. Th' untaught
Live mixed with them,
knowing not Nature's way.
Bhagavad Gita from Book The
Third, Sir Edwin Arnold
Trans

God-realisation is not getting
away from the world, but
looking upon it as the
manifestation of God and

serving Him in all creatures
and beings, in a state of
perfect submission to His Will.
SWAMI RAMADAN

Arjuna: Yet tell me, Teacher!
by what force doth man
Go to his ill, unwilling; as if
one
Pushed him that evil path?

Krishna: Kama it is!
Passion it is! born of the
Darknesses,
Which pusheth him. Mighty
of appetite,
Sinful, and strong is this! -
man's enemy!
As smoke blots the white fire,
as clinging rust
Mars the bright mirror, as the
womb surrounds
The babe unborn, so is the
world of things
Foiled, soiled, enclosed in this
desire of flesh.
The wise fall, caught in it; the
unresting foe
It is of wisdom, wearing
countless forms,
Fair but deceitful, subtle as a
flame.
Sense, mind, and reason -
these, O Kunti's Son!
Are booty for it; in its play
with these

It maddens man, beguiling,
blinding him.
Therefore, thou noblest child
of Bharata!
Govern thy heart! Constrain
th' entangled sense!
Resist the false, soft sinfulness
which saps
Knowledge and judgement!
Yea, the world is strong,
But what discerns it stronger,
and the mind
Strongest; and high o'er all
the ruling Soul.
Bhagavad Gita from Book The
Third, Sir Edwin Arnold Trans

He is suicide who has
somehow achieved human
birth and even manhood and
full knowledge of the
scriptures, but does not strive
for self-liberation, for he
destroys himself by clinging to
the unreal.
SHANKARA from *The Crest
Jewel of Discrimination*, 4

The mind will merge only by
Self-enquiry 'Who am I?' The
thought 'Who am I?' will
destroy all other thoughts and
finally kill itself also. If other
thoughts arise, without trying
to complete them, one must
enquire to whom did this
thought arise. What does it
matter how many thoughts
arise? As each thought arises
one must be watchful and ask
to whom is this thought
occurring. The answer will be
'to me'. If you enquire 'Who
am I?' the mind will return to
its source (on where it issued
from). The thought which
arose will also submerge. As
you practise like this more and
more, the power of the mind
to remain as its source is
increased.
RAMANA MAHARSHI

The wise man who, by means
of concentration on the Self,
realises that ancient, effulgent
One, who is hard to be seen,
unmanifested, hidden, and
who dwells in the *buddhi* and
rests in the body - he, indeed,
leaves joy and sorrow far
behind.
From *The Katha Upanishad*,
I.2.12

You are the one witness of
everything, and are always
completely free. The cause of
your bondage is that you see
the witness as something
other than this.
From *The Ashtavakra Gita*, I.7

What we have to give up is the ego-sense, the idea that we are the doers. God within us is the doer, the sole master of all our activities. If we dedicate all our actions to Him we can destroy our ego-sense and find our supreme union with Him. Surrender does not denote any change in the external mode of life, but a right attitude towards it.
SWAMI RAMADAN

There is the "rightful" doer.
He who acts
Free from self-seeking,
humble, resolute,
Steadfast, in good or evil hap
the same,
Content to do aright - he
"truly" acts.
There is th' "impassioned"
doer. He that works
From impulse, seeking profit,
rude and bold
To overcome, unchastened;
slave by turns
Of sorrow and of joy: of Rajas
he!
And there be evil doers; loose
of heart,
Low-minded, stubborn,
fraudulent, remiss,
Dull, slow, despondent -
children of the "dark".

Bhagavad Gita from Book The Eighteenth, Sir Edwin Arnold Trans

Desirelessness is the greatest happiness - greater than even sovereignty, the heaven, the moon, the spring season, or union with a lovely woman.
From The Yoga Vashista, V.74.44

Brahman pervades equally the open space, the home, and the family. The Supreme Reality has neither attachment nor detachment, neither knowledge nor ignorance. Being the selfsame Brahman, O mind, why do you weep?
From The Avadhuta Gita, V.15

Scripture declares that there is no hope of immortality by means of wealth, so it is evident that 1liberation cannot be brought about by actions.
SHANKARA from The Crest Jewel of Discrimination, 7

Good is the steadfastness whereby a man
Masters his beats of heart, his very breath
Of life, the action of his senses; fixed

In never-shaken faith and
piety:
That is of *Sattwan*, Prince!
"soothfast" and fair!
Stained is the steadfastness
whereby a man
Holds to his duty, purpose,
effort, end,
For life's sake, and the love of
goods to gain,
Arjuna! 'tis of *Rajas*, passion-
stamped!
Sad is the steadfastness
wherewith the fool
Cleaves to his sloth, his
sorrow, and his fears,
His folly and despair. This -
Pritha's Son! -
Is born of *Tamas*, "dark" and
miserable!
Bhagavad Gita from Book The
Eighteenth, Sir Edwin Arnold
Trans

The only way to be always
happy is to submit to God's
will, and leaving everything to
Him, to be contented in the
condition in which He places
us. Surrender means inner
contentment and peace. It
means giving up of the ego-
sense. Until the ego-sense is
completely eliminated, we
cannot realise God.
SWAMI RAMADAN

The body, heaven and hell,
bondage and liberation, and
fear too, all this is pure
imagination. What is there
left to do for me whose very
nature is consciousness?
From *The Ashtavakra Gita*,
II.20

Having realised *Atman*, the
seers become satisfied with
that Knowledge. Their souls
are established in the Supreme
Self, they are free from
passions, and they are tranquil
in mind. Such calm souls ever
devoted to the Self, behold
everywhere the omnipresent
Brahman and in the end enter
into It, which is all this.
From *The Mundaka Upanishad*,
II.2.5

The *Upanishads* - through
their great dictums, such as
"Thou art That" and "I am
Brahman" - have declared that
your inmost *Atman* is the
Reality. You are the all-
embracing Sameness, devoid
of all attributes. Being the
selfsame *Brahman*, O mind,
why do you weep?
From *The Avadhuta Gita*, V.2

Hear from me, Long-armed
Lord! the makings five
Which go to every act, in
Sânkhya taught
As necessary. First the force;
and then
The agent; next, the various
instruments;
Fourth, the especial effort;
fifth, the God.
What work soever any mortal
doth
Of body, mind, or speech, evil
or good,
By these five doth he that.
Which being thus,
Whoso, for lack of knowledge,
seeth himself
As the sole actor, knoweth
nought at all
And seeth nought. Therefore,
I say, if one -
Holding aloof from self - with
unstained mind
Should slay all yonder host,
being bid to slay,
He doth not slay; he is not
bound thereby!
Bhagavad Gita from Book The
Eighteenth, Sir Edwin Arnold
Trans

Embodied beings, having
reached through their heart
(or intellect) that position of
Supreme Bliss, do not value
the visible world, as kings (do
not value) poverty.
From *The Yoga Vashista*,
V.54.72

Proper analysis leads to the
realisation of the reality of the
rope, and this is the end of the
pain of the fear of the great
snake caused by delusion.
SHANKARA from *The Crest
Jewel of Discrimination*, 12

There is "true" Knowledge.
Learn thou it is this:
To see one changeless Life in
all the Lives,
And in the Separate, One
Inseparable.
There is imperfect Knowledge:
that which sees
The separate existences apart,
And, being separated, holds
them real.
There is false Knowledge: that
which blindly clings
To one as if 'twere all, seeking
no Cause,
Deprived of light, narrow, and
dull, and "dark".
Bhagavad Gita from Book The
Eighteenth, Sir Edwin Arnold
Trans

Fools dwelling in darkness, but
thinking themselves wise and

erudite, go round and round,
by various tortuous paths, like
the blind led by the blind.
From *The Katha Upanishad*,
I.2.5

O my dear, the wise men give
up all types of meditation as
well as all types of action -
good or bad. They drink the
nectar of renunciation. I am
by nature blissful and free.
From *The Avadhuta Gita*, IV.24

The instrument of action, the
action, the doer, birth, death
and existence, everything is
only *Brahman*. There is
indeed no other idea without
That.
From *The Yoga Vashista*,
VI/2.60.28

Brahman is not only free from
bondage and liberation, purity
and impurity, union and
separation, but truly It is ever
free. And I am that *Brahman*
- infinite as space.
From *The Avadhuta Gita*, IV.2

By means of a moderate
quantity of *sattwik* (pure) food
(which is superior to all other
rules and regulations of self-
discipline) the *sattwik* or the

pure quality of the mind will
grow and Self-enquiry will be
helped.
RAMANA MAHARSHI

Humbleness, truthfulness, and
harmlessness,
Patience and honour,
reverence for the wise.
Purity, constancy, control of
self,
Contempt of sense-delights,
self-sacrifice,
Perception of the certitude of
ill
In birth, death, age, disease,
suffering, and sin;
Detachment, lightly holding
unto home,
Children, and wife, and all
that bindeth men;
An ever-tranquil heart in
fortunes good
And fortunes evil, with a will
set firm
To worship Me - Me only!
ceasing not;
Loving all solitudes, and
shunning noise
Of foolish crowds; endeavours
a resolute
To reach perception of the
Utmost Soul,
And grace to understand what
gain it were
So to attain, - this is true

Wisdom, Prince!
And what is otherwise is
ignorance!
Bhagavad Gita, from Book The
Thirteenth, Sir Edwin Arnold
Trans

If we control the mind, it does
not matter where we live.
RAMANA MAHARSHI

If only you will remain resting
in consciousness, seeing
yourself as distinct from the
body, then even now you will
become happy, peaceful and
free from bonds.
From *The Ashtavakra Gita*, I.4

Self-surrender means that we
throw the whole burden of
life, our anxieties and sorrows
on the Supreme Lord who is
the Master of all and keep our
mind filled with calmness and
peace that comes from His
constant remembrance.
SWAMI RAMADAN

Clasp Me with heart and
mind! so shalt thou dwell
Surely with Me on high. But
if thy thought
Droops from such height; if
thou be'st weak to set
Body and soul upon Me

constantly,
Despair not! give Me lower
service! seek
To reach Me, worshipping
with steadfast will;
And, if thou canst not
worship steadfastly,
Work for Me, toil in works
pleasing to Me!
For he that laboureth right for
love of Me
Shall finally attain! But, if in
this
Thy faint heart fails, bring Me
thy failure! find
Refuge in Me! Let fruits of
labour go,
Renouncing hope for Me,
with lowliest heart,
So shalt thou come; for,
though to know is more
Than diligence, yet worship
better is
Than knowing, and
renouncing better still.
Near to renunciation - very
near -
Dwelleth Eternal Peace!
Bhagavad Gita fromBook The
Twelfth, Sir Edwin Arnold
Trans

How wonderful it is that in
the Infinite Ocean of myself,
the waves of living beings
arise, collide, play and

disappear, in accordance with their nature.

From *The Ashtavakra Gita*, II.25

Self-surrender means that we throw the whole burden of life, our anxieties and sorrows on the Supreme Lord who is the Master of all and keep our mind filled with calmness and peace that comes from His constant remembrance.

SWAMI RAMADAN

Having known yourself to be That in which the universe appears like waves on the sea, why do you run about like a miserable being?

From *The Ashtavakra Gita*, III.3

Bhakti is not different from *mukti*. Bhakti is being as the Self. One is always that. He realises it by the means he adopts. What is bhakti? To think of God, That means only one thought prevails to the exclusion of all other thoughts. That thought is of God, which is the Self, or it is the self surrendered unto God. When He has taken you up nothing else will assail you.

The absence of thought is bhakti. It is also *mukti*.

RAMANA MAHARSHI

Who hateth nought
Of all which lives, living
himself benign,
Compassionate, from
arrogance exempt,
Exempt from love of self,
unchangeable
By good or ill; patient,
contented, firm
In faith, mastering himself,
true to his word,
Seeking Me, heart and soul;
vowed unto Me, -
That man I love! Who
troubleth not his kind,
And is not troubled by them;
clear of wrath,
Living too high for gladness,
grief, or fear,
That man I love! Who,
dwelling quiet-eyed,
Stainless, serene, well-
balanced, unperplexed,
Working with Me, yet from all
works detached,
That man I love! Who, fixed
in faith on Me,
Dotes upon none, scorns
none; rejoices not,
And grieves not, letting good
or evil hap
Light when it will, and when

it will depart,
That man I love! Who, unto
friend and foe
Keeping an equal heart, with
equal mind
Bears shame and glory; with
an equal peace
Takes heat and cold, pleasure
and pain; abides
Quit of desires, hears praise or
calumny
In passionless restraint,
unmoved by each;
Linked by no ties to earth,
steadfast in Me,
That man I love! But most of
all I love
Those happy ones to whom
'tis life to live
In single fervid faith and love
unseeing,
Drinking the blessèd Amrit of
my Being!
Bhagavad Gita from Book The
Twelfth, Sir Edwin Arnold
Trans

Self-surrender means that we
throw the whole burden of
life, our anxieties and sorrows
on the Supreme Lord who is
the Master of all and keep our
mind filled with calmness and
peace that comes from His
constant remembrance.
SWAMI RAMADAN

Krishna: Whoever serve Me -
as I show Myself -
Constantly true, in full
devotion fixed,
Those hold I very holy. But
who serve -
Worshipping Me The One,
The Invisible,
The Unrevealed, Unnamed,
Unthinkable,
Uttermost, All-pervading,
Highest, Sure -
Who thus adore Me,
mastering their sense,
Of one set mind to all, glad in
all good,
These blessed souls come unto
Me.
Yet, hard
The travail is for such as bend
their minds
To reach th' Unmanifest.
That viewless path
Shall scarce be trod by man
bearing the flesh!
But whereso any doeth all his
deeds
Renouncing self for Me, full of
Me, fixed
To serve only the Highest,
night and day
Musing on Me - him will I
swiftly lift
Forth from Life's ocean of
distress and death,
Whose soul clings fast to Me.

Cling thou to Me!
Bhagavad Gita from Book The
Twelfth, Sir Edwin Arnold
Trans

It is mere fancy to think that
Brahman is bound or released,
that Brahman is created or
uncreated. If Brahman alone
is the indivisible Supreme
Beatitude, how can It be
either mortal or immortal?
From *The Ashtavakra Gita*,
VI.15

"Nought of myself I do!"
Thus will he think - who
holds the truth of truths -
In seeing, hearing, touching,
smelling; when
He eats, or goes, or breathes;
slumbers or talks,
Holds fast or loosens, opens
his eyes or shuts;
Always assured, "This is the
sense-world plays
With senses." He that acts in
thought of Brahm,
Detaching end from act, with
act content,
The world of sense can no
more stain his soul
Than waters mar th'
enamelled lotus-leaf.
Bhagavad Gita from Book The
Fifth, Sir Edwin Arnold Trans

What man of wisdom would
abandon the experience of
supreme bliss to take pleasure
in things with no substance?
When the beautiful moon
itself is shining, who would
want to look at just a painted
moon?
SHANKARA from *The Crest
Jewel of Discrimination*, 522

After hearing of oneself as
pure consciousness and the
supremely beautiful, is one to
go on lusting after sordid
sexual objects?
From *The Ashtavakra Gita*,
III.4

The world is overcome - aye!
even here!
By such as fix their faith on
Unity.
The sinless Brahma dwells in
Unity,
And they in Brahma. Be not
over-glad
Attaining joy, and be not
over-sad
Encountering grief, but, stayed
on Brahma, still
Constant let each abide! The
sage whose soul
Holds off from outer contracts,
in himself
Finds bliss; to Brahma joined

by piety,
His spirit tastes eternal peace.
The joys
Springing from sense-life are
but quickening wombs
Which breed sure griefs: those
joys begin and end!
The wise mind takes no
pleasure, Kunti's Son!
In such as those! But if a man
shall learn,
Even while he lives and bears
his body's chain,
To master lust and anger, he is
blest!
Bhagavad Gita, From: Book
The Fifth, Sir Edwin Arnold
Trans

The splendours of youth are
transient like the shadows of
autumnal clouds. Objects of
sense are pleasing at first sight,
(but) causing pain at the end.
From *The Yoga Vashista*,
VI/2.93.84

My son, you consist of pure
consciousness, and the world
is not separate from you. So
who is to accept or reject it,
and how, and why?
From *The Ashtavakra Gita*,
XV.12

Krishna: When one, O
Pritha's Son! -
Abandoning desires which
shake the mind -
Finds in his soul full comfort
for his soul,
He hath attained the Yog -
that man is such!
In sorrows not dejected, and
in joys
Not overjoyed; dwelling
outside the stress
Of passion, fear, and anger;
fixed in calms
Of lofty contemplation; - such
an one
Is Muni, is the Sage, the true
Recluse!
He who to none and nowhere
overbound
By ties of flesh, takes evil
things and good
Neither desponding nor
exulting, such
Bears wisdom's plainest mark!
He who shall draw
As the wise tortoise draws its
four feet safe
Under its shield, his five frail
senses back
Under the spirit's buckler from
the world
Which else assails them, such
an one, my Prince!
Hath wisdom's mark!
Bhagavad Gita from Book The

Second, Sir Edwin Arnold Trans

There is no satisfaction or elimination of suffering through the experience of unreal things, so experience that non-dual bliss and remain happily content, established in your own true nature.
SHANKARA from *The Crest Jewel of Discrimination*, 523

It is asked why all this creation, so full of sorrow, and evil. All one can say is it is God's will, which is inscrutable. No motive can be attributed to that power, no desire, no end to achieve can be affirmed of that infinite, all-wise and all-powerful Being. God is untouched by activities which take place in His presence. There is no meaning in attributing responsibility and motive to the One before it became many. But God's will for the prescribed course of events is a good solution for the vexed question of free-will. If the mind is worried over what befalls us or what has been committed or omitted by us it is wise to give up the sense of responsibility and free will by regarding ourselves as the ordained instruments of the all-wise and the all-powerful to do and suffer as He pleases. Then He bears all the burdens and gives us peace.
RAMANA MAHARSHI

I am like the mother of pearl and the illusion of the universe is like the silver; this is knowledge. So it has neither to be renounced nor accepted nor destroyed.
From *The Ashtavakra Gita*, VI.3

The wise man should merge his speech in his mind and his mind in his intellect. He should merge his intellect in the Cosmic Mind and the Cosmic Mind in the Tranquil Self.
From *The Katha Upanishad*, I.3.13

Pass your time, noble one, in being aware of your true nature everywhere, thinking of yourself as non-dual, and enjoying the bliss inherent in yourself.
SHANKARA from *The Crest Jewel of Discrimination*, 524

That man alone is wise
Who keeps the mastery of
himself! If one
Ponders on objects of the
sense, there springs
Attraction; from attraction
grows desire,
Desire flames to fierce passion,
passion breeds
Recklessness; then the
memory - all betrayed -
Lets noble purpose go, and
saps the mind,
Till purpose, mind, and man
are all undone.
But , if one deals with objects
of the sense
Not loving and not hating,
making them
Serve his free soul, which rests
serenely lord,
Lo! such a man comes to
tranquillity;
And out of that tranquillity
shall rise
The end and healing of his
earthly pains,
Since the will governed sets
the soul at peace.
The soul of the ungoverned is
not his,
Nor hath he knowledge of
himself; which lacked,
How grows serenity? and,
wanting that,
Whence shall he hope for
happiness?
Bhagavad Gita from Book The
Second, Sir Edwin Arnold
Trans

Let the body last to the end of
the Age, or let it come to an
end right now. What have
you gained or lost, who consist
of pure consciousness?
From *The Ashtavakra Gita*,
XV.10

As flowing rivers disappear in
the sea, losing their names
and forms, so a wise man,
freed from name and form,
attains the *Purusha*, who is
greater than the Great.
From *The Mundaka Upanishad*,
III.2.8

As the primary Absolute
Consciousness alone shines in
itself as world-nature in a
dream, so also, at the
beginning of creation, nothing
other than (*Brahman*) is
produced here.
From *The Yoga Vashista*,
VI/2.176.5

The mind
That gives itself to follow
shows of sense
Seeth its helm of wisdom rent

away,
And, like a ship in waves of whirlwind, drives
To wreck and death. Only with him, great Prince!
Whose senses are not swayed by things of sense -
Only with him who holds his mastery.
Bhagavad Gita from Book The Second, Sir Edwin Arnold Trans

All that is here is mere thought.
From *The Yoga Vashista*, VI/2.210.11

While a man of pure intelligence may achieve the goal by the most casual of instruction, another may seek knowledge all his life and still remain bewildered.
From: *The Ashtavakra Gita*, XV.1

Krishna: thou grievest where no grief should be! thou speak'st
Words lacking wisdom! for the wise in heart
Mourn not for those that live, nor those that die.
Nor I, nor thou, nor any one of these,
Ever was not, nor ever will not be,
For ever and for ever afterwards.
All, that doth live, lives always! To man's frame
As there come infancy and youth and age,
So come there raisings-up and layings-down
Of other and of other life-abodes,
Which the wise know, and fear not. This that irks -
Thy sense-life, thrilling to the elements -
Bringing thee heat and cold, sorrows and joys,
'Tis brief and mutable! Bear with it, Prince!
As the wise bear. The soul which is not moved,
The soul that with a strong and constant calm
Takes sorrow and takes joy indifferently,
Lives in the life undying! That which is
Can never cease to be; that which is not
Will not exist. To see this truth of both
Is theirs who part essence from accident,
Substance from shadow. Indestructible,

Learn thou! the Life is,
spreading life through all;
It cannot anywhere, by any
means,
Be anywise diminished,
stayed, or changed.
But for these fleeting frames
which it informs
With spirit deathless, endless,
infinite,
They perish. Let them perish,
Prince! and fight!
Bhagavad Gita from Book The
Second, Sir Edwin Arnold
Trans

All creatures, of whatever
nature, strive only for
happiness.
From *The Yoga Vashista*,
VI/1.18.20

Arise! Awake! Approach the
great and learn. Like the
sharp edge of a razor is that
path, so the wise say: "hard to
tread and difficult to cross."
From *The Katha Upanishad*,
I.3.14

Cling to the Lord in all
situations. Do not worry
about anything. Have
complete trust in God. Give
up all superstitious notions.
Do not mind the opinions of
the world about you. Court
the society of pure and noble
souls.
SWAMI RAMADAN

This awareness of the truth
makes an eloquent, clever and
energetic man dumb, stupid
and lazy, so it is avoided by
those whose aim is enjoyment.
From *The Ashtavakra Gita*,
XV.3

Never the spirit was born; the
spirit shall cease to be never;
Never was time it was not;
End and Beginning are
dreams!
Birthless and deathless and
changeless remaineth the
spirit for ever;
Death hath not touched it at
all, dead though the house of
it seems!
Bhagavad Gita, From: Book
The Second, Sir Edwin
Arnold Trans

The giving up of the ego (or
the sense of "I" which is the
root of all thoughts) is easier
to perform than even the
splitting off of a flower or the
winking of the eyes. There is
not even a little trouble in
this matter.

From *The Yoga Vashista*,
VI/1.111.31

Your nature is the
consciousness, in which the
whole world wells up, like
waves in the sea. That is
what you are, without any
doubt, so be free of
disturbance.
From *The Ashtavakra Gita*,
XV.7

There lives a Master in the
hearts of men
Maketh their deeds, by subtle
pulling-strings,
Dance to what tune He will.
With all thy soul
Trust Him, and take Him for
thy succour, Prince!
So - only so, Arjuna! - shalt
thou gain -
By grace of Him - the
uttermost repose,
The Eternal Place!
Thus hath been opened thee
This Truth of Truths, the
Mystery more hid
Than any secret mystery.
Meditate!
And - as thou wilt - then act!
Bhagavad Gita from Book The
Eighteenth, Sir Edwin Arnold
Trans

That ego, being looked at,
certainly does not exist at any
time. (When investigated by
inward contemplation, the ego
vanishes). Its knowledge is
only so much. By this
(investigation) alone, it is
destroyed completely.
From *The Yoga Vashista*,
VI/2.8.3

There are no qualifications
necessary to know ones own
name, and the same is true for
the knower of *Brahman*,
knowledge that "I am
Brahman".
SHANKARA, From: *The
Crest Jewel of Discrimination*,
532

Nay! but once more
Take My last word, My utmost
meaning have!
Precious thou art to Me; right
well-beloved!
Listen! I tell thee for thy
comfort this.
Give Me thy heart! adore Me!
serve Me! cling
In faith and love and
reverence to Me!
So shalt thou come to Me! I
promise true,
For thou art sweet to Me!
And let go those -

Rites and writ duties! Fly to
Me alone!
Make Me thy single refuge! I
will free
Thy soul from all its sins! Be
of good cheer!
Bhagavad Gita from Book The
Eighteenth, Sir Edwin Arnold
Trans

Everything is predetermined.
But a man is always free not to
identify himself with the body
and not to be affected by the
pleasures or pains consequent
on the body's activities.
RAMANA MAHARSHI

Have faith, my son, have
faith. Don't let yourself be
deluded in this. You are
yourself the Lord, whose very
nature is knowledge, and you
are beyond natural causation.
From *The Ashtavakra Gita*,
XV.8

A man was in search of a
philosopher's stone. He
happened to find it
accidentally. But he thought
that philosopher's stone was a
too valuable thing to be found
so easily and that he was too
unfortunate to find it so soon.
He therefore threw it away,

thinking it to be a piece of
glass. Throwing it away, he
proceeded further and reached
a forest where, in spite of his
repeated efforts, he finds
nothing but pieces of glass.
From *The Yoga Vashista*, The
story of a Chintamani
(philosopher's stone)

Freed from surroundings,
quiet, lacking nought -
Such an one grows to oneness
with the Brahm;
Such an one, growing one
with Brahm, serene,
Sorrows no more, desires no
more; his soul,
Equally loving all that lives,
loves well
Me, Who have made them,
and attains to Me.
By this same love and worship
doth he know
Me as I am, how high and
wonderful,
And knowing, straightway
enters into Me.
And whatsoever deeds he
doeth - fixed
In Me, as in his refuge - he
hath won
For ever and for ever by My
grace
Th' Eternal Rest! So win
thou! In thy thoughts

Do all thou dost for Me!
Renounce for Me!
Sacrifice heart and mind and
will to Me!
Live in the faith of Me! In
faith of Me
All dangers thou shalt
vanquish, by My grace.
Bhagavad Gita from Book The
Eighteenth, Sir Edwin Arnold
Trans

TWENTY-FOUR

HISTORY

The mark of the historic is the nonchalance with which it picks up an individual and deposits him in a trend, like a house playfully moved in a tornado.
MARY MC CARTHY, *My Confession*, (1961)

Every fact and every work exercises a fresh persuasion over every age and every new species of man. History always enunciates new truths.
FRIEDRICH NIETZSCHE, *The Will to Power*, (1888)

History says, if it pleases, Excuse me, I beg your pardon, it will never happen again if I can help it.
CARL SANDBURG from *Complete Poems*, Good Morning, America, (1950)

History justifies whatever we want it to. It teaches absolutely nothing for it contains everything and gives examples of everything.
PAUL VALÉRY, *Regards sur le monde actuel*, De l'histoire, (1931)

Regrets are idle; yet history is one long regret. Everything

might have turned out so differently!
CHARLES DUDLEY WARNER, *My Summer in a Garden*, (1871)

Human history becomes more and more a race between education and catastrophe.
H.G. WELLS, *The Outline of History*, (1920), 40.4

The historian looks backward. In the end he also believes backward.
FRIEDRICH NIETZSCHE

History is made out of the failure and heroism of each insignificant moment.
FRANZ KAFKA

Not to know what has been transacted in former times is to continue always a child.
CICERO

We must consider how very little history there is; I mean real authentic history. That certain kings reigned, and certain battles were fought, we can depend upon as true; but all the colouring, all the philosophy of history, is

conjecture.
SAMUEL JOHNSON

You cannot understand history without having lived through history yourself.
GOETHE

History would be an excellent thing if only it were true.
LEO TOLSTOY

The one duty we owe to history is to rewrite it.
OSCAR WILDE

History is philosophy from examples.
DIONYSIUS OF HALICARNASSUS, 30-7 BC, *Ars Rhetorica*

If history records good things of good men, the thoughtful hearer is encouraged to imitate what is good; or if it records evil of wicked men, the devout religious listener or reader is encouraged to avoid all that is sinful and perverse.
THE VENERABLE BEDE, AD 673-735, *Ecclesiastical History of the English People*, Preface

Anybody can make history; only a great man can write it.
OSCAR WILDE

Whosoever, in writing a modern history, shall follow truth too near the heels, it may happily strike out his teeth.
WALTER RALEIGH, (circa 1552-1618), *The History of the World*, (1614)

History ... is, indeed, little more than the register of the crimes, follies, and misfortunes of mankind.
EDWARD GIBBON, (1737-94), *The Decline and Fall of the Roman Empire*, (1776-88)

Should the reader discover any inaccuracies in what I have written, I humbly beg that he will not impute them to me, because, as the laws of history require, I have laboured honestly to transmit whatever I could ascertain from common report for the instruction of posterity.
THE VENERABLE BEDE, (AD 673-735), *Ecclesiastical History of the English People*, Preface

History is much decried; it is a tissue of errors, we are told no doubt correctly; and rival historians expose each other's blunders with gratification. Yet the worst historian has a clearer view of the period he studies than the best of us can hope to form of that in which we live.
ROBERT LOUIS STEVENSON

The real history does not get written, because it is not in people's brains but in their nerves and vitals.
ALFRED NORTH WHITEHEAD, *Dialogues*

Perhaps one of the most prolific sources of error in contemporary thinking rises precisely from the popular habit of lifting history out of its proper context and bending it to the values of another age and day. In this way history is never allowed to be itself.
LAURENS VAN DER POST, *The Lost World of the Kalahari*

History never looks like history when you are living through it. It always looks confusing and messy, and it always feels uncomfortable.
JOHN W. GARDNER, *No Easy Victories*

History unfolds itself by strange and unpredictable paths. We have little control over the future; and none at all over the past.
SIR WINSTON CHURCHILL

Working upon us all the while in the darker regions of our nature - in defiance of the power over us of the particular age into which we are born - is always a furtive predilection for some historic era against all the others.
JOHN COWPER POWYS, *The Meaning of Culture*

Man is a history-making creature who can neither repeat his past nor leave it behind.
W.H. AUDEN, (1907-73), *The Dyer's Hand*

History gets thicker as it approaches recent times.
A.J.P. TAYLOR, (1906-90), *English History 1914-45*

It would be a valuable practice for the historian to rise each morning saying to himself three times slowly and with emphasis, "I do not know."
J.L. MARTYN, (1925), *Understanding the Fourth Gospel*, (1991)

We moderns do not believe in demigods, but our smallest hero we expect to feel and act as a demigod.
GOTTHOLD EPHRAIM LESSING, *Laocoön*, (1766), 4

People are trapped in history and history is trapped in them.
JAMES BALDWIN, *Notes of a Native Son*, (1955)

I hold the view that the greatest changes in human history are to be traced back to internal causal conditions, and that they are founded upon internal psychological necessity. For it often seems that external conditions serve merely as occasions on which a new attitude long in preparation becomes manifest.
C.G. JUNG, *Psychological Reflections*

As an antidote to any War I now read history. Histories of Poland, Russia, Austria, Italy, France. One gets a sense of the long line of events. The present sinks into nothingness.
SHERWOOD ANDERSON, *Letters*

Our ignorance of history causes us to slander our own times.
GUSTAVE FLAUBERT, From *In Search of Serenity*

We have constantly to check ourselves in reading history with the remembrance that, to the actors in the drama, events appeared very different from the way they appear to us. We know what they were doing far better than they knew themselves.
RANDOLPH BOURNE, *Youth and Life*

In my old age I have about come to believe that the whole of written history is miscreated and flawed by these discrepancies in the two ideals systems: the one of how we would all like to believe humanity might be, but only

the privileged can afford to believe it; and the one of how we all really know humanity in fact is, but none of us wants to believe it.
JAMES JONES, *World War II*

It would seem as though the great movements of history arose like those sudden broad waves heaving out of the deep sea in calm weather, and rolling forth incomprehensibly under no wind.
HILAIRE BELLOC, A *Conversation with an Angel*

I have always been convinced that individual and collective crimes are closely linked; and in my capacity of journalist I have only tried to make clear that the day to day horrors of our political history are no more than the visible consequences of the invisible history unfolding in the secrecy of the human heart.
FRANCOIS MAURIAC, *An Author and His Work*

It is not the neutrals or the lukewarms who make history.
ADOLF HITLER, Berlin, (1933)

Happy the people whose Annals are blank in History books.
THOMAS CARLYLE, *Life of Frederick the Great*

The historian is a prophet looking backwards.
SCHLEGEL, *Athenaeum*, Berlin, I.2, 20

History is the essence of innumerable Biographies.
THOMAS CARLYLE, *Essays*, On History

History is a gallery of pictures in which there are few originals and many copies.
ALEXIS DE TOCQUEVILLE, (1805-59), *L'Ancien Régime*, (1856)

It has been said that though God cannot alter the past, historians can; it is perhaps because they can be useful to Him in this respect that He tolerates their existence.
SAMUEL BUTLER, (1835-1902(, *Erewhon Revisited*, (1901)

History repeats itself. Historians repeat each other.
PHILIP GUEDALLA, (1889-

1944), *Supers and Supermen,*
(1920)

Since the work of the artist is
openly subjective, and
'feigned' history, what matters
is not what happened to him,
but what he has made his
experience into.
W.H. AUDEN, (1907-73),
History of a Historian, (1955)

History is a gallery of pictures
in which there are few
originals and many copies.
ALEXIS DE
TOCQUEVILLE, *The Ancien
Régime and the Revolution,* page
133

We are never completely
contemporaneous with our
present. History advances in
disguise; it appears on stage
wearing the mask of the
preceding scene, and we tend
to lose the meaning of the
play.
RÉGIS DEBRAY, *Revolution in
the Revolution?,* Chapter 1

History is philosophy drawn
from examples.
DIONYSIUS OF
HALICARNASSUS, *Ars
Rhetorica,* 11.2

Everything which could
possibly enter into the most
disordered of imaginations
might well be said of the
history of the world.
FEODOR DOSTOEVSKY,
Notes from the Underground

History is a child building a
sandcastle by the sea, and that
child is the whole majesty of
man's power in the world.
HERACLITUS, *Fragments,* 24

Historians have been drug
dealers to the addicts of
national self-affirmation.
E.J. HOBSBAWM, (1998)

To all but the saints, who
anyhow have no need of
them, the lessons of history
are totally unavailing.
ALDOUS HUXLEY, *Grey
Eminence,* Chapter 8

Many heroes lived before
Agamemnon, but they are all
unmourned and consigned to
a long night of oblivion,
because they lacked a sacred
bard.
HORACE, *Odes,* Book IV,
Ode 9, line 25

The love of history seems
inseparable from human
nature because it seems
inseparable from self-love.
LORD BOLINGBROKE, *On
the Study of History*, Letter i

So very difficult a matter is it
to trace and find out the truth
of anything by history.
PLUTARCH, *Life of
Themistocles*

Some write a narrative of wars
and feats,
Of heroes little known, and
call the rant
A history. Describe the man,
of whom
His own coevals took but
little note,
And paint his person,
character and views,
As they had known him from
his mother's womb.
WILLIAM COWPER, *The
Task*, Book III, line 139

History a distillation of
Rumour.
THOMAS CARLYLE, *The
French Revolution*, Part I, Book
vii, Chapter v

All those instances to be
found in history, whether real
or fabulous, of a doubtful
public spirit, at which
morality is perplexed, reason is
staggered, and from which
affrighted Nature recoils, are ·
their chosen and almost sole
examples for the instruction of
their youth.
BURKE, *On a Regicide Peace*

World history would be
different if humanity did more
sitting on its rear.
BERTOLT BRECHT, *Drums
in the Night*, (1922)

The historical sense involves a
perception, not only of the
pastness of the past, but of its
presence.
T.S. ELIOT, *Tradition and the
Individual Talent*, (1919)

History is the action and
reaction of these two, nature
and thought - two boys
pushing each other on the
curbstone of the pavement.
RALPH WALDO
EMERSON, *The Conduct of
Life*, Fate, (1860)

That men do not learn very
much from the lessons of
history is the most important
of all lessons that history has

to teach.
ALDOUS HUXLEY, *Collected Essays*, (1959)

History, like a badly constructed concert hall, has occasional dead spots where the music can't be heard.
ARCHIBALD MAC LEISH, (1967)

Hegel says somewhere that all great events and personalities in world history reappear in one way or another. He forgot to add: the first time as tragedy, the second as farce.
KARL MARX, *The Eighteenth Brumaire of Louis Napoleon*, Part 1

The history of the world is the judgement seat of the world.
FRIEDRICH VON SCHILLER, *Resignation*

History has always been a favourite study of those who want to learn something without being put to the effort demanded by the true sciences, which require the exercise of reason.
ARTHUR SCHOPENHAUER, *Essays and Aphorisms*, On Various Subjects, 4

God sometimes sends a famine, sometimes a pestilence, and sometimes a hero for the chastisement of mankind; none of them, surely, for our admiration.
WALTER SAVAGE LANDOR, *The Perpetual Pessimist*

I have read somewhere or other - in Dionysius of Halicarnassus, I think - that History is Philosophy teaching by examples
BOLINGBROKE, *On the Study and Use of History*, Letter ii

Before philosophy can teach by experience, the philosophy has to be in readiness, the experience must be gathered and intelligibly recorded.
THOMAS CARLYLE, *Essays*, On History

History hath triumphed over Time, which besides it, nothing but Eternity hath triumphed over.
SIR WALTER RALEIGH, *The History of the World*, Preface

History that should be a left
hand to us, as of a violinist,
we bind up with prejudice,
warping it to suit our fears as
Chinese women do their feet.
WILLIAM CARLOS
WILLIAMS, quoted in *The
Tragedy of American
Diplomacy*, by William A.
Williams

History may be viewed as a
process of pushing back walls
of inevitability, of turning
what have been thought to be
inescapable limitations into
human possibilities.
HELEN MERRELL LYND,
*On Shame and the Search for
Identity*

All that the historians give us
are little oases in the desert of
time, and we linger fondly in
these, forgetting the vast
tracks between one and
another that were trodden by
the weary generations of men.
J.A. SPENDER, *The
Comments of Bagshot*

Our historic imagination is at
best slightly developed. We
generalise and idealise the past
egregiously. We set up little
toys to stand as symbols for

centuries and the complicated
lives of countless individuals.
JOHN DEWEY, *Characters
and Events*, Volume II

What is History but a register
of the successes and
disappointments, the vices,
the follies, and the quarrels of
those engaged in contention
for power?
PALEY

Where he cannot give
patterns to imitate,
He must give examples to deter.
JUNIUS

Instructed by the antiquary
times,
He must, he is, he cannot but
be wise.
WILLIAM SHAKESPEARE

History makes us some
amends for the shortness of
life.
SKELTON

Her ample page
Rich with the spoils of time.
THOMAS GRAY

History is the complement of
poetry.
SIR J. STEPHENS

History maketh a young man to be old, without either wrinkles or grey hairs, privileging him with the experience of age, without either the infirmities or inconveniences thereof.
FULLER

In histories composed by politicians, they are for drawing up a perpetual scheme of causes and events, and preserving a constant correspondence between the camp and the council table.
THOMAS ADDISON

There is no part of history so generally useful, as that which relates to the progress of the human mind, the gradual improvement of reason, the successive advances of science, the vicissitudes of learning and ignorance, which are the light and darkness of thinking beings, the extinction and resuscitation of arts, and the revolution of the intellectual world. If accounts of battles and invasions are peculiarly the business of princes, the useful or elegant arts are not to be neglected; those who have kingdoms to govern have understandings to cultivate.
SAMUEL JOHNSON

The history of the past is but a mere puppet-show. A little man comes out and blows a little trumpet - and goes in again. You look for something new; and lo! another little man comes out, and blows another little trumpet - and goes in again.
LONGFELLOW

Sin writes history - Goodness is silent.
GOETHE

Everywhere foolish rumour babbles not of what was done, but what was misdone or undone; and History (ever, more or less, the written epitomised synopsis of rumour) knows so little that were not as well unknown. Attila Invasions, Walter-the-Penniless Crusades, Sicilian Vespers, Thirty-Years Wars: mere sin and misery; not work, but hindrance of work! During all this time the Earth was yearly green and yellow with her kind harvests; the hand of the craftsman, the mind of the Thinker rested

not. And so, after all, and in
spite of it all, we still have this
so glorious high-domed
blossoming World; concerning
which History may well ask,
with wonder, Whence it
came? She knows so little of
it, knows so much of what
obstructed it, Whereby that
paradox, "Happy the people
whose annals are vacant."
THOMAS CARLYLE

TWENTY-FIVE

HUMANITY

Chorus of Priests
OH wearisome Condition of
Humanity!
Borne under one Law, to
another bound:
Vainly begot, and yet
forbidden vanity;
Created sicke, commanded to
be sound:
What meaneth Nature by
these diverse Lawes?
Passion and Reason, selfe-
division cause:
Is it the marke or Majesty of
Power
To make offences that it may
forgive?
Nature herselfe doth her owne
selfe defloure,
to hate those errours she her
selfe doth give.
For how should man thinke
that, he may not doe
If Nature did not faile, and
punish too?
Tyrant to others, to her selfe
unjust,
Only commands things
difficult and hard;
Forbids us all things which it
knowes is lust,
Makes easie paines, unpossible
reward.
If Nature did not take delight
in blood,
She would have made more
easie wayes to good.
We that are bound by vowes,
and by Promotion,
With pompe of holy Sacrifice
and rites,
To teach beliefe in good and
still devotion,
To preach of Heaven's
wonders, and delights:
Yet when each of us in his
own heart lookes,
He findes the God there, farre
unlike his Bookes.
FULKE GREVILLE, LORD
BROOKE

The Puppet
By whom was wrought this
puppet?
Where is the puppet's maker?
And where does the puppet
arise?
Where is the puppet stopped?

Not made by self is this
puppet,
Nor is this misfortune made
by others.
Conditioned by cause it comes
to be,
By breaking of cause is it
stopped.

By whom was wrought this
being?
Where is the being's maker?

Where does the being arise?
Where is the being stopped?

Why do you harp on 'being'?
It is a false view for you.
A mere heap of samkharas*,
this -
Here no 'being' is got at.

For as when the parts are
rightly set
We utter the word 'chariot',
So when there are the
khandhas** -
By convention, 'there is a
being' we say.

For it is simply suffering that
comes to be,
Suffering that perishes and
wanes,
Not other than suffering
comes to be,
Naught else than suffering is
stopped.

*Samkharas: characteristics
**Khandhas (or skandhas):
the constituents of personality
Samyutta Nikâya I, 134-35,
from the *Pali*

Our humanity were a poor
thing were it not for the
divinity which stirs within us.
FRANCIS BACON

Man is a rope connecting
animal and superman, - a rope
over a precipice... What is
great in man is that he is a
bridge and not a goal.
FRIEDRICH NIETZSCHE,
Thus Spake Zarathustra,
Section 4

Man is the measure of all
things.
PROTAGORAS, (Diogenes
Laertius, *Protagoras*, Book IX,
Section 51)

Human nature is the same all
over the world; but its
operations are so varied by
education and habit, that one
must see it in all its dresses.
LORD CHESTERFIELD,
Letters, 2 October, 1747

A man ought to compare
advantageously with a river,
an oak, a mountain.
RALPH WALDO
EMERSON, *Conduct of Life*,
Fate

Countless the various species
of mankind,
Countless the shades which
sep'rate mind from mind;
No general object of desire is
know,

Each has his will, and each
pursues his own.
WILLIAM GIFFORD, *Perseus*

A Self-made man; who
worships his creator.
JOHN BRIGHT, of Benjamin
Disraeli

Man is dearer to the gods than
he is to himself.
JUVENAL, *Satires*, Satire X,
line 350

I teach you the Superman.
Man is something which shall
be surpassed.
FRIEDRICH NIETZSCHE,
Also Sprach Zarathustra,
Introduction, Section 1

Nature never rhymes her
children, nor makes two men
alike.
RALPH WALDO
EMERSON, *Essays, Second
Series*, Character

What's he born to be sick, so
always dying,
That's guided by inevitable
fate;
That comes in weeping, and
that goes out crying;
Whose calendar of woes is still
in date;

Whose life's a bubble, and in
length a span;
A concert still in discords?
'Tis a man.
WILLIAM BROWNE,
Britannia's Pastorals, Book I,
Song 2, line 192

A man is a bubble, said the
Greek proverb... descending
from God and the dew of
heaven, from a tear and a drop
of rain.
JEREMY TAYLOR, *Holy
Dying*, Chapter I. Section 1.

For what are men who grasp at
praise sublime,
But bubbles on the rapid
stream of time,
That rise, and fall, that swell,
and are no more,
Born and forgot, ten thousand
in an hour?
YOUNG, *Love of Fame*, Sat.
ii, line 285

We are none other than a
moving row
Of Magic Shadow-shapes that
come and go
Round with the Sun-
illumined Lantern held
In Midnight by the Master of
the Show.
OMAR KHAYYÀM,
Rubáiyát, Stanza 68

God in making man intended
by him to reduce all His
Works back again to Himself.
MATTHEW BARKER,
Natural Theology, page 85

Thou hast made him a little
lower than the angels.
Psalms 8:5

There wanted yet the master
work, the end
Of all yet done; a creature
who, not prone
And brute as other creatures,
but endued
With sanctity of reason, might
erect
His stature, and upright with
front serene
Govern the rest, self-knowing,
and from thence
Magnanimous to correspond
with Heav'n.
MILTON, *Paradise Lost*, Book
VII, line 505

Thus while the mute creation
downward bend
Their sight, and to their
earthy mother tend,
Man looks aloft, and with
erected eyes
Beholds his own hereditary
skies.
OVID, *Metamorphoses*, Book I,
line 84

What a wonderful privilege to
have the weakness of a man
and the serenity of a god!
SENECA, *Epistulae ad
Lucilium*, Epis. 1iii, Section 12

Let each man think himself
an act of God,
His mind a thought, his life a
breath of God.
PHILIP JAMES BAILEY,
Festus, Proëm, line 163

For a man is not as God,
But then most Godlike being
most a man.
ALFRED, LORD
TENNYSON, *Love and Duty*,
line 30

Mankind are earthen jugs
with spirits in them.
HAWTHORNE, *American
Note-Books*, 1842

Upon the potter's flying wheel
the clay
Knows not the purpose of its
plasmic day;
So we upon the blindly-
whirling sphere
Are shaped to ends which do
not yet appear.
JAMES B. KENYON, *The
Potter's Clay*

Human improvement is from within outwards.
FROUDE, *Short Studies on Great Subjects*

Though man sits still and takes his ease,
God is at work on man;
No means, no method unemploy'd,
To bless him, if he can.
YOUNG, *Resignation*, Part I, Stanza 119

Man is his own star; and the soul that can
Render an honest and a perfect man,
Commands all light, all influence, all fate;
Nothing to him falls early or too late.
BEAUMONT AND FLETCHER, *The Honest Man's Fortune*, Epilogue

Love, hope, fear, faith - these make humanity;
These are its sign and note and character.
ROBERT BROWNING, *Paracelsus*, Part III

'Tis the sublime of man,
Our noontide majesty, to know ourselves

Parts and proportions of one wondrous whole!
SAMUEL TAYLOR COLERIDGE, *Religious Musings*, line 127

The way of the superior man is threefold, but I am not equal to it. Virtuous, he is free from anxieties; wise, he is free from perplexities; bold, he is free from fear.
CONFUCIUS, *Analects*, Book XIV, Chapter 30

Every person is a bundle of possibilities and he is worth what life may get out of him before it is through.
HARRY EMERSON FOSDICK, *The Rebirth of Self*

On earth there is nothing great but man; in man there is nothing great but mind.
SIR WILLIAM HAMILTON, *Lectures on Metaphysics*

Man never falls so low that he can see nothing higher than himself.
THEODORE PARKER, *A Lesson for the Day*

How beauteous mankind is!
O brave new world

That has such people in 't!
WILLIAM SHAKESPEARE,
The Tempest, Act V, Scene i,
line 183

Cheerful, for freest action
form'd under the laws divine,
The Modern Man I sing.
WALT WHITMAN, *One's-Self I Sing*

In thy lone and long night-watches, sky above and sea
below,
Thou didst learn a higher
wisdom than the babbling
schoolmen know;
God's stars and silence taught
thee, as His angels only can,
That the one sole sacred thing
beneath the cope of heaven is
Man!
WHITTIER, *The Branded
Hand*, Stanza 9

To you I declare the holy
mystery: There is nothing
nobler than humanity.
MAHÂBHÂRATA, 12, 300, 20

A spectacle unto the world,
and to angels.
1 *Corinthians* 4:9

Drest in a little brief authority,
Most ignorant of what he's
most assur'd,
His glassy essence, like an
angry ape,
Plays such fantastic tricks
before high heaven,
As make the angels weep.
WILLIAM SHAKESPEARE,
Measure for Measure, Act II,
Scene ii, line 117

Each of us inevitable;
Each of us limitless - each of
us with his or her right upon
the earth.
WALT WHITMAN, *Salut au
Monde*, Section 11

What the superior man seeks
is in himself: what the small
man seeks is in others.
CONFUCIUS, *Analects*, Book
XV, Chapter 20

We are the creatures of
imagination, passion and self-will, more than of reason or
even of self-interest ... The
falling of a teacup puts us out
of temper for the day; and a
quarrel that commenced about
the pattern of a gown may end
only with our lives.
WILLIAM HAZLITT,
Winterslow, Essay No. 7

Then say not man's imperfect,
Heav'n in fault;
Say rather man's as perfect as
he ought;
His knowledge measured to
his state and place,
His time a moment, and a
point his space.
ALEXANDER POPE, *Essay
on Man*, Epistle i, line 69

We are children of splendour
and fame,
Of shuddering also, and tears;
Magnificent out of the dust
we came,
And abject from the Spheres.
WILLIAM WATSON, *Ode in
May*

How poor, how rich, how
abject, how august,
How complicate, how
wonderful, is man!
How passing wonder He, who
made him such!
YOUNG, *Night Thoughts*,
Night i, line 68

In the evening, when we
drink together, we are men,
but when daybreak comes, we
arise wild beasts, preying upon
each other.
AUTOMEDON, (*Greek
Anthology*, Book XI, epig. 46)

And Man, whose heav'n-
erected face
The smiles of love adorn -
Man's inhumanity to man
Makes countless thousands
mourn.
ROBERT BURNS, *Man Was
Made to Mourn*, Stanza 7

Man and his littleness perish,
erased like an error and
cancelled;
Man and his greatness survive,
lost in the greatness of God.
WILLIAM WATSON, *Hymn
to the Sea*, Part IV, line 17

Man passes away; his name
perishes from record and
recollection; his history is as a
tale that is told, and his very
monument becomes a ruin.
WASHINGTON IRVING,
*The Sketch Book: Westminster
Abbey*, Conclusion

Mark how fleeting and paltry
is the estate of man, -
yesterday in embryo,
tomorrow a mummy or ashes.
So for the hair's-breadth of
time assigned to thee live
rationally, and part with life
cheerfully, as drops the ripe
olive, extolling the season
that bore it and the tree that

matured it.
MARCUS AURELIUS,
Meditations, Book IV, Section
48

He weaves, and is clothed
with derision;
Sows, and he shall not reap;
His life is a watch or a vision
Between a sleep and a sleep.
ALGERNON SWINBURNE,
Atlanta in Calydon, Chorus

Man that is born of a woman
is of few days and full of
trouble. He cometh forth like
a flower, and is cut down: he
fleeth also as a shadow, and
continueth not.
Job 14:1,2

There is a book into which
some of us are happily led to
look, and to look again, and
never tire of looking. It is the
Book of Man. You may open
that book whenever and
wherever you find another
human voice to answer yours,
and another human hand to
take in your own.
WALTER BESANT, *Books
Which Have Influenced Me*

In human works, tho' labour'd
on with pain,

A thousand movements scarce
one purpose gain;
In God's, one single can its
end produce,
Yet serve to second too some
other use:
So man, who here seems
principal alone,
Perhaps acts second to some
sphere unknown,
Touches some wheel, or verges
to some goal:
'Tis but a part we see, and not
a whole.
ALEXANDER POPE, *Essay
on Man*, Epistle i, line 53

We have to stand upright
ourselves, not be set up.
MARCUS AURELIUS,
Meditations, Book 3, 5

Men must know that, in this
theatre of Man's life, it is
reserved only for God and
angels to be lookers on.
FRANCIS BACON, *The
Advancement of Learning*, Book
2, vii, 5

There is surely a piece of
divinity in us, something that
was before the elements, and
owes no homage unto the sun.
SIR THOMAS BROWNE,
Religio Medici, Part 2, 11

Mankind is not a tribe of animals to which we owe compassion. Mankind is a club to which we owe our subscription.
G.K. CHESTERTON, in the *Daily News*, 10 April 1906

The meaning of man's life consists in proving to himself every minute that he's a man and not a piano key.
FYODOR DOSTOEVSKY, *Notes from the Underground*, Part 1, 8

Man cannot live on the human plane; he must be either above or below it.
ERIC GILL, *Autobiography*

It is because Humanity has never known where it was going that it has been able to find its way.
OSCAR WILDE, *The Critic as Artist*, 1

Man is an embodied paradox, a bundle of contradictions.
C.C. COLTON, *Lacon*, Number 408

A wonderful fact to reflect upon that every human creature is constituted to be that profound secret and mystery to every other.
CHARLES DICKENS, *A Tale of Two Cities*, Chapter 3

It is only the superficial qualities that last. Man's deeper nature is soon found out.
OSCAR WILDE, *Phrases and Philosophies for the Use of the Young*

Men are all inventors sailing forth on a voyage of discovery.
RALPH WALDO EMERSON, *Uncollected Lectures*, Resources

It is not enough to do good; one must do it in the right way.
JOHN MORLEY, *On Compromise*, (1874)

How far that little candle throws his beams! So shines a good deed in a naughty world.

WILLIAM SHAKESPEARE, *The Merchant of Venice*, Act V, Scene 5, Scene i, line 90, (1596-97)

He who wants to do good knocks at the gate; he who

loves finds the gate open.
RABINDRANATH
TAGORE, *Stray Birds*, 83,
(1916)

By nature, men are nearly
alike; by practice, they get to
be wide apart.
CONFUCIUS, *Analects*, (6th
century BC), 17.2

It is to the credit of human
nature, that, except where its
selfishness is brought into
play, it loves more readily
than it hates.
NATHANIEL
HAWTHORNE, *The Scarlet
Letter*, 13, (1850)

Scenery is fine - but human
nature is finer.
JOHN KEATS, letter to
Benjamin Bailey, (1818)

What does reason demand of
a man? A very easy thing - to
live in accord with his own
nature.
SENECA, *Letters to Lucilius*,
41, (1st century AD)

One touch of nature makes
the whole world kin.
WILLIAM SHAKESPEARE,
Troilus and Cressida, Act III.
Scene iii, line 175, (1601-02)

All is disgust when one leaves
his own nature
and does things that misfit it.
SOPHOCLES, *Philoctetes*,
(409 BC)

It is a malady confined to
man, and not seen in any
other creatures, to hate and
despise ourselves.
MONTAIGNE

We can really respect a man
only if he doesn't always *look
out for himself.*
GOETHE

I am fearfully and wonderfully
made.
Psalms 139:14

God hath made man upright;
but they have sought out
many inventions.
Ecclesiastes 7:29

This Being of mine, whatever
it really is, consists of a little
flesh, a little breath, and the
part which governs.
MARCUS AURELIUS,
Meditations, Book II, Section 2

It is a great mistake to think
you are more than you are and

yet to underrate your real value.
GOETHE

Are we not Spirits, that are shaped into a body, into an Appearance; and that fade away again into air and Invisibility? Oh, Heaven, it is mysterious, it is awful to consider that we not only carry a future Ghost within us; but are, in very deed, Ghosts! These Limbs, whence had we them; this stormy Force; this life-blood with its burning Passion? They are dust and shadow; a Shadow system gathered round our ME; wherein, through some moments or years, the Divine Essence is to be revealed in the Flesh.
THOMAS CARLYLE, *Sartor Resartus*

He who doesn't think too much of himself is much more than he thinks.
GOETHE

Man is the only one that knows nothing, that can learn nothing without being taught. He can neither speak nor walk nor eat, and in short he can do nothing at the prompting of nature only, but weep.
PLINY THE ELDER, *Natural History*, Book VII. Section 4

Man is but man; unconstant still, and various;
There's no tomorrow in him, like today.
DRYDEN, *Cleomenes*, Act III, Scene 1

Know then thyself, presume not God to scan:
The proper study of mankind is man.
ALEXANDER POPE, *Essay on Man*, Epistle II, line 1

What hast thou, Man, that thou dar'st call thine own?
What is there in thee, Man, that can be known?
Dark fluxion, all unfixable by thought,
A phantom dim of past and future wrought,
Vain sister of the worm - life, death, soul, clod -
Ignore thyself, and strive to know thy God!
SAMUEL TAYLOR COLERIDGE, *E coelo descendit*

Chaos of thought and passion,
all confused;
Still by himself abused, or
disabused;
Created half to rise, and half
to fall;
Great lord of all things, yet a
prey to all;
Sole judge of truth, in endless
error hurled;
The glory, jest and riddle of
the world.
ALEXANDER POPE, *Essay
on Man*, Epistle II, line 13

A spirit all compact of fire
Not gross to sink, but light
and will aspire.
WILLIAM SHAKESPEARE,
Venus and Adonis

Man seeks his own good at
the whole world's cost.
R. BROWNING, *Luria*, Act I

There's not a man
That lives, who hath not
known his god-like hours,
And feels not what an empire
we inherit
As natural beings in the
strength of nature.
WILLIAM
WORDSWORTH, *The
Prelude*, Book III, line 193

A man is a bundle of
relations, a knot of roots,
whose flower and fruitage is
the world.
RALPH WALDO
EMERSON, *Essays, First
Series*, History

Are not those who nurse their
egos on contempt of humanity
- "the herd in the slime" and
that sort of thing - hurt spirits
who compensate in this way
for a sense of inequality to
life? They may have
remarkable powers, like
Nietzsche, but are never
robust and sane. They lack,
especially, a sense of humour.
CHARLES HORTON
COOLEY, *Life and the Student*

Whenever there is lost the
consciousness that every man
is an object of concern for us
just because he is a man,
civilization and morals are
shaken, and the advance to
fully developed inhumanity is
only a question of time.
ALBERT SCHWEITZER,
quoted in *Man and God*

Man is a whole, but a whole
with an astounding capacity
for living, simultaneously or

successively, in watertight compartments. What happens here has little or no effect on what happens there.
ALDOUS HUXLEY, *Collected Essays*

Man is harder than rock and more fragile than an egg.
YUGOSLAV PROVERB

Ill-adapted for living an easy life, he is well adapted for living a difficult one... Never is he more at home in this universe than when he finds himself "upon an engagement very difficult."
L.P. JACKS, *The Challenge of Life*

Now man cannot live without some vision of himself. But still less can he live without a vision that is true to his inner experience and inner feeling.
D.H. LAWRENCE, *Assorted Articles*

A thousand paths are there which have never yet been trodden; a thousand salubrities and hidden islands of life. Unexhausted and undiscovered is still man and man's world.

FRIEDRICH NIETZSCHE, *Thus Spake Zarathustra*

Man identifies himself with earth or the material ... Spirit is strange to him; he is afraid of ghosts.
HENRY DAVID THOREAU, *Journal*

Man *becomes* man only by the intelligence, but he *is* man only by the heart.
HENRI FRÉDÉRIC AMIEL, *Journal*, April 7, 1851

Man, when perfected, is the best of animals, but, when separated from law and justice, he is the worst of all.
ARISTOTLE, *Politics*, (4th century BC), 1.2

Know, man hath all which Nature hath, but more,
And in that more lie all his hopes of good.
MATTHEW ARNOLD, *To an Independent Preacher*, (1849)

Man is at the bottom an animal, mid-way a citizen, and at the top divine. But the climate of this world is such that few ripen at the top.
HENRY WARD BEECHER,

Proverbs from Plymouth Pulpit, (1887)

So God created man in his own image, in the image of God created he him; male and female created he them.
Genesis 1:27

Everyone is more or less mad on one point.
RUDYARD KIPLING, *Plain Tales from the Hills,* (1888)

Sometimes accidents happen in life from which we have need of a little madness to extricate ourselves successfully.
LA ROCHEFOUCAULD, Maxims, (1665)

Man is not only a contributory creature, but a total creature; he does not only make one, but he is all; he is not a piece of the world, but the world itself; and next to the glory of God, the reason why there is a world.
JOHN DONNE, *Sermons,* No. 35, (1625)

Men are but children of a larger growth.
JOHN DRYDEN, *All for Love,* 4.1, (1678)

The majority of mankind is lazy-minded, incurious, absorbed in vanities, and tepid in emotion, and is therefore incapable of either much doubt or much faith.
T.S. ELIOT, introduction to Pascal's *Pensées,* (1931)

Man as we know him is a poor creature; but he is half-way between an ape and a god, and he is travelling in the right direction.
WILLIAM RALPH INGE, *Outspoken Essay,* Confessio Fidei, (1922)

The Family of Man is more than three billion strong. It lives in more than one hundred nations. Most of its members are not white. Most of them are not Christians. Most of them know nothing about free enterprise, or due process of law or the Australian ballot.
JOHN F. KENNEDY, address, (1963)

[Man] is the only one in whom the instinct of life falters long enough to enable it to ask the question "Why?"
JOSEPH WOOD KRUTCH, *The Modern Temper,* (1929)

For in fact what is man in nature? A Nothing in comparison with the Infinite, an All in comparison with Nothing, a mean between nothing and everything.
PASCAL, Pensées, 72, (1670)

There are three classes of men - lovers of wisdom, lovers of honour, lovers of gain.
PLATO, The Republic, 9, (4th century BC)

A man has many parts, he is virtually everything, and you are free to select in him that part which pleases you.
ANTOINE DE SAINT-EXUPÉRY, The Wisdom of the Sands, 96, (1948)

What a piece of work is man! how noble in reason! how infinite in faculties! in form and moving how express and admirable! in action how like an angel! in apprehension how like a god! the beauty of the world! the paragon of animals!
WILLIAM SHAKESPEARE, Hamlet, Act II, Scene ii, line 315, (1600)

The fish in the water is silent, the animal on the earth is noisy, the bird in the air is singing.
But Man has in him the silence of the sea, the noise of the earth and the music of the air.
RABINDRANATH TAGORE, Stray Birds, 43, (1916)

I am a man; I consider nothing human alien to me.
TERENCE, The Self-Tormentor, (163 BC)

We're all of us guinea pigs in the laboratory of God. Humanity is just a work in progress.
TENNESSEE WILLIAMS, Camino Real, 12, (1953)

TWENTY-SIX

ISLAM

Those unto whom We gave the Scripture recognise (this revelation) as they recognise their sons. But lo! a party of them knowingly conceal the truth.
The Koran

When you speak, speak the truth; perform when you promise; discharge your trust; commit not fornication; be chaste; have no impure desires; withhold your hands from striking, and from taking that which is unlawful and bad. The best of God's servants are those who when seen, remind one of God; and the worst of God's servants are those who carry tales about to do mischief and separate friends, and seek for the defects of the good.
MUHAMMAD

It is the Truth from thy Lord (O Muhammad), so be not thou of those who waver.
The Koran

He who believeth in one God and the Hereafter (i.e. a Muslim) let him speak what is good or remain silent.
MUHAMMAD

And each one hath a goal toward which he turneth; so vie with one another in good works. Wheresoever ye may be, Allah will bring you all together. Lo! Allah is Able to do all things.
The Koran

A true Mu'min is thankful to God in prosperity, and is resigned to His Will in adversity.
MUHAMMAD

And whencesoever thou comest forth (for prayer, O Muhammad) turn thy face toward the inviolable Place of Worship. Lo! it is the Truth from thy Lord. Allah is not unaware of what ye do.
The Koran

It is unworthy of a Mu'min to injure people's reputations; and it is unworthy to curse any one; and it is unworthy to abuse any one; and it is unworthy of a Mu'min to talk vainly.
MUHAMMAD

Whencesoever thou comest forth turn thy face toward the Inviolable Place of Worship;

and wheresoever ye may be (O Muslims) turn your faces toward it (when ye pray) so that men may have no argument against you, save such of them as do injustice - Fear them not, but fear Me! - and so that I may complete My grace upon you, and that ye may be guided.
The Koran

He is not of us who is not affectionate to the little ones and doth not respect the reputation of the old; and he is not of us who doth not order that which is lawful, and prohibit that which is unlawful.
MUHAMMAD

Even as We have sent unto you a messenger from among you, who reciteth unto you Our revelations and causeth you to grow, and teacheth you the Scripture and wisdom, and teacheth you that which ye knew not.
The Koran

The best Muslim house is that in which is an orphan benefited; and the worst Muslim house is that in which

an orphan is ill-treated.
MUHAMMAD

Therefore remember Me, I will remember you. Give thanks to Me, and reject not Me.
The Koran

Whosoever seeks refuge in the name of God, give him refuge; and whoso asks in the name of God, give him; and whoso calls on you, respond to him; and whoso does good to you, return the same to him; and if ye do not find anything to return to him, pray (to God) for him, until ye see that ye have made (him) an ample return.
MUHAMMAD

O ye who believe! Seek help in steadfastness and prayer. Lo! Allah is with the steadfast.
The Koran

Whoso is able and fit, and doth not work for himself or for others, God is not gracious to him.
MUHAMMAD

And call not those who are
slain in the way of Allah
"dead". Nay, they are living,
only ye perceive not.
The Koran

Adore God as thou wouldst if
thou sawest Him; for, if thou
seest Him not, He seeth thee.
MUHAMMAD

I am He whom I love, and He
whom I love is I:
We are two spirits dwelling in
one body.
If thou seest me, thou seest
Him,
And if thou seest Him, thou
seest us both.
HALLÂJ

And surely We shall try you
with something of fear and
hunger, and loss of wealth and
lives and crops; but give glad
tidings to the steadfast,
The Koran

Verily, God is mild, and is
fond of mildness, and He
giveth to the mild what He
doth not give to the harsh.
MUHAMMAD

Who say, when a misfortune
striketh them: Lo! we are

Allah's and lo! unto Him we
are returning.
The Koran

Verily, God is pure and loves
the pure, is clean and loves
the clean, is beneficent and
loves the beneficent, is
generous and loves the generous.
MUHAMMAD

Thy Spirit is mingled in my
spirit even as wine is mingled
with pure water.
When anything touches Thee,
it touches me. Lo, in every
case Thou art I!
HALLÂJ

Such are they on whom are
blessings from their Lord, and
mercy. Such are the rightly
guided.
The Koran

God says: I am with the
thought of My servant
concerning Me; and I am with
him when he remembers Me;
and when he remembers Me
within himself, I remember
him within Myself; and if he
remembers Me in public, I
remember him in a public
better than his own.
MUHAMMAD

Lo! (the mountains) As-Safa
and Al-Marwah are among
the indications of Allah. It is
therefore no sin for him who
is on pilgrimage to the House
(of God) or visiteth it, to go
around them (as the pagan
custom is). And he who
doeth good of his own accord,
(for him) lo! Allah is
Responsive, Aware.
The Koran

Jâmî relates in his *Nafahât al-
Uns* that a certain dervish, a
disciple of the famous
Shihâbuddîn Suhrawardî,
"Was endowed with a great
ecstasy in the contemplation
of Unity and in the station of
passing-away (*fanâ*). One day
he began to weep and lament.
On being asked by the Sheykh
Shihâbuddîn what ailed him,
he answered, 'Lo, I am
debarred by plurality from the
vision of Unity. I am rejected,
and my former state - I cannot
find it!' The Sheykh
remarked that this was the
prelude to the station of
'abiding' (*baqâ*), and that his
present state was higher and
more sublime than the one
which he was in before.
JÂMÎ

If a man draw near to me a
span, I draw near to him a
yard; and if he draw near to
me a yard, I draw near to him
a fathom; and if he comes to
me walking, I come to him
running; and whoso comes to
me with a world of sins, but
associates nothing with me, I
come to him with an equal
front of forgiveness.
MUHAMMAD

Those who hide the proofs
and the guidance which We
revealed, after We had made it
clear in the Scripture: such are
accursed of Allah and
accursed of those who have
the power to curse.
The Koran

He who humbles himself for
(the sake of) God, him will
God exalt; he is small in his
own mind, and great in the
eyes of the people. And he
who is proud and haughty,
God will render him
contemptible, and he is small
in the eyes of the people and
great in his own mind, so that
he becomes more
contemptible to them than a
dog or a swine.
MUHAMMAD

Thy will be done, O my Lord
and Master!
Thy will be done, O my
purpose and meaning!
O essence of my being, O goal
of my desire,
O my speech and my hints
and my gestures!
O all of my all, O my hearing
and my sight,
O my whole and my element
and my particles!
HALLÂJ

Except such of them as repent
and amend and make manifest
(the truth). These it is toward
whom I relent. I am the
Relenting, the Merciful.
The Koran

God saith, 'The person I hold
as a beloved, I am his hearing
by which he heareth, and I am
his sight by which he seeth,
and I am his hands by which
he holdeth, and I am his feet
by which he walketh.'
MUHAMMAD

His love entered and removed
all besides Him and left no
trace of anything else, so that
it remained single even as He
is single.
BÂYAZÎD

Verily God is more
compassionate on His
creatures than a woman on
her own child.
MUHAMMAD

Notwithstanding that the
lovers of God are separated
from Him by their love, they
have the essential thing, for
whether they sleep or wake,
they seek and are sought, and
are not occupied with their
own seeking and loving, but
are enraptured in
contemplation of the Beloved.
It is a crime in the lover to
regard his love, and an outrage
in love to look at one's own
seeking while one is face to
face with the Sought.
BÂYAZÎD

What was in the beginning?
Lord Muhammad said, 'God
was, and nothing was with
Him.'
MUHAMMAD

The story admits of being told
up to this point,
But what follows is hidden,
and inexpressible in words.
If you should speak and try a
hundred ways to express it,
'Tis useless; the mystery

becomes no clearer.
You can ride on saddle and
horse to the sea-coast,
But then you must use a horse
of wood (i.e. a boat).
A horse of wood is useless on
dry land,
It is the special vehicle of
voyagers by sea.
Silence is this horse of wood,
Silence is the guide and
support of men at sea.
JALÂLUDDÎN RÛMÎ from
Masnavî

You will not enter paradise
until you have faith; and you
will not complete your faith
till you love one another.
MUHAMMAD

The best (part) of faith is to
say, 'There is no God but
God,' and the least of it is to
remove all injurious things
from the (public) road.
MUHAMMAD

If ye rely upon God as He
ought to be relied upon, He
will provide you as He
provides the birds: they go out
empty and hungry in the
morning and come back big-
bellied at eventide.
MUHAMMAD

I have put duality away, I have
seen that the two worlds are
one;
One I seek, One I know, One
I see, One I call.
I am intoxicated with Love's
cup, the two worlds have
passed out of my ken;
I have no business save
carouse and revelry.
RÛMÎ from *Divân of Shamsi
Tabrîz*

Go in quest of knowledge
even unto China, i.e. even
unto 'edge of earth'.
MUHAMMAD

Seek knowledge from the
cradle to the grave.
MUHAMMAD

God hath treasuries beneath
the throne, the keys whereof
are the tongues of poets.
MUHAMMAD

With knowledge man riseth to
the heights of goodness and to
a noble position, associateth
with sovereigns in this world,
and attaineth to the
perfection of happiness in the
next.
MUHAMMAD

He is not of us who is not
affectionate to his little ones,
and doth not respect the
reputation of the old; and he
is not of us who doth not
order that which is good, and
prohibit that which is bad.
MUHAMMAD

To gladden the heart of the
weary, to remove the suffering
of the afflicted, hath its own
reward. In the day of trouble,
the memory of the action
cometh like a rush of the
torrent, and taketh our burden
away.
MUHAMMAD

The song of the spheres in
their revolutions
Is what men sing with lute
and voice.
As we all are members of
Adam,
We have heard these melodies
in Paradise.
Though earth and water have
cast their veil upon us,
We retain faint reminiscences
of these heavenly songs;
But while we are thus
shrouded by gross earthly
veils,
How can the tone of the
dancing spheres reach us?

JALÂLUDDÎN RÛMÎ, From
Majnan

From all eternity the Beloved
unveiled His beauty in the
solitude of the unseen;
He held up the mirror to His
own face, He displayed His
loveliness to Himself.
He was both the spectator and
the spectacle; no eye but His
had surveyed the Universe.
All was One, there was no
duality, no pretence of 'mine'
or 'thine'.
The vast orb of Heaven, with
its myriad incomings and
outgoings, was concealed in a
single point.
The Creation lay cradled in
the sleep of non-existence,
like a child ere it has
breathed.
The eye of the Beloved, seeing
what was not, regarded
nonentity as existent.
Although He beheld His
attributes and qualities as a
perfect whole in His own
essence,
Yet He desired that they
should be displayed to Him in
another mirror,
And that each one of His
eternal attributes should
become manifest accordingly

in a diverse form.
Therefore He created the
verdant fields of Time and
Space and the life-giving
garden of the world,
That every branch and leaf
and fruit might show forth His
various perfections.
The cypress gave a hint of His
comely stature, the rose gave
tidings of His beauteous
countenance.
Wherever Beauty peeped out,
Love appeared beside it;
wherever Beauty shone in a
rosy cheek, Love lit his torch
from that flame.
Wherever Beauty dwelt in
dark tresses, Love came and
found a heart entangled in
their coils.
Beauty and Love are as body
and soul; Beauty is the mine
and Love the precious stone.
They have always been
together from the very first;
never have they travelled but
in each other's company.
JÂMÎ

He who helpeth his fellow
creature in the hour of need,
and he who helpeth the
oppressed, him will God help
in the day of travail.
MUHAMMAD

What actions are most
excellent? To gladden the
heart of a human being, to
feed the hungry, to help the
afflicted, to lighten the sorrow
of the sorrowful, and to
remove the wrongs of the
injured.
MUHAMMAD

He who tries to remove the
want of his brother, whether
he be successful or not, God
will forgive his sins.
MUHAMMAD

All God's creatures are His
family; and he is the most
beloved of God who tries to
do most good to God's
creatures.
MUHAMMAD

Creatures are subject to
changing 'states', but the
gnostic has no 'state', because
his vestiges are effaced and his
essence annihilated by the
essence of another, and his
traces are lost in another's
traces.
BÂYAZÎD OF BISTÂM

It is related that Sarî al-Saqatî
said, 'O God, whatever
punishment thou mayst inflict

upon me, do not punish me with the humiliation of being veiled from Thee,' because, if I am not veiled from Thee, my torment and affliction will be lightened by the recollection and contemplation of Thee; but if I am veiled from Thee, even Thy bounty will be deadly to me. There is no punishment in Hell more painful and hard to bear than that of being veiled. If God were revealed in Hell to the people of Hell, sinful believers would never think of Paradise, since the sight of God would so fill them with joy that they would not feel bodily pain. And in Paradise there is no pleasure more perfect than unveiledness. If the people there enjoyed all the pleasures of that place and other pleasures a hundredfold, but were veiled from God, their hearts would be utterly broken. Therefore it is the way of God to let the hearts of those who love Him have vision of Him always, in order that the delight thereof may enable them to endure every tribulation; and they say in their visions, 'We deem all torments more desirable than to be veiled from Thee. When Thy beauty is revealed to our hearts, we take no thought of affliction.'
HUJWÎRÎ from *Kashf al-Mahjûb*

Whoever is kind to His creatures, God is kind to him; therefore be kind to man on earth, whether good or bad; and being kind to the bad, is to withhold him from badness, so that those who are in heaven may be kind to you.
MUHAMMAD

'Who do ye imagine to be strong or powerful?' asked the Prophet. 'He who throws people down,' replied his disciples. 'Nay!' said the Prophet, 'it is he who masters himself when angry.'
MUHAMMAD

There are three things which a man is bound to practise. Whosoever neglects any one of them must needs neglect them all, and whosoever cleaves to any one of them must needs cleave to them all. Strive, therefore, to understand, and consider heedfully. The first is this, that with your mind and your tongue and your actions you declare God to be One; and that, having declared Him to be One, and having declared that none benefits you or harms you except Him, you devote all your actions to Him alone. If you act a single jot of your actions for the sake of another, your thought and speech are corrupt, since your motive in acting for another's sake must be hope or fear; and when you act from hope or fear of other than God, who is the lord and sustainer of all things, you have taken to yourself another god to honour and venerate. While you speak and act in the sincere belief that there is no God except Him, you should trust Him more than the world or money or uncle or father or mother or any one on the face of the earth. Thirdly, when you have established these two things, namely, sincere belief in the unity of God and trust in Him, it behoves you to be satisfied with Him and not to be angry on account of anything that vexes you. Beware of anger! Let your

heart be with Him always, let it not be withdrawn from Him for a single moment.
SHAQIQ OF BALKH

Whoso kills a sparrow for nothing, it will cry aloud to God on the day of resurrection, saying, 'O My Lord! such and such a man killed me for nothing, he never killed me for any good.'
MUHAMMAD

"If My servants ask thee about Me, lo, I am near" (Kor. 2. 182); "We (God) are nearer to him than his own neck-vein" (50. 15); "And in the earth are signs to those of real faith, and in yourselves. What! Do ye not see?" (51. 20-21).
The Koran

Muhammad said: That person will not enter Paradise who hath one atom of pride in his heart. Meekness and modesty are two branches of Iman; and vain talking and embellishing are two branches of hypocrisy.
MUHAMMAD

The taker of usury and the giver of it and the writer of its papers and the witness to it,

are equal in crime.
MUHAMMAD

The holder of monopoly is a sinner and offender.
MUHAMMAD

An adulteress was pardoned, who passed by a dog at a well holding out his tongue from thirst which was nearly killing him; for she took off her short boot and tied it to her wrapper, and pulled water for him; so was she pardoned for that. It was asked, 'Shall we then have any reward for (our behaviour to) the brutes?' 'There are rewards,' said the Prophet, 'for all endued with fresh and tender hearts.'
MUHAMMAD

"Thirty years the high God was my mirror," i.e. according to the explanation given by his biographer, "that which I was I am no more, for 'I' and 'God' is a denial of the unity of God. Since I am no more, the high God is His own mirror."
BÂYAZÎD OF BISTÂM

Once when the Prophet happened to be in a garden belonging to one of the Ansars, a camel came in to the Prophet, and sobbed bitterly, and his eyes shed tears. The Prophet went up to him, and stroked his head and the camel paused. The Prophet said, 'Who is the master of this camel?' A young man of the Ansar said, 'It is mine, O Prophet of God!' The Prophet said, 'Dost thou not fear God with regard to this brute beast which God has given thee to possess? It complains to me that thou dost oppress him and fatigue him.'
MUHAMMAD

We were on a journey with the Prophet when we saw a finch with which were two young ones. We took away the two young ones, and the mother-bird fluttered around. Then the Prophet came and said, 'Who has distressed her by taking away her young ones? Return her young ones to her.' The Prophet also saw the abode of ants which we had burnt, and said, 'Who has burnt this?' We said, 'We (have done this).' The Prophet said, 'It is not meet

that any one should punish (another) by fire unless it be the Lord of fire himself.'
MUHAMMAD

I went from God to God, until they cried from me in me, 'O Thou I!'
BÂYAZÎD OF BISTÂM

To be alone is better than (to have) a bad companion; and a good companion is better than being alone; and dictating the good is better than keeping silence; and silence is better than dictating evil.
MUHAMMAD

God enjoins you to treat women well, for they are your mothers, daughters, and aunts.
MUHAMMAD

The rights of women are sacred. See that women are maintained in the rights attributed to them.
MUHAMMAD

Lord Muhammad said, 'My Cherisher hath ordered me nine things: (1) To reverence Him, externally and internally; (2) to speak true, and with propriety, in prosperity and adversity; (3) moderation in affluence and poverty; (4) to benefit my relations and kindred, who do not benefit me; (5) to give alms to him who refuseth me; (6) to forgive him who injureth me; (7) that my silence should be in attaining knowledge of God; (8) that when I speak, I should mention Him; (9) that when I look on God's creatures, it should be as an example for them.
MUHAMMAD

Seventy Thousand Veils separate Allah, the One Reality, from the world of matter and of sense. And every soul passes before his birth through these seventy thousand. The inner half of these are veils of light: the outer half, veils of darkness. For every one of the veils of light passed through, in this journey towards birth, the soul puts off a divine quality: and for every one of the dark veils, it puts on an earthly quality. Thus the child is born weeping, for the soul knows its separation from Allah, the One Reality. And when the

child cries in its sleep, it is
because the soul remembers
something of what it has lost.
Otherwise, the passage
through the veils has brought
with it forgetfulness (nisyân):
and for this reason man is
called insân. He is now, as it
were, in prison in his body,
separated by these thick
curtains from Allah.

But the whole purpose of
Sûfism, the Way of the
dervish, is to give him an
escape from this prison, an
apocalypse of the Seventy
Thousand Veils, a recovery of
the original unity with The
One, while still in this body.
The body is not to be put off;
it is to be refined and made
spiritual - a help and not a
hindrance to the spirit. It is
like a metal that has to be
refined by fire and transmuted.
And the sheikh tells the
aspirant that he has the secret
of this transmutation. 'We
shall throw you into the fire of
Spiritual Passion,' he says,
'and you will emerge refined.'
W.H.T. GAIRDNER

Whoso desireth that God
should redeem him from the

sorrows and travail of the last
day, must delay in calling on
poor debtors, or forgive the
debt in part or whole.
MUHAMMAD

There is a polish for
everything that taketh away
rust; and the polish for the
heart is the remembrance of
God.
MUHAMMAD

"Love is not to be learned
from men: it is one of God's
gifts and comes of His grace."
"None refrains from the lusts
of this world save him in
whose heart there is a light
that keeps him always busied
with the next world."
"When the gnostic's spiritual
eye is opened, his bodily eye is
shut: he sees nothing but
God."
"If gnosis were to take visible
shape all who looked thereon
would die at the sight of its
beauty and loveliness and
goodness and grace, and every
brightness would become dark
beside the splendour thereof."
"Gnosis is nearer to silence
than to speech."
"When the heart weeps
because it has lost, the spirit

laughs because it has found."
"Nothing sees God and dies,
even as nothing sees God and
lives, because His life is
everlasting: whoever sees it is
thereby made everlasting."
"O God, I never listen to the
cry of animals or to the
quivering of trees or to the
murmuring of water or to the
warbling of birds or to the
rustling wind or to the
crashing thunder without
feeling them to be an
evidence of Thy unity and a
proof that there is nothing
like unto Thee."
"O my God, I invoke Thee in
public as lords are invoked,
but in private as loved ones
are invoked. Publicly I say, 'O
my god!' but privately I say, 'O
my Beloved!' "
R.A. NICHOLSON, *Sayings
of Sufis*

O Lord; grant to me the love
of Thee; grant that I love
those that love Thee; grant
that I may do the deeds that
win Thy love; make Thy love
dearer to me than self, family
or wealth.
MUHAMMAD

TWENTY-SEVEN

JUDAISM

And now, O Israel, what does the Lord your God require of you but to stand in awe of the Lord Your God, walk in all his ways, love him, serve the Lord your God with all your mind and heart, and keep the commands of the Lord and his statutes that I am commanding you today, for your good? ... Do not be stiff-necked any more, for the Lord your God is the God of gods, and the Lord of lords, the great, mighty, and awful God, who is never partial, and never takes a bribe, who secures justice for the orphan and the widow, and loves the resident alien in giving him food and clothing. So you should love the resident alien; for you were once resident aliens yourselves in the land of Egypt.
Deuteronomy 10:12,20

What sort of man is fit to rule? Either a sage who has been invested with power or a king who seeks wisdom.
IBN GABIROL

Happy, indeed, is the man whom God reproves;
So don't reject the instruction of the Almighty.
For he wounds, but he binds up;
He smites, but his hands heal.
He will rescue you from six troubles,
Yes, in seven no harm will touch you.
Job 5:17,19

Man reaches God through truth.
PROVERB

How happy is the man who finds wisdom,
The man who gains understanding!
For her income is better than income of silver,
And her revenue than gold.
She is more precious than corals,
And none of your heart's desires can compare with her.
Long life is in her right hand,
In her left are riches and honour.
Her ways are ways of pleasantness,
And all her paths are peace.
She is a tree of life to those who grasp her,
And happy is every one who holds her fast.

The Lord by wisdom founded
the earth,
By reason he established the
heavens;
By his knowledge the depths
are broken up,
And the clouds drop down
dew.

My son, keep guard on
wisdom and discretion,
Let them not slip from your
sight;
They will be life to you,
And an ornament round your
neck.
Then you may go your way in
security,
Without striking your foot on
a stone;
When you rest, you will not
be afraid,
When you lie down, your
sleep will be sweet;
You will fear no sudden terror,
Nor the storm that falls on the
wicked;

For the Lord will be your
confidence,
And will keep your foot from
the snare.
Book of Proverbs

Man is only wise during the
time that he searches for
wisdom; when he imagines he
has completely attained it, he
is a fool.
IBN GABIROL

I am certain that even the
practical duties cannot be
efficiently performed without
willingness of the heart and
desire of the soul to do them.
If it should enter our mind
that we are under no
obligation to choose and
desire the Service of God, our
bodily organs would be
released from the obligation to
fulfil the practical duties, since
no work is complete without
the assent of the soul. And as
it is clear that the Creator has
imposed upon us external
duties, it would be
unreasonable to suppose that
our mind and heart, the
choicest elements of our
being, should have been
exempted from serving Him to
the extent of their power,
since their co-operation is
requisite for the complete
service of God. Hence, it is
clear that we are under the
obligation of inward as well as
external duties; so that our
service shall be perfect and
complete, and shall engage

mind as well as body.
BAHYA

The world goes on only
because of those who disregard
their own existence.
TALMUD, *Hullin*, 89a

Vanity of vanities ...
Vanity of vanities, all is
vanity!
What does a man gain from
all his toil
At which he toils beneath the
sun?
One generation goes, and
another comes,
While the earth endures
forever.
The sun rises and the sun sets,
And hastens to the place
where he rose.
The wind blows toward the
south,
And returns to the north.
Turning, turning, the wind
blows,
And returns upon its circuit.
All rivers run to the sea,
But the sea is never full;
To the place where the rivers
flow,
There they continue to flow.
All things are wearisome;
One cannot recount them.
The eye is not satisfied with

seeing,
Nor is the ear filled with
hearing.
Whatsoever has been is that
which will be;
And whatsoever has been
done is that which will be
done;
And there is nothing new
under the sun.
Is there a thing of which it is
said, 'Lo, this is new'?
It was already in existence in
the ages
Which were before us.
There is no memory of earlier
people;
And likewise of later people
who shall be,
There will be no memory with
those who are later still.
Ecclesiastes

Hear this, all you peoples;
Give heed, all you dwellers in
the world,
Sons of men, and all mankind,
Both rich and poor.
My mouth speaks wisdom,
And my heart's meditation is
insight.
I incline my ear to proverb;
I solve my riddle on the lyre...
Even wise men die;
The fool and the brutish alike
perish,

And leave their wealth to
others.
Their graves are their
everlasting home,
Their dwelling throughout the
ages,
Though lands are named after
them.
But man is an ox without
understanding;
He is like the beasts that
perish.
This is the fate of those who
are self-sufficient,
And the end of those who are
satisfied with their own words.
Like sheep they are appointed
to Sheol...
KING DAVID, *Psalm* 49

Eloquent silence often is
better than eloquent speech.
PROVERB

The Besht was asked: "What
is the chief point in service to
the Lord, if it be true, as you
teach, that fasting and self-
chastisement are sinful?"
The Besht answered: "The
main thing is to encompass
oneself in the love of God, the
love of Israel, and the love of
the Torah. A man may attain
this if he secures enough
nourishment to preserve his

health, and if he makes use of
his strength to battle against
evil inclinations."
BAAL SHEM-TOV

One who believes that
anything can be accomplished
by money is likely to do
anything for money.
HASIDIC SAYINGS

Of God's purpose, one should
not ask questions.
PROVERB

The sage [Diogenes] was
asked, "Who are greater, the
wise or the rich?" He replied,
"The wise." It was then
objected, "If so, how is it that
there are more wise men at
the doors of the rich than rich
men at he doors of the wise?"
He replied, "Because the wise
appreciate the advantage of
wealth, but the rich do not
appreciate the advantage of
wisdom."
IBN GABIROL

I declare that there is a limit
to man's capacity for
knowledge, since so long as
the mind is in the body, it
cannot know what is beyond
Nature. Therefore when the

mind essays to contemplate what is beyond, it attempts that which is impossible. However, it certainly can know and reflect on all that is in Nature, and should try its utmost to do so.
MOSES MAIMONIDES, *Responsa* II, 23b

It is easier to abandon evil traits today than tomorrow.
HASIDIC SAYINGS

It is our first duty to study the beginning of a human being, his birth, the formation of the parts of his physical frame, the joining together of his limbs, the use of each limb and the necessity which caused his being made in his present form. Next, we should study man's advantages, his various temperaments, the faculties of his soul, the light of his intellect, his qualities - those that are essential and those that are accidental; his desires, and the ultimate purpose of his being. When we have arrived at an understanding of the matters noted in regard to man, much of the mystery of this universe will become clear to us, since the one

resembles the other. And thus some sages declared that philosophy is man's knowledge of himself; that is, knowledge of what has been mentioned in regard to the human being, so that through the evidence of divine wisdom displayed in himself, he will become cognisant of the Creator; as Job said (*Job* 19.26), "From my flesh, I see God."
BAHYA

About tomorrow, let God worry.
PROVERB

The finest quality in man is that he should be an inquirer.
IBN GABIROL

I grew up among wise men and learned that nothing is better than silence.
HILLEL in *Sayings of the Fathers*, line 17

Mind is the foundation of man. If the foundation is solid, the building is secure. By the same token, if a man's mind is filled with holy thoughts, his actions will be sound. But if his mind is occupied with selfish

thoughts, even his good actions are unsound, being built on a weak foundation.
BAAL SHEM-TOV

When I have a difficult subject before me - when I find the road narrow, and can see no other way of teaching a well-established truth except by pleasing one intelligent man and displeasing ten thousand fools - I prefer to address myself to the one man, and to take no notice whatever of the condemnation of the multitude.
MOSES MAIMONIDES,
Guide, Introduction

Even repentance should be attained through joy. We should rejoice so much in God that it will arouse in us regret for having offended Him. Through zealous labour in the performance of a holy deed, we can acquire joy.
God dislikes melancholy and depressed spirits.
Joy is a cure for illnesses caused by melancholy.
It is the duty of the joyful person to endeavour to bring to those in sadness and

melancholy a portion of his mood.
NAHMAN BEN SIMHA,
The Bratzlaver

Fear of a misfortune is worse than a misfortune.
HASIDIC SAYINGS

It is through the intellect that the human being has the capacity of honouring God.
MOSES MAIMONIDES,
Comm. Mishan, Hagigah II, I

Some don't believe in God, yet ask His mercy.
PROVERB

Man should be master of his will and slave of his conscience.
HASIDIC SAYINGS

The wise man is a greater asset to a nation than is a king.
MOSES MAIMONIDES,
Comm. Mishna, Horayot III, end

The Disciples of the Besht were told of a certain man who was known as truly wise. There were several of the Disciples who were prompted to call upon this man in the

town of his residence and to profit by his doctrine. The Master gave them leave, but they inquired: "How shall we know him for a true *Zaddik*?" "Ask him to counsel you," said the Besht, "how to keep your thoughts from going astray when praying or learning. If he offers counsel, you will know that his wisdom is nought; for it is part of man's bondage, until the hour of his death, to wrestle with alien thoughts, time and again, and to subdue them in any ascent of the soul."
BAAL SHEM-TOV

Fear only two: God and the man who has no fear of God.
HASIDIC SAYINGS

Where words abound, sin will not be wanting; but he who holds his tongue acts wisely.
Proverbs 10:19

If I am not for myself, who will be for me? And if I am only for myself, what am I? And if not now - when?
HILLEL in *Sayings of the Fathers*, line 14

The sage was asked, "Why do we never perceive in thee a trace of anxiety?" He replied, "Because I never possessed a thing over which I would grieve had I lost it."
He also said, "Everything requires a fence." He was asked, "What is the fence?" He answered, "Trust." "What is the fence of trust?" he was asked; and he replied, "Faith." To the further question, "What is the fence of faith?" he answered, "To fear nothing."
Who refuses to accept the decree of the Creator, there is no healing to his stupidity. Who is the wisest of men and the most trusting? He who accepts things as they come and go.
IBN GABIROL

A fool says what he knows, a sage knows what he says.
PROVERB

Let us be like the lines leading to the central point of the circle: all come to one point and unite there. But let us not be like the parallel lines, which are always separate.
HASIDIC SAYINGS

Wisdom is the consciousness of Self.
MOSES MAIMONIDES, *Guide*, line 53

The man of piety walks in light and is not afraid to walk alone, whereas the man of impiety walks in darkness and is anxious for company.
HASIDIC SAYINGS

The knowledge that whatever happens to you is for your good raises you to the heights of living in Paradise.
A man should believe in God by virtue of faith rather than miracles.
Be not discouraged by any tribulations which may assail you. The recognition that they are for the good of your soul will aid you to endure them.
If you are your own judge and regret your misdeeds, you will not be judged in Heaven.
Meditation and prayer before God are particularly efficacious in grassy fields and amid the trees, since a man's soul is thereby strengthened, as if every blade of grass and every plant united with him in prayer.

If a man finds that he cannot concentrate upon the theme of his meditation, he should express his thoughts in words. Words are like water which falls continually upon a rock until it breaks it through. In similar fashion they will break through a man's flinty heart.
NAHMAN BEN SIMHA, *The Bratzlaver*

There are two kinds of readers of serious books. One is like the man who squeezes wine grapes with his fingertips. He secures only the watery juice from the ends of the grapes, and, inasmuch as it does not ferment, he complains that the grapes are poor. This type of reader glances hurriedly at the pages of a volume and finds no merit in the writings. The other kind of reader is like the man who squeezes out the full juice from the grapes. It ferments and turns into pleasing wine. This type of reader delves deeply into the words he is reading, and finds delight in the thoughts they convey.
HASIDIC SAYINGS

I am astonished at the person who has not prepared patience for every misfortune, and gratitude for every piece of good fortune.

Worry over what has not occurred is a serious malady. To drink a deadly poison is better than worry.

There is a calamity which, when contrasted with another kind of calamity, appears fortunate. Sometimes a calamity becomes auspicious through fortitude.

Fortitude may be bitter, but it averts injury from those who possess it.

Who is honourable in the sight of the Creator? He who has met with adversity but bravely endures whatever befalls him.
IBN GABIROL

A blow from a sage is better than a kiss from a fool.
PROVERB

It is to be feared that those who become great in riches and comfort generally fall into the vices of insolence and haughtiness, and abandon all good principles.
MOSES MAIMONIDES, *Guide*, III, 39

Silence protects wisdom.
AKIBA in *Sayings of the Fathers*, 3.19

What I want to know is not why I suffer, but whether I suffer for Thy sake.
THE BERDICHEVER RABBI

By the help of God, I mean the fixed and unchangeable order of Nature or the chain of natural events: for I have said before and shown elsewhere that the universal laws of Nature, according to which all things exist and are determined, are only another name for the eternal decrees of God, which always involve eternal truth and necessity.

So that to say that everything happens according to natural laws, and to say that everything is ordained by the decree and ordinance of God, is the same thing. Now since the power in Nature is identical with the power of God, by which alone all things happen and are determined, it follows that whatsoever man, as a part of Nature, provides himself with to aid and preserve his

existence, or whatsoever Nature affords him without his help, is given to him solely by the Divine power, acting either through human nature or through external circumstance. So whatever human nature can furnish itself with by its own efforts to preserve its existence, may be fitly called the inward aid of God, whereas whatever else accrues to man's profit from outward causes may be called the external aid of God.
BARUCH SPINOZA,
Tractatum

What is hateful to thee, never do to thy fellow man: that is the entire Torah; all the rest is commentary.
HILLEL in TALMUD:
Shabbath, 31a

Don't try to bargain with the Lord.
PROVERB

Holiness is of a twofold nature; it begins as a quality of the service rendered to God, but it ends as a reward for such service. It is at first a type of spiritual effort, and then a kind of spiritual gift. A

man must first strive to be holy, and then he is endowed with holiness ...
The most that a man can do to achieve holiness by himself is to make a beginning and to persist in his efforts. Only after having attained all the traits that we have thus far discussed, from watchfulness to the fear of sin, may he "enter the sanctuary" (*Lev* 16.3). For, if he lacks any of them, he is like a stranger, or like one that has a blemish, both of whom are prohibited from entering the sanctuary, as it is said, "A stranger shall not come nigh" (*Num* 18.4). But, if after having passed through all these preliminary stages, he cleaves to God with an ardent love and profound awe by reason of his comprehending God's greatness and majesty, he will gradually break away from all that is physical. In all his doings he will succeed in centring his mind upon the mystery of true communion, until there is poured upon him a spirit from on high, and the name of the Creator, blessed be He, will abide within him as it does within all the holy beings. He will then literally

become a messenger of the Lord ...
MOSES LUZZATTO

When love is strong, a man and woman can make their bed on a sword's blade; when love is weak, a bed of sixty cubits is not wide enough.
TALMUD, Sanhedrin, 7a

It is in the nature of man to strive to gain money and to increase it; and his great desire to add to his wealth and honour is the chief source of misery for man.
MOSES MAIMONIDES, Guide, III,39.

No man is as ugly as the man who is self-satisfied.
HASIDIC SAYING

Absalom was vain about his hair, therefore was he hanged by his hair.
TALMUD, Sotah, 9b

There is no room for God in the man who is filled with himself.
BAAL SHEM-TOV

Dive into the sea of thought, and find there pearls beyond

price.
MOSES IBN EZRA, Shirat Yisrael

For many afflictions, silence is the best remedy.
TALMUD, Megillah, 18a

It is indeed a fact that the transition from trouble to ease gives more pleasure than continual ease.
MOSES MAIMONIDES, Guide, III, 24

If a man does not try to reach wisdom, wisdom will not come to him.
RABBINICAL SAYING

Teach us to apply our hearts unto wisdom.
Psalms 90:12

Wisdom is more precious than pearls.
Proverbs 3:15

Thought serves as a mirror: it shows us the ugliness and the beauty within.
MOSES IBN EZRA, Shirat Yisrael

Words are but the shell; meditation is the kernel.

BAHYA IBN PAQUDA,
Choice of Pearls

Those who are pure of heart
find new thoughts whenever
they meditate.
NACHMAN OF BRATSLAV

The Torah is truth, and the
purpose of knowing it is to
live by it.
MAIMONIDES

If God doesn't approve, a fly
doesn't move.
PROVERB

Wisdom is a tree whose fruit is
virtue.
RABBINICAL SAYING

Without experience there is
little wisdom.
BEN SIRACH, *Ecclesiasticus*

Wisdom, like gold ore, is
mixed with stones and dust.
MOSES IBN EZRA, *Shirat
Yisrael*

Wealth brings anxiety, but
wisdom leads to peace of
mind.
IBN GABIROL

Man makes plans; God
changes them.
PROVERB

To seek perfection in property
or health or character is not a
worthy goal, nor a proper
cause of pride and glory; the
knowledge of God is true
wisdom, and is the only
perfection man should seek.
MAIMONIDES, *Guide for the
Perplexed*, 3.53

The beginning of wisdom is to
desire it.
IBN GABIROL, *Choice Pearls*

Wisdom is God's power in
action; for without it,
everything is but theory.
THE MEZERITZER RABBI

A short life with wisdom is
better than a long life without it.
MOSES IBN EZRA, *Shirat
Yisrael*, 119

Wisdom must not be pursued
with any ulterior motive: to
obtain honours, or to gain
money, or to improve one's
material state by the study of
Torah.
MAIMONIDES, *Mishneh
Torah*

The man who is silent tells us something.
PROVERB

The truly wise man is as liberal with his wisdom as clouds are with their rains.
MOSES IBN EZRA, *Shirat Israel*

Wisdom is the light in man.
MOSES CORDOVERO

If you cling to wisdom, you cannot cling to impure desires.
THE MEZERITZER RABBI

The whole drama of mankind is contained in this, the Book of Books, the Bible. Mahomet called the Jews the 'People of the Book'. That Book is their country. Within its boundaries they live and enjoy inalienable citizenship and cannot be dislodged ... Around them, nations rose and disappeared; states flourished, decayed, vanished; revolutions raged across the world. But the Jews sat pouring over this Book, oblivious to the wild chase of time that rushed over their heads.
HEINRICH HEINE

There is not a verse of the Bible, not a word, but is thick-studded with human emotion.
WALT WHITMAN

The world is new to us every morning - this is God's gift; and every man should believe he is reborn each day.
BAAL SHEM-TOV

If you drop gold and books, pick up the books first, then the gold.
Ecclesiastes 12

My pen is my harp and my lyre; my library is my garden and my orchard.
JUDAH HA-LEVI

The sages would sometimes tie money in a cloth bag and throw it behind their backs for poor men to pick up, so that the poor should not feel shame.
MAIMONIDES, *Mishneh Torah*, 10.1.14

No man is ever impoverished by giving alms, nor is harm ever caused by it.
JOSEPH CARO, *Shulhan Aruk*

When a man has compassion for others, God has compassion for him.
TALMUD, *Bezah*, 32a

Never beat or inflict pain on any animal, beast, bird, or insect.
SEFER HASIDIM

If we do not help a man in trouble, it is as if we caused the trouble.
NACHMAN OF BRATSLAV

The fool has said in his heart, "There is no God."
Psalms 14:1

Guard your tongue as you treasure your wealth.
IBN GABIROL

When dust returns to dust the spirit shall return to God, who gave it.
Ecclesiastes 7

When a sage dies, all men should mourn.
TALMUD, *Shabbath*, 105b

The greatest misers with money are the biggest spendthrifts with desires.
MOSES IBN EZRA, *Shirat Yisrael*

The man who is destined to drown will drown in a glass of water.
TALMUD, *Sanhedrin*, 103a

Israel argues, "Even though we sin, and Thou art angry, Thou shouldst not forsake us: for if the potter makes a jug and leaves a pebble in the clay, is it not inevitable that the jug should leak? Thou didst create in us from our childhood the Evil Inclination, therefore we beseech thee, cause the inclination to pass away so that we may do Thy will." And God replies, "I shall do so - in the world to come."
MIDRASH, *Exodus Rabbah*, 46, 4

What can't be avoided can be welcomed.
TALMUD, *Sanhedrin*, 103a

I know the Lord will help - but help me, Lord, *until* you help.
HASIDIC SAYING

With faith, there are no questions; without faith, there are no answers.
THE CHOFETZ CHAIM

Man must not rely on pure reason; he must mix faith with it.
NACHMAN OF BRATSLAV

True faith needs neither evidence nor research.
HASIDIC SAYING

Faith is not only in the heart; it should be put into words.
NACHMAN OF BRATSLAV

Everything is in God's hands, except the awe of God.
TALMUD, Berakoth, 32b

Whoever fears the Lord is afraid of nothing.
BEN SIRACH, Ecclesiasticus, 34.14

Truth rests with God alone - and a little with me.
PROVERB

Keep me as the apple of Thine eye, and hide me under the shadow of Thy wings.
Psalms 17:8

Man was created to serve God and to cleave to Him, not to accumulate wealth and erect buildings which he must leave behind.
IBN EZRA, Yesod Mora

As man acts, God reacts.
BAAL SHEM-TOV

Man was given two ears and one tongue, so that he may listen more than speak.
HASDAI, Ben ha-Melekh ve-ha-Nazir

It is my desire to do God's will, not that God do my will.
THE GERER RABBI

Don't ask God for what you think is good; ask Him for what he thinks is good for you.
THE CHOFETZ CHAIM

Have not I commanded thee; Be strong and of good courage; be not affrighted, neither be thou dismayed: for the Lord thy God is with thee whithersoever thou goest.
Joshua 1:9

God conceals himself from man's mind, but reveals himself to his heart.
Zohar

Thou art far, farther than the heaven of heavens, and near, nearer than my body is to me.
BAHYA BEN ASHER, Kad ha-Kemah

A house testifies that there was a builder, a dress that there was a weaver, a door that there was a carpenter; so our World by its existence proclaims its Creator, God.
Adapted from RABBI AKIBA, *Midrash Temura*, Chapter 3

Man drives, but it is God who holds the reins.
PROVERB

Wherever you find man's footprints, there God was before you.
Mekilta to Exodus, 17.6

A day in the mind of God is like a millennium in the reckoning of man.
Psalms 90:4

The ways of man are pure in his own eyes; but the Lord weighs the motives.
Proverbs 16:2

Deeds of kindness weigh as much as all the commandments.
TALMUD J, *Pe'ah*, 1.1

Happy is the man whose deeds are greater than his learning.
MIDRASH, *Eliyahu Rabbah*, 17

The man whose good deeds exceed his wisdom is like a tree with few branches and many roots: all the raging winds will not move him.
Sayings of the Fathers, 3.17

That good deed is most meritorious of which no one knows.
Adapted from MAIMONIDES

Naked a man comes into the world, and naked he leaves it; after all his toil, he carries away nothing - except the deeds he leaves behind.
RASHI

Melancholy creates nervous ailments; cheerfulness cures them.
HASIDIC SAYING

Happy is he who knows his place and stands in his own place.
TALMUD

The miserable man is unhappy every day; but the cheerful man enjoys a constant feast.
Proverbs 15:15

The culture of the heart is greater than the culture of the mind.
HASIDIC SAYING

If you want to endure this world, equip yourself with a heart that can withstand suffering.
MIDRASH, Leviticus Rabbah, 30

If silence is good for the wise, how much better it is for fools.
TALMUD, Pesahim, 98b

The heart can ennoble any calling: A kind jailer may exceed the saintly in true merit, and a jester may be first in the kingdom of heaven, if they have diminished the sadness of human lives.
RABBI BAROKA IN TALMUD

A woman prefers poverty with love to riches without love.
Adapted from TALMUD

God knows that the best synagogue is the human heart.
HASIDIC SAYING

The tongue is the pen of the heart.
BAHYA IBN PAQUDA, Duties of the Heart

Words that come from the heart enter the heart.
MOSES IBN EZRA, Shirat Yisrael

Man is a holy Temple, and his heart is the holy of holies.
JONATHAN EIBESCHUTZ, Yaarot Dvash

Many pens are broken, and seas of ink consumed, to describe things that never happened.
MIDRASH, Tanhuma

If you sanctify yourself a little, you are sanctified much.
TALMUD, Yomah, 39a

There are sparks of holiness in everything; they constitute our spirituality.
THE MEZERITZER RABBI

"Love your neighbour as yourself" is the great principle of the Torah.
MIDRASH, Torath Kohanim on Leviticus, 19

To obey out of love is better
than to obey out of fear.
RASHI, *Commentaries*,
Deuteronomy

What you love for yourself,
love also for your fellow man.
FALAQUERA, *Sefer ha-
Mevakesh*

God looks into our hearts
before he looks into our minds.
PROVERB

Man's mind is the Holy of
Holies, and to admit evil
thoughts is like setting up an
idol in the Temple.
THE BERDICHEVER RABBI

You don't have to pray loudly;
just direct your heart to
heaven.
RABBI CHIA

Gold and silver are purified
through fire; if you feel no
sense of improvement after
praying, either you are made
of base metal, or your prayer
lacked heat.
THE KORETSER RABBI

Unless you speak wisely, keep
silent.
IMMANUEL OF ROME

Unless we believe that God
renews creation every day, our
prayers grow habitual and
tedious.
BAAL SHEM-TOV

To flee from god is to flee into
selfishness.
Adapted from PHILO

If I am here, all is here; and if
I am not here, who is here?
HILLEL in TALMUD,
Sukkah, 53a

The I is the soul, which
endures.
NACHMAN OF BRATSLAV

Is not the soul a guest in the
body?
MIDRASH, *Leviticus Rabbah*, 32

The soul is the Lord's candle.
Proverbs 20:27

Wisdom is to the soul as food
is to the body.
ABRAHAM IBN EZRA

Upon death, the soul goes out
of one door and enters
another.
Adapted from BAAL SHEM-
TOV

The heart of fools is in their
mouth; the mouth of the wise
is in their heart.
ANON

TWENTY-EIGHT

JUSTICE

Envy not the glory and riches
of a sinner: for thou knowest
not what his ruin shall be.
Ecclesiasticus, IX. 16

"But," one says, "I see the
noble and good perishing of
hunger and cold." Well, and
do you not see those who are
not noble and good perishing
of luxury and ostentation and
vulgarity?
EPICTETUS

Where Mercy, Love, and Pity
dwell
There God is dwelling too.
WILLIAM BLAKE, *Songs of
Innocence*, The Divine Image,
(1789)

Neither is it possible to
conceal fire in a garment, nor
a base deviation from
rectitude in time.
PYTHAGORIC SAYING

Forsake the outwardness of sin
and the inwardness thereof.
Lo! those who garner sin will
be awarded that which they
have earned.
Qur'ân, VI, 120

Disorder also is subject to the
Master, but he has not yet
imposed order upon it.
HERMES

The rulers of the world
Unmercifully just, who punish
all
To the severest rigours of the
laws,
Are most unjust themselves,
and violate
The laws they seem to guard;
there is a justice
Due to humanity.
CHARLES JOHNSON

Nought is on earth more
sacred or divine,
That gods and men do equally
adore,
Than this same virtue, that
doth right define;
For th' heavens themselves,
whence mortal men implore;
Right in their wrongs, are
rul'd by righteous lore,
Of highest Jove, who doth
true justice deal
To his inferior gods; and
evermore
Therewith contains his
heavenly commonweal;
The skill whereof to prince's
hearts he doth reveal.
SPENSER

We hand folks over to God's mercy, and show none ourselves.
GEORGE ELIOT, *Adam Bede*, 42, (1859)

Poise the cause in justice's equal scales,
Whose beam stands sure, whose rightful cause prevails.
WILLIAM SHAKESPEARE

Justice is passionless and therefore sure;
Guilt for a while may flourish; virtue sink
'Neath the shade of calumny and ill; justice
At last, like the bright sun, shall break majestic forth,
The shield of innocence, the guard of truth.
J.F. SMITH

Man is unjust, but God is just; and finally justice triumphs.
LONGFELLOW

Justice from violence must be exempt;
But fraud's her only object of contempt;
Fraud in the fox, force in the lion dwells;
But justice both from human hearts expels;

But he's the greatest monster, without doubt,
Who is a wolf within, a sheep without.
DENHAM

Of all the virtues justice is the best;
Valour without it is a common pest;
Pirates and thieves, too oft with courage graced,
Show us how ill the virtue may be placed,
'Tis our complexion makes us chaste or brave:
Justice from reason and from heaven we have;
All other virtues dwell but in the blood,
That's in the soul and gives the name of good.
WALLER

Justice consists in doing no injury to men; decency in giving them no offence.
TULLY

Sound judgement is the ground of writing well.
ROSCOMMON

Pour not water on a drowning mouse.
THOMAS FULLER, M.D., *Gnomologia*, 3915, (1732)

In forming a judgement, lay your hearts void of foretaken opinions; else, whatsoever is done or said, will be measured by a wrong rule; like them who have the jaundice, to whom everything appeareth yellow.
SIR PHILIP SIDNEY

He that judges without informing himself to the utmost that he is capable, cannot acquit himself of judging amiss.
LOCKE

Do not your juries give their verdict
As if they felt the cause, not heard it?
BUTLER

Yet shall the axe of justice hew him down,
And level with the root his lofty crown.
SANDYS

Justice like lightning, ever should appear
To few men's ruin, but to all men's fear.
SWETNAM

Teach me to feel another's woe,
To hide the fault I see;
That mercy I to others show,
That mercy show to me.
ALEXANDER POPE, *The Universal Prayer*, 10, (1738)

Justice discards party, friendship, kindred, and is always therefore represented as blind.
THOMAS ADDISON

Ay, justice, who evades her?
Her scales reach every heart;
The action and the motive,
She weigheth each apart;
And none who swerve from right or truth
Can 'scape her penalty.
MRS. HALE

Justice, though moving with a tardy pace, has seldom failed of overtaking the wicked in their flight.
HORACE

Of mortal justice if thou scorn the rod,
Believe and tremble, thou art judged of God.
SWETNAM

If strict justice be not the rudder of all our other virtues, the faster we sail, the farther we shall find ourselves from that 'haven where we should be.'
COLTON

Be just and fear not;
Let all the ends thou aim'st at be thy country's,
Thy God's, and truth's.
WILLIAM SHAKESPEARE

When a man's life is under debate,
The judge can ne'er too long deliberate.
DRYDEN

Clemency is the support of justice.
RUSSIAN PROVERB

A wise judge, by the craft of the law, was never seduced from its purpose.
SOUTHEY

Yet show some pity -
I show it most of all when I show justice,
For then I pity those I do not know,
Which a dismiss'd offence would after gall;

And do him right that,
answering one foul wrong,
Lives not to act another.
WILLIAM SHAKESPEARE

If we look more closely, we shall find
Most have the seeds of judgement in their mind.
ALEXANDER POPE

Judging is balancing an account, and determining on which side the odds lie.
LOCKE

Men are not to be judged by their looks, habits, and appearances; but by the character of their lives and conversations, and by their works. 'Tis better that a man's own works, than that another man's words should praise him.
L'ESTRANGE

Forbear to judge, for we are sinners all.
WILLIAM SHAKESPEARE

How little do they see what is, who frame
Their hasty judgement upon that which seems.
SOUTHEY

Every one complains of the badness of his memory, but nobody of his judgement.
LA ROCHEFOUCAULD

Sweet mercy is nobility's true badge.
WILLIAM SHAKESPEARE, *Titus Andronicus*, Act I, Scene i, line 119 (1592-93)

Four things belong to a judge: to hear courteously, to answer wisely, to consider soberly, and to decide impartially.
SOCRATES

Though justice be thy plea, consider this, that in the course of justice none of us should see salvation.
WILLIAM SHAKESPEARE

It is because men are prone to be partial towards those they love, unjust to those they hate, servile to those above them, and either harsh or over-indulgent to those below them in station, poverty or distress, that it is difficult to find any one capable of forming a sound judgement with respect to the qualities of others.
CONFUCIUS

Have we not always found in our past experience that, on the whole, our kind interpretations were truer than our harsh ones?
FABER

Hear one side, and you will be in the dark; hear both sides, and all will be clear.
HALIBURTON

The most generous and merciful in judgement upon the faults of others, are usually the most free from faults themselves.
AUGHEY

The mercy of the Lord is from everlasting to everlasting upon them that fear Him.
Psalms 103:17

As the torrent that rushes down the mountain destroys all that is borne away by it, so does common opinion overwhelm reason in him who accepts it without first asking: "What is the foundation?" See that what you receive as Truth is not merely the shadow of it; for what you acknowledge as convincing is often but plausible.

Do not say that the event proves the wisdom of the action; remember that man is not above the reach of accidents.

Do not condemn the judgement of another because it differs from your own; for, may you not both be in error?
DANDEMIS

There is no better ruler than judgement; no safer guardian than justice; no stronger sword than right; no ally surer than truth.

Justice is an unassailable fortress built on the brow of a mountain which cannot be overthrown by the violence of torrents, nor demolished by the force of armies.
From *Arabic Sayings*

Men are often unjust because they form the habit of supposing that if they respect the rights and meet the claims which are protected and enforced by law, they have done all that in strict justice can be required of them; Christ has warned us that there is a judgement to come, and that when this life is over we shall be judged by a law more searching and more equitable, and sustained by more terrible sanctions, than any that human tribunals can administer.
R.D.DALE, *Laws of Christ for Common Life*, Chapter III

Augustus Caesar was sitting in judgement when Mecaenas, the patron of Horace, was present. Seeing that the emperor was about to pass sentence of death unjustly, Mecaenas tried to get near him, but failing on account of the crowd, he wrote on a piece of paper, "Rise, Executioner" (*Surge, Carnifex*), and threw the note into Caesar's lap. Caesar immediately rose without condemning any person to death, and far from being offended, was troubled at having given cause for the rebuke.
PERCY ANECDOTES

Justice without power is inefficient; power without justice is tyranny.
BLAISE PASCAL, *Pensées*

A man should never be ashamed to own he has been

in the wrong, which is but saying, in other words, that he is wiser today than he was yesterday.
JONATHAN SWIFT, *Thoughts on Various Subjects*

What is Truth?, said jesting Pilate; And would not stay for an Answer.
SIR FRANCIS BACON, *Essays*, Of Truth

We must take care to do Right Things Rightly: for a just Sentence may be unjustly executed.
WILLIAM PENN, *Some Fruits of Solitude*

Revenge is a kinde of Wilde Justice; which the more Mans nature runs to, the more ought Law to weed it out. For as for the first Wrong, it doth but offend the Law; but the Revenge of that Wrong, putteth the Law out of Office.
SIR FRANCIS BACON, *Essays*, Of Revenge

Truth is its [justice's] handmaid, freedom is its child, peace is its companion, safety walks in its steps, victory follows in its train; it is the brightest emanation from the gospel; it is the attribute of God.
SYDNEY SMITH, *Lady Holland's Memoir*, Volume I, page 29

Justice is truth in action.
BENJAMIN DISRAELI, Speech, February 11, 1851

Justice without wisdom is impossible.
FROUDE, *Short Studies on Great Subjects*, Party Politics

Who redeemeth thy life from destruction; who crowneth thee with loving kindness and tender mercies.
Psalms 103:4

The spirits of just men made perfect.
Hebrews 12:23

Justice, though moving with tardy pace, has seldom failed to overtake the wicked in their flight.
HORACE, *Carmina*, III, 2, 31

Just are the ways of God, And justifiable to men.
MILTON, *Samson Agonistes*, line 293

The path of the just is as the shining light, that shineth more and more unto the perfect day.
Proverbs 4:18

Justice is itself the great standing policy of civil society; and any eminent departure from it, under any circumstances, lies under the suspicion of being no policy at all.
BURKE, *Reflections on the Revolution in France*

Justice extorts no reward, no kind of price: she is sought, therefore, for her own sake.
CICERO, *De Legibus*, I, 18

Justice does not descend from its pinnacle.
DANTE, *Purgatorio*, VI, 37

The one great principle of the English law is, to make business for itself.
CHARLES DICKENS, (1812-70), *Bleak House*, (1853)

When constabulary duty's to be done,
A policeman's lot is not a happy one.
W.S. GILBERT, (1836-1911), *The Pirates of Penzance*, (1879)

No poet ever interpreted nature as freely as a lawyer interprets the truth.
JEAN GIRAUDOUX, (1882-1944), *La Guerre de Troie n'aura pas lieu*, (1935)

Bowels of mercies, kindness, humbleness of mind, meekness, long-suffering.
Colossians 3:12

Let us remember that justice must be observed even to the lowest.
CICERO, *De Natura Deorum*, III, 15

A verbal contract isn't worth the paper it is written on.
SAM GOLDWYN, (1882-1974), *The Great Goldwyn*, (1937)

Every society gets the kind of criminal it deserves. What is equally true is that every community gets the kind of law enforcement it insists on.
ROBERT KENNEDY, (1925-68), *The Pursuit of Justice*, (1964)

Loopholes are not always of a fixed dimension. They tend to enlarge as the numbers that

pass through wear them away.
HAROLD LEVER, (1914-95),
Speech to Finance Bill
Committee, (1968)

The Court's opinion will
accomplish the seemingly
impossible feat of leaving this
area of the law more confused
than it found it.
WILLIAM H. REHNQUIST,
(1924-), Opinion in Roe v.
Wade 1973

The devil makes his
Christmas pies of lawyers'
tongues and clerks' fingers.
LATE 16TH-CENTURY
SAYING

A man who is his own lawyer
has a fool for his client.
EARLY 19TH- CENTURY
SAYING

Open thy bowels of
compassion.
CONGREVE, The Mourning
Bride, Act IV, Scene 7

No one should be judge in his
own cause.
MID 15TH-CENTURY
SAYING

The journalists have
constructed for themselves a
little wooden chapel, which
they also call the Temple of
Fame, in which they put up
and take down portraits all
day long and make such a
hammering you can't hear
yourself speak.
GEORG CHRISTOPH
LICHTENBERG, (1742-99),
Georg Christoph Lichtenberg
Aphorismen, (1904)

There are laws to protect the
freedom of the press's speech,
but none that are worth
anything to protect the people
from the press.
MARK TWAIN, (1835-
1910), License of the Press,
(1873)

A mistake in judgement isn't
fatal, but too much anxiety
about judgement is.
PAULINE KAEL, (1965)

Youth is the period of harsh
judgements, and a man seldom
learns until he reaches thirty
that human nature is made up
not of simples, but of
compounds.
ELLEN GLASGOW, The
Miller of Old Church, (1911)

I learned early in life not to judge others. We outcasts are very happy and content to leave that job to our social superiors.
ETHEL WATERS, *His Eye Is on the Sparrow*, (1951)

We need not be too strict in seeing
The failings of a fellow being.
MARY LAMB, *The Rook and the Sparrows*, (1809)

Crime takes but a moment but justice an eternity.
ELLEN O'GRADY, From *Woman Police Deputy Is Writer of Poetry*, (1918)

Someone
will take the ball
from the hands that play
the game of terror.
NELLY SACHS, *O the Chimneys*, Someone, (1967)

Justice is mercy's highest Self.
FRANCES HODGSON BURNETT, *A Lady of Quality*, (1896)

Blessed are the merciful: for they shall obtain mercy.
Matthew Verse 7
A lawyer has no business with the justice or injustice of the cause which he undertakes, unless his client asks his opinion, and then he is bound to give it honestly. The justice or injustice of the cause is to be decided by the judge.
SAMUEL JOHNSON, *Tour to the Hebrides*, (J. Boswell)

Under a government which imprisons any unjustly, the true place for a just man is also a prison.
HENRY DAVID THOREAU, (1817-62), *Civil Disobedience*

You shall judge of a man by his foes as well as by his friends.
JOSEPH CONRAD, (1857-1924), *Lord Jim*, Chapter 34

Force, if unassisted by judgement, collapses through its own mass.
HORACE, *Odes*, III

The place of justice is a hallowed place.
FRANCIS BACON, (1561-1626), *Essays*, Of Judicature

Are you going to hang him *anyhow* - and try him afterward?

MARK TWAIN, (1835-1910), *Innocents at Home*, Chapter 5

Who will not mercie unto others show,
How can he mercie ever hope to have?
SPENSER, *The Faerie Queene*, Book IV, Canto i, Stanza 42

The supernatural virtue of justice consists of behaving exactly as though there were equality when one is the stronger in an unequal relationship.
SIMONE WEIL, (1909-43), *Waiting on God*, Forms of the Implicit Love of God

Don't let your opinion sway your judgement.
SAM GOLDWYN, quoted by Sidney Skotsky

The price of justice is eternal publicity.
ARNOLD BENNETT, *Things That Have Interested Me*

Moderation in the pursuit of justice is no virtue.
SENATOR BARRY GOLDWATER, Republican National Convention, (1964)

I would rather be British than just.
REV. IAN PAISLEY, quoted, *Sunday Times*, (1971)

Rigid justice is the greatest injustice.
THOMAS FULLER, M.D., *Gnomologia*, 4055, (1732)

A great deal may be done by severity, more by love, but most by clear discernment and impartial justice.
GOETHE, quoted in Johann Peter Eckermann's *Conversations with Goethe*, March 22, 1825

Justice delayed is democracy denied.
ROBERT F. KENNEDY, *The Pursuit of Justice*, (1964)

In matters of government, justice means force as well as virtue.
NAPOLEON 1, *Maxims*, (1804-15)

We praise or blame as one or the other affords more opportunity for exhibiting our power of judgement.
FRIEDRICH NIETZSCHE, *Human, All Too Human*, 86, (1878)

Knowledge is the treasure, but judgement the treasurer of a wise man.
WILLIAM PENN, *Some Fruits of Solitude*, line 162, (1693)

Such as every man is inwardly so he judgeth outwardly.
THOMAS À KEMPIS, *The Imitation of Christ*, 2. 4, (1426)

Many have justice in their hearts, but slowly it is let fly, for it comes not without council to the bow.
DANTE, *Purgatorio*, 6, The Divine Comedy, (circa 1300-21)

When one observes oneself as one actually is, then either one is moved to despair because one considers oneself as hopeless, ugly, miserable; or one looks at oneself without any judgement. And to look at oneself without any judgement is of the greatest importance, because this is the only way you can understand yourself and know about yourself.
J. KRISHNAMURTI, *You Are the World*

Distrust all those who talk much of their justice! Verily, in their souls not only honey is lacking.
FRIEDRICH NIETZSCHE, Thus Spake Zarathustra

Justice. To be ever ready to admit that another person is something quite different from what we read when he is there (or when we think about him), Or rather, to read in him that he is certainly something different, perhaps something completely different from what we read in him.
SIMONE WEIL, *Gravity and Grace*

We are always giving things absolutely arbitrary characters. This thing is good, that thing is bad, we say; but badness or goodness, beauty or ugliness are not in things themselves, but in the ways those things relate themselves to us.
PHILLIPS BROOKS, *Visions and Tasks*

The duty of judges is to dispense justice; their profession is to delay it. Some of them know their duty, and

practise their profession.
JEAN DE LA BRUYÈRE,
Characters, Of Certain
Customs, 33

How strange that it is easier
for us to be just toward men
than toward God!
JOSEPH DE MAISTRE, *The
Saint Petersburg Dialogues*, 1

Passing judgement on people,
or characters in a book, means
making silhouettes of them.
CESARE PAVESE, *Diary
1935-1950*, This Business of
Living, (1939)

It is much more difficult to
judge oneself than to judge
others.
ANTOINE DE SAINT-
EXUPÉRY, *The Little Prince*,
Chapter 10

Judges don't age. Time
decorates them.
ENID BAGNOLD, *The Chalk
Garden*, Act 2

As the judge of the people is
himself, so are his officers; and
what manner of man the ruler
of the city is, such are all they
that dwell therein.
Apocrypha Ecclesiasticus, 10.2

No man can justly censure or
condemn another, because
indeed no man truly knows
another.
SIR THOMAS BROWNE,
Religio Medici, Part 2, 4

We judge other people by
what they say and do,
ourselves by what we think
and intend.
COMTESSE DIANE, *Maxims
of Life*, page 49

Portia: The quality of mercy is
not strain'd;
It droppeth, as the gentle rain
from heaven
Upon the place beneath: it is
twice bless'd;
It blesseth him that gives, and
him that takes:
'Tis mightiest in the mightiest;
it becomes
The throned monarch better
than his crown:
His sceptre shows the force of
temporal power,
The attribute to awe and
majesty,
Wherein doth sit the dread
and fear of kings;
But mercy is above the
sceptred sway;
It is enthronéd in the hearts of
kings,

It is an attribute to God
himself;
And earthly power doth then
show likest God's,
When mercy seasons justice:
Therefore, Jew,
Though justice be thy plea,
consider this,
That in the course of justice,
none of us
Should see salvation: we do
pray for mercy.
WILLIAM SHAKESPEARE,
The Merchant of Venice

Nothing is more unsatisfactory
than a mature judgement
adopted by an immature mind.
JOHANN WOLFGANG
VON GOETHE, quoted in
Edward Fitzgerald, *Polonius*, A
Persian Legend

The seat of knowledge is in
the head; of wisdom, in the
heart. We are sure to judge
wrong if we do not feel right.
WILLIAM HAZLITT,
Characteristics, 388

In the strange heat all
litigation brings to bear on
things, the very process of
litigation fosters the most
profound misunderstandings
in the world.
RENATA ADLER, *Reckless
Disregard*

TWENTY-NINE

LEISURE

If you are losing your leisure,
look out! You may be losing
your soul.
LOGAN PEARSALL
SMITH, *Afterthoughts*

Leisure and solitude are the
best effect of riches, because
mother of thought. Both are
avoided by most rich men,
who seek company and
business; which are signs of
being weary of themselves.
SIR W. TEMPLE

Let's to billiards.
WILLIAM SHAKESPEARE,
Antony and Cleopatra, Act II,
Scene v, line 3

In green old gardens, hidden
away
From sight of revel and sound
of strife, ...
Here may I live what life I
please,
Married and buried out of
sight.
VIOLET FANE, *In Green Old
Gardens*

This is a sport which makes
the body's very liver curl with
enjoyment.
MARK TWAIN, *Life on the
Mississippi*

The holiest of all holidays are
those
Kept by ourselves in silence
and apart;
The secret anniversaries of the
heart,
When the full river of feeling
overflows; -
The happy days unclouded to
their close;
The sudden joys that out of
darkness start
As flames from ashes; swift
desires that dart
Like swallows singing down
each wind that blows!
LONGFELLOW, *Holidays*

With ecstasies so sweet
As none can even guess,
Who walk not with the feet
Of joy in idleness.
ROBERT BRIDGES, *Spring*,
Ode I, Stanza 10

Time for work, - yet take
Much holiday for art's and
friendship's sake.
GEORGE JAMES DE
WILDE, *On the Arrival of
Spring*

That indolent but delightful
condition of doing nothing.
PLINY THE YOUNGER,
Epistles, Book VIII, Epistle 9

There is one piece of advice, in a life of study, which I think no one will object to; and that is, every now and then to be completely idle, - to do nothing at all. Indeed this part of a life of study is commonly considered so decidedly superior to the rest that it has almost obtained an exclusive preference.
SYDNEY SMITH, *Lectures on Moral Philosophy*, Number 19

You will soon break the bow if you keep it always stretched.
PHAEDRUS, *Fables*, Book III, Fable 14.1.10; PUBLILIUS SYRUS, *Sententiae*, Number 388

Extreme *busyness*, whether at school or college, kirk or market, is a symptom of deficient vitality; and a faculty for idleness implies a catholic appetite and a strong sense of personal identity.
R.L. STEVENSON, *An Apology for Idlers*

Life does not agree with philosophy: there is no happiness without idleness, and only the useless is pleasurable.
TCHEKHOV, *Note-Books*

It is well to lie fallow for a while.
M.F. TUPPER, *Proverbial Philosophy*, Of Recreation

I am happiest when I am idle. I could live for months without performing any kind of labour, and at the expiration of that time I should feel fresh and vigorous enough to go right on in the same way for numerous more months.
ARTEMUS WARD, *Natural History*, Chapter 3

Take up and read, take up and read.
ST. AUGUSTINE, (AD 354-430), *Confessions* (AD 397-8)

I loafe and invite my soul, I lean and loafe at my ease observing a spear of summer grass.
WALT WHITMAN, *Song of Myself*, Section 1

What makes a garden
And why do gardens grow?
Love lives in gardens -
God and lovers know!
CAROLYN GILTINAN, *The Garden*

You should do nothing that did not absolutely *please* you. Be idle, be very idle! The habits of your mind are such that you will necessarily do much; but be as idle as you can.
SAMUEL TAYLOR COLERIDGE, *Letter to Southey*, 1799

Increased means and increased leisure are the two civilisers of man.
BENJAMIN DISRAELI, Speech to the Conservatives of Manchester, (1872)

A life of leisure and a life of laziness are two things.
BENJAMIN FRANKLIN, *Poor Richard*, 1746

Leisure is the mother of Philosophy.
THOMAS HOBBES, *Leviathan*, Part IV, Chapter 46

Give time to your friends, leisure to your wife, relax your mind, give rest to your body, so that you may the better fulfil your accustomed occupation.
PHAEDRUS, *Fables*, Book III, Prol. 1.12

How various his employments whom the world
Calls idle; and who justly, in return,
Esteems that busy world an idler too!
WILLIAM COWPER, *The Task*, Book III, line 352

Leisure without study is death; it is a tomb for the living man.
SENECA, *Epistulae ad Lucilium*, Epistle 1 xxxii 3

Leisure is the best of all possessions.
SOCRATES, from DIOGENES LAERTIUS *Socrates* II, Section 30

A man ought to read just as inclination leads him; for what he reads as a task will do him little good.
SAMUEL JOHNSON, from James Boswell *Life of Samuel Johnson* (1791)

He enjoys true leisure who has time to improve his soul's estate.
H.D. THOREAU, *Journal*, 11 February 1840

God loves an idle rainbow,
No less than labouring seas.
RALPH HODGSON,
A Wood Song

What is more delightful than
lettered ease?
CICERO, Tusculanarum
Disputationum, Boo. V,
Chapter 36, Section 105

Is there no road now to
Leisurely Lane? We travelled
it long ago!
A place for the lagging of
leisurely steps, sweet and
shady and slow.
VIRGINIA WOODWARD
CLOUD, Leisurely Lane

Play so that you may be
serious.
ANACHARSIS (circa 600
BC), in Aristotle's
Nicomachean Ethics (4th
century BC), 10.6

The true object of all human
life is play. Earth is a task
garden; heaven is a
playground.
G.K. CHESTERTON, Oxford
from Without, All Things
Considered, (1908)

Game, noun: any unserious
occupation designed for the
relaxation of busy people and
the distraction of idle ones; it's
used to take people to whom
we have nothing to say off our
hands, and sometimes even
ourselves.
ETIENNE BONNOT, ABBÉ
DE CONDILLAC,
Dictionnaire des Synonymes,
Oeuvres Philosophique, Verse 3

It is a happy talent to know
how to play.
RALPH WALDO
EMERSON, Journals, 1834

There are toys for all ages.
ENGLISH PROVERB

Yes, in the poor man's garden
grow
Far more than herbs and
flowers -
Kind thoughts, contentment,
peace of mind,
And joy for weary hours.
MARY HOWITT, The Poor
Man's Garden

Our minds need relaxation,
and give way
Unless we mix with work a
little play.

MOLIÈRE, *The School for Husbands*, (1661)

In our play we reveal what kind of people we are.
OVID, *The Art of Love*, 3, (circa AD 8)

To the art of working well a civilized race would add the art of playing well.
GEORGE SANTAYANA, *Little Essays*, 61, (1920)

It is not abstinence from pleasures that is best, but mastery over them without being worsted.
ARISTIPPUS (5th - 4th century BC) quoted in Diogenes Laertius' *Lives and Opinions of Eminent Philosophers* (3rd century AD)

A broad margin of leisure is as beautiful in a man's life as in a book.
H.D. THOREAU, *Journal*, 28 December 1852

Nothing gives rest but the sincere search for truth.
PASCAL, *Pensées*, 907, (1670)

The time to read is any time: no apparatus, no appointment of time and place, is necessary.
JOHN AIKIN, (1747-1822), *Letters from a Father to his Son* (1796)

The Soul is restless and furious, it wants to tear itself apart, and cure itself of being human.
UGO BETTI, *Goat Island*, 1.4, (1946), editor Gino Rizzo

I have sought for happiness everywhere, but I have found it nowhere except in a little corner with a little book.
THOMAS À KEMPIS, (circa 1380-1471), attributed, Gerald Donaldson *Books* (1981)

To withdraw is not to run away, and to stay is no wise action, when there's more reason to fear than to hope.
CERVANTES, *Don Quixote*, 1.3.9, (1605-15)

One cannot rest except after steady practice.
GEORGE ADE, *Forty Modern Fables*, The Man Who Was Going to Retire, (1901)

It is better to have loafed and lost than never to have loafed at all.

JAMES THURBER, *Fables for Our Time*, The Courtship of Arthur and Al, (1943)

To do nothing at all is the most difficult thing in the world, the most difficult and the most intellectual.
OSCAR WILDE, *Intentions*, The Critic as Artist (1891)

The hardest work is to go idle.
Yiddish Proverbs, (1949), editor Hanan J. Ayalti

Nor should I regard leisure and freedom from trouble as a good; for what has more leisure than a worm?
SENECA, *Epistulae ad Lucilium*, Epistle 1, xxxvii

Consider the lilies of the field, how they grow; they toil not, neither do they spin: And yet I say unto you, That even Solomon in all his glory was not arrayed like one of these.
Matthew 6:28-29

It is because artists do not practise, patrons do not patronize, crowds do not assemble to reverently worship the great work of Doing Nothing, that the world has lost its philosophy and even failed to invent a new religion.
G.K. CHESTERTON, *Generally Speaking*, On Leisure, (1928)

Fair Quiet, have I found thee here,
And Innocence, thy sister dear?
ANDREW MARVELL, *The Garden*

To be at ease is better than to be at business. Nothing really belongs to us but time, which even he has who has nothing else.
BALTASAR GRACIÁN, *The Art of Worldly Wisdom*, 247, (1647)

Leisure and curiosity might soon make great advances in useful knowledge, were they not diverted by minute emulation and laborious trifles.
SAMUEL JOHNSON, *The Rambler*, 177, (1750-52)

Read in order to live.
GUSTAVE FLAUBERT, (1821-80), Letter to Mademoiselle de Chantepie, June 1857

Lie down and listen to the
crabgrass grow,
The faucet leak, and learn to
leave them so.
MARYA MANNES, *But Will
It Sell?*, Controversy, (1955-64)

In itself and in its
consequences the life of
leisure is beautiful and
ennobling in all civilised
men's eyes.
THORSTEIN VEBLEN, *The
Theory of the Leisure Class*, 3,
(1890)

Friendship requires more time
than poor busy men can
usually command.
RALPH WALDO
EMERSON, *The Conduct of
Life*, Behaviour, (1860)

God Almighty first planted a
garden. And, indeed, it is the
purest of human pleasures. It
is the greatest refreshment to
the spirits of man; without
which buildings and palaces
are but gross handiwork; and a
man shall ever see that when
ages grow to civility and
elegancy, men come to build
stately gardens sooner than to
garden finely: as if gardening
were the greater perfection.

FRANCIS BACON, *Essays*,
Of Gardens

The bow that's always bent
will quickly break;
But if unstrung 'twill serve you
at your need.
So let the mind some
relaxation take
To come back to its task with
fresher heed.
PHAEDRUS, *Fables*, Book III,
Fable 14

Albess: Sweet recreation
barred, what doth ensue
But moody and dull
melancholy,
Kinsman to grim and
comfortless despair;
And at her heels a huge
infectious troop
Of pale distemperatures, and
foes to life?
WILLIAM SHAKESPEARE,
Comedy of Errors, Act V,
Scene i, line 92

Better to hunt in fields for
health unbought,
Than fee the doctor for a
nauseous draught.
The wise for cure on exercise
depend;
God never made His work for
man to mend.

DRYDEN, *Epistle to John Dryden of Chesterton*, line 92

To cure the mind's wrong bias, spleen,
Some recommend the bowling-green;
Some hilly walks; all exercise;
Fling but a stone, the giant dies.
MATTHEW GREEN, *The Spleen* line 90

On the books she was planning to read:
I have not had time yet. But I look at them as a child looks at a cake, - with glittering eyes and watering mouth, imagining the pleasure that awaits him!
ELIZABETH GASKELL, (1810-65), Letter to George Smith, 4 August 1859

It is impossible to enjoy idling thoroughly unless one has plenty of work to do.
JEROME K. JEROME, *Idle Thoughts of an Idle Fellow*, On Being Idle

Sometimes we are clarified and calmed healthily, as we never were before in our lives, not by an opiate, but by some unconscious obedience to the all-just laws, so that we become like a still lake of purest crystal and without an effort our depths are revealed to ourselves. All the world goes by us and is reflected in our deeps.
HENRY DAVID THOREAU, *Journal*

The art of leisure lies, to me, in the power of absorbing without effort the spirit of one's surroundings; to look, without speculation, at the sky and sea; to become part of a green plain; to rejoice, with a tranquil mind, in the feast of colour in a bed of flowers.
DION CALTHROP, *The Charm of Gardens*

Leisure only means a chance to do other jobs that demand attention.
OLIVER WENDELL HOLMES, JR., *Holmes-Pollock Letters*, Volume II

Now, when so many have leisure, they have become detached from themselves, not merely from the earth. From all the widened horizons of our greater world a thousand

voices call us to come near, to understand, and to enjoy, but our ears are not trained to hear them. The leisure is ours but not the skill to use it. So leisure becomes a void, and from the ensuing restlessness men take refuge in delusive excitations or fictitious visions, returning to their own earth no more.
ROBERT MACIVER, Man Alone

An intention to write never turns into a letter. A letter must happen to one like a surprise, and one may not know where in the day there was room for it to come into being.
RAINER MARIA RILKE, Letters of Rainer Maria Rilke, (1892-1910)

There is no ancient gentlemen but gardeners.
WILLIAM SHAKESPEARE, Hamlet, Act V, Scene i, line 33

Well, your letter makes up for today's bad weather; within me the sun is shining from a blue sky, outside there is fog and drizzle.
SIGMUND FREUD, The Letters of Sigmund Freud

Some minds learn most when they seem to learn least. A certain placid, unconscious, equable taking-in of knowledge suits them, and alone suits them.
WALTER BAGEHOT, Literary Studies, Volume 1

Leisure is time at personal risk.
A.M. SULLIVAN, The Three-Dimensional Man

As peace is the end of war, so to be idle is the ultimate purpose of the busy.
SAMUEL JOHNSON, The Idler, Number 1

Leisure is indeed an affair of mood and atmosphere rather than simply of the clock. It is not a chronological occurrence but a spiritual state. It is unhurried pleasurable living among one's native enthusiasms.
IRWIN EDMAN, The Uses of Philosophy

Reading maketh a full man.
FRANCIS BACON, (1561-1626), *Essays*, Of Studies, (1625)

To be for one day entirely at leisure is to be for one day an immortal.
CHINESE PROVERB

Leisure, like its sister peace, is among those things which are internally felt rather than seen from the outside.
VERNON LEE, *Limbo and Other Essays*

It is in his pleasure that a man really lives, it is from his leisure that he constructs the true fabric of self.
AGNES REPPLIER, *Essays in Idleness*

And leave us leisure to be good.
GRAY, *Hymn*, Adversity, Scene 3

No blessed leisure for Love or Hope,
But only time for Grief.
HOOD, *The Song of the Shirt*

That in trim gardens takes his pleasure.
MILTON, *Il Penseroso*, line 49

Must be out-of-doors enough to get experience of wholesome reality, as a ballast to thought and sentiment. Health requires this relaxation, this aimless life.
HENRY DAVID THOREAU, *Journal*

Mend when thou canst; be better at thy leisure.
WILLIAM SHAKESPEARE, *King Lear*, Act II, Scene iv, line 232

What is this life if, full of care, We have no time to stand and stare.
W.H. DAVIES, (1871-1940), *Leisure*, (1911)

Oh, Adam was a gardener, and God who made him sees That half a proper gardener's work is done upon his knees. So when your work is finished, you can wash your hands and pray
For the Glory of the Garden that it may not pass away!
And the glory of the Garden it shall never pass away!
RUDYARD KIPLING, *The Glory of the Garden*

To be able to fill leisure intelligently is the last product of civilization.
BERTRAND RUSSELL, (1872-1970), *The Conquest of Happiness* (1930)

It was Einstein who made the real trouble. He announced in 1905 that there was no such thing as absolute rest. After that there never was.
STEPHEN LEACOCK, (1869-1944), *The Boy I Left Behind Me* (1947)

We are closer to the ants than to the butterflies. Very few people can endure much leisure.
GERALD BRENAN, (1894-1987), *Thoughts in a Dry Season*, (1978)

If I am doing nothing, I like to be doing nothing to some purpose. That is what leisure means.
ALAN BENNETT, (1934-), *A Question of Attribution*, (1989)

All work and no play makes Jack a dull boy.
MID 17TH-CENTURY SAYING

The thing which is the most outstanding and chiefly to be desired by all healthy and good and well-off persons, is leisure with honour.
CICERO, (106-43 BC), *Pro Sestio*

No country can reach a high stage of civilization without a leisure class.
GERTRUDE ATHERTON, *Can Women Be Gentlemen?* (1938)

People who know how to employ themselves, always find leisure moments, while those who do nothing are forever in a hurry.
MARIE-JEANNE ROLAND, (1792), *Memoirs of Madame de Staël and of Madame Roland*, (1847)

What we lack is not so much leisure to do as time to reflect and time to feel. What we seldom "take" is time to experience the things that have happened, the things that are happening, the things that are still ahead of us.
MARGARET MEAD AND RHODA METRAUX, *A Way of Seeing*, (1970)

Leisure is gone - gone where the spinning-wheels are gone, and the pack-horses, and the slow wagons, and the peddlers who brought bargains to the door on sunny afternoons.
GEORGE ELIOT, Adam Bede (1859)

The multi-billion-dollar entertainment and leisure industries notwithstanding, Americans have not learned how to use large amounts of leisure in noncompulsive, personally satisfying ways.
JANET SALTZMAN CHAFETZ, Masculine/Feminine or Human? (1974)

That is well said, replied Candide, but we must cultivate our garden.
VOLTAIRE, Candide, Chapter 30

There is always time for a nap.
SUZY BECKER, All I Need to Know I Learned From My Cat, (1990)

Leisure requires the evidence of our own feelings, because it is not so much a quality of time as a peculiar state of mind ... What being at leisure means is more easily felt than defined.
VERNON LEE, Limbo, About Leisure, (1908)

Leisure, some degree of it, is necessary to the health of every man's spirit.
HARRIET MARTINEAU, Society in America, Volume 3 (1837)

Reading is to the mind what exercise is to the body.
RICHARD STEELE, (1672-1729), Tatler, (1710)

Leisure and the cultivation of human capacities are inextricably interdependent.
MARGARET MEAD, in Redbook, (1963)

The wisdom of a learned man cometh by opportunity of leisure and he that hath little business shall become wise. How can he get wisdom that holdeth the plough and that glorieth in the goad, that driveth oxen, and is occupied in their labours, and whose talk is of bullocks?
Ecclesiasticus, 38, 24-25

Hey! Mr. Tambourine Man,
play a song for me,
I'm not sleepy and there is no
place I'm going to.
BOB DYLAN (Robert Allen
Zimmerman, 1941-),
Mr. Tambourine Man

I am interested in leisure in
the way that a poor man is
interested in money. I can't
get enough of it.
PRINCE PHILIP, (1921-),
Attributed

A god gave us this leisure.
VIRGIL, (70-19 BC), *Eclogue*,
1.6

THIRTY

LITERATURE

If anyone doubts the *reality* of our Art, he should read the books of those ancient Sages whose good faith no one ever yet called in question, and whose right to speak on this subject cannot be challenged. If you will not believe *them*, I am not so foolish as to enter into a controversy with one who denies first principles.
MICHAEL SENDIVOGIUS

And quoted odes, and jewels five-words long,
That on the stretched forefinger of all Time
Sparkle for ever.
ALFRED, LORD TENNYSON, *Princess*, c. 2, 355

The truth I tell is writ on many a page of the writers of the Holy Spirit.
DANTE, *Paradiso*, XXXIX, 40

Poetry is the consolation of mortal men.
RALPH WALDO EMERSON, *Poetry and Imagination*

Experience enables me to depose to the comfort and blessing that literature can prove in seasons of sickness and sorrow; - how powerfully intellectual pursuits can help in keeping the head from crazing, and the heart from breaking.
THOMAS HOOD

Such a superiority do the pursuits of literature possess above every other occupation, that even he who attains but a mediocrity in them merits the pre-eminence above those that excel the most in the common and vulgar professions.
DAVID HUME

Poetry is the handmaid to Imagination and Fancy.
KEBLE, *Lectures on Poetry*, Number I

The place that does contain my books, the best companions, is to me a glorious court, where hourly I converse with the old sages and philosophers; and sometimes for variety, I confer with kings and emperors, and weigh their counsels.
FLETCHER

They give new views to life, and teach us how to live; they soothe the grieved, the stubborn they chastise, fools they admonish, and confirm the wise: their aid they yield to all: they never shun the man of sorrow, nor the wretch undone: unlike the hard, the selfish and the proud, they fly not sullen from the suppliant crowd; nor tell to various people various things, but show to subjects what they show to kings. Silent they are, but, though deprived of sound, here all the living languages abound; here all that live no more, preserved they lie in tombs that open to the curious eye. Blessed be the gracious Power who taught mankind to stamp a lasting image of the mind.
CRABBE

A good book is the precious life-blood of a master spirit, embalmed and treasured up on purpose, to a life beyond life.
MILTON

All good poetry is the spontaneous overflow of powerful feelings.
WILLIAM

WORDSWORTH, Preface to Second Edition of *Lyrical Ballads*, (1800)

A library is true fairyland, a very palace of delight, a haven of repose from the storms and troubles of the world. Rich and poor can enjoy it alike, for here, at least, wealth gives no advantage.
AVEBURY

Let us deem the glorious art of Poetry a kind of medicine divinely bestowed upon man.
KEBLE, *Lectures on Poetry*, Number I

Hymns to the gods and the praises of worthy actions are the only sort of poetry to be admitted to our state. For if you were to admit the pleasurable muse also, in songs or verses, we should have pleasure and pain reigning in our state instead of law.
PLATO, *Republic*, Book 10, 8

Poetry is the devil's wine.
ST. AUGUSTINE

In my garden I spend my days; in my library I spend my nights. With the flowers I am

with the present; with my books I am in the past. I go into my library, and all history unrolls before me. I breathe morning air of the world while the scent of Eden's roses yet lingered in it, while it vibrated only to the world's first brood of nightingales, and to the laugh of Eve. I see the Pyramids building; I hear the shoutings of the armies of Alexander; I feel the ground shake beneath the march of Cambyses. I sit as in a theatre - the stage is Time, the play is the Play of the World. What a spectacle it is! O men and women, so far separated, yet so near, so strange, yet so well known. By what miraculous power do I know ye all! Books are the true Elysian fields where the spirits of the dead converse, and into these fields a mortal may venture unappalled. What King's Court can boast such company? What school of Philosophy such wisdom? Seated in my library at night, and looking on the silent faces of my books, I am occasionally visited by a strange sense of the supernatural. They are not collections of printed pages, they are ghosts. I take one down, and it speaks to me of men and things not now known on Earth. I call myself solitary, but sometimes I think I misapply the term; for no man sees more company than I do. I travel with mightier cohorts around me than ever did Timour or Genghis Khan on their fiery marches. I am a Sovereign in my library; but it is the dead, not the living, that attend my levees.
ALEXANDER SMITH

Language put to its best purpose, used at its utmost power and with the greatest skill, and recorded that it may not pass away, evaporate and be forgotten, is what we call, for want of a better word, literature.
J.W. MACKAIL, *Classical Studies*, page 214

Poetry is of all humane learning the most ancient and of most fatherly antiquity, as from whence all other learnings have taken their beginnings.
SIR P. SYDNEY, *Apologie for Poetrie*

O souls, perplexed by hood
and cowl,
Fain would you find a teacher;
Consult the lark and not the
owl,
The poet, not the preacher.
A. AUSTIN, *The Owl and the
Lark*

Great literature is simply
language charged with
meaning to the utmost
possible degree.
EZRA POUND, *How to Read*,
Part II

To turn events into ideas is
the function of literature.
GEORGE SANTAYANA,
Little Essays, page 138

Literature must be an analysis
of experience and a synthesis
of the findings into a unity.
REBECCA WEST, *Ending in
Earnest*

There is no such thing as
either literature or poetry for
the masses.
JEAN COCTEAU, *Le Rappel
à l'Ordre*, page 136

Our high respect for a well-
read man is praise enough of
literature.

RALPH WALDO
EMERSON, *Letters and Social
Aims*, Quotations

Gie me ae spark o' Nature's
fire!
That's a' the learning I desire;
Then, though I trudge
through dub an' mire -
At plough or cart,
My Muse, though hamely in
attire,
May touch the heart.
ROBERT BURNS, *Epistle to
John Lapraik*

It is life that shakes and rocks
us; it is literature which
stabilizes and confirms.
H.W. GARROD, *Profession of
Poetry*, page 257

Verse has more power to
soothe than prose.
KEBLE, *Lectures on Poetry*,
Number 6

It is the dull man who is
always sure, and the sure man
who is always dull. The more
a man dreams, the less he
believes. A great literature is
thus chiefly the product of
doubting and inquiring minds
in revolt against the
immovable certainties of the

nation.
H.L. MENCKEN, (1880-
1956), Prejudices, (2nd series,
1920)

Any writer worth his salt
knows that only a small
proportion of literature does
more than partly compensate
people for the damage they
have suffered in learning to
read.
REBECCA WEST, (1892-
1983), Path from a White Horse

All high poetry is infinite; it is
as the first acorn, which
contained all oaks potentially.
PERCY BYSSHE SHELLEY,
Defence of Poetry, (1821)

Among the values I would
like passed on to the next
millennium, there is this
above all: a literature that has
absorbed the taste for mental
orderliness and exactitude, the
intelligence of poetry, but at
the same time that of science
and of philosophy.
ITALO CALVINO, (1923-
85), Six Memos for the Next
Millennium, (1992)

The illusion of art is to make
one believe that great

literature is very close to life,
but exactly the opposite is
true. Life is amorphous,
literature is formal.
FRANÇOISE SAGAN,
(1935-), Writers at Work,
(1958) 1st series

The virtue of much literature
is that it is dangerous and may
do you extreme harm.
JOHN MORTIMER, (1923-),
C.H. Rolph, Books in the Dock

Poetry is the first and last of
all knowledge - it is as
immortal as the heart of man.
WILLIAM
WORDSWORTH, Preface to
Second Edition of Lyrical
Ballads, (1800)

It takes a great deal of history
to produce a little literature.
HENRY JAMES, (1843-
1916), Hawthorne, (1879)

Ideas are to literature what
light is to painting.
PAUL BOURGET, (1852-
1935), La Physiologie de
l'Amour Moderne, (1890)

Literature always anticipates
life. It does not copy it, but
moulds it to its purpose. The

nineteenth century, as we know it, is largely an invention of Balzac.
OSCAR WILDE

I doubt if anything learnt at school is of more value than great literature learnt by heart.
SIR RICHARD LIVINGSTONE, *On Education*

All literature, all art, best seller or worst, must be sincere, if it is to be successful ... Only a person with a Best Seller mind can write Best Sellers; and only someone with a mind like Shelley's can write *Prometheus Unbound*. The deliberate forger has little chance with his contemporaries and none at all with posterity.
ALDOUS HUXLEY, *Essays New and Old*

Nothing goes by luck in composition. It allows of no tricks. The best you can write will be the best you are.
THOREAU, *Journal*, February 28 1841

Ideally, the writer needs no audience other than the few who understand. It is immodest and greedy to want more.
GORE VIDAL, *Encounter, Theories of the New Novel*, (1967)

There is no royal path to good writing; and such paths as exist do not lead through neat critical gardens, various as they are, but through the jungles of self, the world, and of craft.
JESSAMYN WEST, *Saturday Review*, (1957)

To speak in literature with the perfect rectitude and insouciance of the movements of animals and the unimpeachableness of the sentiment of trees in the woods and grass by the roadside is the flawless triumph of art.
WALT WHITMAN, preface to Leaves *of Grass*, (1855)

Not marble, nor the gilded monuments
Of princes, shall outlive this powerful rhyme.
WILLIAM SHAKESPEARE, Sonnet 55

For the creation of a master-work of literature two powers must concur, the power of the man and the power of the moment.
MATTHEW ARNOLD, *The Function of Criticism*, (1864)

What is so wonderful about great literature is that it transforms the man who reads it towards the condition of the man who wrote, and brings to birth in us also the creative impulse.
E.M. FORSTER, *Two Cheers for Democracy*, Anonymity: An Enquiry, (1951)

The literary sensibility is geared to the timeless, that is, to the now only as an avenue by which all time can be reached.
JOHN SIMON, Should Albee Have Said 'No Thanks'?, *The New York Times*, (1967)

A novel is a mirror walking along a main road.
STENDHAL, *Scarlet and Black*, Chapter 49

The ancient historians gave us delightful fiction in the form of fact; the modern novelist presents us with dull facts in the guise of fiction.
OSCAR WILDE, *The Decay of Lying*

A good novel tells us the truth about its hero; but a bad novel tells us the truth about its author.
G.K. CHESTERTON, *Heretics*, Chapter 15

By its very nature, the novel indicates that we are becoming. There is no final solution. There is no last word.
CARLOS FUENTES, *Guardian*, (1989)

A poem is the very image of life expressed in its eternal truth.
PERCY BYSSHE SHELLEY, *Defence of Poetry*, (1821)

Fiction was invented the day Jonah arrived home and told his wife that he was three days late because he had been swallowed by a whale.
GABRIEL GARCIA MÁRQUEZ, *Guardian*, (1999)

Every novelist has something in common with a spy: he

watches, he overhears, he seeks motives and analyses character, and in his attempt to serve literature he is unscrupulous.
GRAHAM GREENE, A *Sort of Life*, Chapter 7

The only part of a story that is true is the part the listener believes.
HERMANN HESSE, *Reflections*, 400: Reality and Imagination

Great novels are always a little more intelligent than their authors. Novelists who are more intelligent than their books should go into another line of work.
MILAN KUNDERA, *The Art of the Novel*, Jerusalem Address

There is no life that can be recaptured wholly; as it was. Which is to say that all biography is ultimately fiction.
BERNARD MALAMUD, *Dulin's Lives*, 1

A novelist is, like all mortals, more fully at home on the surface of the present than in the ooze of the past.

VLADIMIR NABOKOV, *Strong Opinions*, 20

Parcels have always exercised an odd fascination for me - one always expects something of a sensational nature, and one is always disappointed. In that respect they resemble the modern novel.
PETER ACKROYD, *The Last Testament of Oscar Wilde*, 14 August 1900

You can't get at the truth by writing history; only the novelist can do that.
GERALD BRENAN, *Times Literary Supplement*, (1986)

Fairy tales are the only true accounts that man has ever given of his destiny.
G.K. CHESTERTON, in *The World*, (1902)

Beneath the rule of men entirely great
The pen is mightier than the sword.
(1ST) LORD LYTTON, *Richelieu*

Charles James Fox thought, "Poetry the great refreshment of the human mind, - the only

thing, after all; that men first found out that they had minds by making and tasting poetry."
RALPH WALDO EMERSON, *Poetry and Imagination*

The Sibyl, uttering sentences all full of serious thought and meaning, continues her voice a thousand years, through the favour of the divinity that speaks within her.
PLUTARCH, *Of the Pythian Oracle*

The essence of all poetry is to be found, not in high-wrought subtlety of thought, nor in pointed cleverness of phrase, but in the depths of the heart and the most sacred feelings of the men who write.
KEBLE, *Lectures on Poetry*, Number 28

Captains and conquerors leave a little dust,
And Kings a dubious legend of their reign;
The swords of Caesar's, they are less than rust;
The poet doth remain.
SIR W. WATSON, *Lachrymae Musarum*, 114

A great poem is a fountain for ever overflowing with the waters of wisdom and delight.
PERCY BYSSHE SHELLEY, *Defence of Poetry*, (1821)

If evil does not exist, what is going to happen to literature?
V.S. PRITCHETT, *Mr. Beluncle*, 23

Literature happens to be the only occupation in which wages are not given in proportion to the goodness of the work done.
ANTHONY TROLLOPE, speech on 10 April 1869, St. George's Hall, Liverpool, for Dicken's farewell tour

What is the difference between literature and journalism? Oh! Journalism is unreadable and literature is not read.
OSCAR WILDE, *The Critic as Artist*, 1

Half of literature was about it: young women struggling to escape from under the weight of old men, for the sake of the species.
J.M. COETZEE, *Disgrace*, 21

Literature is the art of writing something that will be read twice; journalism what will be grasped at once.
CYRIL CONNOLLY, *Enemies of Promise*, Chapter 3

Look in thy heart and write.
SIR PHILIP SIDNEY, William Gray's *Life of Sir Philip Sidney*

The great and good do not die, even in this world. Embalmed in books, their spirits walk abroad. The book is a living voice. It is an intellect to which one still listens.
SAM'L SMILES, *Character*, Chapter X

So must a writer, whose productions should
Take with the vulgar, be of vulgar mould.
EDMUND WALLER, *Epistle to Mr. Killegrew*

Some future strain, in which the muse shall tell
How science dwindles, and how volumes swell.
How commentators each dark passage shun,
And hold their farthing candle to the sun.
YOUNG, *Love of Fame*, Satire VII, line 95

It may be glorious to write
Thoughts that shall glad the two or three
High souls, like those far stars that come in sight
Once in a century.
LOWELL, *An Incident in a Railroad Car*

The most glorious poetry that has ever been communicated to the world is probably a feeble shadow of the original conceptions of the poet.
PERCY BYSSHE SHELLEY, *Defence of Poetry*, (1821)

He who writes prose builds his temple to Fame in rubble; he who writes verses builds it in granite.
BULWER-LYTTON, *Caxtoniana*, Essay XXVII, The Spirit of Conservatism

You do not publish your own verses, Laelius; you criticise mine. Pray cease to criticise mine, or else publish your own.
MARTIAL, *Epigrams*, Book I, Epigram 91

The ink of the scholar is more
sacred than the blood of the
martyr.
MOHAMMED, *Tribute to
Reason*

Writings survive the years; it
is by writings that you know
Agamemnon, and those who
fought for or against him.
OVID, *Epistolae Ex Ponto*, IV.
8. 51

Devise, wit; write, pen; for I
am for whole volumes in folio.
WILLIAM SHAKESPEARE,
Love's Labour's Lost, Act I,
Scene ii, line 190

Written with a pen of iron,
and with the point of a
diamond.
Jeremiah 17:1

The chief glory of every
people arises from its authors.
SAMUEL JOHNSON, *Preface
to Dictionary*

Damn the age; I will write for
Antiquity.
CHARLES LAMB, *Bon Mots
by Charles Lamb*

Perhaps the greatest lesson
which the lives of literary men

teach us is told in a single
word: Wait!
LONGFELLOW, *Hyperion*,
Book I, Chapter VIII

All great writing comes by the
grace of God, and all doing
and having.
RALPH WALDO
EMERSON, *Essays*, Of
Experience

Write to the mind and heart,
and let the ear Glean after
what it can.
BAILEY, *Festus*, Sc. Home

Poetry is the record of the best
and happiest moments of the
happiest and best minds.
PERCY BYSSHE SHELLEY,
Defence of Poetry, (1821)

There is probably no hell for
authors in the next world -
they suffer so much from
critics and publishers in this.
BOVEE, *Summaries of Thought*

The book that he has made
renders its author this service
in return, that so long as the
book survives, its author
remains immortal and cannot
die.

RICHARD DE BURY,
Philobiblon, Chapter I, 21

But words are things, and a
small drop of ink,
Falling, like dew, upon a
thought produces
That which makes thousands,
perhaps millions think.
BYRON, *Don Juan*, Canto III,
Stanza 88

There is first the literature of
knowledge, and secondly, the
literature of *power*. The
function of the first is - to
teach; the function of the
second is - to *move*, the first is
a rudder, the second an oar or
a sail. The first speaks to the
mere discursive understanding;
the second speaks ultimately,
it may happen, to the higher
understanding or reason, but
always *through* affections of
pleasure and sympathy.
THOMAS DE QUINCEY,
Essays on the Poets, Alexander
Pope

The proper study of mankind
is books.
ALDOUS HUXLEY, (1894-
1964), *Chrome Yellow*

The idea of going to a writers'
congress in Moscow was
rather like attending a human
rights conference in Nazi
Germany.
DAVID MARKSTEIN,
Member of the Writers' Guild
of Great Britain

God forbid people should read
our books to find the juicy
passages.
GRAHAM GREENE, (1904-
91), *The Observer*, Sayings of
the Week, (1979)

The mysteries of divine Truth
supplied the place of poetry
among our forefathers, while
now the present generation
readily foregoes that higher
wisdom, satisfied as it would
seem with that poetry which
is but a shadow of it.
KEBLE, *Lectures on Poetry*,
Number 30

Literature and butterflies are
the two sweetest passions
known to man.
VLADIMIR NABOKOV,
(1899-1977), *Radio Times*, Oct
1962

Literature is my Utopia. Here
I am not disfranchised. No

barrier of the senses shuts me out from the sweet, gracious discourse of my book-friends. They talk to me without embarrassment or awkwardness.
HELEN KELLER, *The Story of My Life*, (1902)

When literature becomes deliberately indifferent to the opposition of good and evil it betrays its function and forfeits all claim to excellence.
SIMONE WEIL, *On Science, Necessity, and the Love of God*, (1968)

Coroners' inquests by learned societies can't make Shakespeare a dead man.
ELLEN TERRY, *The Story of My Life*, (1908)

No author ever drew a character, consistent to human nature, but what he was forced to ascribe to it many inconsistencies.
BULWER-LYTTON, *What Will He Do With It?*, Book IV, Chapter XIV, Heading

A best-seller is the golden tomb of a mediocre talent.
LOGAN PEARSALL

SMITH, (1865-1946), *Afterthoughts*, (1931)

Poetry ever communicates all the pleasure which men are capable of receiving; it is ever still the light of life; the source of whatever of beautiful or generous or true can have place in an evil time.
PERCY BYSSHE SHELLEY, *Defence of Poetry*, (1821)

Books cannot be killed by fire. People die, but books never die. No man and no force can abolish memory ... In a war, we know, books are weapons. And it is a part of your dedication always to make them weapons for man's freedom.
FRANKLIN D. ROOSEVELT, (1882-1945), Message to the Booksellers of America, (1942)

Russian literature saved my soul. When I was a young girl in school and I asked what is good and what is evil, no one in that corrupt system could show me.
IRINA RATUSHINSKAYA, (1954-), in *Observer*, (1989)

What literature can and should do is change the people who teach the people who don't read the books.
A.S. BYATT, (1936-), interview in *Newsweek*, 5 June 1995

The pencil of the Holy Ghost hath laboured more in describing the afflictions of Job than the felicities of Solomon.
FRANCIS BACON, (1561-1626), *Essays*, Of Adversity, (1625)

We present you with this Book, the most valuable thing that this world affords. Here is wisdom; this is the royal Law; these are the lively Oracles of God.
Coronation Service 1689: The Presenting of the Holy Bible

The English Bible, a book which, if everything else in our language should perish, would alone suffice to show the whole extent of its beauty and power.
LORD MACAULAY, (1800-59), *John Dryden*, (1828)

An apology for the Devil: It must be remembered that we have only heard one side of the case. God has written all the books.
SAMUEL BUTLER, (1835-1902), *Notebooks* (1912)

He set out seriously to describe the indescribable. That is the whole business of literature, and it is a hard row to hoe.
G.K. CHESTERTON, (1874-1936), *All I Survey*, On Literary Cliques

It is a clear, or at least a probable hypothesis, that ... poetry was providentially destined to prepare the way for Revealed Truth itself.
KEBLE, *Lectures on Poetry*, Number 40

National literature no longer means very much, the age of world literature is due.
JOHANN WOLFGANG VON GOETHE, (1749-1832), *Conversations with Eckermann*, 31 January 1827

If God exists, what's the good of literature? If God does not exist, what's the point of

writing?
EUGENE IONESCO, (1912-
94), interview in *Guardian*,
(1990)

All art is full of magic and
trickery, but in a novel the
whole thing can subside into
an ocean of reflection and
continuous thought - at least
in a traditional novel -
whereas in theatre you are
really jumping from place to
place like a mountain goat.
IRIS MURDOCH, (1919-),
interview in *Weekend
Guardian*, (1989)

I'm happy the great ones are
thriving
But what puzzles my head
Is the thought that they
needed reviving
I had never been told they
were dead.
PHYLLIS McGINLEY, *The
Prevalence of Literary Revival*

Poetry, which has been
defined as the harmonious
unison of man with nature.
THOMAS CARLYLE, *Early
German Literature*

England produced
Shakespeare: the British

Empire the six-shilling novel.
GEORGE MOORE, *Hail and
Farewell*, (1911)

Literature is not about
something: it is the thing
itself, the quiddity.
VLADIMIR NABOKOV,
Lectures on Literature

When I am dead, I hope it
may be said:
'His sins were scarlet but his
books were read'.
HILAIRE BELLOC, *Epigram
on his Books*

The only biography that is
really possible is
autobiography. To recount
the actions of another man is
not biography, it is zoology,
the noting down of the habits
of a new and outlandish
animal. It is most valuable
and interesting, but it does
not deal with the spring and
spirit of a man's existence.
G.K. CHESTERTON, *A
Handful of Authors*

Reference books are like wives
- it's only when you have
taken them home and lived
with them a bit that you really
find out what they are like.

BRIAN W. ALDISS, *The Brightfount Diaries*

... the sarcastic reply of Porson, who hearing some one observe that 'certain modern poets would be read and admired when Homer and Virgil were forgotten', made answer - 'And not till then!'
WILLIAM HAZLITT, *The English Comic Writers*, On Wit and Humour

The poet is the priest of the invisible.
WALLACE STEVENS, (1879-1955), *Adagia*, (1957)

It is harder to make one's name by a perfect work than it is for a mediocre one to win esteem through the name one already has.
JEAN DE LA BRUYÈRE, (1645-96), *Les Caractères ou les moeurs de ce siècle*, (1688)

Prose - words in their best order; poetry - the best words in the best order.
SAMUEL TAYLOR COLERIDGE, *Table Talk*

There can be nothing so gratifying to an author as to arouse the respect and esteem of the reader. Make him laugh and he will think you a trivial fellow, but bore him in the right way and your reputation is assured.
W. SOMERSET MAUGHAM, *Gentleman in the Parlour*, (1930)

Poetry is the breath and finer spirit of all knowledge; it is the impassioned expression which is in the countenance of all science.
WILLIAM WORDSWORTH, Preface to Second Edition of *Lyrical Ballads*, (1800)

THIRTY-ONE

LOVE

Immature love says: 'I love you because I need you.' Mature love says: 'I need you because I love you.'
ERICH FROMM, (1900-1980), *The Art of Loving*, (1956)

All things work together for good to them that love God, to them who are the called according to his purpose.
Romans 8:28

The wound's invisible
That love's keen arrows make.
WILLIAM SHAKESPEARE

It requires infinitely a greater genius to make love, than to make war.
NINON DE L'ENCLOS, *The Memoirs of Ninon de L'Enclos*, Volume 1, (1778)

We can sometimes love what we do not understand, but it is impossible completely to understand what we do not love.
MRS. JAMESON

God and every one that loveth is born of God, and knoweth God.
He that loveth not knoweth not God, for God is love.
1 *John* 4:7-8

An old, a grave discreet man, is fittest to discourse of love matters; because he hath likely more experience, observed more, hath a more staid judgement, can better discern, resolve, discuss, advise, give better cautions and more solid precepts, better inform his auditors in such a subject, and by reason of his riper years, sooner divert.
BURTON

A lover is a man who, in his anxiety to possess another, has lost possession of himself.
BULWER

Why love among the virtues is not known?
It is, that love contracts them all in one.
JOHN DONNE

When love comes it comes without effort, like perfect weather.
HELEN YGLESIAS, *Family Feeling*, (1976)

God - love must be seized with a discontent which never

ceases until the goal is reached.
SWAMI RAMDAS, *Holy War*, 405

Love seizes on us suddenly, without giving warning, and our disposition, or our weakness, favours the surprise; one look, one glance from the fair fixes and determines us. Friendship on the contrary, is a long time in forming, it is of slow growth, through many trials and months of familiarity.
LA BRUYERE

Love is strong as death. Many waters cannot quench love, neither can the floods drown it; if a man would give all the substance of his house for love, it would utterly be condemned.
Song of Solomon 8:6, 6

All thoughts, all passions, all delights,
Whatever stirs this mortal frame,
All are but ministers of love,
And feed his sacred flame.
SAMUEL TAYLOR COLERIDGE

It is the secret sympathy,
The silver link, the silken tie
Which heart to heart, and mind to mind
In body and in soul can bind.
SCOTT

And what do all the great words come to in the end, but that? - I love you - I am at rest with you - I have come home.
DOROTHY L. SAYERS, *Busman's Honeymoon*, (1937)

The most powerful symptom of love is a tenderness which becomes at times almost insupportable.
VICTOR HUGO

Love is not love
Which alters when it alteration finds -
Love alters not with his brief hours and weeks,
But bears it out even to the edge of doom.
If this be error, and upon me prov'd,
I never writ, nor no man ever lov'd.
WILLIAM SHAKESPEARE

As the hart panteth after the water brooks, so panteth my soul after thee, O God.
Psalms 42:1

Heaven's harmony is universal love.
WILLIAM COWPER

Love is the great instrument of nature, the bond and cement of society, the spirit and spring of the universe. Love is such an affection as cannot so properly be said to be in the soul, as the soul to be in that: it is the whole nature wrapped up into one desire.
SOUTHEY

We don't believe in rheumatism or true love until we have been attacked by them.
MARIE VON EBNER-ESCHENBACK, Aphorisms, (1893)

Like Diana's kiss, unask'd, unsought,
Love gives itself, but is not bought.
LONGFELLOW

The science of love is the philosophy of the heart.
CICERO

The first sound in the song of love,
Scarce more than silence is,
and yet a sound.
Hands of invisible spirits touch the strings
Of that mysterious instrument, the soul,
And play the prelude of our fate.
LONGFELLOW

Love conquers all things, and let us yield to love.
VIRGIL

To love deeply in one direction makes us more loving in all others.
ANNE-SOPHIE SWETCHINE, The Writings of Madame Swetchine, (1869)

They say, base men being in love, have then
A nobility in their natures more
Than is native to them.
WILLIAM SHAKESPEARE

Love is omnipresent in nature as motive and reward. Love is our highest word, and the synonym of God. Every promise of the soul has innumerable fulfilments; each of its joys ripens into a new want. Nature, uncontainable, flowing, forelooking, in the

first sentiment of kindness, anticipates already a benevolence which shall lose all particular regards in its general light. The introduction of this felicity is in a private and tender relation of one to one, which is the enchantment of human life; which, like a certain divine rage and enthusiasm, seizes on man at one period, and works a revolution in his mind and body; unites him to his race, pledges him to the domestic and civil relations, carries him with new sympathy into nature, enhances the power of the senses, opens the imagination, adds to his character heroic and sacred attributes, establishes marriage, and gives permanence to human society.
RALPH WALDO EMERSON

What *is* a mother's love?
A noble, pure, and tender flame
Enkindled from above.
JAMES MONTGOMERY

When God's nearness takes possession of a man's heart, it overwhelms all else, both the inward infiltrations of the purposes and the outward motions of the members. Thereafter that man continues, going or coming, taking or giving; there prevails in him the purpose which has ruled his mind, namely, the love of God and His nearness.
AHMAD B. 'ÎSÂ AL-KHARRÂZ

Love, that is first and last of all things made,
The light that has the living world for shade,
The spirit that for temporal veil has on
The souls of all men woven in unison,
One fiery raiment with all lives inwrought
And lights of sunny and starry deed and thought,
And alway through new act and passion new
Shines the divine same body and beauty through,
The body spiritual of fire and light
That is to worldly noon as noon to night;
Love, that is flesh upon the spirit of man
And spirit within the flesh whence breath began;
Love, that keeps all the choir

of lives in chime;
Love, that is blood within the
veins of time;
That wrought the whole world
without stroke of hand,
Shaping the breadth of sea,
the length of land,
And with the pulse and
motion of his breath
Through the great heart of the
earth strikes life and death,
The sweet twain chords that
make the sweet tune live
Through day and night of
things alternative,
Through silence and through
sound of stress and strife,
And ebb and flow of dying
death and life;
Love, that sounds loud or light
in all men's ears,
Whence all men's eyes take
fire from sparks of tears,
That binds on all men's feet or
chains or wings;
Love, that is root and fruit of
terrene things;
Love, that the whole world's
waters shall not drown,
The whole world's fiery forces
not burn down;
Love, that what time his own
hands guard his head
The whole world's wrath and
strength shall not strike dead;
Love, that if once his own

hands make his grave
The whole world's pity and
sorrow shall not save;
Love, that for very life shall
not be sold,
Nor bought nor bound with
iron nor with gold;
So strong that heaven, could
love bid heaven farewell,
Would turn to fruitless and
unflowering hell;
So sweet that hell, to hell
could love be given,
Would turn to splendid and
sonorous heaven;
Love that is fire within thee
and light above,
And lives by grace of nothing
but of love.
ALGERNON SWINBURNE,
from *Prelude to Tristram of
Lyonesse*

I bless
all knowledge of love, all ways
of publishing it.
MONA VAN DUYN, *To See,
To Take*, Open Letter From a
Constant Reader, (1970)

Love is the purification of the
heart from self; it strengthens
and ennobles the character,
gives higher motive and a
nobler aim to every action of
life, and makes both man and

woman strong, noble, and
courageous; and the power to
love truly and devotedly is the
noblest gift with which a
human being can be endowed;
but it is a sacred fire that must
not be burnt to idols.
MISS JEWSBURY

It is possible that a man can
be so changed by love that
one could not recognise him
as the same person.
TERENCE

Love has no power to act
when curbed by jealousy.
HILL

Love! thou hast every bliss in
store;
'Tis friendship, and 'tis
something more;
Each other every wish they
give:
Not to know love is not to
live.
GAY

Love is not in our choice, but
in our fate.
DRYDEN

What is love that naught can
countervail?
Naught save itself, ev'n such a

thing is love
And worldly wealth in worth
as far doth fail
As lowest earth doth yield to
heav'n above,
Divine is love, and scorneth
worldly pelf
And can be bought with
nothing but with self.
SIR W. RALEIGH

They who live without Love
are dead.
But the worst of all deaths is
this -
That the loving soul be
cowardly toward Love;
For perfect Love is never
cowardly.
HADEWIJCH, *The Need of
All Needs*, (13th century)

A single atom of the love of
God in a heart is worth more
than a hundred thousand
paradises.
BÂYAZID AL-BISTÂMI

Love one human being purely
and warmly, and you will love
all. The heart in this heaven,
like the wandering sun, sees
nothing, from the dew drop to
the ocean, but a mirror which
it warms and fills.
RICHTER

Love is ever busy with his shuttle;
Is ever weaving into life's dull warp
Bright gorgeous flowers, and scenes Arcadian
Hanging our gloomy prison-house about
With tapestries, that make its walls dilate
In never-ending vistas of delight.
LONGFELLOW

Love demands expression. It will not stay still, stay silent, be good, be modest, be seen and not heard, no. It will break out in tongues of praise, the high note that smashes the glass and spills the liquid.
JEANETTE WINTERSON, *Written on the Body*, (1992)

It is better to have loved and lost,
Than never to have loved at all.
ALFRED, LORD TENNYSON

Thou demandest what is love? It is that powerful attraction toward all that we conceive, fear, or hope beyond ourselves, when we find within our own thoughts the chasm of an insufficient void, and seek to awaken in all things that are, a community with what we experience within ourselves.
PERCY BYSSHE SHELLEY

Love that has nothing but beauty to keep it in good health is short lived, and apt to have ague fits.
ERASMUS

I think I know what love is for, although I'm not quite sure. I think that love is given us so that we can see a soul. And this soul we see is the highest conception of excellence and truth we can bring forth: this soul is our reflected self. And from seeing what one soul is, we imagine what all souls may be - and thus we reach God, who is the Universal Soul.
HUBBARD

Love is that which exists to *do* good, not merely to *get good*.
VICTORIA WOODHULL, (1873)

As Plato sometimes speaks of the divine love, it arises not out of indigency, as creature

love does, but out of fulness and redundancy: it is an overflowing fountain, and that love which descends upon created being is a free efflux from the almighty source of love: and is well pleasing to him that those creatures which he hath made should partake of it.
JOHN SMITH THE PLATONIST

Didst thou but know the inly touch of love thou wouldst as soon go kindle fire with snow, as seek to quench the fire of love with words.
WILLIAM SHAKESPEARE

By love subsists all lasting grandeur; that gone, we are as dust.
WILLIAM WORDSWORTH

The important thing is not to think much but to love much; do, then, whatever most arouses you to love.
ST. TERESA OF AVILA, (1577)

As for the phenomena of Love permeating all the living creation, they express the mortal nature seeking to become deathless by the one possible process of generation. Sexual love is the expression of this craving for immortality in the physical organism; and the work of all creative art is its intellectual issue.

In whatsoever field this desire of immortality by propagation moves us, we must be attracted by the beautiful, and by beauty of soul more divinely than by beauty of form.

He who would love rightly must from the beginning seek to hold intercourse with beautiful forms, and love one wherein he would generate intellectual beauty. Thus he would be led up to the contemplation of universal beauty, which is eternal, without beginning, at all times, utterly, and to all. This is that to which they attain who advance by these steps from the contemplation of beauty in particulars to the revelation of the supreme beauty. Such a one is at last in contact not with shadows but with the ultimate reality, and if immortality be at all given to human beings, he is thereby become immortal.
SOCRATES

Love has nothing to do with
what you are expecting to get
- only with what you are
expecting to give - which is
everything.
KATHARINE HEPBURN,
Me, (1991)

It is to summon all that is
beautiful in earth, heaven or
soul, to the banquet of love.
It means that the least gesture
will call forth the presence of
the soul with all its treasure.
It means that the beauty that
turns into love is
undistinguishable from the
love that turns into beauty. It
means to be able no longer to
tell where the ray of a star
leaves off and the kiss of an
ordinary thought begins. It
means that each day will
reveal to us a new beauty in
that mysterious angel, and
that we shall walk together in
a goodness that shall ever
become more and more living,
loftier and loftier.
MAETERLINCK

But be our experience in
particulars what it may, no
man ever forgot the visitations
of that power to his heart and
brain, which created all things
new; which was the dawn in
him of music, poetry and art;
which made the face of nature
radiant with purple light, the
morning and the night varied
enchantments; when a single
tone of one voice could make
the heart bound, and the most
trivial circumstance associated
with one form is put in the
amber of memory; when he
became all eye when one was
present, and all memory when
one was gone; when no place
is too solitary, and none too
silent, for him who has richer
company and sweeter
conversation in his new
thoughts than any old friends
can give him; for the figures,
the motions, the words of the
beloved object are not like
other images written in water,
but, as Plutarch said,
'enamelled in fire' and make
the study of midnight. 'Thou
art not gone being gone,
where'er thou art; thou leavest
in him thy watchful eyes, in
him thy loving heart.'
RALPH WALDO EMERSON

We are pieces of steel, and thy
love is the magnet.
DIVÂNI SHAMSI TABRIZ,
XXXII

To renounce your individuality, to see with another's eyes, to hear with another's ears, to be two and yet but one, to so melt and mingle that you no longer know you are you or another, to constantly absorb and constantly radiate, to reduce earth, sea and sky and all that in them is to a single being, to give yourself to that being so wholly that nothing whatever is withheld, to be prepared at any moment for sacrifice, to double your personality in bestowing it: that is love.
GAUTIER

Love comes unseen - we only see it go.
DOBSON

I do not think reading the mystics would hurt you myself. You say you must avoid books which deal with 'feelings' - but the mystics don't deal with *feelings* but with *love* which is a very different thing. You have too many 'feelings', but not nearly enough love.
EVELYN UNDERHILL, (1909), *The Letters of Evelyn Underhill*, (1943)

He brought me to the banqueting house, and his banner over me was love. Stay me with flagons, comfort me with apples: for I am sick of love.
His left hand is under my head, and his right hand doth embrace me.
Song of Solomon 2:4-6

Love is not bought - 'tis of the soul the noblest element, the spirit-bond that links the angel with humanity. As well mightest thou attempt to purchase heaven, to vend the stars, make traffic of the skies, or measure out what is immeasurable, as count each feeling in the pulse of love!
SWAIN

To fear love is to fear life, and those who fear life are already three parts dead.
BERTRAND RUSSELL, *Marriage and Morals*

Let me not to the marriage of true minds
Admit impediments. Love is not love
Which alters when it alteration finds,
Or bends with the remover to

remove.
O, no! it is an ever-fixed mark,
That looks on tempests and is never shaken.
WILLIAM SHAKESPEARE, *Sonnet* 116

Love is above the laws, above the opinion of men; it is the truth, the flame, the pure element, the primary idea of the moral world.
GERMAINE DE STAËL, (1766-1817), *Zulma, and Other Tales*

Thou (Wisdom) lovest all things that are, and hatest none of the things which thou hast made: for thou didst not appoint or make any thing hating it.
RUMI, *Wisdom*, XI. 25

All, everything that I understand, I understand only because I love.
LEO TOLSTOY, (1828-1910), *War and Peace*, Book VII, Chapter 16

Grumbling is the death of love.
MARLENE DIETRICH, *Marlene Dietrich's ABC*, (1962)

Beware you be not swallowed up in books! An ounce of love is worth a pound of knowledge.
JOHN WESLEY, (1703-91), *Life of Wesley*, Chapter 16 (R. Southey)

Love fled
And paced upon the mountains overhead
And hid his face amid a crowd of stars.
W.B. YEATS, (1865-1939), *When you are Old*

For aught that I could ever read,
Could ever hear by tale or history,
The course of true love never did run smooth.
WILLIAM SHAKESPEARE, *A Midsummer Night's Dream*, Act I, Scene i

Love is my religion - I could die for that.
JOHN KEATS, (1795-1821), Letter to Fanny Brawne, 13 October 1819

When a man is in love he endures more than at other times; he submits to everything.

FRIEDRICH WILHELM
NIETZSCHE, (1844-1900),
The Antichrist

Ye gods! annihilate but space
and time.
And make two lovers happy.
ALEXANDER POPE, (1688-
1744), *The Art of Sinking in
Poetry*, 11

Love cannot survive if you
just give it scraps of yourself,
scraps of your time, scraps of
your thoughts.
MARY O'HARA, *Green
Grass of Wyoming*, (1946)

Love looks not with the eyes,
but with the mind;
And therefore is wing'd Cupid
painted blind.
WILLIAM SHAKESPEARE,
A Midsummer Night's Dream,
Act I, Scene i

As a devotee cannot live
without God, so also God
cannot live without His
devotee. Then the devotee
becomes the sweetness, and
God its enjoyer. The devotee
becomes the lotus, and God
the bee. It is the Godhead
that has become these two in
order to enjoy Its own Bliss.

That is the significance of the
episode of Radha and Krishna.
SRI RAMAKRISHNA,
Creation, 48

Love has a hem to her
garment that reaches the very
dust. It sweeps the stains from
the streets and lanes, and
because it can, it must.
MOTHER TERESA, *The Love
of Christ*, (1982)

Come live with me, and be
my love,
And we will some new
pleasures prove
Of golden sands, and crystal
brooks,
With silken lines, and silver
hooks.
JOHN DONNE, (1573-1631),
The Bait

Love one another, but make
not a bond of love:
Let it rather be a moving sea
between the shores of your
souls.
Fill each other's cup but drink
not from one cup.
Give one another of your
bread but eat not from the
same loaf...
And stand together yet not
too near together:

For the pillars of the temple stand apart,
And the oak tree and the cypress grow not in each other's shadow.
KABIL GIBRAN, *The Prophet*

Love has the quality of informing almost everything - even one's work.
SYLVIA ASHTON WARNER, *Myself*, (1967)

Love is the wisdom of the fool and the folly of the wise.
SAMUEL JOHNSON, (1709-84), *Johnsonian Miscellanies*, Volume II

What will survive of us is love.
PHILIP LARKIN, (1922-85), *The Whitsun Weddings*, An Arundel Tomb

Love is, above all, the gift of oneself.
JEAN ANOUILH, *Ardèle*

When it comes, will it come without warning
Just as I'm picking my nose?
Will it knock on my door in the morning,
Or tread in the bus on my toes?
Will it come like a change in the weather?
Will its greeting be courteous or rough?
Will it alter my life altogether?
O tell me the truth about love.
W.H. AUDEN, (1907-73), *Twelve Songs*, XII

He that loveth not knoweth not God: for God is love ... He that dwelleth in love dwelleth in God, and God in him.
1 John 4:8,16

Love sought is good, but given unsought is better.
WILLIAM SHAKESPEARE, *Twelfth Night*, Act III, Scene i

In expressing love we belong among the undeveloped countries.
SAUL BELLOW, (1915-), in *Lover's Quotation Book*

Is it not by love alone that we succeed in penetrating to the very essence of a being?
IGOR STRAVINSKY, *An Autobiography*, 5, (1936)

Let the dead have the immortality of fame, but the living the immortality of love.
RABINDRANATH TAGORE, Stray Birds, 279, (1916)

There is no fear in love; but perfect love casteth out fear: because fear hath torment. He that feareth is not made perfect in love.
1 John 4:18

Love is a great thing, a great good in every wise; it alone maketh light every heavy thing and beareth evenly every uneven thing.
THOMAS À KEMPIS, The Imitation of Christ, 2.6, (1426)

If it is your time love will track you like a cruise missile. If you say, "No! I don't want it right now," that's when you'll get it for sure. Love will make a way out of no way. Love is an exploding cigar which we willingly smoke.
LYNDA BARRY, Big Ideas, (1983)

There is no remedy for love but to love more.
THOREAU, Journal, 25 July 1839

The Love-god inflames more fiercely those he sees are reluctant to surrender.
TIBULLUS, Elegies, 1.8, (1st century BC)

One cannot be strong without love. For love is not an irrelevant emotion; it is the blood of life, the power of reunion of the separated.
PAUL TILLICH, The Eternal Now, 3.1.3.2, (1963)

Love is something far more than desire for sexual intercourse; it is the principal means of escape from the loneliness which afflicts most men and women throughout the greater part of their lives.
BERTRAND RUSSSELL, Marriage and Morals, The Place of Love in Human Life, (1929)

Love's gift cannot be given, it waits to be accepted.
RABINDRANATH TAGORE, Fireflies, (1928)

The invisible path of gravity liberates the stone. The invisible slope of love liberates man.

ANTOINE DE SAINT-
EXUPÉRY, *Flight to Arrras*, 23,
(1942)

Not to believe in love is a
great sign of dullness. There
are some people so indirect
and lumbering that they think
all real affection must rest on
circumstantial evidence.
GEORGE SANTAYANA,
*The Life of Reason: Reason in
Society*, 1, (1905-06)

True love's the gift which God
has given
To man alone beneath the
heaven.
SIR WALTER SCOTT, *The
Lay of the Last Minstrel*, 5.8.,
(1805)

Free love is too expensive.
BERNADETTE DEVLIN, *The
Price of My Soul*, (1969)

Love is the astrolabe* of the
mysteries of God.
RUMI
*An instrument used by early
astronomers to measure the
altitude of stars and planets
and also as a navigational aid.

In one sense, the opposite of
fear is courage, but in the
dynamic sense the opposite of
fear is love, whether this be
love of man or love of justice.
ALAN PATON, *Saturday
Review*, The Challenge of
Fear, (1967)

[Love is] the joy of the good,
the wonder of the wise, the
amazement of the gods;
desired by those who have no
part in him, and precious to
those who have the better part
in him.
PLATO, *The Symposium*, (4th
century BC)

The greatest love is a
mother's; then comes a dog's;
then comes a sweetheart's.
POLISH PROVERB

For one human being to love
another: that is perhaps the
most difficult of all our tasks,
the ultimate, the last test and
proof, the work for which all
other work is but preparation.
RAINER MARIA RILKE,
Letters to a Young Poet, 14 May
1904

Love has no continuity; it
cannot be carried over to
tomorrow; it has no future.
What has is memory, and

memories are ashes of everything dead and buried. Love has no tomorrow; it cannot be caught in time and made respectable. It is there when time is not. It has no promise, no hope; hope breeds despair. It belongs to no god and so to no thought and feeling. It is not conjured up by the brain. It lives and dies each minute. Is a terrible thing, for love is destruction. It is destruction without tomorrow. Love is destruction.
J. KRISHNAMURTI

Love refines
The thoughts, and heart enlarges, hath his seat
In reason, and is judicious, is the scale
By which to heavenly love thou mayest ascend.
MILTON, Paradise Lost, VIII, line 589, (1667)

Love is more afraid of change than destruction.
FRIEDRICH NIETZSCHE, Miscellaneous Maxims and Opinions, 280, (1879)

Love is a driver, bitter and fierce if you fight and resist him,

Easy-going enough once you acknowledge his power.
OVID, The Loves, 1.2, (circa AD 8)

It was a great holiness, a religion, as all great loves must be.
ELSIE DE WOLFE, After All, (1935)

Love does not cause suffering: what causes it is the sense of ownership, which is love's opposite.
ANTOINE DE SAINT-EXUPÉRY, The Wisdom of the Sands, 49, (1948)

Love should be a tree whose roots are deep in the earth, but whose branches extend into heaven.
BERTRAND RUSSELL, Marriage and Morals, Sex and Individual Well-Being, (1929)

There is no harvest for the heart alone;
The seed of love must be Eternally
Resown.
ANNE MORROW LINDBERGH, The Unicorn and Other Poems, Second Sowing, 1935-1955, (1956)

Born at the banquet of the gods, Love has of necessity been eternally in existence, for it springs from the intention of the Soul towards its best, towards the Good: as long as Soul has been, Love has been.
PLOTINUS

That love for one, from which there doth not spring
Wide love for all, is but a worthless thing.
JAMES RUSSELL LOWELL, Sonnet 3, (1840)

The souls of all our brethren are ever hovering about us, craving for a caress, and only waiting for the signal.
MAURICE MAETERLINCK, The Treasures of the Humble, The Invisible Goodness, (1896)

It is love, not reason, that is stronger than death.
THOMAS MANN, The Magic Mountain, 6.7, (1924)

We are not the same persons this year as last; nor are those we love. It is a happy chance if we, changing, continue to love a changed person.

W. SOMERSET MAUGHAM, The Summing Up, 77, (1938)

Jesus said unto him, Thou shalt love the Lord thy God with all thy heart, and with all thy soul, and with all thy mind.
This is the first and great commandment.
And the second is like unto it.
Thou shalt love thy neighbour as thyself.
On these two commandments hang all the law and the prophets.
Matthew 22:37-40

My love for you is the sole image
Of God a human is allowed.
ELSE LASKER-SCHÜLER, To My Child, (1920)

When one loves somebody, everything is clear - where to go, what to do - it all takes care of itself and one doesn't have to ask anybody about anything.
MAXIM GORKY, The Zykovs, 4, (1914)

As selfishness and complaint pervert and cloud the mind, so

love with its joy clears and sharpens the vision.
HELEN KELLER, My Religion, (1927)

Though a man excels in everything, unless he has been a lover his life is lonely, and he may be likened to a jewelled cup which can contain no wine.
YOSHIDA KENKÔ, The Harvest of Leisure (Tsure-Zure Gusa, circa 1330-35)

Where love finds the soul he neglects the body, and only turns to it in his idleness as to an afterthought. Its best allurements are but the nuts and figs of the divine repast.
WALTER SAVAGE LANDOR, Imaginary Conversations, Scipio, Polybius, and Panaetius, (1824-53)

Love is a naked child: do you think he has pockets for money?
OVID, The Loves, 1.10, (circa AD 8)

It is impossible to repent of love. The sin of love does not exist.

MURIEL SPARK, The Mandelbaum Gate, (1965)

Truth seeth God, and Wisdom beholdeth God, and of these two cometh the third: that is, a holy marvelling delight in God; which is Love. Where Truth and Wisdom are verily, there is Love verily, coming of them both.
JULIAN OF NORWICH, Knowledge, 761

Love is not an emergency.
Anonymous operator to a would-be caller during a telephone strike in France, in Simone de Beauvoir, Force of Circumstance, (1963)

Love compels cruelty To those who do not understand love.
T.S. ELIOT, The Family Reunion, 2.2, (1939)

Love is all we have, the only way that each can help the other.
EURIPIDES, Orestes, (408 BC)

To love nothing is not to live; to love but feebly is to languish rather than live.
FÉNELON, À un homme du monde, (1699)

Try to reason about love, and you will lose your reason.
FRENCH PROVERB

Love all the people you can. The sufferings from love are not to be compared to the sorrows of loneliness.
SUSAN HALE, (1868), *Letters of Susan Hale*, (1918)

Love knows hidden paths.
GERMAN PROVERB

Even as love crowns you so shall he crucify you. Even as he is for your growth so is he for your pruning.
KAHLIL GIBRAN, *The Prophet*, On Love, (1923)

A life without love, without the presence of the beloved, is nothing but a mere magic-lantern show. We draw out slide after slide, swiftly tiring of each, and pushing it back to make haste for the next.
GOETHE, *Elective Affinities*, 27, (1809)

Nay, what is more, it is the 'Truth' who is Himself at once the lover and the beloved, the seeker and the sought. He is loved and sought in His character of the 'One who is all': and He is lover and seeker when viewed as the sum of all particulars and plurality.
JÂMI, *Reality*, 775

Unable are the Loved to die For Love is Immortality.
EMILY DICKINSON, poem, (circa 1864)

Being got it [love] is a treasure sweet,
Which to defend, is harder than to get:
And ought not be profaned on either part,
For though 'tis got by chance, 'tis kept by art.
JOHN DONNE, *Elegy*, 17, The Expostulation, (1635)

Pains of love be sweeter far Than all other pleasures are.
JOHN DRYDEN, *Tyrannic Love*, 4.1, (1669)

Who would give a law to lovers?
Love is unto itself a higher law.
BOETHIUS, *The Consolation of Philosophy*, 3, (AD 524)

Whoso loves
Believes the impossible.

ELIZABETH BARRETT
BROWNING, *Aurora Leigh*, 5.
409, (1856)

O Lyric Love, half angel and
half bird,
And all a wonder and a wild
desire.
ROBERT BROWNING, *The
Ring and the Book*, 1, (1868-
69)

Eternal Love doth keep
In his complacent arms, the
earth, the air, the deep,.
WILLIAM CULLEN
BRYANT, *The Ages*, (1821)

I believe in the curative
powers of love as the English
believe in tea or Catholics
believe in the Miracle of
Lourdes.
JOYCE JOHNSON, *Minor
Characters*, (1983)

Love is Nature's second sun.
GEORGE CHAPMAN, *All
Fools*, 1.1, (circa 1599)

The absolute value of love
makes life worthwhile, and so
makes Man's strange and
difficult situation acceptable.
Love cannot save life from
death, but it can fulfil life's
purpose.
ARNOLD J. TOYNBEE, *Why
and How I Work*, (1969)

If a man say, I love God, and
hateth his brother, he is a liar:
for he that loveth not his
brother whom he hath seen,
how can he love God whom
he hath not seen?
1 *John* 4:20

Love is the child of freedom,
never that of domination.
ERICH FROMM, *The Art of
Loving*

In the divisions of love, there
always abides the unity of him
who loves.
JOHN DEWEY, *Characters
and Events*, Volume 1

But to love is quite another
thing: it is to will an object for
itself, to rejoice in its beauty
and goodness for themselves,
and without respect to
anything other than itself.
ETIENNE GILSON, *The
Spirit of Medieval Philosophy*

We learn it at last - that the
one gift in our treasure house
is love - love - love. If we
may not give it, if no one

looks into our eyes and asks our gift - we may indeed collect ourselves and offer our second-best to the world, and the world may applaud. But the vital principle is gone from our lives.
RUTH BENEDICT, *An Anthropologist at Work*, Margaret Mead

In the last resort we must begin to love in order that we may not fall ill, and must fall ill, if in consequence of frustration, we cannot love.
SIGMUND FREUD, quoted in *Life Against Death* by Norman O. Brown

Love doesn't just sit there, like a stone, it has to be made, like bread; re-made all the time, made new.
URSULA K. LE GUIN, *The Lathe of Heaven*, (1971)

We receive love - from our children as well as others - not in proportion to our demands or sacrifices or needs, but roughly in proportion to our own capacity to love.
ROLLO MAY, *Man's Search for Himself*

We find rest in those we love, and we provide a resting place in ourselves for those who love us.
SAINT BERNARD OF CLAIRVAUX, *Letters*

God lies in wait for us therefore with nothing so much as with love. For love is like the fisherman's hook. To the fisherman falls no fish that is not caught on his hook. Once it takes the hook the fish is forfeit to the fisherman; in vain it twists hither and thither, the fisherman is certain of his catch. And so I say of love: he who is caught thereby has the strongest of all bonds and yet a pleasant burden. He who bears this sweet burden fares further, gets nearer therewith than by using any harshness possible to man. Moreover, he can cheerfully put up with whatever befalls, cheerfully suffer what God inflicts. Naught makes thee so much God nor God so much thine own as this sweet bond. He who has found this way will seek no other. He who hangs on this hook is so fast caught that foot and hand, mouth, eyes and heart and all that is man's is bound to be God's ... Who is caught in this net, who walks in this way, whatsoever he works is wrought by love, whose alone the work is: busy or idle it matters nothing ... Await thou therefore this hook, so thou be happily caught, and the more surely caught so much the more surely freed. That we may be thus caught and freed, help us O thou who art love itself.

ECKHART

To be loved for what one is, is the greatest exception. The great majority love in another only what they lend him, their own selves, their version of him.

GOETHE, *Wisdom and Experience*

Whatever you are doing, love yourself for doing it. Whatever you are thinking, love yourself for thinking it.

THADDEUS GOLAS, *The Lazy Man's Guide to Enlightenment*

There's so much of the child in me yet, and life to me

means love just as it does to a child - love of many kinds and degrees, but each and all helping us on our way and bringing the journey's end a little nearer the knowledge of God.

ELLEN GLASGOW, *Letters*

Where love rules, there is no will to power; and where power predominates, there love is lacking. The one is the shadow of the other.

C.G. JUNG, *Psychological Reflections*

That love is all there is, Is all we know of Love.

EMILY DICKINSON

Heaven be thanked, we live in such an age, When no man dies for love, but on the stage.

JOHN DRYDEN, Epilogue to *Mithridates*, (1678)

Love does not recognise the difference between peasant and mikado.

JAPANESE PROVERB

My beloved is mine, and I am his: he feedeth among the lilies.

Until the day break, and the
shadows flee away, turn my
beloved, and be thou like a
roe or a young hart upon the
mountains of Bether.
Song of Solomon 2:16-17

When you really want love
you will find it waiting for
you.
OSCAR WILDE, *De Profundis*

Love is like butter, it goes well
with bread.
YIDDISH PROVERB

If you do not let love reside in
the body it is homeless.
MARTIN ALLWOOD,
Something Like Aphorisms, I
Myself

Love, after all, is but the
antithesis of hatred; and
hatred is egotism turned inside
out.
MINNA ANTRIM, *The
Wisdom of the Foolish*, page 8

Nuptial love maketh
mankind; friendly love
perfecteth it; but wanton love
corrupteth and embaseth it.
FRANCIS BACON, *Essays*,
Of Love

Better is a dinner of herbs
where love is, than a stalled
ox and hatred therewith.
Proverbs 15:17

If an individual is able to love
productively, he loves himself
too; if he can love only others,
he cannot love at all.
ERICH FROMM, *The Art of
Loving*, Chapter 2, Section 3

The story of a love is not
important - what is important
is that one is capable of love.
It is perhaps the only glimpse
we are permitted of eternity.
HELEN HAYES, in
Guideposts, (1960)

Few of us love others for what
they really are. Most of us
love what they imagine in
others; they love their own
idea in someone else.
JOHANN WOLFGANG
VON GOETHE, *Goethe's
Opinions*, page 58

I shall show you love philtre
compounded without drug or
herb or witches' spell. It is
this: if you wish to be loved,
love.
HECATO, quoted in Seneca,
Letters from a Stoic, 9

It is the same with love as with art: the man who can love great things just a little is poorer than the man who can love the little things passionately.
HERMANN HESSE, Reflections, 613, Love

Love means never having to say you're sorry.
ERICH SEGAL, Love Story, Chapter 13

Love it the way it is.
THADDEUS GOLAS, The Lazy Man's Guide to Enlightenment

Love is an endless mystery, for it has nothing else to explain it.
RABINDRANATH TAGORE, Fireflies, page 140

Love is a disease that kills nobody, but one whose time has come.
MARGUERITE DE VALOIS, in J. de Finod, A Thousand Flashes of French Wit

Love is to the moral nature exactly what the sun is to the earth.
HONORÉ DE BALZAC

Blissful is the dawn of Wisdom, like the virgin's wedding night;
Till experienced none can know it as it is, O Tingri folk.
PHADAMPA SANGAY

Doubt of the reality of love ends by making us doubt everything.
FRÉDÉRIC AMIEL

The best way to know God is to love many things.
VINCENT VAN GOGH

He who comes to do good knocks at the gate; he who loves finds the door open.
RABINDRANATH TAGORE

Everyone admits that love is wonderful and necessary, yet no one can agree on what it is.
DIANE ACKERMAN, A Natural History of Love

The real value of love is the increased general vitality it produces.
PAUL VALÉRY

Love consists in this that two solitudes protect and touch

and greet each other.
RAINER MARIA RILKE

The ideal story is that of two
people who go into love step
for step, with a fluttered
consciousness, like a pair of
children venturing together
into a dark room.
ROBERT LOUIS
STEVENSON, *Virginibus*
Puerisque, El Dorado, (1881)

From women's eyes this
doctrine I derive:
They are the ground, the
books, the academes,
From whence doth spring the
true Promethean fire.
WILLIAM SHAKESPEARE,
Love's Labour's Lost, (1595)

How do I love thee? Let me
count the ways.
I love thee to the depth and
breadth and height
My soul can reach.
ELIZABETH BARRETT
BROWNING, *Sonnets from*
the Portuguese, Number 43,
(1850)

And now abideth faith, hope,
love, these three; but the
greatest of these is love.
1 *Corinthians*

You who seek an end of love,
love will yield to business: be
busy, and you will be safe.
OVID, (43 BC - AD circa 17)
Remedia Amoris

Lord, make me an instrument
of Your peace!
Where there is hatred let me
sow love.
ST. FRANCIS OF ASSISI,
(1181-1226), *Prayer of St.*
Francis

The love that moves the sun
and the other stars.
DANTE ALIGHIERI, (1265-
1321), *Divina Commedia*
Paradiso

Love is the extremely difficult
realisation that something
other than oneself is real.
IRIS MURDOCH, *The*
Sublime and the Good

But true love is a durable fire,
In the mind ever burning,
Never sick, never old, never
dead,
From itself never turning.
WALTER RALEGH, (circa
1552-1618), *Walsinghame*

Love is the only weapon we
need.

REVEREND H.R.L. SHEPPARD, *The Human Parson*

It is love that I am seeking for
But of a beautiful unheard of kind
That is not in the world.
W.B. YEATS, *The Shadowy Waters*

The whole world is a market-place for Love,
For naught that is, from Love remains remote.
The Eternal Wisdom made all things in Love:
On Love they all depend, to Love all turn.
The earth, the heavens, the sun, the moon, the stars
The centre of their orbit find in Love.
By Love are all bewildered, stupefied,
Intoxicated by the Wine of Love.
From each, a mystic silence Love demands,
What do all seek so earnestly? 'Tis Love.
Love is the subject of their inmost thoughts,
In Love no longer 'Thou' and 'I' exist,
For self has passed away in the

Beloved.
Now will I draw aside the veil from Love,
And in the temple of mine inmost soul
Behold the Friend, Incomparable Love.
He who would know the secret of both worlds
Will find the secret of them both, is Love.
ATTÂR

Many a man in love with a dimple makes the mistake of marrying the whole girl.
STEPHEN LEACOCK, *Literary Lapses*, (1910)

Love seeketh not itself to please,
Nor for itself hath any care,
But for another gives its ease,
And builds a Heaven in Hell's despair.
WILLIAM BLAKE, (1757-1827), *Songs of Experience*, The Clod and the Pebble

Falling in love is one of the activities forbidden that tiresome person, the consistently reasonable man.
SIR ARTHUR EDDINGTON, (1932)

Lovers re-create the world.
CARTER HEYWARD, *Our
Passion for Justice*, (1984)

This is the miracle that
happens every time to those
who really love: the more they
give, the more they possess of
that precious nourishing love
from which flowers and
children have their strength
and which could help all
human beings if they would
take it without doubting ...
RAINER MARIA RILKE

Through love bitter things
seem sweet,
Through love bits of copper
are made gold.
Through love dregs taste like
pure wine,
Through love pains are as
healing balms.
Through love thorns become
roses,
And through love vinegar
becomes sweet wine.
Through love the stake
becomes a throne,
Through love reverse of
fortune seems good fortune.
Through love a prison seems a
rose bower,
Without love a grate full of
ashes seems a garden.

Through love burning fire is
pleasing light,
Through love the Devil
becomes a Houri.
Through love hard stones
become soft as butter,
Without love soft wax
becomes hard iron.
Through love grief is a joy,
Through love Ghouls turn
into angels.
Through love stings are as
honey,
Through love lions are
harmless as mice.
Through love sickness is
health,
Through love wrath is as
mercy.
Through love the dead rise to
life,
Through love the king
becomes a slave.
Even when an evil befalls you,
have due regard;
Regard well him who does you
this ill turn.
The sight which regards the
ebb and flow of good and ill
Opens a passage for you from
misfortune to happiness.
Thence you see the one state
moves you into the other,
One opposite state generating
its opposite in exchange.
RUMI, *The Mathnawi*

The final word is love.
DOROTHY DAY, *The Long
Loneliness*, (1952)

THIRTY-TWO

MANKIND

Man is not only a contributory creature, but a total creature; he does not only make one, but he is all; he is not a piece of the world, but the world itself; and next to the glory of God, the reason why there is a world.
JOHN DONNE, *Sermons*, Number 35, (1625)

Men are but children of a larger growth.
JOHN DRYDEN, *All for Love*, 4.1, (1678)

Man doth not live by bread only, but by every word that proceedeth out of the mouth of the Lord doth man live.
Deuteronomy 8:3, also *Matthew* 4:4 and *Luke* 4:4

Man is a simple being. And however rich, varied, and unfathomable he may be, the cycle of his situations is soon run through.
GOETHE, quoted in Johann Peter Eckermann's *Conversations with Goethe*, 1 May 1825

[Man] is the only one in whom the instinct of life falters long enough to enable it to ask the question, "Why?"
JOSEPH WOOD KRUTCH, *The Genesis of a Mood*, (1929)

Whatever profits man, that is the truth. In him all nature is comprehended, in all nature only he is created, and all nature only for him. He is the measure of all things, and his welfare is the sole and single criterion of truth.
THOMAS MANN, *The Magic Mountain*, 6.3, (1924)

Man becomes man only by the intelligence, but he is man only by the heart.
HENRI FRÉDÉRIC AMIEL, *Journal*, 7 April 1851

Man is at the bottom an animal, mid-way a citizen, and at the top divine. But the climate of this world is such that few ripen at the top.
HENRY WARD BEECHER, *Proverbs from Plymouth Pulpit*, (1887)

Man, **n.** An animal so lost in rapturous contemplation of what he thinks he is as to overlook what he indubitably ought to be.
AMBROSE BIERCE, *The Devil's Dictionary*, (1881-1911)

What characterises man is the richness and subtlety, the variety and versatility of his nature.
ERNST CASSIRER, *An Essay on Man, The Crisis in Man's Knowledge of Himself*, (1944)

All men are bizarre and inexplicable composites of contraries; that is what those fellows who turn out novels and plays refuse to understand. Their men are all of one piece. There are no such creatures. There are ten men in one man, and often they all show themselves within one hour, under certain circumstances.
EUGÈNE DELACROIX

And the Lord God formed man of the dust of the ground, and breathed into his nostrils the breath of life; and man became a living soul.
Genesis 2:7

Man is God's highest present development. He is the latest thing in God.
SAMUEL BUTLER

Every man is the descendant of every king and every slave that ever lived.
KAHLIL GIBRAN

He who exalts himself does not rise high.
LAO-TSE

Man is a passion which brings a will into play, which works an intelligence.
HENRI FRÉDÉRIC AMIEL, *Journal*, 28 December 1880

Man is a whole, but a whole with an astounding capacity for living, simultaneously or successively, in watertight compartments. What happens here has little or no effect on what happens there.
ALDOUS HUXLEY, *Collected Essays*

Man is harder than rock and more fragile than an egg.
YUGOSLAV PROVERB

Man uses his intelligence less in the care of his own species than he does in his care of anything else he owns or governs.
ABRAHAM MEYERSON, *Speaking of Man*

The devotion to what men at their best may be, to what at their best they make of the world, constitutes a love that is nothing less than religious.
IRWIN EDMAN, *The Uses of Philosophy*

Ill-adapted for living an easy life, he is well adapted for living a difficult one... Never is he more at home in this universe than when he finds himself 'upon an engagement very difficult'.
L.P. JACKS, *The Challenge of Life*

When I inquire about the future of man, I must, if my questions are seriously meant, disregard all mere aspects, be they splendid or be they dispiriting, and thus dig down to the sources of the possible where man, equipped with the fullest attainable knowledge, strives to make his own future, and not merely to contemplate it.
KARL JASPERS, *Man in the Modern Age*

Now man cannot live without some vision of himself. But still less can he live without a vision that is true to his inner experience and inner feeling.
D.H. LAWRENCE, *Assorted Articles*

Man is born unto trouble, as the sparks fly upward.
Job 5:7

A thousand paths are there which have never yet been trodden; a thousand salubrities and hidden islands of life. Unexhausted and undiscovered is still man and man's world.
FRIEDRICH NIETZSCHE, *Thus Spake Zarathustra*

Strange inhabitants are we of a world, so strange that at one moment the heart aches at its loveliness, and another aches at its miseries, so strange that when we think of death we are in love with life, when of life we are enamoured of death. What kind of beings are we in fact? Whatever we are, never forget that we are nature's children, her contradictions are ours, ours also her talents and graces.
W. MACNEILE DIXON, *The Human Situation*

To satisfy his deeper social instincts and intuitions, a man must be able to get away from his family altogether, and foregather in the communion of men.
D.H. LAWRENCE, *Assorted Articles*

They are so obsessed by public affairs that they see the world as by moonlight, which shows the outlines of every object but not the details indicative of their nature.
REBECCA WEST, quoted in *Rebecca West*

Men build bridges and throw railroads across deserts, and yet they contend successfully that the job of sewing on a button is beyond them. Accordingly, they don't have to sew buttons.
HEYWOOD BROUN, *Seeing Things at Night*

Every modern male has, lying at the bottom of his psyche, a large, primitive being covered with hair down to his feet. Making contact with this Wild Man is the step the Eighties male or the Nineties male has yet to take.

ROBERT BLY, (1926-), *Iron John*, (1990)

A man is as old as he feels, and a woman as old as she looks.
ANON

Just such disparity
As is 'twixt air and angels' purity,
'Twixt women's love, and men's will ever be.
JOHN DONNE, (1572-1631), *Air and Angels*

Of all human struggles there is none so treacherous and remorseless as the struggle between the artist man and the mother woman.
GEORGE BERNARD SHAW, (1856-1950), *Man and Superman*

Most men are reasonably useful in a crisis. The difficulty lies in convincing them that the situation has reached a critical point.
ELIZABETH PETERS, *Curse of the Pharaohs*, (1981)

A woman who has known but one man is like a person who has heard only one composer.

ISADORA DUNCAN, *My Life*, (1927)

Mankind is not a tribe of animals to which we owe compassion. Mankind is a club to which we owe our subscription.
G.K. CHESTERTON, (1906)

Man would be otherwise. That is the essence of the specifically human.
ANTONIO MACHADO, *Juan de Matrena*, (1943)

Man, unlike any other thing organic or inorganic in the universe, grows beyond his work, walks up the stairs of his concepts, emerges ahead of his accomplishments.
JOHN STEINBECK, *The Grapes of Wrath*, (1939)

What a piece of work is man! How noble in reason! how infinite in faculties! in form and moving, how express and admirable! in action, how like an angel! in apprehension, how like a god! the beauty of the world! the paragon of animals! And yet, to me, what is this quintessence of dust? Man delights not me - no, nor woman neither.
WILLIAM SHAKESPEARE, (1504-1616), *Hamlet*, Act II, Scene ii

Thou hast made him a little lower than the angels.
Psalms 8:5

The fish in the water is silent, the animal on the earth is noisy, the bird in the air is singing. But Man has in him the silence of the sea, the noise of the earth and the music of the air.
RABINDRANATH TAGORE, (1861-1914), *Stray Birds*, 43

We're all of us guinea pigs in the laboratory of God. Humanity is just a work in progress.
TENNESSEE WILLIAMS, (1911-83), *Camino Real*, 12

He is a poor creature who does not believe himself to be better than the whole world else. No matter how ill we may be, nor how low we may have fallen, we should not change identity with any other person.
SAMUEL BUTLER

It is the best thing in life that each should have everything in himself: his fate, his future, his whole expanse and world.
RAINER MARIA RILKE

A wonderful fact to reflect upon, that every human creature is constituted to be that profound secret and mystery to every other.
CHARLES DICKENS, (1812-70), A Tale of Two Cities, 1

Any man's death diminishes me, because I am involved in Mankind; And therefore never send to know for whom the bell tolls; it tolls for thee.
JOHN DONNE, (1573-1631), Devotions, 17

Human beings are like timid punctuation marks sprinkled among the incomprehensible sentences of life.
JEAN GIRAUDOUX, (1882-1944), Siegfried, 2

Man as we know him is a poor creature; but he is halfway between an ape and a god and he is travelling in the right direction.
DEAN W.R. INGE, (1860-1954), Outspoken Essays

I am fearfully and wonderfully made.
Psalms 139:14

There are one hundred and ninety-three living species of monkeys and apes. One hundred and ninety-two of them are covered with hair. The exception is a naked ape self-named Homo sapiens.
DESMOND MORRIS, The Naked Ape, Introduction

Man, as he is, is not a genuine article. He is an imitation of something, and a very bad imitation.
P.D. OUSPENSKY, (1878-1947), The Psychology of Man's Possible Evolution, Chapter 2

The proper study of Mankind is Man.
ALEXANDER POPE, (1688-1744), An Essay on Man, Epistle II

Man is Heaven's masterpiece.
FRANCIS QUARLES, (1592-1644), Emblems, Book II

Man when perfected, is the best of animals, but, when separated from law and justice,

he is the worst of all.
ARISTOTLE, *Politics*, Book I

And God said, Let us make
man in our image, after our
likeness: and let them have
dominion over the fish of the
sea, and over the fowl of the
air, and over the cattle, and
over all the earth, and over
every creeping thing that
creepeth upon the earth. So
God created man in his own
image, in the image of God
created he him; male and
female created he them.
And God blessed them, and
God said unto them, Be
fruitful, and multiply, and
replenish the earth, and
subdue it: and have dominion
over the fish of the sea, and
over the fowl of the air, and
over every living thing that
moveth upon the earth.
Genesis 1:26-28

There is surely a piece of
divinity in us, something that
was before the elements, and
owes no homage unto the sun.
THOMAS BROWNE,
Religio Medici

Man is the shuttle, to whose
winding quest

And passage through these
looms
God ordered motion, but
ordained no rest.
HENRY VAUGHAN, (1622-
95), *Man*

The children of God should
not have any other country
here below but the universe
itself, with the totality of all
the reasoning creatures it ever
has contained, contains, or
ever will contain. That is the
native city to which we owe
our love.
SIMONE WEIL, (1909-43),
Waiting on God, Letter VI

We need more understanding
of human nature, because the
only real danger that exists is
man himself ... We know
nothing of man, far too little.
His psyche should be studied
because we are the origin of
all coming evil.
C.G. JUNG, (1875-1961),
BBC TV *Face to Face*

Every creature of God is good.
1 *Timothy* 4:4

Man's ultimate love for man?
Yes, yes, but only in the
separate darkness of man's

love for the present,
unknowable God.
D.H. LAWRENCE, *Kangaroo*,
Chapter 17

Man is the measure of all
things.
PROTAGORAS, (circa 485-
415 BC), quoted by Plato in
Theaetetus, 160 AD

Lord, what fools these mortals
be!
WILLIAM SHAKESPEARE,
A Midsummer Night's Dream,
Act III, Scene ii, page 115

How many roads must a man
walk down
Before you call him a man?
BOB DYLAN, *Blowin' in the
Wind*

I am a little world made
cunningly
Of elements, and an angelic
spright.
JOHN DONNE, (1571-1631),
Holy Sonnets, 5

We need words to keep us
human. Being human is an
accomplishment like playing
an instrument. It takes
practice.
MICHAEL IGNATIEFF,

(1947-), *The Needs of
Strangers*, Chapter 4

Men are like wine. Some turn
to vinegar, but the best
improve with age.
POPE JOHN XXIII, (1881-
1963)

I teach you the superman.
Man is something that is to be
surpassed.
FRIEDRICH NIETZSCHE,
(1844-1900), *Thus Spake
Zarathustra*, Prologue,
Chapter 3

The miracle of man is not
how far he has sunk but how
magnificently he has risen.
We are known among the
stars by our poems, not our
corpses.
ROBERT ARDREY, (1908-
80), *African Genesis*

Thus we are men and we
know not how: there is
something in us that can be
without us, and will be after us.
SIR THOMAS BROWNE,
(1605-82), *Religio Medici*, I.35

Thou turnest man to
destruction; and sayest,
Return, ye children of men.

For a thousand years in thy
sight are but as yesterday
when it is past, and as a watch
in the night.
Thou carriest them away as
with a flood; they are as a
sleep: in the morning they are
like grass which groweth up...
So teach us to number our
days, that we may apply our
hearts unto wisdom.
Psalms 90:3-5,12

We do not need, and indeed
never will have, all the
answers before we act... It is
often only through taking
action that we can discover
some of them.
CHARLOTTE BUNCH, *Not
by Degrees*, (1987)

Heaven and earth are ruthless,
and treat the myriad creatures
as straw dogs; the sage is
ruthless, and treats the people
as straw dogs.
Is not the space between
heaven and earth like a
bellows?
It is empty without being
exhausted:
The more it works the more
comes out.
Much speech leads inevitably
to silence.

Better to hold fast to the void.
LAO TZU, from *Tao Te Ching*

Man with all his noble
qualities, with sympathy that
feels for the most debased,
with benevolence which
extends not only to other men
but to the humblest living
creature, with his god-like
intellect which has penetrated
into the movements and
constitution of the solar
system - with all these exalted
powers - still bears in his
bodily frame the indelible
stamp of his lowly origin.
CHARLES DARWIN, (1809-
82), *The Descent of Man*,
Conclusion

This is an absurd position for
man the heir of all the ages to
be in, hag-ridden by the flimsy
creatures of his own brain. If
a pebble in our boot torments
us we expel it. We take off
the boot and shake it out.
And once the matter is fairly
understood it is just as easy to
expel an intruding and
obnoxious thought from the
mind. About this there ought
to be no mistake; no two
opinions. The thing is
obvious, clear and

unmistakable. It should be as easy to expel an obnoxious thought from your mind as to shake a stone out of your shoe; and until a man can do that it is just nonsense to talk about his ascendancy over Nature and all the rest of it. He is a mere slave and a prey to the batwinged phantoms that flit through the corridors of his own brain.
EDWARD CARPENTER

The chief end of man is to realise his highest ideal by intelligent and persevering work in the face of difficulty, obstruction and danger.
BLACKIE

All human evil comes from a single cause, man's inability to sit still in a room.
BLAISE PASCAL

Do not vaunt your body or your brain; for is not the Master of the house more honourable than the walls of the house? As ground must be prepared before corn is planted, and the potter must build his furnace before he can make his porcelain, so let your Spirit actuate and direct your flesh. Is not your hand a miracle in itself? Why was it given to you but that you might stretch it out to the assistance of one another. Why, of all things living, are you, alone, made capable of blushing, unless it be that if you allow your soul to do a shameful thing the world shall be able to read the shame upon your face. Why do fear and dismay rob your face of its natural colour? Avoid guilt, and then you, and the whole world, shall know that fear is beneath you, and that, to you, dismay is unmanly. You, alone, of all creatures of the earth, have the power of speech. Be thankful for your glorious privilege; and pay to Him who gave you speech a welcome and a rational praise.
DANDEMIS

THIRTY-THREE

MEDIEVAL
PHILOSOPHY

Natural things are intermediate between God's knowledge and ours. For we get our knowledge from natural things of which God, through His knowledge, is the cause.
ST. THOMAS AQUINAS, *Summa Theologiae*, I, Part 1.2, qu. 14, a. 8

The members of the [New Platonic] Academy maintained: (1) where matters of philosophy are concerned - and Carneades disowned interest in anything else - man can know nothing for certain. Despite this, he can be wise and the total task of a wise man is to search for truth. From this it follows: (2) a wise man will not assent to anything. If he did, he would inevitably fall into error, which is something wicked in a wise man ...
Since it would seem to follow that one who assents to nothing will do nothing, the position of the academicians provoked considerable animosity ... Consequently, they proposed their theory of the 'probable' or 'truth-like', as they called it, insisting that

the wise man does not desert his duties at all since he has some norm to follow. Truth as such, however, remains hidden either because it is shrouded or obfuscated by a kind of opacity of nature or because of its indistinguishable resemblance to falsity. Actually, they insist, it is a great achievement for the wise man to withhold his assent, or to suspend judgement as it were ...
ST. AUGUSTINE

To know God's nature one would have to be God Himself.
JOSEPH ALBO, (circa 1380-1444), *Sefer ha-Ikkarim*, 2.30

As St. Augustine puts it: "A principal point about man's salvation is the belief and teaching that philosophy or the pursuit of wisdom is not something other than religion, for those whose teaching we disapprove of are precisely those who do not share our religion." What is the practice of philosophy but explaining the rules of the true religion in which God,

the supreme and principal cause of all things, is humbly worshiped and rationally investigated? It follows from this that true philosophy is true religion, and conversely, true religion is true philosophy. Every type of perfect and godly teaching wherein the rational grounds for anything is sought most earnestly and found most clearly stated is in that branch of learning the Greeks customarily call philosophy ...
JOHN SCOTES ERUGERIA

The will of God is truly the cause of the existence of all things, whether visible or invisible, in that all created things, before appearing in their visible forms, were already truly and essentially alive in the will of their Creator. "All that came to be," says John, "had life in him" (John 1.4). And he testified in the Apocalypse to the same statement by the twenty-four elders: "You are worthy, O Lord our God, to receive glory and honour and power, because you created all things; by your will they have their being and were created"

(Apoc. 4.11). In the first place it is said, "they have their being," and then that, "they were created," because the things that were externally expressed by their making, already existed internally in the providence and in the design of the Creator.
ST. PETER DAMIAN

It is indeed by faith that we enter upon the knowledge of those things of which it is correctly said, "Unless you believe, you will not understand." But we must not just stand there at the entrance, but with all zeal and diligence hasten onward to master their deeper and more interior aspects so that day by day we may advance in our understanding of those things we hold by faith. For it is in the full knowledge and perfect grasp of such things that we obtain eternal life. To know such things is of the greatest benefit. To contemplate them brings the greatest joy. They are our supreme treasure. The pleasure they bring never ends. To taste such is the height of sweetness. To enjoy

them is infinite delight.
RICHARD OF ST. VICTOR

It is plain that the
immateriality of a thing is the
reason that it can have
knowledge, and the ability to
know corresponds to the
degree of immateriality.
Hence it is said that on
account of their materiality
plants do not have knowledge.
The senses can know because
they receive the likenesses of
things without the matter.
The intellect is even more
able to have knowledge
because it is more separated
from matter and unmixed, as
Aristotle says. So since God
is immaterial to the highest
degree, it follows that He has
knowledge to the highest
degree.
ST. THOMAS AQUINAS,
Summa Theologiae, I, Part 1,
qu. 14, a. 1

It is the supreme Self as
apparently delimited by the
adjuncts of body, sense, lower
mind, intellect and so on
which is falsely referred to by
the ignorant as 'the embodied
one'... And the empirical
distinctions such as 'I am the

agent and this is the object of
my act', which depend on this
false notion, are not
contradicted until the truth
declared in the text 'That
thou art' that only the Self
exists has been directly
apprehended. But when there
has once been a direct
apprehension of the fact that
only the Self exists, all
empirical notions, such as
those of bondage and
liberation, cease."
ADI SHANKARA

In the name of God, the
Merciful, the Compassionate.
Someone asked the eminent
shaykh Abû 'Ali b. Sinâ (may
God the Exalted have mercy
on him) the meaning of the
Sûfî saying, 'He who knows
the secret of destiny is an
atheist'. In reply he stated
that this matter contains the
utmost obscurity, and is one of
those matters which may be
set down only in enigmatic
form and taught only in a
hidden manner, on account of
the corrupting effects its open
declaration would have on the
general public. The basic
principle concerning it is
found in a Tradition of the

Prophet (God bless and safeguard him): 'Destiny is the secret of God; do not declare the secret of God'. In another Tradition, when a man questioned the Prince of the Believers, 'Alî (may God be pleased with him), he replied, 'Destiny is a deep sea; do not sail out on it'. Being asked again he replied, 'It is a stony path; do not walk on it'. Being asked once more he said, 'It is a hard ascent; do not undertake it'.
AVEROËS

It is necessary to assume something which is necessary of itself, and has no cause of its necessity outside itself but is rather the cause of necessity in other things. And this all men call God.
ST. THOMAS AQUINAS, (c. 1225-1274), *Summa Theologiae*, 1, Part 1, qu. 2, a. 3

For the common throng cannot continue anything that is perfect; would that it were avoiding error in life and in pursuit. We see that such is the case among the professors of philosophy as well as in the truth of our faith. For the wise have always been divided from the multitude, and they have veiled the secrets of wisdom not only from the world at large but also from the rank and file of those devoting themselves to philosophy.
ROGER BACON

It follows necessarily from the twenty-fifth premise that there is a mover, which has moved the matter of that which is subject to generation and corruption so that it received form. If now it is asked: what moved this proximate mover? - it follows of necessity that there exists for it another mover either of its own species or of a different species; for motion exists in four categories, and sometimes these different kinds of change are called motion in a general way, as we have mentioned in the fourth premise. Now this does not go to infinity, as we have mentioned in the third premise. For we have found that every movement goes back, in the last resort, to the movement of the fifth body,

and no further. It is from this movement that every mover and predisposer in the whole lower world proceeds and derives.
MOSES MAIMONIDES

For a creature is related to God as a footprint (*vestigium*), as an image (*imago*) and as a likeness (*similitudo*). Insofar as it is a footprint, it is compared to God as a principle; as an image, it is related to God as to its object; but as a likeness, it is united to God as to an infused gift. And therefore every creature that comes from God is a footprint; every one that knows God is an image; and each creature in whom God dwells, and only such, is a likeness. Corresponding to this triple degree of relatedness there is a threefold degree of divine cooperation.
ST. BONAVENTURE

The power of God over things surpasses the power of our intellect. Now our intellect can understand a creature apart from God. Much more therefore can God make a creature able of itself to keep itself in existence ... The more perfect the agent the more perfect an effect can it produce. Now natural agents can produce effects which are able to remain in existence without their causes. Therefore *a fortiori* God can do it.
ST. THOMAS AQUINAS

Augustine: Well I believe the soul's proper habitation, its homeland so to speak, is the God himself who created it. As for its substance, I am at a loss for a name. For I certainly do not believe it is made of any ordinary or familiar elements known to us such as earth, water, air, or fire, or of any combination thereof. Should you ask: What is a tree made of? I would list these four elements that we regard all such things to be composed of. But if you ask further: And what is earth itself, or air or fire made of? I would be unable to answer. In similar fashion, should you ask what man is made of, I could say: Of body and soul. Likewise, if you were to ask about the composition of the body, I would refer you to the same four elements. But since the soul seems simple and of a substance all its own, when you ask me what it is made of, I am as lost for an answer as when you ask what earth is composed of.

Evodius: I don't understand why you claim it has a substance all its own when you admit it was made by God.

Augustine: I can't deny earth was made by God, but I am unable to say what further bodies constitute it, so to speak. For earth is something simple by the very fact that it is earth. That is why it is called an element of anything composed of the four elements. There is nothing incompatible about our saying that the soul has a nature proper to itself and yet is made by God. For he himself made this nature that is peculiarly its own even as he made the distinctive natures of fire, air, earth, and water, - the elements of which all other things are composed.
ST. AUGUSTINE

Divine providence does not watch in an equal manner over all the individuals of the human species, but providence is graded as their human perfection is graded.
MOSES MAIMONIDES, *The Guide of the Perplexed*, page 475

Since we cannot know what God is, but only what He is not, we must consider the ways in which He is not rather than the ways in which He is.
ST. THOMAS AQUINAS, (c. 1225-1274), *Summa Theologiae*, 1, Part 1, qu. 3, introduction

The supreme good for man should be his in terms of his highest power, and not according to the vegetative soul, which is also found in plants, nor according to the sensitive soul, which is also found in animals and from which their sensual pleasures arise. But man's highest power is his reason and intellect. For this is the supreme director of human life both in the order of speculation and in the order of action. Therefore, the supreme good attainable by man must be his by means of

his intellect. Therefore, men who are so weighed down by sense pleasures that they lose intellectual goods should grieve. For they never attain their supreme good. It is insofar as they are given to the senses that they do not seek that which is the good of the intellect itself. Against these the Philosopher protests, saying: "Woe to you men who are numbered among beasts and who do not attend to that which is divine within you!" He calls the intellect that which is divine in man. For if there is anything divine in man, it is right for it to be the intellect. Just as that which is best among all beings is divine, so also that which is best in man we call divine.
JOHN DUNS SCOTIUS

It seems that God's inability to perform the impossible is the prior characteristic for the following reason. That God can make what is possible is prior to the possible's capacity to be made by God. In the same vein then God's inability to make the impossible should be prior to the impossible's inability to be made by God.

The antecedent is evident from the fact that everything that pertains to God is prior to anything that pertains to a creature, and consequently also to anything that the creature gets from God. Therefore, since the ability to make the possible is a divine characteristic, this should pertain to God in some prior fashion than that the impossibility of being made by God should be a characteristic of a thing other than God. To the contrary: Nothing that suggests any lack of perfection can be a primary attribute of God.
WILLIAM OCKHA

First as to the unfolding of the true principle. The mind has two doors from which issue its activities. One leads to a realisation of the mind's Pure Essence, the other leads to the differentiations of appearing and disappearing, of life and death. Through each door passes all the mind's conceptions so interrelated that they never have been separated and never will be.

What is meant by the Pure Essence of Mind? It is the

ultimate purity and unity, the all-embracing wholeness, the quintessence of Truth. Essence of Mind belongs to neither death nor rebirth, it is uncreated and eternal. The concepts of the conscious mind are being individualised and discriminated by false imaginations. If the mind could be kept free from discriminative thinking there would be no more arbitrary thoughts to give rise to appearances of form, existencies and conditions. Therefore from the beginning, all concepts have been independent of individuation, of names and mental moods and conditions. They are in their essential nature of an equal sameness, neither variable nor breakable nor destructible. As they are of one suchness, of one purity, it is spoken of as Mind-essence. ASHVAGHOSHA, from *Awakening of Faith*

For if there be something superior to truth, then this would rather be God, but if not, then truth itself is God. But whichever be the case, you cannot deny that God exists. And this was the question we set out to discuss. Now if it bothers you that we have it on faith, from Christ's sacred teaching, that there is a 'Father of Wisdom', remember it is also a tenet of our faith that this be accepted for the present as settled by faith and let us question it no further. For [our present concern is that] God exists and he does so in the truest and highest sense of the word. It is not only by faith that we regard this beyond doubt but also, I think, by a certain, though tenuous form of knowledge.
ST. AUGUSTINE

Future contingents cannot be certain to us, because we know them *as* future contingents. They can be certain only to God whose understanding is in eternity above time. In the same way a man going along a road does not see those who come behind him; but the man who sees the whole road from a height sees simultaneously all those who are going along the road.
ST. THOMAS AQUINAS, (circa 1225-1274), *Summa Theologiae*, 1, Part 1, qu. 14, a 13

In sentences such as 'That thou art,' the meaning of the sentence will not become clear until there has first been a discrimination of the meaning of the word 'thou' as the pure 'I', ever liberated. Reasoning by the method of agreement and difference is required for discrimination of the meaning of the word 'thou' and not for anything else. For when discrimination has once determined the meaning of the word 'thou', the meaning of the sentence becomes as clear as a bilva fruit held in the palm of the hand. In this way the meaning of the holy text 'That thou art' as bare 'I' becomes clear from the meaning of the words that compose it, since the inmost Self (of the hearer) is determined as the meaning through the cancellation of the false notion of the Self as sufferer. When the meaning (of the text 'That thou art') is capable of being made out (rationally) in this way, it is no longer possible for those genuinely expert in the meanings of sentences and words to assume meanings which are not the meaning of the Veda and which would undermine that meaning.
ADI SHANKARA

A great disparity subsists between the knowledge an artificer has of the thing he has made and the knowledge someone else has of the artifact in question.
MOSES MAIMONIDES (1135-1204), *The Guide of the Perplexed*, page 484

Laws can be unjust because they are contrary to the divine good, for example, the laws of tyrants which promote idolatry or whatever else is against divine law. In no way is it permissible to observe them.
ST. THOMAS AQUINAS, *Summa Theologiae*, I, Part 1.2, qu. 96, a. 4

All religions, as we have said, agree on the fact that souls experience states of happiness or misery after death, but they disagree in the manner of symbolising these states and explaining their existence to men. And it seems that the [kind of] symbolisation which is found in this religion of ours is the most perfect means of explanation to the majority of men, and provides the greatest stimulus to their souls to [pursue the goals of] the life beyond; and the primary concern of religions is with the majority. Spiritual symbolisation, on the other hand, seems to provide less stimulus to the souls of the masses towards [the goals of] the life beyond, and the masses have less desire and fear of it than they do of corporeal symbolisation. Therefore it seems that corporeal symbolisation provides a stronger stimulus to [the goals of] the life beyond than spiritual; the spiritual [kind] is more acceptable to the class of debating theologians, but they are the minority.

AVEROËS

For the differentiations of words are but false notions with no basis in reality. They have in their falsity only a relative existence as false imaginations and thoughts arise and pass away. Even as applying to Mind-essence

words have no value, for in Mind-essence there is nothing to be grasped nor named. But we use words to get free from words until we reach the pure wordless Essence. In Essence of Mind there is nothing that can be taken away and nothing that can be added. All concepts are an undivided part of Reality; they are not artificial but are unchangeable and ineffable and unthinkable. They are the Essence of Mind itself.

ASHVAGHOSHA, from *Awakening of Faith*

I state, therefore, that God must exist just as this fact must be proved in metaphysics: second, that God's existence is naturally known to every man; and third, that God is of infinite power and of infinite goodness, and coupled with this that he is of infinite substance and essence, so that it follows that he is best, wisest, and most powerful. Fourth, that God is one in essence and not more than one. Fifth, that not only is God one in essence but triune in another way, which must in

general be explained by the
metaphysician, but here must
be unfolded in special
doctrinal form. Sixth, that he
has created all things and rules
in the realm of nature.
Seventh, that besides
corporeal things he has
created spiritual substances
which we call intelligences
and angels; because
intelligence is a term denoting
a nature, but angel is a term
denoting an office.
ROGER BACON

We have found the definition
of 'person', namely, 'an
individual substance of a
rational nature'.
BOETHIUS, (circa 480-524),
Contra Eutychen, Loeb
Classical Library, Number 74,
page 84

We call the intention good
which is right in itself, but the
action is good, not because it
contains within it some good,
but because it issues from a
good intention. The same act
may be done by the same man
at different times. According
to the diversity of his
intention, however, this act
may be at one time good, at

another bad.
PETER ABELARD, (1079-
1142), Abailard's Ethics, page 46

All that I have written seems
to me like straw compared to
what has now been revealed
to me.
ST. THOMAS AQUINAS,
(c. 1225-1274), quoted in J.A.
Weisheipl, Friar Thomas
d'Aquino, page 322

It is not the case ... that
because God foreknew what
would be in the power of our
wills, there is for that reason
nothing in the power of our
wills. For He Who forknew
this did not foreknow nothing
... If He Who foreknew what
would be in the power of our
wills did not forknow nothing,
but something, assuredly, even
though He did forknow, there
is something in the power of
our wills.
ST. AUGUSTINE, City of
God, Book 5, Chapter 10

I have no hope but in your
great mercy. Grant what you
command and command what
you will.
J.L. AUSTIN, Confessions,
Book 10, Section 29

There are certain individual goods which have not a necessary connection with happiness, because without them a man can be happy, and to such the will does not adhere of necessity. But there are some things which have a necessary connection with happiness, by means of which things man adheres to God, in Whom alone true happiness consists. Nevertheless, until through the certitude of the Divine Vision, the necessity of such connection be shown, the will does not adhere to God of necessity, nor to those things which are of God ... It is therefore clear that the will does not desire of necessity whatever it desires.

ST. THOMAS AQUINAS,
Summa Theologiae, I, Part 1, qu. 10, a. 2

THIRTY-FOUR

MODERN PHILOSOPHY

Properly written texts are like spiders' webs: tight, concentric, transparent, well-spun and firm. They draw into themselves all the creatures of the air. Metaphors flitting hastily through them become their nourishing prey. Subject matter comes winging towards them. The soundness of a conception can be judged by whether it causes one quotation to summon another. Where thought has opened up one cell of reality, it should, without violence by the subject, penetrate the next. It proves its relation to the object as soon as other objects crystallize around it. In the light that it casts on its chosen substance, others begin to glow.
THEODOR ADORNO, (1903-1969), *Minima Moralia*

Wise men weigh the advantages of any course of action against its drawbacks, and move not an inch until they can see what the result of their action will be; but while they are deep in thought, the men with self-confidence 'come and see and conquer'.
AHAD HA-AM (ASHER GINZBERG), (1856-1927), A *Biography*

The connotation of courage, which we now feel to be a quality of the hero, is in fact already present in a willingness to speak at all, to insert one's Self into the world and begin to be one's own.
HANNAH ARENDT, (1906-1975), *The Human Condition*

I conclude then that the necessary and sufficient conditions for knowing that something is the case are first that what one is said to know be true, secondly that one be sure of it, and thirdly that one should have the right to be sure. This right may be earned in various ways; but even if one could give a complete description of them it would be a mistake to try to build it into the definition of knowledge, just as it would be a mistake to try to incorporate our actual standards of goodness into a definition of good.

Either it is an accident that I choose to act as I do or it is not. If it is an accident, then it is merely a matter of chance that I did not choose otherwise; and if it is merely a matter of chance that I did not choose otherwise, it is surely irrational to hold me morally responsible for choosing as I did. But if it is not an accident that I choose to do one thing rather than another, then presumably there is some causal explanation of my choice: and in that case we are led back to determinism.

A.J. AYER, *The Problem of Knowledge* and *Philosophical Essays*

Those who have handled sciences have been either men of experiment or men of dogmas. The men of experiment are like the ant; they only collect and use; the reasoners resemble spiders, who make cobwebs out of their own substance. But the bee takes the middle course; it gathers its material from the flowers of the garden and of the field, but transforms and digests it by a power of its own. Not unlike this is the true business of philosophy.

It is true, that a little Philosophy inclineth Mans Minde to *Atheisme*; But depth in Philosophy, bringeth Mens Mindes about to *Religion* ...

FRANCIS BACON, (1561-1626) *The Philosophical Works of Francis Bacon and Essays*

Nature has placed mankind under the governance of two sovereign masters, *pain* and *pleasure*. It is for them alone to point out what we ought to do, as well as to determine what we shall do. On the one hand the standard of right and wrong, on the other the chain of causes and effects, are fastened to their throne. They govern us in all we do, in all we say, in all we think; every effort we can make to throw off our subjection will serve but to demonstrate and confirm it. In words a man may pretend to abjure their empire: but in reality he will remain subject to it all the while. The *principle of utility* recognises this subjection, and assumes it for the foundation of that system, the object of which is to rear the fabric of felicity by the hands of reason and of law. Systems which

attempt to question it deal in sounds instead of sense, in caprice instead of reason, in darkness instead of light.
JEREMY BENTHAM, (1748-1832), An Introduction to the Principles of Morals and Legislation

The human spirit is in prison. Prison is what I call this world, the given world of necessity.
... man is not only of this world but of another world; not only of necessity, but of freedom.
NICOLAS BERDYAEV, The Meaning of the Creative Act

We see only the appearances, and not the real qualities of things ... for aught we know, all we see, hear, and feel, may be only phantom and vain chimera, and not at all agree with the real things, existing in rerum natura. All this scepticism follows, from our supposing a difference between things and ideas, and that the former have a subsistence without the mind, or unperceived. It were easy to dilate on this subject, and shew how the arguments urged by sceptics in all ages, depend on the supposition of external objects.

For as we have shewn the doctrine of matter or corporeal substance, to have been the main pillar and support of scepticism, so likewise upon the same foundation have been raised all the impious schemes of atheism and irreligion. Nay so great a difficulty hath it been thought, to conceive matter produced out of nothing, that the most celebrated among the ancient philosophers, even of these who maintained the being of a God, have thought matter to be uncreated and coeternal with him. How great a friend material substance hath been to atheists in all ages, were needless to relate. All their monstrous systems have so visible and necessary a dependence on it, that when this corner-stone is once removed, the whole fabric cannot choose but fall to the ground; insomuch that it is no longer worth while, to bestow a particular consideration on the absurdities of every wretched sect of atheists.

But if we attentively consider the constant regularity, order, and concatenation of natural things, the surprising magnificence, beauty, and perfection of the larger, and the exquisite contrivance of the smaller parts of the creation, together with the exact harmony and correspondence of the whole, but above all, the never enough admired laws of pain and pleasure, and the instincts or natural inclinations, appetites, and passions of animals, I say if we consider all these things, and at the same time attend to the meaning and import of the attributes, one, eternal, infinitely wise, good, and perfect, we shall clearly perceive that they belong to the aforesaid spirit, who works all in all, and by whom all things consist.

GEORGE BERKELEY, *A Treatise Concerning the Principles of Human Knowledge*

There is a line among the fragments of the Greek poet Archilochus which says: 'The fox knows many things, but the hedgehog knows one big thing'. Scholars have differed about the correct interpretation of these dark words, which may mean no more than that the fox, for all his cunning, is defeated by the hedgehog's one defence. But, taken figuratively, the words can be made to yield a sense in which they mark one of the deepest differences which divide writers and thinkers, and, it may be, human beings in general.

If social and psychological determinism were established as an accepted truth, our world would be transformed more radically than was the teleological world of the classical and middle ages by the triumphs of mechanistic principles or those of natural selection. Our words - our modes of speech and thought - would be transformed in literally unimaginable ways; the notions of choice, of responsibility, of freedom, are so deeply embedded in our outlook that our new life, as creatures in a world genuinely lacking in these concepts, can, I should maintain, be

conceived by us only with the greatest difficulty. But there is, as yet, no need to alarm ourselves unduly.
ISAIAH BERLIN, *Four Essays on Liberty*

We find that the essence of human society consists in a common self, a life and a will, which belong to and are exercised by the society as such, or by the individuals in society as such; it makes no difference which expression we choose. The reality of this common self, in the action of the political whole, receives the name of the 'general will'
...
BERNARD BOSANQUET, (1848-1923), *The Philosophical Theory of the State*

Metaphysics is the finding of bad reasons for what we believe upon instinct; but to find these reasons is no less an instinct.

The way of taking the world which I have found most tenable is to regard it as a single Experience, superior to relations and containing in the fullest sense everything which is. Whether there is any particular matter in this whole which falls outside of any finite centre of feeling, I cannot certainly decide; but the contrary seems perhaps more probable. We have then the Absolute Reality appearing in and to finite centres and uniting them in one experience. We can, I think, understand more or less what, in order for this to be done, such an experience must be. But to comprehend it otherwise is beyond us and even beyond all intelligence ... Those for whom philosophy has to explain everything need therefore not trouble themselves with my views.
F.H. BRADLEY, *Appearance and Reality*

Every mental act is conscious; it includes within it a consciousness of itself. Therefore, every mental act, no matter how simple, has a double object, a primary and a secondary object. The simplest act, for example the act of hearing, has as its primary object the sound, and for its secondary object, itself, the mental phenomenon in which the sound is heard.

And now we have found what we have been looking for. We have arrived at the source of our concepts of the good and the bad, along with that of our concepts of the true and the false. We call a thing *true* when the affirmation relating to it is correct. We call a thing *good* when the love relating to it is correct. In the broadest sense of the term, the good is that which is worthy of love, that which can be loved with a love that is correct.
FRANZ BRENTANO, *The Origin of our Knowledge of Right and Wrong*

It is worth remembering (though there is nothing that we can do about it) that the world as it really is may easily be a far nastier place than it would be if scientific materialism were the whole truth and nothing but the truth about it.
C.D. BROAD, (1887-1971), *Lectures on Psychical Research*

When *Thou* is spoken, the speaker has no thing for his object. For where there is a thing, there is another thing.

Every *It* is bounded by others; *It* exists only through being bounded by others. But when *Thou* is spoken, there is no thing. *Thou* has no bounds. When *Thou* is spoken, the speaker has no *thing*; he has indeed nothing. But he takes his stand in relation.
All real living is meeting.
MARTIN BUBER, *I and Thou*

... change ... alters the substance of the objects themselves, and gets rid of all their essential good as well as the accidental evil annexed to them. Change is novelty, and whether it is to operate any one of the effects of reformation at all, or whether it may not contradict the very principle upon which reformation is desired, cannot be certainly known beforehand. Reform is not a change in the substance or in the primary modification of the objects, but a direct application of a remedy to the grievance complained of. So far as that is removed, all is sure. It stops there; and if it fails the substance which underwent the operation, at the very worst, is but where it

was.
EDMUND BURKE, (1729-
1797), *Letter to a Noble Lord,
The Philosophy of Edmund
Burke*

... nothing can be more
evident, than that, exclusive
of revelation, man cannot be
considered as a creature left by
his Maker to act at random,
and live at large up to the
extent of his natural power, as
passion, humour, wilfulness,
happen to carry him; which is
the condition brute creatures
are in; but that, *from his make,
constitution, or nature, he is, in
the strictest and most proper
sense, a law to himself.* He
hath the rule of right within:
what is wanting is only that
he honestly attend to it.
    But, allowing that mankind
hath the rule of right within
himself, yet it may be asked,
'What obligations are we
under to attend and follow it?
... Your obligation to obey
this law, is its being the law of
your nature. That your
conscience approves of and
attestts to such a course of
action, is itself alone an
obligation. Conscience does
not only offer itself to show us

the way we should walk in,
but it likewise carries its own
authority with it, that it is our
natural guide, the guide
assigned us by the Author of
our nature ...
JOSEPH BUTLER, *Sermons,*
Number iii

In wonder all philosophy
began, in wonder it ends, and
admiration fills up the
interspace; but the first
wonder is the offspring of
ignorance, the last is the
parent of adoration.
SAMUAL TAYLOR
COLERIDGE

Until a man has expressed his
emotion, he does not yet
know what emotion it is. The
act of expressing it is therefore
an exploration of his own
emotions. He is trying to find
out what these emotions are.
R.G. COLLINGWOOD,
(1889-1943), *The Principles of
Art*

Man stands face to face with
the irrational. He feels within
him his longing for happiness
and for reason. The absurd is
born of this confrontation
between the human need and

the unreasonable silence of the world.
ALBERT CAMUS, (1913-1960), *The Myth of Sisyphus*

Belief in the God of Christian faith is an expression of allegiance to a particular set of values, and the experience of the God of Christian faith is experience of the impact of those values in one's life.

So it would seem that religion forbids that there should be any extra-religious reality of God. The most we can say is that it is religiously appropriate to think that there may be beyond the God of religion a transcendent divine mystery witnessed to in various ways by the faith of mankind. But we cannot say anything about it. Any possibility of non-religious knowledge of this mystery would weaken the stringency and the saving power of the religious requirement.
DON CUPITT, (1934-), *Taking Leave of God*

I have noticed certain laws which God has so established in nature, and of which he has implanted such notions in our minds, that after adequate reflection we cannot doubt that they are exactly observed in everything which exists or occurs in the world.

This will not seem at all strange to those who know how many kinds of automatons, or moving machines, the skill of man can construct with the use of very few parts, in comparison with the great multitude of bones, muscles, nerves, arteries, veins and all the other parts that are in the body of any animal. For they will regard this body as a machine which, having been made by the hand of God, is incomparably better ordered than any machine that can be devised by man, and contains in itself movements more wonderful than those in any such machine.

When we know how much the beasts differ from us, we understand much better the arguments which prove that our soul is of a nature entirely independent of the body, and consequently that it is not bound to die with it. And since we cannot see any other causes which destroy the soul, we are naturally led to conclude that it is immortal.

It is quite evident that existence can no more be separated from the essence of God than the fact that its three angles equal two right angles can be separated from the idea of a triangle, or than the idea of a mountain can be separated from the idea of a valley. Hence it is just as much of a contradiction to think of God (that is, a supremely perfect being) lacking existence (that is, lacking a perfection), as it is to think of a mountain without a valley.
RENÉ DESCARTES, *Discourses and Fifth Meditation*

... the whole history of science, art and morals proves that the mind that appears *in* individuals is not as such individual mind. The former is in itself a system of belief, recognitions, and ignorances, of acceptances and rejections, of expectancies and appraisals of meanings which have been instituted under the influence of custom and tradition.

Character is the interpenetration of habits.
JOHN DEWEY, *The Late Works and Human Nature and Conduct*

Quantum mechanics is certainly imposing. But an inner voice tells me that it is not yet the real thing. The theory says a lot, but does not really bring us any closer to the secret of the 'old one'. I, at any rate, am convinced that *He* is not playing dice.
ALBERT EINSTEIN, (1879- 1955), *The Born - Einstein Letters*

Attend to yourself: turn your attention away from everything that surrounds you and towards your inner life; this is the first demand that philosophy makes of its disciple. Our concern is not with anything that lies outside you, but only with yourself.

What sort of philosophy one chooses depends, therefore, on what sort of man one is; for a philosophical system is not a dead piece of furniture that we can reject or accept as we wish; it is rather a thing animated by the soul of the person who holds it. A person indolent by nature or dulled and distorted by mental servitude, learned luxury, and vanity will never raise himself to the level of idealism.

Our task is to *discover* the primordial, absolutely unconditioned first principle of all human knowledge ... It is intended to express that *Act* which does not and cannot appear among the empirical states of our consciousness, but rather lies at the basis of all consciousness and alone makes it possible.
J.G. FICHTE, *Science of Knowledge*

Historians of civilization appear to be at one in assuming that powerful components are acquired for every kind of cultural achievement by this diversion of sexual instinctual forces from sexual aims and their direction to new ones - a process which deserves the name of 'sublimation'.
... it often seems that the poet's derisive comment is not unjustified when he says of the philosopher: 'With his nightcaps and the tatters of his dressing-gown he patches up the gaps in the structure of the universe'.
SIGMUND FREUD, *The Theory of Sexuality and New Introductory Lectures on Psychoanalysis*

Man is a machine. All his actions, words, thoughts, feelings, opinions and habits are the results of external influences, external impressions. Out of himself a man cannot produce a single thought, a single action. Everything he says, does, thinks, feels - all this happens. To establish this fact for oneself, to be convinced of its truth, means getting rid of a thousand illusions about man, about his being creative and consciously organising his own life, and so on. But it is one thing to understand with the mind and another thing to feel with one's 'whole mass', to be really convinced that it is so and never forget it.
It is possible to stop being a machine, but for that it is necessary first of all to *know* the machine. A machine, a real machine, does not know itself and cannot know itself. When a machine knows itself it is then no longer a

machine, at least, not such a machine as it was before. It already begins to be *responsible* for its actions.

Man has no permanent and unchangeable I. Every thought, every mood, every desire, every sensation says 'I'. And in each case it seems to be taken for granted that this I belongs to the Whole, to the whole man, and that a thought, a desire, or an aversion is expressed by this Whole. In actual fact, there is no foundation whatever for this assumption. Man's every thought and desire appears and lives quite separately and independently of the Whole. And the Whole never expresses itself, for the simple reason that it exists, as such, only physically as a thing, and in the abstract as a concept.
G.I. GURDJIEFF, (1866-1949), quoted in P.D. Ouspensky, *In Search of the Miraculous*

The Absolute is Mind (Spirit) - this is the supreme definition of the Absolute. To find this definition and to grasp its meaning and burden was, we may say, the ultimate purpose of all education and all philosophy: it was the point to which turned the impulse of all religion and science; and it is this impulse that must explain the history of the world. The word 'Mind' (Spirit) - and some glimpse of its meaning - was found at an early period: and the spirituality of God is the lesson of Christianity. It remains for philosophy in its own element of intelligible unity to get hold of what was thus given as a mental image, and what implicitly is the ultimate reality ...
G.W.F. HEGEL, (1770-1831), *Encyclopaedia*

Do we in our time have an answer to the question of what we really mean by the word 'being'? Not at all. So it is fitting that we should raise anew *the question of the meaning of Being*. But are we nowadays even perplexed at our inability to understand the expression 'Being'? Not at all. So first of all we must reawaken an understanding for the meaning of this question.

We are too late for the gods
and too early for Being.
Being's poem,
just begun, is man.

Is Being a mere word and
its meaning a vapour, or does
what is designated by the word
'Being' hold within it the
historical destiny of the West?
MARTIN HEIDEGGER,
*Being and Time; Poetry,
Language, Thought, and An
Introduction to Metaphysics*

... there is no such thing as
perpetual tranquillity of mind,
while we live here; because
life itself is but motion, and
can never be without desire,
nor without fear, no more
than without sense.
　　... he that will do anything
for his pleasure, must engage
himself to suffer all the pains
annexed to it; and these pains,
are the natural punishments of
those actions, which are the
beginning of more harm than
good. And hereby it comes to
pass that intemperance is
naturally punished with
diseases; rashness with
mischances; injustice with the
violence of enemies: pride,
with ruin; cowardice, with
oppression; negligent

government of princes, with
rebellion; and rebellion, with
slaughter.
THOMAS HOBBES,
Leviathan, English Works

All the perceptions of the
human mind resolve
themselves into two distinct
kinds, which I shall call
IMPRESSIONS and IDEAS.
The difference betwixt these
consists in the degrees of force
and liveliness, with which
they strike upon the mind,
and make their way into our
thought or consciousness.
Those perceptions, which
enter with most force and
violence, we may name
impressions; and under this
name I comprehend all our
sensations, passions and
emotions, as they make their
first appearance in the soul.
By *ideas* I mean the faint
images of these in thinking
and reasoning.
　　'Tis not, therefore, reason,
which is the guide of life, but
custom.
　　... experience only teaches
us, how one event constantly
follows another; without
instructing us in the secret
connexion, which binds them

together, and renders them inseparable.

So that, upon the whole, there appears not, throughout all nature, any one instance of connexion which is conceivable by us. All events seem entirely loose and separate. One event follows another; but we never can observe any ties between them. They seem *conjoined*, but never *connected.* And as we can have no idea of any thing which never appeared to our outward sense or inward sentiment, the necessary conclusion *seems* to be that we have no idea of connexion or power at all, and that these words are absolutely without any meaning, when employed either in philosophical reasonings or common life. But there still remains one method of avoiding this conclusion, and one source which we have not yet examined.

DAVID HUME, A *Treatise on Human Nature and An Enquiry Concerning Human Understanding*

Consciousness, then, does not appear to itself chopped up in bits. Such words as 'chain' or 'train' do not describe it fitly as it presents itself in the first instance. It is nothing jointed; it flows. A 'river' or a 'stream' are the metaphors by which it is most naturally described.

... the rigorously impersonal view of science might one day appear as having been a temporarily useful eccentricity rather than the definitively triumphant position, which the sectarian scientist at present so confidently announces it to be.

... that which produces effects within another reality must be termed a reality itself, so I feel as if we had no philosophic excuse for calling the unseen or mystical world unreal.

... that here is a continuum of cosmic consciousness, against which our individuality builds, but accidental fences, and into which our several minds plunge as into a mother-sea or reservoir ... fitful influences from beyond leak in, showing otherwise unverifiable common connection.

WILLIAM JAMES, *The Principles of Psychology; The Varieties of Religious Experience and Essays in Religion and Morality*

Awakening to myself, in my situation ... I must *search for being* if I want to find my real self. But it is not till I fail in this search for intrinsic being that I begin to philosophize.
KARL JASPERS, (1883-1969), *Philosophy*

I have therefore found it necessary to deny knowledge in order to make room for faith.

What objects may be in themselves, and apart from all this receptivity of our sensibility, remains completely unknown to us.

Synthesis in general ... is the mere result of the power of imagination, a blind but indispensable function of the soul, without which we should have no knowledge whatsoever, but of which we are scarcely ever conscious.

Psychologists have hitherto failed to realise that imagination is a necessary ingredient of perception itself.

I have no knowledge of myself as I am, but merely as I appear to myself.

Moral theology ... is a conviction of the existence of a supreme being - a conviction which bases itself on moral laws.

Belief in God and in another world is so interwoven with my moral sentiment that as there is little danger of my losing the latter, there is equally little cause for fear that the former can ever be taken from me.

If we judge objects merely according to concepts, then all representation of beauty is lost. Thus there can be no rule according to which anyone is to be forced to recognise anything as beautiful.

Two things fill the mind with ever new and increasing admiration and awe, the oftener and more steadily we reflect on them: *the starry heavens above and the moral law within.*

We do not need science and philosophy to know what we should do to be honest and good, yea, even wise and virtuous.

There will always be metaphysics in the world, and what is more in everyone, especially in every thinking man.
IMMANUEL KANT, *Critique of Pure Reason; Critique of Judgement; Critique of Practical Reason and Prolegomena to Any Future Metaphysics*, page 136

The greatest hazard of all, losing one's self, can occur very quietly in the world, as if it were nothing at all. No other loss can occur so quietly; any other loss - an arm, a leg, five dollars, a wife, etc. - is sure to be noticed.

Without risk there is no faith. Faith is precisely the contradiction between the infinite passion of the individual's inwardness and the objective uncertainty. If I am capable of grasping God objectively, I do not believe, but precisely because I cannot do this I must believe. If I wish to preserve myself in faith I must constantly be intent upon holding fast to the objective uncertainty, so as to remain out upon the deep, over seventy thousand fathoms of water, still

preserving my faith.

The paradox in Christian truth is invariably due to the fact that it is truth as it exists for God. The standard of measure and the end is super-human; and there is only one relationship possible: faith.
SOREN KIERKEGAARD, *The Sickness Unto Death; Concluding Unscientific Postscript and The Journals of Soren Kierkegaard*

Philosophy of science without history of science is empty; history of science without philosophy of science is blind.
IMRE LAKATOS, (1922- 1974), *Boston Studies in the Philosophy of Science*

All things are understood by God *a priori*, as eternal truths; for he does not need experience, and yet all things are known by him adequately. We, on the other hand, know scarcely anything adequately, and only a few things *a priori*; most things we know by experience, in the case of which other principles and other criteria must be applied.

As there is an infinite number of possible universes

in the ideas of God, and as only one can exist, there must be a sufficient reason for God's choice, to determine him to one rather than to another. And this reason can only be found in the *fitness*, or in the degrees of perfection, which these worlds contain.

This connection or adaption of all created things with each, and of each with all the rest, means that each simple substance has relations which express all the others, and hence is a perpetual living mirror of the universe.

There is a world of created beings - living things, animals, entelechies, and souls - in the least part of matter ... Thus there is nothing waste, nothing sterile, nothing dead in the universe; no chaos, no confusions, save in appearance.

Everything is regulated in all things once for all with as much order and agreement as possible, since supreme wisdom and goodness cannot act without perfect harmony: the present is big with the future, what is to come could be read in the past, what is distant expressed in what is near. The beauty of the Universe could be learnt in each soul, could one unravel all its folds which develop perceptibly only with time.

This supreme wisdom, united to a goodness that is no less infinite, cannot but have chosen the best ... There would be something to correct in the actions of God if it were possible to do better ... So it may be said that if this were not the best of all possible worlds, God would not have created any.
GOTTFRIED WILHELM LEIBNIZ, *Universal Synthesis and Analysis; Monadology; Principles of Nature and Grace and Theodicy*

What am I? What ought I to do? What may I hope and believe? To this everything in philosophy may be reduced. It were to be wished that other things might be thus simplified; at least we ought to try whether everything that we intend to treat of in a book cannot at once be so epitomized.
GEORG CHRISTOPH LICHTENBERG, *The Reflections of Lichtenberg*

... the *nominal Essence* of *Gold,* is that complex *Idea* the word *Gold* stands for, let it be, for instance, a Body yellow, of a certain weight, malleable, fusible, and fixed. But the *real Essence* is the constitution of the insensible parts of that Body, on which those Qualities, and all the other Properties of *Gold* depend. How far these two are different, though they are both called *Essence,* is obvious, at first sight, to discover.
JOHN LOCKE, *An Essay Concerning Human Understanding,* Book 3, Chapter 6.2

In reality, the other is not shut up inside my perspective of the world, because this perspective itself has no definite limits, because it slips spontaneously into the other's, and because both are brought together in one single world in which we all participate as anonymous subjects of perception.
It is true that I do not feel that I am the constituting agent either of the natural or of the cultural world ... Yet the fact remains that I am the one by whom they are experienced ,... the indeclinable *I* ... Consciousnesses present themselves with the absurdity of a multiple solipsism.
Solipsism would be strictly true only of someone who managed to be tacitly aware of his existence without being or doing anything, which is impossible, since existing is being in and of the world. The philosopher cannot fail to draw others with him into his reflective retreat, because in the uncertainty of the world, he has for ever learned to treat them as *consorts,* and because all his knowledge is built on this datum of opinion.
MAURICE MERLEAU-PONTY, *Phenomenology of Perception*

... desiring a thing and finding it pleasant, aversion to it and thinking of it as painful, are phenomena entirely inseparable, or rather two parts of the same phenomenon; in strictness of language, two different modes of naming the same psychological fact... to desire anything, except in proportion as the idea of it is pleasant, is a physical and metaphysical impossibility.

It is better to be a human being dissatisfied than a pig satisfied; better to be Socrates dissatisfied than a fool satisfied. And if the fool, or the pig, is of a different opinion, it is because they only know their own side of the question.

The modern mind is, what the ancient mind was not, brooding and self-conscious; and its meditative self-consciousness has discovered depths in the human soul which the Greeks and Romans did not dream of, and would not have understood. But what they had got to express, they expressed in a manner which few even of the greatest moderns have attempted to rival.

JOHN STUART MILL,
Utilitarianism and Inaugural Address

There are no facts, only interpretations.

Physicists believe in a 'true world' in their own fashion ... But they are in error. The atom they posit is inferred according to the logic of the persepctivism of consciousness - and is therefore itself a subjective fiction. This world picture they sketch differs in no essential way from the subjective world picture: it is only construed with more extended sense, but with *our* senses nonetheless.

[Anything which] is a living and not a dying body ... will have to be an incarnate will to power, it will strive to grow, spread, seize, become predominant - not from any morality or immorality but because it is *living* and because life simply *is* will to powe r... 'Exploitation' ... belongs to the *essence* of what lives, as a basic organic function; it is a consequence of the will to power, which is after all the will of life.

I teach you the Superman. Man is something that should be overcome.

Man is a rope, tied between beast and Superman - a rope over an abyss.

All instincts that do not discharge themselves outwardly *turn inward* - this is what I call the *internalisation* of man: thus it was that man first developed what was later called his 'soul'. The entire inner world, originally as thin as if it were stretched between two membranes, expanded and extended itself, acquired depth, breadth and height, in the same measure as the outward discharge was *inhibited*.

All psychology so far has got stuck in moral prejudices and fears; it has not dared to descend into the depths.

Philosophy, as I have so far understood and lived it, means living voluntarily among ice and high mountains, - seeking out everything strange and questionable in existence, everything so far placed under a ban by morality.

Those thinkers in whom all stars move in cyclic orbits are not the most profound. Whoever looks into himself as into vast space and carries galaxies in himself, also knows how irregular all galaxies are; they lead into the chaos and labyrinth of existence.

I tell you: one must have chaos in one, to give birth to a dancing star.
FRIEDRICH NIETZSCHE, *Nachlass; The Will to Power; Beyond Good and Evil; On The Genealogy of Morals; Ecce Homo; The Gay Science; Thus Spoke Zarathustra*

Man is only a reed, the weakest in nature, but he is a thinking reed. There is no need for the whole universe to take up arms to crush him: a vapour, a drop of water is enough to kill him. But even if the universe were to crush him, man would still be nobler than his slayer, because he knows that he is dying and the advantage the universe has over him. The universe knows none of this.

Thus all our dignity consists in thought. It is on thought that we must depend for our recovery, not on space and time, which we could never fill. Let us then strive to think well; that is the basic principle of morality.
BLAISE PASCAL, (1623-1662), *Pensées*, Number 200

There is a reality behind the world as it appears to us, possibly a many-layered reality, of which the appearances are the outermost

layers. What the great scientist does is boldly to guess, daringly to conjecture, what these inner realities are like. This is akin to myth making ... The boldness can be gauged by the distance between the world of appearance and the conjectured reality, the explanatory hypotheses.
KARL POPPER, (b. 1902), *The Philosophy of Karl Popper*, Replies to my Critics

I have been accused of denying consciousness, but I am not conscious of having done so. Consciousness is to me a mystery, and not one to be dismissed. We know what it is like to be conscious, but not how to put it into satisfactory scientific terms. Whatever it precisely may be, consciousness is a state of the body, a state of nerves.
WILLARD V.O. QUINE, *Quiddities: An Intermittently Philosophical Dictionary*

Yea is the beginning. Nay cannot be the beginning for it could only be a Nay of the Nought. This, however, would presuppose a negatable Nought, a Nay, therefore, that had already decided on a Yea. Therefore Yea is the beginning.
FRANZ ROSENZWEIG, (1886-1929), *The Star of Redemption*

Man was born free, and he is everywhere in chains. Those who think themselves the masters of others are indeed greater slaves than they. How did this transformation come about? I do not know. How can it be made legitimate? That question I believe I can answer.
... social man lives constantly outside himself, and only knows how to live in the opinion of others, so that he seems to receive the consciousness of his own existence merely from the judgement of others concerning him ... everything being reduced to appearances, there is but art and mummery in even honour, friendship, virtue and often vice itself, of which we at length learn the secret of boasting; ... in short ... always asking others what we are, and never daring to ask ourselves,

... we have nothing to show for ourselves but a frivolous and deceitful appearance, honour without virtue, reason without wisdom, and pleasure without happiness.
JEAN-JAQUES ROUSSEAU, *The Social Contract and A Discourse on the Origin of Inequality*

When you have taken account of all the feelings roused by Napoleon in writers and readers of history, you have not touched the actual man; but in the case of Hamlet you have come to the end of him. If no one thought about Hamlet, there would be nothing left of him; if no one had thought about Napoleon, he would soon have seen to it that someone did. The sense of reality is vital in logic, and whoever juggles with it by pretending that Hamlet has another kind of reality is doing a disservice to thought. A robust sense of reality is very necessary in framing a correct analysis of propositions about unicorns, golden mountains, round squares, and other such pseudo-objects.
BERTRAND RUSSELL, *Introduction to Mathematical Philosophy*

... I am the self which I will be, in the mode of not being it.
Nothingness is not, Nothingness 'is made-to-be' ... The being by which Nothingness comes to the world must be its own Nothingness.
... This *nothing* is human reality itself as the radical negation by means of which the world is revealed ... human reality is that which causes *there to be* nothing outside of being.
... every action, no matter how trivial, is not the simple effect of the prior psychic state and does not result from a linear determinism but rather is integrated as a secondary structure in global structures and finally in the totality which I am.
JEAN-PAUL SARTRE, *Being and Nothingness*

The eternal, timeless act of self-consciousness which we call Self is that which gives all things existence.
F.W.J. SCHELLING, (1775-1854), *Systems of Transcendental Idealism*

'The world is my representation': this is a truth valid with reference to every living and knowing being, although man alone can bring it into reflective, abstract consciousness. If he really does so, philosophical discernment has dawned on him. It then becomes clear and certain to him that he does not know a sun and an earth, but only an eye that sees a sun, a hand that feels an earth; that the world around him is there only as representation, in other words, only in reference to another thing, namely that which represents, and this is himself.

The concept of *will* is of all possible concepts the only one that has its origin *not* in the phenomenon, *not* in the mere representation of perception, but which comes from within, and proceeds from the most immediate consciousness of everyone. In this consciousness each one knows and at the same time is himself his own individuality according to its nature immediately, without any form, even the form of subject and object, for here knower and known coincide.
ARTHUR SCHOPENHAUER, *The World as Will and Representation*

God is the cause of all things, which are in him.

In nature there is nothing contingent, but all things have been determined from the necessity of the divine nature to exist and produce an effect in a certain way.

By *natura naturata* I understand whatever follows from the necessity of God's nature.

The will cannot be called a free cause, but only a necessary one.

The human mind is part of the infinite intellect of God. Therefore, when we say the human mind perceives this or that, we are saying nothing but that God, not insofar as he is infinite, but insofar as he is explained through the nature of the human mind... has this or that idea.
BENEDICT SPINOZA, *Ethics*, Parts I and II

Opposed elements stand to each other in mutual

requirement. In their unity,
they inhibit or contrast. God
and the World stand to each
other in this opposed
requirement. God is the
infinite ground of all
mentality, the unity of vision
seeking physical multiplicity.
The World is the multiplicity
of finites, actualities seeking a
perfected unity. Neither God,
nor the World, reaches static
completion. Both are in the
grip of the ultimately
metaphysical ground, the
creative advance into novelty.
Either of them, God and the
World, is the instrument of
novelty for the other.
ALFRED NORTH
WHITEHEAD, *Process and
Reality*

What is your aim in
philosophy? - To shew the fly
the way out of the fly-bottle.
  There is no such thing as
the subject that thinks or
entertains ideas.
If I wrote a book called *The
World as I found it*, I should
have to include a report on
my body, and should have to
say which parts were
subordinate to my will, and
which were not, etc., this

being a method of isolating
the subject, or rather of
showing that in an important
sense there is no subject; for it
alone could *not* be mentioned
in that book. The subject
does not belong to the world:
rather, it is a limit of the
world.
  The sense of the world
must lie outside the world. In
the world everything is as it is,
and everything happens as it
does happen: in it no value
exists - and if it did exist, it
would have no value.
LUDWIG WITTGENSTEIN,
*Philosophical Investigations and
Tractatus Logico-Philosophicus*

THIRTY-FIVE

MUSIC

Sacred music causes flight to sadness and to the evil spirits because the spirit of Jehovah sings happily in a heart filled with holy joy.
HEINRICH KHUNRATH

Musical harmony is a most powerful conceiver. It allures the celestial influences and changes affections, intentions, gestures, notions, actions, and dispositions ... Fish in the lake of Alexandria are delighted with harmonious sounds; music has caused friendship between dolphins and men. The playing of the harp affects the Hyperborean swans. Melodious voices tame the Indian elephants. The elements themselves delight in music.
CORNELIUS AGRIPPA

Yea, music is the Prophet's art
Among the gifts that God hath sent,
One of the most magnificent!
LONGFELLOW, Christus,
Part III, Second Interlude,
Stanza 5

Music ... in remote times was not only cultivated, but venerated to such an extent that the same men were regarded as musicians, poets and sages, among whom Orpheus and Linus ... Because he tamed savage and unruly spirits by charming them. Orpheus gained a reputation not only for moving wild beasts, but even rocks and trees.
QUINTILIAN

Allah has not sent a Prophet except with a beautiful voice.
MUHAMMAD

The purpose of music, considered in relation to God, is to arouse longings for Him and passionate love towards Him and to produce states in which He reveals Himself and shows His favour, which are beyond description and are known only by experience, and, by the Sûfis, these states are called 'ecstasy'. The heart's attainment of these states through hearing music is due to the mystic relationship which God has ordained between the rhythm of music and the spirit of man. The human spirit is so affected by that rhythm, that music is the cause to it of

longing and joy and sorrow and 'expansion' (*inbisât*) and 'contraction' (*inqibâd*), but he who is dull of hearing and unresponsive and hard of heart, is debarred from this joy.
AL-GHAZÂLÎ

Serious music preserves and restores the consonance of the parts of the Soul, as Plato and Aristotle say and as we have experienced frequently.
MARSILIO FICINO

Music was created for the consummation of concord in human nature, not to be the cause of voluptuousness.
HUAI NAN TZÛ

Music does not give rise, in the heart, to anything which is not already there: so he whose inner self is attached to anything else than God is stirred by music to sensual desire, but the one who is inwardly attached to the love of God is moved, by hearing music, to do His will... The common folk listen to music according to nature, and the novices listen with desire and awe, while the listening of the saints brings them a vision of the Divine gifts and graces, and these are the gnostics to whom listening means contemplation. But finally, there is the listening of the spiritually perfect, to whom, through music, God reveals Himself unveiled.
AL-SUHRAWARDÎ

There let the pealing organ blow,
To the full voiced quire below,
In service high, and anthems clear,
As may with sweetness, through mine ear,
Dissolve me into ecstasies,
And bring all heaven before mine eyes.
MILTON, *Il Penseroso*, line 161

Harmony, which has motions akin to the revolutions of our souls, is not regarded by the intelligent votary of the Muses as given by them with a view to irrational pleasure, which is deemed to be the purpose of it in our day, but as meant to correct any discord which may have arisen in the courses of the soul, and to be our ally in bringing her into harmony

and agreement with herself;
and rhythm too was given by
them for the same reason, on
account of the irregular and
graceless ways which prevail
among mankind generally, and
to help us against them.
PLATO, *Timaeus*, 47 C

The singers have hushed their
notes of clear song:
The red sleeves of the dancers
are motionless.
Hugging his lute, the old
harper of Chao
Rocks and sways as he touches
the five chords.
The loud notes swell and
scatter abroad:
'Sa, sa,' like wind blowing the
rain.
The soft notes dying almost to
nothing:
'Ch'ieh, ch'ieh,' like the voice
of ghosts talking.
Now as glad as the magpie's
lucky song:
Again bitter as the gibbon's
ominous cry.
His ten fingers have no fixed
note:
Up and down - 'kung,' chih,
and yü.
And those who sit and listen
to the tune he plays
Of soul and body lose the

mastery.
And those who pass that way
as he plays the tune,
Suddenly stop and cannot
raise their feet.

Alas, alas that the ears of
common men
Should love the modern and
not love the old.
Thus it is that the harp in the
green window
Day by day is covered deeper
with dust.
PO CHÜ-I, *The Harper of
Chao*

The Pythagoreans said, that
an harmonic sound is
produced from the motion of
the celestial bodies; and they
scientifically collected this
from the analogy of their
intervals; since not only the
ratios of the intervals of the
sun and moon, and Venus and
Mercury, but also of the other
stars, were discovered by
them.
SIMPLICIUS

I cannot dance O lord, unless
Thou lead me.
If Thou wilt that I leap
joyfully
Then must Thou Thyself first

dance and sing!
Then will I leap for love
From love to knowledge.
From knowledge to fruition,
From fruition to beyond all
human sense.
There will I remain
And circle evermore.
MECHTHILD OF
MAGDEBURG

The ancient kings were ever
careful about things that
affected the human heart.
They tried therefore to guide
the people's ideals and
aspirations by means of li*,
establish harmony in sounds
by means of music, regulate
conduct by means of
government, and prevent
immorality by means of
punishments. Li*, music,
punishments and government
have a common goal, which is
to bring about unity in the
people's hearts and carry out
the principles of political
order.
Music rises from the human
heart. When the emotions
are touched, they are
expressed in sounds, and when
the sounds take definite forms,
we have music. Therefore the
music of a peaceful and
prosperous country is quiet
and joyous, and the
government is orderly; the
music of a country in turmoil
shows dissatisfaction and
anger, and the government is
chaotic; and the music of a
destroyed country shows
sorrow and remembrance of
the past, and the people are
distressed. Thus we see music
and government are directly
connected with one another.
CONFUCIUS
*Li can mean ritual, propriety,
tradition, depending on the
context.

He has moved a little nearer
To the Master of all music.
LONGFELLOW, Hiawatha,
Part XV, line 56

The whole Pythagoric school
produced certain appropriate
songs, usefully conducting the
dispositions of the soul to
passions contrary to those
which it before possessed. For
when they went to bed they
purified the reasoning power
from the perturbations and
noises to which it had been
exposed during the day, by
certain odes and peculiar
songs, and by this means

procured for themselves
tranquil sleep, and few and
good dreams. But when they
rose from bed, they again
liberated themselves from the
torpor and heaviness of sleep,
by songs of another kind.
Sometimes, also, by musical
sounds alone, unaccompanied
with words, they healed the
passions of the soul and
certain diseases, enchanting,
as they say, in reality. And it
is probable that from hence
this name *epode*, i.e.
enchantment, came to be
generally used. After this
manner, therefore, Pythagoras
through music produced the
most beneficial correction of
human manners and lives.
IAMBLICHUS

Music expresses the harmony
of the universe, while rituals
express the order of the
universe. Through harmony
all things are influenced, and
through order all things have
a proper place. Music rises
from heaven, while rituals are
patterned on the earth. To go
beyond these patterns would
result in violence and disorder.
In order to have the proper
rituals and music, we must
understand the principles of
Heaven and Earth.
CONFUCIUS

Since the celestial spheres
revolve and the planets and
stars are moved, it follows that
they must have musical notes
and expressions with which
God is glorified, delighting the
souls of the angels, just as in
the corporeal world our souls
listen with delight to melodies
and obtain relief from care
and sorrow. And inasmuch as
these melodies are but echoes
of heavenly music, they recall
to us the spacious gardens of
Paradise and the pleasures
enjoyed by the souls dwelling
there; and then our souls long
to fly up thither and rejoin
their mates.
THE RASÂ'IL OF THE
IKHWÂNU 'I-SAFÂ

Our songs are the same as His
songs.
Chândogya Upanishad, I. vii. 5

The Powers which are in all
things sing within me also.
HERMES

Three sorts of Persons are led
to God, the *Musician* by

Harmony, the *Philosopher* by the *beam* of *Truth*, the *Lover* by the *light of Beauty*. All these *Conductors* to the *supream Being* meet in this *Love*, of which we speak; the *first* and *only true Beauty*, being the *first Birth*, the first *Effulgency*, the *essential Image* of the *supream Goodness*, is also the *first*, the *supream*, the *only Truth*; the *Original*, the *measure*, the *end of all Truth*; which by its amiable attractive Light, conducteth all Understandings in the search of Truth, and giveth them rest only in its transparent and blissful Bosom. This also is the *first*, the *only*, the *universal Harmony*, the *Musick* of all things in Heaven and on Earth; the Musick, in which all things of Earth and of Heaven, meet to make *one melodious* Consort.
PLATO

In relating the things of the earth to the celestial, and those of heaven to the inferior, the Chaldeans have shown in the mutual affections between these parts of the universe (which are separated in space but not in essence) the harmony that unites them in a sort of musical accord.
PHILO OF ALEXANDRIA

All songs are a part of Him, who wears a form of sound.
VISHNU PURÂNA

'Tis said, the pipe and lute
that charm our ears
Derive their melody from
rolling spheres ...
We, who are parts of Adam,
heard with him
The song of angels and of
seraphim.
Our memory, though dull and
sad, retains
Some echo still of those
unearthly strains.
Oh, music is the meat of all
who love,
Music uplifts the soul to
realms above.
The ashes glow, the latent
fires increase:
We listen and are fed with joy
and peace.
RÛMÎ

Untwisting all the chains that
tie the hidden soul of
harmony.
MILTON, *L'Allegro*, line 143

Music draws to itself the human spirits (senses), which are principally vapours of the heart, as it were, so that they almost cease to act: so entirely is the soul one thing when it listens, and the power of all (the rest of the senses) seems to fly to that sensible spirit which receives sound.
DANTE, Il Convito, II. xiv. 11

By continuous practice of the Saman chants, in the prescribed manner and with concentration of mind, a man attains the Supreme Brahman ... The practice of these is indeed liberation. He who knows the inner meaning of the sound of the lute, who is expert in intervals and in modal scales and knows the rhythms, travels without effort upon the way of liberation.
YÂJÑAVALKYÂ SMRITI, III. iv. 112-115

And it came to pass, when the minstrel played, that the hand of the Lord came upon him.
II Kings 3:15

I will strike every chord in seeking spiritual transmutation, like the lute-

player whose plectrum moves up and down the strings. That, from playing the sahûr tune in this fashion, the seas of Divine mercy may surge to scatter their pearls and lavish their bounty.
RÛMÎ

Allâh listens more intently to a man with a beautiful voice reading the Qur'ân than does a master of a singing-girl to her singing.
MUHAMMAD

The music which is called Gândharva (Mârga) is that which has been from time immemorial, practised by the Gandharvas (celestial singers) and which leads surely to Moksa (liberation), while the Gâna (Desî) music is that which has been invented by composers.
RÂMÂMÂTYA

Musical innovation is full of danger to the whole State, and ought to be prohibited. So Damon tells me, and I can quite believe him: - he says that when modes of music change the fundamental laws of the State always change

with them.
PLATO, *Republic* IV. 424 BC

The music of Cheng is lewd and corrupting, the music of Sung is soft and makes one effeminate, the music of Wei is repetitious and annoying, and the music of Ch'i is harsh and makes one haughty. These four kinds of music are all sensual music and undermine the people's character, and that is why they cannot be used at the sacrifices. The *Book of Songs* says, 'The harmonious sounds are *shu* and *yung* and my ancestor listened to them.' *Shu* means 'pious' and *yung* means 'peaceful'. If you have piety and peacefulness of character, you can do everything you want with a country.
CONFUCIUS

The soul continues as an instrument of God's harmony, a tuned instrument of divine joy for the Spirit to strike on.
BOEHME

Beauty addresses itself chiefly to sight; but there is a beauty for the hearing too, as in certain combinations of words and in all kinds of music, for melodies and cadences are beautiful; and minds that lift themselves above the realm of sense to a higher order are aware of beauty in the conduct of life, in actions, in character, in the pursuits of the intellect; and there is the beauty of the virtues.
PLOTINUS

Sound produced from ether is known as 'unstruck'. In this unstruck sound the Gods delight. The Yogis, the Great Spirits, projecting their minds by an effort of the mind into this unstruck sound, depart, attaining Liberation.
Struck sound is said to give pleasure, 'unstruck' sound gives Liberation.
This (unstruck sound) having no relation with human enjoyment does not interest ordinary men.
Sañgîtā Makarandā 1.4-6; *Nārandâ Purânā*; *Shivā tattvā Ratnākarâ*, 6, 7, 12

Consequently the most perfect, faultless harmony cannot be perceived by the ear, for it exists not in things

sensible but only as an ideal conceived by the mind ... No man can hear it while still in the body, for it is wholly spiritual and would draw to itself the essence of the soul, as infinite light would attract all light to itself. Such infinitely perfect harmony, in consequence, would be heard only in ecstasy by the ear of the intellect, once the soul was free from the things of sense.
NICHOLAS OF CUSA

(Pythagoras) fixed his intellect in the sublime symphonies of the world, he alone hearing and understanding, as it appears, the universal harmony and consonance of the spheres, and the stars that are moved through them, and which produce a fuller and more intense melody than any thing effected by mortal sounds. This melody also was the result of dissimilar and variously differing sounds, celerities, magnitudes, and intervals, arranged with reference to each other in a certain most musical ratio, and thus producing a most

gentle, and at the same time variously beautiful motion and convolution.
IAMBLICHUS

Since the drum is often the only instrument used in our sacred rites, I should perhaps tell you here why it is especially sacred and important to us. It is because the round form of the drum represents the whole universe, and its steady strong beat is the pulse, the heart, throbbing at the centre of the universe. It is as the voice of *Wakan-Tanka*, and this sound stirs us and helps us to understand the mystery and power of all things.
BLACK ELK

God hath men who enter Paradise through their flutes and drums.
MUHAMMAD

When you see the type of a nation's dance, you know its character.
CONFUCIUS

All the dancer's gestures are signs of things, and the dance is called rational, because it

aptly signifies and displays
something over and above the
pleasure of the senses.
ST. AUGUSTINE

The Supreme Intelligence
dances in the soul ... for the
purpose of removing our sins.
By these means, our Father
scatters the darkness of
illusion (*maya*), burns the
thread of causality (*karma*),
stamps down evil (*mala,
anava, avidya*), showers Grace,
and lovingly plunges the soul
in the ocean of Bliss (*ananda*).
They never see rebirths, who
behold this mystic dance.
Unmai Vilakkam, v. 32.37.39

The movement of whose body
is the world, whose speech the
sum of all language,
Whose jewels are the moon
and stars - to that pure Siva I
bow!
Abhinaya Darpana

Why should not every Sûfî
begin to dance, like a mote,
In the sun of eternity, that it
may deliver him from decay?
Dîvâni Shamsi Tabrîz, XXXIX

God can be served in different
ways. An ecstatic lover of
God enjoys Him in different
ways. Sometimes he says, 'O
God, You are the lotus and I
am the bee,' sometimes God
says, 'I am Your dancing-girl.'
He dances and sings before
Him. He thinks of himself
sometimes as the friend of
God and sometimes as His
handmaid. He looks on God
sometimes as a child, as did
Yasodâ, and sometimes as
husband or sweetheart, as did
the gopis.
SRI RAMAKRISHNA

But who would dare to say
that music is in essence an
architectural representation
when, on the contrary, this
only enters the field of sound
as the depiction of our
phenomenal world? To aim at
architecture is to remain
outside the states that
constitute the very being of
music. It is vain to object
that Bach and the early
composers [*primitifs*],
Beethoven and his successors,
and Wagner and César Franck
built on the traditions of
perfect architectures. Who
cannot see that Beethoven
surpasses at every moment the

rational data of form, and by adapting them to his vision, smashes the sacred moulds?
ALBERT TROTROT, from *Review of Les Entretiens Idealistes*, (1906)

George Herbert's love to music was such, that he usually went twice a week, at certain appointed days, to the Cathedral at Salisbury; and at his return, would say, - "That the time spent in prayer and cathedral-music elevated his soul, and was his heaven upon earth." But before his return thence to Bemerton (his parish) he would usually sing, and play his part, at an appointed private music-meeting.
ALFRED SINDALL

Musical training is a more potent instrument than any other, because rhythm and harmony find their way into the inward places of the soul, on which they mightily fasten, imparting grace, and making the soul of him who is rightly educated graceful, or of him who is ill-educated ungraceful.
PLATO, *Republic*, III. 401 D

When I was employed upon the Oratorio of "The Creation," I felt myself so penetrated with religious feeling, that before I sat down to the pianoforte I prayed to God with earnestness that He would enable me to praise Him worthily.
HAYDN

Tones rise from the human heart, and music is connected with the principles of human conduct. Therefore the animals know sounds but do not know tones, and the common people know tones but do not know music. Only the superior man is able to understand music. Thus from a study of the sounds, one comes to understand the tones; from a study of the tones, one comes to understand music; and from the study of music, one comes to understand the principles of government and is thus fully prepared for being a ruler.
CONFUCIUS

Music is the art of the prophets, the only art that can *calm* the agitations of the soul; it is one of the most

magnificent and delightful
presents God has given us.
LUTHER

For *Musicke* is the *Handmaid*
of the LORD,
And for his *Worship* was at
first ordayned;
Yea therewithall she fitly doth
accord;
And where *Devotion* thriveth
is retayned,
Still, by a naturall power, doth
helpe to raise,
The *Mind* to God when joyful
Notes are sounded:
And *Passions* fierce
distemperatures alaies,
When by grave *Tones* and
Melody is bounded.
GEORGE WITHER, *Emblem*, 3

Praise ye the Lord. Praise
God in his Sanctuary: praise
him in the firmament of his
power.
Praise him for his mighty acts:
praise him according to his
excellent greatness.
Praise him with the sound of
the trumpet: praise him with
the psaltery and harp.
Praise him with the timbrel
and dance: praise him with
stringed instruments and
organs.

Praise him upon the loud
cymbals: praise him upon the
high sounding cymbals.
Let every thing that hath
breath praise the Lord. Praise
ye the Lord.
Psalms 150

Music is the only sensual
gratification which mankind
may indulge in to excess
without injury to their moral
or religious feelings.
THOMAS ADDISON

There is in souls a sympathy
with sounds,
And as the mind is pitch'd,
the ear is pleas'd
With melting airs of martial,
brisk or grave.
Some chord in unison with
what we hear
Is touch'd within us, and the
heart replies.
WILLIAM COWPER

Music exalts each joy, allays
each grief
Expels disease, softens every
pain,
Subdues the rage of poison
and of plague.
ARMSTRONG

To know the science of music is nothing else than this - to know how all things are ordered, and how God's design has assigned to each its place; for the ordered system in which each and all by the supreme Artist's skill are wrought together into a single whole yields a divinely musical harmony, sweet and true beyond all melodious sounds.
HERMES

Music so softens and disarms the mind
That not an arrow does resistance find.
WALLER

And in their motions harmony divine
So smoothes her charming tones, that God's own ear
Listens delighted.
MILTON, *Paradise Lost*, Book, Verse 620

Of all the arts beneath the heaven,
That man has found, or God has given,
None draws the soul so sweet away,
As music's melting, mystic lay;

Slight emblem of the bliss above,
It soothes the spirit all to love.
HOGG

There's music in the sighing of a reed;
There's music in the gushing of a rill;
There's music in all things, if men had ears
Their earth is but an echo of the spheres.
BYRON

Music moves us, and we know not why; we feel the tears, but cannot trace their source. Is it the language of some other state, born of its memory? For what can wake the soul's strong instinct of another world, like music?
LANDON

From harmony, from heavenly harmony, this universal frame began: when Nature underneath a heap of jarring atoms lay, and could not heave her head, the tuneful voice was heard from high, Arise, ye more than dead! Then cold, and hot, and moist, and dry in order to their stations leap, and Music's

power obey. From harmony, from heavenly harmony this universal frame began; from harmony to harmony through all the compass of the notes it ran, the diapason closing full in Man.
As from the power of sacred lays the spheres began to move, and sung the great Creator's praise to all the blest above; so when the last and dreadful hour this crumbling pageant shall devour, the trumpet shall be heard on high, the dead shall live, the living die, and Music shall untune the sky.
DRYDEN

How sweet the moonlight sleeps upon this bank! Here we will sit, and let the sounds of music creep in our ears: soft stillness and the night become the touches of sweet harmony...
Such harmony is in immortal souls; but, whilst this muddy vesture of decay doth grossly close it in, we cannot hear it.
WILLIAM SHAKESPEARE

There is music in all things, if men had ears.
BYRON

Music is the universal language of mankind.
LONGFELLOW

The meaning of song goes deep. Who is there that, in logical words, can express the effect music has on us? It is a kind of inarticulate, unfathomable speech, which leads us to the edge of the Infinite, and lets us for a moment gaze into that!
THOMAS CARLYLE

Long ago the Egyptians appear to have recognised the very principle of which we are now speaking - that their young citizens must be habituated to forms and strains of virtue. These they fixed, and exhibited the patterns of them in their temples; and no painter or artist is allowed to innovate upon them, or to leave the traditional forms and invent new ones. To this day, no alteration is allowed either in these arts, or in music at all. And you will find that their works of art are painted or moulded in the same forms which they had ten thousand years ago... A law-giver may institute

melodies which have a natural truth and correctness without any fear of failure. To do this, however, must be the work of God, or of a divine person; in Egypt they have a tradition that their ancient chants which have been preserved for so many ages are the composition of the Goddess Isis ... The love of novelty which arises out of pleasure in the new and weariness of the old, has not strength enough to corrupt the consecrated song and dance, under the plea that they have become antiquated.
PLATO, *Laws* II, 656 D

Music is the fourth great material want of our natures - first food, then raiment, then shelter, then music.
BOVEE

Music is a thing of the soul - a rose-lipped shell that murmurs of the eternal sea: a strange bird singing the songs of another shore.
HOLLAND

The essentially active function of music may force the listener into such a state of passivity that his faculty of musical perception will crave only pieces which offer no resistance whatever, which in every respect satisfy his basest instincts - music which is nothing but a cheap and trashy amenity, an opiate always and everywhere available. Our present era, in which the majority of listeners is constantly subject to this kind of music, has, in my opinion, reached a point below which a further degeneration of the Boethian attitude is impossible.

In spite of this gloomy statement, I do not mean that the situation is hopeless. There still are, and always will be, composers who are more than mere arrangers of sounds. Among the multitudes of listeners there exist large groups who demand more from music than a permanent lulling accompaniment to their most banal activities. And not all performers are as godforsaken as many of our virtuosi with their limited repertoire of circus tricks. Finally, in that science which deals with the essence, the effects, and the history of

music, one observes a growing tendency to replace the predominantly materialistic methods of the past with ways of research and communication the impulses of which stem from a closer inclination towards an Augustinian interpretation of music and its functions. The durable values of music are not forgotten; they are as alive as they were thousands of years ago, and we as musicians can do nothing better than to accept them as the guiding principles for our work.
PAUL HINDSMITH, from A Composer's World

Listen to music religiously, as if it were the last strain you might hear.
HENRY DAVID THOREAU

The best sort of music is what it should be - sacred; the next best, the military, has fallen to the lot of the devil.
SAMUEL TAYLOR COLERIDGE

MUSIC belongs to the reality-systems that depend on EMOTION, and specifically on the system where the GOOD PRINCIPLE of the world manifests through emotion, i.e., the SUBJECTIVE FINALITY of creation constituting BEAUTY. We will later see, in particular, that the special beauty consisting of a simple ESTHETIC CAUSALITY or sensible expression, and manifesting through the EMBODIMENT OF INTELLIGENCE IN TONES, is the object of MUSIC. - Such, then, following this absolute generation of different reality-systems that make up the universe, is the PHILOSOPHICAL DEFINITION OF MUSIC, in which we discover immediately that the FIRST PRINCIPLE of this art, considered as a science, consists of the esthetic modifications of TIME, which alone constitutes a priori an embodiment of the spirit or intelligence forming the object of music.
COUNT CAMILLE DURIETTE, from Esthétique Musicale

Music is the universal language of mankind.

LONGFELLOW, *Ancient Spanish Ballads*, Outre-Mer

Mathematics and music are the principles of the measured harmonies known to us. They are also eminently the divine language: mathematics for justice [*justice*], music for accuracy [*justesse*]. Where would the systematic unity of the universe be if our passions were excluded from this measured harmony, which is in our eyes the seal of divine and material justice?
CHARLES FOURIER, from *Des Séries Mesurées*

When I hear music I fear no danger, I am invulnerable, I see no foe. I am related to the earliest times, and to the latest.
HENRY DAVID THOREAU

Harmonies unheard create the harmonies we hear and wake the soul to the consciousness of beauty, showing it the one essence in another kind; for the measures of our music are not arbitrary, but are determined by the Principle whose labour is to dominate matter and bring pattern into being.
PLOTINUS

Lorenzo:
How sweet the moonlight
sleeps upon this bank!
Here will we sit, and let
the sounds of music
Creep in our ears: soft
stillness and the night
Become the touches of
sweet harmony.
Sit, Jessica: look how the
floor of heaven
Is thick inlaid with patines
of bright gold;
There's not the smallest
orb which thou behold'st
But in his motion like an
angel sings,
Still quiring to the young-
eyed cherubins:
Such harmony is in
immortal souls;
But whilst this muddy
vesture of decay
Doth grossly close it in, we
cannot hear it.
Come, ho, and wake Diana
with a hymn!
With sweetest touches
pierce your mistress' ear,
And draw her home with
music.

Jessica:
I am never merry when I
hear sweet music.

Lorenzo:
The reason is, your spirits
are attentive:
For do but note a wild and
wanton herd,
Or race of youthful and
unhandled colts,
Fetching mad bounds,
bellowing, and neighing
loud,
Which is the hot condition
of their blood;
If they but hear perchance
a trumpet sound,
Or any air of music touch
their ears,
You shall perceive them
make a mutual stand,
Their savage eyes turn'd to
a modest gaze
By the sweet power of
music: therefore the poet
Did feign that Orpheus
drew trees, stones, and
floods;
Since nought so stockish,
hard, and full of rage,
But music for the time
doth change his nature.
That man that hath no
music in himself,
Nor is not moved with

concord of sweet sounds,
Is fit for treasons,
stratagems, and spoils,
The motions of his spirit
are dull as night,
And his affections dark as
Erebus;
Let no such man be
trusted. - Mark the music
...

Nerissa:
It is your music, madam, of
the house.

Portia:
Nothing is good, I see,
without respect;
Methinks it sounds much
sweeter than by day.

Nerissa:
Silence bestows that virtue
on it, madam.
WILLIAM SHAKESPEARE,
The Merchant of Venice

One man with a dream, at
pleasure,
Shall go forth and conquer a
crown
And three with a new song's
measure
Can trample a kingdom down.
A.W.E. O'SHAUGHNESSY,
Music Makers

Do you know how to begin?
Take the string or the reed,
And grow old with it in your
hand.
Wake in the night
To feel if you hold it with
freedom.
Let your mornings be heavy
With wonder if your
suppleness remains;
And the day a long labour,
And the years a fear of
stiffness.
Then perhaps towards the
end,
Time frosting your joints,
You will make music,
Shake hills,
Drag men in their multitudes
As the moon drags the sea.
RICHARD CHURCH

See deep enough, and you see
musically; the heart of nature
being everywhere music, if you
can only reach it.
THOMAS CARLYLE, *Heroes
and Hero-Worship*, Lecture 3

Music remains the only art,
the last sanctuary, wherein
originality may reveal itself in
the face of fools, and not
pierce their mental opacity.
JAMES HUNEKER,
Iconoclasts, page 142

Music, the mosaic of the Air.
ANDREW MARVELL,
Music's Empire

We agree, then, that music is
nothing other than the
perfected natural language;
that its expression is
independent of any kind of
human convention; that this
sublime and mysterious
expression, like that of nature
itself (whose accents it
imitates) is engraved in living
lines on all hearts; that it
embraces everything that
arises from feeling; that it can
only feebly be translated into
words; that it extends beyond
the limits of the imagination;
and that it has not been given
to us to be shut up within the
narrow boundaries of thought.
We agree, finally, that the
language of music is the
language of all living beings,
whether rational or not.
G.A. VILLOTEAU, *La
Musique de l'Ancienne Egypte*

The dancing foot, the sound
of the tinkling bells,
The songs that are sung, and
the various steps,
The forms assumed by our
Master as He dances,

Discover these in your own heart, so shall your bonds be broken.
TRIMÛLAR (on Natarâja, representing Siva's cosmic dance)

Melody is the part that really makes music what it is; it gives it its life and movement; it is from melody that music gets its physiognomy and character; by its means, music paints, touches, and conquers the senses. Harmony is nothing but a garment, more or less diaphanous, more or less suitable, which one throws over a beautiful body like a gauze, silk, linen or wool, allowing one to discern its forms and outlines, disguising them, or altogether suppressing them. Melody without harmony is always something; harmony without melody is nothing. The one is a lovable nymph who pleases despite her nakedness; the other, a rich drapery that can only please to the degree that it is worn with grace. Lastly, nature gives only the first, while the second is a product of art.
FABRE D'OLIVET, from *Correspondence*, 553

Musical form is nothing less than the revelation in space and time of the formal and static essence [*l'en-soi*] of the world.
ARTHUR SCHOPENHAUER, from *Metaphysics of Music*

It is at the Opera that all the faculties of the sciences and arts unite to give us the active picture of material unities, the image of the passional unities for which we are reserved. Thus the Opera will be a sacred function among the Harmonians, as the emblem of the general unity that God knows how to establish in the mechanism of the universe, and which should rule in the same way in the social unities of the globe.
CHARLES FOURIER, II, 357

The human voice is thus the magic wand of the regeneration of a people by the power of harmony, a vibrant and magnetic power which propagates in concentric rings with instantaneous speed and produces those unanimous explosions, those spontaneous

repercussions, that are the only worthy reward of noble imaginations.
H. USMAR BONNAIRE, 20

A man is alone, and in the midst of deepest calm. Not only is music nothing to him, but even the air does not exist as far as sound is concerned, since it carries none. Such a man takes his lyre, or sings; and without stirring from his place, he goes on to develop all around him the hidden riches of the air, the liveliness of tones laden with emotion, the active treasures of harmony and the magic power of chords, the still more penetrating powers of melody, whereby his inner self paints its deepest emotions. In fine, he links his inner self with the musical powers of the air, and the powers of the air with his inner self, so as to make it communicate with that pure and superior region with which music is contiguous. Thus by this performance he not only lifts his own being to the divine region, but also makes this divine region descend into his whole being.
LOUIS CLAUDE DE SAINT

MARTIN, from *De l'Esprit des Choses*

Hell is full of musical amateurs. Music is the brandy of the damned.
BERNARD SHAW, *Man and Superman*, Act III

Among all the arts, music alone can be purely religious.
MADAME DE STAËL, *Corinne*, Book VIII, Chapter 3

In periods of disorder, rites are altered and music is licentious. Then sad sounds are lacking in dignity, joyful sounds lack in calm ... When the spirit of opposition manifests itself, indecent music comes into being ... When the spirit of conformity manifests itself, harmonious music appears ... So that, under the effect of music, the five social duties are without admixture, the eyes and ears are clear, the blood and the vital spirits are balanced, habits are reformed, customs are improved, the Empire is in complete peace.
CONFUCIUS

Music is the true universal language which is understood

everywhere, so that it is ceaselessly spoken in all countries and throughout all the centuries with great zeal and earnestness, and a significant melody which says a great deal soon makes its way round the entire earth, while one poor in meaning which says nothing straightaway fades and dies: which proves that the content of a melody is very well understandable. Yet music speaks not of things but of pure weal and woe, which are the only realities for the *will*: that is why it speaks so much to the heart, while it has nothing to say *directly* to the head and it is a misuse of it to demand that it should do so, as happens in all *pictorial* music ... For expression of the passions is one thing, depiction of things another.
ARTHUR SCHOPENHAUER, from *Aphorisms on Aesthetics*

But God has a few of us whom he whispers in the ear;
The rest may reason and welcome: 'tis we musicians know.
ROBERT BROWNING, *Abt Vogler*

The language of tones belongs equally to all mankind, and melody is the absolute language in which the musician speaks to every heart.
RICHARD WAGNER, *Beethoven*

He who does not dance in remembrance of the Friend has no friend.
MUHAMMAD

God has endowed sound-vibrations, which are the highest pleasure of the ear, with such complete harmonic properties that the study of music is enough to teach one, at least in their elements, the laws of Harmony in general: laws whose finest application is in organising human societies.
VICTOR HENNEQUIN, from *La Religion*

As I went under the new telegraph-wire, I heard it vibrating like a harp high overhead. It was as the sound of a far-off glorious life, a supernal life, which came down to us, and vibrated the lattice-work of this life of ours.

H.D. THOREAU, *Journal*, 3 September 1851

There's sure no passion in the human soul
But finds its food in music.
GEORGE LILLO, *Fatal Curiosity*, Act I, Scene ii

All music is what awakes from you when you are reminded by the instruments,
It is not the violins and the cornets, it is not the oboe nor the beating drums, nor the score of the baritone singer singing his sweet romanza, nor that of the men's chorus, nor that of the women's chorus
It is nearer and farther than they.
WALT WHITMAN, *A Song for Occupations*, Part IV

I pant for the music which is divine;
My heart in its thirst is a dying flower;
Pour forth the sound like enchanted wine,
Loosen the notes in a silver shower;
Like a herbless plain, for the gentle rain,
I gasp, I faint, till they wake again.

PERCY BYSSHE SHELLEY, *Music*

Music bright as the soul of light, for wings an eagle, for notes a dove.
SWINBURNE, *Bothwell*, Act II, line 13

The music had the heat of blood,
A passion that no words can reach;
We sat together, and understood
Our own heart's speech.
ARTHUR SYMONS, *During Music*

Where light and shade repose, where music dwells
Lingering - and wandering on as loth to die;
Like thoughts whose very sweetness yieldeth proof
That they were born for immortality.
WILLIAM WORDSWORTH,
Ecclesiastical Sonnets, Part III, Number 43

Music religious heat inspires,
It wakes the soul, and lifts it high,
And wings it with sublime

desires,
And fits it to bespeak the
Deity.
THOMAS ADDISON, A
Song for St. Cecilia's Day,
Stanza 4

God is its author, and not
man; he laid
The key-note of all
harmonies; he planned
All perfect combinations, and
he made
Us so that we could hear and
understand.
J.G. BRAINARD, Music

And sure there is music even
in the beauty, and the silent
note which Cupid strikes, far
sweeter than the sound of an
instrument; for there is music
wherever there is harmony,
order, or proportion; and thus
far we may maintain the
music of the spheres.
SIR THOMAS BROWNE,
Religio Medici, Part II, Section IX

Music is well said to be the
speech of angels.
THOMAS CARLYLE, Essays,
The Opera

When the morning stars sang
together, and all the sons of

God shouted for joy.
Job 38:7

Heard melodies are sweet, but
those unheard
Are sweeter; therefore, ye soft
pipes, play on;
Not to the sensual ear, but,
more endear'd,
Pipe to the spirit ditties of no
tone.
KEATS, Ode on a Grecian Urn

Music is in all growing things;
And underneath the silky
wings
Of smallest insects there is
stirred
A pulse of air that must be
heard;
Earth's silence lives, and
throbs, and sings.
LATHROP, Music of Growth

Writ in the climate of heaven,
in the language spoken by
angels.
LONGFELLOW, The Children
of the Lord's Supper, line 262

Ring out ye crystal spheres!
Once bless our human ears,
If ye have power to touch our
senses so:
And let your silver chime
Move in melodious time;

And let the base of Heaven's
deep organ blow,
And with your ninefold
harmony,
Make up full consort to the
angelic symphony.
MILTON, *Hymn on the
Nativity*, Stanza 13

We are the music-makers,
And we are the dreamers of
dreams,
Wandering by lone sea-
breakers,
And sitting by desolate
streams;
World-losers and world-
forsakers,
Of whom the pale moon
gleams:
Yet we are the movers and
shakers
Of the world for ever, it seems.
A.W.E. O'SHAUGHNESSY,
Music Makers

Light quirks of music, broken
and uneven,
Make the soul dance upon a
jog to Heav'n.
ALEXANDER POPE, *Moral
Essays*, Ep. IV, line 143

We hanged our harps upon
the willows in the midst
thereof.
Psalms 138:2

Music is the poetry of the air.
JEAN PAUL RICHTER

You would play upon me; you
would seem to know my stops;
you would pluck out the heart
of my mystery; you would
sound me from my lowest note
to the top of my compass.
WILLIAM SHAKESPEARE,
Hamlet, Act III, Scene ii, line
379

Life without Music would be a
mistake.
FRIEDRICH NIETZSCHE,
Twilight of the Idols

[Music] opens within us the
region of our inner faculties,
where God himself has
inscribed or drawn his own
image. When God sees this
sign of our alliance coming
from us, he cannot ignore it:
he regards it with
complaisance, and this merest
glance from him produces a
holy harmony. It makes of the
man a being who can no
longer show himself without
all the signs of election, light,
and power, and who can no
longer utter a single tone
without giving birth to a
miracle.

LOUIS CLAUDE DE SAINT MARTIN, from *L'Esprit des Choses*

The first sentence in Boethius' work can be regarded as the principal thesis of his philosophy. It says: "Music is a part of our human nature; it has the power either to improve or to debase our character." In the relationship of music and the human mind the position of forces has now changed: music has become the active partner; our mind is a passive receiver and is impressed and influenced by the power music exerts. No wonder, then, that music abandons its role as a modest aid to moral growth and assumes gubernatorial rights.
PAUL HINDSMITH, from *A Composer's World*

Opera in English, is, in the main, just about as sensible as baseball in Italian.
FRANK MUIR, *The Frank Muir Book*

If music be the food of love, play on;
Give me excess of it, that, surfeiting,

The appetite may sicken, and so die.
That strain again! it had a dying fall:
O, it came o'er my ear like the sweet sound
That breathes upon a bank of violets,
Stealing and giving odour.
WILLIAM SHAKESPEARE, *Twelfth Night*, Act I, Scene i, line 1

THIRTY-SIX

PATIENCE

People will endure their tyrants for years, but they tear their deliverers to pieces if a millennium is not created immediately.
WOODROW WILSON, (1856-1924), in John Dos Passos, Mr. W.'s War

Let every man be swift to hear, slow to speak, slow to wrath.
James 1:19

Our patience will achieve more than our force.
EDMUND BURKE, (1729-97), Reflections on the Revolution in France

Patience and perseverance at length
Accomplish more than anger and brute strength.
JEAN DE LA FONTAINE, (1621-95), Fables, II.11

Patience, to prevent
That murmur, soon replies,
God doth not need
Either man's work or his own gifts; who best
Bear his mild yoke, they serve him best; his state
Is kingly; thousands at his bidding speed,

And post o'er land and ocean without rest,
They also serve who only stand and wait.
JOHN MILTON, (1608-74), Sonnet On His Blindness

Though patience be a tired mare, yet she will plod.
WILLIAM SHAKESPEARE, (1564-1616), Henry V, Act II, Scene i, line 25

Always remember that the future comes one day at a time.
DEAN ACHESON, Sketches From Life

Suffer us not to mock ourselves with falsehood
Teach us to care and not to care
Teach us to sit still.
T.S. ELIOT, Ash Wednesday, (1930)

It is but reasonable to bear that accident patiently, which God sends, since impatience does but entangle us, like the fluttering of a bird in a net, but cannot at all ease our trouble, or prevent the accident; it must be run through, and therefore it were

better we compose ourselves
to a patient than to a
troublous and miserable
suffering.
JEREMY TAYLOR

Patience makes that more
tolerable which it is
impossible to prevent or
remove.
HORACE

Patience -
Of whose soft grace, I have
her sovereign aid,
And rest myself content.
WILLIAM SHAKESPEARE

All is equal to the sage: he is
established in quietude and
tranquillity;
If a thing does not accord with
him, it still accords with the
will of God.
ANGELUS SILESIUS

Patience is bitter, but its fruit
is sweet.
J.J. ROUSSEAU

Patience sat by him, in an
angel's garb,
And held out a full bowl of
rich content,
Of which he largely quaff'd.
HAVARD

E'en the best must own,
Patience and resignation are
the pillars
Of human peace on earth.
YOUNG

Patience, my lord! why 'tis the
soul of peace;
Of all the virtues 'tis the
nearest kin to heaven;
It makes men look like gods:
the best of men
That e'er wore earth about
him, was a sufferer,
A soft, meek, patient, humble,
tranquil spirit,
The first true gentleman that
ever breath'd.
DECKER

A man said to the prophet,
'Give me a command.' He
said, 'Do not get angry.'
MUHAMMAD

If thou intendest to vanquish
the greatest, the most
abominable and wickedest
enemy, who is able to do thee
mischief, both in body and
soul, and against whom thou
preparest all sorts of weapons,
but cannot overcome, then
know that there is a sweet and
loving physical herb to serve
thee, named *patience*.
LUTHER

Attempt the end, and never
stand to doubt;
Nothing's so hard but search
will find it out.
HERRICK, Seek and Find

He that would have a cake out
of the wheat must tarry the
grinding.
WILLIAM SHAKESPEARE

All God wants of man is a
peaceful heart; then he
performs within the soul an
act too Godlike for creature to
attain to or yet see. The
divine Wisdom is discretely
fond and lets no creature watch.
ECKHART

Or arm th' obdured breast
With stubborn patience as
with triple steel.
MILTON, Paradise Lost, Book
II, line 568

Immured in sense, with
fivefold bonds confined,
Rest we content if whispers
from the stars
In waftings of the incalculable
wind
Come blown at midnight
through our prison-bars.
WILLIAM WATSON,
Epigrams

If the single man plant himself
indomitably on his instincts,
and there abide, the huge
world will come round to him.
RALPH WALDO
EMERSON, Addresses and
Lectures, The American
Scholar

I propose to fight it out on
this line, if it takes all summer.
GENERAL GRANT, Despatch
to Washington

Passion is overcome only by
him who has won through
stillness of spirit the perfect
vision. Knowing this, I must
first seek for stillness; it comes
through the contentment that
is regardless of the world.
What creature of a day should
cling to other frail beings,
when he can never again
through thousands of births
behold his beloved?
SÂNTI-DEVA

Patience and the mulberry leaf
becomes a silk gown.
CHINESE PROVERB

Let him that hath no power of
patience retire within himself,
though even there he will
have to put up with himself.

BALTASAR GRACIAN, *The Art of Worldly Wisdom*, 159, (1647)

You can't set a hen in one morning and have chicken salad for lunch.
GEORGE HUMPHREY, *Time*, Jan. 26, 1953

Verily in the remembrance of Allah do hearts find rest.
Qur'ân, XIII.28

If you wait, there will come nectar-like fair weather.
JAPANESE PROVERB

We shall sooner have the fowl by hatching the egg than by smashing it.
ABRAHAM LINCOLN, speech, (1865)

Only with winter-patience can we bring
The deep-desired, long-awaited spring.
ANNE MORROW LINDBERGH, *The Unicorn and Other Poems*, (1939)

Patience and diligence, like faith, remove mountains.
WILLIAM PENN, *Some Fruits of Solitude*, 1. 234, (1693)

He who has patience may accomplish anything.
RABELAIS, *Gargantua and Pantagruel*, 4.48, (1532-64)

Whoever has no patience has no wisdom.
SA'DI, *Gulistan*, 3.1, (1258)

To be patient is sometimes better than to have much wealth.
TALMUD

Wise people, after they have listened to the laws, become serene, like a deep, smooth, and still lake.
Dhammapada, VI. 82

Patience serves as a protection against wrongs as clothes do against cold. For if you put on more clothes as the cold increases it will have no power to hurt you. So in like manner you must grow in patience when you meet with great wrongs, and they will then be powerless to vex your mind.
LEONARDO DA VINCI

Of all the qualities of an excellent character patience is enough for us.
MONTAIGNE

Have patience with all things, but chiefly have patience with yourself. Do not lose courage in considering your own imperfections, but instantly set about remedying them - every day begin the task anew.
ST. FRANCIS DE SALES

A man who is master of patience is master of everything else.
LORD HALIFAX

He that can have patience can have what he will.
BENJAMIN FRANKLIN

All Sadhanas are done with a view to still the mind. The perfectly still mind is the Universal Spirit.
SWAMI RAMDAS

How poor are they that have not patience!
What wound did ever heal but by degrees?
WILLIAM SHAKESPEARE, Othello, Act III, Scene ii, line 379

Adopt the pace of nature: her secret is patience.
RALPH WALDO EMERSON

The principal part of faith is patience.
GEORGE MACDONALD

The most useful virtue is patience.
JOHN DEWEY

Every day I learn, with pains, for which I am grateful:
Patience is everything!
RAINER MARIA RILKE

Patience accomplishes its object, while hurry speeds to its ruin.
SA'DI, Gulistan, 8.37, (1258)

How poor are they who have not patience!
What wound did ever heal, but by degrees?
WILLIAM SHAKESPEARE

The most powerful prayer, one wellnigh omnipotent, and the worthiest work of all is the outcome of a quiet mind.
ECKHART

Patience is needed with everyone, but first of all with ourselves.
ST. FRANCIS DE SALES

I am managing more and more
to make use of that long
patience you taught me by
your tenacious example; that
patience which,
disproportionate to everyday
life that seems to bid us haste,
puts us in touch with all that
surpasses us.
RAINER MARIA RILKE,
Letters of Rainer Maria Rilke

Never, above all, let anxiety
gain the upper hand with
thee, for if thou becomest
agitated, the demon will be
content and will come off
victorious.
SISTER CONSOLATA

A fool uttereth all his mind:
but a wise man keepeth it in
till afterwards.
Proverbs 29:11

All this talk and turmoil and
noise and movement and
desire is outside of the veil;
within the veil is silence and
calm and rest.
BÂYAZID AL-BISTÂMI

Perhaps there is only one
cardinal sin: impatience.
Because of impatience they
were expelled, because of
impatience they do not return.
FRANZ KAFKA, *Collected
Aphorisms*, 3

It is easy to maintain a
situation while it is still
secure;
It is easy to deal with a
situation before symptoms
develop;
It is easy to break a thing
when it is yet brittle;
It is easy to dissolve a thing
when it is yet minute.
Deal with a thing while it is
still nothing;
Keep a thing in order before
disorder sets in.
A tree that can fill the span of
a man's arms
Grows from a downy tip;
A terrace nine storeys high
Rises from hodfuls of earth;
A journey of a thousand miles
Starts from beneath one's feet.
Whoever does anything to it
will ruin it; whoever lays hold
of it will lose it.
Therefore the sage, because he
does nothing, never ruins
anything; and, because he
does not lay hold of anything,
loses nothing.
In their enterprises the people
Always ruin them when on
the verge of success.

Be as careful at the end as at
the beginning
And there will be no ruined
enterprises.
Therefore the sage desires not
to desire
And does not value goods
which are hard to come by.
LAO TZU, *Tao Te Ching*

Men must endure
Their going hence, even as
their coming hither:
Ripeness is all.
WILLIAM SHAKESPEARE,
King Lear, Act V,
Scene ii line 9

Expect nothing. Live frugally
on surprise.
ALICE WALKER, *Expect
Nothing*

This vertu [Patience] maketh
a man lyk to God, and maketh
him Goddes owene dere child,
as seith Crist.
CHAUCER, *Parson's Tale*,
Section 50

The man who lacks patience
also lacks philosophy.
SA'DI

Children, that peace which is
found in the spirit and the

inner life is well worth our
care, for in that peace lies the
satisfaction of all our wants.
In it the Kingdom of God is
discovered and His
righteousness is found. This
peace a man should allow
nothing to take from him,
whatever betide, come weal or
woe, honour or shame.
TAULER

Though patience be a tired
mare, yet she will plod.
WILLIAM SHAKESPEARE,
Henry V, Act II, Scene i

God's ways seem dark, but
soon or late
They touch the shining hills
of day;
The evil cannot brook delay,
The good can well afford to
wait.
WHITTIER, *Lines to Friends*

Ye have heard of the patience
of Job.
James 5:2

A high hope for a low heaven:
God grant us patience!
WILLIAM SHAKESPEARE,
Love's Labour's Lost, Act I,
Scene i, line 195

Patience is the greatest prayer.
HINDU PROVERB, (a saying
of Buddha)

Patience is the key of
Paradise.
TURKISH PROVERB

All fruits do not ripen in one
season.
LAURE JUNOT, DUCHESSE
DE ABRANTÈS, Mémoires
Historiques, (1835)

Satisfaction is quietness of
heart under the course of
destiny.
AL-MUHÂSIBÎ

What is so certain of victory
as patience?
SELMA LAGERLÖF, The
Story of Gösta Berling, (1891)

With strength and patience all
his grievous loads are borne,
And from the world's rose-bed
he only asks a thorn.
WM. R. ALGER, Oriental
Poetry, Mussud's Praise of the
Camel

I worked with patience, which
means almost power.
E.B. BROWNING, Aurora
Leigh, Book, III, line 205

Patience and shuffle the cards.
CERVANTES, Don Quixote,
Part II, Book I, Chapter VI

Patience is a necessary
ingredient of genius.
BENJAMIN DISRAELI,
Contarini Fleming, Part IV,
Chapter V

Peace is in that heart in which
no wave of desire of any kind
rises.
SWAMI RAMDAS

Rule by patience, Laughing
Water!
LONGFELLOW, Hiawatha,
Part X, Hiawatha's Wooing

Patience, thou young and
rose-lipped cherubim!
WILLIAM SHAKESPEARE,
Othello, Act IV, Scene ii

A watched pot never boils.
ANON

Let patience have her perfect
work.
James

Let nothing trouble you,
nothing frighten you. All
things are passing; God never
changes. Patient endurance

attains all things. Whoever
possesses God lacks nothing:
God alone suffices.
ST. TERESA OF AVILA,
(1512-82)

Our patience will achieve
more than our force.
EDMUND BURKE, (1729-
97), *Reflections on the
Revolution in France*, (1790)

When a man has restrained
the turbulent passions of his
breast by the power of right
judgement, and has spread the
garment of soft compassion
and sweet content over his
heart and mind, let him then
worship divine serenity within
himself.
YOGA-VASISHTHA

Be the day weary or be the day
long, at last it ringeth to
evensong.
ANON

Still achieving, still pursuing,
Learn to labour and to wait.
LONGFELLOW, *A Psalm of
Life*, Stanza 9

Endurance is the crowning
quality,
And patience all the passion

of great hearts.
LOWELL, *Columbus*, line 241

And makes us rather bear
those ills we have
Than fly to others that we
know not of?
WILLIAM SHAKESPEARE,
Hamlet, Act III, Scene I, line 81

Persevere and preserve
yourselves for better
circumstances.
VIRGIL, Aeneid, line 207

All men commend patience,
although few be willing to
practise it.
THOMAS À KEMPIS,
Imitation of Christ, Book III,
Chapter 12

It is a long lane that has no
turning.
ANON

All things come round to him
who will but wait.
LONGFELLOW, *Tales of a
Wayside Inn*, The Student's
Tale, Part 1

Every cup should be sweet to
you which extinguishes thirst.
SEXTUS THE
PYTHAGOREAN

The longest way round is the
shortest way home.
ANON

I will with patience hear, and
find a time
Both meet to hear and answer
such high things.
'Till then, my noble friend,
chew upon this.
WILLIAM SHAKESPEARE,
Julius Caesar, Act I, Scene ii,
line 169

Every misfortune is to be
subdued by patience.
VIRGIL, Aeneid, Verse 710

Sufferance is the badge of all
our tribe.
WILLIAM SHAKESPEARE,
Merchant of Venice, Act I,
Scene iii, line 111

THIRTY-SEVEN

PRACTICALITY

In all our resolves we must decide which is the line of conduct that presents the fewest drawbacks and then follow it out as being the best one, because one never finds anything perfectly pure and unmixed, or exempt from danger.
MACHIAVELLI

Perfect things teach hope.
FRIEDRICH NIETZSCHE

A committee is a group that keeps the minutes and loses hours.
MILTON BERLE, (1954)

Life is mostly froth and bubble
Two things stand like stone
Kindness in another's trouble
Courage in your own.
ADAM LINDSAY GORDON
(1833-1870) Ye Wearie
Wayfarer, Fytte,8

The indefatigable pursuit of an unattainable perfection, even though it consists in nothing more than in the pounding of an old piano, is what alone gives a meaning to our life on this unavailing star.
LOGAN PEARSALL SMITH

He who neglects to drink of the spring of experience is likely to die of thirst in the desert of ignorance.
LING PO, Epigram

Pedantry prides herself on being wrong by rules; while common sense is contented to be right without them.
CHARLES CALEB
COLTON, Lacon, line 48,
(1825)

When one has finished building one's house, one suddenly realises that in the process one has learned something that one really needed to know in the worst way - before one began.
FRIEDRICH NIETZSCHE,
Beyond Good and Evil, 277,
(1886)

That which we have not been forced to decipher, to clarify by our own personal effort, that which was made clear before, is not ours.
MARCEL PROUST,
Remembrance of Things Past:
The Sweet Cheat Gone, (1913-27)

Logic is one thing and commonsense another.
ELBERT HUBBARD, *The Note Book*, (1927)

In practice, such trifles as contradictions in principle are easily set aside; the faculty of ignoring them makes the practical man.
HENRY ADAMS, *The Education of Henry Adams*, 3, (1907)

Only when you have crossed the river can you say the crocodile has a lump on his snout.
ASHANTI PROVERB

Each believes naught but his experience.
EMPEDOCLES, *Fragments*, No. 2, 1.5

Good intentions are useless in the absence of common sense.
JAMI, *Baharistan*, The Camel and the Rat, (15th century)

The authentic insight and experience of any human soul, were it but insight and experience in hewing of wood and drawing of water, is real knowledge, a real possession and acquirement.
THOMAS CARLYLE, *Corn-Law Rhymes*, (1832)

In this world we must either institute conventional forms of expression or else pretend that we have nothing to express; the choice lies between a mask and a fig-leaf.
GEORGE SANTAYANA, *Soliloquies in England*, Carnival, (1922)

Every act of courage
Is a manifestation
Of the ground of being,
However questionable
The content of the act may be.
PAUL TILLICH, *The Courage to Be*

Precision of communication is important, more important than ever, in our era of hair-trigger balances, when a false, or misunderstood word may create as much disaster as a sudden thoughtless act.
JAMES THURBER, *Lanterns and Lances*, (1961)

A mariner must have his eye upon rocks and sands, as well as upon the North Star.
THOMAS FULLER, M.D., *Gnomologia*, 319, (1732)

A strong and well-constructed man digests his experiences (deeds and misdeeds) just as he digests his meats, even when he has some tough morsels to swallow.
FRIEDRICH NIETZSCHE, *The Genealogy of Morals*, 3.16, (1887)

I had rather ride on an ass that carries me than a horse that throws me.
GEORGE HERBERT, *Jacula Prudentum*, (1651)

What man would be wise, let him drink of the river
That bears on its bosom the record of time;
A message to him every wave can deliver
To teach him to creep till he knows how to climb.
JOHN BOYLE O'REILLY, *Rules of the Road*

A rational man acting in the real world may be defined as one who decides where he will strike a balance between what he desires and what can be done.
WALTER LIPPMANN, *The Public Philosophy*, 4.2, (1955)

The barber learns his trade on the orphan's chin.
ARABIC PROVERB

The knowledge of the world is only to be acquired in the world, and not in a closet.
LORD CHESTERFIELD, *Letters to His Son*, October 4, 1746

Thou shalt know by experience how salt the savour is of other's bread, and how sad a path it is to climb and descend, another's stairs.
DANTE, *Paradiso*, Canto XVII, line 58

However much thou art read in theory, if thou hast no practice thou art ignorant.
SA'DI, *Gulistan*, 8.3, (1258)

Somebody said it couldn't be done,
But he with a chuckle replied
That "maybe it couldn't," but he would be one
Who wouldn't say so till he'd tried.
EDGAR A. GUEST, *It Couldn't Be Done*

Experience, next, to thee I owe,

Best guide; not following thee,
I had remain'd
In ignorance; thou open'st
wisdom's way,
And giv'st access, though
secret she retire.
MILTON, *Paradise Lost*, Book
IX, line 807

He was a self-made man who
owed his lack of success to
nobody.
JOSEPH HELLER, *Catch-22*,
Chapter 3

Our very business in life is not
to get ahead of others, but to
get ahead of ourselves.
THOMAS L. MONSON

What is more mortifying than
to feel that you have missed
the plum for want of courage
to shake the tree?
LOGAN PEARSALL
SMITH, *Afterthoughts*

The only place where success
comes before work is in a
dictionary.
VIDAL SASSOON, BBC radio

Experience is a comb which
nature gives us when we are
bald.
CHINESE PROVERB

By their fruits ye shall know
them.
Matthew 7:20

Management is efficiency in
climbing the ladder of success;
leadership determines whether
the ladder is standing against
the right wall.
STEPHEN R. COVEY, *The 7
Habits of Highly Effective
People*

It's damn pleasant. I think,
abstractly, it adds to one's
ability to act and to tackle any
job, whether related to one's
field or not. This is both
helpful and dangerous, but in
general, I would say that
unless one has enough success
at something to trust oneself
... one is poorly off.
ELIZABETH JANEWAY,
Open Secrets, by Barbaralee
Diamonstein

The cure for all the illness of
life is stored in the inner
depth of life itself, the access
to which becomes possible
when we are alone. This
solitude is a world in itself, full
of wonders and resources
unthought of. It is absurdly
near; yet so unapproachably

distant.
RABINDRANATH
TAGORE, *Letters to a Friend*

Only the wearer knows where
the shoe pinches.
ENGLISH PROVERB

It is often wonderful how
putting down on paper a clear
statement of a case helps one
to see, not perhaps the way
out, but the way in.
A.C. BENSON, *Excerpts from
the Letters of Dr. A.C. Benson
to M.E.A.*

Love your neighbours, but
don't pull down the fence.
CHINESE PROVERB

You often get a better hold
upon a problem by going away
from it for a time and
dismissing it from your mind
altogether.
DR. FRANK CRANE, *Essays*

If a man write a better book,
preach a better sermon, or
make a better mouse-trap than
his neighbour, tho he build his
house in the woods, the world
will make a beaten path to his
door.
RALPH WALDO EMERSON

We always carry out by
committee anything in which
any one of us alone would be
too reasonable to persist.
FRANK MOORE COLBY,
The Colby Essays, Subsidising
Authors, V.I, (1926)

A great man is one who seizes
the vital issue in a complex
question, what we might call
the "jugular vein" of the
whole organism, - and spends
his energies upon that.
JOSEPH RICKABY, *An Old
Man's Jottings*

And he gave it for his
opinion, that whoever could
make two ears of corn, or two
blades of grass, to grow upon a
spot of ground where only one
grew before, would deserve
better of mankind and do
more essential service to his
country, than the whole race
of politicians put together.
SWIFT, *Gulliver's Travels*,
Voyage to Brobdingnag, Part
II, Chapter VII

I know by my own pot how
the others boil.
FRENCH PROVERB

It is hard for thee to kick
against the pricks.
Acts 9:5

I have always observed that to
succeed in the world one
should appear like a fool but
be wise.
MONTESQUIEU, *Pensées
Diverses*

Either do not attempt at all,
or go through with it.
OVID, *Ars Amatoria*, Book I,
389

It is best for man not to seek
to climb too high, lest he fall.
NICHOLAS BACON

To climb steep hills
Requires slow pace at first.
WILLIAM SHAKESPEARE,
Henry VIII, Act I, Scene i,
line 131

Courage is required not only
in a person's occasional crucial
decision for his own freedom,
but in the little hour-to-hour
decisions which place the
bricks in the structure of his
building of himself into a
person who acts with freedom
and responsibility.
ROLLO MAY, *Man's Search
for Himself*

Successfully to accomplish any
task it is necessary not only
that you should give it the
best there is in you, but that
you should obtain for it the
best there is in those under
your guidance.
GEORGE W. GOETHALS,
(1918)

He who has once burnt his
mouth always blows his soup.
GERMAN PROVERB

The African lions rush to
attack bulls; they do not
attack butterflies.
MARTIAL, *Epigrams*, Book
XII, 62.5

The success of most things
depends upon knowing how
long it will take to succeed.
MONTESQUIEU, *Pensées
Diverses*

That low man seeks a little
thing to do,
Sees it and does it:
This high man with a great
thing to pursue,
Dies ere he knows it.
That low man goes on adding
one to one,
His hundred's soon hit;
This high man aiming at a

million,
Misses an unit.
ROBERT BROWNING,
Grammarian's Funeral

The spirited horse, which will
of itself strive to beat in the
race, will run still more swiftly
if encouraged.
OVID, *Epistolae Ex Ponto*,
II.11.21

If a man has good corn, or
wood, or boards, or pigs to
sell, or can make better chairs
or knives, crucibles, or church
organs, than anybody else, you
will find a broad, hard-beaten
road to his house, tho it be in
the woods. And if a man
knows the law, people will
find it out, tho he live in a
pine shanty, and resort to him.
And if a man can pipe or sing,
so as to wrap the prisoned soul
in an elysium; or can paint
landscape, and convey into
oils and ochres all the
enchantments of spring or
autumn; or can liberate or
intoxicate all people who hear
him with delicious songs and
verses, 'tis certain that the
secret can not be kept: the
first witness tells it to a
second, and men go by fives

and tens and fifties to his
door.
RALPH WALDO
EMERSON, *Journal*, Works,
Volume VIII, page 528,
(1855)

You know more of a road by
having travelled it than by all
the conjectures and
descriptions in the world.
WILLIAM HAZLITT, *Literary
Remains*, On the Conduct of
Life, (1836)

We learn courageous actions
by going forward whenever
fear urges us back. A little
boy was asked how he learned
to skate. "Oh, by getting up
every time I fell down," he
answered.
DAVID SEABURY, *How to
Worry Successfully*

When all you have is a
hammer, everything looks like
a nail.
LATE 20TH-CENTURY
SAYING, (North American)

I shall the effect of this good
lesson keep,
As watchman to my heart.
WILLIAM SHAKESPEARE,
Hamlet, Act I, Scene iii, line 45

Few [problems] are difficult of solution. The difficulty, all but invariable, is in confronting them. We know what needs to be done; for reasons of inertia, pecuniary interest, passion or ignorance, we do not wish to say so.
J.K. GALBRAITH, *The Age of Uncertainty*, (1977)

Our problems are man-made, therefore they may be solved by man. And man can be as big as he wants. No problem of human destiny is beyond human beings.
PRESIDENT JOHN F. KENNEDY, speech, (1963)

No problem is insoluble given a big enough plastic bag.
TOM STOPPARD, *Jumpers*

It isn't that they can't see the solution. It is that they can't see the problem.
G.K. CHESTERTON, (1874-1936), *The Scandal of Father Brown*, The Point of a Pin

Who heeds not experience, trust him not.
JOHN BOYLE O'REILLY, *Rules of the Road*

What we're saying today is that you're either part of the solution or you're part of the problem.
ELDRIDGE CLEAVER, (1935-), speech (1968)

It is quite a three-pipe problem.
ARTHUR CONAN DOYLE, (1859-1930), *The Adventures of Sherlock Holmes*, The Red-healed League

The basic problems facing the world today are not susceptible to a military solution.
PRESIDENT JOHN F. KENNEDY, (1917-63), speech

Be wise today: 'tis madness to defer.
EDWARD YOUNG (1683-1765), *Night Thoughts*, Night I, 390

Experience is by industry achieved
And perfected by the swift course of time.
WILLIAM SHAKESPEARE, *The Two Gentlemen of Verona*, Act I, Scene iii, line 22

If you are the summit of a volcano the least you can do is smoke.
WINSTON CHURCHILL, *Great Contemporaries*, The Ex-Kaiser, 1937

In almost everything, experience is more valuable than precept.
QUINTILIAN, *De Institutione Oratoria*, Book V, Chapter 10

Men of power have not time to read; yet men who do not read are unfit for power.
MICHAEL FOOT, *Debts of Honour*

If I go a week without practice the audience notices it. If I go a day without practice I notice it.
ARTHUR RUBENSTEIN

If the Creator had
a purpose in equipping
us with a neck,
He surely meant us
to stick it out.
ARTHUR KOESTLES, *Encounter*, May 1970

God is on the side not of the heavy battalions, but of the best shots.
VOLTAIRE, *Notebooks*

Talk to him of Jacob's ladder, and he would ask the number of the steps.
DOUGLAS WILLIAM JERROLD, (1803-57)

Probable impossibilities are to be preferred to improbable possibilities.
ARISTOTLE, (384-322 BC), *Poetics*

How often have I said to you that when you have eliminated the impossible, whatever remains, however improbable, must be the truth?
ARTHUR CONON DOYLE, (1859-1930), *The Sign of Four*, (1890)

Einstein was a man who could ask immensely simple questions. And what his life showed, and his work, is that when the answers are simple too, then you hear God thinking.
JACOB BRONOWSKI, (1908-74), *The Ascent of Man*, (1973)

Forgetting those things which are behind, and reaching forth unto those things which are before,

I press toward the mark.
Philippians

If a problem is too difficult to solve, one cannot claim that it is solved by pointing at all the efforts made to solve it.
HANNES ALFVEN, (1908-95)

Not to go back, is somewhat to advance,
And men must walk at least before they dance.
ALEXANDER POPE, (1688-1744), *Imitations of Horace*

Men are wise in proportion, not to their experience, but to their capacity for experience.
BERNARD SHAW, *Maxims for Revolutionists*

Nothing in progression can rest on its original plan. We may as well think of rocking a grown man in the cradle of an infant.
EDMUND BURKE, (1729-97), *Letter to the Sheriffs of Bristol*, (1777)

The people I respect must behave as if they were immortal and as if society was eternal.

E.M. FORSTER, *Two Cheers for Democracy*, (1951)

His years but young, but his experience old;
His head unmellow'd, but his judgement ripe.
WILLIAM SHAKESPEARE, *The Two Gentlemen of Verona*, Act II, Scene iv, line 69

The great virtue in life
is real courage,
that knows how to face facts
and live beyond them.
D.H. LAWRENCE, *Selected Letters*

Believe one who has proved it. Believe an expert.
VIRGIL, *Aeneid*, Book XI, line 283

I know
The past, and thence I will essay to glean
A warning for the future, so that man
May profit by his errors, and derive
Experience from his folly.
PERCY BYSSHE SHELLEY, *Queen Mab*, Part III, line 6

It is contrary to human nature to court privations. We know

that the saints did court them, and valued them as avenues to grace ... We ourselves are not hunting assiduously for hardships; but which of us has not summoned up courage enough to laugh in the face of disaster?
AGNES REPPLIER,
Americans and Others

Courage is rightly esteemed the first of human qualities because it is the quality which guarantees all others.
WINSTON S. CHURCHILL

He that climbs the tall tree has won right to the fruit. He that leaps the wide gulf should prevail in his suit.
SIR WALTER SCOTT,
Talerina, Blondel's Song, Chapter 26

My dear thing, it all comes back, as everything always does, simply to personal pluck. It's only a question, no matter when or where, of having enough.
HENRY JAMES, *The Awkward Age*

The highest courage is not to be found in the instinctive acts of men who risk their lives to save a friend or slay a foe; the physical fearlessness of a moment or an hour is not to be compared with immolation of months or years for the sake of wisdom or art.
JOSEPH H. ODELL,
Unmailed Letters

Pick yourself up,
Dust yourself down,
And start all over again.
FRANK SINATRA

What do you mean by guts?
DOROTHY PARKER

Grace under pressure.
ERNEST HEMINGWAY

By experience we find out a shorter way by a long wandering. Learning teacheth more in one year than experience in twenty.
ROGER ASCHAM, *The Scholemaster*

Courage is required not only in a person's occasional crucial decision for his own freedom, but in the little hour-to-hour decisions which place the bricks in the structure of his building of himself into a

person who acts with freedom and responsibility.
ROLLO MAY, *Man's Search for Himself*

We learn courageous actions by going forward whenever fear urges us back. A little boy was asked how he learned to skate. "Oh, by getting up every time I fell down," he answered.
DAVID SEABURY, *How to Worry Successfully*

If thou shouldst never see my face again,
Pray for my soul. More things are wrought by prayer
Than this world dreams of. Wherefore, let thy voice
Rise like a fountain for me night and day.
For what are men better than sheep or goats
That nourish a blind life within the brain,
If, knowing God, they lift not hands of prayer
Both for themselves and those who call them friend?
For so the whole round earth is every way
Bound by gold chains about the feet of God.
ALFRED LORD TENNYSON, Poet Laureate (1809-92), from *Idylls of the King*

We must assume our existence as *broadly* as we in any way can; everything, even the unheard-of, must be possible in it. That is at bottom the only courage that is demanded of us: to have courage for the most extraordinary, the most singular and the most unexplicable that we may encounter.
RAINER MARIA RILKE, *Letters to a Young Poet*

Experience teaches slowly, and at the cost of mistakes.
J.A. FROUDE, *Short Studies on Great Subjects*, Party Politics

What is a committee? A group of the unwilling, picked from the unfit, to do the unnecessary.
RICHARD HARKNESS, *New York Herald Tribune*, June 15, 1960

Take no thought for your life, what ye shall eat, or what ye shall drink: nor yet for your body, what ye shall put on. Is

not the life more than meat,
and the body than raiment?
... Consider the lilies of the
field, how they grow; they toil
not, neither do they spin; and
yet I say unto you, That even
Solomon in all his glory was
not arrayed like one of these.
Wherefore, if God so clothe
the grass of the field, which to
day is, and to morrow is cast
into the oven, shall he not
much more clothe you, O ye
of little faith?
'... Your heavenly Father
knoweth that ye have need of
all these things.
But seek ye first the kingdom
of God, and his righteousness,
and all these things shall be
added unto you.
JESUS CHRIST, from
Matthew 6:25 forward

To show the world what long
experience gains,
Requires not courage, though
it calls for pains;
But at life's outset to inform
mankind
Is a bold effort of a valiant
mind.
GEORGE CRABBE, *The
Borough*, Letter VII, line 47

I have come to the borders of
sleep,
The unfathomable deep
Forest where all must lose
Their way, however straight,
Or winding, soon or late;
They cannot choose.

Many a road and track
That, since the dawn's first
crack,
Up to the forest brink,
Deceived the travellers
Suddenly now blurs,
And in they sink.

Here love ends,
Despair, ambition ends,
All pleasure and all trouble,
Although most sweet or bitter,
Here ends in sleep that is
sweeter
Than tasks most noble.

There is not any book
Or face of dearest look
That I would not turn from
now
To go into the unknown
I must enter and leave alone
I know not how.

The tall forest towers,
Its cloudy foliage lowers
Ahead, shelf above shelf,
Its silence I hear and obey

That I may lose my way
And myself.
EDWARD THOMAS,
English Poet, (1878-1917)

Time's glory is to calm
contending kings,
To unmask falsehood, and
bring truth to light.
WILLIAM SHAKESPEARE,
(1564-1616), from *The Rape of
Cicero*

No coward soul is mine,
No trembler in the world's
storm -
troubled sphere:
I see Heaven's glories shine,
And faith shines equal,
arming me
from fear.
EMILY BRONTE, from *No
Coward Soul is Mine*, (1846)

The soul, secured in her
existence,
Smiles at the drawn dagger
And defies its point.
THOMAS ADDISON, *Cato*,
Act I, Sc iv

Be steadfast as a tower
That doth not bend
Its stately summit
To the tempest's shock.
DANTE, *Purgatorio*, Verse 14

Courage is not simply one of
the virtues but the form of
every virtue at the resting
point, which means at the
point of highest reality.
C.S. LEWIS, (1898-1963),
quoted in *The Unquiet Grave*,
Chapter 3

Lo! I am ready with even
mind to suffer all that God
has decreed concerning me,
whether unto life or unto
death. Nothing is better,
more salutary, or more
pleasant to me, nor do I
choose or desire anything else
than that He should find me
ever ready to accept the
judgement of His will.
JAN VAN RUYSHROECK,
(1293-1381), from *The
Adornment of the Spiritual
Marriage*, Watkins Publishing,
1951

His head was silver'd o'er with
age,
And long experience made
him sage.
JOHN GAY, *Fables*,
Introduction, line 3

Courage is the price
that life exacts
for granting peace,

the soul that knows it not,
knows no release
from little things;
knows not the livid loneliness
of fear,
nor mountain heights
where bitter joy can hear
the sound of wings.
AMELIA EARHART, U.S.
Aviator, (1897-1937), from
The Sound of Wings, Chapter 1

He who knows others is
clever;
He who knows himself has
discernment.
He who overcomes others has
force;
He who overcomes himself is
strong.
He who knows contentment is
rich;
He who perseveres is a man of
purpose;
He who does not lose his
station will endure;
He who lives out his days has
had a long life.
LAO TZU, from *Tao Te
Ching*, line 33

THIRTY-EIGHT

RELATIONSHIP

He who, silent, loves to be with us - he who loves us in our silence - has touched one of the keys that ravish hearts.
ANON

Familiar acts are beautiful through love.
PERCY BYSSHE SHELLEY, *Prometheus Unbound*, 4, (1818-19)

When brothers agree, no fortress is so strong as their common life.
ANTISTHENES, (5th-4th century BC), quoted in Diogenes Laertius' *Lives and Opinions of Eminent Philosophers*

Manny a man that cud rule a hundherd millyon sthrangers with an ir'n hand is careful to take off his shoes in th' front hallway whin he comes home late at night.
FINLEY PETER DUNNE, *Mr. Dooley On Making a Will, Famous Men*, (1919)

If woman is to recapture the lost companionship with man and child, she must once more forget herself, as she did in the old pioneer days, and follow them into the world.
PEARL S. BUCK, *To My Daughters, With Love*, (1967)

Govern a family as you would cook a small fish - very gently.
CHINESE PROVERB

The parents' age must be remembered, both for joy and anxiety.
CONFUCIUS, *Analects*, (6th century BC), 4.21

No loss by flood and lightning, no destruction of cities and temples by the hostile forces of nature, has deprived man of so many noble lives and impulses as those which his intolerance has destroyed.
HELEN KELLER, *Optimism*, 2, (1903)

It is the heart always that sees, before the head can see.
THOMAS CARLYLE, *Chartism*, 5, (1839)

Women, as most susceptible, are the best index of the coming hour.
RALPH WALDO EMERSON, *The Conduct of Life*, Fate, (1860)

In about the same degree as you are helpful, you will be happy.
KARL REILAND, (1961)

'Tis not enough to help the feeble up,
But to support him after.
WILLIAM SHAKESPEARE, *Timon of Athens*, Act I, Scene I, line 107, (1607-08)

Knowing sorrow well, I learn the way to succour the distressed.
VIRGIL, *Aeneid*, (30-19 BC), line 630

The sum which two married people owe to one another defies calculation. It is an infinite debt, which can only be discharged through all eternity.
GOETHE, *Elective Affinities*, 9, (1809)

The strong and the weak cannot keep company.
AESOP, *Fables*, The Two Pots, (6th century BC?)

Whoever touches pitch will be defiled.
Apocrypha, Ecclesiasticus, 13.1

A wise man associating with the vicious becomes an idiot; a dog travelling with good men becomes a rational being.
ARABIC PROVERB

A man is known by the company he organises.
AMBROSE BIERCE, *The Devil's Dictionary*, (1881-1911)

Tell me thy company, and I'll tell thee what thou art.
CERVANTES, *Don Quixote*, 2.3.23, (1605-15)

As, when there is sympathy, there needs but one wise man in a company and all are wise, so, a blockhead makes a blockhead of his companion.
RALPH WALDO EMERSON, *The Conduct of Life*, Considerations by the Way, (1860)

He that takes the Devil into his boat must carry him over the sound.
ENG LISH PROVERB

There are six requisites in every happy marriage. The first is Faith and the remaining five are Confidence.

ELBERT HUBBARD, *The Note Book*, (1927)

Better fare hard with good men than feast it with bad.
THOMAS FULLER, M.D., *Gnomologia*, 893, (1732)

He that lies down with dogs shall rise up with fleas.
LATIN PROVERB

By associating with good and evil persons a man acquires the virtues and vices which they possess, even as the wind blowing over different places takes along good and bad odours.
Panchatantra, 1, (circa 5th century AD)

Our unconscious is like a vast subterranean factory with intricate machinery that is never idle, where work goes on day and night from the time we are born until the moment of our death.
MILTON R. SAPIRSTEIN, *Paradoxes of Everyday Life*, 8, (1955)

Things and men have always a certain sense, a certain side by which they must be got hold of if one wants to obtain a solid grasp and a perfect command.
JOSEPH CONRAD, *Under Western Eyes*, 4.1, (1911)

It takes a long time to understand nothing.
EDWARD DAHLBERG, *Reasons of the Heart*, On Wisdom and Folly, (1965)

No man knows what the wife of his bosom is until he has gone with her through the fiery trials of this world.
WASHINGTON IRVING, *The Sketch Book of Geoffrey Crayon*, (1819-20)

Between
Our birth and death we may touch understanding
As a moth brushes a window with its wing.
CHRISTOPHER FRY, *The Boy with a Cart*, (1945)

Understanding is the beginning of approving.
ANDRÉ GIDE, *Journals*, (1902)

A moment's insight is sometimes worth a life's experience.

OLIVER WENDELL
HOLMES, SR., *The Professor
at the Breakfast Table*, (1860)

I would advise no man to
marry who is not likely to
propogate understanding.
SAMUEL JOHNSON,
Johnsonian Miscellanies, V.1,
(1897)

Time which diminishes all
things increases understanding
for the aging.
PLUTARCH, *Moralia*, The
Education of Children, (circa
AD 100)

To understand is to forgive,
even oneself.
ALEXANDER CHASE,
Perspectives, (1966)

If you do not understand a
man you cannot crush him.
And if you do understand
him, very probably you will
not.
G.K. CHESTERTON, *All
Things Considered*,
Humanitarianism and
Strength, (1908)

Grieve not that men and
women do not know you;
grieve that you do not know

men and women.
CONFUCIUS, *Analects*, (6th
century BC), 1.16

Herein lies the tragedy of the
age: not that men are poor, -
all men know something of
poverty; not that men are
wicked, - who is good? not
that men are ignorant, - what
is truth? Nay, but that men
know so little of men.
W.E.B. DU BOIS, *The Souls of
Black Folk*, 12, (1903)

It is impossible for one person
to know another so well that
he can dispense with belief.
FRIEDRICH
DÜRRENMATT, *The
Marriage of Mr. Mississippi*, 2,
(1952)

The men that women marry,
And why they marry them,
will always be
A marvel and a mystery to the
world.
LONGFELLOW, *Michael
Angelo*, line 6, (1883)

All persons are puzzles until at
last we find in some word or
act the key to the man, to the
woman; straightway all their
past words and actions lie in

light before us.
RALPH WALDO
EMERSON, *Journals*, (1842)

Each of us really understands
in others only those feelings
he is capable of producing
himself.
ANDRÉ GIDE, *Journal of the
Counterfeiters*, (1921)

It is profound philosophy to
sound the depths of feeling
and distinguish traits of
character. Men must be
studied as deeply as books.
BALTASAR GRACIAN, *The
Art of Worldly Wisdom*, 157,
(1647)

No one can understand unless,
holding to his own nature, he
respects the free nature of
others.
GRAFFITO written during
French student revolt, May
1968

The deep sea can be
fathomed, but who knows the
hearts of men?
MALAY PROVERB

There is no more lovely,
friendly and charming
relationship, communion or
company than a good
marriage.
MARTIN LUTHER, *Table
Talk*, (1569)

Until we know what
motivates the hearts and
minds of men we can
understand nothing outside
ourselves, nor will we ever
reach fulfilment as that
greatest miracle of all, the
human being.
MARYA MANNES, *More in
Anger*, 2.2, (1958)

A man, to be greatly good,
must imagine intensely and
comprehensively; he must put
himself in the place of
another, and of many others;
the pains and pleasures of his
species must become his own.
PERCY BYSSHE SHELLEY,
A Defence of Poetry, (1821)

Hail, wedded love, mysterious
law, true source
Of human offspring.
MILTON, *Paradise Lost*, Book
IV, line 750, (1667)

One learns peoples through
the heart not the eyes or the
intellect.
MARK TWAIN, *What Paul
Bourget Thinks of Us*, (1895)

I don't ask for your pity, but just your understanding - not even that - no. Just for your recognition of me in you, and the enemy, time, in us all.
TENNESSEE WILLIAMS, *Sweet Bird of Youth*, 3, (1959)

A man should always consider how much he has more than he wants, and how much more unhappy he might be than he really is.
JOSEPH ADDISON, The Spectator, 574, (1714)

Nothing is miserable unless you think it so.
BOETHIUS, *The Consolation of Philosophy*, 2, (AD 524)

It is not possible for one to teach others who cannot teach his own family.
CONFUCIUS

We are made for co-operation, like feet, like hands, like eyelids, like the rows of the upper and lower teeth. To act against one another is contrary to nature.
MARCUS AURELIUS, *Meditations*, Book 2.1
Marriage is the perfection which love aimed at, ignorant of what it sought.
RALPH WALDO EMERSON, *Journals*, (1850)

When marrying one should ask oneself this question: Do you believe that you will be able to converse well with this woman into your old age?
FRIEDRICH NIETZSCHE, *Human, All Too Human*, 406, (1878)

Men love women, women love children, children love hamsters, hamsters don't love anybody.
ALICE THOMAS ELLIS, TV programme, *Bookmark*, (Dec 1987)

The opinions which we hold of one another, our relations with friends and kinsfolk are in no sense permanent, save in appearance, but are as eternally fluid as the sea itself.
MARCEL PROUST, *Remembrance of Things Past*, The Guermantes Way, (1913-27)

Every deed and every relationship is surrounded by an atmosphere of silence. Friendship needs no words - it

is solitude delivered from the anguish of loneliness.
DAG HAMMARSKJÖLD, *Markings*, Thus It Was

We keep passing unseen through little moments of other people's lives.
ROBERT M. PIRSIG, *Zen and the Art of Motorcycle Maintenance*, Part 3, Chapter 24

There's no vocabulary
For love within a family, love that's lived in
But not looked at, love within the light of which
All else is seen, the love within which
All other love finds speech.
This love is silent.
T.S. ELIOT, *The Elder Statesman*, 2, (1958)

Never marry but for love; but see that thou lovest what is lovely.
WILLIAM PENN, *Some Fruits of Solitude*, line 79, (1693)

Bringing up a family should be an adventure, not an anxious discipline in which everybody is constantly graded for performance.

MILTON R. SAPIRSTEIN, *Paradoxes of Everyday Life*, 3, (1955)

A fanatic is one who can't change his mind and won't change the subject.
SIR WINSTON CHURCHILL, *The New York Times*, (July 1954)

Relationship is life, and this relationship is a constant movement, a constant change.
J. KRISHNAMURTI, *You Are the World*

Time necessarily brings changed in any relation, and one must be prepared to recognise these changes and to grow and to change with time. But if one can believe that it is possible for the greater knowledge that two persons may acquire of each other in the course of time to bring also greater respect and love, then - beyond the inevitabilities of human life cycles - one need not fear time.
HELEN MERRELL LYND, *On Shame and the Search for Identity*

A good marriage is that in which each appoints the other guardian of his solitude.
RAINER MARIA RILKE, *Letters*, (1892-1926)

Relationships are things that have their good times and bad times. I try to cope with the bad times by projecting myself into the character of the other person - to consider how that person feels, and try to imagine myself in that person's position. It's not a painful process - it helps you. I think if you can manage to do that, at least you don't run into terrible trouble with people.
TENNESSEE WILLIAMS, *Close-up*, by John Gruen

No matter how genuine a relationship may be, there will always be stresses and storms, to bring unexpected words, to make one impotent and afraid, to make one feel the terribleness of not being able to count on the other person, to create the despairing feeling that breaks in love can never be repaired. But one lives and loves, and suffers and forgets, and begins again - perhaps even thinking that this time, this new time, is to be permanent. But man is not permanent and man is not predictable.
CLARK MOUSTAKAS, *Creativity and Conformity*

A friend is a person who knows all about you - and still likes you.
HUBBARD

The only way to have a friend is to be one.
RALPH WALDO EMERSON, *Essays*, Of Friendship

Romance calls for 'the faraway love' of the troubadours; marriage for love of 'one's neighbour as thyself'.
DENIS DE ROUGEMONT, *Love in the Western World*, 7.7, (1939)

The firmest friendships have been formed in mutual adversity: iron is most strongly united in the fiercest flame.
COLTON

Friends are much better tried in bad fortune than in good.
ARISTOTLE

Yea, the poor wretch on bed of straw that lies, if she find favour in her husband's eyes, enjoys a happiness unknown to one, rich in all else, but poor in love alone. A loving wife is ever hard to find, as is a man that to his wife is kind.
BUDDHA

Marry by all means. If you get a good wife you will become very happy; if you get a bad one you will become a philosopher - and that is good for every man!
SOCRATES

The friendships which last are those wherein each friend respects the other's dignity to the point of not really wanting anything from him.
CYRIL CONNOLLY, The Unquiet Grave, (1945)

I always felt that the great high privilege, relief and comfort of friendship was that one had to explain nothing.
KATHERINE MANSFIELD, Antony Alpen, Katherine Mansfield, (1954)

It takes patience to appreciate domestic bliss; volatile spirits

prefer unhappiness.
GEORGE SANTAYANA, The Life of Reason, Reason in Society, 2, (1905-06)

Money can't buy friends, but you can get a better class of enemy.
SPIKE MILLIGAN, Puckoon

Each friend represents a world in us, a world possibly not born until they arrive, and it is only by this meeting that a new world is born.
ANAÏS NIN, Diary, (March 1937)

You can measure the social caste of a person by the distance between the husband's and wife's apartment.
ALFONSO XIII OF SPAIN

Seldom, or perhaps never, does a marriage develop into an individual relationship smoothly and without crises; there is no coming to consciousness without pain.
CARL JUNG, Contributions to Analytical Psychology, (1928)

Only the strong of heart can be well married, since they do

not turn to marriage to supply what no other human being can ever get from another - a sure sense of the fortress within himself.
MAX LERNER, *The Unfinished Country*, (1929)

In every marriage there is a selfish and an unselfish partner. A pattern is set up and soon becomes inflexible, of one person always making the demands and one person always giving way.
IRIS MURDOCH, *A Severed Head*, (1961)

It isn't silence you can cut with a knife any more, it's interchange of ideas. Intelligent discussion of practically everything is what is breaking up modern marriage.
E.B. WHITE, *Every Day Is Saturday*

All the unhappy marriages came from the husband having brains.
P.G. WODEHOUSE, *Adventures of Sally*, (1920)

Woe to the house where the hen crows and the rooster keeps still.
SPANISH PROVERB

Don't let your marriage go stale
Change the bag on the Hoover of life.
VICTORIA WOOD, ITV, (1982)

No human relation gives one possession in another, every two souls are absolutely different, in friendship or in love, the two side by side raise hands together to find what one cannot reach alone.
KAHIL GIBRAN, (1883-1931), *Beloved Prophet: the love letters of Kahil Gibran and Mary Haskell*

The married state, with and without the affection suitable to it, is the compleatest image of heaven and hell we are capable of receiving in this life.
RICHARD STEELE, *The Spectator*, 479, (1711-12)

The meeting of two personalities is like the contact of two chemical substances: if there is any reaction, both are

transformed.
CARL GUSTAV JUNG,
Modern Man in Search of a
Soul, (1933)

It is easier to live through
someone else than to become
complete yourself.
BETTY FRIEDAN, The
Feminine Mystique, (1963)

Oh I get by with a little help
from my friends,
Mm, I get high with a little
help from my friends.
JOHN LENNON, (1940-80),
and PAUL McCARTNEY,
(1942-)

A fanatic is a man that does
what he thinks th' Lord wud
do if He knew th' facts iv th'
case.
FINLEY PETER DUNNE, Mr.
Dooley's Philosophy, Casual
Observations, (1900)

If you cannot have your dear
husband for a comfort and a
delight, for a breadwinner and
a crosspatch, for a sofa, chair
or a hot-water bottle, one can
use him as a Cross to be
Borne.
STEVIE SMITH, (1902-71),
Novel on Yellow Paper, (1936)

The value of marriage is not
that adults produce children
but that children produce
adults.
PETER DE VRIES, The
Tunnel of Love, (1954)

I think we explored the
further reaches of 'for better or
for worse'.
MARY ARCHER, (1944-),
on her marriage with Jeffrey
(29 June 2001)

An ideal wife is any woman
who has an ideal husband.
BOOTH TARKINGTON,
Looking Forward to the Great
Adventure, (1926)

The awe and dread with
which the untutored savage
contemplates his mother-in-
law are amongst the most
familiar facts of anthropology.
JAMES GEORGE FRAZER,
(1854-1941), The Golden
Bough

Having one child makes you a
parent; having two you are a
referee.
DAVID FROST, (1939-),
Independent, (1989)

What greater thing is there for two human souls, than to feel that they are joined for life - to strengthen each other in all labour, to rest on each other in all sorrow, to minister to each other in all pain, to be one with each other in silent unspeakable memories at the moment of the last parting?
GEORGE ELIOT, Adam Bede, (1859)

Union is only possible to those who are units. To be fit for relations in time, souls, whether of man or woman, must be able to do without them in the spirit.
MARGARET FULLER, Woman in the Nineteenth Century, (1845)

In true marriage lies
Nor equal, nor unequal. Each fulfils
Defect in each and always thought in thought,
Purpose in purpose, will in will, they grow,
The single pure and perfect animal,
The two-celled heart beating with one full strike, Life.
ALFRED, LORD TENNYSON, The Princess: A Medley, 7, (1851)

Human relations just are not fixed in their orbits like the planets - they're more like galaxies, changing all the time, exploding into light for years, then dying away.
MAY SARTON, Crucial Conversations, (1975)

Do we really know anybody? Who does not wear one face to hide another?
FRANCES MARION, Westward the Dream, (1948)

When you hug someone, you learn something else about them. An important something else.
E.I. KONIGSBURG, From the Mixed-Up Files of Mrs. Basil E. Frankweiler, (1967)

If one is out of touch with oneself, then one cannot touch others.
ANNE MORROW LINDBERGH, Gift From the Sea, (1955)

Love seems the swiftest, but it is the slowest of all growths. No man or woman really knows what perfect love is until they have been married a quarter of a century.

MARK TWAIN, *Notebook*, (1935)

A relationship isn't meant to be an insurance policy, a life preserver or a security blanket. DIANE CROWLEY, (1992)

What is missing in him is probably necessary for what is missing in you. Let us not to the marriage of true impediments admit minds. JEAN KERR, *Mary, Mary*, (1963)

My one regret in life is that I am not someone else. WOODY ALLEN, (1935-)

We don't really go that far into other people, even when we think we do. We hardly ever go in and bring them out. We just stand at the jaws of the cave, and strike a match, and ask quickly if anybody's there. MARTIN AMIS, (1949-), *Money*, page 310

I move on feeling and have learned to distrust those who don't. NIKKI GIOVANNI, *Poems of Angela Yvonne Davis*, (1970)

In marriage do thou be wise: prefer the person before money, virtue before beauty, the mind before the body; then thou hast a wife, a friend, a companion, a second self. WILLIAM PENN, *Some Fruits of Solitude*, 1.92, (1693)

I do not believe in things: I believe in relationships. GEORGES BRAQUE, (1883-1963), in J. Culler, *Saussure*, Chapter 4

Industrial relations are like sexual relations. It's better between two consenting parties. VIC FEATHER, (1908-76), *Guardian Weekly*, (1976)

We have flown the air like birds and swum the sea like fishes, but have yet to learn the simple act of walking the earth like brothers. MARTIN LUTHER KING, JR., (1929-68), *Guardian*, (1983)

Better to be without logic than without feeling. CHARLOTTE BRONTË, *The Professor*, (1846)

Moving up the steep hill of a relationship had to be easier on tandem than unicycle, especially if the other person wasn't pedalling in the opposite direction.
SUSAN SUSSMAN, (1942-), The Dieter, Chapter 23

'Tis thus that on the choice of friends
Our good or evil name depends.
GAY, Old Woman and Her Cats, Part 1

We never know the true value of friends. While they live, we are too sensitive of their faults; when we have lost them, we only see their virtues.
J.C. and A.W. HARE, Guesses at Truth

Two friends, two bodies with one soul inspir'd.
HOMER, Iliad, Book XVI, line 267

I desire so to conduct the affairs of this administration that if at the end, when I come to lay down the reins of power, I have lost every other friend on earth, I shall at least have one friend left, and that friend shall be down inside of me.
LINCOLN, Reply to Missouri Committee of Seventy, (1864)

Our feelings are our most genuine paths to knowledge.
AUDRE LORDE, in Black Women Writers at Work, (1983)

A friend is, as it were, a second self.
CICERO, De Amicilia, XXI. 80

I would not enter on my list of friends
(Though graced with polish'd manners and fine sense,
Yet wanting sensibility) the man
Who needlessly sets foot upon a worm.
WILLIAM COWPER, The Task, Book VI, line 560

Forsake not an old friend, for the new is not comparable unto him. A new friend is as new wine: when it is old thou shalt drink it with pleasure.
Ecclesiasticus, IX. 10

Animals are such agreeable friends - they ask no

questions, they pass no criticisms.
GEORGE ELIOT, Mr. *Gilfil's Love-Story*, Chapter VII

I have loved my friends as I do virtue, my soul, my God.
SIR THOMAS BROWNE, *Religio Medici*, Part II, Section V

There is no man so friendless but what he can find a friend sincere enough to tell him disagreeable truths.
BULWER-LYTTON, *What Will He Do With It?*, Book II, Chapter XIV

Human relations are built on feeling, not on reason or knowledge. And feeling is not an exact science; like all spiritual qualities, it has the vagueness of greatness about it.
AMELIA E. BARR, *The Belle of Bowling Green*, (1904)

Manners are the shadows of virtues; the momentary display of those qualities which our fellow-creatures love and respect. If we strive to become, then, what we strive to appear, manners may often

be rendered useful guides to the performance of our duties.
SIDNEY SMITH

The best time for marriage will be towards thirty, for as the younger times are unfit, either to choose or to govern a wife and family, so, if thou stay long, thou shalt hardly see the education of thy children, who, being left to strangers, are in effect lost; and better were it to be unborn than ill-bred; for thereby thy posterity shall either perish, or remain a shame to thy name.
SIR WALTER RALEIGH

Domestic happiness, thou only bliss
Of paradise that has survived the fall.
WILLIAM COWPER

Take the daughter of a good mother.
FULLER

Like the one-tenth of our brain that we currently use, I think now that most if not all of us have access to about one-tenth of our possible feelings.

SONIA JOHNSON, *The Ship That Sailed Into the Living Room*, (1991)

Thus grief still treads upon the heels of pleasure,
Marry'd in haste, we may repent at leisure.
CONGREVE

Strong are the instincts with which God has guarded the sacredness of marriage.
MARIA M'INTOSH

He that hath wife and children hath given hostages to fortune; for they are impediments to great enterprises, either of virtue or mischief.
FRANCIS BACON, *Essays*, Of Marriage and Single Life

A holy family that make Each meal a Supper of the Lord.
LONGFELLOW, *The Golden Legend*, Part 1

It is unwise to feel too much if we think too little.
AGNES REPPLIER, (1957)

He that flies from his own family has far to travel.

PETRONIUS, *Satyricon*, Section 43

The bonds that unite another person to oneself exist only in our mind.
MARCEL PROUST, *Remembrance of Things Past*, The Sweet Cheat Gone, (1913-27)

Man is a knot, a web, a mesh into which relationships are tied. Only those relationships matter.
ANTOINE DE SAINT-EXUPÉRY, *Flight to Arras*, 19, (1942)

When the moon is not full, the stars shine more brightly.
UGANDA PROVERB

Atrophy of feeling creates criminals.
ANAÏS NIN, (1940), *The Diary of Anaïs Nin*, Volume 3, (1969)

If we say that a thing is great or small by its own standard of great or small, then there is nothing in all creation which is not great, nothing which is not small.

CHUANG TZU, *Works*, 2.2,
(4th-3rd century BC)

Without wearing any mask we
are conscious of, we have a
special face for each friend.
OLIVER WENDELL
HOLMES, SR., *The Professor
at the Breakfast Table*, 8,
(1860)

THIRTY-NINE

SCIENCE

To refuse the conduct of the light of nature (*luminis naturalis*) is not merely foolish but even impious.
ST. AUGUSTINE, *De Trinitate*, Book.4, Chapter 6

Science is nothing else but perception.
PLATO, *Theaetetus*, 46

The learned is happy nature to explore;
The fool is happy that he knows no more.
ALEXANDER POPE, *Essay on Man*, Ep. 2, 261

True is it Nature hides
Her treasures less and less.
Man now presides
In power, where once he trembled in his weakness;
Science advances with gigantic strides;
But are we aught enriched in love and meekness?
WILLIAM WORDSWORTH, *Miscellaneous Sonnets*, Part 3.41

Science is meaningless because it gives no answer to our question, the only question important for us:

'What shall we do and how shall we be?'
LEO TOLSTOY, (1828-1910)

Every good poem, in fact, is a bridge built from the known, familiar side of life over into the unknown. Science too, is always making expeditions into the unknown. But this does not mean that science can supersede poetry. For poetry enlightens us in a different way from science; it speaks directly to our feelings or imagination. The findings of poetry are no more and no less true than science.
C. DAY-LEWIS, (1904-72), *Poetry for You*, (1944)

Science and religion, religion and science, put it as I may, they are two sides of the same glass, through which we see darkly until these two, focusing together, reveal the truth.
PEARL S. BUCK, A *Bridge for Passing*, 3, (1962)

Shakespeare would have grasped wave functions, Donne would have understood complementary and relative time. They would have been

excited. What richness! They would have plundered this new science for their imagery. And they would have educated their audiences too. But you 'arts' people, you're not only ignorant of these magnificent things, you're rather proud of knowing nothing.
IAN MC EWAN, (1948-), *The Child in Time*, (1987)

The villagers seldom leave the village; many scientists have limited and poorly cultivated minds apart from their speciality.
SIMONE WEIL, *On Science, Necessity, and the Love of God*, (1968)

One of the disabling weaknesses of current Western literature is its unwillingness or inability to engage with the dance of the spirit in the sciences. Music and the arts are equipped to do better.
GEORGE STEINER, (1929-), *A Festival Overture*

Every man has a scheme that won't work.
E.W. HOWE

It seems to me that those sciences which are not born of experience, the mother of all certainty, and which do not end in known experience - that is to say, those sciences whose origin or process or end does not pass through any of the five senses - are vain and full of errors.
LEONARDO DA VINCI

The Germans, and not they alone, have a gift for making science inaccessible.
GOETHE

Science is true judgement in conjunction with reason.
PLATO, *Theaetetus*, 141

If the labours of the men of science should ever create any material revolution, direct or indirect, in our condition, and in the impressions which we habitually receive, the poet will sleep no more than at present, but he will be ready to follow the steps of the man of science, not only in those general indirect effects, but he will be at his side, carrying sensation into the midst of the objects of the science itself.

The remotest discoveries of the chemist, the botanist, or mineralogist, will be as proper objects of the poet's art as any upon which it can be employed, if the time should ever come when these things shall be familiar to us, and the relations under which they are contemplated by the followers of these respective sciences shall be manifestly and palpably material to us as enjoying and suffering beings.
WILLIAM WORDSWORTH, (1770-1850), preface to *Lyrical Ballads*, (1800)

Alas! Can we ring the bells backward? Can we unlearn the arts that pretend to civilise, and then burn the world? There is a march of science; but who shall beat the drums for its retreat?
CHARLES LAMB

If they [scientists] are worthy of the name, they are indeed about God's path and about his bed and spying out all his ways.
SAMUEL BUTLER, *Note-Books*

The greatest and saddest defect is not credulity, but our habitual forgetfulness that our science is ignorance.
HENRY DAVID THOREAU

It is the unscientific who are the materialists, whose intellect is not quickened, and the divinity which is everywhere eludes their stupid gaze.
G.W. RUSSELL (AE)

To expect a man to retain everything that he has ever read is like expecting him to carry about in his body everything that he has ever eaten.
ARTHUR SCHOPENHAUER, *Parerga and Paralipomena*

A science which does not bring us nearer to God is worthless.
SIMONE WEIL

Science is always simple and always profound. It is only the half-truths that are dangerous.
GEORGE BERNARD SHAW, *The Doctor's Dilemma*, 1, (1913)

Science is the most intimate school of resignation and humility, for it teaches us to bow before the seemingly most insignificant of facts.
MIGUEL DE UNAMUNO, *Tragic Sense of Life*, (1913)

Sweet is the lore which Nature brings;
Our meddling intellect
Mis-shapes the beauteous forms of things: -
We murder to dissect.
WILLIAM WORDSWORTH, *The Tables Turned*, (1798)

Science always departs from life and returns to it by a detour.
GOETHE

I am sorry to say that there is too much point to the wisecrack that life is extinct on other planets because their scientists were more advanced than ours.
PRESIDENT JOHN F. KENNEDY, (1959)

Nominally a great age of scientific inquiry, ours has actually become an age of superstition about the infallibility of science; of almost mystical faith in its non mystical methods; above all ... of external verities; of traffic-cop morality and rabbit-test truth.
LOUIS KRONENBERGER, *Company Manners*, line 4, (1954)

'Faith' is a fine invention
When Gentlemen can *see*
But *Microscopes* are prudent
In an Emergency.
EMILY DICKINSON, poem, (circa 1860)

Science has always promised two things not necessarily related - an increase first in our powers, second in our happiness or wisdom, and we have come to realise that it is the first and less important of the two promises which it has kept most abundantly.
JOSEPH WOOD KRUTCH, *The Modern Temper*, The Disillusion with the Laboratory, (1929)

The quick harvest of applied science is the usable process, the medicine, the machine. The shy fruit of pure science is Understanding.

LINCOLN BARNETT, (1950)

There's always wan encouragin' thing about th' sad scientific facts that come out ivry week in th' pa-apers. They're usually not thrue.
FINLEY PETER DUNNE, Mr. Dooley On Making a Will, (1919)

'Tis a short sight to limit our faith in laws to those of gravity, of chemistry, of botany, and so forth.
RALPH WALDO EMERSON, The Conduct of Life, Worship, (1860)

Scientist alone is true poet he gives us the moon
he promises the stars he'll make us a new universe if it comes to that.
ALLEN GINSBERG, Poem Rocket, (1961)

As soon as any one belongs to a narrow creed in science, every unprejudiced and true perception is gone.
GOETHE, quoted in Eckermann's Conversations with Goethe, (1824)

One science only will one genius fit,
So vast is art, so narrow human wit.
ALEXANDER POPE, Essay on Criticism, Part I, line 60

If it [science] tends to thicken the crust of ice on which, as it were, we are skating, it is all right. If it tries to find, or professes to have found, the solid ground at the bottom of the water, it is all wrong.
SAMUEL BUTLER, 2 Notebooks, Science, 20

God does not play dice.
ALBERT EINSTEIN

The religion that is afraid of science dishonours God and commits suicide.
RALPH WALDO EMERSON, Journals, (1831)

When one longs for a drink, it seems as though one could drink a whole ocean - that is faith; but when one begins to drink, one can only drink altogether two glasses - that is science.
ANTON CHEKHOV, Notebooks

One could count on one's fingers the number of scientists throughout the world with a general idea of the history and development of their particular science: there is none who is really competent as regards sciences other than his own. As science forms an indivisible whole, one may say that there are no longer, strictly speaking, scientists, but only drudges doing scientific work.
SIMONE WEIL, Oppression and Liberty, (1955)

Poetry is not the proper antithesis to prose, but to science. Poetry is opposed to science, and prose to metre.
SAMUEL TAYLOR COLERIDGE, Lectures and Notes of 1818

Biology is the study of complicated things that give the appearance of having been designed for a purpose. Physics is the study of simple things that do not tempt us to invoke design.
RICHARD DAWKINS, The Blind Watchmaker, Chapter 1

There is more religion in men's science, than there is science in their religion.
HENRY DAVID THOREAU

Every abstract is simply juggling with symbols.
DENIS DIDEROT, D'Alembert's Dream, page 221

Science is what a machine can do; art is what it will never do.
JOHN FOWLES, The Aristos, Chapter 9, line 41

Scientific knowledge helps us mainly because it makes the wonder to which we are called by nature rather more intelligible.
JOHANN WOLFGANG VON GOETHE, Maxims and Reflections

The way to do research is to attack the facts at the point of greatest astonishment.
CELIA GREEN, The Decline and Fall of Science, Aphorisms

Natural science does not simply describe and explain nature; it is part of the interplay between nature and ourselves; it describes nature

as exposed to our method of questioning.
WERNER HEISENBERG,
Physics and Philosophy,
Chapter 6

The ideal scientist thinks like a poet and works like a book-keeper.
EDWARD O. WILSON,
Consilience, Chapter 4

Man has to awake to wonder - and so perhaps do peoples. Science is a way of sending him to sleep again.
LUDWIG WITTGENSTEIN,
Culture and Value

Science investigates; religion interprets. Science gives man knowledge which is power; religion gives man wisdom which is control.
MARTIN LUTHER KING, JR., *Strength to Love*, line 1, (1963)

To have one favourite study and live in it with happy familiarity, and cultivate every portion of it diligently and lovingly, as a small yeoman proprietor cultivates his own land, this, as to study at least, is the most enviable

intellectual life.
PHILIP G. HAMERTON,
The Intellectual Life

There is one thing even more vital to science than intelligent methods; and that is, the sincere desire to find out the truth, whatever it may be.
CHARLES SANDERS PEIRCE

Love not the flower they pluck and know it not,
And all their botany is Latin names.
RALPH WALDO EMERSON, *Blight*

Put by the Telescope!
Better without it man may see,
Stretch'd awful in the hush'd midnight,
The ghost of his eternity.
COVENTRY PATMORE, *The Unknown Eros*

The true definition of science is this: the study of the beauty of the world.
SIMONE WEIL, *The Need for Roots*, (1949)

Science, like art, religion, political theory, or

psychoanalysis - is work that holds out the promise of philosophic understanding, excites in us the belief that we can 'make sense of it all'.
VIVIAN GORNICK, Women in Science, (1983)

If you do something once, people will call it an accident. If you do it twice, they call it a coincidence. But do it a third time and you've just proven a natural law.
GRACE MURRAY HOPPER, Mothers of Invention, (1988)

Almost anyone can do science; almost no one can do good science.
L.L. LARISON CUDMORE, The Center of Life, (1977)

We especially need imagination in science. It is not all mathematics, nor all logic, but it is somewhat beauty and poetry.
MARIA MITCHELL, (1866)

Good science is almost always so very simple. After it has been done by someone else, of course.
L.L. LARISON CUDMORE, The Center of Life

After your death you will be what you were before your birth.
ARTHUR SCHOPENHAUER, Parerga and Paralipomena

He who has science and art has religion too.
GOETHE

The effort to reconcile science and religion is almost always made, not by theologians, but by scientists unable to shake off altogether the piety absorbed with their mother's milk.
H.L. MENCKEN, Minority Report, 232, (1956)

It is only when science asks why, instead of simply describing how, that it becomes more than technology. When it asks why, it discovers Relativity. When it only shows how, it invents the atomic bomb.
URSULA K. LE GUIN, Language of the Night, (1979)

God is subtle but he is not malicious.
ALBERT EINSTEIN

We assume that knowledge of science is the prerogative of only a small number of human beings, isolated and priestlike in their laboratories. This is not true. The materials of science are the materials of life itself. Science is part of the reality of living; it is the what, the how, and the why of everything in our experience.
RACHEL CARSON, *The House of Life*, (1952)

Science is not neutral in its judgements, nor dispassionate, nor detached.
KIM CHERNIN, *The Obsession*, (1981)

Our science is like a store filled with the most subtle intellectual devices for solving the most complex problems, and yet we are almost incapable of applying the elementary principles of rational thought.
SIMONE WEIL, *The Power of Words*

Science is only an episode of religion - and an unimportant one at that.
CHRISTIAN MORGENSTERN

Whatever a scientist is doing - reading, cooking, talking, playing - science thoughts are always there at the edge of the mind. They are the way the world is taken in; all that is seen is filtered through an ever present scientific musing.
VIVIAN GORNICK, *Women in Science*, (1983)

The scientist in his laboratory is not only a technician: he is also a child placed before natural phenomena which impress him like a fairy tale.
MARIE CURIE, (1993), *Madame Curie*, (1938)

Science may be described as the art of systematic over simplification.
KARL POPPER

That is the essence of science; ask an impertinent question and you are on the way to a pertinent answer.
J. BRONOWSKI, *The Ascent of Man*

When a distinguished elderly scientist says something is possible, he is probably right; when he says something is impossible he is probably wrong.
ARTHUR C. CLARKE

Man is slightly nearer to the atom than the stars. From his central position he can survey the grandest works of Nature with the astronomer, or the minutest works with the physicist.
SIR ARTHUR EDDINGTON, *Stars and Atoms*

Science has 'explained' nothing; the more we know the more fantastic the world becomes and the profounder the surrounding darkness.
ALDOUS HUXLEY, *Views of Holland*

The wallpaper with which the men of science have covered the world of reality is falling to tatters.
HENRY MILLER, *Tropic of Cancer*, (1934)

Every formula which expresses a law of nature is a hymn of praise to God.
MARIA MITCHELL, (1818-89)

When this circuit learns your job, what are you going to do?
MARSHALL MC LUHAN, (1911-80)

Inanimate objects are classified scientifically into three major categories - those that don't work, those that break down, and those that get lost.
RUSSELL BAKER, (1925-)

The first rule of intelligent tinkering is to save all the parts.
PAUL RALPH EHRLICH, (1932-)

Any sufficiently advanced technology is indistinguishable from magic.
ARTHUR C. CLARKE (1917-), *The Lost Worlds of 2001*

The thing with high-tech is that you always end up using scissors.
DAVID HOCKNEY, (1937-)

Give me but one firm spot on which to stand, and I will move the earth.
ARCHIMEDES, (circa 287-212 BC), on the action of a lever

'Twas thus by the glare of false science betray'd,
That leads to bewilder, and dazzles to blind.
BEATTIE, *The Hermit*

Man is a tool-using animal ... Without tools he is nothing, with tools he is all.
THOMAS CARLYLE, (1795-1881), Sartor Resartus

One machine can do the work of fifty ordinary men. No machine can do the work of one extraordinary man.
ELBERT HUBBARD, (1859-1915), Thousand and One Epigrams, (1911)

Your worship is your furnaces,
Which, like old idols, lost obscenes,
Have molten bowels; your vision is
Machines for making more machines.
GORDON BOTTOMLEY, To Ironfounders and Others, (1912)

When you see something that is technically sweet, you go ahead and do it and you argue about what to do about it only after you have had your technical success. That is the way it was with the atomic bomb.
J. ROBERT OPPENHEIMER, (1904-67)

Technology ... the knack of so arranging the world that we need not experience it.
MAX FRISCH, (1911-91), Homo Faber, (1957)

Science is for the cultivation of religion, not for worldly enjoyment.
SADI, (circa 1213-91), The Rose Garden, (1258)

It is God who is the ultimate reason of things, and the knowledge of God is no less the beginning of science than his essence and will are the beginning of beings.
GOTTFRIED WILHELM LEIBNIZ, (1646-1716)

The atoms of Democritus
And Newton's particles of light
Are sands upon the Red Sea shore
Where Israel's tents do shine so bright.
WILLIAM BLAKE, (1757-1827), MS Note-Book

There are reverent minds who ceaselessly scan the fields of Nature and the books of Science in search of gaps - gaps which they will fill up

with God. As if God lived in gaps?
HENRY DRUMMOND, (1851-97), *The Ascent of Man*

Science without religion is lame, religion without science is blind.
ALBERT EINSTEIN, (1879-1955), *Science, Philosophy and Religion*

We have grasped the mystery of the atom and rejected the Sermon on the Mount.
OMAR BRADLEY, (1893-1981)

Increasing knowledge of science without a corresponding growth of religious wisdom only increases our fear of death.
SIR SARVEPALLI RADHAKRISHNAN

There is no evil in the atom; only in men's souls.
ADLAI STEVENSON

I ask you to look both ways. For the road to a knowledge of the stars leads through the atom; and important knowledge of the atom has been reached through the

stars.
ARTHUR EDDINGTON, (1882-1944), *Stars and Atoms*, (1928)

It is much easier to make measurements than to know exactly what you are measuring.
J.W.N. SULLIVAN, (1886-1937)

The aim of science is not to open the door to infinite wisdom, but to set a limit to infinite error.
BERTOLT BRECHT, Life of Galileo, (1939)

In effect, we have redefined the task of science to be the discovery of laws that will enable us to predict events up to the limits set by the uncertainty principle.
STEPHEN HAWKING, (1942-)

Lucky is he who has been able to understand the causes of things.
VIRGIL, (70-19 BC), *Georgics*

That all things are changed, and that nothing really perishes, and that the sum of

matter remains exactly the same, is sufficiently certain.
FRANCIS BACON, (1561-1626), Cogitationes de Natura Rerum

The changing of bodies into light, and light into bodies, is very conformable to the course of Nature, which seems delighted with transmutations.
ISAAC NEWTON, (1642-1727), Opticks, (1730 edition)

Natural science does not simply describe and explain nature, it is part of the interplay between nature and ourselves.
WERNER HEISENBERG, (1901-76), Physics and Philosophy

Science should leave off making pronouncements: the river of knowledge has too often turned back on itself.
JAMES JEANS, (1887-1946), The Mysterious Universe, Chapter 1

Our scientific power has outrun our spiritual power. We have guided missiles and misguided men.
MARTIN LUTHER KING,

JR., (1929-68), Strength of Love, Chapter 7

Science, at bottom, is really anti-intellectual. It always distrusts pure reason, and demands the production of objective fact.
H.L. MENCKEN, (1880-1956), Minority Report, 412

Traditional scientific method has always been at the very best, twenty-twenty hindsight. It's good for seeing where you've been.
ROBERT M. PIRSIG, (1928-), Zen and the Art of Motorcycle Maintenance, Part III, Chapter 24

The highest wisdom has but one science - the science of the whole - the science explaining the whole creation and man's place in it.
LEO TOLSTOY, (1828-1910), War and Peace, V, Chapter 2

Science appears but what in truth she is,
Not as our glory and our absolute boast,
But as a succedaneum, and a prop

To our infirmity.
WILLIAM
WORDSWORTH, (1770-
1850), *The Prelude*, II, 212

Scientists, therefore, are
responsible for their research
not only intellectually but also
morally ... the results of
quantum mechanics and
relativity theory have opened
up two very different paths for
physics to pursue. They may
lead us - to put it in extreme
terms - to the Buddha or to
the bomb, and it is up to each
of us to decide which path to
take.
FRITJOF OF CAPRA, (1939-
), *The Turning Point*, II, 3

Every genuine scientist must
be ... a metaphysician.
GEORGE BERNARD
SHAW, *Back to Methuselah*,
Preface

Religion will not regain its old
power until it can face change
in the same spirit as does
science. Its principles may be
eternal, but the expression of
those principles requires
continual development.
ALFRED NORTH
WHITEHEAD, *Science and the
Modern World*, 12, (1925)

Had he not been an untidy
man and apt to leave his
cultures exposed on the
laboratory table the spore of
hyssop mould, the *penicillin
notatum*, might never have
floated in from Praed Street
and settled on his dish of
staphylococci.
ANDRÉ MAUROIS, (Émile
Herzog: 1885-1967), *Life of
Alexander Fleming*

Science robs men of wisdom
and usually converts them
into phantom beings loaded
up with facts.
MIGUEL DE UNAMUNO Y
JUGO, (1864-1936), *Essays
and Soliloquies*

Whenever science makes a
discovery, the devil grabs it
while the angels are debating
the best way to use it.
ALAN VALENTINE

As long as vitalism and
spiritualism are open questions
so long will the gateway of
science be open to mysticism.
RUDOLF VIRCHOW, (1821-
1902)

Far out in the uncharted
backwaters of the

unfashionable end of the Western Spiral arm of the Galaxy lies a small unregarded yellow sun. Orbiting this at a distance of roughly ninety-two million miles is an utterly insignificant little blue green planet whose ape-descended life forms are so amazingly primitive that they still think digital watches are a pretty neat idea.
DOUGLAS ADAMS, (1952-), *The Hitch Hiker's Guide to the Galaxy*

Scientists are treated like gods handing down new commandments. People tend to assume that religion has been disproved by science. But the scientist may tell us how the world works, not why it works, not how we should live our lives, not how we face death or make moral decisions.
SUSAN HOWATCH, (1940-)

I do not know what I may appear to the world, but to myself I seem to have been only like a boy playing on the seashore, and diverting myself in now and then finding a smoother pebble or a prettier shell than ordinary, whilst the great ocean of truth lay all undiscovered before me.
ISAAC NEWTON, (1642-1727)

Do you really believe that the sciences would ever have originated and grown if the way had not been prepared by magicians, alchemists, astrologers and witches whose promises and pretensions first had to create a thirst, a hunger, a taste for *hidden* and *forbidden* powers? Indeed, infinitely more had to be *promised* than could ever be fulfilled in order that anything at all might be fulfilled in the realms of knowledge.
FRIEDRICH WILHELM NIETZSCHE, (1844-1900), *The Gay Science*

We have no right to assume that any physical laws exist, or if they have existed up to now, that they will continue to exist in a similar manner in the future.
MAX PLANCK, (1858-1947), *The Universe in the Light of Modern Physics*

Science without conscience is the death of the soul.
FRANÇOIS RABELAIS, (1483-1553)

When we have found how the nucleus of atoms are built-up we shall have found the greatest secret of all - except life. We shall have found the basis of everything - of the earth we walk on, of the air we breathe, of the sunshine, of our physical body itself, of everything in the world, however great or however small - except life.
ERNEST RUTHERFORD, (1871-1937), *Passing Show 24*

O star-eyed Science, hast thou wander'd there,
To waft us home the message of despair?
CAMPBELL, *Pleasures of Hope*, Part II, line 325

An undevout astronomer is mad.
EDWARD YOUNG, *Night Thoughts*, 9.771, (1742-46)

If all the arts aspire to the condition of music, all the sciences aspire to the condition of mathematics.

GEORGE SANTAYANA, (1863-1952)

Science is always wrong. It never solves a problem without creating ten more.
GEORGE BERNARD SHAW, (1856-1950)

Art and religion first, then philosophy; lastly science. That is the order of the great subjects of life, that's their order of importance.
MURIEL SPARK, (1918-)

Fifty-five crystal spheres geared to God's crankshaft is my idea of a satisfying universe. I can't think of anything more trivial than quarks, quasars, big bangs and black holes.
TOM STOPPARD, (1937-)

Mystics always hope that science will some day overtake them.
BOOTH TARKINGTON, (1869-1946), *Looking Forward to the Great Adventure*

The thing-in-itself, the will-to-live, exists whole and undivided in every being, even in the tiniest; it is

present as completely as in all that ever were, are, and will be, taken together.
ARTHUR SCHOPENHAUER, *Parerga and Paralipomena*

The microbe is so very small
You cannot make him out at all,
But many sanguine people hope
To see him through a microscope.
His jointed tongue that lies beneath
A hundred curious rows of teeth;
His seven tufted tails with lots
Of lovely pink and purple spots,
On each of which a pattern stands
Composed of forty separate bands;
His eyebrows of a tender green;
But Scientists, who ought to know,
Assure us that they must be so...
Oh! let us never, never doubt
What nobody is sure about!
HILAIRE BELLOC, *Cautionary Verses*, The Microbe
No one should approach the temple of science with the soul of a money changer.
THOMAS BROWNE, (1605-82)

There was a young lady named Bright,
Whose speed was far faster than light;
She set out one day
In a relative way,
And returned home the previous night.
ARTHUR HENRY REGINALD BULLER, (1874-1944)

Human pride
Is skilful to invent most serious names
To hide its ignorance.
PERCY BYSSHE SHELLEY, *Queen Mab*, VII

Putting on the spectacles of science in expectation of finding the answer to everything looked signifies inner blindness.
FRANK DOBIE, (1888-1964), *The Voice of Coyote*

And new Philosophy calls all in doubt,
The Element of fire is quite put out;

The Sun is lost, and th' earth,
and no man's wit
Can well direct him where to
look for it.
JOHN DONNE, (1573-1631),
An Anatomy of the World, 205

When you are courting a nice
girl an hour seems like a
second. When you sit on a
red-hot cinder a second seems
like an hour. That's relativity.
ALBERT EINSTEIN, (1879-
1955)

All the world is a laboratory
to the inquiring mind.
MARTIN H. FISCHER,
(1879-1962), Fischerisms

To some physicists chaos is a
science of process rather than
state, of becoming rather than
being.
JAMES GLEICK, Chaos

Thus I saw that most men
only care for science so far as
they get a living by it, and
that they worship even error
when it affords them a
subsistence.
GOETHE, (1749-1832),
Conversations with Goethe,
(Eckermann)

Many persons nowadays seem
to think that any conclusion
must be very scientific if the
arguments in favour of it are
derived from twitching of
frogs' legs - especially if the
frogs are decapitated - and
that - on the other hand - any
doctrine chiefly vouched for
by the feelings of human
beings - with heads on their
shoulders - must be benighted
and superstitious.
WILLIAM JAMES, (1842-
1910), Pragmatism

Life exists in the universe only
because the carbon atom
possesses certain exceptional
properties.
JAMES JEANS, (1877-1946),
The Mysterious Universe,
Chapter 1

Water is H2O, hydrogen two
parts, oxygen one, but there is
also a third thing that makes
it water and nobody knows
what that is.
D.H. LAWRENCE, (1885-
1930), The Third Thing

Science conducts us, step by
step, through the whole range
of creation, until we arrive, at
length, at God.

MARGUERITE OF VALOIS,
(1553-1615), *Memoirs*, (1594-
1600), Letter XII

FORTY

SELF-
KNOWLEDGE

To know oneself - this was the first principle and the first demand of old psychological schools. We still remember these words, but have lost their meaning. We think that *to know ourselves*, means to know our peculiarities, our desires, our tastes, our capacities and our intentions, when in reality it means to know ourselves as machines, that is to know the *structure* of one's machine, its *parts*, functions of different parts, the conditions governing their work and so on. We realise in a general way that we cannot know any machine without studying it. We must remember this in relation to ourselves and must study our own machines as machines. The means of study is *self-observation*. There is no other way and no one can do this work for us. We must do it ourselves. But before this we must learn *how* to observe. I mean, we must understand the technical side of observation: we must know that it is necessary to observe *different functions* and distinguish between them, remembering, at the same time, about *different states of consciousness*, about *our sleep*, and about the *many 'I's' in us*.
P.D. OUSPENSKY, *Man's Possible Evolution*

Ye people that labour the
worlde to mesure,
Thereby to knowe the regyons
of the same,
Knowe firste yourself, that
knowledge is moste sure.
For certaynly it is rebuke and
shame
For man to labour onely for a
name,
To knowe the compasse of all
the worlde wyde
Nat knowynge hymselfe, nor
how he sholde him gyde.
A BARCLAY, from *Ship of Fools*

There is a god within us, and
we have intercourse with
heaven. That spirit comes
from abodes on high.
OVID

The soul is a much better
thing than all the others
which you possess. Can you
then show me in what way
you have taken care of it? For
it is not likely that you, who
are so wise a man,

inconsiderately and carelessly allow the most valuable thing that you possess to be neglected and to perish!
EPICTETUS

We cannot describe the natural history of the soul, but we know that it is divine. I cannot tell if these wonderful qualities which house to-day in this mortal frame shall ever reassemble in equal activity in a similar frame, or whether they have before had a natural history like that of this body you see before you; but this one thing I know, that these qualities did not now begin to exist, cannot be sick with my sickness, nor buried in any grave; but that they circulate through the Universe: before the world was, they were. Nothing can bar them out, or shut them in, they penetrate the ocean and land, space and time, form and essence, and hold the key to universal nature. I draw from this, faith, courage, and hope. All things are known to the soul. It is not to be surprised by any communication. Nothing can be greater than it. Let those fear and those fawn who will.

The soul is in her native realm, and it is wider than space, older than time, wide as hope, rich as love. Pusillanimity and fear she refuses with a beautiful scorn: they are not for her who putteth on her coronation robes, and goes out through universal love to universal power.
RALPH WALDO EMERSON

It is the soul itself which sees and hears, and not those parts which are, as it were, but windows to the soul.
CICERO

Our birth is but a sleep and a forgetting; the soul that rises with us - our life's star, hath had elsewhere its setting, and cometh from afar; not in entire forgetfulness, and not in utter nakedness, but trailing clouds of glory do we come from God who is our home.
WILLIAM WORDSWORTH

'Tis the divinity that stirs within us.
THOMAS ADDISON

There has been added to your body Something which you

cannot see, and this
Something speaks to you in a
way that is different from your
senses.
The body remains after this
unseen part has fled, so it is
no part of the body. It is
immaterial, therefore eternal.
It is free to act, therefore
accountable for its actions.
Know Yourself, therefore, as
the pride of Earth's creatures.
You are the link uniting
Divinity and matter. There is
a part of God Himself in you;
therefore, remember your own
dignity. Be faithful to the
Divine spark which is You.
DANDEMIS

He that knows himself, knows
others; and he that is ignorant
of himself, could not write a
very profound lecture on other
men's heads.
COLTON

The most difficult thing in life
is to know yourself.
THALES

Explore the dark recesses of
the mind,
In the soul's honest volume
read mankind,
And own, in wise and simple,

great and small,
The same grand leading
principle in all,
And by whatever name we call
The ruling tyrant, self is all in
all.
J. CHURCHILL

Life is the soul's nursery.
THACKERAY

The soul on earth is an
immortal guest,
Compell'd to starve at an
unreal feast:
A spark, which upward tends
by nature's force:
A stream diverted from its
parent source;
A drop dissever'd from the
boundless sea;
A moment, parted from
eternity;
A pilgrim panting for the rest
to come;
An exile, anxious for his
native home.
HANNAH MORE

The soul, of origin divine,
God's glorious image, freed
from clay,
In heaven's eternal sphere
shall shine
A star of day!
The sun is but a spark of fire,

A transient meteor in the sky;
The soul, immortal as its sire,
Shall never die.
MONTGOMERY

Whatever that be, which
thinks, which understands,
which wills, which acts, it is
something celestial and
divine; and, upon that
account, must necessarily be
eternal.
CICERO

I am positive I have a soul;
nor can all the books with
which materialists have
pestered the world, ever
convince me to the contrary.
STERNE

Blessed is the person who
utterly surrenders his soul for
the name of YHWH to dwell
therein and to establish
therein its throne of glory.
ZOHAR

That which has a beginning
must also end... Realisation is
not acquisition of anything
new nor is it a new faculty. It
is only removal of all
camouflage... The ultimate
Truth is so simple. It is
nothing more than being in

the pristine state... Mature
minds alone can grasp the
simple Truth in all its
nakedness.
SRI RAMANA MAHARSHI

How is it possible to find
oneself when seeking others
rather than oneself?... By not
taking the mind to be
naturally a duality, and
allowing it, as the primordial
consciousness, to abide in its
own place, beings attain
deliverance.
PADMA-SAMBHAVA

Our original Buddha-Nature
is, in highest truth, devoid of
any atom of objectivity. It is
void, omnipresent, silent,
pure; it is glorious and
mysterious peaceful joy - and
that is all. Enter deeply into
it by awaking to it yourself.
That which is before you is it,
in all its fullness, utterly
complete. There is naught
beside. Even if you go
through all the stages of a
Bodhisattva's progress towards
Buddhahood, one by one;
when at last, in a single flash,
you attain to full realisation,
you will only be realising the
Buddha-Nature which has

been with you all the time; and by all the foregoing stages you will have added to it nothing at all. You will come to look upon those aeons of work and achievement as no better than unreal actions performed in a dream. That is why the Tathâgata said: 'I truly attained nothing from complete, unexcelled Enlightenment.'
HUANG PO

Realise what is present here and now. The sages did so before and still do that only. Hence they say that is looks as if newly got. Once veiled by ignorance and later revealed, Reality looks as if newly realised. But it is not new.
SRI RAMANA MAHARSHI

It is of course nothing new that you gain. God is already within you, but you had forgotten Him and so temporarily lost Him. When any external matter enters your eye, you feel terrible irritation. When it is removed, your pain is relieved and you feel as if you have gained something new. In fact, you did not gain anything new. You only got back to the normal state you had lost temporarily.
SWAMI RAMDAS

To be satisfied in God is the highest difficulty in the whole world, and yet most easy... because God is. For God is not a being compounded of body and soul, or substance and accident, or power and act, but is all act, pure act, a Simple Being whose essence is to be, whose Being is to be perfect.
THOMAS TRAHERNE

When true sanctity and purity shall ground (a man) in the knowledge of divine things, then shall the inward sciences, that arise from the bottom of his own soul, display themselves; which indeed are the only true sciences: for the soul runs not out of itself to behold temperance and justice abroad, but its own light sees them in the contemplation of its own being, and that divine essence which was before enshrined within itself.
PLOTINUS

Stop talking, stop thinking,
and there is nothing you will
not understand.
Return to the Root and you
will find the Meaning;
Pursue the Light, and you will
lose its source ...
There is no need to seek
Truth: only stop having views.
SENG-TS'AN

One loses science when losing
the purity of the heart.
NICHOLAS VALOIS

The end reached by the
theologian, is the beginning of
the way for the dervish.
'ABD AL-WAHHÂB AL-
SHA'RÂNÎ

With all their science, those
people at Paris are not able to
discern what God is in the
least of creatures - not even in
a fly!
ECKHART

I feel within me a consuming
fire of heavenly love which
has burned up in my soul
everything that was contrary
to itself and transformed me
inwardly into its own nature.
WILLIAM LAW, (spoken on
his deathbed)

The Self being illumined by
meditation, and then burning
with the fire of Knowledge, is
delivered from all accidents,
and shines in its own
splendour, like gold which is
purified in the fire.
SRI SANKARÂCHÂRYA

The mind becomes a blank
sheet; then the Yogi destroys
this sheet and becomes
identified with the Self, the
supreme Being, from whom
the mind derives all its light.
He thus obtains omniscience
and final emancipations.
These are things which are so
much Greek to our Western
psychologists; this is why they
grope in darkness. They have
no idea of the perfect Being or
Purusha, witness of the mind's
activities.
SWAMI SIVANANDA

Either the thoughts are
eliminated by holding on to
the root-thought 'I' or one
surrenders oneself
unconditionally to the Higher
Power. These are the only
two ways for Realisation.
SRI RAMANA MAHARSHI

When you come to a certain point of the so-called expansion of your love and vision, it undergoes a sudden and lightning change into the Universal Consciousness. It is Jiva realising that it is Brahman. Jiva is the individual soul. As soon as the ignorance which has obsessed the soul is removed, that instant it realises that it is the Supreme Spirit. In regard to this transformation, there are no intermediary stages. The stages are only, Ramdas repeats, in the process of self-purification which helps to break the barriers between us and God and grants us the knowledge that we are one with Him.
SWAMI RAMDAS

Thou art but an atom, He, the great whole; but if for a few days Thou meditate with care on the whole, thou becomest one with it.
JÂMI

When you wake up you will find that this whole world, above and below, is nothing other than a regarding of oneself.
HAKUIN

Men do not know themselves, and therefore they do not understand the things of their inner world. Each man has the essence of God, and all the wisdom and power of the world (germinally) in himself; he possesses one kind of knowledge as much as another, and he who does not find that which is in him cannot truly say that he does not possess it, but only that he was not capable of successfully seeking for it.
PARACELSUS

Children, ye shall not seek after great science. Simply enter into your own inward principle, and learn to know what you yourselves are, spiritually and naturally.
TAULER

Duke (in disguise): I pray you, sir, of what disposition was the duke?
Escalus: One that, above all other strifes, contended especially to know himself.
WILLIAM SHAKESPEARE, *Measure for Measure*, Act III, Scene ii, line 50

It may not be too difficult to accept the fact that enlightenment or Self-realisation, or whatever, is not something to be achieved by an individual because the basis of what is desired by an individual is the annihilation of that very individuality, the sense of volition. It may also not be too difficult to accept the fact that Self-realisation is a sudden spontaneous happening that is not the culmination of acquiring conceptual knowledge by the individual.

What is difficult to accept is that the sudden happening of Self-realisation does not need at least some groundwork to be prepared by the very ego who yearns for the happening. In other words, surely some kind of spiritual practice is not only necessary but inevitable, and also, such practice, whatever may be the path, can only be done by the ego. In other words, when Ramana Maharshi says, "find out 'Who am I?'," surely he is asking the ego to find out. This cannot be denied.

The problem basically is that such necessary groundwork cannot be prepared by the discursive methods usually suggested and employed. We must sit at the feet of the accepted Masters, like Ramana Maharshi, who are not personally interested in handing out the necessary spiritual guidance. Such Masters have the fundamental understanding that reaching the heart of the seekers is not their personal responsibility, and that whether the teaching reaches a particular seeker depends entirely on the receptivity of the particular seeker as provided in the relative programming of that body-mind organism, over which the concerned individual has had absolutely no control. In other words, success will happen only if it is supposed to happen according to God's Will or the Cosmic Law.

RAMESH BALSEKAR, from *The Ultimate Understanding*

I AM,
Without beginning, without end,
Older than night or day,
Younger than the babe new-born,

Brighter than light,
Darker than darkness,
Beyond all things and
creatures,
Yet fixed in the heart of every
one.

From me the shining worlds
flow forth,
To me all at last return,
Yet to me neither men nor
angels
May draw nigh,
For I am known only to
myself.

Ever the same is mine inmost
being;
Absolutely one, complete,
whole, perfect;
Always itself;
Eternal, infinite, ultimate;
Formless, indivisible, changeless.
PAUL FOSTER CASE, from
The Book of Tokens

The Knowledge of one's
identity with the pure Self
that negates the (wrong)
notion of the identity of the
body and the Self sets a man
free even against his will
when it becomes as firm as the
belief of the man that he is a
human being.
SRI SANKARÂCHÂRYA

This above all, to thine own
Self be true.
WILLIAM SHAKESPEARE,
Hamlet

If thou know not thyself, O
fairest among women, go
forth, and follow after the
steps of the flocks.
Canticle of Canticles 1.7

If you will know yourselves,
then you will be known and
you will know that you are the
sons of the living Father. But
if you do not know yourselves,
then you are in poverty and
you are poverty.
The Gospel according to
Thomas, Log. 3

No one can be saved without
self-knowledge.
ST. BERNARD

Let us enter the cell of self-
knowledge.
ST. CATHERINE OF SIENA

Jesus said: Whoever knows the
All but fails to know himself
lacks everything.
The Gospel according to
Thomas, Log. 67

And when he (Apollonius) had taken his seat, he (a Brahman sage) said: 'Ask whatever you like, for you find yourself among people who know everything.' Apollonius then asked him whether they knew themselves also, thinking that he, like the Greeks, would regard self-knowledge as a difficult matter. But the other, contrary to Apollonius' expectations, corrected him and said: 'We know everything, just because we begin by knowing ourselves; for no one of us would be admitted to this philosophy unless he first knew himself.' And Apollonius remembered what he had heard Phraotes say, and how he who would become a philosopher must examine himself before he undertakes the task; and he therefore acquiesced in this answer, for he was convinced of its truth in his own case also.
THE LIFE OF APOLLONIUS OF TYANA

You ought, O Soul, to get sure knowledge of your own being, and of its forms and aspects. Do not think that any one of the things of which you must seek to get knowledge is outside of you; no, all things that you ought to get knowledge of are in your possession, and within you. Beware then of being led into error by seeking (elsewhere) the things which are in your possession.
HERMES

He who reflects upon himself, reflects upon his own original.
PLOTINUS

God hath stamped a copy of his own archetypal loveliness upon the soul, that man by reflecting into himself might behold there the glory of God.
JOHN SMITH THE PLATONIST

If a man knows himself, he shall know God.
CLEMENT OF ALEXANDRIA

(The Pythagoreans) investigated, not what is *simply* good, but what is *especially* so; nor what is difficult, but what is most difficult; for a man to know himself.
IAMBLICHUS

When one's mind is thus known in its nakedness, this Doctrine of Seeing the Mind Naked, this Self-Liberation, is seen to be exceedingly profound.
Seek, therefore, thine own Wisdom within thee.
It is the Vast Deep.
PADMA-SAMBHAVA

'Seek within - know thyself,' these secret and sublime hints come to us wafted from the breath of Rishis through the dust of ages.
SWAMI RAMDAS

The soul which is attempting to rise to the height of knowledge must make self-knowledge its first and chief concern. The high peak of knowledge is perfect self-knowledge.
RICHARD OF SAINT-VICTOR

You never know yourself till you know more than your body. The Image of God was not seated in the features of your face, but in the lineaments of your Soul. In the knowledge of your Powers, Inclinations, and Principles, the knowledge of yourself chiefly consisteth.
THOMAS TRAHERNE

Thou knowest Myself in thyself, and from this knowledge thou wilt derive all that is necessary.
ST. CATHERINE OF SIENA

Man must first of all know his own soul before he can know his Lord; for his knowledge of the Lord is as the fruit of his knowledge of himself.
IBN 'ARABI

I say, no man knows God who knows not himself first.
ECKHART

You ought to know yourself as you really are, so that you may understand of what nature you are and whence you have come to this world and for what purpose you were created and in what your happiness and misery consist.
AL-GHAZÂLÎ

The enquiry 'Who am I?' is the only method of putting an end to all misery and ushering in supreme Beatitude.
SRI RAMANA MAHARSHI

Only the truly intelligent understand this principle of the identity of all things. They do not view things as apprehended by themselves, subjectively; but transfer themselves into the position of the things viewed. And viewing them thus they are able to comprehend them, nay, to master them; - and he who can master them is near. So it is that to place oneself in subjective relation with externals, without consciousness of their objectivity, - this is TAO.
CHUANG-TSE, Chapter II

When we're identified with Awareness, we're no longer living in a world of polarities. Everything is present at the same time.
From *Ram Dass: One Liners*

Thoroughly to know oneself, is above all art, for it is the highest art. If thou knowest thyself well, thou art better and more praiseworthy before God, than if thou didst not know thyself, but didst understand the course of the heavens and of all the planets and stars, also the virtue of all herbs, and the structure and dispositions of all mankind, also the nature of all beasts, and, in such matters, hadst all the skill of all who are in heaven and on earth.
Theologia Germanica, IX

And is self-knowledge such an easy thing, and was he to be lightly esteemed who inscribed the text on the temple at Delphi?
PLATO, *Alcibiades*, I, 129 A

Thou believest thyself to be nothing, and yet it is in thee that the world resides.
AVICENNA

Self-knowledge is the shortest road to the knowledge of God. When 'Ali asked Mohammad, 'What am I to do that I may not waste my time?' the Prophet answered, 'Learn to know thyself.'
'AZÎZ IBN MUHAMMAD AL-NASAFÎ

He who knows others is wise; He who knows himself is enlightened.
TAO TE CHING, XXXIII

Origen says the soul's quest of God comes by self-observation. If she knew herself she would know God also.
ECKHART

The final aim of knowledge is to hold that we know nothing. He alone being wise, who is also alone God.
PHILO

To know and yet not to do is in fact not to know.
WANG YANG-MING

Knowledge without action is not knowledge.
HUJWÎRÎ

But be ye doers of the word, and not hearers only, deceiving your own selves.
James 1:22

Those who love the Truth in each thing are to be called lovers of wisdom and not lovers of opinion.
PLATO, *Republic* V, 480 B

One momentary glimpse of Divine Wisdom, born of meditation, is more precious than any amount of knowledge derived from merely listening to and thinking about religious teachings.
GAMPOPA

Mere performance of spiritual austerity is its progress also. Steadiness is what is required.
SRI RAMANA MAHARSHI

Any one in whose soul God shall put the touchstone, he will distinguish certainty from doubt.
RÛMÎ

Those who desire progress along the Way must first cast out the dross acquired through heterogeneous learning.
HUANG PO

Light seeking light doth light of light beguile.
WILLIAM SHAKESPEARE, *Love's Labour's Lost*, Act I, Scene i, line 77

O foolish people, and without understanding; which have eyes, and see not; which have ears, and hear not.
Jeremiah, Verse 21

I would rather die of pure love than let God escape from me in dark wisdom.
MECHTHILD OF MAGDEBURG

He who is learned is not wise; He who is wise is not learned.
TAO TE CHING, LXXXI

Any knowledge that does not bring us this supreme bliss and freedom is not worth acquiring. We stuff our minds with knowledge of so many facts and things gained from all and sundry, or reading all kinds of books. The brain becomes a repository of learning about all the ephemeral and passing phases of life. Naturally, such a man becomes a restless being - unbalanced, confused and erratic in his behaviour and conduct. Seek, therefore, to know the true source of your life, - God. That is why you are here.
SWAMI RAMDAS

If a man had all that sort of knowledge that ever was, he would not be at all the wiser; he would only be able to play with men, tripping them up and oversetting them with distinctions of words. He would be like a person who pulls away a stool from some one when he is about to sit down, and then laughs and makes merry at the sight of his friend overturned and laid on his back.
PLATO, *Euthydemus*, 278 C

For wisdom will not enter into a malicious soul, nor dwell in a body subject to sins.
Wisdom, I.4

Without self-knowledge, experience breeds illusion; with self-knowledge, experience, which is the response to challenge, does not leave a cumulative residue as memory. Self-knowledge is the discovery from moment to moment of the ways of the self, its intentions and pursuit, its thoughts and appetites. There can never be "your experience" and "my experience", the very term "my experience" indicates ignorance and the acceptance of illusion.
J. KRISHNAMURTI, from *Daily Meditation, January 25*

In thinking, "This is I" and
"That is mine" one binds
himself with himself, as does a
bird with a snare!
Maitri Upanishad 6.30

Consciousness is pure, eternal
and infinite; it does not arise
nor cease to be. It is ever
there in the moving and
unmoving creatures, in the
sky, on the mountain and in
fire and air. When life-breath
(prana) ceases, the body is
said to be "dead" or "inert".
The life-breath returns to its
source - air - and
consciousness freed from
memory and tendencies
remains as the self.
YOGA VASISHTHA 3.55

There is no greater mystery
than this,
that being the Reality
ourselves,
we seek to gain Reality.
SRI RAMANA MAHARSHI

To reach the realms of light,
we have to pass through the
clouds. Some men stop there;
others are able to pass beyond.
From *The Pretty Wit of Joseph
Joubert*

They talk, says Sheridan one
day to Lord Holland, of
avarice, lust, ambition, as
great passions. It is a mistake;
they are little passions.
Vanity is the great
commanding passion of all. It
is this that produces the most
grand and heroic deeds, or
impels to the most dreadful
crimes. Save me from this
passion, and I can defy the
others. They are mere
urchins, but this is a giant.
TOM MOORE, *Journal* (5
August 1824)

Acquire a firm will and the
utmost patience.
ANANDA MOYI

If each moment wasted in the
pursuit of non-Self be utilised
for the pursuit of the Self,
realisation of the Self will very
soon ensue.
SRI RAMANA MAHARSHI

FORTY-ONE

SEXUALITY

Sexuality is a sacrament.
STARHAWK, *The Spiral Dance*, (1979)

He (the sacrificer) then offers a dish of clotted curds to Mitra and Varuna. Now he who performs this (Agni-kayana) rite comes to be with the gods; and these two, Mitra and Varuna are a divine pair. Now, were he to have intercourse with a human woman without having offered this (oblation), it would be a descent, as if one who is divine would become human; but when he offers this dish of clotted curds to Mitra and Varuna, he thereby approaches a divine mate: having offered it, he may freely have intercourse in a befitting way.
Satapatha-Brâhmana, IX.V. line 54

All forms of sexual loving become acceptable if the lovers wear togas or wolfskins.
NAOMI MITCHISON, (1897-), *Writing Lives*, (1988)

I know the very difference that lies
'Twixt hallow'd love and base unholy lust;
I know the one is as a golden spur,
Urging the spirit to all noble aims;
The other but a foul and miry pit,
O'erthrowing it in midst of its career.
FANNY KEMBLE BUTLER

Brahmacharya is 'living in Brahman'. It has no connection with celibacy as commonly understood... Celibacy is certainly an aid to realisation among so many other aids... It is a matter of fitness of mind. Married or unmarried, a man can realise the Self, because that is here and now.
SRI RAMANA MAHARSHI

Sex divorced from love is the thief of personal dignity.
CAITLIN THOMAS, *Not Quite Posthumous Letter to My Daughter*, (1963)

Sex as something beautiful may soon disappear. Once it was a knife so finely honed the edge was invisible until it was touched and then it cut deep. Now it is so blunt that

it merely bruises and leaves ugly marks.
MARY ASTOR, A *Life on Film*

For the bewitching of naughtiness doth obscure things that are honest; and the wandering of concupiscence doth undermine the simple mind. He, being made perfect in a short time, fulfilled a long time.
Wisdom, 4.12-13

Sex annihilates identity, and the space given to sex in contemporary novels is an avowal of the absence of character.
MARY MC CARTHY, *On the Contrary*

Did my heart love till now? forswear it, sight!
For I ne'er saw true beauty till this night.
WILLIAM SHAKESPEARE, *Romeo and Juliet*, Act I, Scene v, line 56

The price of shallow sex may be a corresponding loss of capacity for deep love.
SHANA ALEXANDER, *Talking Woman*

More divorces start in the bedroom than in any other room in the house.
ANN LANDERS, *Since You Ask Me*

Consumerism is what physical lust is really about.
CAROLE STEWART MC DONNELL, in *Life Notes*

Sex is only the liquid centre of the great Newberry Fruit of friendship.
JILLY COOPER, (1937-), *Super-Jilly*, jacket

Continental people have sex life; the English have hot-water-bottles.
GEORGE MIKES, (1912-87), *How to be an Alien*

It is better to marry than to burn.
I *Corinthians* 7:9

You cannot call it love; for at your age
The hey-day in the blood is tame, it's humble
And waits upon the judgement.
WILLIAM SHAKESPEARE, (1564-1616), *Hamlet*, Act III, Scene iii, line 68

Full near I came unto where
dwelleth
Laila, when I heard her call.
That voice is sweet beyond
compare.
I would that it might never
cease.
She favoured me and drew me
to her,
took me in, into her precinct.
With discourse intimate
addressed me,
sat me face to face with her.
Closer drew herself towards
me,
raised the cloak that hid her
from me,
Made me marvel to
distraction,
bewildered me with all her
beauty.
She took me and amazed me,
and hid me in her inmost self.
Until I thought that she was I,
and my life she took as
ransom.
SHAYKH AHMAD AL-'
ALAWÎ

Sex itself must always, it
seems to me, come to us as a
sacrament and be so used or it
is meaningless. The flesh is
suffused by the spirit, and it is
forgetting this in the act of
love-making that creates

cynicism and despair.
MAY SARTON, *Recovering*,
(1980)

I have never yet seen anyone
whose desire to build up his
moral power was as strong as
sexual desire.
CONFUCIUS, (551-479 BC),
Analects

Not tonight, Josephine.
NAPOLEON I, *The History of
Napoleon*, (1841)

While we think of it, and talk
of it
Let us leave it alone,
physically, keep apart.
For while we have sex in the
mind, we truly have none in
the body.
D.H. LAWRENCE, *Leave Sex
Alone*, (1929)

I think Lawrence tried to
portray this [sex] relation as in
a real sense an act of holy
communion. For him flesh
was sacramental of the spirit.
BISHOP JOHN ROBINSON,
(1919-83), *The Times*, (1960)

Blissful is the dawn of
Wisdom, like the virgin's
wedding night;

Till experienced none can
know it as it is, O Tingri folk.
PHADAMPA SANGAY

Traditionally, sex has been a
very private, secretive activity.
Herein perhaps lies its
powerful force for uniting
people in a strong bond. As
we make sex less secretive, we
may rob it of its power to hold
men and women together.
THOMAS SZASZ, (1920-),
The Second Sin, (1973)

Sexuality is the lyricism of the
masses.
CHARLES BAUDELAIRE,
(1821-67), French Poet,
Journaux Intimes, 93

It doesn't matter what you do
in the bedroom as long as you
don't do it in the street and
frighten the horses.
MRS PATRICK CAMPBELL,
in *The Duchess of Jermyn Street*

As one embraced by a darling
bride knows naught of 'I' and
'thou', so self embraced by the
foreknowing (solar) Self
knows naught of a 'myself'
within or a 'thyself' without.
Brihad-Âranyaka Upanishad,
IV. iii. 21

Ignorance of the necessity for
sexual intercourse to the
health and virtue of both man
and woman, is the most
fundamental error in medical
and moral philosophy.
GEORGE DRYSDALE, *The
Elements of Social Science*

No sex is better than bad sex.
GERMAINE GREER,
attributed

No sex without responsibility.
LORD LONGFORD, *The
Observer*, (1954)

It has to be admitted that we
English have sex on the brain,
which is a very unsatisfactory
place to have it.
MALCOLM MUGGERIDGE,
Sayings of the Decade, (1964)

Love is not the dying moan of
a distant violin - it's the
triumphant twang of a
bedspring.
S.J. PERELMAN, (1904-79),
*Quotations for Speakers and
Writers*

I tend to believe that cricket
is the greatest thing that God
ever created on earth ...
certainly greater than sex,

although sex isn't too bad
either.
HAROLD PINTER, (1930-),
The Observer, (1980)

Lo! the God-fearing are in a
state secure,
Amid gardens and
watersprings,
Attired in silk and gold
brocade, facing one another;
Thus: and We shall wed them
in houris with wide lovely
eyes.
Qur'ân, XLIV. 51-54

Sex is the tabasco sauce which
an adolescent national palate
sprinkles on every course in
the menu.
MARY DAY WINN, (1888-
1965), *Adam's Rib*

Freud found sex an outcast in
the outhouse and left it in the
living room an honoured
guest.
W. BERAN WOLFE, *The
Great Quotations*

Pornography is the attempt to
insult sex, to do dirt on it.
D.H. LAWRENCE, *Phoenix*,
Pornography and Obscenity,
(1936)

There are two things in this
world which delight me:
women and perfumes. These
two things rejoice my eyes,
and render me more fervent in
devotion.
MUHAMMAD

When Lust
By unchaste looks, loose
gestures, and foul talk,
But most by lewd and lavish
act of sin,
Lets in defilement to the
inward parts,
The soul grows clotted by
contagion,
Imbodies and imbrutes.
JOHN MILTON, *Comus*, line
463

To be carnally minded is
death.
Romans 8:6

Love indeed (I may not deny)
first united provinces, built
cities, and by a perpetual
generation makes and
preserves mankind; but if it
rage it is no more love, but
burning lust, a disease, frenzy,
madness, hell... It subverts
kingdoms, overthrows cities,
towns families; mars, corrupts,
and makes a massacre of men;

thunder and lightning, wars,
fires, plagues, have not done
that mischief to mankind, as
this burning lust, this brutish
passion.
ROBERT BURTON, *Anatomy
of Melancholy*, Part III, Section
2, Mem. 1, Subs. 2

There are no instincts less
harmful or more productive of
delight in the whole range of
human instinct and emotion
than the desire for sex-love
and the desire for children.
DORA RUSSELL, *The Right
to Be Happy*

The most intense and perfect
contemplation of God is
through women, and the most
intense union (in the sensory
realm, which serves as support
for this contemplation) is the
conjugal act.
IBN' ARABÎ

Love comforteth like sunshine
after rain,
But Lust's effect is tempest
after sun;
Love's gentle spring doth
always fresh remain,
Lust's winter comes ere
summer half be done;
Love surfeits not. Lust like a

glutton dies;
Love is all truth, Lust full of
forged lies.
WILLIAM SHAKESPEARE,
Venus and Adonis, line 799

What men call gallantry, and
gods, adultery,
Is much more common where
the climate's sultry.
BYRON, *Don Juan*, Canto I,
Stanza 63

For everything created
In the bounds of earth and
sky,
Hath such longing to be
mated,
It must couple or must die.
G.J. WHYTE-MELVILLE,
Like to Like

Making love, we are all more
alike than we are when we are
talking or acting. In the
climax of the sexual act,
moreover, we forget ourselves;
that is commonly felt to be
one of its recommendations.
Sex annihilates identity, and
the space given to sex in
contemporary novels is an
avowal of the absence of
character.
MARY MC CARTHY, *On the
Contrary*

In that conjunction of the two sexes, or, to speak more truly, that fusion of them into one, which may be rightly named Eros, or Aphrodite, or both at once, there is a deeper meaning than man can comprehend. It is a truth to be accepted as sure and evident above all other truths, that by God, the Master of all generative power, has been devised and bestowed upon all creatures, this sacrament of eternal reproduction, with all the affection, all the joy and gladness, all the yearning and the heavenly love that are inherent in its being.
HERMES

As in all other experiences, we always have the sexual experience we deserve, depending on our loving kindness towards ourselves and others.
THADDEUS GOLAS, The Lazy Man's Guide to Enlightenment

Th' expense of spirit in a waste of shame
Is lust in action; and till action, lust
Is perjur'd, murd'rous, bloody, full of blame,
Savage, extreme, rude, cruel, not to trust;
Enjoy'd no sooner but despised straight.
WILLIAM SHAKESPEARE, (1564-1616), Sonnet 129

Today the emphasis is on sex, and very little on the beauty of sexual relationship. Contemporary books and films portray it like a contest, which is absurd.
HENRY MILLER, Supertalk

However muted its present appearance may be, sexual dominion obtains nevertheless as perhaps the most pervasive ideology of our culture and provides its most fundamental concept of power.
KATE MILLET, Sexual Politics

Woman, verily, O Gautama, is a sacrificial fire. In this case the sexual organ is the fuel; when one invites, the smoke; the vulva, the flame; when one inserts, the coals; the sexual pleasure, the sparks. In this fire the gods offer semen. From this oblation arises a person (purusa).
Chândogya Upanishad, V. viii, 2

Brihad Âranyaka Upanishad,
VI. ii, 13

The body searches for that
which has injured the mind
with love.
LUCRETIUS, (1st century
BC), *On the Nature of
Things*, 4

Most creatures have a vague
belief that a very precarious
hazard, a kind of transparent
membrane, divides death from
love; and that the profound
idea of nature demands that
the giver of life should die at
the moment of giving.
MAURICE MAETERLINCK,
The Life of the Bee, (1901)

The degree and kind of a
man's sexuality reach up into
the ultimate pinnacle of his
spirit.
FRIEDRICH NIETZSCHE,
Beyond Good and Evil, 75,
(1886)

Civilised people cannot fully
satisfy their sexual instinct
without love.
BERTRAND RUSSELL,
Marriage and Morals, The
Place of Love in Human Life,
(1929)

The sex instinct is one of the
three or four prime movers of
all that we do and are and
dream, both individually and
collectively.
PHILIP WYLIE, *Generation of
Vipers*, 6, (1942)

This procreation is the union
of man and woman, and is a
divine thing: for conception
and generation are an
immortal principle in the
mortal creature.
PLATO, *Symposium*, 206 C

It is my thesis that the core of
the problem for women today
is not sexual but a problem of
identity - a stunting or evasion
of growth that is perpetuated
by the feminine mystique. It
is my thesis that as the
Victorian culture did not
permit women to accept or
gratify their basic sexual
needs, our culture does not
permit women to accept or
gratify their basic need to
grow and fulfil their
potentialities as human
beings, a need which is not
solely defined by their sexual
role.
BETTY FRIEDAN, *The
Feminine Mystique*

Making love is one
demonstration of how space
relations ask us to surrender in
love, and absorb the
differences and imperfections
and beauties of other human
beings.
THADDEUS GOLAS, *The
Lazy Man's Guide to
Enlightenment*

The sexual embrace can only
be compared with music and
with prayer.
HAVELOCK ELLIS, *Essays of
Love and Virtue*, On Life and
Sex, 1, (1937)

The true sexual union is the
union of the Parashakti
(*kundalinî*) with Atman;
anything else is but carnal
connection with women.
Kulârnava Tantra, V. 111-112

Answering questions is a
major part of sex education.
Two rules cover the ground.
First, always give a truthful
answer to a question; secondly,
regard sex knowledge as
exactly like any other
knowledge.
BERTRAND RUSSELL

Passionate love (*al'-ishq*) is
not peculiar to the human
species, for it penetrates
through all existing things -
celestial, elemental, vegetable
and mineral.
AVICENNA

FORTY-TWO

SPORT

The real adherent of the
sporting ethic knows that
when he's wet, cold, hungry,
sore, exhausted, and perhaps a
little frightened, he's having a
marvellous time.
MRS. FALK FEELEY, *A
Swarm of Wasps*

Sport strips away personality,
letting the white bone of
character shine through.
RITA MAE BROWN, *Sudden
Death*

I was brought up very strictly.
No drugs, nothing. I wasn't
even allowed to drink *tea*
when I was young because of
the caffeine. My mother
wouldn't have a celebration
drink on her eightieth
birthday. She's a Christian
and so am I. Prayer is
important to me - not that I
pray for seven wickets or
anything so specific. If it was
that simple everyone would be
praying for things they want
and we'd all be happy for the
rest of our lives. Very often
I've had the feeling that I'm
getting outside help. Some
people call it a sixth sense. I
believe it's something that's
been put there by someone.

MICHAEL HOLDING, from
The Zen of Cricket

There are boxers possessed of
such remarkable intuition,
such uncanny prescience, one
would think they were
somehow recalling their fights,
not fighting them as we
watch.
JOYCE CAROL OATES, *On
Boxing*

Power-lifting as a competitive
sport is about as interesting for
spectators as watching cows
chew their cud.
GRACE LICHTENSTEIN,
Machisma

Time spent in a casino is time
given to death, a foretaste of
the hour when one's flesh will
be diverted to the purposes of
the worm and not of the will.
REBECCA WEST, *The
Thinking Reed*

To bowl quick is to revel in
the glad arrival action; to
thrill in physical prowess and
to enjoy a certain sneaking
feeling of superiority over the
other mortals who play the
game. No batsman likes quick
bowling and this knowledge

gives one a sense of
omnipotence.
MIKE TYSON, from *The Zen
of Cricket*

Then ye returned to your
trinkets; then ye contented
your souls
With the flannelled fools at
the wicket or the muddied
oafs at the goals.
RUDYARD KIPLING, (1865-
1936), *The Islanders*, (1903)

It's awfully bad luck on Diana
Her ponies have swallowed
their bits;
She fished down their throats
with a spanner
And frightened them all into
fits.
SIR JOHN BETJEMAN

Casino owners spoke more
loudly than any of the other
kings of industry to defend
their contribution to society.
They could speak more loudly
because theirs was the purest
activity of civilised man.
They had transcended the
need for a product. They
could maintain and advance
life with machines that made
nothing but money.
JANE RULE, *The Desert of the
Heart*

By sports like these are all
their cares beguil'd,
The sports of children satisfy
the child.
GOLDSMITH, *The Traveller*,
line 153

When I play with my cat, who
knows whether I do not make
her more sport, than she
makes me?
MONTAIGNE, *Apology for
Raimond de Sebonde*

For when the One Great
Scorer comes
To write against your name,
He marks - not that you won
or lost -
But how you played the game.
GRANTLAND RICE, (1880-
1954), *Alumnus Football*

You must lose a fly to catch a
trout.
HERBERT, *Jacula Prudentum*

To survive in grand prix
racing, you need to be afraid.
Fear is an important feeling.
It helps you to race longer and
live longer.
AYRTON SENNA, (1960-
94), Brazilian motor racing
driver

I wanted a play that would paint the full face of sensuality, rebellion and revivalism. In South Wales these three phenomena have played second fiddle only to the Rugby Union which is a distillation of all three.
GWYN THOMAS, (1913-81), *Jackie the Jumper*

There's no secret. You just press the accelerator to the floor and steer left.
BILL VUKOVICH, (1918-55), US motor racing driver

The heroes of ancient and modern fame ... have treated life and fortune as a game to be well and skilfully played, but the stake not to be so valued but that any time it could be held a trifle light as air, and thrown up.
RALPH WALDO EMERSON, *Essays, Second Series*, New England Reformers

Float like a butterfly
Sting like a bee.
MUHAMMAD ALI, (Cassius Clay, 1942-)

While we least think it, he prepares his Mate.
Mate, and the King's pawn played, it never ceases,
Though all the earth is dust of taken pieces.
JOHN MASEFIELD, *The Widow in the Bye Street*, Part I, last lines

Sport, like a sonnet, forces beauty within its own system.
RITA MAE BROWN, *Sudden Death*

The game isn't over till it's over.
YOGI BERRA (1925-), US baseball player

Life's too short for chess.
HENRY JAMES BYRON, (1834-84), *Our Boys*, I

I just forgot to duck.
JACK DEMPSEY, (1895-1983), US boxer, (1926)

There is plenty of time to win this game, and to thrash the Spaniards too.
FRANCIS DRAKE, (1540-96), British navigator and admiral, (1588)

Swearing at the polo club? It's a load of bollocks.
MAJOR RONALD FERGUSON

Bullfighting is the only art in which the artist is in danger of death and in which the degree of brilliance in the performance is left to the fighter's honour.
ERNEST HEMINGWAY, (1899-1961), *Death in the Afternoon*, Chapter 9

I find it more satisfying to be a bad player at golf. The worse you play, the better you remember the occasional good shot.
NUBAR GULBENKIAN, *Daily Telegraph*, (1972)

It is unbecoming for a cardinal to ski badly.
JOHN PAUL II

I am sorry I have not learned to play at cards. It is very useful in life: it generates kindness and consolidates society.
SAMUEL JOHNSON, (1709-84), *Tour to the Hebrides*, (J. Boswell)

It was an old, old, old, old lady,
And a boy who was half-past three;
And the way they played together
Was beautiful to see.
H.C. BUNNER, *One, Two, Three*

It [angling] deserves commendations; ... it is an art worthy the knowledge and practice of a wise man.
IZAAK WALTON, *The Compleat Angler*, Part I, Chapter 1

Golf is a game whose aim is to hit a very small ball into an even smaller hole, with weapons singularly ill-designed for the purpose.
WINSTON CHURCHILL

Oh, he's football crazy, he's football mad
And the football it has robbed him o' the wee bit sense he had.
And it would take a dozen skivvies, his clothes to wash and scrub,
Since our Jock became a member of that terrible football club.

JIMMIE MC GREGOR, (1932-), *Football Crazy*

Life will always remain a gamble, with prizes sometimes for the imprudent, and blanks so often to the wise.
JEROME K. JEROME

Defeat doesn't finish a man - quit does. A man is not finished when he's defeated. He's finished when he quits.
RICHARD NIXON

Canst thou draw out leviathan with an hook?
Job 41:1

A man able to think isn't defeated - even when he is defeated.
MILAN KUNDERA, (1929-)

The moment of victory is much too short to live for that and nothing else.
MARTINA NAVRATILOVA, (1956-)

Winning is everything. The only ones who remember you when you come second are your wife and your dog.
DAMON HILL, (1960-)

One more such victory and we are lost.
PYRRHUS, (319-272 BC), Plutarch *Parallel Lives*

Know ye not that they which run in a race run all, but one receiveth the prize.
I *Corinthians*

EVERYBODY has won, and all must have prizes.
LEWIS CARROLL, (1832-98), *Alice's Adventures in Wonderland*, (1865)

Some people think football is a matter of life and death ... I can assure them it is much more serious than that.
BILL SHANKLY, (1914-81)

We may say of angling as Dr. Boteler said of strawberries: "Doubtless God could have made a better berry, but doubtless God never did"; and so, (if I might be judge,) God never did make a more calm, quiet, innocent recreation than angling.
IZAAK WALTON, *The Compleat Angler*, Part I, Chapter V

As a rule, the game of life is worth playing, but the struggle is the prize.
DEAN W.R. INGE, *Wit and Wisdom of Dean Inge*, No. 199

We are not interested in the possibilities of defeat; they do not exist.
QUEEN VICTORIA, (1819-1901)

New Yorkers love it when you spill your guts out there. Spill your guts at Wimbledon and they make you stop and clean it up.
JIMMY CONNORS, (1952-)

A horse is dangerous at both ends and uncomfortable in the middle.
IAN FLEMING

Everything about sport is derived from the hunt: there is no sport in existence that does not base itself either on the chase or on aiming, the two key elements of primeval hunting.
DESMOND MORRIS, (1928-), *The Animal Contract*

Give me mine angle, we'll to the river; there,

My music playing far off, I will betray
Tawny-finn'd fishes; my bended hook shall pierce
Their slimy jaws.
WILLIAM SHAKESPEARE, *Antony and Cleopatra*, Act II, Scene v, line 10

On practice ranges today you see player after player obviously working on an exaggerated in-to-out swing path to cure their slices (without avail, I might add) because they have read or been told that the slice is caused by an out-to-in swing path, as opposed to an open club-face. My remedy is to tee up to a ball, set the player square to it and say: "Now I want you to hit that ball forty-five degrees to the left." The immediate result is that the player clears his hips and swings from in-back-to-in which squares the club-face and the ball flies straight in spite of his exaggerated feel of an out-to-in swing path. Arsenic might not be the prescribed cure for arsenical poisoning. But the cure for one man's slice is very often a thought that causes another

man's slice. Nearly fifty years ago when I first started to teach golf most slices were out-to-in: right shoulder high and the club-face open at impact. Not so today. More likely the swing is in-to-out with the right shoulder too low, producing a push-fade. The club-face squares when the arc is in-back-to-in.
JOHN JACOBS, from *Golf in a Nutshell*

When we have matched our rackets to these balls,
We will in France, by God's grace, play a set
Shall strike his father's crown into the hazard.
WILLIAM SHAKESPEARE, (1564-1616), *Henry V*, (1599)

We are in the world like men playing at tables; the chance is not in our power, but to play it is; and when it is fallen, we must manage it as we can.
JEREMY TAYLOR, *Holy Living and Dying*, Of Contentedness, Section 2

The nice aspect about football is that, if things go wrong, it's the manager who gets the blame.
GARY LINEKER, (1960-)

If you watch a game, it's fun.
If you play it, it's recreation.
If you work at it, it's golf.
BOB HOPE, (1903-2003)

What I know most surely about morality and the duty of man I owe to sport.
ALBERT CAMUS, (1913-60)

It [poker] exemplifies the worst aspects of capitalism that have made our country so great.
WALTER MATTHAU, (1920-), *The Biggest Game in Town*

'A clear fire, a clean hearth, and the rigour of the game.' This was the celebrated wish of old Sarah Battle (now with God), who, next to her devotions, loved a good game at whist.
CHARLES LAMB, (1775-1834), *Essays of Elia*, Mrs. Battle's Opinions on Whist

A professor of anatomy once declared that there are only fourteen types of woman - young women, women who are really wonderful all things considered, and the twelve most famous women in history

- and the same applies to Bridge partners. Over and above this, they are usually either so good that you lose all your self-confidence, or so bad that you lose all your money.
W.D.H. MC CULLOUGH, (1901-78), Aces Made Easy

Jogging is very beneficial. It's good for your legs and your feet. It's also very good for the ground. It makes it feel needed.
(SNOOPY) CHARLES SCHULZ, (1922-), in Peanuts

One of the foulest cross-country runs that ever occurred outside Dante's Inferno.
P.G. WODEHOUSE, (1881-1975), Psmith Journalist, Chapter 30

The pleasant'st angling is to see the fish
Cut with her golden oars the silver stream,
And greedily devour the treacherous bait.
WILLIAM SHAKESPEARE, Much Ado About Nothing, Act III, Scene i, line 26

The most important thing in the Olympic Games is not to win but to take part, just as the most important thing in life is not the triumph but the struggle.
PIERRE DE COUBERTIN, (1863-1937), (1908)

The bigger they come, the harder they fall.
BOB FITZSIMMONS, (1862-1917), (1899)

Any cyclist will confirm that in hilly country the slope is always steeper the side you are going up. This is one of the great mysteries of Nature.
PHILIPPA GREGORY, (1954-), Guardian, (1985)

And upon all that are lovers of virtue; and dare trust in his providence; and be quiet; and go a-angling.
IZAAK WALTON, The Compleat Angler, Part I, Chapter XXI

The life of man is like a game with dice: if you don't get the throw you want, you must show your skill in making the best of the throw you do get.
TERENCE, Adelphi, 1.739

By archery in the traditional sense, which he esteems as an art and honours as a national heritage, the Japanese does not understand a sport but, strange as this may sound at first, a religious ritual. And consequently, by the 'art' of archery he does not mean the ability of the sportsman, which can be controlled, more or less, by bodily exercises, but an ability whose origin is to be sought in spiritual exercises and whose aim consists in hitting a spiritual goal, so that fundamentally the marksman aims at himself and may even succeed in hitting himself ...

The 'Great Doctrine' of archery tells us something very different. According to it, archery is still a matter of life and death to the extent that it is a contest of the archer with himself; and this kind of contest is not a paltry substitute, but the foundation of all contests outwardly directed - for instance with a bodily opponent. In this contest of the archer with himself is revealed the secret essence of this art, and instruction in it does not suppress anything essential by waving the utilitarian ends to which the practice of knightly contests was put.
EUGENE HERVIGEL, from *Zen in the Art of Archery*

Pro football is like nuclear warfare. There are no winners, only survivors.
FRANK GIFFORD

A golf course is the epitome of all that is purely transitory in the universe, a space not to dwell in, but to get over as quickly as possible.
JEAN GIRAUDOUX, *The Enchanted*, 1, (1933)

Ideally, the umpire should combine the integrity of a Supreme Court justice, the physical agility of an acrobat, the endurance of Job and the imperturbability of Buddha. From *Time*, The Villains in Blue

While the golfer can play tricks with his mind, this is a two-way process and the mind can equally play tricks with the golfer. At one stage in his career whenever Max Faulkner surveyed a putt he was horrified to see the hole

filling up with cement and he had to take a hurried stab to get the ball up to the hole while there was still a hole for it to fall into. When that happens it is time to leave the clubs in the cupboard for a bit.
JOHN JACOBS, from *Golf in a Nutshell*

Bodily exercise profiteth little; but godliness is profitable unto all things.
1 *Timothy* 4:8

Oh, the wild joys of living! the leaping from rock up to rock,
The strong rending of boughs from the fir-tree, the cool silver shock
Of the plunge in a pool's living water.
ROBERT BROWNING, *Men and Women*, Saul, 9, (1855)

Angling may be said to be so like the mathematics that it can never be fully learnt.
ISAAK WALTON, *The Compleat Angler*, Author's Preface

Golf may be played on Sunday, not being a game within the view of the law, but

being a form of moral effort.
STEPHEN LEACOCK, *Other Fancies*, Why I Refuse to Play Golf

The natural state of the football fan is bitter disappointment, no matter what the score.
NICK HORNBY, (1957-), *Fever Pitch*

We are under-exercised as a nation. We look instead of play. We ride instead of walk. Our existence deprives us of the minimum of physical activity essential for healthy living.
PRESIDENT JOHN F. KENNEDY, address, National Football Foundation

Bodily exercises are to be done discreetly; not to be taken evenly and alike by all men.
THOMAS À KEMPIS, *The Imitation of Christ*, line 19, (1426)

Regimen is superior to medicine, especially from time immemorial.
VOLTAIRE, *Philosophical Dictionary*, Physicians, (1764)

To behold the Englishman at
his *best* one should watch him
play tip-and-run.
RONALD FIRBANK, The
Flower Beneath the Foot,
Chapter 14

Chess, Game of: simulates
military tactics. All the great
generals were good chess-
players. Too serious for a
game, too frivolous for a
science.
GUSTAVE FLAUBERT, *The
Dictionary of Received Ideas*

Cricket is first and foremost a
dramatic spectacle. It belongs
with the theatre, ballet, opera
and the dance.
C.L.R. JAMES, *Beyond a
Boundary*, Chapter 16

Who plays for more
Than he can lose with
pleasure, stakes his heart.
HERBERT, *The Temple: The
Church Porch*, Stanza 33

But helpless Pieces of the
Game He plays
Upon this Chequer-board of
Nights and Days;
Hither and thither moves, and
checks , and slays,
And one by one back in the

Closet lays.
OMAR KHAYYÁM,
Rubáiyát, Stanza 69

Cards were at first for benefits
designed,
Sent to amuse, not to enslave
the mind.
GARRICK, *Epilogue to Ed.
Moore's Gamester*

Dare to err and to dream; a
higher meaning often lies in
childish play.
SCHILLER, *Thekla*

In play there are two pleasures
for your choosing -
The one is winning, and the
other losing.
BYRON, *Don Juan*, Canto
XIV, Stanza 12

Councillors of state sit
plotting and playing their
high chess-game whereof the
pawns are men.
THOMAS CARLYLE, *Sartor
Resartus*, Book I, Chapter 3

The horse, the horse! The
symbol of surging potency and
power of movement, of action,
in man.
D.H. LAWRENCE, *Apocalypse*

We are puppets, Man in his pride, and Beauty fair in her flower;
Do we move ourselves, or are moved by an unseen hand at a game
That pushes us off from the board, and others ever succeed?
Ah yet, we cannot be kind to each other here for an hour;
We whisper and hint, and chuckle, and grin at a brother's shame
However we brave it out, we men are a little breed.
ALFRED, LORD TENNYSON, Maud, Part IV, Stanza 5

Lovell: The faith they have in tennis and tall stockings.
WILLIAM SHAKESPEARE, King Henry VIII, Act I, Scene iii, line 30

Football is an art more central to our culture than anything the Arts Council designs to recognise.
GERMAINE GREER, (1939-)

Man only plays when he is fully a human being, and is only fully human when he plays.
FRIEDRICH VON SCHILLER, On the Aesthetic Education of Man, 15

Solitaire is the only thing in life that demands absolute honesty.
HUGH WHEELER, A Little Night Music, Stephen Sondheim

Life is a game of whist. From unseen sources
The cards are shuffled, and the hands are dealt.
Blind are our efforts to control the forces
That, though unseen, are no less strongly felt.
I do not like the way the cards are shuffled,
But yet I like the game and want to play;
And through the long, long night will I, unruffled,
Play what I get, until the break of day.
EUGENE F. WARE, Whist

The outside of a horse is good for the inside of a man.
LT. COL. HARRY LLEWELLYN

There is excitement in the game, but little beauty except

in the long-limbed 'pitcher', whose duty it is to hurl the ball rather further than the length of a cricket-pitch, as bewilderingly as possible. In his efforts to combine speed, mystery, and curve, he gets into attitudes of a very novel and fantastic, but quite obvious beauty.
RUPERT BROOKE, *Letters from America*

Baseball's clock ticks inwardly and silently, and a man absorbed in a ball game is caught in a slow, green place of removal and concentration and in a tension that is screwed up slowly and ever more tightly with each pitcher's windup and with the almost imperceptible forward lean and little half-step with which the fielders accompany each pitch. Whatever the pace of the particular baseball game we are watching, whatever its outcome, it holds us in its own continuum and mercifully releases us from our own.
ROGER ANGELL, *The Summer Game*

A cunning gamester never plays the card which his adversary expects, and far less that which he desires.
BALTASAR GRACIAN, *The Oracle*

If you must play, decide upon three things at the start: the rules of the game, the stakes, and the quitting time.
CHINESE PROVERB

Nine gamblers could not feed a single rooster.
YUGOSLAV PROVERB

There is enough energy wasted in poker to make a hundred thousand successful men every year.
ARTHUR BRISBANE, *The Book of Today*

Betting and gambling would lose half their attractiveness, did they not deceive us with the fancy that there may be an element of personal merit in our winnings. Our reason may protest, but our self-love is credulous.
ROBERT LYND, *The Peal of Bells*

For the wholesome-minded person, with a keen sense of life and a broad sympathy

with its interests, there is ever
a fascination in watching the
chances of a gaming table.
Fortune seems to come down
and give a private exhibition
of her wheel. The great
universe seems to stand still
for a while, and only this
microcosm to be subjected to
its chances.
WILLIAM J. LOCKE, A
Study in Shadows

Doubt not but angling will
prove to be so pleasant, that it
will prove to be, like virtue, a
reward to itself.
ISAAK WALTON, The
Compleat Angler, Part I,
Chapter I

I do much of my creative
thinking while golfing. If
people know you are working
at home they think nothing of
walking in for a cup of coffee.
But they wouldn't dream of
interrupting you on the golf
course.
HARPER LEE, To Kill a
Mocking Bird

Go anywhere in England
where there are natural,
wholesome, contented and
really nice English people, and

what do you always find?
That the stables are the real
centre of the household.
GEORGE BERNARD
SHAW, Heartbreak House,
Preface, (1920)

Tennis is not just a game of
physical ability, techniques,
and tactics. As you gain in
experience, you will discover
that 75 per cent of the game is
in the mind. Develop these
skills to help your game.
- Concentration: Learn to
focus your attention like a
champion.
- Self-belief: Build up your
self-confidence by visualising
success.
- Motivation: The extent of
your desire to play and
succeed is the measure of the
progress you make.
With mind-training exercises
you can improve your mental
skills in the same way as you
practice on court to improve
your game.
- Visualise yourself as a calm
player in control of your game,
and repeat a short phrase to
inspire confidence.
- Set yourself goals to increase
your motivation. Make them
challenging, attainable, and

performance-related.
- Practise concentrating - on
your opponent's serve, or on
the height of the ball as it
crosses the net.
PAUL DOUGLAS, from
Tennis

There's something wrong with
a young chap who doesn't play
games. Not even snooker.
BERNARD HOLLOWOOD,
Scowle in the Sixties

Games always cover
something deep and intense,
else there would be no
excitement in them, no
pleasure, no power to stir us.
ANTOINE DE SAINT-
EXUPÉRY, *Airman's Odyssey*

FORTY-THREE

SUCCESS

Success, which is something so simple in the end, is made up of thousands of things, we never fully know what.
RAINER MARIA RILKE, *Letters of Rainer Maria Rilke,* (1892-1910)

If the plow cannot reach it, the harrow can.
CHINESE PROVERB

'Twixt failure and success the point's so fine
Men sometimes know not when they touch the line.
Just when the pearl was waiting one more plunge,
How many a struggler has thrown up the sponge!...
Then take this honey from the bitterest cup:
"There is no failure save in giving up!"
HENRY AUSTIN, *Perseverance Conquers All*

May he grant you your heart's desire and crown all your plans with success!
Psalms 20:4

I've often thought that success comes to her by the spirit in her that dares and defies her idea not to prove the right one. One has seen it so again and again, in the face of everything, become the right one.
HENRY JAMES, *The Wings of the Dove*

If at first you do succeed, don't take any more chances.
KIN HUBBARD

There is only one success - to be able to spend your life in your own way.
CHRISTOPHER MORLEY, *Where the Blue Begins,* (1922)

If a man be self-controlled, truthful, wise, and resolute, is there aught that can stay out of the reach of such a man?
Panchatantra, 3, (circa 5th century)

Success abides longer among men
when it is planted by the hand of God.
PINDAR, *Odes,* Nemea 8, (5th century BC)

There is no success without hardship.
SOPHOCLES, *Electra,* (century 418-14 BC)

The key to success isn't much good until one discovers the right lock to insert it in.
TEHYI HSIEH, *Chinese Epigrams Inside Out and Proverbs*, 7

Take care of minutes: for hours will take care of themselves.
EARL OF CHESTERFIELD, *Letters to His Son*, 6 November 1747

Being Number One isn't everything to me, but for those few hours on the court it's way ahead of whatever's in second place.
BILLIE JEAN KING

To tend, unfailingly, unflinchingly, towards a goal, is the secret of success.
ANNA PAVLOVA, *Pages of My Life*

The secret of success is concentration; wherever there has been a great life, or a great work, that has gone before. Taste everything a little, look at everything a little; but live for one thing.
RALPH IRON, *The Story of an African Farm*, (1883)

It isn't success after all, is it, if it isn't an expression of your deepest energies?
MARILYN FRENCH, *The Bleeding Heart*

Without counsel, plans go wrong, but with many advisers they succeed.
Proverbs 15:22

I personally measure success in terms of the contributions an individual makes to her or his fellow human beings.
MARGARET MEAD, in *Redbook*

A hundred shots and a hundred hits.
CHINESE PROVERB

I've never sought success in order to get fame and money: it's the talent and the passion that count in success.
INGRID BERGMAN, in *Limelighters*

People seldom see the halting and painful steps by which the most insignificant success is achieved.
ANNIE SULLIVAN, in Helen Keller, *The Story of My Life*, (1902)

There is a small number of men and women who think for all the others, and for whom all the rest talk and act.
JEAN-JACQUES ROUSSEAU, *Julie ou la nouvelle Héloise*, Part 2, Letter 14

'Thinkers' are people who re-think; who think that what was thought before was never thought *enough*.
PAUL VALÉRY, *Suite*, Thinkers

Method of investigation: as soon as we have thought something, try to see in what way the contrary is true.
SIMONE WEIL, *Gravity and Grace*, Contradiction

To be successful, a woman has to be much better at her job than a man.
GOLDA MEIR, *L'Europeo*

Even a stopped clock is right twice every day. After some years, it can boast of a long series of successes.
MARIE VON EBNER-ESCHENBACH, *Aphorisms*, (1893)

If the axe is dull and its edge unsharpened, more strength is needed but skill will bring success.
Ecclesiastes 10:10

Veni, vidi, vici.
I came, I saw, I conquered.
JULIUS CAESAR, (100-44 BC)

For what shall it profit a man, if he shall gain the whole world, and lose his own soul?
Mark

Success is a science; if you have the conditions, you get the result.
OSCAR WILDE, (1854-1900), (1883)

One's religion is whatever he is most interested in, and yours is Success.
JAMES BARRIE, (1860-1937), *The Twelve-pound Look*, I

We never do anything well till we cease to think about the manner of doing it.
WILLIAM HAZLITT, (1778-1830), *On Prejudice*

To burn always with this hard, gem-like flame, to maintain this ecstasy, is success in life.
WALTER PATER, (1839-94), *The Renaissance*, Conclusion

It's just as difficult to overcome success as it is to overcome failure.
WILLIAM WALTON, (1902-83), in *WW: Behind the Façade*, Chapter 16

I started at the top and worked my way down.
ORSON WELLES, (1915-85), in *The Filmgoer's Book of Quotes*

Success - "the bitch-goddess Success" in William James' phrase - demands strange sacrifices from those who worship her.
ALDOUS HUXLEY, *Proper Studies*, (1927)

Unless a man has been taught what to do with success after getting it, the achievement of it must inevitably leave him prey to boredom.
BERTRAND RUSSELL, *The Conquest of Happiness*, (1930)

To attain ... the Unattainable.
ALFRED, LORD TENNYSON, *Timbuctoo*, line 196

Those things which are not practicable are not desirable. There is nothing in the world really beneficial that does not lie within the reach of an informed understanding and a well-directed pursuit.
EDMUND BURKE, *Speech on the Plan for Economical Reform*, (1780)

Presence of mind and courage in distress
Are more than armies to procure success.
DRYDEN, *Aureng-Zebe*, Act II

The religious man is the only successful man.
FREDERICK WILLIAM FABER

Be studious in your profession, and you will be learned. Be industrious and frugal, and you will be rich. Be sober and temperate, and you will be healthy. Be in general virtuous, and you will be happy. At least, you will, by such conduct, stand the best

chance for such consequences.
BENJAMIN FRANKLIN,
Letter to John Alleyn

To know how to wait is the great secret of success.
DE MAISTRE

The success of most things depends upon knowing how long it will take to succeed.
MONTESQUIEU, *Pensées Diverses*

By their fruits ye shall know them.
Matthew 7:20

Success don't konsist in never making blunders, but in never making the same one the seckond time.
JOSH BILLINGS, *Wit and Humour*, Affurisms, Mollassis Kandy

Management is efficiency in climbing the ladder of success; leadership determines whether the ladder is standing against the right wall.
STEPHEN R. COVEY, *The 7 Habits of Highly Effective People*

Be nice to people on your way up because you'll meet 'em on your way down.
WILSON MIZNER, in *The Legendary Mizners*, Chapter 4

Our very business in life is not to get ahead of others, but to get ahead of ourselves.
THOMAS L. MONSON

Ask, and it shall be given you; seek, and ye shall find; knock, and it shall be opened unto you: For every one that asketh receiveth; and he that seeketh findeth; and to him that knocketh it shall be opened.
Matthew 7:7-8

Success consists of getting up just one more time than you fall.
OLIVER GOLDSMITH

In all your undertakings let a reasonable assurance animate your endeavours; and remember that if you despair of success you cannot hope to succeed.
Do not terrify your soul with vain fears; neither let your heart sink because of the phantoms of imagination.

Remember that as fear invites failure, so he that hopes helps himself.
If you believe a thing impossible, your despondency will make it so; but, if you persevere, you will overcome all difficulties.
In all your desires, let reason go before you, and do not set your hopes beyond the bounds of probability; so shall success attend all your undertakings, and your heart will not be vexed with disappointments.
DANDEMIS

The men whom I have seen succeed best in life have always been cheerful and hopeful men, who went about their business with a smile on their faces, and took the changes and chances of this mortal life like men, facing rough and smooth alike as it came.
CHARLES KINGSLEY

The men who try to do something and fail are infinitely better than those who try to do nothing and succeed.
LLOYD JONES

'Tis not in mortals to command success; but we'll do more, Sempronius, we'll deserve it.
THOMAS ADDISON

Ch'ing, the chief carpenter, was carving wood into a stand for hanging musical instruments. When finished, the work appeared to those who saw it as though of supernatural execution. And the prince of Lu asked him, saying, "What mystery is there in your art?"
"No mystery, your Highness," replied Ch'ing; "and yet there is something. When I am about to make such a stand, I guard against any diminution of my vital power. I first reduce my mind to absolute quiescence. Three days in this condition, and I become oblivious of any reward to be gained. Five days, and I become oblivious of any fame to be acquired. Seven days, and I become unconscious of my four limbs and my physical frame. Then, with no thought of the Court present to my mind, my skill becomes concentrated, and all disturbing elements from

without are gone. I enter some mountain forest. I search for a suitable tree. It contains the form required, which is afterwards elaborated. I see the stand in my mind's eye, and then set to work. Otherwise, there is nothing. I bring my own natural capacity into relation with that of the wood. What was suspected to be of supernatural execution in my work was due solely to this."
CHUANG-TSE, Chapter XIX

Let us work as if success depended on ourselves alone, but with the heartfelt conviction that we are doing nothing and God everything.
ST. IGNATIUS OF LOYOLA

Self-reverence, self-knowledge, self-control: these three alone lead life to sovereign power.
ALFRED, LORD TENNYSON

Skillfulness in action is called Yoga.
Bhagavad-Gitâ, II.50

One with such a concentrated mind rises above the tumult of the subjective as well as of the objective world. He is like the arrow-maker, who while fashioning his arrows is conscious only of his task.
SRIMAD BHAGAVATAM, XI, iii

Put your heart, mind, intellect and soul even to your smallest acts. This is the secret of success.
SWAMI SIVANANDA

If you wish success in life make perseverance your bosom friend, experience your wise counsellor, caution your elder brother, and hope your guardian genius.
THOMAS ADDISON

Fortune, success, position are never gained, but by piously, determinedly, bravely striking, growing, living to a thing. One line, - a line fraught with Instruction, includes the secret of Lord Kenyon's final success, - he was prudent, he was patient, and he persevered.
TOWNSEND

The person who succeeds is not the one who holds back,

fearing failure, nor the one who never fails ... but rather the one who moves on in spite of failure.
CHARLES R. SWINDOLL

The talent of success is nothing more than doing what you can do well, and doing well whatever you do, without a thought of fame.
LONGFELLOW

The man who forged swords for the Minister of War was eighty years of age. Yet he never made the slightest slip in his work.
The Minister of War said to him, "Is it your skill, Sir, or have you any method?"
"It is *concentration*," replied the man. "When twenty years old, I took to forging swords. I cared for nothing else. If a thing was not a sword, I did not notice it. I availed myself of whatever energy I did not use in other directions in order to secure greater efficiency in the direction required. Still more of that which is never without use (*Tao*); so that there was nothing which did not lend its aid."
CHUANG-TSE, Chapter XXII

FORTY-FOUR

SUFFERING

Extraordinary afflictions are not always the punishment of extraordinary sins, but sometimes the trial of extraordinary graces.
HENRY

So grief and care oft cloud our early hours, then, like the tempest, spirits flee away and leave all bright and blest our closing day.
MITCHELL

In adversity man sees himself abandoned by others; he finds that all his hopes are centred within himself; he rouses his soul; he encounters his difficulties, and they yield before him.
In prosperity he fancies himself safe: he thinks he is beloved by all who smile upon him; he grows careless and remiss; he does not see the dangers before him; he trusts to others, and, in the end, they deceive him.
Better is the sorrow that leads to contentment, than the joy that renders a man unable to endure distress and afterwards plunges him into it.
Be upright in your whole life: be content in all its changes.

And remember that he who despairs of the end shall never attain unto it.
DANDEMIS

Prosperity, as is truly asserted by Seneca, very much obstructs the knowledge of ourselves. No man can form a just estimate of his own powers by inactive speculation. That fortitude which has encountered no dangers, that prudence which has surmounted no difficulties, that integrity which has been attacked by no temptations, can at best be considered but as gold not yet brought to the test, of which, therefore, the true value cannot be assigned.
SAMUEL JOHNSON

The liquid drops of tears, that you have shed,
Shall come again; transformed to orient pearl;
Advantaging their loan with interest
Of ten-times-double gain of happiness.
WILLIAM SHAKESPEARE,
King Richard III, Act IV,
Scene iv

No matter what we have come through, or how many perils we have safely passed, or how imperfect and jagged - in some places perhaps irreparably - our life has been, we cannot in our heart of hearts imagine how it could have been different. As we look back on it, it slips in behind us in orderly array, and, with all its mistakes, acquires a sort of eternal fitness, and even, at times, of poetic glamour.
RANDOLPH BOURNE, *Youth and Life*

If every man's internal care
Were written on his brow,
How many would our pity share
Who raise our envy now.

The fatal secret, when reveal'd,
Of every aching breast,
Would prove, that only while conceal'd
Their lot appear'd the best.
METASTASIO

A sublime thing.
O fear not in a world like this,
And thou shalt know ere long,
Know how sublime a thing it is
To suffer and be strong.
LONGFELLOW

Courage! Suffering when it climbs highest, lasts not long.
AESCHYLUS, *Fragments*, Fragment 190

For I reckon that the sufferings of this present time are not worthy to be compared with the glory which shall be revealed in us.
Romans VIII, 18

The suffering man ought really to consume his own smoke; there is no good in emitting smoke till you have made it into fire.
THOMAS CARLYLE, *On Heroes, Hero-Worship and the Heroic in History*, 5, (1841)

We cannot live, sorrow or die for somebody else, for suffering is too precious to be shared.
EDWARD DAHLBERG, *Because I Was Flesh*

Either the human being must suffer and struggle as the price of a more searching vision, or his gaze must be shallow and without intellectual revelation.
THOMAS DE QUINCEY, *Suspiria de Profundis*, Vision of Life, (1845)

A *Wounded* Deer - leaps
highest.
EMILY DICKINSON, poem,
(circa 1860)

Duke: Sweet are the uses of
adversity;
Which, like a toad, ugly and
venomous,
Wears yet a precious jewel in
his head:
And this our life, exempt from
public haunt,
Finds tongues in trees, books
in the running brooks,
Sermons in stones, and good
in every thing! -
I would not change it.
Amiens: Happy is your grace,
That can translate the
stubbornness of fortune
Into so quiet and so sweet a
style!
WILLIAM SHAKESPEARE,
As You Like It, Act II, Scene i

Every man has his own
destiny: the only imperative is
to follow it, to accept it, no
matter where it leads him.
HENRY MILLER, *The
Wisdom of the Heart*

Much of your pain is self-
chosen.
It is the bitter potion by
which the physician within
you heals your sick self.
KAHLIL GIBRAN, *The
Prophet*, On Pain, (1923)

He who fears he shall suffer,
already suffers what he fears.
MONTAIGNE, *Essays*, Of
Experience, (1580-88)

This is Daddy's bedtime secret
for today: Man is born broken.
He lives my mending. The
grace of God is glue.
EUGENE O'NEILL, *The
Great God Brown*, (1926)

Pain makes man think.
Thought makes man wise.
Wisdom makes life endurable.
JOHN PATRICK, *The
Teahouse of the August Moon*,
(1953)

Man never reasons so much
and becomes so introspective
as when he suffers; since he is
anxious to get at the cause of
his sufferings, to learn who has
produced them, and whether
it is just or unjust that he
should have to bear them.
LUIGI PIRANDELLO, *Six
Characters in Search of an
Author*, 3, (1921)

To a great extent, suffering is a sort of need felt by the organism to make itself familiar with a new state, which makes it uneasy, to adapt its sensibility to that state.
MARCEL PROUST, *Remembrance of Things Past: The Guermantes Way*, (1913-27)

A man who suffers before it is necessary, suffers more than is necessary.
SENECA, *Letters to Lucilius*, 98, (1st century)

Clergymen and people who use phrases without wisdom sometimes talk of suffering as a mystery. It is really a revelation.
OSCAR WILDE, *De Profundis*, (1905)

How much further suffering goes in psychology than psychology!
MARCEL PROUST

We shall draw from the heart of suffering itself the means of inspiration and survival.
WINSTON S. CHURCHILL

Experience is valuable only when it has brought suffering and when the suffering has left its mark upon both body and mind.
ANDRÉ MAUROIS

The more a man loves, the more he suffers. The sum of possible grief for each soul is in proportion to its degree of perfection.
FRÉDÉRIC AMIEL

All those who suffer in the world do so because of their desire for their own happiness.
SHANTIDEVA, (c. 685-763), *Bodhicaryavatara*, Chapter 8, Verse 129

If you bear the cross gladly, it will bear you.
THOMAS À KEMPIS, (circa 1380-1471), *The Imitation of Christ*

How amusing it is to see the fixed mosaic of one's little destiny being filled out by tiny blocks of events, - the enchainment of minute consequences with the illusion of choice weathering it all!
ALICE JAMES, *Diary*

Be grateful for, not blind to

the many, many sufferings which thou art spared; thou art no better than those who have been searched out and racked by them.
ORCHOTH ZADIKKIM, (circa 15th century)

I am the only man in the world who cannot commit suicide.
REVEREND CHAD VARAH

[Suffering is] a form of gratitude to experience or an opportunity to experience evil and change it into good.
SAUL BELLOW, Herzog

A cause is like champagne and high heels - one must be prepared to suffer for it.
ARNOLD BENNETT, The Title, (1918)

We are healed of a suffering only by experiencing it to the full.
MARCEL PROUST, Remembrance of Things Past, The Fugitive, (1925)

Thank you, madam, the agony is abated.
LORD MACAULAY, (1800-59), aged four, having had hot coffee spilt over his legs, Life and Letters of Lord Macaulay, (1876)

Sorrow and silence are strong, and patient endurance is godlike.
HENRY WADSWORTH LONGFELLOW, (1807-82), Evangeline, (1847)

What does not kill me makes me stronger.
FRIEDRICH NIETZSCHE, (1844-1900), Twilight of the Idols, (1889)

Who never ate his bread with tears, who never sat through the sorrowful night, weeping upon his bed, does not know you, O heavenly powers.
JOHANN WOLFGANG VON GOETHE, (1749-1832), Wilhelm Meister, ii. 13

The quality of mercy is not strain'd;
It droppeth as the gentle rain from heaven
Upon the place beneath. It is twice blest;
It blesseth him that gives and him that takes.
WILLIAM SHAKESPEARE,

(1564-1616), *The Merchant of Venice*, Act IV, Scene i

A man who fears suffering is already suffering from what he fears.
MICHEL DE MONTAIGNE, (1533-92), *Essays*, III, 13

One nail drives out another. But four nails make a cross.
CESARE PAVESE, (1908-50), *This Business of Living: A Diary*, (1935-1950)

I would have killed myself but I was in analysis with a strict Freudian and if you kill yourself ... they make you pay for the sessions you miss.
WOODY ALLEN, (1935-), in *Annie Hall*

Then the eighty-year-old lady with a sparkle,
A Cambridge lady, hearing of the latest
Suicide, said to her friend, turning off
TV for tea, "Well, my dear, doesn't it seem
A little like going where you haven't been invited?
RICHARD EBERHART, (1904-), *How It Is*

Suffering has always been with us, does it really matter in what form it comes? All that matters is how we bear it and how we fit it into our lives.
ETTY HILLESUM, (1942), *An Interrupted Life*, (1983)

True knowledge comes only through suffering.
ELIZABETH BARRETT BROWNING, (1844), in *The Complete Works of Elizabeth Barrett Browning*, (1900)

That there should be a purpose to suffering, that a person should be chosen for it, special - these are houses of the mind, in which whole peoples have found shelter.
GISH JEN, *Typical American*, (1991)

Although the world is full of suffering, it is full also of the overcoming of it.
HELEN KELLER, *Optimism*, (1903)

We are not permitted to choose the frame of our destiny. But what we put into it is ours.
DAG HAMMARSKJÖLD, *Markings*

Pain is inevitable. Suffering is optional.
M. KATHLEEN CASEY, in *The Promise of a New Day*, (1985)

Pain is an event ... Suffering, on the other hand, is the nightmare reliving of unscrutinised and unmetabolized pain.
AUDRE LORDE, *Sister Outsider*, Eye to Eye

Suffering raises up those souls that are truly great; it is only small souls that are made mean-spirited by it.
ALEXANDRA DAVID-NEEL, (1889), *La Lampe de Sagesse*

So much that was beautiful and so much that was hard to bear. Yet whenever I showed myself ready to bear it, the hard was directly transformed into the beautiful.
ETTY HILLESUM, *An Interrupted Life*

As adversity leads us to think properly of our state, it is most beneficial to us.
SAMUEL JOHNSON

Adversity has the effect of eliciting talents, which in prosperous circumstances would have lain dormant.
HORACE

The good are better made by ill,
As odors crush'd are sweeter still.
ROGERS

One day Hasan of Basra and Mâlik son of Dinâr and Shakik of Balkh came to see Râbi'a (al-Adawîya) when she was ill. Hasan said, "None is sincere in his claim (to love God) unless he patiently endure the blows of his Lord." Râbi'a said, "This smalls of egoism." Shakik said, "None is sincere in his claim unless he give thanks for the blows of his Lord." Râbi'a said, "This must be bettered." Malik son of Dinâr said, "None is sincere in his claim unless he delight in the blows of his Lord." Râbi'a said, "This still needs to be improved." They said, "Do thou speak." She said, "None is sincere in his claim unless he forget the blows in beholding his Lord."
'ATTÂR

There have been times when I've thought about suicide - but with my luck it would probably turn out to be only a temporary solution.
WOODY ALLEN, (1935-), in *Apt and Amusing Quotations*, Death

Man, if thou art faithful to God, and desirest nought but Him,
The harshest affliction will be for thee a Paradise.
ANGELUS SILESIUS

When sadness and suffering become intense and intolerable, know for certain that a new era is going to dawn bringing signal progress.
SWAMI RAMDAS

The appointed thing comes at the appointed time in the appointed way.
MYRTLE REED, *Master of the Vineyard*

Wouldst thou know for certain whether thy sufferings are thine own or God's? Tell by these tokens. Suffering for thyself, in whatever way, the suffering hurts thee and is hard to bear. But suffering for God and God alone thy suffering hurts thee not nor does it burden thee, for God bears the load. Believe me, if there were a man willing to suffer on account of God and of God alone, then though he fell a sudden prey to the collective sufferings of all the world it would not trouble him nor bow him down, for God would be the bearer of his burden.
MAESTER ECKHART

Despise not the chastening of the Lord; neither be weary of his correction.
Proverbs 3:11

For whom the Lord loveth he chasteneth, and scourgeth every son whom he receiveth. If ye endure chastening, God dealeth with you as with sons; for what son is he whom the father chasteneth not? But if ye be without chastisement, whereof all are partakers, then are ye bastards, and not sons.
Hebrews 12:6-8

As many as I love, I rebuke and chasten: be zealous therefore, and repent.
Revelation 3:19

Just as an unshapen stone can be fashioned into a beautiful image worthy of adoration and worship only after it has received many a stroke of the chisel, so also a distorted and inharmonious life has to pass through many a trial, suffering and tribulation, before a great change could come over it, before the life of ignorance could be transmuted into a life of immortal splendour and joy, fit to be revered and adored.
SWAMI RAMDAS

Blessed are they which are persecuted for righteousness' sake: for theirs is the kingdom of heaven.
Matthew 5:10

Nay, good my fellows, do not please sharp fate
To grace it with your sorrows;
bid that welcome
Which comes to punish us,
and we punish it
Seeming to bear it lightly.
WILLIAM SHAKESPEARE,
Antony and Cleopatra, Act IV,
Scene xii, line 135

Empty honour is deaf and blind before God,
Undeserved contempt sanctifies all God's children.
MECHTHILD OF MAGDEBURG

Allâh tasketh not a soul beyond its scope.
Qur'ân, II, 286

God is faithful, who will not suffer you to be tempted above that ye are able.
I *Corinthians* 10:13

One meets his destiny often in the road he takes to avoid it.
FRENCH PROVERB

God sends us nothing that is too hard or too painful to bear. He proportions all to our strength and abilities. Our trials are suited to our needs as the glove to the hand of the wearer. All things will contribute to our sanctifications if we but co-operate with the designs of Divine Providence.
ST. ALPHONSUS LIGUORI

But who may abide the day of his coming? and who shall stand when he appeareth? for he is like a refiner's fire, and like fullers' soap:
And he shall sit as a refiner

and purifier of silver: and he shall purify the sons of Levi, and purge them as gold and silver, that they may offer unto the Lord an offering in righteousness.
Malachi 3:2,3

The purpose of this discipline and this rough treatment is that the furnace may extract the dross from the silver.
The testing of good and bad is in order that the gold may boil and bring the scum to the top.
RÛMÎ

Let not poverty and misfortune distress you; for as gold is tried in the fire, the believer is exposed to trials.
'ALÎ

Bear that which is necessary, as it is necessary.
SEXTUS THE PYTHAGOREAN

We may rest assured that nothing whatever happens on earth without God's permission. What a source of consolation to know that even the sufferings and adversities which God sends us are for our very best, and have in

view our eternal salvation. Ah, how great will be our shame when we stand before the judgement-seat of God and see clearly the loving intention of Divine Providence in sending us those trials which we tried to evade, thus battling against our own salvation!
ST. ALPHONSUS LIGUORI

And the light of Israel shall be for a fire, and his Holy One for a flame: and it shall burn and devour his thorns and his briers in one day.
Isaiah 10:17

Whoever blames God, despises his mercy.
BOEHME

How often has it happened that what we consider a punishment and chastisement of God, was a special work of grace, an act of His infinite mercy!
ST. ALPHONSUS LIGUORI

And when man faces destiny, destiny ends and man comes into his own.
ANDRÉ MALRAUX, *The Voices of Silence*

One must know that misfortune, being the means of leading one to the Doctrine, is also a *guru*.
GAMPOPA

The soul that is without suffering does not feel the need of knowing the ultimate cause of the universe. Sickness, grief, hardships, etc., are all indispensable elements in the spiritual ascent.
ANANDA MOYÎ

And he that taketh not his cross, and followeth after me, is not worthy of me.
Matthew 10:38

It is better, if the will of God be so, that ye suffer for well doing, than for evil doing.
I *Peter* 3:17

I say that next to God there is no nobler thing than suffering ... I hold, if anything were nobler than suffering, God would have saved mankind therewith, for we might well accuse him of being unfriendly to his Son if he knew of something superior to suffering ... Further, I maintain, no man apart from

God has ever been so holy or so good as to deserve the least nobility, such as the smallest suffering would give ... I tell you, right suffering is the mother of all virtues, for right suffering so subdues the heart, it cannot rise to pride but perforce is lowly.
MAESTER ECKHART

If we want to be without any sort of pain, we must ascertain first the cause of pain. A little consideration will make it clear to us that the root cause of all sorrow is the mistaken identification of the Self with the body ... Ignorance alone is the prime cause of all misery.
SRI CHANDRASEKHARA BHÂRATI SWÂMIGAL

So long as you consider yourself the body you see the world as external. The imperfection appears to you. God is perfection. His work is also perfection. But you see it as imperfection because of your wrong identification.
SRI RAMANA MAHARSHI

Those to whom Love draws nigh are the most severely proven.
'ATTÂR

The world is afflicted with death and decay, therefore the wise do not grieve, knowing the terms of the world.
BUDDHAGHOSA

Miseries, though belonging to the world of dreams, are of a certainty painful, and do not vanish until we cease our dreaming. Nor does this dream of life come to an end for him whose thoughts are engrossed in transitory, sensuous things.
Srimad Bhagavatam, XI, xv

Yea, though I walk through the valley of the shadow of death, I will fear no evil: for thou art with me; thy rod and thy staff they comfort me.
Psalm 23:4 (KJV)

If suffering went out of life, courage, tenderness, pity, faith, patience, and love in its divinity would go out of life, too.
FR. ANDREW

Out of suffering have emerged the strongest souls; the most massive characters are seared with scars.
EDWIN HUBBEL (E.H.) CHAPIN

We often learn more of God under the rod that strikes us, than under the staff that comforts us.
STEPHEN CHARNOCK

One sees great things from the valley; only small things from the peak.
G.K. CHESTERTON

We have already had to re-think so many of our conceptions of motion, we will also gradually learn to realise that that which we call destiny goes forth from within people, not from without into them.
RAINER MARIA RILKE, *Letters to a Young Poet*

Adversity is the diamond dust Heaven polishes its jewels with.
ROBERT LEIGHTON

When pain is to be borne, a little courage helps more than much knowledge, a little human sympathy more than much courage, and the least tincture of the love of God more than all.
C.S. LEWIS, *Problem of Pain*

Afflictions are but the shadow of God's wings.
GEORGE MAC DONALD

Every painful event contains in itself a seed of growth and liberation.
ANTHONY DE MELLO

There has never yet been a man in our history who led a life of ease whose name is worth remembering.
THEODORE ROOSEVELT

Suffering makes one more sensitive to the pain in the world. It can teach us to put forth a greater love for everything that exists.
DOROTHEE SOELLE

Then there came to him all his brothers and sisters and all who had known him before, and they ate bread with him in his house; they showed him sympathy and comforted him for all the suffering that the Lord had brought upon him.
Job 42:11

It is of the Lord's mercies that we are not consumed, because his compassions fail not. They are new every morning:

great is thy faithfulness.
Lamentations 3:22-23

Blessed are the merciful, for they will receive mercy.
Matthew 5:7

Trials enable people to rise above Religion to God.
FR. ANDREW

The brightest crowns that are worn in heaven have been tried, and smelted, and polished, and glorified, through the furnace of tribulation.
EDWIN HUBBEL

Problems are the cutting-edge that distinguishes between success and failure. Problems ... create our courage and our wisdom. It is only because of problems that we grow mentally and spiritually.
M. SCOTT PECK

In shunning a trial we are seeking to avoid a blessing.
CHARLES HADDON SPURGEON

Human beings are born to trouble just as sparks fly upward.
Job 5:7

As there is design and symmetry in nature, I believe there is also design and symmetry in human experience if we will learn to yield ourselves to our destinies.
KATHARINE BUTLER HATHAWAY, *The Journals and Letters of the Little Locksmith*

Let us belong to God even in the thick of the disturbance stirred up round about us by the diversity of human affairs. True virtue is not always nourished in external calm any more than good fish are always found in stagnant waters.
ST. FRANCIS DE SALES

Tribulation: God's fastest road to patience, character, hope, confidence, and genuine love.
BILL GOTHARD

There is no man in the world without some troubles or affliction, though he be a king or a pope.
THOMAS À KEMPIS

Trouble is the structural steel that goes into character building.
DOUGLAS MEADOR

Nothing influences the quality of our life more than how we respond to trouble.
ERWIN G. TIEMAN

The secret of sorrow is, men think God has a plan for them. He only has a plan through them.
PANIN

FORTY-FIVE

TAOISM

What cannot be seen is called
evanescent;
What cannot be heard is
called rarefied;
What cannot be touched is
called minute.
These three cannot be
fathomed
And so they are confused and
looked upon as one.
Its upper part is not dazzling;
Its lower part is not obscure.
Dimly visible, it cannot be
named
And returns to that which is
without substance.
This is called the shape that
has no shape,
The image that is without
substance.
This is called indistinct and
shadowy.
Go up to it and you will not
see its head;
Follow behind it and you will
not see its rear.
Hold fast to the way of
antiquity
In order to keep in control the
realm of today.
The ability to know the
beginning of antiquity
Is called the thread running
through the way.
LAO TZE, *Tao Te Ching*

In its original cosmic sense,
the Tao is the ultimate,
undefinable reality and as
such it is the equivalent of the
Hinduist Brahman and the
Buddhist Dharmakaya. It
differs from these Indian
concepts, however, by its
intrinsically dynamic quality
which, in the Chinese view, is
the essence of the universe.
The Tao is the cosmic process
in which all things are
involved; the world is seen as
a continuous flow and change.
FRITZJ OF CAPRA

The kind man discovers it and
calls it kind. The wise man
discovers it and calls it wise.
The people use it day by day
and are not aware of it, for the
way of the superior man is
rare.
Tao reveals itself differently to
each individual, according to
his own nature. The man of
deeds, for whom kindness and
the love of his fellow man are
supreme, discovers the tao of
cosmic events and calls it
supreme kindness - "God is
love". The contemplative
man, for whom calm wisdom
is supreme, discovers the tao
of the universe and calls it

supreme wisdom. The common people live from day to day, continually borne and nourished by tao, but they know nothing of it; they see only what meets the eye. For the way of the superior man, who sees not only things but the tao of things, is rare. The tao of the universe is indeed kindness and wisdom; but essentially tao is also beyond kindness and wisdom.
R WILHELM, *I Ching*

He who conforms to the course of the Tao, following the natural processes of Heaven and Earth, finds it easy to manage the whole world.
HUAI NAN TZU

The knowledge of the ancients reached the highest point - the time before anything existed. This is the highest point. It is exhaustive. There is no adding to it.
CHUANG-TSE, Chapter XXIII

Organic molecules from cosmic clouds,
Millions of years in the midst of eternity.
We sprang from the primordial;
Our spirituality came in the evolution.
DENG MING-DAO

Rest only in inaction and all things will transform themselves. Relax your body, expel your intelligence, forget your natural relationships, and you will be in complete harmony with boundless cosmic forces. Release both mind and spirit, negate the soul, and all things will return to their root. When each one has returned to its root and is without perception, to the end of its days it will not be separated from that state which is turbid and undifferentiated. For when you perceive a thing you become separated from it. Do not inquire into its name. Do not probe into its nature. For all things live unto themselves.
CHUANG-TZU

The key to Chuang Tzu's thought is the complementarity of opposites, and this can be seen only when one grasps the central 'pivot' of Tao which passes squarely through both 'Yes' and 'No', 'I' and 'Not-I'. Life is a continual development. All beings are in a state of flux. Chuang Tzu would have agreed with Herakleitos. What is impossible today may suddenly become possible tomorrow. What is good and pleasant today may, tomorrow, become evil and odious. What seems right from one point of view may, when seen from a different aspect, manifest itself as completely wrong.

THOMAS MERTON

What, then, are the patterns of the cosmic Way which human beings have to recognise? The principal characteristic of the Tao is the cyclic nature of its ceaseless motion and change. "Returning is the motion of the Tao," says Lao Tzu, and "Going far means returning." The idea is that all developments in nature, those in the physical world as well as those of human situations, show cyclic patterns of coming and going, of expansion and contraction.

FRITZJ OF CAPRA

Of old he who was well versed in the way
Was minutely subtle, mysteriously comprehending,
And too profound to be known.
It is because he could not be known
That he can only be given a makeshift description:
Tentative, as if fording a river in winter,
Hesitant, as if in fear of his neighbours;
Formal like a guest;
Falling apart like thawing ice;
Vacant like a valley;
Murky like muddy water.
Who can be muddy and yet, settling, slowly become limpid?
Who can be at rest and yet, stirring, slowly come to life?
He who holds fast to this way Desires not to be full.
It is because he is not full That he can be worn and yet newly made.

LAO TZE, *Tao Te Ching*

The sage embraces heaven and earth and his favour extends to all the world. Yet

his lineage is not known. Therefore in life he holds no titles, and in death no posthumous honours. He does not accumulate material things, nor seek to establish his fame. Such may be called a Great Man.
CHUANG-TZU

Yang Chu's friend Chi Liang fell ill. After seven days, when the crisis arrived, his sons stood in a circle round him weeping and asking him to call a doctor. "Look how foolish my sons are!" Chi Liang said to Yang Chu. "Why don't you compose a song for me which will help them to understand?"
Yang Chu sang:

"What heaven does not know
How can man discern?
Blessings do not come from heaven,
Nor calamities from the sins of men.
Is it you and I who are ignorant?
Do doctors and shamans understand?"

Chi Liang's sons did not see the point, and finally called

three doctors named Chiao, Yü and Lu to feel his pulse and diagnose the illness.

Mr. Chiao said to Chi Liang:

"Your temperature, and the filling and emptying of your vital forces, are out of order. The illness is due to irregular meals, sexual over-indulgence, and worrying too much. It is not the work of heaven or of spirits, and although critical it can be cured."

"The usual sort of doctor!" said Chi Liang. "Get rid of him at once."

Mr Yü said:

"At birth there was too little vital fluid in your mother's womb and too much milk in your mother's breast. The illness is not a matter of one morning or evening; its development has been gradual and is irreversible."

"A good doctor!" said Chi Liang. "Let him stay for dinner."

Mr. Lu said:

"Your illness is not from heaven, nor from man, nor from spirits. Ever since you were endowed with life and a body, you have known what it is that governs them. What can medicine and the needle do for you?"

"A diving doctor!" said Chi Liang. "Send him off with a rich present."

Soon afterwards Chi Liang's illness mended of itself.

Valuing life cannot preserve it, taking care of the body cannot do it good; scorning life cannot shorten it, neglecting the body cannot do it harm. Hence some who value life do not live, some who scorn it do not die, some who take care of the body do it no good, some who neglect it do it no harm. This seems unreasonable, but it is not; in these cases life and death, good and harm, come of themselves.

Some value life and live, some scorn it and die, some take care of the body and do it good, some neglect it and do it harm. This seems only reasonable but it is not; in these cases also life and death, good and harm, come of themselves.

LIEH TZU

It manifests itself as kindness but conceals its workings. It gives life to all things, but it does not share the anxieties of the holy sage. Its glorious power, its great field of action, are of all things the most sublime.

The movement from within outward shows tao in its manifestations as the force of supreme kindness. At the same time it remains mysterious even in the light of day. The movement from without inward conceals the results of its workings. It is just as when in spring and summer the seeds start growing, and with it there is at work that quiet power which conceals within the seed all the results of growth and in hidden ways prepares what the coming year is to bring. Tao works tirelessly and eternally in this way. Yet this life-giving activity, to which all beings owe their existence, is something purely spontaneous. It is not like the conscious anxiety of man, who strives for the good with inward toil.

R. WILHELM, *I Ching*

However, the wise man lives in harmony with others without being led astray by them. How wholesome is his virtue!
He establishes himself in the middle way without leaning towards either side. How intelligent is his virtue!
When propitious practices prevail in public affairs, he remains undeviating in his private life. How reliable is his virtue!
When vicious practices prevail in public affairs, he still retains his virtuous habits without modification even in the face of death.
How enduring is his virtue!

CONFUCIUS

You should not search through others,
Lest the Truth recede farther from you.
When alone I proceed through myself,
I meet him wherever I go.

He is the same as me,
Yet I am not he!
Only if you understand this
Will you identify with
*tathata.**

LIANG-CHIEH

*Things as they are in Absolute Reality

Activity is essential, but exhausting.
And its importance is only on the surface.
Withdraw into Tao at the end of the day.
Returning is renewal.

DENG MING-DAO

It possesses everything in complete abundance: this is its great field of action. It renews everything daily: this is its glorious power.
There is nothing that tao may not possess, for it is omnipresent; everything that exists, exists in and through it. But it is not lifeless possessing; by reason of its eternal power, it continually renews everything, so that each day the world becomes as glorious again as it was on the first day of creation.

R. WILHELM, *I Ching*

I do my utmost to attain
emptiness;
I hold firmly to stillness.
The myriad creatures all rise
together
And I watch their return.
The teaming creatures
All return to their separate
roots.
Returning to one's roots is
known as stillness.
This is what is meant by
returning to one's destiny.
Returning to one's destiny is
known as the constant.
Knowledge of the constant is
known as discernment.
Woe to him who wilfully
innovates
While ignorant of the
constant,
But should one act from
knowledge of the constant
One's action will lead to
impartiality,
Impartiality to kingliness,
Kingliness to heaven,
Heaven to the way,
The way to perpetuity,
And to the end of one's days
one will meet with no danger.
LAO TZE, *Tao Te Ching*

In the Beginning of
Beginnings was Void of Void,
the Nameless.

And in the Nameless was the
One, without body, without
form.
This One - this Being in
whom all find power to exist -
Is the Living.
From the Living, comes the
Formless, the Undivided.
From the act of this Formless,
come the Existents, each
according
To its inner principle. This is
Form. Here body embraces
and cherishes spirit.
The two work together as one,
blending and manifesting
their
Characters. And this is
Nature.
But he who obeys Nature
returns through Form and
Formless to the Living,
And in the Living
Joins the unbegun Beginning.
The joining is Sameness. The
sameness is Void. The Void is
infinite.
The bird opens is beak and
sings its note
And then the beak comes
together again in Silence.
So Nature and the Living
meet together in Void.
Like the closing of the bird's
beak
After its song.

Heaven and earth come
together in the Unbegun,
And all is foolishness, all is
unknown, all is like
The lights of an idiot, all is
without mind!
To obey is to close the beak
and fall into Unbeginning.
CHUANG TZU

Endeavour said to Destiny:

"How can your effect be as
great as mine?"

"What effect on things do you
have, that you should wish to
compare yourself with me?"

"Whether a man lives long or
dies young, succeeds or fails,
has high rank or low, is poor
or rich, all this is within the
reach of my endeavour."

"P'eng Tsu was no wiser than
Yao and Shun, yet he lived
eight hundred years; Yen Yüan
was no less talented than
ordinary men, yet he died at
eighteen. Confucius was no
less virtuous than the feudal
lords, but they distressed him
in Ch'en and Ts'ai; the Yin
Emperor Chou did not behave
better than the three good

ministers he executed, but he
sat on the throne. Chi Cha
had no rank in Wu, yet T'ien
Heng became sole master of
the state of Ch'i. Po Yi and
Shu Ch'i starved to death on
Mount Shou-yang, but the
Chi family grew richer than
Chan Ch'in. If all this is
within the reach of your
endeavour, why did you give
long life to one and early
death to the other, why did
you permit the sage to fail and
villains to succeed, demean an
able man and exalt a fool,
impoverish good men and
enrich a bad one?"

"If it is as you say, certainly I
have no effect on things. But
is it you who directs that
things should be so?"

"When we say that a thing is
destined, how can there be
anyone who directs it? I push
it when it is going straight, let
it take charge when it is going
crooked. Long life and short,
failure and success, high rank
and low, wealth and poverty,
come about of themselves.
What can I know about it?
What can I know about it?"
LIEH-TZU

What, then, should the wise man do? Should he simply remain indifferent and treat right and wrong, good and bad, as if they were all the same? Chuang Tzu would be the first to deny that they were the same. But in so doing, he would refuse to grasp one or the other and cling to it as to an absolute. When a limited and conditioned view of 'good' is erected to the level of an absolute, it immediately becomes an evil, because it excludes certain complementary elements which are required if it is to be fully good. To cling to one partial view, one limited and conditioned opinion, and to treat this as the ultimate answer to all questions is simply to 'obscure the Tao' and make oneself obdurate in error.
THOMAS MERTON

To investigate the mysterious and to perform the spectacular for the sake of future reputation is something which I will not do.
The wise man emulates Nature in all his ways. To do so in only some ways is not enough.
The wise man accepts his genuine nature. Even though he may be completely unknown, ignored by everyone, he lives without remorse. Only one who is saintly can do this.
CONFUCIUS

As begetter of all begetting, it is called change.
The dark begets the light and the light begets the dark in ceaseless alternation, but that which begets this alternation, that to which all life owes its existence, is tao with its law of change.
R. WILHELM, *I Ching*

The best of all rulers is but a shadowy presence to his subjects.
Next comes the ruler they love and praise;
Next comes one they fear;
Next comes one with whom they take liberties.
When there is not enough faith, there is lack of good faith.
Hesitant, he does not utter words lightly.
When his task is

accomplished and his work
done
The people all say, "It
happened to us naturally."
LAO TZE, *Tao Te Ching*

Each day I forge my body into
steel
And fold in bright strands of
consciousness.
Piling up ripe fruit and
fragrant flowers,
Lighting red candles and
incense,
Serving tea, rice, and wine.
Anointing with aromatic oils,
Offering heart and bones,
The altar is my anvil, sun and
moon the coals,
Discipline the hammer, lungs
the bellows.
DENG MING DAO

He who grasps the central
pivot of Tao, is able to watch
'Yes' and 'No' pursue their
alternating course around the
circumference. He retains his
perspective and clarity of
judgement, so that he knows
that 'Yes' is 'Yes' in the light
of the 'No' which stands over
against it. He understands
that happiness, when pushed
to an extreme, becomes
calamity. That beauty, when

overdone, becomes ugliness.
THOMAS MERTON

Man's body (microcosm) is
noble.
Therefore the Tao opened a
path,
Bequeathing chieh rules,
ching canons, and wen scripts,
Whereby the bodily state
could be transcended,
By a higher state of union
with the Tao.
By preserving life essences,
Through performing the
rituals,
And promising to fulfil the
moral commandments,
The heart is quiet and
contemplates darkness (yin);
The will (chih) is fixed on
undivided brightness (yang);
All thought is reduced to the
one (hun-tun),
The six fu administrative
centres of the microcosm
By centring (in the Yellow
Court) are without sensation,
Inside and outside, pure and
empty,
Joined as one with all of
nature.
Then one offers incense, and
pronounces the vows,
Causing the heart to ascend to
the heavens,

And all the heavenly spirits to
come down to earth,
To hear the music of the
sacred liturgy, and
To answer the prayers of all
men,
According to how they have
kept the moral precepts,
And followed the way of the
eternal Tao.
KO HUNG

The heart and the mind must
be as one,
Purified from any sullied
desires.
Only the pure of mind can
touch the heavens
Only the upright of heart can
assemble spirits.
Nature obeys the upright and
(Cheng) orthodox.
CHUANG TZU

As that which completes the
primal images, it is called the
Creative; as that which
imitates them, it is called the
Receptive.
This is based on the view
expressed likewise in the Tao
Te Ching, namely, that
underlying reality there is a
world of archetypes, and
reproductions of these make
up the real things in the
material world. The world of
archetypes is heaven, the
world of reproductions is the
earth: there energy, here
matter; there the Creative,
here the Receptive. But it is
the same tao that is active
both in the Creative and in
the Receptive.
R. WILHELM, *I Ching*

Among the old masters there
were quite a few who
transmitted to us their
teachings, which are helpful.
For example, Master Hsüeh-
fêng said, "The entire great
earth is nothing but yourself."
Master Chia-shan said, "Find
me on top of a hundred blades
of grass and recognise the king
in the noisy market place."
Master Lo-p'u said, "When
you hold a grain of dust, you
are holding the great earth in
your hand. A hairy lion, all of
it, is you." Take these sayings
and reflect on them again and
again. After days, years, you
will find your entrance.
YUN MEN

With one stroke, all previous
knowledge is forgotten.
No cultivation is needed for
this.

This occurrence reveals the ancient way
And is free from the track of quiescence.
No trace is left anywhere.
Whatever I hear and see does not conform to rules.
All those who are enlightened
Proclaim this to be the greatest action.
The Master came to the assembly and said, "The Tao is attained by one's inner awakening; it does not depend upon words. Look at the invisible and boundless. Where can you find any intermittence? How can you reach it by the labour of the intellect? It is simply the reflection of illumination, and that is your whole daily task. Only those who are ignorant will go in the opposite direction."
HSIANG YEN

In the world there is nothing more submissive and weak than water. Yet for attacking that which is hard and strong nothing can surpass it. This is because there is nothing that can take its place.
That the weak overcomes the strong,
And the submissive overcomes the hard,
Everyone in the world knows yet no one can put this knowledge into practice.
Therefore the sage says,
One who takes on himself the humiliation of the state
Is called a ruler worthy of offering sacrifices to the gods of earth and millet;
One who takes on himself the calamity of the state
Is called a king worthy of dominion over the entire empire.
Straightforward words
Seem paradoxical.
LAO TZE, *Tao Te Ching*

The glass of everything,
Emptiness, stillness, tranquillity, tastelessness,
Silence, non-action: this the level of heaven and earth.
This is perfect Tao. Wise men find here
Their resting place.
Resting, they are empty.

From emptiness comes the unconditioned.
From this, the conditioned, the individual things.
So from the sage's emptiness, stillness arises;

From stillness, action. From
action attainment.
From their stillness comes
their non-action, which is also
action
And is, therefore, their
attainment.
For stillness is joy. Joy is free
from care
Fruitful in long years.
Joy does all things without
concern:
For emptiness, stillness,
tranquillity, tastelessness,
Silence, and non-action
Are the root of all things.
CHUANG TZU

In that it serves for exploring
the laws of number and thus
for knowing the future, it is
called revelation. In that it
serves to infuse an organic
coherence into the changes, it
is called the work.
The future likewise develops
in accordance with the fixed
laws, according to calculable
numbers. If these numbers are
known, future events can be
calculated with perfect
certainty. This is the thought
on which the Book of
Changes is based. This world
of the immutable is the
demonic world, in which
there is no free choice, in
which everything is fixed. It
is the world of yin. But in
addition to this rigid world of
number, there are living
trends. Things develop,
consolidate in a given
direction, grow rigid, then
decline; a change sets in,
coherence is established once
more, and the world is one
again. The secret of tao in
this world of the mutable, the
world of light - the realm of
yang - is to keep the changes
in motion in such a manner
that no stasis occurs and an
unbroken coherence is
maintained. He who succeeds
in endowing his work with
this regenerative power
creates something organic,
and the thing so created is
enduring.
R. WILHELM, *I Ching*

"According to what you say, I
cannot see your original
master." The Master then
continued: "Is there anyone
who does not show his
gratitude to the 'Four Graces'*
and the 'Three Existences'**?"
If he does not understand the
meaning of these, how can he
be free from the suffering of

the beginning and end of existence? Every thought he has in his mind should be free from attachment to things, and also every step he takes should be free from attachment to his dwelling place. When he keeps on in such a way without interruption, he will be close to the answer."
LIANG
*Grace of Parents, all Beings, The Ruler, Buddhism.
** (1) body-mind, (2) the future state (3) after death -
CHIEH

To be poured into without becoming full, and pour out without becoming empty, without knowing how this is brought about, - this is the art of 'Concealing the Light.'
CHUANG-TSE, Ch. II

When peace is made between great enemies,
Some enmity is bound to remain undispelled.
How can this be considered perfect?
Therefore the sage takes the left-hand tally, but exacts no payment from the people.
The man of virtue takes charge of the tally;
The man of no virtue takes charge of exaction.
It is the way of heaven to show no favouritism.
It is for ever on the side of the good man.
LAO TZE, *Tao Te Ching*

Nature harmonises with the reliable rhythms of heaven above, and is consistent with the regularities in the earth and water below.
In their inclusiveness and sustainingness, and in their comprehensiveness and protectiveness, they are comparable to Heaven and Earth.
In the orderliness of procedures, they are comparable to day and night and the four seasons. Nature shows how all things flourish together without harming each other. Each thing follows its own nature (*tao*) without interfering with others. Lesser things such as rivulets follow their own courses, while at the same time greater processes such as day and night and the four seasons pursue their tremendous transformations.

This is why Nature is so magnificent.
CONFUCIUS

In ancient times the true man did not rebel against penury, was not ambitious to succeed, and did not scheme and plan. That being so, if he committed an error he did not make it a subject for vain regret. When he accomplished something he did not consider this achievement as anything special. And so, he would climb heights without fear, enter water without being soaked, and fire without being burnt. With knowledge such as his one could mount up to be with Tao.
CHUANG-TZU

This notion of dynamic balance is essential to the way in which the unity of opposites is experienced in Eastern mysticism. It is never a static identity, but always a dynamic interplay between two extremes. This point has been emphasized most extensively by the Chinese sages in their symbolism of the archetypal poles yin and yang.

They called the unity lying behind yin and yang the Tao and saw it as a process which brings about their interplay: 'That which lets now the dark, now the light appear is Tao.'
FRITZJ OF COPRA

The Principle is an infinity which nothing can augment or diminish.
CHUANG-TSE, Chapter XXII

Which lies closest, fame or self? Which counts for most, self or goods? Which is worse, gaining or losing? Therefore, the more things are cherished and the greater the trouble. The more things are hoarded the heavier the loss. He who is contented will not suffer humiliation. He who stays put will not be in danger. He will be able to remain for a long time.
LAO TZE, *Tao Te Ching*

The true character of wu wei is not mere inactivity but *perfect action* - because it is act without activity. In other words, it is action not carried out independently of Heaven and earth and in conflict with the dynamism of the whole, but in perfect harmony with the whole. It is not mere passivity, but it is action that seems both effortless and spontaneous because performed 'rightly', in perfect accordance with our nature and with our place in the scheme of things. It is completely free because there is in it no force and no violence. It is not 'conditioned' or 'limited' by our own individual needs and desires, or even by our own theories and ideas.

THOMAS MERTON

To be without tranquillity and contentment is to lack virtue. Without virtue no man on earth can survive for long.

CHUANG TZU

He who knows others is clever;
He who knows himself has discernment.
He who overcomes others has force;
He who overcomes himself is strong.
He who knows contentment is rich;
He who perseveres is a man of purpose;
He who does not lose his station will endure;
He who lives out his days has had a long life.

LAO TZE, *Tao Te Ching*

Where is Tao right now?
You say that it is all around me, but I
Only see my surroundings, only feel my own heartbeat.
Can you show me Tao without reasoning it out in my mind?
Can you help me see it here and now?
Can you help me feel it as doubtlessly as I touch?
You argue that Tao is beyond the senses,
But how do I know it exists?
You say that Tao is beyond definitions,
Then how will I understand it?
It is hard enough understanding the economy, my relationships,
The bewilderment of world events, violence, crime,
Drug abuse, political repression, and war,
With all these things requiring years to fathom,
How can I understand

something that is
Colourless, nameless,
flavourless, intangible, and
silent?
Show me Tao! Show me Tao!
DENG MING-DAO

That aspect of it which
cannot be fathomed in terms
of the light and the dark is
called spirit.
In their alternation and
reciprocal effect, the two
fundamental forces serve to
explain all the phenomena in
the world. Nonetheless, there
remains something that
cannot be explained in terms
of the interaction of these
forces, a final why. This
ultimate meaning of tao is the
spirit, the divine, the
unfathomable in it, that
which must be revered in
silence.
R. WILHELM, *I Ching*

The sage observes nature but
does not assist it. Though
complete in virtue he does not
accumulate it. Emanating
from Tao he does not contrive
plans. Being in accord with
benevolence he does not
presume upon it. Cleaving to
justice he does not accumulate

it. He accords with the rituals
and does not shun their use.
He takes affairs in hand and
does not excuse himself. He
orders things by law and
allows no confusion. He
depends upon people and does
not make light of them. He
relies on material things and
does not discard them. As
regards things, though none
are fit for use, one cannot but
use them.
CHUANG-TZU

"The difference between
Buddhism and Taoism lies
simply in their names. Should
we not bring out their
teachings?" Ch'u replied,
"What teachings do you want
to discuss?" Master Liang-
chieh gave his illustration by a
quotation: "When ideas are
obtained, words are
forgotten." Ch'u challenged
him saying, "You are letting
the teachings stain your
mind." The Master then said,
"How much more you are
staining your mind by talking
about Buddhism and Taoism!"
It is said that the reverend
monk Ch'u died because of
this challenge.
LIANG CHIEH

Only the most sage person in the world can unite in himself the quickness, clarity, breadth, and depth of understanding needed for guiding men; the magnanimity, generosity, benevolence, and gentleness needed for getting along with others; the attentiveness, strength, stability, and tenacity needed for maintaining control; the serenity, seriousness, unwaveringness, and propriety needed for commanding respect; and the well-informedness, methodicalness, thoroughness, and penetration needed for exercising sound judgement.
Because he exercises his abilities when they are needed, he is able to do all kinds of things, to serve wide areas, to penetrate deeply, and to flow on perpetually.
CONFUCIUS

The Emperor T'ang of Yin asked Chi of Hsia: "Have there always been things?"

"If once there were no things, how come there are things now? Would you approve if the men who live after us say there are no things now?"

"In that case, do things have no before and after?"

"The ending and starting of things
Have no limit from which they began.
The start of one is the end of another,
The end of one is the start of another.
Who knows which came first?

But what is outside things, what was before events, I do not know."

"In that case, is everything limited and exhaustible above and below and in the eight directions?"

"I do not know."

When T'ang pressed the question, Chi continued:

"It is Nothing which is limitless, Something which is inexhaustible. How do I know this?... But also there is nothing limitless outside what is limitless, and nothing inexhaustible within what is inexhaustible.

"There is no limit, but neither is there anything limitless; there is no exhausting, but neither is there anything inexhaustible. That is why I know that they are limitless and inexhaustible, yet do not know whether they may be limited and exhaustible."
LIEH TZU

As regards the quietude of the sage, he is not quiet because quietness is said to be good. He is quiet because the multitude of things cannot disturb his quietude. When water is still one's beard and eyebrows are reflected in it. A skilled carpenter uses it in a level to obtain a measurement. If still water is so clear, how much more are the mental faculties! The mind of a sage is the mirror of heaven and earth in which all things are reflected.
CHUANG-TZU

Why do you scorn others?
Can it be that you are that proud?
No matter how accomplished you are,
There are people ahead of you and behind you.
All beings on the path,
All victims of the same existence,
All with body, mind, and spirit
No one is better than the next person.
Help others for all the times that you have been ignored.
Be kind to others, for all the times that you have been scorned.
DENG MING DAO

The way is broad, reaching left as well as right.
The myriad creatures depend on it for life yet it claims no authority.
It accomplishes its task yet lays claim to no merit.
It clothes and feeds the myriad creatures yet lays no claim to being their master.
For ever free of desire, it can be called small; yet, as it lays no claim to being master when the myriad creatures turn to it, it can be called great.
It is because it never attempts itself to be great that it succeeds in becoming great.
LAO TZE, *Tao Te Ching*

"How does the true man of Tao
Walk through walls without obstruction,
Stand in fire without being burnt?"

Not because of cunning
Or daring;
Not because he has learned,
But because he has unlearned.

All that is limited by form, semblance, sound, colour,
Is called *object*.
Among them all, man alone
Is more than an object.
Though, like objects, he has form and semblance,
He is not limited to form. He is more.
He can attain to formlessness.
CHUANG TZU

Chuang Tzu saw that one basic characteristic of the sage is that he recognises himself to be *as other men are*. He does not set himself apart from others and above them. And yet there is a difference; he differs '*in his heart*' from other men, since he is centred on Tao and not on himself. But 'he does not know in what way he is different'. He is also aware of his relatedness to others, his union with them, but he does not 'understand' this either. He merely lives it.
THOMAS MERTON

The Changes is a book
From which one may not hold aloof.
Its tao is forever changing -
Alteration, movement without rest,
Flowing through the six empty places;
Rising and sinking without fixed law,
Firm and yielding transform each other.
They cannot be confined within a rule;
It is only change that is at work here...

They also show care and sorrow and their causes.
Though you have no teacher,
Approach them as you would your parents.
R. WILHELM, *I Ching*

In old times the perfect man of Tao was subtle, penetrating and so profound that he can hardly be understood ...
Going back to the origin is called peace;

It means reversion to destiny.
Reversion to destiny is called
eternity.
He who knows eternity is
called enlightened ...
Being supreme he can attain
Tao.
He who attains Tao is
everlasting.
Though his body may decay
he never perishes.
LAO TZE, *Tao Te Ching*, XV,
XVI

The non-action of the wise
man is not inaction.
It is not studied. It is not
shaken by anything.

The sage is quiet because he is
not moved,
Not because he *wills* to be
quiet.
Still water is like glass.
You can look in it and see the
bristles on your chin.
It is a perfect level;
A carpenter could use it.
If water is so clear, so level,
How much more the spirit of
man?
The heart of the wise man is
tranquil.
It is the mirror of heaven and
earth.
CHUANG-TZU

FORTY-SIX

UNIVERSE

He is from eternity to eternity,
and to him nothing may be
added,
Nor can he be diminished,
and he hath no need of any
counsellor.
Ecclesiasticus, XLII, 21-22

The man who doesn't know
what the universe is doesn't
know where he lives.
MARCUS AURELIUS

The Universe is the mirror of
God - the mirror in which His
majesty and perfection are
reflected, the mirror in which
He sees Himself - and the
heart of man is the mirror of
the Universe; if the Traveller
then would know God, he
must look into his own heart.
'AZIZ IBN MUHAMMAD
AL-NASAFÎ

The good writer seems to be
writing about himself, but has
his eye always on that thread
of the universe which runs
through himself, and all things.
RALPH WALDO EMERSON

I am a part of all that I have
met.
ALFRED, LORD
TENNYSON, *Ulysses*

The Mind like a mirror is
brightly illuminating and
knows no obstructions,
It penetrates the vast universe
to its minutest crevices;
All its contents, multitudinous
in form, are reflected in the
Mind,
Which, shining like a perfect
gem, has no surface, nor the
inside.
YOKA DAISHI

When I saw into myself I saw
God in me and everything
God ever made in earth and
heaven. Let me explain it
better. As you know right
well, anyone who faces God in
the mirror of truth sees
everything depicted in that
mirror: all things, that is to
say.
ECKHART

A thing appears in the world
and then goes to destruction.
If it has no true existence,
how may it appear again?
If it is free from both
manifestation and destruction,
what then arises?
Stay! Your master has spoken.
SARAHA

He bowed the heavens also, and came down: and darkness was under his feet.
Psalms 18:9

The Shaikh (may God be well pleased with him) says in the *Fass i Shu'aibî*, that the universe consists of accidents all pertaining to a single substance, which is the Reality underlying all existences. This universe is changed and renewed unceasingly at every moment and at every breath. Every instant one universe is annihilated and another resembling it takes its place, though the majority of men do not perceive this, as God most glorious has said: "But they are in doubt regarding the new creation" (*Qur'ân*, L. 15)... They have not grasped the fact that the universe, together with all its parts, is nothing but a number of accidents, ever changing and being renewed at every breath, and linked together in a single substance, and at each instant disappearing and being replaced by a similar set. In consequence of this rapid succession, the spectator is deceived into the belief that the universe is a permanent existence.
JÂMÎ

Now they say that the world is unreal. Of what degree of unreality is it? Is it like that of a son of a barren mother or a flower in the sky, mere words without any reference to facts? Whereas the world is a fact and not a mere word. The answer is that it is a superimposition on the one Reality, like the appearance of a snake on a coiled rope seen in dim light.
SRI RAMANA MAHARSHI

He who lives in harmony with his own self, his daemon, lives in harmony with the universe; for both the universal order and the personal order are nothing but different expressions and manifestations of a common underlying principle.
MARCUS AURELIUS

Man is not born to solve the problems of the universe, but to find out where the problems begin, and then to take his stand within the

limits of the intelligible.
GOETHE

The universe is true for all of us and different for each of us.
MARCUS PROUST

Everything in the universe goes by indirection. There are no straight lines.
RALPH WALDO EMERSON, Society and Solitude

The moon is nothing
But a circumambulatory aphrodisiac
Divinely subsidised to provoke the world
Into a rising birth rate.
CHRISTOPHER FRY, The Lady's Not for Burning, Act 3

As milk is spontaneously changed into curds and water into ice, so Brahma modifies Itself in diverse ways, without the aid of instruments or external means of any kind whatever. Thus the spider spins its web out of its own substance, subtle beings take diverse forms, and the lotus grows from marsh to marsh without organs of locomotion.
Brahma-Sûtra, II, i

I do not wonder at a snowflake, a shell, a summer landscape, or the glory of the stars; but at the necessity of beauty under which the universe lies.
RALPH WALDO EMERSON, The Conduct of Life, Fate, (1860)

Do not think of the water failing; for this water is without end.
Dîvâni Shamsi Tabrîz, XII

The atoms of the universe may be counted, but not so my manifestations; for eternally I create innumerable worlds.
Srimad Bhagavatam, XI, x

The fire which serves as pyre for the Phoenix, and cradle where he resumes a new life... draws its origins from the highest mountain on earth... This fire is the source of all light which illumines this vast universe: it imparts heat and life to all beings..., a Flame that is never consumed.
MICHAEL MAIER

Unfathomable as the sea, wondrously ending only to

begin again, informing all
creation without being
exhausted, the *Tao* of the
perfect man is spontaneous in
its operation.
CHUANG-TSE, Chapter
XXII

Verily His command, when
He intendeth a thing, is that
He saith unto it: Be! and it is.
Qur'ân, XXXVI. 82

The force with which God
works is his will; and his very
being consists in willing the
existence of all things ... For
God wills things to be, and, in
that way, these things also
have existence.
HERMES

There is speculation. Then
there is wild speculation.
Then there is cosmology.
MARTYN HARRIS, *Odd
Man Out*, a Brief History of
Hawking

Even sleepers are workers and
collaborators in what goes on
in the universe.
HERACLITUS, *Fragments*, 124

The children of God should
not have any other country

here below but the universe
itself, with the totality of all
the reasoning creatures it ever
has contained, contains, or
ever will contain. That is the
native city to which we owe
our love.
SIMONE WEIL, *Waiting on
God*, Letter 6

I live not in myself, but I
become
Portion of that around me.
BYRON, *Childe Harold's
Pilgrimage*, Canto III, Stanza 25

Law rules throughout
existence, a Law which is not
intelligent but Intelligence.
RALPH WALDO
EMERSON, *The Conduct of
Life*, Fate, (1860)

Nature, it seems, is the
popular name
for milliards and milliards and
milliards
of particles playing their
infinite game
of billiards and billiards and
billiards.
PIET HEIN, *Grooks*,
Atomyriades

The whole visible world is
only an imperceptible atom in

the ample bosom of nature.
No idea approaches it.
PASCAL, Pensées, 72, (1670)

All are but parts of one
stupendous whole,
Whose body Nature is, and
God the soul.
ALEXANDER POPE, An
Essay on Man, line 267,
(1733-34)

To be happy in this world,
especially when youth is past,
it is necessary to feel oneself
not merely an isolated
individual whose day will soon
be over, but part of the stream
of life flowing on from the
first germ to the remote and
unknown future.
BERTRAND RUSSELL, The
Conquest of Happiness, 13

Thou canst not stir a flower
Without troubling of a star.
FRANCIS THOMPSON, The
Mistress of Vision, (1897)

I do not value any view of the
universe into which man and
the institutions of man enter
very largely and absorb much
of the attention. Man is but
the place where I stand, and
the prospect hence is infinite.

THOREAU, Journal, 2 April
1852

'Tis very puzzling on the brink
Of what is called Eternity to
stare,
And know no more of what is
here, than there.
BYRON, Don Juan, 10.20

The fairest thing we can
experience is the mysterious.
It is the fundamental emotion
which stands at the cradle of
true art and true science.
ALBERT EINSTEIN, title
essay, The World As I See It,
(1934)

Between the idea
And the reality
Between the motion
And the act
Falls the Shadow.
T.S. ELIOT, The Hollow Men,
5, (1925)

All is riddle, and the key to a
riddle is another riddle.
RALPH WALDO
EMERSON, The Conduct of
Life, Illusions, (1860)

Grieve not, because thou
understandest not life's
mystery; behind the veil is

concealed many a delight.
HAFIZ, ghazals from the
Divan, 18, (14th century)

Would there be this eternal
seeking if the found existed?
ANTONIO PORCHIA,
Voces, (1968)

We are ignorant of the
Beyond because this ignorance
is the condition *sine qua non*
of our own life. Just as ice
cannot know fire except by
melting, by vanishing.
JULES RENARD, *Journal*,
September 1890

In the depths of the world, of
the sky, there's a rhythm that
must be listened to. Anybody
can. One day ... that beat
may seep down from your
wrist to your pen. Like blood
- which has no ultimate sex.
*One must give back the stare of
the universe.* Anybody can.
HORTENSE CALISHER,
Herself

The universe is to be valued
because there is truth in it and
beauty in it; and we live to
discover the truth and beauty
no less than to do what is
right. Indeed, we cannot

attain to that state of mind in
which we shall naturally do
what is right unless we are
aware of the truth and the
beauty of the universe.
A. CLUTTON BROCK, *The
Ultimate Belief*

The conflict of forces and the
struggle of opposing wills are
of the essence of our universe
and alone hold it together.
HAVELOCK ELLIS, *Selected
Essays*

I discover everywhere in the
smallest things, that
omnipotent hand which
supports the heavens and the
earth, and which seems as it
were in sport while it
conducts the universe.
FRANÇOIS FÉNELON,
Reflections and Meditations

The universe is built on a plan
the profound symmetry of
which is somehow present in
the inner structure of our
intellect.
PAUL VALÉRY, in *Rectitude*
by Antonin G. Sertillanges

Of the 'real' universe we know
nothing, except that there
exist as many versions of it as

there are perceptive minds.
Each man lives alone in his
private universe.
GERALD BULLETT, *Dreaming*

A grain of sand includes the
universe.
SAMUEL TAYLOR
COLERIDGE, *Additional Table
Talk*, Thought

Space is the stature of God.
JOUBERT, *Pensées*, No. 183

All that is in tune with thee,
O Universe, is in tune with
me!
MARCUS AURELIUS,
Meditations, Book IV, Section 23

It is an infinite sphere whose
centre is everywhere, its
circumference nowhere.
BLAISE PASCAL, *Pensées*,
Section II, number 72

Great is this organism of mud
and fire, terrible this vast,
painful, glorious experiment.
GEORGE SANTAYANA,
Little Essays, page 86

The universe is a thought of
God.
SCHILLER, *Essays: Aesthetical
and Philosophical*, Letter 4

Let your soul stand cool and
composed before a million
universes.
WALT WHITMAN, *Song of
Myself*, Section 48

Face to face with the universe,
man will be the sole evidence
of his audacious dreams of
divinity, since the God he
vainly sought is himself.
GEORGES CLEMENCEAU,
In the Evening of My Thought

Teach me, by this stupendous
scaffolding,
Creation's golden steps to
climb to Thee.
YOUNG, *Night Thoughts*,
Night, ix, line 592

O God, I am thinking Thy
thoughts after Thee.
JOHANNES KEPLER, when
studying astronomy
Has God any dwelling-place
save earth and sea, the air of
heaven and virtuous hearts?
Why seek the Deity further?
Whatever we see is God, and
wherever we go.
LUCAN, *De Bello Civili*, Book
IX, line 578

Know first, the heaven, the
earth, the main,

The moon's pale orb, the
starry train,
Are nourished by a soul,
A bright intelligence, whose
flame
Glows in each member of the
frame,
And stirs the mighty whole.
VIRGIL, *Aeneid*, Book VI,
line 724

What, but God?
Inspiring God! who, boundless
Spirit all,
And unremitting Energy,
pervades,
Adjusts, sustains and agitates
the whole.
THOMSON, *The Seasons*,
Spring, line 852

Who coverest thyself with
light as with a garment: who
stretchest out the heavens like
a curtain: Who layeth the
beams of his chambers in the
waters: who maketh the
clouds his chariot: who
walketh upon the wings of the
wind: Who maketh his angels
spirits; his ministers a flaming
fire.
Psalms 104:2-4

One Universe made up of all
things; and one God in it all,

and one principle of Being,
and one Law, one Reason
shared by all thinking
creatures, and one Truth.
MARCUS AURELIUS,
Meditations, Book VII,
Section 9

Between the birthday and the
grave,
Teaching the tender heart be
brave,
He woos our better from our
worse,
The Artist of the Universe.
PAUL SHIVELL, *The Studios
Photographic*

God never meant that man
should scale the heav'ns
By strides of human wisdom.
In his works
Though wondrous, he
commands us in his word
To seek him rather where his
mercy shines.
WILLIAM COWPER, *The
Task*, Book III, line 221

Who thou art I know not,
But this much I know:
Thou hast set the Pleiades
In a silver row.
HARRY KEMP, *God, the
Architect*

Only God is permanently interesting. Other things we may fathom, but he out-tops our thought and can neither be demonstrated nor argued down.
J.F. NEWTON, My *Idea of God*, page 5

Every conjecture we can form with regard to the works of God has as little probability as the conjectures of a child with regard to the works of a man.
THOMAS REID, *Intellectual Powers*, Volume I

Who fathoms the Eternal Thought?
Who talks of scheme and plan?
The Lord is God! He needeth not
The poor device of man.
J.G WHITTIER, *The Eternal Goodness*, Stanza 4

In this unbelievable universe in which we live there are no absolutes. Even parallel lines, reaching into infinity, meet somewhere yonder.
PEARL BUCK, A *Bridge for Passing*

The cosmos is about the smallest hole that a man can hide his head in.
G.K. CHESTERTON, *Orthodoxy*, Chapter 1

Anyone informed that the universe is expanding and contracting in pulsations of eighty billion years has a right to ask, "What's in it for me?"
PETER DE VRIES, *The Glory of the Hummingbird*, Chapter 1

The universe begins to look more like a great thought than like a great machine.
JAMES JEANS, *The Mysterious Universe*

In my youth I regarded the universe as an open book, printed in the language of physical equations, whereas now it appears to me as a text written in invisible ink, of which in our rare moments of grace we are able to decipher a small fragment.
ARTHUR KOESTLER, *Bricks to Babel*, Epilogue

Out of all possible universes, the only one which can exist, in the sense that it can be known, is simply the one

which satisfies the narrow conditions necessary for the development of intelligent life.
BERNARD LOVELL, *In the Centre of Immensities*

My theology, briefly, is that the universe was dictated but not signed.
CHRISTOPHER MORLEY

As I walk ... as I walk ...
The universe ... is walking with me ...
Beautifully ... it walks before me ...
Beautifully ... on every side ...
As I walk ... I walk with beauty.
MARY AUSTIN, *Everyman's Genius*, (1925)

So loving is the universe, so joyful, so determined to give us everything we need and to love us and show us the way to live, too, that we are beaten to the ground, boiled by God's waves, as we play in the surf.
SOPHY BURNHAM, *A Book of Angels*, (1990)

What if the universe
is *not about*
us? Then what?
What
is it about
and what
about
us?
MAY SWENSON, *To Mix With Time*, The Universe, (1963)

The universe and I exist together, and all things and I are one.
ZHUANGZI, (circa 369-286 BC), *Chuang Tzu*, Chapter 2

The eternal silence of these infinite spaces terrifies me.
BLAISE PASCAL, (1623-62), *Pensées*, (1670)

I suspect that there are more things in heaven and earth than are dreamed of, or can be dreamed of, in any philosophy.
WILLIAM SHAKESPEARE, *Hamlet*

The eternal mystery of the world is its comprehensibility ... The fact that it is comprehensible is a miracle.
ALBERT EINSTEIN, in *Franklin Institute Journal*, Physics and Reality
Space isn't remote at all. It's only an hour's drive away if

your car could go straight upwards.
FRED HOYLE

The Greeks said God was always doing geometry, modern physicists say he's playing roulette, everything depends on the observer, the universe is a totality of observations, it's a work of art created by us.
IRIS MURDOCH, *The Good Apprentice*

What is it that breathes fire into the equations and makes a universe for them to describe... Why does the universe go to all the bother of existing?
STEPHEN HAWKING, *A Brief History of Time*

I think it is likely that there is life out there. I fear we shall never know about it.
RICHARD DAWKINS, *Seven Wonders of the World*, BBC TV, (1997)

Universe is the aggregate of all humanity's consciously apprehended and communicated non-simultaneous and only partially overlapping experiences.
R. BUCKMINSTER FULLER, *Synergetics*

If at that moment [one second after beginning to expand] the rate of expansion had been reduced by only a part in a thousand billion, then the universe would have collapsed after a few million years.
SIR BERNARD LOVELL, *In the Centre of Immensities*

The universe is transformation; our life is what our thoughts make it.
MARCUS AURELIUS, *Meditations*, Book IV, Section 3

I laid my heart open to the benign indifference of the universe.
ALBERT CAMUS, *The Outsider*, II, 5

Sweep away the illusion of Time; glance, if thou have eyes, from the near moving-cause to its far distant Mover. Oh, could I transport thee direct from the Beginnings to the Endings, how were thy eyesight unsealed, and thy heart set flaming in the Light-

sea of celestial wonder! Then sawest Thou that this fair Universe, were it in the meanest province thereof, is in very deed the star-domed City of God; that through every star, through every grass-blade, and most through every living Soul, the glory of a present God still beams. But Nature, which is the Time-vesture of God, reveals Him to the wise, and hides Him from the foolish.
THOMAS CARLYLE

There is no object on earth which cannot be looked at from a cosmic point of view. DOSTOEVSKY, *Critical Articles*: Introduction, Polnoye Sobraniye Sochinyeni, (Complete Collected Works, 1895) Volume 9

FORTY-SEVEN

WIT

Wit is the bedfellow of
wisdom.
JONAS CABAL

No man ... who has wrestled
with a self-adjusting card table
can ever quite be the man he
once was.
JAMES THURBER, *Let Your
Mind Alone*

Not by wrath, does one kill
but by laughter.
FRIEDRICH NIETZSCHE,
Thus Spoke Zarathustra, On
Reading and Writing, 1,
(1883-92)

Sarah said, "God has made me
laugh. Now everyone will
laugh with me."
Genesis 21:6 (CEV)

If you're not allowed to laugh
in heaven, I don't want to go
there.
MARTIN LUTHER

Too bad all the people who
know how to run the country
are busy driving taxi cabs and
cutting hair.
GEORGE BURNS

Falstaff: The brain of this
foolish-compounded clay man,

is not able to invent anything
that tends to laughter, more
than I invent or is invented
on me: I am not only witty in
myself, but the cause that wit
is in other men.
WILLIAM SHAKESPEARE,
II. Henry IV, Act I, Scene ii,
line 6

One morning I shot an
elephant in my pajamas.
How he got into my pajamas
I'll never know.
GROUCHO MARX, *Animal
Crackers*

Laugh not too much; the witty
man laughs least:
For wit is news only to
ignorance.
Less at thine own things
laugh; lest in the jest
Thy person share, and the
conceit advance.
HERBERT, *The Temple*,
Church Porch, Stanza 39

We must laugh before we are
happy, or else we may die
before we ever laugh at all.
LA BRUYÈRE, *Characters*, Of
the Heart

Care to our coffin adds a nail,
no doubt;

And every Grin, so merry,
draws one out.
JOHN WOLCOT (Peter
Pindar), *Expostulatory Odes*, 15

Wit is nothing worth till it be
dear bought.
HENRY MEDWALL, *Nature*,
Part II, line 1292, (circa 1500)

Wit when temperate is
pleasing, when unbridled it
offends.
PHAEDRUS, *Fables*, Book V,
fable 5, line 41

Wit is folly unless a wise man
hath the keeping of it.
JOHN RAY, *English Proverbs*,
page 174

Wit rules the heavens,
discretion guides the skies.
TASSO, *Gerusalemme*, Book
X, Stanza 20

Melancholy men of all others
are most witty.
ARISTOTLE, Burton,
Anatomy of Melancholy, I, iii,
line 3

It is the soul that is not yet
sure of its God that is afraid to
laugh in His presence.
GEORGE MAC DONALD

All this is but a web of the
wit; it can work nothing.
FRANCIS BACON, *Essays*,
Of Empire

I could dance with you till the
cows come home.
Better still, I'll dance with the
cows and *you* come home.
GROUCHO MARX, *Duck Soup*

An ounce of wit is worth a
pound of sorrow.
RICHARD BAXTER, *Of Self-
Denial*

Good wits jump; a word to the
wise is enough.
CERVANTES, *Don Quixote*,
Part II, Chapter 37

A time to weep and a time to
laugh, a time to mourn and a
time to dance.
Ecclesiastes 2:4 (NIV)

It is wit to pick a lock and
steal a horse, but it is wisdom
to let them alone.
THOMAS FULLER,
Gnomologia, Number 3031

The fox that waited for the
chickens to fall off their perch
died of hunger.
GREEK PROVERB

Even in laughter the heart is sorrowful; and the end of mirth is heaviness.
Proverbs 14:13

The man who cannot laugh is not only fit for treasons, stratagems, and spoils; but his whole life is already a treason and a stratagem.
THOMAS CARLYLE, *Sartor Resartus*, line 4, (1833-34)

Pain is deeper than all thought; laughter is higher than all pain.
ELBERT HUBBARD, *The Philistine*, (1895-1915)

It is a sign of old age when one starts to shave with the mobile and call up a friend on the Remington.
JONAS CABAL

In laughter all that is evil comes together, but is pronounced holy and absolved by its own bliss.
FRIEDRICH NIETZSCHE, *Thus Spoke Zarathustra*, The Seven Seals, 1, (1883-92)

We are in the world to laugh. In purgatory or in hell we shall no longer be able to do so. And in heaven it would not be proper.
JULES RENARD, *Journal*, June 1907

Clumsy jesting is no joke.
AESOP, *Fables*, The Ass and the Lapdog, (6th century BC?)

A sense of humour keen enough to show a man his own absurdities, as well as those of other people, will keep him from the commission of all sins, or nearly all, save those that are worth committing.
SAMUEL BUTLER, *Note-Books*, Lord, What Is Man?, (1912)

Laughter is able to mediate between the infinite magnitude of our tasks and the limitation of our strengths.
JÜRGEN MOLTMANN

Humour is an affirmation of dignity, a declaration of man's superiority to all that befalls him.
ROMAIN GARY, *Promise at Dawn*

The humorist has a good eye for the humbug; he does not

always recognise the saint.
W. SOMERSET
MAUGHAM, *The Summing
Up*, 20

Go - and never darken my
towels again.
GROUCHO MARX, *Duck
Soup*

Keep company with the more
cheerful sort of the godly;
there is no mirth like the
mirth of believers.
RICHARD BAXTER

A jest's prosperity lies in the ear
Of him that hears it, never in
the tongue
Of him that makes it.
WILLIAM SHAKESPEARE,
Love's Labour's Lost, Act V,
Scene ii line 70, (1594-95)

Humour is emotional chaos
remembered in tranquillity.
JAMES THURBER

Humour is the first of the gifts
to perish in a foreign tongue.
VIRGINIA WOOLF, *On Not
Knowing Greek*, (1925)

All's good in a famine.
THOMAS FULLER, M.D.,
Gnomologia, 545, (1732)

There's a hell of a distance
between wisecracking and wit.
Wit has truth in it;
wisecracking is simply
callisthehenics with words.
DOROTHY PARKER, *Writers
at Work*

All Nature wears one
universal grin.
FIELDING, *Tom Thumb the
Great*, Act I, Scene 1

How much lies in Laughter:
the cipher-key, wherewith we
decipher the whole man.
THOMAS CARLYLE, *Sartor
Resartus*, Book I, Chapter iv

The world would not be in
such a snarl, had Marx been
Groucho instead of Karl.
IRVING BERLIN

Laughter is the most beautiful
and beneficial therapy God
ever granted humanity.
CHARLES R. SWINDOLL

I remain just one thing, and
one thing only - and that is a
clown.
It places me on a far higher
plane than any politician.
CHARLIE CHAPLIN

No mind is thoroughly well
organised that is deficient in a
sense of humour.
SAMUEL TAYLOR
COLERIDGE, (1772-1834)
Table Talk

Many a time I wanted to stop
talking and find out what I
really believe.
WALTER LIPPMAN

Mirth is the sweet wine of
human life. It should be
offered sparkling with zestful
life unto God.
HENRY WARD BEECHER

How old would you be if you
didn't know how old you was.
SATCHEL PAIGE

Advertisements contain the
only truths to be relied on in a
newspaper.
THOMAS JEFFERSON

Don't cry because it's over;
smile because it happened.
ANON

Total absence of humour
renders life impossible.
COLETTE, *Chance
Acquaintances*

As for the Freudian, it is a
very low, Central European
sort of humour.
ROBERT GRAVES,
Occupation: Writer

There's a wonderful family
called Stein,
There's Gert and there's Epp
and there's Ein;
Gert's poems are bunk,
Epp's statues are junk,
And no one can understand Ein.
ANON

Humour iz wit with a roosters
tail feathers stuck in its cap,
and wit iz wisdom in tight
harness.
JOSH BILLINGS, *Wit and
Humour*, Hints to Comik
Lekturers

True humour springs not more
from the head than from the
heart; it is not contempt, its
essence is love: it issues not in
laughter, but in still smiles,
which lie far deeper. It is a
sort of inverse sublimity,
exalting, as it were, into our
affections what is below us,
while sublimity draws down
into our affections what is
above us.
THOMAS CARLYLE

It is a splendid thing to laugh inwardly at yourself. It is the best way of regaining your good humour and of finding God without further anxiety.
HENRI DE TOURVILLE

I don't have a photograph, but you can have my footprints. They are upstairs in my socks.
GROUCHO MARX, A Night At the Opera

Men show their character in nothing more clearly than by what they think laughable.
GOETHE

Laugh and grow strong.
ST. IGNATIUS OF LOYOLA

He who laughs best today, will also laugh last.
FRIEDRICH NIETZSCHE, Twilight of the Idols, Maxims and Missiles, 43, (1888)

Conquered people tend to be witty.
SAUL BELLOW, Mr. Sammler's Planet, Chapter 2

What he has is wit, not humour, and wit alone never turns inwards.
ROBERTSON DAVIES, The Rebel Angels, Second Paradise, VI

I shall ne'er be ware of mine own wit till I break my shins against it.
WILLIAM SHAKESPEARE, As You Like It, Act II, Scene iv, line 59

Wit will shine
Through the harsh cadence of a rugged line.
JOHN DRYDEN, To the Memory of Mr. Oldham, (1684)

A man who could make so vile a pun would not scruple to pick a pocket.
JOHN DENNIS, in The Gentleman's Magazine, (1781)

What is an Epigram? a dwarfish whole,
Its body brevity, and wit its soul.
SAMUEL TAYLOR COLERDIGE, Epigram, (1809)

Those who cannot miss an opportunity of saying a good thing ... are not to be trusted with the management of any great question.
WILLIAM HAZLITT, Characteristics, (1823)

It is better to be witty and wise than witty and otherwise.
DOUGLAS JERROLD

Satire must not be a kind of superfluous ill will, but ill will from a higher point of view.
PAUL KLEE, *Diaries 1898-1918*, Diary III, 420

Humour will never destroy anything that is genuine. All it can do is puncture balloons.
KENNETH L. WILSON

He must have wit who understands he is a fool.
PUBLILIUS SYRUS, *Moral Sayings*, 451

Dr. Strabismus (Whom God Preserve) of Utrecht is carrying out research work with a view to crossing salmon with mosquitoes. He says it will mean a bite every time for fishermen.
J.B. MORTON, *By the Way*

Shared laughter creates a bond of friendship. When people laugh together, they cease to be young and old, master and pupils, worker and driver. They have become a single group of human beings, enjoying their existence.
WILLIAM GRANT LEE

What is perfectly true is imperfectly witty.
WALTER SAVAGE LANDOR, *Imaginary Conversations*, Diogenes and Plato, (1824-53)

In the midst of the fountain of wit there arises something bitter, which stings in the very flowers.
LUCRETIUS, *On the Nature of Things*, 4, 1133, (1st century BC)

The strains of Verdi will come back to you tonight, and Mrs. Claypool's cheque will come back to you in the morning.
GROUCHO MARX, *A Night at the Opera*

I have ever thought so superstitiously of wit, that I fear I have committed idolatry against wisdom.
JOHN LYLY, *Euphues: The Anatomy of Wit*, (1579)

It is not enough to possess wit. One must have enough of it to avoid having too much.
ANDRÉ MAUROIS, *De la conversation*, (1921)

Wit is the rarest quality to be met with among people of education, and the most common among the uneducated.
WILLIAM HAZLITT

Wit and Humour - if any difference it is in duration - lightning and electric light. Same material, apparently; but one is vivid, and can do damage - the other fools along and enjoys elaboration.
MARK TWAIN

Don't try to be witty in the writing, unless it's natural - just true and real.
F. SCOTT FITZGERALD, letter (1938)

Please accept my resignation. I don't want to belong to any club that will accept me as a member.
GROUCHO MARX, resigning from Friar's Club, Hollywood

Methinks sometimes I have no more wit than a Christian or an ordinary man has; but I am a great eater of beef, and I believe that does harm to my wit.
WILLIAM SHAKESPEARE, (1564-1616), *Twelfth Night*, Act I, Scene iii, line 90

Satire is alive and well and living in the White House.
ROBIN WILLIAMS, *Rolling Stone*, (1985)

As the crackling of thorns under a pot, so is the laughter of the fool.
Ecclesiastes 7:6

And unextinguish'd laughter shakes the skies.
HOMER, *Iliad*, Book I, line 771

It is often just as sacred to laugh as it is to pray.
CHARLES R. SWINDOLL

Wit is the epitaph of an emotion.
FRIEDRICH NIETZSCHE, *Menschliches, Allzumenschliches*, (1867-80)

Now am I a tin whistle Through which God blows, And I wish to God I were a trumpet
- But why, God only knows.
J.C. SQUIRE, *A Fresh Morning*

An epigram is a flashlight of a
truth; a witticism, truth
laughing at itself.
MINNA THOMAS
ANTRIM, *Naked Truth and
Veiled Illusions*, (1901)

Mingle a little folly with your
wisdom; a little nonsense now
and then is pleasant.
HORACE

FORTY-EIGHT

WOMAN

Oh, woman! lovely woman!
Nature made thee to temper
man; we had been brutes
without you!
OTWAY

The world was sad, the garden
was a wild; and Man, the
hermit, sighed, till Woman
smiled.
CAMPBELL

A handsome woman is a
jewel; but a good woman is a
treasure.
SAADI

A creature not too bright or
good
For human nature's daily food;
For transient sorrows, simple
wiles,
Praise, blame, love, kisses,
tears, and smiles:
A Being breathing thoughtful
breath,
A traveller between life and
death;
The reason firm, the
temperate will,
Endurance, foresight, strength
and skill;
A perfect Woman, nobly
planned,
To warn, to comfort, and
command;

And yet a Spirit still and
bright
With something of angelic
light.
WILLIAM WORDSWORTH

Kindness in woman, not her
beauteous looks, shall win my
love.
WILLIAM SHAKESPEARE

Women have more of what is
termed good sense than men.
They cannot reason wrong, for
they do not reason at all.
They have fewer pretensions,
are less implicated in theories,
and judge of objects more
from their immediate and
involuntary impression on the
mind, and therefore more
truly and naturally.
HAZLITT

A grandam's name is little less
in love,
Than is the doting title of a
mother.
WILLIAM SHAKESPEARE,
Richard III, Act IV, Scene iv,
line 299

I have oftimes noted, when
women receive the doctrine of
the gospel, they are far more
fervent in faith, they hold to

it more stiff and fast than men do; as we see in the loving Magdalen, who was more hearty and bold than Peter.
LUTHER

A man without religion is to be pitied, but a Godless woman is a horror above all things.
MISS EVANS

Earth's noblest thing, a woman perfected.
J.R. LOWELL

A beautiful and chaste woman is the perfect workmanship of God, the true glory of angels, the rare miracle of earth, and the sole wonder of the world.
HERMES

The man that lays his hand upon a woman
Save in the way of kindness, is a wretch
Whom 'twere gross flattery to name a coward.
TOBIN

What manly eloquence could produce such an effect as a woman's silence.
MICHELET

Women are the poetry of the world, in the same sense as the stars are the poetry of heaven. Clear, light-giving, harmonious, they are the terrestrial planets that rule the destinies of mankind.
HARGRAVE

The man who bears an honourable mind will scorn to treat a woman lawlessly.
WILLIAM SHAKESPEARE

And yet believe me, good as well as ill,
Woman's at best a contradiction still.
Heaven when it strives to polish all it can
Its last best work, but forms a softer man.
ALEXANDER POPE

Woman is something between a flower and an angel.
There is in every true woman's heart a spark of heavenly fire, which beams and blazes in the dark hours of adversity.
WASHINGTON IRVING

Verily the best of women are those who are content with little.
MOHAMMED

For my part I distrust all generalisations about women, favourable and unfavourable, masculine and feminine, ancient and modern.
BERTRAND RUSSELL

A virtuous woman is a crown to her husband: but she that maketh ashamed is as rottenness in his bones.
Proverbs 12:4

Yet when I approach
Her loveliness, so absolute she seems,
And in herself complete; so well to know
Her own, that what she wills to do or say,
Seems wisest, virtuousest, discreetest, best.
MILTON, *Paradise Lost*, Book VIII, line 546

There will be a singing in your heart,
There will be a rapture in your eyes;
You will be a woman set apart,
You will be so wonderful and wise.
You will sleep, and when from dreams you start,
As of one that wakes in Paradise,

There will be a singing in your heart,
There will be a rapture in your eyes.
ROBERT W. SERVICE, *The Mother*

She was a phantom of delight
When first she gleamed upon my sight,
A lovely apparition, sent
To be a moment's ornament.
WILLIAM WORDSWORTH, *She Was a Phantom of Delight*

Variability is one of the virtues of a woman. It avoids the crude requirement of polygamy. So long as you have one good wife you are sure to have a spiritual harem.
G.K. CHESTERTON, *The Glory of Grey*, (1910)

Women never use their intelligence - except when they need to prop up their intuition.
JACQUES DEVAL, from *News Summaries*

The entire being of a woman is a secret which should be kept.
ISAK DINESEN, *Last Tales*, Of Hidden Thoughts and of Heaven

Women are like the arts,
forced unto none
Open to all searchers,
unprized, if unknown.
JOHN DONNE, Elegy 3,
Change, (1635)

Happy he
With such a mother! Faith in
womankind
Beats with his blood, and trust
in all things high
Comes easy to him, and tho'
he trip and fall
He shall not blind his soul
with clay.
ALFRED, LORD
TENNYSON, The Princess,
Part VII, 1ine 308

Women have simple tastes.
They can get pleasure out of
the conversation of children
in arms and men in love.
H.L. MENCKEN, A Book of
Burlesques, Sententiae, (1920)

Woman's reason is in the milk
of her breasts.
GEORGE MEREDITH, The
Ordeal of Richard Feveral, 43,
(1859)

There is no such thing as an
old woman. Any woman of
any age, if she loves, if she is

good, gives a man a sense of
the infinite.
JULES MICHELET, L'Amour,
v.4, (1859)

Let man fear woman when she
loves: then she makes any
sacrifice, and everything else
seems without value to her.
FRIEDRICH NIETZSCHE,
Thus Spoke Zarathustra, On
Little Old and Young
Women, 1

What one beholds of a woman
is the least part of her.
OVID, Love's Cure,
(circa AD 8)

It is a high distinction for a
homely woman to be loved for
her character rather than for
beauty.
PLUTARCH, Moralia,
Marriage Counsel, (circa AD
100)

Women see through each
other, but they rarely look
into themselves.
THEODOR REIK, Of Love
and Lust, 4, 48

And say to mothers what a
holy charge
Is theirs - with what a kingly

power their love
Might rule the fountains of
the new-born mind.
LYDIA HUNTLY
SIGOURNEY, *The Mother of
Washington*, line 33

Women prefer poverty with
love to luxury without it.
HAGGADAH, *Palestinian
Talmud*, (4th century)

The ability to find joy in the
world of sorrow and hope at
the edge of despair is woman's
witness to courage and her gift
of new life to all.
MIRIAM THERESE
WINTER

Woman's basic fear is that she
will lose love.
SIGMUND FREUD,
Civilization and Its Discontents

When three women join
together the stars come out in
broad daylight.
TELAGU PROVERB

Spiritually a woman is better
off if she cannot be taken for
granted.
GERMAINE GREER, *The
Female Eunuch*

'Tis beauty that doth oft make
women proud;
'Tis virtue, that doth make
them most admired;
'Tis modesty, that makes them
seem divine.
WILLIAM SHAKESPEARE

Oh fairest of creation! last and
best
Of all God's works! creature in
whom excell'd
Whatever can to sight or
thought be form'd,
Holy, divine, good, amiable, or
sweet!
MILTON, *Paradise Lost*, Book
IX, line 896

No man, as a general rule,
shows his soul to another
man; he shows it only to a
woman.
LAFCADIO HEARN, *Life
and Letters*

Two different things wanteth
the true man: danger and
diversion. Therefore wanteth
he woman, as the most
dangerous plaything.
FRIEDRICH NIETZSCHE,
Thus Spake Zarathustra

Charm is deceptive and
beauty fleeting; but the

woman who fears the Lord is
honoured.
Proverbs 31:30

Much of what we as women
do is in a supportive role, but
imagine what would happen
to a building if its support
pillars were removed.
JUDY HUBBEKK

It was to a virgin woman that
the birth of the Son of God
was announced. It was to a
fallen woman that his
resurrection was announced.
FULTON JOHN SHEEN

How can a woman be
expected to be happy with a
man who insists on treating
her as if she were a perfectly
natural being?
OSCAR WILDE

Think what cowards men
would be if they had to bear
children. Women are an
altogether superior species.
GEORGE BERNARD SHAW

Most women would rather be
loved too well than too wisely.
MINNA ANTRIM, *The
Wisdom of the Foolish*, page 3

Women are really supposed to
be much nicer than men.
That's what they're here for.
W.H. AUDEN, *Table Talk of
W.H. Auden*

Children are the anchors that
hold a mother to life.
SOPHOCLES, *Phaedra*,
Fragment 619

Remember that woman never
speaks more forcibly than
when she is silent, nor acts
with more energy than when
in repose.
HONORÉ DE BALZAC

Feminism is an insurrection,
not a coffee morning.
GERALDINE BEDELL

There is a tide in the affairs of
women,
Which, taken at the flood,
leads - God knows where.
LORD BYRON,
Don Juan, VI, 12

You don't know a woman
until you've had a letter from
her.
ADA LEVERSON,
Tenterhooks, Chapter 7

A woman is as old as she looks before breakfast.
EDGAR WATSON HOWE, *Country Town Sayings*, (1911)

The bearing and the training of a child
Is woman's wisdom.
ALFRED, LORD TENNYSON, *The Princess*, Part V, line 456

So for the mother's sake the child was dear,
And dearer was the mother for the child!
SAMUEL TAYLOR COLERIDGE, *Sonnet: To a Friend Who Asked How I Felt when the Nurse First Presented My Infant to Me*

'Tis hers to pluck the amaranthine flower
Of faith, and round the sufferer's temple bind
Wreaths that endure affliction's heaviest shower,
And do not shrink from sorrow's keenest wind.
WILLIAM WORDSWORTH, *Weak is the Will of Man*

Without woman's hopes, without her fears, without the home that plighted love endears, without the smiles from plighted beauty won, oh! what were man? - a world without a sun.
CAMPBELL

Women wish to be loved without a why or a wherefore; not because they are pretty, or good, or well-bred, or graceful, or intelligent, but because they are themselves.
HENRI FRÉDÉRIC AMIEL, *Journal*, March 1868

With women, the heart argues, not the mind.
MATTHEW ARNOLD, *Merope*, (1858)

As a jewel of gold in a swine's snout, so is a fair woman which is without discretion.
Proverbs 11:22

A woman is a creature who has discovered her own nature.
JEAN GIRAUDOUX, *Judith*, 2, (1931)

A woman prefers a man without money to money without a man.
GREEK PROVERB

Women never reason, and therefore they are (comparatively) seldom wrong.
WILLIAM HAZLITT, *Characteristics*, (1823)

Until women assume the place in society which good sense and good feeling alike assign to them, human improvement must advance but feebly.
FRANCES WRIGHT, *Course of Popular Lectures*, Of Free Enquiry, (1829)

Woman's normal occupations in general run counter to creative life, or contemplative life, or saintly life.
ANNE MORROW LINDBERGH, *Gift From the Sea*, (1955)

The most wasteful 'brain drain' in America today is the drain in the kitchen sink.
ELIZABETH GOULD DAVIS, *The First Sex*

They say that man is mighty,
He governs land and sea,
He wields a mighty sceptre
O'er lesser powers that be;
But a mightier power and stronger
Man from his throne has hurled,
For the hand that rocks the cradle
Is the hand that rules the world.
WILLIAM ROSS WALLACE, *What Rules the World*, (circa 1865)

Consider the 'new' woman, ... Clearly a conflict of interest. She's supposed to be a ruthless winner at work and a bundle of nurturing sweetness at home.
RITA MAE BROWN, *In Her Day*

I didn't fight to get women out from behind the vacuum cleaner to get them onto the board of Hoover.
GERMAINE GREER

Today the problem that has no name is how to juggle work, love, home and children.
BETTY FRIEDAN, *The Second Stage*

Feminism is the most revolutionary idea there has ever been. Equality for

women demands a change in
the human psyche more
profound than anything Marx
dreamed of. It means valuing
parenthood as much as we
value banking.
POLLY TOYNBEE, in
Guardian, (1987)

A whistling woman and a
crowing hen are neither fit for
God nor men.
PROVERB, (early 18th
century)

I could have stayed home and
baked cookies and had teas.
But what I decided was to
fulfil my profession, which I
entered before my husband
was in public life.
HILLARY RODHAM
CLINTON

Whoever has a daughter and
does not bury her alive, nor
insult her nor favour his son
over her, Allah will enter him
into Paradise.
AHMAD IBN HANBAL,
(780-855), Musnad No. 1957

And what is bettre than
wisedoom?
Womman. And
what is bettre than a good

womman?
Nothyng.
GEOFFREY CHAUCER,
(circa 1343-1400), The
Canterbury Tales, The Tale of
Melibee

The weaker sex, to piety more
prone.
WILLIAM ALEXANDER,
EARL OF STIRLING, (circa
1567-1640), Doomsday 5th
Hour, (1637)

Eternal Woman draws us
upward.
JOHANN WOLFGANG
VON GOETHE, (1749-
1832), Faust, Part 2

Only the male intellect,
clouded by sexual impulse,
could call the undersized,
narrow-shouldered, broad-
hipped, and short-legged sex
the fair sex.
ARTHUR
SCHOPENHAUER, On
Women, (1851)

The freedom women were
supposed to have found in the
Sixties largely boiled down to
easy contraception and
abortion: things to make life
easier for men, in fact.

JULIE BURCHILL, *Damaged Goods*

Thou, while thy babes around thee cling,
Shalt show us how divine a thing
A woman may be made.
WILLIAM WORDSWORTH, *To a Young Lady*

You can now see the Female Eunuch the world over ... spreading herself wherever blue jeans and Coca-Cola may go. Wherever you see nail varnish, lipstick, brassieres, and high heels, the Eunuch has set up her camp.
GERMAINE GREER

There is no female Mozart because there is no female Jack the Ripper.
CAMILLE PAGLIA

Basically my wife was immature, I'd be at home in the bath and she'd come in and sink my boats.
WOODY ALLEN, (1935-), in *Nudge Nudge, Wink Wink*

It is better to dwell in a corner of the housetop, than with a brawling woman in a wide house.
Proverbs 21:9

I ... chose my wife, as she did her wedding gown, not for a fine glossy surface, but such qualities as would wear well.
OLIVER GOLDSMITH, (1728-74), *The Vicar of Wakefield*, Chapter 1

For a light wife doth make a heavy husband.
WILLIAM SHAKESPEARE, *The Merchant of Venice*, Act V, Scene i, line 130

The female woman is one of the greatest institooshuns of which this land can boste.
ARTEMUS WARD, (1834-67), *A W His Book*, Woman's Rights

I do not wish them to have power over men; but over themselves.
MARY WOLLSTONECRAFT, (1759-97), *A Vindication of the Rights of Women*, 4

Women were brought up to believe that men were the answer. They weren't. They

weren't even one of the
questions.
JULIAN BARNES, *Staring at
the Sun*, Part 2

So God created man in his
own image, in the image of
God created he him; male and
female created he them.
Genesis 1:27

The mother's heart is the
child's schoolroom.
HENRY WARD BEECHER,
Life Thoughts

Man and woman are two
locked caskets, of which each
contains the key to the other.
ISAK DINESEN, *Winter's
Tales*, A Consolatory Tale

Now, Watson, the fair sex is
your department.
SHERLOCK HOLMES, *The
Second Stain*

That is the great distinction
between the sexes. Men see
objects, women see
relationship between objects.
Whether the objects need
each other, love each other,
match each other. It is an
extra dimension of feeling we
men are without and one that

makes war abhorrent to all
real women - and absurd.
JOHN FOWLES, *The Magus*,
Chapter 52, revised edition
edition

When Eve ate this particular
apple, she became aware of
her own womanhood,
mentally. And mentally she
began to experiment with it.
She has been experimenting
ever since. So has man.
D.H. LAWRENCE, *Fantasia of
the Unconscious*, Chapter 7

As unto the bow the cord is,
So unto the man is woman;
Though she bends him, she
obeys him,
Though she draws him, yet
she follows;
Useless each without the
other!
H.W. LONGFELLOW, (1807-
82), *The Song of Hiawatha*, 10

First the sweetheart of the
nation, then the aunt, woman
governs America because
America is a land of boys who
refuse to grow up.
SALVADOR DE
MADARIAGA, in *The
Perpetual Pessimist*

Happy is the man with a wife to tell him what to do and a secretary to do it.
LORD MANCROFT

Any man who says he can see through a woman is missing a lot.
GROUCHO MARX

It's the little questions from women about tappets that finally push men over the edge.
PHILIP ROTH, *Letting Go*, Part I, Chaper 1

A woman without a man is like a fish without a bicycle.
GLORIA STEINEM

A mother is a mother still, The holiest thing alive.
SAMUEL TAYLOR COLERIDGE, *The Three Graves*, Stanza 10

The cocks may crow, but it's the hen that lays the egg.
MARGARET THATCHER, (1987)

Sometimes I think if there was a third sex men wouldn't get so much as a glance from me.
AMANDA VAIL, *Love Me Little*, Chapter 6

God could not be everywhere and therefore he made mothers.
JEWISH PROVERB

Whoever rightly considers the order of things may plainly see the whole race of woman-kind is by nature, custom, and the laws, made subject to man, to be governed according to his discretion: therefore it is the duty of every one of us that desires to have ease, comfort, and repose, with those men to whom we belong, to be humble, patient, and obedient, as well as chaste ...
GIOVANNI BOCCACCIO, (1313-75), *Decameron*, Ninth Day

The sons of God saw the daughters of men, that they were fair.
Genesis 6:2

We are unimportant. We are here to serve, to heal the wounds and give love.
MARIKE DE KLERK

A man is in general better pleased when he has a good dinner upon his table, than when his wife talks Greek.

SAMUEL JOHNSON,
Johnsonian Miscellanies,
Volume II

People are just not very
ambitious for women still.
Your son you want to be the
best he can be. Your daughter
you want to be happy.
ALEXA CANADY, in *I
Dream a World*

I'm all for women myself. I
believe they're the comin'
man.
JULIE M. LIPPMANN,
Martha By-the-Day, (1912)

The dogma of woman's
complete historical subjection
to man must be rated as one of
the most fantastic myths ever
created by the human mind.
MARY RITTER BEARD,
Woman As a Force in History

The future destiny of the child
is always the work of the
mother.
NAPOLEON BONAPARTE,
Sayings of Napoleon

Every man who is high up
likes to feel that he has done
it himself; and the wife smiles,
and lets it go at that. It's our

only joke. Every woman
knows that.
J.M. BARRIE, *Peter Pan*

Simply having children does
not make mothers.
JOHN A. SHEDD, *Salt from
My Attic*, page 38

And the Lord God caused a
deep sleep to fall upon Adam,
and he slept: and he took one
of his ribs, and closed up the
flesh instead thereof;
And the rib, which the Lord
God had taken from man,
made he a woman, and
brought her unto the man.
And Adam said, "This is now
bone of my bones, and flesh of
my flesh: she shall be called
Woman, because she was
taken out of Man.
Therefore shall a man leave
his father and his mother, and
shall cleave unto his wife: and
they shall be one flesh.
And they were both naked,
the man and his wife, and
were not ashamed.
Genesis 2:21-25

It is an unfortunate fact that
where two ladies get in the
same kitchen it is often a
recipe for disaster.

GRAHAM DAVIS, 22 May 1994

It is only the women whose eyes have been washed clear with tears who get the broad vision that makes them little sisters to all the world.
DOROTHY DIX, Her Book, Introduction

The happiest women, like the happiest nations, have no history.
GEORGE ELIOT, The Mill on the Floss, Chapter 6

She is abstract femininity ... the prototype of a galactic New Woman.
FEDERICO FELLINI, referring to Kim Basinger

And Adam called his wife's name Eve; because she was the mother of all living.
Genesis 3:20

Who can find a virtuous woman? for her price is far above rubies.
The heart of her husband doth safely trust in her, so that he shall have no need of spoil. She will do him good and not evil all the days of her life.

Proverbs 31:10-12

The great question ... which I have not been able to answer, despite my thirty years of research into the feminine soul, is 'What does a woman want?'
SIGMUND FREUD, (1856-1939)

A woman's preaching is like a dog's walking on his hinder legs. It is not done well; but you are surprised to find it done at all.
SAMUEL JOHNSON, Life of Johnson, Volume I, (J. Boswell)

When the Himalayan peasant meets the he-bear in his pride,
He shouts to scare the monster, who will often turn aside,
But the she-bear thus accosted rends the peasant tooth and nail
For the female of the species is more deadly than the male.
RUDYARD KIPLING, The Female of the Species

If you educate a man you educate a person, but if you educate a woman you educate a family.

RUBY MANIKAN, (20th century), Indian Church leader

American women expect to find in their husbands a perfection that English women only hope to find in their butlers.
W. SOMERSET MAUGHAM, A Writer's Notebook

Thousands of American women know far more about the subconscious than they do about sewing.
H.L. MENCKEN, Prejudices

I expect that Woman will be the last thing civilised by Man.
GEORGE MEREDITH, (1828-1909), The Ordeal of Richard Feverel, Chapter 1

Confusion has seized us, and all things go wrong,
The women have leaped from 'their spheres',
And, instead of fixed stars, shoot as comets along,
And are setting the world by the ears!
MARIA CHAPMAN, The History of Woman Suffrage, Volume 1, (1881)

Whatever women do they must do twice as well as men to be thought half as good. Luckily, this is not difficult.
CHARLOTTE WHITTON, in Canada Month

Mother is the name for God in the lips and hearts of little children.
THACKERAY, Vanity Fair, Volume II, Chapter 12

Now that you have touched the women, you have struck a rock, you have dislodged a boulder, and you will be crushed.
SOUTH AFRICAN CHANT

Let me not be sad because I am born a woman
In this world; many saints suffer in this way.
JANABAI, (circa 1340)

If ... society will not admit of woman's free development, then society must be remodelled.
ELIZABETH BLACKWELL, (1848)

I shrug my shoulders in despair at women who moan at the lack of opportunities and then

take two weeks off as a result
of falling out with their
boyfriends.
SOPHIE MIRMAN

Don't aim to be an earthly
Saint, with eyes fixed on a
star,
Just try to be the fellow that
your Mother thinks you are.
WILL S. ADKIN, *Just Try to
Be the Fellow*

In a matriarchy men should be
encouraged to take it easy, for
most women prefer live
husbands to blocks of shares
and seats on the board.
J.B. PRIESTLEY, *Thoughts in
the Wilderness*
I know that a woman is a dish
for the gods, if the devil dress
her not.
WILLIAM SHAKESPEARE,
(1564-1616), *Antony and
Cleopatra*, Act V, Scene ii

When a woman behaves like a
man, why doesn't she behave
like a nice man?
DAME EDITH EVANS

Women are equal because
they are not different any
more.
ERIC FROMM, *The Art of
Loving*

A woman is like a tea bag.
Only when in hot water do
you realise how strong she is.
NANCY REAGAN

FORTY-NINE

WORLD

In such communion, while yet a child, had I perceived the presence and the power of greatness. Early had I learned to reverence the volume that displays the mystery - the life which cannot die; but in the mountains did I feel my faith. All things, responsive to the writing, there breathed immortality; revolving life, and greatness still revolving - infinite! There littleness was not: the least of things seemed infinite. Low desires, low thoughts had there no place: yet was my heart lowly, for I was meek in gratitude.
WILLIAM WORDSWORTH

Now these pilgrims, as I said, must needs go through this fair ...
But that which did not a little amuse the merchandisers was, that these pilgrims set very light by all their wares; they cared not so much as to look upon them; and, if they called upon them to buy, they would put their fingers in their ears, and cry, "Turn away mine eyes from beholding vanity!" and look upwards, signifying that their trade and traffic was in heaven.

JOHN BUNYAN, *The Pilgrim's Progress*

Accuse not nature, she hath done her part; do thou but thine!
MILTON

All those who love Nature she loves in return, and will richly reward, not perhaps with the good things as they are commonly called, but with the best things of this world - not with money and titles, horses and carriages, but with bright and happy thoughts, contentment and peace of mind.
AVEBURY

This is human happiness! Its secret and its evidence are writ in the broad book of Nature. 'Tis to have attentive and believing faculties; to go abroad rejoicing in the joy of beautiful and well-created things; to love the voice of waters, and the sheen of silver fountains leaping to the sea; to thrill with the rich melody of birds living their life of music; to be glad in the gay sunshine, reverent in the storm; to see a beauty in the

stirring leaf and find calm
thoughts beneath the
whispering tree; to see, and
hear, and breathe the
evidence of God's deep
wisdom in the natural world!
WILLIS

Lovely indeed the mimic
works of art - but Nature's
works, far lovelier.
WILLIAM COWPER

And this our life, exempt from
public haunt,
Finds tongues in trees, books
in the running brooks,
Sermons in stones, and good
in everything.
WILLIAM SHAKESPEARE,
As You Like It, (1599)

What is this world?
What but a spacious burial
field unwall'd;
The very turf on which we
tread once lived.
BLAIR Add Christian
name??

This world is like a mint, we
are no sooner
Cast into the fire, taken out
again,
Hammer'd, stamp'd, and made
current, but

Presently we are chang'd.
DECKER AND WEBSTER

Above me are the Alps - the
palaces of Nature, whose vast
walls have pinnacled in clouds
their snowy scalps, and
throned Eternity in icy halls
of cold sublimity; where forms
and falls the avalanche - the
thunderbolt of snow!
All that expands the spirit, yet
appals, gather round these
summits, as to show how
Earth may pierce to Heaven,
yet leave vain man below.
LORD BYRON

The noblest employment of
the mind of man is the study
of the works of his Creator.
To him whom the science of
Nature delights, every object
brings a proof of his God; and
everything that proves this
gives cause for adoration.
Cast your eyes towards the
cloud. Do you not find the
heavens full of wonders? Look
down at the Earth. Does not
the worm proclaim to you:
"Could less than
Omnipotence have formed
me?" The planets follow their
courses; the sun remains in his
place; the comet wanders

through space and returns to his destined road again. What but an Infinite Wisdom could have appointed them their laws? Can the meanest fly create itself? - could you have fashioned it?

You who see the whole as admirable as its parts cannot better employ your eye in tracing out your Creator's greatness in them; or your mind than in examining the wonders of Creation.

What is the study of words compared with this? Wherein is Knowledge, but in the study of Nature?
DANDEMIS

Clouds, mists, rocks and sapphire sky confused: commingled, mutually inflamed, molten together - each lost in each, a marvellous array vast in size, in abundance glorified; in vision, forms uncouth of mightiest power for admiration and mysterious awe.
WILLIAM WORDSWORTH

However, you're a man, you've seen the world -
The beauty and the wonder and the power,

The shapes of things, their colours, lights and shades, Changes, surprises - and God made it all!
ROBERT BROWNING, *Fra Lippo Lippi*, II, 276-9

The created world is but a small parenthesis in eternity, and a short interposition for a time, between such a state of duration as was before it, and may be after it.
SIR THOMAS BROWNE

Ay, beauteous is the world, and many a joy
Floats through its wide dominion. But, alas, When we would seize the winged good, it flies, And step by step, along the path of life,
Allures our yearning spirits to the grave.
GOETHE

All the ways of this world are as fickle and unstable as a sudden storm at sea.
THE VENERABLE BEDE

The world's a wood, in which all lose their way,
Though by a different path each goes astray.
BUCKINGHAM

There is one's trade and one's family, and beyond it seems as if the great demon of worldly-mindedness would hardly allow one to bestow a thought or care.
MATTHEW ARNOLD

Oh who would trust this world, or prize what's in it That gives and takes, and chops and changes ev'ry minute.
QUARLES

A good man and a wise man may at times be angry with the world, at times grieved for it; but be sure no man was ever discontented with the world who did his duty in it.
SOUTHEY

There always are in the world a few inspired men whose acquaintance is beyond price, and who spring up quite as much in ill-ordered as in well-ordered cities. These are they whom the citizens of a well-ordered city should be ever seeking out, going forth over sea and over land to find him who is incorruptible.
PLATO, *Laws*, XII, 951 B

This bit of earth here under us is but a handful of dirt. Yet when considered in its breadth and depth, it supports heavy mountains without strain and retains rivers and oceans without letting them drain away.
This mountain here before us looks like a mere pile of rocks; yet on its broad slopes grow grass and trees, birds and animals make their homes on it, and stores of valuable minerals abound within it.

This lake here before us seems like a mere dipperful; yet in its bottomless depths swim myriads of fishes and turtles and sharks. Bountiful resources swarm within it.
In the *Book of Verses* it is written: 'The provisions of Heaven! How plenteous and unfailing!' This means that such plenitude and endless supply is what makes Heaven Heaven, or the nature of Nature.
CONFUCIUS

In the beginning, before there was any division of subject and object, there was one existence, Brahman alone, One without a second. That

time is called the Krita yuga, or the golden age, when people skilled in knowledge and discrimination realised that one existence... Men had but one caste, known as Hamsa. All were equally endowed with knowledge, all were born knowers of Truth; and since this was so the age was called Krita, which is to say, 'Attained'.
Srimad Bhagavatam, XI, xvii and xi

He created the heavens and the earth with truth, and He shaped you and made good your shapes.
Qur'ân, LXIV, 3

Gratiano: You have too much respect upon the world:
They lose it that do buy it with much care.
WILLIAM SHAKESPEARE, *Merchant of Venice*, Act I, Scene i, line 74

Each planet, each plant, each butterfly, each moth, each beetle, becomes doubly real to you when you know its name. Lucky indeed are those who from their earliest childhood have heard all these things

named.
JOHN COWPER POWYS, *The Meaning of Culture*

It is an outcome of faith that nature - as she is perceptible to our five senses, - takes the character of such a well formulated puzzle.
ALBERT EINSTEIN, *Out of my Later Years*

The happiest man is he who learns from Nature the lesson of worship.
RALPH WALDO EMERSON

There is a pleasure in the pathless woods; there is a rapture on the lonely shore; there is society where none intrudes, by the deep sea, and music of its roar. I love not man the less, but Nature more.
LORD BYRON

Come forth into the light of things,
Let Nature be your Teacher.
WILLIAM WORDSWORTH, *The Tables Turned*

O chestnut tree, great rooted blossomer,

Are you the leaf, the blossom
or the bole?
O body swayed to music; O
brightening glance,
How can we know the dancer
from the dance?
W.B. YEATS, *Among School
Children*

Be not blind, but open-eyed,
to the great wonders of Nature,
familiar, everyday objects
though they be to thee. But
men are more wont to be
astonished at the sun's eclipse
than at his unfailing rise.
ORCHOTH ZADIKKIM,
(circa 15th century)

I believe a leaf of grass is no
less than the journey-work of
the stars,
And the pismire is equally
perfect, and a grain of sand,
and the egg of the wren,
And the tree toad is a chef-
d'oeuvre for the highest,
And the running blackberry
would adorn the parlours of
heaven.
WALT WHITMAN, *Song of
Myself*, (1855)

Nature is not a temple, but a
workshop, and man's the
workman in it.

IVAN TURGENEV, *Fathers
and Sons*, (1862)

In nature there are neither
rewards nor punishments -
there are consequences.
ROBERT G. INGERSOLL,
Some Reasons Why, (1881)

Christianity deposes Mother
Nature and begets, on her
prostrate body, Science, which
proceeds to destroy Nature.
TED HUGHES, in *Your
Environment*

People thought they could
explain and conquer nature -
yet the outcome is that they
destroyed it and disinherited
themselves from it.
VÁCLAV HAVEL

Nothing is further than Earth
from Heaven: nothing is
nearer than Heaven to Earth.
JULIUS AND AUGUSTUS
HARE, *Guesses at Truth*, 2

Our labour here is brief, but
the reward is eternal. Do not
be disturbed by the clamour of
the world, which passes like a
shadow. Do not let the false
delights of a deceptive world
deceive you.
ST. CLARE OF ASSISI

The world is but a school of inquiry.
MICHEL DE MONTAIGNE, *Essays*, Book 3, Chapter 8

The world is the sum-total of our vital possibilities.
JOSÉ ORTEGA Y GASSET, *The Revolt of the Masses*, Chapter 4

All the world's a stage,
And all the men and women merely players:
They have their exits and their entrances;
And one man in his time plays many parts.
WILLIAM SHAKESPEARE, *As You Like It*, Act II, Scene vii, line 139

The world is the totality of facts not of things.
LUDWIG WITTGENSTEIN, *Tractatus Logico-philosophicus*, 1, 1

The earth is the Lord's, and the fulness thereof; the world, and they that dwell therein.
Psalms 24:1

There may be heaven; there must be hell;
Meantime, there is our earth here - well!
ROBERT BROWNING, *Time's Revenges*

The worlds revolve like ancient women
Gathering fuel in vacant lots.
T.S. ELIOT, *Preludes*, IV

It's a funny old world - a man's lucky if he gets out of it alive.
W.C. FIELDS, in *You're Telling Me*

To persons standing alone on a hill during a clear midnight such as this, the roll of the world eastward is almost a palpable movement.
THOMAS HARDY, (1840-1928), *Far from the Madding Crowd*, Chapter 2

The world is charged with the grandeur of God.
GERARD MANLEY HOPKINS, (1844-89), *God's Grandeur*

I see the world as a football, kicked about by the higher powers, with me clinging on by my teeth and toenails to the laces.
DAN LENO, (1860-1904), *Theatre*

The world is everything that is the case.
LUDWIG WITTGENSTEIN, *Tractatus Logico-philosophicus*, 1, 1

The world is one vast graveyard of defunct cities, all destroyed by the shifting of markets they could not control, and all compressed by literature into a handful of poems.
ALASDAIR GRAY, *The Emperor's Injustice*

The world's great age begins anew,
The golden years return,
The earth doth like a snake renew
Her winter weeds outworn.
PERCY BYSSHE SHELLEY, *Hellas*, line1060

The world is too much with us; late and soon,
Getting and spending we lay waste our powers;
Little we see in Nature that is ours.
WILLIAM WORDSWORTH, *Miscellaneous Sonnets*

This fine old world of ours is but a child
Yet in the go-cart. Patience! Give it time
To learn its limbs: there is a hand that guides.
ALFRED, LORD TENNYSON, *The Princess*, Conclusion

This world's no blot for us,
Nor blank; it means intensely, and means good:
To find its meaning is my meat and drink.
ROBERT BROWNING, *Fra Lippo Lippi*, II, 307-9

The world waits
For help. Beloved, let us love so well,
Our work shall still be better for our love,
And still our love be sweeter for our work,
And both commended, for the sake of each,
By all true workers and true lovers born.
ELIZABETH BARRETT BROWNING, *Aurora Leigh*

No man is born into the world whose work
Is not born with him. There is always work,

And tools to work withal, for
those who will;
And blessed are the horny
hands of toil.
LOWELL, A *Glance Behind the
Curtain*

Then I began to think, that it
is very true which is
commonly said, that the one-
half of the world knoweth not
how the other half liveth.
RABELAIS, *Works*, Book II,
Chapter xxxii

Hamlet: How weary, stale, flat,
and unprofitable
Seem to me all the uses of this
world!
Fye on't! oh, fye! 'tis an
unweeded garden,
That grows to seed; things
rank, and gross in nature,
Possess it merely.
WILLIAM SHAKESPEARE,
Hamlet, Act I, Scene ... line
133

A boundless continent,
Dark, waste, and wild, under
the frown of night
Starless expos'd.
MILTON, *Paradise Lost*, Book
III, line 423

The world is a comedy to
those who think, a tragedy to
those who feel.
HORACE WALPOLE, *Letter
to Sir Horace Mann*, 1770

Nature never set forth the
earth in so rich tapestry as
diverse poets have done ... her
world is brazen, the poets only
deliver a golden one.
PHILIP SIDNEY, *The Defence
of Poetry*, (1595)

We must look upon all things
of this world as none of ours,
and not desire them. This
world and that to come are
two enemies. We cannot
therefore be friends to both;
but we must resolve which we
would forsake and which we
would enjoy.
ST. CLEMENT I OF ROME

Poems are made by fools like
me,
But only God can make a tree.
JOYCE KILMER, *Trees*,
(1914)

My own habitual feeling is
that the world is so extremely
odd, and everything in it so
surprising. Why *should* there
be green grass and liquid

water, and *why* have I got
hands and feet?
DOM JOHN CHAPMAN,
Spiritual Letters

He who wants a new world
must first buy the old.
DUTCH PROVERB

Man does not come to know
the world by that which he
extorts from it, but rather by
that which he adds to it:
himself.
PAUL CLAUDEL, *Poetic Art*

Remoteness from the world
gives an inward distinction;
but immersion, on the other
hand, awakens all that is
human in selfhood. The
former demands self-
discipline; but the latter is
love.
KARL JASPERS, *Man in the
Modern Age*

The world is a sure teacher,
but it requires a fat fee.
FINNISH PROVERB

In the evening, the gentleness
of the world on the bay.
There are days when the
world lies, days when it tells
the truth. It is telling the

truth this evening - with what
sad and insistent beauty.
ALBERT CAMUS, *Notebooks*

The world is the world, and
teaches all of us, more or less,
one lesson.
OSCAR W. FIRKINS, *Oscar
Firkins: Memoirs and Letters*

Enlightenment is not for the
Quietists and Puritans who, in
their different ways, deny the
world, but for those who have
learned to accept and
transfigure it.
ALDOUS HUXLEY, *Collected
Essays*

A day like today I realise what
I've told you a hundred
different times - that there's
nothing wrong with the world.
What's wrong is our way of
looking at it.
HENRY MILLER, *A Devil in
Paradise*

What one thinks, what one
feels, the agony, the suffering,
the ambition, the envy, the
extraordinary confusion one is
in, that is the world.
J. KRISHNAMURTI, *You Are
the World*

The world pays us what it owes us oftener than we pay what we owe the world.
JOSH BILLINGS, *His Works Complete*

Man draws the nearer to God as he withdraws further from the consolations of this world.
THOMAS À KEMPIS

Every man's nose will not make a shoehorn. Let us leave the world as it is.
CERVANTES

You should live in the world so as it may hang about you like a loose garment.
LORD HALIFAX

When I reflect back upon what I have seen, what I have heard, and what I have done myself, I can hardly persuade myself that all that frivolous hurry and bustle, and pleasures of the world, had any reality; but they seem to have been the dreams of restless nights.
LORD CHESTERFIELD

The world only exists in your eyes - your conception of it. You can make it as big or as small as you want to.
F. SCOTT FITZGERALD, *The Crack-Up*

The world is a bride of surpassing beauty - but remember that this maiden is never bound to anyone.
HAFIZ, ghazals from the *Divan*, 34, (14th century)

Pistol: Why, then, the world's mine oyster,
Which I with sword will open.
WILLIAM SHAKESPEARE, *Merry Wives of Windsor*, Act II, Scene ii, line 2

Books are a world in themselves, it is true; but they are not the only world. The world itself is a volume larger than all the libraries in it.
WILLIAM HAZLITT, *On the Conversation of Authors*, (1826)

The unrest which keeps the never stopping clock of metaphysics going is the thought that the nonexistence of this world is just as possible as its existence.
WILLIAM JAMES, *Some Problems of Philosophy*, The Problem of Being, (1911)

Set the foot down with distrust upon the crust of the world - it is thin.
EDNA ST. VINCENT MILLAY, Huntsman, What Quarry?, Underground System

For in and out, above, about, below,
'Tis nothing but a Magic Shadow-show,
Played in a Box whose Candle is the sun,
Round which we Phantom Figures come and go.
OMAR KHAYYÁM, Rubáiyát, 46, (11th-12th century)

We read the world wrong and say that it deceives us.
RABINDRANATH TAGORE, Stray Birds, 75, (1916)

The world is a gambling-table so arranged that all who enter the casino must play and all must lose more or less heavily in the long run, though they win occasionally by the way.
SAMUEL BUTLER, (d. 1902), Note-Books, Lord, What Is Man? (1912)

This world, after all our science and sciences, is still a miracle; wonderful, inscrutable, magical and more, to whosoever will think of it.
THOMAS CARLYLE, On Heroes, Hero-Worship and the Heroic in History, 1, (1841)

Just as the cloud of unknowing lies above you, between you and your God, so you must fashion a cloud of forgetting beneath you, between you and every created thing.
ANON, The Cloud of Unknowing, (14th century)

The world is a great volume, and man the index of that book; even in the body of man, you may turn to the whole world.
JOHN DONNE, Sermons, Numer 42, (1626)

This is the way the world ends
Not with a bang but a whimper.
T.S. ELIOT, The Hollow Men, 5

In seventy or eighty years, a man may have a deep gust of the world; know what it is, what it can afford, and what

'tis to have been a man.
SAMUEL TAYLOR
COLERIDGE

The world is wide; no two
days are alike, nor even two
hours; neither was there ever
two leaves of a tree alike since
the creation of the world; and
the genuine productions of
art, like those of nature, are all
distinct from each other.
JOHN CONSTABLE

Here is the world, sound as a
nut, not the smallest piece of
chaos left, never a stitch nor
an end, not a mark of haste, or
botching, or second thought;
but the theory of the world is
a thing of shreds and patches.
RALPH WALDO EMERSON

It is no part of God's scheme
that any very large number of
people in this world should be
positively wise, good, and
well-to-do. If it had been He
would have taken measures to
ensure that such should be the
case.
SAMUEL BUTLER

One is happy in the world
only when one forgets the
world.
ANATOLE FRANCE

A man's feet should be
planted in his country, but his
eyes should survey the world.
GEORGE SANTAYANA

The world was not created
once and for all for each of us.
In the course of life things
that we never even imagined
are added to it.
MARCEL PROUST

God rules the world not from
the outside, not by gravity and
chemical affinity, but in the
hearts of men: as your soul is,
so is the fate of the world you
live in and move in. Nothing
is outside.
EGON FRIEDELL

Happy those who live in the
dream of their own existence,
and see all things in the light
of their own minds; who walk
by faith and hope; to whom
the guiding star of their youth
still shines from afar, and into
whom the spirit of the world
has not entered!
WILLIAM HAZLITT

Everything in the world is
alive. Everything that seems
to us dead seems so only
because it is either too large

or, on the contrary, too small.
We do not see microbes, and
heavenly bodies seem dead to
us, for the same reason we
seem dead to an ant. The
earth is undoubtedly alive,
and a stone on the earth is the
same as a nail on the finger.
LEO TOLSTOY

Call the world if you Please
"The vale of Soul-making".
Then you will find out the use
of the world (I am speaking
now in the highest terms for
human nature admitting it to
be immortal which I will here
take for granted for the
purpose of showing a thought
which has struck me
concerning it) I say 'Soul
making' Soul as distinguished
from an Intelligence - There
may be intelligences or sparks
of the divinity in millions -
but they are not souls till they
acquire identities, till each
one is personally itself.
I[n]telligences are atoms of
perception - they know and
they see and they are pure, in
short they are God - how then
are Souls to be made? How
then are these sparks which
are God to have identity
given them - so as ever to

possess a bliss peculiar to each
ones individual existence?
How, but by the medium of a
world like this?

... Do you not see how
necessary a World of Pains
and troubles is to school an
Intelligence and make it a
soul? A Place where the heart
must feel and suffer in a
thousand diverse ways! Not
merely is the Heart a
Hornbook, It is the Minds
Bible, it is the Minds
experience, it is the teat from
which the Mind or
intelligence sucks its identity -
As various as the Lives of Men
are - so various become their
Souls, and thus does God
make individual beings, Souls,
Identical Souls of the sparks of
his own essence.
... I mean, I began by seeing
how man was formed by
circumstances - and what are
circumstances? - but
touchstones of his heart -? and
what are touchstones? but
proovings of his heart? - and
what are proovings of his
heart but fortifiers or alterers
of his nature? and what is his
altered nature but his soul? -
and what was his soul before it

came into the world and had
These provings and alterations
and perfectionings? - An
intelligence - without Identity
- and how is this Identity to
be made? Through the
medium of the Heart? And
how is the heart to become
this Medium but in a world of
Circumstances?
JOHN KEATS, *A Letter*

FIFTY

ZEN

Studying Zen under a teacher is just like this. What you obtain at first is the nature with which man is innately endowed. It is the true face of the unique One Vehicle of the Lotus. What I have obtained is this very same nature, innate from the outset, this one and only true face of the One Vehicle of the Lotus. This is called seeing into one's own nature. This nature does not change in the slightest degree from the time one first starts in the Way until complete intuitive wisdom is perfected. It is like the metal refined by the Great Metal-maker. Therefore it has been said: "At the time that one first conceives the desire to study Buddhism, enlightenment has already been attained." In the teaching schools this is the first of the ten stages. But even more so, it is also the very last barrier. Who can tell how far in the distance the garden of the Patriarchs lies? CHANG LU

What is the attitude adopted through judo and aikido? It can, perhaps, be explained by using two examples. When an enraged person threatens us, there are two possibilities open. The first is to resist the aggressive force. Although this is the most common reaction, it is the wrong one. The action of self-defence comes from the mind and the brain. Following this, mental reactions such as anger and fear occur. We expend considerable energy in resisting the force of attack of the adversary. Should we be stronger than our assailant, the challenge is not troublesome, but if the aggressor is stronger, we are easily overcome.

However, in this situation another possibility is open to us, and this alternative is the one advocated by the judo instructors. We should not be dictated to by our mental habits nor by our brain but by *Hara* or the centre of instinctive wisdom in the body. Instead of resisting the attack, we should draw it in as a willow accommodates snow and wind. We should remain detached and fearless. We should not resist. Judo and aikido provide us with certain

holds which in this situation should be used against the adversary himself. The more violent his aggressiveness, the more violent his fall. We have seen *black belt* holders overcome men of great strength like this. Even without moving, by making some imperceptible gesture, the master of judo can defeat the aggressor. He does not combat force with force.
ROBERT LINSEN, from *Zen*

Many times the mountains have turned from green to yellow -
So much for the capricious earth!
Dust in your eyes, the triple world is narrow;
Nothing on the mind, your chair is wide enough.
MUSO (1275-1351)

The Subtlety of Zen
To learn the subtlety of Zen, you must clarify your mind and immerse your spirit in silent
exercise of inner gazing.
When you see into the source of reality, with no obstruction whatsoever, it is open and formless, like water in

autumn, clear and bright, like the moon taking away the darkness of night.
HONGZHI

Snow still remains on the hills,
The plum flower does not yet smile.
Ice in the creek begins to melt.
The willow tree is about to show new growth.
Very few people walk the road of Nirvana,
While demons and devils laugh and jump along the way.
SOYEN SHAKU

Smell of autumn-
heart longs
for the four-mat room.
BASHO

Meditation yields its significance
After the person has experienced it
Not when he tries
To understand it by means of examination.

He should be prepared to encounter
Unexpected states of consciousness

And be willing
To go where he is led
Without expectations.

In spiritual life
Even a sincere mistake
Taken seriously
May have more value
Than half-hearted allegiance
to theoretical truth.
MEHER BABA

Spontaneous Knowledge
All realms of phenomena arise
from one mind. When the one
mind is quiescent, all
appearances
end. Then which is other,
which is self?
Because there are no
differentiated appearances at
such a time, nothing at all is
defined, not a
single thought is produced -
you pass before birth and after
death; the mind becomes a
point of
subtle light, round and
frictionless, without location,
without traces.
Then your mind cannot be
obscured.
This point where there can be
no obscuration is called
spontaneous knowledge. Just
this realm of

spontaneous knowledge is
called the original attainment.
Nothing whatsoever is
attained from
outside.
HONGZHI

There are some blind, bald
idiots who stand in a calm,
unperturbed, untouchable
place and consider that the
state of mind produced in this
atmosphere comprises seeing
into their own natures. They
think that to polish and
perfect purity is sufficient, but
have never even in a dream
achieved the state [of the
person described above].
People of this sort spend all
day practicing non-action and
end up by having practiced
action all the while; spend all
day practicing non-creating
and end up by having
practiced creating all the
while. Why is this so? It is
because their insight into the
Way is not clear, because they
cannot arrive at the truth of
the Dharma-nature.
HAKVIN

Arid fields,
the only life -
necks of cranes.
SHIKO

Can Zen help us with valuable solutions to the problems engendered by our modern civilisation? It is difficult to say, though Zen can bring, when it is practised seriously, an inner relaxation amidst the most intense outside activity, and this of course is one of its most precious benefits and one which has prompted many Westerners to adopt Zen. Another cause for Zen's increased popularity could be that people now question the values which preside in western civilisation and are searching for an inspiration.
ROBERT LINSEN, from *Zen*

Finding Out for Oneself
    The mind originally is detached from objects, reality basically has no explanation. This is why a classical Zen master said, "Our school has no slogans, and no doctrine to give people."
    Fundamentally it is a matter of people arriving on their own and finding out for themselves; only then can they talk about it.
HONGZHI

A monk in Old China dwelt on a rocky road by a spring.
He raised his empty fist when he met another monk.
I will not follow him, but will quit everything for good.
My gate is shut from the dust of the world,
And from the entanglement of ivy -
And I sleep as I please without any disturbance.
JAKUSHITSU

Today Rakan, riding an iron horse
Backwards, climbs Mount Sumeru.
Galloping through Void,
I'll leave no trace.
RAKAN-KEINAN

On his deathbed
Buddha taught his disciples
To practice forbearance.
Man should act like the willow branches,
Which bend gently against the wind.
Three times we have commemorated
Buddha's Nirvana Day in this plateau.
We did not learn much during the past three years.
We are ready, however,

To face the world with
equanimity,
Taking smilingly the
snowstorm of abuse
As well as the sunshine of
honeyed words.
Praise be to the Buddha, the
Enlightened One.
NYOGEN SENZAKI,
February 13

At last I've broken Unmon's
barrier!
There's exit everywhere - east,
west; north, south.
In at morning, out at evening;
neither host nor guest.
My every step stirs up a little
breeze.
DAITO (1282-1337)

Evening rain washes away the
dust of the world.
When my train starts, I leave
everything behind.
Though I may pass through
mountains
Or cross new waters on my
journey,
The waning moon and soft
wind
Will bring me new dreams,
one by one!
SOYEN SHAKU

Skylark
sings all day,
and day not long enough.
BASHO

For us the comprehension of
Zen means that we must adapt
ourselves so that a kind of
inner bond can be realised
within ourselves. The inner
voyage undertaken to learn
the wisdom of Zen is perhaps
the healthiest and most vital
of all adventures. According
to the eastern sages, we travel
to 'the other bank of the
ocean of the Being, at the
heart of ourselves'. Unknown
horizons are revealed to us,
where the divine and the
human are the same.
ROBERT LINSEN, *As Zen*

Zen Mind
Just wash away the dust and
dirt of subjective thoughts
immediately. When the dust
and dirt are washed away, your
mind is open, shining brightly,
without boundaries, without
centre or extremes.
Completely whole, radiant
with light, it shines through
the universe, cutting through
past,
present and future.

This is inherent in you, and does not come from outside. This is called the state of true reality. One who has experienced this can enter into all sorts of situations in response to all sorts of possibilities, with subtle function that is marvellously effective and naturally uninhibited.
HONGZHI

What a shame it is that they spend in vain this one birth as a human being, a birth so difficult to obtain. They are like blind turtles wandering pointlessly in empty valleys, like demons who guard the wood used for coffins. That they return unreformed in suffering to their old homes in the three evil ways is because their practice was badly guided, and from the outset they had not truly seen their own natures. They have exhausted the strength of their minds in vain and have in the end been able to gain no benefit at all. This is regrettable indeed.
HAKVIN

First snow -
head clear,
I wash my face.
ETSUJIN (1656-1739)

The
Secrets
Of
Spiritual
Life
Are
Opened
To
Those
Who
Venture

Not
To
Those
Who
Seek
Guarantees
For
Every
Step.
MEHER BABA

"In the spring garden of discipline,
Perseverance blooms its first flower."
So the Buddha said in his last teaching.
Hundred thousand brothers and sisters!

You have pined long enough.
NYOGEN SENZAKI

Zen Mastery
The action and repose of
those who have mastered Zen
are like flowing clouds,
without
self-consciousness, like the full
moon, reflected everywhere.
People who have mastered
Zen are not stopped by
anything: though clearly in
the midst of all things, still
they are highly aloof; though
they encounter experiences
according to circumstances,
they are not tainted or mixed
up by them.
HONGZHI

Zen Buddhists talk about 'just
sitting', a meditative practice
in which the idea of a duality
of self and object does not
dominate one's consciousness.
What I'm talking about here
in motorcycle maintenance is
'just fixing', in which the idea
of a duality of self and object
doesn't dominate one's
consciousness. When one
isn't dominated by feelings of
separateness from what he's
working on, then one can be
said to 'care' about what he's
doing. That is what caring
really is, a feeling of
identification with what one's
doing. When one has this
feeling then he also sees the
inverse side of caring, Quality
itself.
ROBERT M. PIRSIG, from
Zen and the Art of Motorcycle
Maintenance

Love the world
As your own self
Then you can truly
Care for all things.

It is more important
To see the simplicity
To realise one's true nature
To cast off selfishness
And temper desire.

Creating yet not possessing
Working yet not taking credit
Work is done then forgotten
Therefore it lasts forever.
LAO TSU

Everyone's Zen
Ever since the time of the
Buddha and the founders of
Zen, there has never been any
distinction
between ordained and lay
people, in the sense that
everyone who has accurate

personal experience of true realization is said to have entered the school of the enlightened mind and penetrated the source of religion.
HONGZHI

This fellow, perfect in men's eyes,
Utters the same thing over
And over, fifty-six years. Now
Something new - spear trees, sword hills!
IKUO-JOUN

The age of technology has brought with it disadvantages for man. This is not to throw discredit on the achievements of science in our age. But Zen advocates (as Socrates did) the necessity to know ourselves fully in order to establish in ourselves a psychological maturity. This should be emphasised just as much as progress in technology. The proper use of such power as atomic energy depends on our inner evolution. Zen and modern psychology teach us that ignorance of ourselves and the deep nature of all things orients us towards abnormal and inadequate behaviour. Our sense of spiritual values are degraded under the influence of a too intellectualised development. Intellectuality and spirituality are not synonymous.
ROBERT LINSEN, from *Zen*

He walks freely in the world,
And goes just one way.
From the eternal past to the eternal future,
He is alone,
No one accompanies him.
If you ask him how old he is,
He will look at you with a smile,
And point to the endless sky.
JAKUSHITSU

June rain,
hollyhocks turning
where sun should be.
BASHO

I moved across the Dharma-nature,
The earth was buoyant, marvellous.
That very night, whipping its iron horse,
The void galloped into Cloud Street.
GETSUDO (1285-1361)

Nightingale -
my clogs
stick in the mud.
BONCHO (circa 1714)

Lust, greed, and anger
respectively have
Body, heart, and mind
As their vehicles of
expression.
Selfishness seeks fulfilment
Through desires
But succeeds only in
increasing
Unsatisfied desires.
MEHER BABA

Aloof of the Tumult
When you understand and
arrive at the emptiness of all
things, then you are
independent of every
state of mind, and transcend
every situation. The original
light is everywhere, and you
then adapt
to the potential at hand;
everything you meet is Zen.
While subtly aware of all
circumstances, you are empty
and have no subjective stance
towards
them. Like the breeze in the
pines, the moon in the water,
there is a clear and light
harmony. You

have no coming and going
mind, and you do not linger
over appearances.
The essence is in being
inwardly open and
accommodating while
outwardly responsive without
unrest. Be like spring causing
the flowers to bloom, like a
mirror reflecting images, and
you will
naturally emerge aloof of all
tumult.
HONGZHI

When Buddha passed from
the world,
Ananda and most of the good
monks
Wept in grief.
While Subhadra and a few
bad ones
Felt relief from discipline.
The cremation was over
before sundown.
The people of ten countries
built ten towers
Enshrining Buddha's
remaining ashes.
The vines which cover a
window of our Zendo
Show us Nirvana today with
their new buds.
NYOGEN SENZAKI

The Fifth Patriarch told a new monk,
"Southern monkeys have no Buddha nature."
That monk proved that he had Buddha nature
By becoming the Sixth Patriarch!
In any part of the globe
Where there is air, a fire can burn.
SOYEN SHAKU

Zen Experience
When you are empty and spontaneously aware, clean and spontaneously clear, you are capable of
panoramic consciousness without making an effort to grasp perception, and you are capable of
discerning understanding without the burden of conditioned thought. You go beyond being and nothingness, and transcend conceivable feelings.
This is only experienced by union with it - it is not gotten from another.
HONGZHI

Dozing on horseback,
smoke from tea-fires
drifts to the moon.
BASHO

There will be a feeling within you
You will feel a separation
You will know a oneness.

And you will awaken
And you will speak
And your actions will transform the world
And your love
Will reach into the core of all things.

Some will be afraid.
Let them know this great love
Through you

Speak out
Take action
Without
And within.
ANON

The fundamental principle of the Universe is inexpressible. Spiritual perfection cannot be cultivated (it cannot result from an act of will of the ego nor of its intellectual construction, since this ego, such as we know it, is only illusion and ignorance).
In the final analysis, nothing is achieved (we are and have always been the supreme Reality, but we do not know

it, because of our fundamental distraction).

There is nothing else of much importance in Buddhism. The simple fact of drawing water and breaking wood encloses the marvellous mystery of Zen.
ROBERT LINSEN, Zen

Normalcy
The time when you "see the sun in daytime and see the moon at night," when you are not deceived, is the normal behaviour of a Zen practitioner, naturally without edges or seams. If you want to attain this kind of normalcy, you have to put an end to the subtle pounding and weaving that goes on in your mind.
HONGZHI

What is 'to let go your hold when hanging from a sheer precipice'? Supposing a man should find himself in some desolate area where no man has ever walked before. Below him are the perpendicular walls of a bottomless chasm. His feet rest precariously on a patch of slippery moss, and there is no spot of earth on which he can steady himself. He can neither advance nor retreat; he faces only death. The only things he has on which to depend are a vine that he grasps by the left hand and a creeper that he holds with his right. His life hangs as if from a dangling thread. If he were suddenly to let go his dried bones would not even be left.

So it is with the study of the Way. If you take up one koan and investigate it unceasingly your mind will die and your will will be destroyed. It is as though a vast, empty abyss lay before you, with no place to set your hands and feet. You face death and your bosom feels as though it were afire. Then suddenly you are one with the koan, and both body and mind are cast off. This is known as the time when the hands are released over the abyss.
HAKVIN

Late spring:
paling rose,
bitter rhubarb.
SODO (1641-1716)

No more heavy burdens on
your shoulders
You walk out freely.
East, West, South, North,
You may go wherever you like.
This morning I part from you
without a word.
The voice of pattering rain
against the window.
SOYEN SHAKU

Zen Life, Zen Action
The worldly life of people who
have mastered Zen is buoyant
and unbridled, like clouds
making
rain, like the moon in a
stream, like an orchid in a
recondite spot, like spring in
living beings.
Their action is not self-
conscious, yet their responses
have order. This is what those
who have
mastered Zen do.
It is also necessary to turn
back to the source, to set foot
on the realm of peace, plunge
into
the realm of purity, and stand
alone, without companions,
going all the way through the
road
beyond the Buddhas. Only
then can you fully
comprehend the centre and

the extremes, penetrate the
very top and the very bottom,
and freely kill and enliven,
roll up and roll out.
HONGZHI

Love is its own reason for
being.
It is complete in itself.

When love is present
The path to truth is joyous.

In love, all is spontaneous.
Spontaneity belongs to
spirituality.
The state of unlimited
spontaneity,
In which there is
uninterrupted

Self knowledge.
MEHER BABA

Melon
in morning dew -
mud-fresh
BASHO

Enlightened Awareness
Buddhas and Zen masters do
not have different realizations;
they all teach the point of
cessation, where past, present
and future are cut off and all
impulses stop, where there is

not
the slightest object.
Enlightened awareness shines
spontaneously, subtly
penetrating the root
source.
HONGZHI

The cause of our current social
crises, he would have said, is a
genetic defect within the
nature of reason itself. And
until this genetic defect is
cleared, the crises will
continue. Our current modes
of rationality are not moving
society forward into a better
world. They are taking it
further and further from that
better world. Since the
Renaissance these modes have
worked. As long as the need
for food, clothing and shelter
is dominant they will
continue to work. But now
that for huge masses of people
these needs no longer
overwhelm everything else,
the whole structure of reason,
handed down to us from
ancient times, is no longer
adequate. It begins to be seen
for what it really is -
emotionally hollow,
esthetically meaningless and
spiritually empty. That, today,

is where it is at, and will
continue to be at for a long
time to come.
ROBERT M. PIRSIG, *Zen and
the Art of Motorcycle
Maintenance*

No more head shaving,
Washing flesh.
Pile high the wood,
Set it aflame!
CHITSU

"Those who live without
unreasonable desires
Are walking on the road of
Nirvana."
So Buddha said on his
deathbed.
Evacuees who follow him,
learning contentment,
Should attain peace of mind
Even in this frozen desert of
internment.
See a break in the clouds in
the East!
The winter sun rises calmly,
Illuminating the light of
wisdom.
NYOGEN SENZAKI

In immeasurable time,
Through eternal space,
Do not say that a certain
Buddha
Lives in a certain country.

After all, the world wherein
you live,
Is your own Paradise.
SOYEN SHAKU

Vainly I dug for a perfect sky,
Piling a barrier all around.
then one black night, lifting a
heavy
Tile, I crushed the skeletal
void!
MUSO

Forty-nine years -
What a din!
Eighty-seven springs -
What pleasures!
What's having? not having?
Dreaming, dreaming.
Plum trees snow-laden,
I'm ready!
UNCHO

Autumn and Spring
When Zen practice is
completely developed, there is
no centre, no extremes, there
are no edges
or corners. It is perfectly
round and frictionless.
It is also necessary to be
empty, open, unpolluted, so
"the clear autumn moon cold,
its shining
light washes the night.
Brocade clouds flower prettily,

the atmosphere turns into
spring."
HONGZHI

Bodhidharma brought
together the principal
Buddhist leaders in China, in
the presence of the emperor
Wu, and explained to them
his conceptions of the living
Buddhism. He found himself
facing total uncomprehension.
He was greatly saddened and
withdrew for nine years in a
monastery in northern China.
Enriched with a much deeper
spiritual illumination, he
resumed his campaign in
favour of a renaissance of the
living Buddhism. He defined
the spirit and the aim of
Ch'an in the following way:

An oral transmission without
scriptures.
No dependence on words and
letters.
A direct search aimed at the
essence of man.
To see into one's own nature
and attain the perfect
awakening.
ROBERT LINSEN, from *Zen*

Small fish-boats,
after what

as snow covers my hat?
SHIKO

The Twenty-eighth Patriarch,
Bodhidharma, borne by the
living body of the bodhisattva
Kannon, endured endless
stretches of raging waves to
come to China, a land that
already possessed the sacred
scriptures in abundance, to
transmit the seal of the
Buddha mind that had been
handed down from the
Tathagata. Hearing of this,
and wondering what Great
Matter he had to impart,
people wiped their eyes,
adjusted their garments, and
came longing for instruction.
And what he had to teach was
only the one thing - seeing
into one's own nature and
becoming Buddha. Although
he set up six gates, including
the 'Breaking through Form'
and the 'Awakened Nature',
ultimately they all come down
to the one thing - seeing into
one's own nature.
HAKVIN

Life is a sort of dance. The
children of the world are
playing their game - all kinds
of games. They form a group
and dance around their own
maypole. When I lived in
San Fransisco I used to watch
the happy dancing of children
around the maypole every
May Day. It was my
optimistic viewpoint of the
karmic world.
I see, however, the people of
the world clinging fatally to
their maypoles. When they
fall, they dumbfoundedly lose
their entire interest in life.
They want to stay as children
the rest of their lives. Such
people are clinging to the
delusion of individual soul,
the existence of which
Buddhism denies strongly.
They do not want to think.
They should act as grown men
and women and dance around
the world freely, without
fastening themselves to the
maypole.
NYOGEN SENZAKI

I love sickness because it is my
attendant monk.
There is no devil, no Buddha -
Both are gone.
Where is the real source to be
returned unto?
Great emptiness hangs over
this small hut!
SOYEN SHAKU

Crow's
abandoned nests,
a plum tree.
BASHO

The Light of Mind
When material sense doesn't
blind you, all things are seen
to be the light of the mind.
You
transcend with every step, on
the path of the bird, no
tarrying anywhere. You respond
to the world with clarity, open
awareness unstrained.
HONGZHI

It is better to study god than
to be ignorant about him.
It is better to feel for god than
to study him.
It is better to experience god
than to feel for him.
It is better to become god
than to experience him.
MEHER BABA

We know now how ridiculous
it is to consider a living being,
thing or object from the point
of view of isolation or
independence of any kind.
Nothing is independent or
isolated. Everything holds
together. To claim the
isolation of an object, a metal
paper knife for example,
simply because the senses of
sight and touch endow it with
definite and precise contours
is, in fact, a childish
simplification which we must
learn to condemn. The action
of the atoms of this paper
knife extends across all of the
interstellar worlds. It fills the
entire Universe of billions of
light-years with the
potentiality of its presence.
And reciprocally, something
of each of the atoms situated
in the farthest confines of the
galaxies is found in the heart
of this apparently isolated
paper knife. It is very
probable that if this
something of very distant
origin were not present a
noticeable modification of the
plural organisation of the
atoms and molecules would
take place and make the
appearance of our paper knife
utterly unrecognizable.
ROBERT LINSEN, from *Zen*

To slice through Buddhas,
Patriarchs
I grip my polished sword.
One glance at my mastery,
The void bites its tusks!
DAITO

Piled for burning,
brushwood
starts to bud.
BONCHO

Shedding Your Skin
The experience described as
shedding your skin,
transcending reflections of
subjective
awareness, where no mental
machinations can reach, is not
transmitted by sages. It can
only be
attained inwardly, by profound
experience of spontaneous
illumination. The original
light destroys the darkness,
real illumination mirrors the
infinite. Subjective
assessments of what is or is not
are all transcended.
HONGZHI

O

is a symbol of the world,
of oneness and unity. O Books
explores the many paths of wholeness
and spiritual understanding which
different traditions have developed down
the ages. It aims to bring this knowledge
in accessible form, to a general readership,
providing practical spirituality to today's seekers.

For the full list of over 200 titles covering:

- CHILDREN'S PRAYER, NOVELTY AND GIFT BOOKS
- CHILDREN'S CHRISTIAN AND SPIRITUALITY
- CHRISTMAS AND EASTER
- RELIGION/PHILOSOPHY
- SCHOOL TITLES
- ANGELS/CHANNELLING
- HEALING/MEDITATION
- SELF-HELP/RELATIONSHIPS
- ASTROLOGY/NUMEROLOGY
- SPIRITUAL ENQUIRY
- CHRISTIANITY, EVANGELICAL
AND LIBERAL/RADICAL
- CURRENT AFFAIRS
- HISTORY/BIOGRAPHY
- INSPIRATIONAL/DEVOTIONAL
- WORLD RELIGIONS/INTERFAITH
- BIOGRAPHY AND FICTION
- BIBLE AND REFERENCE
- SCIENCE/PSYCHOLOGY

Please visit our website,
www.O-books.net

SOME RECENT O BOOKS

GOOD AS NEW
A radical re-telling of the Christian Scriptures
John Henson

This radical new translation conveys the early Christian scriptures in the idiom of today. It is "inclusive," following the principles which Jesus adopted in relation to his culture. It is women, gay and sinner friendly. It follows principles of cultural and contextual translation, and returns to the selection of books that the early Church held in highest esteem. It drops Revelation and includes the Gospel of Thomas,

"a presentation of extraordinary power." Rowan Williams, Archbishop of Canterbury
"I can't rate this version of the Christian scriptures highly enough. It is amazingly fresh, imaginative, engaging and bold." Adrian Thatcher, Professor of Applied Theology, College of St Mark and St John, Plymouth

"I found this a literally shocking read. It made me think, it made me laugh, it made me cry, it made me angry and it made me joyful. It made me feel like an early Christian hearing these texts for the first time." Elizabeth Stuart, Professor of Christian Theology, King Alfred's College, Winchester

John Henson, a retired Baptist minister, has co-ordinated this translation over the last 12 years on behalf of *ONE for Christian Exploration*, a network of radical Christians and over twenty organisations in the UK

1-903816-74-2
£19.99 $29.95 hb

THE THOUGHTFUL GUIDE TO THE BIBLE
Roy Robinson

Most Christians are unaware of the revolution in how the Bible may be understood that has taken place over the last two hundred years. This book seeks to share the fruits of the Biblical revolution in an easily accessible manner. It seeks to inform you of its main features and to encourage you to do your own thinking and come to your own conclusions.

Roy Robinson is a United Reformed Church minister, now retired and living in England. A former missionary in Zaire this work arises from a lifetime of study and Bible teaching at the Oxted Christian Centre, which he founded.

1-903816-75-0
£14.99 $19.95

LET THE STANDING STONES SPEAK
Messages from the Archangels revealed
Natasha Hoffman with Hamilton Hill

The messages encoded in the standing stones of Carnac in Brittany, France, combine and transcend spiritual truths from many disciplines and traditions, even though their builders lived thousands of years before Buddha, Christ and MuhammAd. The revelations received by the authors as they read the stones make up a New Age Bible for today.

"an evergreen..a permanent point of reference for the serious seeker."
Ian Graham, author of *God is Never Late*

Natasha Hoffman is a practising artist, healer and intuitive, and lives with her partner Hamilton in Rouziers, France.

1-903816-79-3
£9.99 $14.95

BRINGING GOD BACK TO EARTH
John Hunt

Religion is an essential part of our humanity. We all follow some form
of religion, in the original meaning of the word. But organised religion
establishes definitions, boundaries and hierarchies which the founders
would be amazed by. If we could recover the original teachings and
live by them, we could change ourselves and the world for the better.
We could bring God back to earth.

"The best modern religious book I have read. A masterwork." Robert
Van de Weyer, author of *A World Religions Bible*

"Answers all the questions you ever wanted to ask about God and some
you never even thought of." Richard Holloway, former Primus
Episcopus and author of *Doubts and Loves*

John Hunt runs a publishing company of which O Books is an
imprint.

1-903816-81-5
£9.99 $14.95

ZEN ECONOMICS
Robert Van de Weyer

Just as Zen sages taught that attitudes and behaviour can suddenly
alter, Van de Weyer combines economic analysis with social and
philosophical insight to reveal how the entire world is on the verge of
an economic and social transformation. The thrift practised by the
Japanese, which has caused their economy to stagnate, will soon
spread to all affluent countries, because it is the rational response to
the economic, social and spiritual challenges that affluent people are
now facing.

But thrift on a global scale, far from causing stagnation, will enable
many of the world's most intractable problems to be solved. Van de
Weyer offers practical financial and personal advice on how to
participate in and cope with this global change. This book carries

several messages of hope, which are linked by the theme of saving and investing. It's single most important message is that in the western world most of us have reached a point of prosperity where the investment with the highest rate of return is investing in the self.

Robert Van de Weyer lectured in Economics for twenty years at Cambridge University, England. He has written and edited over fifty books on a variety of themes, including economics, religion and history.

1-903816-78-5
£9.99 $12.95

TORN CLOUDS
Judy Hall

Drawing on thirty years experience as a regression therapist and her own memories and experiences in Egypt, ancient and modern, *Torn Clouds* is a remarkable first novel by an internationally-acclaimed MBS author, one of Britain's leading experts on reincarnation. It features time-traveller Megan McKennar, whose past life memories thrust themselves into the present day as she traces a love affair that transcends time. Haunted by her dreams, she is driven by forces she cannot understand to take a trip to Egypt in a quest to understand the cause of her unhappy current life circumstances. Once there, swooning into a previous existence in Pharaonic Egypt, she lives again as Meck'an'ar, priestess of the Goddess Sekhmet, the fearful lion headed deity who was simultaneously the Goddess of Terror, Magic and Healing.

Caught up in the dark historical secrets of Egypt, Megan is forced to fight for her soul. She succeeds in breaking the curse that had been cast upon her in two incarnations.

Judy Hall is a modern seer who manages the difficult task of evoking the present world, plus the realm of Ancient Egypt, and making them seem real. There is an energy behind the prose, and a power in her imagery which hints that this is more than just a story of character and plot, but an outpouring from another age, a genuine glimpse into beyond-time

Mysteries which affect us all today. Alan Richardson, author of *Inner Guide to Egypt.*

Judy Hall has been a karmic counsellor for thirty years. Her books have been translated into over fourteen languages.
1 903816 80 7
£9.99/$14.95

HEALING HANDS
David Vennells

Hand reflexology is one of the most well-known and respected complementary therapies, practised in many hospitals, surgeries, hospices, health and healing centres, and is enjoying a growing popularity. *Healing Hands* explains the simple techniques of Hand Reflexology so clearly, with the aid of illustrations, that "within a few days the reader could be competently treating themselves or others." It is aimed at those interested in learning the practical techniques (how to give yourself and others a full treatment), and also includes the fascinating history of reflexology, how it works with the hands and the various things we can do to support the healing process. As the reader learns the techniques step by step, they can gradually increase their knowledge of anatomy and physiology, together with developing a more accurate awareness of the hand reflexes and how to treat them accurately and successfully.

David Vennells is a Buddhist teacher of Reiki and the author of *Reiki Mastery* (O Books).
1 903816 81 5
£9.99/$16.95